The End of the Old Order in Rural Europe

The End of the Old Order in Rural Europe

Jerome Blum

Princeton University Press
Princeton, New Jersey

Library of Congress Cataloging in Publication Data will
be found on the last printed page of this book

This book has been composed in VIP Aldus

Printed in the United States of America
by Princeton University Press, Princeton, New Jersey

To E. T. B.
with affection and admiration

PREFACE

A long-standing interest in the history of rural Europe, and especially in the relationship between the seigniors and the peasants, led to the writing of this book. It begins with a study of the internal structure and the economic activities of the rural societies of the eighteenth and nineteenth centuries in those states whose inhabitants were divided into an hierarchy of orders, and where most of the people were peasants who were subservient to the seigniors who owned the land. The second part of the book concerns itself with forces and elements, old and new, ranging from absolute monarchs to village rioters and revolutionaries, whose demands and actions and innovations ultimately undermined the hierarchical order that had persisted for so many centuries. The third section deals with the emancipations—the first one in the duchy of Savoy in 1771 and the last in the new state of Romania in 1864—that freed the peasantry, and thereby cleared the way for a new kind of social arrangement: the class society.

The task of writing the book was made easier by the generous assistance given me. Much of the research and writing was done at the Library of Congress. I owe a great deal to the thoughtfulness and cooperation of the staff of that great institution. I wish particularly to acknowledge the consideration shown me by Dudley Ball, William Sartain, Roland C. Maheu and Anne Hallstein, by Dr. Robert V. Allen and above all, by Miss Constance Carter, whose truly remarkable skills as a reference librarian saved me many hours of searching. Fellowships from the John Simon Guggenheim Memorial Foundation and from the National Endowment for the Humanities allowed me the luxury of two years of leave during which I was able to work uninterruptedly on the book. Finally, I am deeply indebted to Professors Joseph R. Strayer of Princeton, Marc Raeff of Columbia, and Robert Forster of Johns Hopkins, all of whom read the manuscript and provided me with valuable critical judgments and suggestions.

JEROME BLUM

TABLE OF CONTENTS

Contents

Contents

Part Three: Emancipation

LIST OF ILLUSTRATIONS

The Servile Lands of Europe, 18th-19th centuries.

The End of the Old Order in Rural Europe

INTRODUCTION

In the last quarter of the eighteenth century over a hundred million people, or about two-thirds of the population of all Europe, lived in the lands about which this book concerns itself: France, Savoy, Switzerland, Germany, Denmark, Schleswig-Holstein, the Hapsburg Monarchy, the Danubian Principalities of Moldavia and Wallachia (Romania), Poland, Lithuania, the Baltic provinces of Russia, and Russia itself. Of these many millions at least seven, and in some countries more than nine, out of every ten persons lived on the land.[1] Nearly all of these country dwellers drew their living from agriculture; a relatively small number were occupied in other callings, such as handicraft production, forest industries, mining, and the like. Whatever the source of their livelihoods, they belonged to that order of society known as the peasantry. Through the accident of their birth into that lowest of estates, they were denied by the society in which they lived freedoms and privileges possessed by members of orders with higher status, compelled to be subservient to and dependent upon persons in these higher status groups, and required to render certain payments and services demanded of no other order of the society. The degree of their subservience, the extent of their dependence, and the weight of their obligations formed a spectrum from relatively light restrictions and impositions in western and parts of central Europe, to oppressive and time-consuming services demanded in eastern Europe. Peasants in western Europe enjoyed much personal freedom but were not truly free. Most of them still lived in dependence upon, and owed servile obligations to, their seigniors. Those who lived in eastern Europe endured a serfdom that often was scarcely distinguishable from chattel slavery. Whether mild or onerous, servility, the submissiveness of the great majority to a few, distinguished the societies of these lands, and I will call them, collectively, the servile lands.

The social structure of each of these lands was divided into orders, or estates, that were arranged in a descending scale of status and privilege. Law and custom defined the orders, and law and custom established the hierarchy of privileges and obligations that characterized the society. This was the traditional order, the old regime, that had prevailed for centuries.

---

[1] Population data from Urlanis (1941), 414-415. Estimated ratios of rural populations: France, 85 per cent in 1789, Soboul (1970), 1, 44; Switzerland, 68 per cent in 1800, Hauser (1961) 245; Germany, 80 per cent in 1800, Franz (1970a), 13; Denmark, 80 per cent in 1769, *Statistik Aarbog* (1916), table 5; Poland, 72 per cent *ca.* 1800, Rusiński (1973), 84; Hungary, over 90 per cent *ca.* 1800, Macartney (1962), 105; Estonia, 84 per cent in 1782, *Studia historica . . . Hans Kruus* (1971), 256; Russia, 92 per cent in 1851, Miliukov (1896), 1, 79.

Unlike modern society, there was no common body of rights and duties shared by everyone by virtue of their membership in the society. The words that the Russian historian, N. M. Karamzin, used in 1811 to describe the situation in his homeland, could have been said of all of the servile lands. Russians, he said, had no civil rights, properly speaking. "We have only . . . the specific rights of the various estates of the realm; we have gentry, merchants, townfolk, peasants, and so forth—they all enjoy their specific rights, but they have no right in common, save for that of calling themselves Russians."[2]

Each order was itself divided into many layers of social status. The grandee who owned immense stretches of field and forest and who had thousands and even tens of thousands of peasants in his villages, and the petty nobleman who plowed his own fields, belonged to the same estate and could claim the same privileges. In theory they were *una eademque nobilitas*, one and the same nobility, to use the phrase of the sixteenth-century codifier of Hungarian feudal law. In reality they were worlds apart in social status, and in economic and political power. The same gulf separated the powerful archbishop or the abbot of a wealthy monastery from the rural parish priest, and the wealthy merchant from the obscure town artisan. The peasantry, too, had its stratification of status groups, though in the narrow world of the village the contrasts were not as sharp, nor the distances between groups as striking, as they were in the great world.

Some vertical mobility was possible within an order. Great families sometimes declined into poverty and obscurity, and men of less distinguished ancestry rose to high places and to great power. There was movement between orders, too; for example, if a bourgeoise married a peasant she descended into the order of the peasantry, or if a peasant youth became a cleric he ascended into the estate of the clergy. But these and similar transfers were exceptional and unimportant perturbations of the social structure, a structure so rigid that changes in status had to be by legal or official act, as when a serf was freed or a commoner ennobled.

The hierarchical arrangement of the orders rested upon the esteem accorded by the society to the functions performed by each estate. These functions had no necessary connection with the production of goods or with any other economic activity. This was especially true of the ruling orders, the clergy and the nobility, who owed their leadership to their priestly and warrior roles. The ownership of wealth, in principle at least, was not considered to be a qualification for status. In the long run, however, it almost always turned out to be of much importance in the establishment of the relative positions of the members of the ruling orders. In the lower estates, economic role had much to do with the determination of status. The order of merchants and craftsmen, who together formed the bourgeoisie of the

[2] Pipes (1959), 185.

towns, was distinguished from the estate of the peasants, who lived out in the countryside and drew their living from the land.

The hierarchical structure provided the mechanism by which society governed itself. Each member of the society occupied a fixed place in the social structure, and each knew his superiors and gave them his loyalty and obedience. Each was supposed to serve those above him. As the Parlement of Paris explained in a remonstrance to the throne in 1776, the harmony of civil society rested "only on that gradation of powers, authorities, preeminences and distinctions which holds each man in his place and guarantees all stations against confusion."[3]

The persistence of the hierarchical order was explained in large part by the traditional acceptance of the authority of kings and nobles. "Habit," William James observed, "is the enormous flywheel of society, its most precious conservative agent." The persistence of the traditional society was explained, too, by the low level of productivity in economic life, the resulting need to allocate most human and material resources to agriculture, and the dependence of the peasants upon the higher orders for the land they needed. There were, of course, challenges to this social structure, expressions of discontent with the injustices of its system of values, and sporadic outbursts of violent protest. The established order rarely had any difficulty in putting down these assaults upon it. Indeed, the inequalities of power, privilege, and honor that characterized the traditional society never seemed greater than they were in the last century of the old order. Then, at what seemed to be the apogee of its long history, the hierarchical structure, along with many other institutions of the traditional society, began to crumble. Too rigid to adjust to new pressures and new demands put upon it, the old order entered into an era of dislocation out of which emerged the age in which we now live.

In modern society the individual does not belong to a legally defined order or estate into which he has been born, nor does he have hereditary privileges or obligations that raise or lower his status in comparison with his fellows. Modern society is a class society. Membership in each class is determined by the role the individual plays in the production of goods and services, by the opportunity he has to acquire material goods, and by the amount of wealth he commands. Those with comparable incomes, or with what Max Weber called comparable "market situations," form a class with a common way of life. Thus the possession of wealth is of central importance in the class society. In earlier times, as Sombart pointed out, wealth followed upon the possession of power. Men became rich because they belonged to the ruling elite of their society. In the modern class society, power follows upon the possession of wealth.

Like the orders in the traditional society, the classes are arranged hierar-

---

[3] Palmer (1959), I, 451.

chically. One commonly uses the terms upper, middle, and lower class; there are recognized strata within each of these categories; and persons are born into the class of which their parents are members. There is, however, an all-important difference between the hierarchy of the society of orders and that of the modern class society. The society of orders presupposed the natural inequality of men. The class society presupposes the natural equality of men. Members of every class are equally citizens of the state, are judged by the same laws and the same courts, and no one class is legally defined as superior to another class. No one is compelled, by virtue of the status he acquired at birth, to serve another man of a higher class, to pay him dues and obligations, and to be judged by him. The distinctions among the strata of the class society are not established by law or custom. And in contrast to the rigidity and exclusiveness of the orders in the traditional society, the classes are relatively open and fluid. The law ignores class distinctions, and so there are no legal obstacles to passage from one class to another.[4]

There are dimensions other than class by which people are ranked and differentiated. Among them is Max Weber's model of social stratification, which included status and party, in addition to class. By status he referred to the prestige or standing a person enjoyed in his community because of the position he occupied. Party referred to membership in a group that sought to promote the interests of its members through political power.[5] T. H. Marshall proposed the concept of "citizenship," by which he meant a status that included civil, political, and social rights. In pre-modern society, citizenship in this sense was restricted to a small elite. The extension of citizenship to strata of society hitherto excluded from it modernized and finally destroyed the old order; the equality implicit in the concept of citizenship was incompatible with the principle of inequality upon which the traditional order rested.[6]

The transition from the old order to modern society, from a society of status to a class society, is what this book is about. Beginning with an examination of the traditional order, it seeks to tell when the transition happened, why it happened, and why it happened when it did. Because of the overwhelming importance of agriculture in the pre-industrial world, because the overwhelming majority of the population consisted of peasants who were held in a servile and dependent status, because the burden of supporting the state and the privileged orders rested largely upon these peasants, and because of the leading role of the landed proprietors, the interrelationships of peasants, lord, and land assumed critical importance in

---

[4] Lhomme (1960), 1-2; Marshall (1964), 85; Toennies (1953), 50; Sombart (1928), I, ii, 585-586; Weber (1953), 65-66.
[5] Weber (1953), 63-75.
[6] Marshall (1964), 71-85.

the passage to modern society. The primary instrument by which this transition was effected was the process of the emancipation of the peasantry in country after country in the century from the 1770's to the 1860's. During that century the many millions of peasants who lived in the servile lands were freed from the restrictions and the legal inequalities of the old order.

The history of the movement that liberated the peasants has hitherto always been told country by country. The first of these studies was published in St. Petersburg in 1861. Its author was a self-educated private scholar named Samuel Sugenheim who lived in Frankfurt-am-Main. His groundbreaking book, which received a prize from the Imperial Russian Academy, devoted successive sections to accounts of the emancipation of the peasants in Spain and Portugal, France, Italy, Great Britain, Ireland, Germany, Scandinavia, Switzerland, and the Low Countries. Each section reached far back in time, in some cases to the origins of servility, in each of these lands. The immense learning, the detailed and careful research, and the wealth of data that distinguish the book have given it a long and useful life, so useful, indeed, that is was reprinted in Germany in 1966. From the 1880's to the early 1900's students and former students of the seminar conducted by Georg Friedrich Knapp at the University of Strassburg published a series of monographs on rural conditions and on the emancipations in a number of German lands and in a few neighboring states. Professor Knapp himself wrote what has long been the standard text on the peasant emancipation in Prussia. The works of his students are valuable, but, with one exception, are not of the same quality (nor length) as the book of their master. The one exception was Carl Grünberg's study of the emancipation in Bohemia, Moravia, and Silesia, a classic that rivals Knapp's work, on which it was closely modeled. The studies of Knapp and his school, reflecting the interests of the time, viewed the emancipations from the standpoint of government policy. They concentrated on the legal and administrative aspects of the movement that prepared the way for the emancipation of the peasantry, and that finally liberated them from their servility. It is as if they were always looking down from the elevated position of the central government upon the institutions of agrarian life. They neglected or overlooked demographic, economic, technological, and social changes, and the impact of these changes upon the relationships between lord and peasant, and upon the positions lord and peasant occupied in their societies.

The Knapp school was given the opportunity to present a much more complete coverage of the emancipation movement in the third edition of the *Handwörterbuch der Staatswissenschaften*, published in 1909-1911. The editors of this great encyclopedia, one of the monuments of imperial German scholarship, commissioned outstanding scholars to write lengthy essays on the liberation of the peasantry, and that meant men who had studied with Knapp or been influenced by his work. Knapp himself wrote the piece on the eastern provinces of Prussia; Carl Grünberg was the author of the articles on Austria, Hungary, and Romania; Carl J. Fuchs did the essays on the emancipations in a number of lesser German states; W. G. Simkhowitsch contributed the articles on Russia, and on the Baltic provinces; and so on. In addition to these lands there were long articles on Denmark, the Low Countries, Norway, Sweden, Great Britain, France—and Japan. Together, the essays, all under the heading of *Bauernbefreiung*, and their inclusive bibliographies, took up eighty-six double-columned pages of small type. Published separately, they would have formed a sizable book.

The next venture at a comprehensive history of the emancipation appeared in 1921. That was when Henri Sée published a volume he called *Esquisse d'un histoire du régime agraire en Europe aux xviiᵉ et xixᵉ siècles.* He explained that his purpose was to trace the essential features of a comparative history of the agrarian regimes, and of the condition of the rural population of Europe in the eighteenth and nineteenth centuries. In the first, and longest, part of the book he devoted individual chapters to rural conditions in France, southwest Germany, northwest Germany, England, Ireland, Electoral Saxony and Prussia, the Baltic lands, Austria and Russia. The second part recounts the history of the emancipations in Savoy, France, Germany, the Baltic lands, Austria, and Russia. It is a thin book, well below the quality of other works that came from the pen of the prolific M. Sée. He provided skimpy treatments of most of the countries he discussed, he omitted much, and he did not avail himself of important monographic materials.

The present study views the process of agrarian change and of emancipation as a European experience. National boundaries serve only to identify aspects of a shared historical transformation that lasted for over a century. The book presents a synoptic reconstruction of that transformation, rather than a comparative study of country after country; it proposes to construct what Arthur Spiethoff called a real type, that is "a totality pattern that is as close as possible a representation of some historical reality."[7] This method of presentation rests upon the conviction that the social structure of the lands dealt with in this book followed a common pattern of transition from the traditional order to the modern class society. The method of presentation rests, too, upon the conviction that, at any given time, these lands were at different stages of what was essentially the same course of social and economic development. That conviction, in turn, allows a release from the constraints imposed by the conventions of chronology, so that similar events in two or more lands, though separated in time by decades, can be employed to illustrate or document a stage in the process of the transition from the old order to the modern world.

[7] Lane and Riemersma (1953), 441.

Part One
The Traditional Order

CHAPTER 1
The Seigniors

I

A thin and privileged stratum formed the uppermost layer of the social order of servile Europe. It was made up of the people who owned the land. They were the seigniors, the lords. Most of the seigniors, and in some of the servile lands just about all of them, belonged to the order of the nobility. That meant that they were members of an hereditary caste, composed of families who enjoyed rights and privileges denied to the other members of their societies.

Among English-speaking peoples, the understanding of the rank of nobility is nearly always based upon the example of the English peerage. Actually, the English concept of nobility was peculiar to that land, and differed significantly from the concept that prevailed in the servile lands. Indeed, in the continental sense, England had no nobility. For, unlike the servile lands, in England the nobility did not form a legally defined order with specific prerogatives guaranteed by law and tradition in such matters as taxation, ownership of land, monopolies, judicial authority, and other attributes (all discussed in later pages) that were possessed by the nobility of the servile lands. Aside from the right to sit in the House of Lords, the privileges of the English nobility were, as the opening sentence of the Introduction to the earliest volumes of Burke's *Peerage* put it, "very unimportant, and minister much more to the pomp than the power of the possessor." They included the right to be tried by their peers when indicted for high treason or a felony, exemption from jury service, personal access to the sovereign, the right to appoint chaplains, and the ancient (but no longer exercised) privilege that allowed lords, when passing through the King's forests to or from a session of Parliament, to kill one or two of the King's deer "in view of the forester if he be present, or on blowing a horn, if he be absent, that he may not seem to take the King's venison by stealth."[1]

In the servile lands, all descendants of a nobleman, or at least all descendants in the male line, were themselves noble, and children of titled families bore their parents' title while their parents were still alive. In England only the eldest in the male line inherited nobility. All other family members were commoners, though they were accorded so-called courtesy titles. That was why the English nobility was so small. At the end of the eighteenth century there were fewer than two hundred peers. In England every nobleman had a title, whether duke, marquis, earl, viscount, or

---

[1] Palmer (1907), 144-152.

baron. On the continent the majority of the nobility, including many of the greatest families, had no title, nor did they need them. Their special privileges sufficed to mark them off from the rest of their societies. In Germany and in France nobles did add a "von" or "zu," or "de" to their surnames, and some in France adopted the title of marquis, or count, or baron.[2]

There was no difference, however, in the self-image harbored by the nobility of England and of the continent. They thought of themselves as special beings, possessed of qualities that merited the respect and the deference of the lesser mortals among whom they lived. A consciousness of their superiority never deserted them; pride was to them a virtue. To guarantee that their superiority would always be acknowledged, they created a code of behavior that distinguished them from those beneath them in the social pyramid.

The lesser orders, for their part, did indeed acknowledge the nobility's claim to superiority, admired the demeanor and the way of life of the nobility, and accepted their own inferiority. Goethe's Wilhelm Meister spoke for his age when in a letter to his brother Werner he wrote: "I know not how it is in foreign countries, but in Germany, a universal, and, if I may say so, personal cultivation is beyond the reach of anyone except a nobleman. A burgher may acquire merit; by excessive efforts he may even educate his mind; but his personal qualities are lost, or worse than lost, let him struggle as he will. . . . A certain stately grace in common things, a sort of gay elegance in earnest and important ones, becomes [the nobleman] well; for it shows him to be everywhere in equilibrium. He is a public person; and the more cultivated his movements, the more sonorous his voice, the more staid and measured his whole being is, the more perfect is he. . . . [W]hatever else there may be in him or about him, capacities, talents, wealth, all seem gifts or superrogation."[3]

Wilhelm Meister could have learned from his real-life near-contemporary Adam Smith, that it was the same in other lands as it was in Germany. Smith, in his *Theory of Moral Sentiments*, first published in 1759, asked by what important accomplishments did the nobleman "render himself worthy of that superiority over his fellow citizens, to which the virtue of his ancestors had raised him?" He answered his own question by explaining that it was not by knowledge, industry, patience, self-denial, or by personal merit of any kind. Rather the nobleman "learns an habitual regard to every circumstance of ordinary behavior, and studies to perform all those small duties with the most exact propriety. . . . His air, his manner, his deportment, all mark that elegant and graceful sense of his own superiority, which those who are born to inferior status can hardly ever

[2] Bluche (1973), 13.
[3] Goethe (1901), ii, 13 (Book v, ch. iii).

arrive at: these are the arts by which he proposes to make mankind more easily submit to his authority, and to govern their inclinations according to his own pleasure: and in this he is seldom disappointed."[4]

Neither Goethe nor Smith, both of bourgeois origins, were content with society's arbitrary assignment of superiority to the nobleman. Goethe, however (or at least his fictional hero Wilhelm Meister), seemed resigned to it, suggesting that it was due neither to the encroachments of the nobility nor to the submissiveness of the burghers, but to the constitution of society itself. In contrast, Smith bristled with resentment, even though he, too, seemed to place the responsibility upon the nature of society. "This disposition to admire, and almost to worship, the rich and the powerful," he wrote, "and to despise, or at least, to neglect, persons of poor and mean condition, though necessary both to establish and to maintain the distinction of ranks and the order of society, is, at the same time, the great and the most universal cause of the corruption of our moral sentiments."[5]

In the everyday life of the traditional society there were constant symbolic reminders of the superior status of the nobility. Nobles took precedence at all gatherings. They sat in the places of honor at church services, they received communion before the rest of the congregation, and in France (and doubtless in other lands) they prescribed the time for mass in the village church, and the priest waited for their arrival before he began the service. At the theater they sat in boxes—a method of segregation that originated in Paris—or in the front seats. At concerts in Germany a space separated the quality from the common people; at court concerts great nobles were surrounded by a sea of empty chairs whose number was in direct proportion to the eminence of the grandee. In the German universities the nobles sat on separate benches, and in the few schools in which nobles and commoners were fellow students, the nobles ate, slept, and bathed apart from their schoolmates. At dances and garden parties a rope separated the nobility from the burghers; that custom continued on at small German courts into the nineteenth century, and persisted in Bavaria until shortly before the outbreak of World War I.[6] Only nobles could have coats of arms, only they could carry a sword, and only they could decorate their hats with plumes, clothe their servants in livery, use special seals, and a host of other such external evidences of their status. To the considerable annoyance of noblemen, commoners sometimes adopted these signs of nobility, thereby giving rise to many a duel between a noble angered by these pretensions and the offending commoner. People of the lesser orders used respectful forms of address when they spoke to a nobleman, with appropriate gradations scaled to the rank of the nobleman. In some of the eastern lands peas-

[4] Smith (1969), 75 (part i, sect. iii, ch. ii).
[5] *Ibid.*, 84 (part i, sect. iii, ch. iii).
[6] Bruford (1935), 57-58; Bramsted (1964), 154.

ants kissed the hand of the seignior, and took off their hats and bowed to the ground when they accosted a lord (or even when a carriage that they presumed carried a nobleman drove by, as William Coxe discovered when he visited Poland).[7]

Symbols of his status distinguished the nobleman even when he ran afoul of the law. Men of other orders could be sentenced to be whipped or pilloried, but, to quote Adam Smith again, "To scourge a person of quality, or to set him in the pillory, upon account of any crime whatever, is a brutality of which no European government, except that of Russia, is capable."[8] Three years after Smith's book appeared, even Russia exempted its nobility from corporal punishment. And as the last respect paid to the honor that the nobility prized so highly, a noble condemned to death was beheaded rather than hanged, and was thereby spared the indignity of being executed in the same manner as a commoner.

The symbolic expressions of superiority did not cease at the line between nobles and commoners. There were recognized strata within the order of the nobility itself, each with its special marks of distinction and its proper form of address. Sometimes these status symbols bordered on the ridiculous or the comic, such as the sole right of French duchesses to carry parasols in the Corpus Christi procession, or the sole right of Wallachian boiars of the first rank to wear full beards, or the rule that at masked balls at the court of the Hapsburgs only the higher nobility could remain masked, while all others had to unmask upon arrival.

The high status and the abundant privileges of the nobility had been justified originally by their role as the protectors of the other members of the society from internal and external dangers. By the last century of the old order, that justification no longer had the pertinence it once possessed. Yet the aura remained. A pattern had established itself that satisfied what someone has called the hunger for hierarchy in human breasts. Adam Smith explained this widespread human failing with his customary elegance of language and keeness of perception. "When we consider the condition of the great," he wrote, "in those delusive colors in which the imagination is apt to paint it, it seems to be almost the abstract idea of a perfect and happy state. It is the very state which, in all our waking dreams and idle reveries, we had sketched out to ourselves as the final object of all our desires. We feel, therefore, a peculiar sympathy with the satisfaction of those who are in it. . . . Upon this disposition of mankind to go along with all the passions of the rich and the powerful, is founded the distinction of ranks and the order of society. Our obsequiousness to our superiors more frequently arises from our admiration for the advantages of their situation, than from any expectation of benefit from their good will. Their benefits

---

[7] Bruford (1935), 54; Coxe (1802), I, 347.
[8] Smith (1969), 82 (part I, sect. III, ch. II).

can extend but to a few; but their fortunes interest almost everybody. We are eager to assist them in completing a system of happiness that approaches so near to perfection; and we desire to serve them for their own sake, without any other recompense but the vanity or the honor of obeying them."[9]

Their societies still presumed that in return for their status and privileges the nobles would make certain contributions to the common weal. As a document presented to the Estates held at Orleans in 1560 explained, the privileges granted to the nobility were given them "not only to serve to repulse and attack enemies, but also to help and sustain the other orders and to keep them in peace and quiet under the authority of the king."[10] In eighteenth-century Prussia and Russia, legislation spelled out the responsibility of the nobility to society. "It is incumbent upon the nobility," said the Prussian law code of 1794, "as the first order in the state, and by the nature of its calling, to defend the state, as well as to support its external dignity and its internal organic law." In Russia, Peter I in 1722 had made nobility itself dependent upon service in the armed forces or in the bureaucracy. The requirement to serve was abolished forty years later, but, as the Charter of the Nobility, granted by Empress Catherine II in 1785, explained, the nobleman was expected when called upon "to spare neither effort, nor life itself, in the service of the state."[11]

Many noblemen took the responsibility assigned to them with great seriousness and devoted themselves to public careers. In every land they filled the higher ranks of the military and the bureaucracy, and often many of the lesser posts. Certainly the desire for personal glory, the glamour of life at court, and the power and sometimes the wealth that came with high office, had much to do with their decision to devote themselves to military or civil service. Nonetheless, dedication to their duties and concern for the welfare of their societies were common among them. Many other nobles, however, and indeed, the greatest majority of them in every land, showed neither interest in, nor aptitude for, the military and bureaucratic roles assigned to their order. Yet they continued to enjoy all the prerogatives of the noble estate.

Though pride of family lay at the heart of the hereditary nobility, few could boast of long-distinguished lineage whose first ennoblement lay far in the past. Most noble families were of recent creation. The number of nobles in France is estimated to have doubled between 1715 and 1789, while population increased by about 15 per cent. Prussia experienced a large inflation of honors in the latter half of the eighteenth and first part of the nineteenth century. In Russia, where Peter I had established a Table of Ranks in 1722

---

[9] *Ibid.*, 72-74.
[10] Chérin (1788), pt. 2, 40.
[11] *Allgemeines Landrecht* (1970), part II, title 9, art. 1; *Polnoe sobranie zakonov*, 1st series, XXII, 348, art. 20.

that gave nobility to those who rose to a specified grade in the armed forces or in the civil bureaucracy, there was a steady accretion to the nobility. Just between 1825 and 1845 some 20,000 men became hereditary nobles through promotions in the imperial service. In the Danubian Principalities only a very few of the noble families could trace their origins farther back than the early years of the eighteenth century. Many, and quite possibly the majority, of the noble families of the Austrian Monarchy were established in the course of the seventeenth and eighteenth centuries. After the conquest of Bohemia in 1620 a new Catholic nobility replaced the Protestant lords there. The many wars and the territorial expansion of the Hapsburg empire, and the administrative reorganizations, created a need for officers and bureaucrats who were often rewarded for their labors by patents of nobility. Many of the new Hapsburg nobles came from other lands and were already nobles. They were drawn to the service of the Hapsburgs by opportunities for fame and fortune that were lacking in their homelands. Of the 37 men appointed to the rank of field marshal during the Thirty Years' War, 34 were foreigners. Of the 157 men who served as field marshals in the Austrian army during the eighteenth century, only 16 had been born in the Monarchy. In Denmark, too, there was an influx of foreign nobles after the coup of 1665, which established royal absolutism there. The sovereigns apparently were uncertain of the complete loyalty of the native nobility, and the native nobility for its part was reluctant to serve the throne that had so severely reduced the nobles' power in the management of the state.[12]

The progenitors of many recently established noble families had purchased their nobility. The sale of patents of nobility, or of posts in the government that carried with it membership in the order of the nobility, had been a common practice of money-hungry sovereigns, especially but far from exclusively in France. A contemporary estimated that by the end of the *ancien régime* in France as many as 150 persons a year became nobles by purchasing public offices. During the reign of Emperor Joseph II of Austria (1780-1790) there was practically a fixed scale of prices for titles. It cost about 20,000 gulden to be named a count, 6,000 to gain the title of baron, and 386 to become an untitled nobleman.[13] The families of older creation considered themselves the social superiors of those of more recent vintage. However, it did not take long to overcome the handicap of new arrival in the ranks of the nobility; in France as few as three generations, from grandfather to grandson, sufficed for a family to be counted among the *ancienne noblesse*.[14]

[12] France, Gruder (1968), 177-178; Prussia, Martiny (1938), 75-80; Russia, Korelin (1971), 60; Danubian Principalities, Wilkinson (1971), 56-57; Austrian Monarchy, Siegert (1971), 31-32; Denmark, Andrews (1774), 125-140.

[13] Goodwin (1965), 359; Bruford (1935), 61.

[14] Gruder (1968), 118.

In the principal cantons of Switzerland, urban patriciates, made up of the leading burgher families, occupied the role filled by the nobility elsewhere in Europe. These patriciates, whose rise began in the fifteenth century, actually became more powerful and more exclusive than the nobilities of other lands. They ruled over both city and country by occupying most or all of the seats in the Great Councils, in which resided the sovereign power of the cantons. They were also the leading officeholders, merchants, manufacturers, and military commanders in their respective cantons. As for their exclusivity, they closed their ranks against the entry of new families. In Bern families that died out were not replaced, so that over the years the size of patriciate dwindled. Around 1700 the Bernese patriciate included 452 families; by 1787 that number had fallen to 243. Moreover, a much smaller inner circle of families held all of the 299 seats on the Great Council of Bern. Some of these families had 10 to 16 of their members on the Council. In Fribourg, in the last years of the eighteenth century, 71 families monopolized all of the income-producing offices in the cantonal government. In Solothurn the patriciate in 1682 declared itself closed to new additions. In 1550 in that canton 70 families were represented among 89 members of the Great Council; by 1778 members of just 12 families held 136 seats. In Lucerne the number of families privileged to hold office was set "once and for all" in 1798 at 29. In Zurich in 1798 half of the seats on the Great Council were held by members of 13 families. In Basel two-thirds of the seats in the Great Council and two-thirds of the offices in the cantonal government were occupied by members of the families of the patriciate.[15]

II

The high status accorded members of the nobility was the symbolic recognition by society of their superiority. There were also material privileges that attached themselves to the noble condition. Among these privileges the most important concerned land and taxes.

In agricultural societies land is the single most important commodity and those who control it dominate the society. That was why the right to own rural land was often limited by law to the state, the church, and the nobility, and in some sovereignties to cities as corporate entities and to institutions such as universities or charitable foundations. And just as these restrictions on the ownership of land mirrored the traditional order's hierarchy of privilege, so too did the emergence in the last decades of the old order of burghers and even of peasants as landowners in those states where that had been prohibited give evidence of the disintegration of the *ancien régime*. In the kingdom of Prussia the law forbade commoners to own noble estates, that is, properties to which adhered uniquely noble

[15] Gitermann (1941), 241-246; Coxe (1789), I, 224-226, 248-250, II, 171-178, 221-226.

privileges that included exemption from land taxes and the right to a seat in the provincial estates. In the last third of the eighteenth century, however, a lively trade developed in these properties, in the course of which commoners acquired noble manors. Sometimes they evaded the law by using a noble as a strawman between seller and buyer, or they disguised the purchase by calling it a lease, and sometimes they openly bought the property in their own name. By 1800 commoners owned 13 per cent of all the noble estates in Brandenburg and between 4 and 10 per cent of the noble properties in Pomerania. A survey conducted between 1783 and 1795 in Silesia found that 1,200 to 1,300 noble families and about 250 bourgeois families owned manors there. Bourgeois landowners did not penetrate into every province of the kingdom. In East Prussia at the end of the eighteenth century, out of some 10 million *morgen* in productive use, the state owned 65 per cent, the nobility around 30 per cent, and cities 5 per cent. The state rented out two-thirds of its great holdings to peasants, and another 25 per cent was held by free peasants who were called proprietors but whose land was included in the rubric of state lands.[16] Often, manors that belonged to the crown, noblemen, and cities were rented to burghers. Some of these lessees took over large complexes, especially those belonging to the state, for which they paid large rents. In addition, the renter of crown land had to post a security, usually of 25 per cent or more of the annual rent. Only men of considerable means could assume these costs, and, indeed, the wealth of the bourgeois lessees of royal domain became proverbial among contemporaries. Some of them used the money they made to buy land from nobles and even from the crown, and a few of them gained admission to the nobility.[17]

In Denmark crown and nobility shared the monopoly on land ownership until 1660. Then a monarchical *coup d'état*, supported by the clegy and the burghers, transformed the king into a hereditary and absolute ruler and reduced the power of the nobility. Commoners were now allowed to own rural property. In the years that followed, the crown sold much of its land to raise money. In 1660 the holdings of the crown had covered an estimated 50 per cent of the kingdom. By the second half of the eighteenth century the state owned only 20 per cent of the Danish land, nobles owned 60 per cent, and commoners 20 per cent.[18]

In the German and Slav provinces of the Hapsburg Monarchy, restrictions on the right to own manors broke down in the course of the eighteenth century. In Bohemia, for example, in 1802 nobles owned 640 estates and non-nobles 168 (another 111 properties belonged to cities). In Hungary

[16] Martiny (1938), 34-36, 114; Eggert (1965), 15n.; Ziekursch (1927), 47-48; Stein (1918), I, 291-292. The Prussian *morgen* was equal to .2553 hectares or .631 acres.
[17] Müller (1965), 171-179, 185-192.
[18] Nielsen (1933), 175; Jensen (1937), 41.

the nobility had greater success in preserving its special right, which dated back to 1514, to own rural land. In the 1780's, of the 9,921 inhabited places, nobles owned 86.5 per cent, the church 12 per cent, royal free cities a bit more than 1 per cent, and free peasants about .4 per cent. The restrictions on landownership continued until 1844, when new legislation allowed commoners to own rural property.[19]

The right of the Russian nobility to own land to the exclusion of non-nobles, granted in the seventeenth century, had not been complete. Then, beginning in the 1730's, a series of decrees deprived non-nobles of the right to own rural real property and serfs, and by 1762 nobles were in sole possession of this privilege. Their monopoly lasted until 1801. That was when Tsar Alexander I decreed that any of his subjects except serfs could own land on which no serfs lived. Only nobles could own serf-populated land. Serfs could acquire land in the name of their masters until 1841. Then a new law allowed them to own unpopulated land in their own names if their masters gave approval. These laws made only a minor dent in the landowning monopoly of the nobility. In 1858 over one-half of the 1.9 million square miles of European Russia belonged to private landowners, nearly all of them noblemen. The rest belonged to the state.[20]

In Livonia the restriction of landowning to the nobility was of recent origin. It had been introduced by Russia when in 1710 that power had supplanted Sweden as ruler of Livonia. To win and hold the allegiance of the Livonian nobility, the Russian conquerors gave back to the Livonian seigniors the land that the Swedish crown had taken from them in the so-called "reductions" of the last part of the seventeenth century. In 1687 the Swedish crown had owned six times as much land in Livonia as had the nobles. By 1758 the nobles owned five times as much land as did their new sovereign. Most Livonian nobles held their land as fiefs from the tsar, could not alienate them without imperial approval, and could lose their manor if the crown decided to dispossess the holder of the fief. These disabilities were terminated when on 3 May 1783 Empress Catherine II decreed that all her Livonian fiefs were henceforth the alodial properties of their occupants. However, the efforts to establish and preserve a monopoly on landownership for the Livonian nobility proved unsuccessful. Many proprietors there had been impoverished by the Great Northern War, which had raged through their land in the first two decades of the eighteenth century. Hard up for cash, they mortgaged their land with the only capital-owning people in the region, the merchants of Riga. When, as often happened, the borrower could not meet his payments, the merchant lender took possession of the estate. The legal fiction of noble proprietorship was preserved by the

[19] Grünberg (1894), I, 39n.; Kübeck (1909), I, pt. 1, 88; Feigl (1964), 51-52; Richter (1964), 60; Revesz (1964), 10; Demian (1809), II, 284.
[20] Zaionchkovskii (1968), 25; Blum (1961), 358-362.

new owner's describing himself as the holder of the mortgage, rather than the hereditary lord of the manor.[21]

In Poland laws of 1496, 1538, and 1611 had forbidden the ownership of land by commoners, and the restriction persisted until almost the end of Poland's existence as an independent state. At the time of the first partition in 1772 the nobility owned 78 per cent of the land, the crown 13 per cent, and the church 9 per cent. The Constitution of 1791, adopted in the desperate effort of patriots to save their state from disintegration, along with other reforms gave burghers the right to own rural property. Four years later Austria, Russia, and Prussia swallowed what was left of Poland and applied their own laws to the territories they annexed.[22]

In the mid-nineteenth century over three-quarters of the Danubian Principalities was owned by nobles and by monasteries. Most of this land belonged to nobles, though the monasteries, all of them of the Greek Orthodox persuasion, were great proprietors in their own right (they owned an estimated one-quarter of Moldavia and one-third of Wallachia). The rest of the land was the property of the state, institutions, communities, and free peasant proprietors. The state owned a relatively small amount until just before the end of the servile order in the Principalities, when late in 1863 it secularized the monastic lands and took them over for its own uses.[23]

In much of France, in the plateauland of Switzerland, in Savoy, and in much of western Germany the feudal principle of *nulle terre sans seigneur* had managed to survive, apparently largely through the artifices of lawyers and the acquiescence of the government. That meant that the seignior had the legal ownership—or the *dominium directum*, as the lawyers called it—of the land within his fief or seigniory. Those peasants who held land in the seigniory by hereditary tenure had most of the rights of ownership. In popular speech, in government reports, and even in legal texts they were called proprietors. Actually they owned only the right to use the land, the *dominium utile*. In recognition of the superior ownership of the seignior, the occupant of the land owed certain obligations to the lord and stood in a servile relationship to him. The land over which the seignior had both *dominium directum* and *dominium utile*, called in France his *domaine* or *réserve*, was distinct from his seigniory. Some seigniors had no *domaine*, nor were all seigniors noblemen. In France on the eve of the Revolution noble *domaine* took up about one-fifth of all the cultivated land in the kingdom. The church owned 10 per cent, members of the bourgeoisie 30 per cent, and 35 per cent was in the hands of those peasants who had the *dominium utile* of the land they occupied. These country-wide estimates concealed wide variations among the different parts of the realm. Depend-

21 Schwabe (1928), 257; Transehe-Roseneck (1890), 132-133, 172-173.
22 Maçzak (1967), 119-121; Leskiewicz (1965), 239, 243.
23 Georgescu-Buzău (1965), 17; Riker (1931), 354; Emerit (1937) 238.

ing upon the region, noble *domaine* took up from 9 to 44 per cent of the land, the clergy had from 1 to 20 per cent, the bourgeoisie from 12 to 45 per cent, and the peasants from 22 to 70 per cent.[24]

In Savoy, where until 1771 the law forbade the ownership of rural property by burghers, and in western Germany, the seignior was usually a nobleman, though sometimes the church or the sovereign was the chief proprietor. In Bavaria the Catholic church in 1760 owned 56 per cent of the 29,807 peasant holdings there, the nobility owned 24 per cent, and the sovereign 13 per cent. In some of the smaller principalities, such as Baden or Hohenlohe, the ruler owned nearly all of the land. In most of the cantons of Switzerland, the nobility had long since faded into insignificance. It had been dispossessed of most of its property by the sovereign cities in the late Middle Ages. Only in Vaud, the southwestern corner of the country, annexed by Bern from Savoy in 1536, did the nobility still form a distinct order, albeit with neither power nor wealth and usually saddled with heavy debts. The cities, charitable foundations, the Catholic church, and prosperous burghers owned seigniorial rights over much of the Vaudois countryside.[25]

Certain privileges attached themselves to the ownership of property recognized as noble land. One of the most valuable of these privileges concerned taxation. In Hungary, the Danubian Principalities, Livonia, Poland, Electoral Saxony, much of the kingdom of Prussia, Lower Saxony, and Denmark, the state levied no taxes on land registered in the rolls as noble land. Taxes were imposed on land registered as peasant land, and seigniors had to pay the tax if they dispossessed the peasant occupant and added the land to their demesne. Conversely, land registered as noble land remained tax-free regardless of the social order to which its subsequent proprietors belonged. In short, the privilege of exemption from taxation adhered to the land rather than to the person of its proprietor. In some of the servile lands, however, special fiscal immunities adhered to the person of the nobleman, so that he did not have to pay taxes demanded of members of other orders. In Hungary nobles paid no taxes, tolls, tariffs, or tithes. Their immunity from all levies was one of the three cardinal privileges granted to the Magyar nobility by the Golden Bull of King Andreas II in 1222. In the other servile lands exemptions were not as complete. They often included freedom from tariffs and tolls but not from other levies.[26]

[24] Ashley (1913), 175; Lütge (1957), 89-90; Meier (1908), II, 117-118; Soboul (1958), 57-58; Soboul (1960), 105.

[25] Savoy, Darmstaedter (1897), 51; Germany, Wittich (1896), 192-193, Carsten (1959), 352, Liebel (1965), 42, Schremmer (1963), 5; Switzerland, Rappard (1912), 153, 201; Chevallez (1949), 200.

[26] Hungary, Király (1969), 70; Danubian Principalities, Haufe (1939), 81; Livonia, Tobien (1899), I, 4; Poland, Warszawski (1914), 55-56; Electoral Saxony, Blaschke (1955), 100-102; Prussia, Korth (1953), 151n., Martiny (1938), 10; Goldschmidt (1910), 27; Lower Saxony, Meyer (1965), 21, Wittich (1896), 4-5, 186-187; Denmark, Andrews (1774), II, 426-429, 434-435.

In southern and western Germany and in the German and Slav crown-lands of the Austrian Monarchy, rulers had managed to impose taxes on land that belonged to nobles and to the church. The tax rate, however, was nearly always much lower than that charged for peasant land. In seventeenth-century Bohemia, for example, the rate on noble land was about one-seventh of that levied on peasant land. It was increased in the next century but was still considerably less than that paid by peasants. At that, noble proprietors in Bohemia and the other provinces of the Austrian Monarchy evaded some of the tax they should have paid. The land registers of the seventeenth and eighteenth centuries, which provided the basis for assessments until well into the nineteenth century, were based upon statements provided by the noble proprietors themselves, and apparently many of them did not report the full extent of their holdings.[27]

In France, too, the government succeeded in clipping some of the fiscal immunities of the nobility. Nobles normally did not have to pay the *taille*, the direct tax that everyone else had to pay. If, however, they used hired labor to farm above a certain amount of land on their own account—the amount varied among the different parts of France—they were subject to the *taille*. In that part of the kingdom in which the *taille* was levied only on land, the so-called *pays de taille réele* (in the rest of France the tax was levied on all property), the nobles had to pay the *taille* on non-noble land that they used. They also had to pay the poll tax from 1659 on, and from 1750 a tax on income. This latter impost, called the *vingtième* because it was originally intended to be a levy of one-twentieth, or 5 per cent, on net income, was later increased to 10 and then to 15 per cent. It fell almost entirely on land, since this was the one source of income that could be assessed with some approximation to accuracy. The government had intended for these taxes to bear with equal weight upon nobles and commoners, but in the regime of privilege that was old France the nobles easily contrived to avoid paying their fair share. The church paid no taxes and even the private property of churchmen was exempted. Since the mid-sixteenth century, however, the church periodically made a *don gratuit*, a "free gift," to the state. In the eighteenth century the church made this payment every five years. The "gift" averaged out to about 3.6 millions livres a year.[28]

The Charter of the Nobility granted by Catherine II in 1785 had formally exempted the Russian nobility from direct taxes. A few years later Tsar Paul (1796-1801) imposed a tax on the nobility that his son and successor Alexander I quickly repealed. In 1799 the government required nobles to pay duties on exports of grain and on certain imported luxury wares. In 1812 a progressive tax on income from landed property was introduced.

[27] Lütge (1967), 174; Carsten (1959), 419; Revesz (1964), 251; Feigl (1964), 52n., 100-102; Rosdolski (1961), 11.
[28] Soboul (1960), I, 62-64; Marion (1968), 186-187, 556-559; Behrens (1963), 458-464.

The rate was low and the proprietor himself made the assessment of his property for the purpose of the tax. Nonetheless, the levy aroused the hostility of the nobility, who regarded it as a serious violation of their rights, and it was repealed in 1828.[29]

The rulers of the small duchy of Savoy probably came the closest to ending the fiscal immunities of church and nobility. After the completion of a cadastre drawn up between 1728 and 1738, the then duke ordered the nobility to pay taxes on their land except that part which they could prove had belonged to their ancestors before 1584. In 1783 another ducal order required the church to pay taxes on two-thirds of the land that it had owned before 1584.[30]

Complete or partial exemption from taxation was not an exclusive privilege of the nobility. In France thousands of commoners who held state offices (which often they had purchased precisely for this reason) did not have to pay the *taille*. In many parts of the servile lands, elected or appointed officials of village communities did not pay taxes while occupying their offices, and often parish priests were also exempted. In most cases the number of tax-exempt non-nobles and the total extent of their property must have been trivial compared to the area of noble-owned land that went untaxed. Sometimes, though, the exemption of non-nobles assumed significant proportions. In upper Hungary the holdings of the tax-exempt parish priests often equalled four or five peasant holdings of average size. That could mean that as much as one-tenth or even more of the peasant land in a village did not pay taxes. It also meant that the villagers had to pay a larger tax on their land to make up for the tax that the priest did not pay. In the Danubian Principalities, employees of the state and a number of other groups, including certain categories of peasants, were exempted from taxes. An estimate made in 1844 reported that there were 2.6 million tax-payers in the Principalities and 757,000 others who were exempt.[31]

Despite these fiscal immunities, noblemen became involved in the tax system. During the seventeenth and eighteenth centuries the government in Denmark, Poland, Russia, the Austrian Monarchy, and in many parts of eastern Germany made the seigniors responsible for the collection and the guarantee of taxes levied by the state on their peasants. That meant that the lord had to pay the tax if he could not squeeze it out of his peasants. In light of the tax arrears that piled up in Russia, it would appear that at least the Russian government did not press the seigniors to pay up for their delinquent serfs. Moreover, some seigniors or their agents in Poland and in Austria (and probably in other lands, too) profited from their fiscal respon-

[29] Florinsky (1953), 699; Blum (1961), 464.
[30] Bruchet (1908), xiii.
[31] Marion (1968), 528-529; Revesz (1964), 301; Blum (1971b), 559; Goldschmidt (1910), 25; Emerit (1937), 280-281; cf. Raeff (1966), 175, n. 10.

sibilities by levying more than the state asked for and pocketing the surplus, or used it to pay taxes on peasant land which they had added to their demesnes.[32]

III

Privileges are of little moment unless they are restricted to a minority of the body politic; their value is in inverse proportion to the numbers who are privileged. The members of the noble order formed a small fraction of the population of their respective countries, ranging from as little as 1 per cent in European Russia (including the Baltic, White Russia, and Lithuanian provinces) in 1858, about 1.5 per cent in France before the Revolution, about 4 per cent in Hungary in the 1820's, to around 8 per cent in Poland before the first partition of that state in 1772.[33] This small sector of the population was subdivided into many strata of wealth, of status, and of power. The uppermost layer, which formed a miniscule portion of the entire nobility, controlled a huge share of the wealth and power. The wealthiest and the most powerful of these grandees lived in central and western Europe. In Poland 40 to 50 families owned enormous stretches of land and had vast incomes. In the later years of the eighteenth century Prince Charles Radziwill had an annual income of five million Polish florins and maintained a private army that in 1764 had 6,000 men in it. Count Felix Potocki's properties covered 17,000 square kilometers, an area equal to over half the size of the Netherlands. His annual income amounted to three million Polish florins. He maintained a court with 400 people in it—more than were at the court of Poland's elected king. In 1770 Prince Stanislaus Lubomirski owned 25,000 square kilometers (an area four-fifths as large as Belgium) on which there were 31 cities and 728 villages.[34] In the last decades of the eighteenth century an estimated one-third of all the land in the Austrian Monarchy, after Russia the largest state in Europe, belonged to a few hundred families. Their special strongholds were Bohemia and Hungary. In Bohemia in 1788 there were 174 noble families, 15 of them princes, 79 counts, and 96 barons and knights. Data of a few years earlier showed that the princes owned land valued at 465 million florins. The property of the counts added up to 119 million florins, and that of the barons and knights was worth only 17.6 million florins. The manors of the

[32] Andrews (1774), II, 368-369; Revesz (1964), 251; Raeff (1966), 96, 206n.; Blum (1961), 464-465; Feigl (1964), 100-102.

[33] Russia: 609,973 hereditary nobles out of a population of 59.3 million; Tsentral'nyi statisticheskii komitet (1863), 174, 267. France: *ca.* 350,000 out of a population of *ca.* 24-25 million; Soboul (1960), I, 40-41. Other estimates of the number of French nobles are as low as 120,000; Bluche (1973), 12. Hungary: *ca.* 400,000 nobles out of a population of about 10 million; Barany (1968), 149. Poland: over 1 million in a population of 11.4 million; Roos (1971), 42.

[34] *Encyclopédie polonaise* (1920), II, 103; Rutkowski (1926), 499-500.

Schwarzenbergs alone, richest of the princes, were valued at 14.4 million florins. At the time of the emancipation in 1848, the Schwarzenbergs owned 1.6 million acres in Bohemia with 230,000 peasants.[35] In the 1790's in Hungary 40 per cent of the land belonged to 150 or so families. In the 1840's Prince Paul Anton Esterházy, greatest of the Hungarian magnates, had around 700,000 peasants, about 6.5 per cent of Hungary's entire population. Another 6.5 per cent lived on the lands of the next eight wealthiest proprietors. Esterházy's annual income ran from 800,000 to 1.7 million florins. The combined holdings of Esterházy and four others of the wealthiest proprietors, Prince Batthyány, Count Károlyi, Count Széchenyi and Baron von Sina, took up almost 14 per cent of the entire surface of Hungary.[36]

In Russia, where property was measured not by land area but by the number of adult male serfs, 3 per cent of the serfowners in 1858 owned 44 per cent of the serfs. The wealth of some of these proprietors reached staggering proportions. In the mid-nineteenth century Count D. N. Sheremetev owned almost 300,000 serfs of both sexes and over 1.9 million acres of land. Concentration of ownership reached its apogee, however, in the Danubian Principalities. In the first half of the nineteenth century 15 to 20 families owned over one-third of all the land in Moldavia and Wallachia.[37]

At the other end of the scale were thousands of petty nobles whose holdings were often no larger than those of neighboring peasants or who owned no land at all. In Brandenburg a large and growing number of nobles in the last third of the eighteenth century were at or below the poverty line. They had to rely on pensions, welfare payments, and employment provided by the state, and apparently sometimes on begging; at least a law of 1789 forbade army officers to beg. In Farther Pomerania (Pomerania east of the Oder River) there were entire villages of petty nobles whose way of life was the same as that of neighboring villages of peasants.[38] Poland, too, had villages of petty nobles who were distinguishable from peasants only by their pretensions and their ability to read and write. Many poverty-striken nobles took service as domestics in the manor houses and palaces of wealthier nobles. Some lived by begging and brigandage. By the mid-nineteenth century there were in Congress Poland (that part of partitioned Poland under Russian rule) 33,360 petty noble proprietors, compared with 7,204 middle and large landowners. These small proprietors owned on the average 21 *morgi* (29 acres) or about enough land to support a peasant household.[39] In

---

[35] Kerner (1932), 70-71; Stölzl (1971), 35.

[36] Revesz (1964), 10, 13; Marczali (1910), 112-113; Katus (1961), 140; Blum (1948), 36.

[37] Shchepetov (1947), 20-21, 26; Troinitskii (1861), 67; Emerit (1937), 240.

[38] Martiny (1938), 67-71; Goldschmidt (1910), 62.

[39] Zajaczkowski (1963), 90-91; Rutkowski (1926), 498; Leslie (1956), 14; Kostiushko (1954), 208. The *morga* equalled 1.38 acres or .56 hectares.

Hungary thousands of nobles, forming the largest single segment of the nobility, lived like peasants. They were sometimes called sandal nobles because, unable to afford boots, they, like the peasants, wore half-shoes strapped over the instep. In principle they had the same privileges as the higher strata of the nobility. In practice they often had to pay taxes, and the landless among them sometimes took over a peasant holding from a prosperous nobleman and paid him all the dues in labor, kind, and cash that a peasant had to pay.[40]

France, too, had its squireens, its *hobereaux*, people like the impoverished noble families who, according to Arthur Young, lived on 50 or even 25 *louis* a year. In Russia there were many thousands of noblemen who lived in straitened circumstances, engaged in an endless struggle to make ends meet. In 1858, 40 per cent of all noble landowners had less than 21 male serfs, the lowest rubric in the official statistics on serfowning. In the Little Russian provinces of Chernigov and Poltava, 65 per cent, and in five other provinces from 48 to 60 per cent, of all serfowners were in this category. In the Danubian Principalities owners of less than 150 hectares were considered petty proprietors. They were found mainly in the hill country, usually had no peasants on their property, lived and dressed like their peasant neighbors, and often were less well-off than prosperous peasants. However, they ardently defended their right to the status and privileges of nobles.[41]

Many of the landowners, whether large, middling or small, had their properties broken into scattered pieces, so that often an individual proprietor did not own an entire village. Instead, the village, with its fields and woods, was divided among several owners. This had resulted from inheritance when the testator split his property among several heirs, from sales when an owner sold part of his property, and in earlier times from the creation of new fiefs by feudal lords. In the Austrian province of Styria, only one tenth of the villages belonged to a single proprietor; the other nine-tenths had multiple owners. In France many large and medium-sized landowners had their *domaine* dispersed through eight or even fourteen to sixteen different parishes. In Russia it was not uncommon for even a small property to have as many as ten to twenty owners. A knowledgeable contemporary wrote in 1776 that most Russian villages belonged to two to seven or more proprietors, and a traveler in the 1840's heard of one village of 260 people that had 83 proprietors.[42]

[40] Király (1969), 34-35; Barany (1968), 154-155; Marczali (1910), 128.
[41] Young (1970), i, 51, 58; Lacroix (1963), 42-43; Carré (1920), 119-131; Troinitskii (1861), 45, 67; Emerit (1937), 248, 250, 386-387.
[42] Bloch (1966), 285-286; Stolz (1936), 168; Louchitsky (1911), 51-54; Confino (1969), 104-105; Haxthausen (1847), ii, 126-127, iii, 59; Chepko (1964), 389; *cf.* Wittich (1896), 6; Ziekursch (1927), 62-63; Skrubbeltrang (1953), 8.

IV

Periodic convocations of assemblies, or estates, or diets, dominated by the nobility, had once been of importance to the governance of the old order. Some of them still met regularly during the last century of the traditional society; others were convened rarely or never. In Savoy the Estates-General met for the last time in 1560. The rulers had established their power so firmly that they no longer needed the support or approval of the assembly. As a French diplomat reported in 1776, the central authority in Savoy was "an arbitrary power without limits and which keeps each order of its subjects in that condition which it judges fit for it to be assigned." In France the Estates-General met last in 1614, and did not assemble again until the very end of the *ancien régime* in that country. Provincial estates met in the eighteenth century in only five provinces, and only in two were they of any significance. Estates had been established in most of the German principalities in the late middle ages, and had enjoyed much influence in the sixteenth century. In many parts of southern Germany, however, noblemen gained the status of free imperial knights and withdrew from the diets, which henceforth were attended only by the representatives of the clergy and of the towns. In other principalities the nobility remained in the assemblies. In the seventeenth and eighteenth centuries the power of these bodies declined. In Bavaria the diet was convoked only three times in the seventeenth century, and did not meet at all during the entire eighteenth century. In other German states the assemblies continued to meet, and although their powers to participate in governing were severely restricted, rulers often consulted with them about proposed legislation. Not infrequently the estates themselves provided the initiative for legislative action, made clear to the prince their opposition to proposed reforms in the lord-peasant relationship, and pointed out the advantages to the state of the status quo.[43]

In the German and Slav crownlands of the Austrian Monarchy the once potent provincial estates had been stripped of nearly all of their authority during the eighteenth century by the centralizing reforms of Empress Maria Theresa and of Joseph II. Nonetheless they continued to meet, and in fact were reconstituted after 1815 in provinces in which they had been abolished during the French occupation of Austrian territories in the Napoleonic era. However, attendance was poor and proceedings routine until the 1840's. Then, in these last years of the old order in the Hapsburg realm, the estates of several provinces became centers of noble agitation and discontent. In Hungary the national Diet and the county assemblies had a major voice in the government of the kingdom. Nobles and repre-

[43] Bruchet (1908), xiv, xv-xvi; Palmer (1959), 41; Carsten (1959), 423-424.

sentatives of the royal free cities sat in the lower house of the Diet, and magnates and prelates in the upper house. The Diet could reject royal proposals of legislation submitted to it, and could originate measures that became law when signed by the monarch. Until 1825 the requirement that the king must convene the Diet at least once every three years had been more often disregarded than observed. Thereafter the Diet met at the designated interval, and up to the end of the old order, and its own demise, in 1848, it provided the vehicle for intense political activity by the Hungarian nobility. The county assemblies, called congregations, were responsible for the administration of all local political and judicial matters. They chose the county officials and the representatives to the lower house of the Diet from their own ranks, and had to give their consent to the decrees of the Diet before they could be applied within the county.[44]

In Poland, noblemen and high churchmen held all of the seats in both houses of the Sejm, the national diet; the towns had been excluded in the sixteenth century. The deputies to the lower house were chosen by the regional assemblies, called dietines, of the local nobility. Each delegate, as the representative of his regional assembly, or more precisely, of the magnate who controlled the assembly, could force the dissolution of the Sejm by merely rising and announcing *sic nolo, sic veto*. Forty-eight of the 55 diets held between 1653 and 1764 were "exploded" by this so-called *liberum veto*. Rivalries and jealousies among great lords and ministers of state, who used the deputies as their pawns, had reduced the Sejm to a political farce. Governmental authority actually rested with the regional assemblies. They had the power to levy taxes, maintain armed forces, and supervise the administration of their regions. In effect, Poland was a confederation of about 50 small noble republics.[45] In Russia, Catherine II's Charter of the Nobility of 1785 had ordered the hereditary nobility of each province and local district to organize itself into assemblies, and had given the assemblies authority over much of the local and provincial administration. In practice, the assemblies were firmly controlled by the central government, whose chief representative, the governor of the province, had nearly unlimited authority in the administration of the province. Most nobles showed scant interest in the assemblies; the meetings were sparsely attended and became little more than social occasions at which old acquaintanceships could be renewed.[46]

[44] Marczali (1910), 142-144; Blum (1948), 23-28, 37-39.
[45] Palmer (1959), 416-417.
[46] Raeff (1957), 44-45, 234; Ruffmann (1961), 173; Engelmann (1884), 283-284.

CHAPTER 2

The Peasants

I

WITH the ownership of land went power and authority over the peasants who lived on the land. There were a multitude of variations in the nature of that authority and in the nature of the peasants' subservience to their seigniors, in the compass of the seigniors' supervision and control, and in the obligations that the peasants had to pay their lords. The peasants themselves were known by many different names, and so, too, were the obligations they owed the seigniors. But, whatever the differences, the status of the peasant everywhere in the servile lands was associated with unfreedom and constraint. In the hierarchical ladder of the traditional order he stood on the bottom rung. He was "the stepchild of the age, the broad, patient back who bore the weight of the entire social pyramid . . . the clumsy lout who was deprived and mocked by court, noble and city."[1]

In all of the servile lands there were peasants who enjoyed full or partial freedom from seigniorial authority. Many of these people traced their free status to forebearers who had settled as colonists in newly opened regions, drawn there by the promise of freedom for themselves and their dependants. Others owed their liberty to emancipation freely given by the seigniors or purchased by the peasants. In the Swiss cantons of Uri, Schwyz, Unterwalden, Appenzell, Glarus, the Toggenberg district of St. Gall, and the uplands of Bern, the peasants had never paid servile obligations, or had freed themselves of these payments long ago.[2] In France an undetermined but not extensive amount of peasant land, located especially in the center and south, had managed to evade the seigniorial net, despite seigniorial and governmental efforts to enforce the rule of *nulle terre sans seigneur*.[3] In western Germany there were settlements of free peasants called imperial villages. Created centuries before, these villages, like the imperial cities, recognized only the Holy Roman Emperor as their lord. By the eighteenth century, however, most of the imperial villages had fallen under the control of local rulers and had lost their special status. Other free peasants lived along the French-German border. In medieval times, lords had freed these people to keep them from leaving to become colonists elsewhere, or because as borderers they had special military value. All together, the free peasantry made up a small fraction of the rural population of western Germany,

---

[1] Carl Hinrichs quoted in Abel (1967), 256.
[2] Rappard (1912), 128, 131, 169.
[3] Soboul (1960), 110; Goubert (1969), 83; Sée (1906), 60n.

and despite their free status most of them had to pay dues and fees to seigniors who had established authority over them.[4]

Eastern Germany, and especially East Prussia, had a much larger free peasant population than did the west. In 1798 in East Prussia 12,790 (21 per cent) out of 61,301 peasant holdings belonged to free peasants. They were the descendants of the colonists of earlier centuries, or of the autochtonous pagan inhabitants who had won freedom by immediate conversion to Christianity when the Teutonic Knights conquered the region in the thirteenth century. In East Prussia freemen were called *Kölmer* because the Knights had given them the same privileges they gave to the city of Kulm (and Thorn) in 1223. Free peasants in other parts of eastern Germany were known by other names, but with time *Kölmer* came into frequent use as the generic name for all of them.

The *Kölmer* occupied a category of their own in the rural social hierarchy, midway between the mass of the peasantry and the nobility; a status mirrored in the Prussian army, in which their sons served as noncommissioned officers, the sons of the nobility became the commissioned officers, and the sons of the unfree peasants served in the ranks. Though they were called proprietors of their holdings and could alienate them as they pleased, they did not have full ownership. Their land was considered part of the state's domain, and they paid a fee to the sovereign and performed services on the royal demesne in recognition of his superior ownership. Those freemen who rented land from private seigniors sometimes had to pay dues in kind and labor in addition to a money rent. They often lived in their own villages or on isolated farmsteads. Increasingly, however, manorial land encircled their holdings, they became fellow-villagers of the seigniorial peasants, and by the eighteenth century some of the *Kölmer* had lost much of their freedom to the lords in whose villages they now lived. The seigniors compelled them to pay some of the same dues demanded of the unfree peasants, and they had to have the lord's consent to sell their holding. And, because many of them often lacked documents to prove their special status, they lived in constant peril of loss of their land to a grasping seignior and of being reduced to the serfdom that bound most the peasants of eastern Germany.[5]

In Denmark, too, free peasants often found themselves at the mercy of seigniors. Their number, never large, fell sharply after the establishment of royal absolutism in 1660. By the end of the seventeenth century they made up less than 1 per cent of the peasant population in most of the kingdom; a few districts had from 3 to 7-8 per cent. Free peasants who rented

---

[4] Franz (1970a), 76-79; Lütge (1949), 79-80; Lütge (1957), 85-89; Lütge (1967), 195-196; Wittich (1896), 21; Schremmer (1963), 22; Knapp (1902), 56-58.
[5] Knapp (1887), I, 14, II, 8; Stein (1919), I, 136, 373-374; Henning (1969), 7-8n.; Dessmann (1904), 68-69; Czybulka (1949), 56-61.

land from seigniors had to perform labor services for their landlords. The "Danish Law" of 1685, which codified the legislation of the new absolutism, had ordered the restriction of these labor services to one-fourth of those demanded of serfs. The free peasants, however, found it difficult and often impossible to secure this right, and royal charters, in defiance of the king's own law, often permitted seigniors to increase the labor services of their free tenants.[6]

Most of the Austrian Monarchy had only a sprinkling of free peasants. In the Slav provinces of Bohemia, Moravia, and Silesia they comprised scarcely 1 per cent of the rural population. In Moravia, for example, in the second half of the eighteenth century it was estimated that not more than 20 peasants a year gained their freedom. Liberty came typically through individual acts of emancipation, usually in return for a money payment by the peasant. Other so-called free peasants actually were runaway serfs. They settled on the manor of another lord who chose to evade his legal responsibility to return the fugitives to their rightful masters because he wanted to keep them as renters or farm hands.[7] A like dearth of free peasants prevailed in the German crownlands, with the striking exception of Tyrol and Vorarlberg. The peasants there had won their freedom from all seigniorial bonds in the fifteenth and sixteenth centuries. A few pockets of unfreedom had persisted until the Hapsburg sovereigns had abolished them during the seventeenth and first half of the eighteenth centuries.[8]

The peasants in the 450-square-mile duchy of Cracow had been freed when that territory had been part of Napoleon's grand duchy of Warsaw. After Napoleon's fall, Cracow had become a free state under Russian, Prussian, and Austrian protection until 1846, when Austria annexed it. Unlike their fellows in other parts of the short-lived grand duchy of Warsaw whose freedom turned out to be a chimera (pp. 231-233), the peasants of Cracow remained truly free.[9]

Hungary had about 250,000 free peasants in the 1820's out of a rural population of about nine million. Some of these freemen were prosperous farmers, others had no land at all and earned meager livings as hired workers of noblemen and of landed peasants. They were unevenly dispersed, with apparently a heavy concentration in southern Hungary and Croatia, while in Transylvania, the easternmost part of Hungary, there were only 94 villages of free peasants (many of them German colonists who were called Saxonians) out of the 1,960 villages there in 1848.[10]

In eighteenth- and nineteenth-century Russia serfs won freedom by vol-

[6] Nielsen (1933), 178; Skrubbeltrang (1953), 165-166; Andrews (1974), II, 359.
[7] Henning (1969), 56; Stark (1952), 357-358; Dessmann (1904), 68-69.
[8] Buchinger (1952), 78; Feigl (1964), 59; Stolz (1940), 24-26.
[9] Kieniewicz (1969), 120.
[10] Barany (1968), 188; Revesz (1964), 13-14; Georgescu-Buzău (1965), 15.

untary emancipation by their seigniors, or by purchasing their freedom, or by military service. A handful of wealthy peasants, who had gained their riches through trade and industry and who paid heavy prices for their emancipation, became members of the bourgeoisie. The others, once freed, were enrolled in the category of state peasants and so remained in an unfree status, albeit one not as constraining nor as degrading as that of the serf. In the second half of the eighteenth century the government offered special privileges to foreigners to persuade them to colonize unpeopled regions of European Russia. The colonists, most of them Germans, whose descendants numbered nearly half a million by the 1850's, had much more freedom than did state peasants but still had certain external restraints placed upon them. Finally, a few hundred peasants in northern Russia whose ancestors had performed some unusual service for royalty were entirely free of servile obligations and restrictions. There had been many free peasants in the Lithuanian provinces annexed by Russia in the third partition of Poland in 1795. In 1806 there were 114,722 adult male free peasants in the province of Vilna alone, about one-fourth of the adult male peasant population there. These free peasants rented land from seigniors who then proceeded to reduce them to the status of serfs. Official data from the 1830's showed that 131,013 free adult male peasants had been enserfed in the provinces of Vilna and Kovno. The government, always inimical to Polish nobles whose loyalty it (rightly) suspected, established a special office to help these people regain their lost freedom. It was not an especially successful effort; between 1836 and 1850 only 18,986 adult males, or less than 15 per cent, were restored to freedom.[11]

Among all the servile lands, Poland and the Danubian Principalities had the largest proportions of free peasants in their populations. In Poland at the end of the eighteenth century between 20 and 30 per cent of about one million holdings were held by freemen. Many of these people came from neighboring lands, especially runaways from Pomerania and Silesia. They were welcomed by Polish landowners, who asked no questions and demanded only a small quitrent of the newcomers. Others were residents of towns that in the sixteenth and seventeenth centuries had received city privileges. This allowed the townsmen to hold land on free tenures. Many of these so-called towns were really villages, or were decayed urban centers that had become villages, with most of their inhabitants engaged in rural pursuits. Still other freemen were runaway serfs who enjoyed freedom in their new places of residence so long as their owners did not reclaim them. Not all free peasants, however, remained in that status. Many of them voluntarily became serfs of a lord. Some did this in return for the seignior's assumption of the debts of the peasant, some to find peace and security or seigniorial protection from criminal prosecution, but by far the largest

<hr>

[11] Pokhilevich (1966), 395; Blum (1961), 481-485; Neupokoev (1962), 390-394.

number became serfs because they married a serf and thereby acquired the status of their spouse.[12]

An estimated 107,000 or about one-fifth of the more than 500,000 peasant families in the Danubian Principalities were free. Most of these people lived in the hill country, where they owned their land and where they had rights to the use of forests and pastures. The Principalities also had peasant colonists who cleared and settled seigniorial land in return for special privileges stipulated in written agreements. Generally, these people came from Transylvania (which, though part of Hungary, was populated chiefly by Romanians) and from south of the Danube, as well as from within the Principalities themselves. They agreed to do only three to six days of labor a year for the seignior and most of them had the right to commute this small obligation into a cash payment. They received the right to the perpetual use of the land they cleared. The state levied a reduced tax on their land and allowed them to pay it directly to the state treasury, and thereby escape the extortions inflicted on other peasants by the agents of the treasury. In a land where official extortion and corruption was a way of life that was a valuable concession.[13]

The peasants of western Europe, save for a relatively small number, had long ago thrown off the bonds that held them in serfdom. Nonetheless, they still owed servile obligations to seigniors, and they were still subject, to a greater or lesser extent depending upon the locality, to the jurisdiction and punitive authority of seigniors. Some historians have made much of the fact that the dependence or servility of these peasants was not attached to their persons (as it was to the person of a serf). Rather, they argue that the dependence adhered to the land. It became part of the price the peasant paid for the use of his holding to the seignior who had the superior ownership of the land. Since nearly all of the land in these societies belonged to seigniors—whether prince, nobleman, institution, or burgher—nearly all of the peasants owed servile obligations. It seems to me to be a matter of little practical consequence, except perhaps to nationalistic historians, whether the servility and dependence adhered to the person or to the land. If, however, the argument must be pursued, there is much that shows that servility often did adhere to the person. Thus, peasants who were landless and who earned their livings as hired farm laborers or as artisans were under seigniorial jurisdiction and had to pay servile obligations, albeit in smaller amounts than peasants with land. In many parts of central and western Europe, peasants owed services and obedience to other seigniors in addition to the seignior who had the superior ownership of the land on which the peasant lived. Indeed, in some places the payments owed to the superior landowner counted among the lesser obligations of the peasant.

[12] Rutkowski (1926), 123, 488-489, 505; Henning (1969b), 65; Revesz (1964), 100-101.
[13] Jonescu (1909), 1; Oțetea (1960), 301.

[33]

The other seigniors could include a lord who had jurisdiction over the peasant, another to whom he had to pay a share of his produce, and a so-called *Vogtherr*, or patron. It was quite common to have one or more of these seigniorial roles divided among several people who had acquired their partial ownership through purchase, inheritance, gift, or exchange. Usually, one individual filled several of these roles, or joint owners consolidated their claims through exchange or purchase, so that probably few peasants had a different person in each of these seignioral roles. Two or three seemed the usual pattern, though in southwestern Germany it was not uncommon for a peasant to have four separate seigniors. An aura of utility tinged certain of these seigniorial functions. Others were functionless vestiges of days long gone. Thus, the *Vogtherr* had appeared in Germany and Austria in troubled medieval times when peasants, unable to defend themselves and their property, had placed themselves under the protection of a lord. In return for his protection they paid him dues and services. The need for protection had long since disappeared, but the *Vogtherr* still received his payment though he did nothing.[14]

The fact was that peasants in the western lands were dependent upon seigniors and stood in a servile relationship to them. Surely it made no difference to the individual peasant whether that dependence was acquired by birth into the peasantry, or by virtue of occupation of a certain piece of land. The dependence was still there. Even peasants who were recognized as fully free and who were alodial proprietors of their holdings had to pay obligations to seigniors that were not demanded of property owners who belonged to other orders. Sidney Herbert put it succinctly when he wrote: "Could a medieval lawyer have been transported into the France of 1790 and told that Jacques Bonhomme, a peasant, was bound to carry his corn to the lord's mill, to perform so many *corvées* during the year, to pay *rachat* or *acapte* at each mutation of property, and that his land was subject to *champart* and *lods et ventes*, he would have unhesitatingly proclaimed him a serf, and would have been filled with amazement to hear that he was nothing of the sort, but a free man."[15] The peasants themselves recognized their unfreedom and servility. The *cahiers* of grievances they sent to Paris on the eve of the Revolution were filled with complaints and anger at the servile obligations and the seigniorial privileges that oppressed and confined them.[16] The judgment of a Swiss scholar that "the principle of the absolute freedom of the human person was not generally recognized"[17] before the emancipations of the peasantry was true not only of his homeland, but of all the servile societies of western Europe.

[14] Knapp (1919), 132; Schremmer (1963), 5-6, 8; Darmstaedter (1897), 10; Wittich (1896), 183; Lütge (1949), 43, 56-57; Lütge (1957), 103; Feigl (1964), 108-109, 111-112, 253-254; Revesz (1964), 130-131.
[15] Herbert (1969), 130.   [16] Marion (1902), 349.
[17] Rappard (1912), 138.

II

The relatively small number of serfs in western Europe were called *main-mortables* in French-speaking lands and *Leibeigene* or *Eigenhörige* in German-speaking ones. Their serfdom was vestigal, a remnant of the serf-dom once so common in western Europe, and with little resemblance to the far harsher serfdom that prevailed in eastern Europe. Peasants acquired the stain of serfdom in several ways. One, of course, was through inherit-ance—in Germany through the mother's side only. Residence in certain towns and villages automatically converted people into serfs of the local sei-gnior, who in some instances was the town itself as a corporate entity. It was said of such places that "Luft macht eigen," a reversal of the medieval dic-tum "Stadtluft macht frei." Württemberg and Baden contained a number of these towns and villages. They were less common elsewhere in south-western Germany and in Hesse-Cassel, Burgundy, and Lorraine. People became serfs, too, after they had occupied for a specified period, such as a year and a day, a holding that carried with it the status of serf. This kind of serfdom, found in parts of Swabia, Hannover, northwest Lorraine, parts of Luxembourg, and in Franche-Comté, was called *Realleibeigenschaft* or *mainmorte réelle*, because the serfdom adhered to the land.[18]

Some regions held a high concentration of serfs, others had smaller numbers or none at all. In France about 400,000 of the estimated one mil-lion *mainmortables* in that country lived in Franche-Comté, where in 1784 a contemporary estimated that they made up half of the population. In 1781 in Burgundy 3,421 of the 9,331 communities were of *mainmortables*. Smaller numbers were scattered through other parts of eastern and central France and there were peasants in Brittany whose status, called *quevaise*, closely resembled *mainmorte*. In Savoy the majority of the peasants were *mainmortables*. Among the German states, Baden and Hannover had rela-tively large concentrations—in the duchies of Hoya and Diepholz in Han-nover serfs outnumbered other peasants. Lesser densities occurred in other states of western Germany; central Germany had almost no serfs. Several of the Swiss cantons had *mainmortables* among their population, with siz-able numbers in a few places in St. Gall and Thurgau.[19]

Serfs could legally be bought, sold, exchanged, or given away by their owner. Nearly always such transactions involved the alienation by the serfowner of his seigniory, and with it his rights over the serfs who lived there. The only effect this sale had on the serfs was that now they had a

[18] Wittich (1896), 243, 246; Rudloff (1915), 802-803; Schremmer (1963), 15, 19; Lütge (1949), 70; Knapp (1902), 88; Knapp (1919), I, 131; Knapp (1964), 365; Herbert (1969), 4; Stolz (1940), 29; Aulard (1919), 6-7; Darmstaedter (1897), 162, 166, 171.
[19] Millot (1937), 180; Roupnel (1922), 237n., Sée (1939), I, 182-183; Sée (1906), 8-9, 10-23; Darmstaedter (1897), 2; Herbert (1969), 10; Wittich (1896), 243; Brentano (1899), 238, Jordan-Rozwadowski (1900), 359; Borcke-Stargordt (1954), 322n.; Lütge (1957), 9-14; Henne am Rhyn (1903), I, 454-455.

new lord to whom they owed their obligations. There were instances, however, in which serfowners sold or exchanged their serfs without land, as if they were chattels. The serf then had to move to the seigniory of his new owner. Such sales remained legal in a number of German principalities up to the end of the servile order, though in practice they seem rarely to have taken place.[20]

The western European serf could own land in his own name, or hold land on hereditary tenure from a lord of whom he was not the serf. Like other peasants, he could have several seigniors to whom he owed obligations. Like other hereditary tenants, he could buy, sell, exchange, mortgage, or bequeath his land at will. However, none of these conditions applied to land he held from the seignior whose serf he was. He had to have his master's consent to alienate or mortgage the holding, or face confiscation and eviction. When lords gave their serfs permission to alienate, they demanded a fee. In Franche-Comté the charge was one-twelfth of the sale price, but sometimes seigniors demanded as much as one-half. The serf could not bequeath his holding and his personal property to whomever he pleased. Again he had to have his master's consent. In France and in Savoy he could leave his property only to those children who lived with him. Failing such heirs, all of his property escheated to the seignior. Some serfowners in France and Savoy even claimed as their own the property of those of their serfs who lived away from the lord's seigniory and who died leaving heirs. A royal decree of 8 August 1779 had ordered the end in France of this practice, called *droit de suite*. However, the *parlement* of Besançon in Franche-Comté, most of whose members owned serfs, refused to register the decree until 1787, and then only after the king compelled it, so that *droit de suite* persisted there almost to the Revolution.[21]

In southwest Germany the lord once had claimed all of the property of a deceased serf on the ground that all which the serf possessed belonged to the lord, who out of grace had permitted the peasant to own and use the property during his lifetime. Traces of this persisted into the eighteenth century, when the seignior claimed all of the property at the death of a childless serf. In general, however, the lord took only a set percentage of the serf's property, or his best animal, or his best garment, or a small cash payment, and allowed the serf to bequeath the rest of his property as he wished. In northwest Germany the lord customarily took half of the movables of the decedent and his second best animal. In Switzerland the seigniors in Basel and Solothurn no longer took a share of the property of

---

[20] Brünneck (1902), 133-134; Knapp (1902), 88; Knapp (1964), 70-71; Schremmer (1963), 16; Meier (1908), II, 118; Lütge (1949), 70-71.

[21] Millot (1937), 18, 39, 41, 44, 55, 134; St. Jacob (1960), 38-39; Roupnel (1922), 237n.; Bruchet (1908), xliv, xlv; Darmstaedter (1897), 122; Wittich (1896), 223, 243-244; Schremmer (1963), 18; Knapp (1919), 67; Lütge (1949), 69, 70.

their deceased serfs, but in Schaffhausen the practice continued, with the payment usually made in cash.

In principle the serf could not leave the seigniory of his owner, but it had been a long time since lords had been able to enforce that rule. Now the serf could leave if he received permission from the lord and met certain conditions. In Franche-Comté and in Lorraine if the serf left without authorization the lord could take the income from the departed peasant's hereditary holding. If he did not return within a specified period—ten years in Franche-Comté—the holding escheated to the seignior. In many places the peasant who wanted to leave had to pay an exit fee to his lord. Sometimes the fee was a fixed sum, and sometimes it was a percentage of the value of the peasant's property that could be as much as 10 per cent but more often was 2.5 to 3 per cent. By paying the exit fee the peasant freed himself from serfdom. If he left without paying the fee, he remained a serf and his lord had a claim on his property when he died. If the departing peasant who left without paying was a woman, she not only remained a serf, but in the Germanic lands her children were legally serfs of her lord, no matter where they were born or where they lived.[22]

Serfs did not have to leave the seigniory in order to gain their freedom. They could purchase it if their owner was willing, and remain in their homes. The price was set by agreement between lord and serf, although in some places it was a fixed amount. On occasion an entire village bought its liberty at what must sometimes have been a great financial sacrifice. The people of Pusey in Franche-Comté paid their lord 50,000 livres and ceded a meadow to him in return for their emancipation from serfdom and from the obligations they owed him. In Bavaria, and after 1701 in Lorraine, serfs who entered the priesthood or who married a noble or who were ennobled (these two latter events must have been most unusual) were automatically freed.

Nearly everywhere seigniors required their serfs, male and female alike, to make a small annual payment, usually presented in person, as an acknowledgment of their serfdom. Sometimes, too, the serfs had to do homage and take an oath of loyalty to the lord, either periodically or when the serf became the occupant of a holding. In Württemberg the serfs made their payments and took their oath of loyalty on 26 December, St. Stephen's Day. After the ceremony the seignior gave his serfs a feast that usually cost him more than the dues he had just received from them, thereby showing that the dues were not a source of revenue but rather a recognition of his lordship. Some serfs were excused from the payment, as, for example, in the duchy of Hohenlohe the servants of the seignior and

---

[22] Millot (1937), 37-39, 49-50; Darmstaedter (1897), 71, 165, 169; Schremmer (1963), 15, 19; Sée (1921), 55; Rudloff (1915), 802; Brünneck (1890), 130; Wittich (1896), 223, 229, 244, 245; Knapp (1919), 130.

poor peasants. In parts of Lorraine only serfs who lived outside the seigniory had to make the payment.[23]

The degree of freedom enjoyed by the serfs of western Europe, especially when compared with that of the serfs of eastern Europe, has persuaded some historians to maintain that their serfdom was "nothing more than a special kind of taxation" and a device to increase seigniorial revenues. It is said that their obligations were no more onerous, and sometimes less onerous, than those of other peasants, and that their status was neither degrading nor socially incapacitating, so that serfs rose to high rank in church and state and remained serfs.[24] If, indeed, the obligations and status of serfdom made so little difference, it becomes difficult to understand why serfs bothered to redeem themselves from it, at sometimes excessively heavy prices. It is worth noting, too, that as a rule serfs who rose to high office were allowed to redeem themselves. Only exceptionally did they remain serfs. In Baden many higher officials of the margrave were also his serfs, until in 1764 they were freed.[25] The fact that legally serfs could be bought, sold, exchanged, or given away certainly distinguished—and degraded—their status as compared with other peasants of western Europe. And it seems clear that serfs themselves considered their position as both demeaning and intolerable. They ran away to escape it and they entered lawsuits against their lords, as did the six serf communities whose case against their owner, the abbé of St. Claude, was made famous by the support given it by Voltaire. Some lords shared the aversion of their serfs. In 1775 the abbot of Luxeuil in Franche-Comté wanted to free the 8,936 serfs who belonged to the abbey. In his memorial to the royal council he called serfdom a kind of slavery that humiliated and dispirited the serfs, made them less efficient than other peasants, and even impelled them not to marry because they did not want "to reproduce their slavish race." Their attitude and their inefficiency produced economic loss to their seigniors and the lawsuits they brought against their lords often proved financially ruinous for both parties.[26]

III

In general the status of the peasantry worsened as one moved eastward across the continent and it reached its nadir in the lands that lay on the other side of the Elbe River. Most of the peasants there were held in a serf-

[23] Aulard (1919), 35-36, 36n.; Roupnel (1922), 237; Knapp (1902), 89-90; Knapp (1919), 129; Wittich (1896), 223, 246; St. Jacob (1960), 38-40; Lütge (1949), 71; Schremmer (1963), 15; Darmstaedter (1897), 18, 71, 140, 163, 167.
[24] Knapp (1902), 99; Lütge (1955), 650; Jordan-Rozwadowski (1960), 361; Schremmer (1963), 17; Stolz (1940), 31-32.
[25] Knapp (1919), 129; Franz (1970a), 227.
[26] Millot (1937), 144-145; Aulard (1919), 27-30.

dom that was far more onerous and far more degrading than the vestigal serfdom of western Europe. In the last part of the eighteenth century the term *Leibeigenschaft*, slavery, came into use in German-speaking lands as the name for serfdom, instead of the more accurate *Erbuntertänigkeit*, hereditary subjection. It was employed especially by reformers in the hope that the use of the odious word "slavery" would lend force to their arguments for change. Actually, serfdom in eastern Europe was not slavery (though sometimes it seemed scarcely different from it), if only because the serf was recognized as a legal individual, within certain limitations could initiate and participate in court actions, and possessed certain individual, albeit severely, restricted rights.

There were, of course, differences among the eastern lands in the extent to which the peasants were "servile subjects of the manor" (as they were described in the Pomeranian Royal Peasant Order of 30 December 1764). In Russia, Livonia, Poland, Schleswig-Holstein, Denmark, and in much of eastern Germany, especially in Mecklenburg, Swedish Pomerania, and Upper Lusatia in Electoral Saxony, the law placed few limits upon the authority of the seignior. Often the only effective restraint on the lord was his knowledge that his demands might reach the point at which his serfs would run away to escape them. The peasants in the Austrian Monarchy and in Electoral Saxony (except for Upper Lusatia) and other lands of east-central Germany were considerably less dependent upon the will and whim of their seigniors. Reforms of the second half of the eighteenth century had given the peasants of the Hapsburg realm many rights they had not before possessed. They still bore "the marks of the yokes and chains of their earlier slavery,"[27] for they remained the hereditary servile subjects of their lords. But now the central government had established norms that curbed the powers the lord once had over his peasants. For example, he could not now demand more labor services than the laws specified, nor could he prevent his peasants from leaving, providing they complied with the complex provisions set out in the legislation, nor could he evict them from their holdings without proper cause. The nobles of Saxony had never succeeded in establishing as much control over their peasants as their fellow lords in neighboring lands. Most important, the taint of serfdom adhered to the land, like the *Realleibeigenschaft* or *mainmorte réelle* of the west, and not to the person. The Saxon peasant owed dependence and obligations to a seignior only so long as he held land from the seignior.[28]

Serfdom in the Danubian Principalities differed from the serfdom of the other eastern lands, notably in that the seignior had neither civil nor criminal jurisdiction over his peasants. In practice, however, the serf there had no real protection against excessive demands and harsh treatment by his

[27] Kübeck (1909), I, pt. 1, 88-89.
[28] Blum (1948), 45-46; Mailath (1830), 49-50; Blaschke (1965), 239-240, 256-257.

1. Polish peasant children. Painting by J.-P. Norblin, 1745-1830.
(H. Vautrin, La Pologne du xviiᵉ siècle, Paris, 1966.)

seignior. In 1746 and then in 1749 Prince Constantine Mavrocordato, hospodar successively of Wallachia and Moldavia, compelled the boyars of each principality to agree to reforms that, supposedly, abolished serfdom. However, the peasants still remained in servile dependence upon their lords, and as the decades went by that dependence increased, as did their exploitation by the seigniors.[29]

The alienation of serfs without land, often involving the break-up of families, reveals the depth of the degradation to which serfs had been reduced in many of the eastern lands. They were sold, mortgaged, exchanged, and gambled away. This concept of the serf as a chattel, a thing that could be made over to another person, apparently was a phenomenon largely of the seventeenth and especially of the eighteenth century. The practice assumed especially large proportions in Russia. The law code of 1649 had forbidden the sale of serfs, but serfowners quickly and freely disregarded the ban. The central government did nothing to stop them. Instead, it gave its tacit recognition by such legislation as a ban on the use of the hammer by auctioneers at public sales of serfs, or in 1833, and again in 1841, outlawing the separation of parents and their unwed children by sale or gift.[30] In 1761 the Livonian diet gave legal sanction to the sale of serfs without land, though it forbade their sale for export and the separation of a married couple. A contemporary in the 1770's reported that serfs and their children were exchanged for horses and dogs. When famine struck in the winter of 1788-1789, seigniors in one district of Livonia, in order to save on the support they had to provide their serfs, were reported to have sold orphan girls of six to twelve for a pittance and even given them away.[31] In Mecklenburg, where peasants probably suffered worse treatment than anywhere else in Germany, there was an active and open trade in serfs from the mid-seventeenth century on, though it did not receive official sanction from the government until 1757. Johann Heinrich Voss (1751-1826), Mecklenburg poet and German patriot, who came of peasant stock, accused the seigniors of Mecklenburg of selling serfs as recruits for the Prussian army.[32]

A law of 1681 allowed the sale of serfs without land in Brandenburg under certain conditions, but reportedly the trade never assumed large proportions there. In 1759 the government ordered an end to the active commerce in serfs in Prussian Silesia. The ban seems not to have been entirely effective, since sales continued there until as late as 1795. By a decree of 8 November 1773 Frederick II expressly forbade the sale of serfs without land in East Prussia. In contrast, in Swedish Pomerania as late as the 1780's legislation specifically permitted the sale of serfs without land and mortgag-

[29] Oțetea (1955), 302-307. [30] Blum (1961), 424-428.
[31] Transehe-Roseneck (1890), 193-194, 196-197, 200.
[32] Mager (1955), 178-179.

ing and exchanging them. A writer in 1784 compared the traffic there in serfs with the African slave trade. In Schleswig-Holstein the law forbade the sale of serfs without land, but serfowners paid no heed to the prohibition. Reports told of a lord who exchanged a serf for two dogs and of serfowners who used their serfs as stakes in gambling at cards.[33]

In Poland the law was silent on the right of lords to sell their serfs without land, and eighteenth-century jurists decided that they did have the right. Until after World War II, however, historians had found so few records of such sales that they assumed that they were highly exceptional.[34] Then a collection of sources published in 1958 contained 2,788 cases of the alienation of serfs without land, and presumably these sources recorded only a portion of the total number of sales. Some of the transactions broke up families. Some were made on the condition, insisted upon by the church, that the serfs had to remain Catholics. If they did not, the seller had the right to demand back his serfs. Most of the sales were to nearby lords, but sometimes the serfs were sold to more distant masters and even to buyers from Germany.[35]

In Hungary and Transylvania, too, the laws said nothing about the sale of serfs without land. Lords there bought, sold, mortgaged, exchanged, and gave away serfs from the sixteenth to the late eighteenth centuries. The last known sale of a serf without land in Hungary occurred in 1773 and in Transylvania in the 1780's. In fact, the nobles of Transylvania demanded an indemnity for the loss of a valued privilege when the reforms of Joseph II ended the sale of serfs without land. In Bohemia, too, in the seventeenth century, and in the eighteenth century up to the time of the reforms of Joseph II in the 1780's, proprietors sold peasants without land. Some of them veiled the transaction by arranging for the purchaser to buy "freedom" for the serfs and then the "freed" serf in gratitude became the serf of his "benefactor." Others made no effort at concealment. The lords of Bohemia, and in Hungary, too, usually did restrict their sales to landless serfs, such as farmhands, day laborers, and children; they did not sell, without land, peasants who had holdings. In Bukovina, before its annexation by Austria in 1775 a part of Moldavia, lords in the seventeenth and eighteenth centuries freely bought and sold serfs without land, despite laws that forbade such transactions.[36]

[33] Brandenburg, Jordan-Rozwadowski (1900), 366; Prussian Silesia, Ziekursch (1927), 97-101; East Prussia, Brünneck (1887), 56-57, 63-64; Swedish Pomerania, Fuchs (1888), 177-180; Mager (1955), 170; Schleswig-Holstein, Hanssen (1861), 15-16, 16n.; Russia, Kulischer (1932), 2-3.

[34] Rutkowski (1926), 487-488. But *cf.* Warszawski (1914), 77, who suspected that serf sales were far more frequent than the then known sources indicated.

[35] Revesz (1964), 123-125.

[36] Revesz (1964), 142-145, 148-150; Stark (1952), 359-360; Grünberg (1901), 27; Grünberg (1909), ii, 597.

The Peasants

In Russia there were servile peasants other than the serfs of private proprietors. By far the most numerous of these people were the state peasants.
Early in the eighteenth century Peter I had created the state peasantry as a
separate legal and social category, as part of his program to simplify administrative procedures such as the collection of taxes and other obligations. He formed the core of the new category from peasants who had never
been enserfed, the *odnodvortsy*, descendants of minor servitors who had
been settled on the frontiers, migrants to Siberia, and the non-Slavic
peoples of the Volga basin and beyond. Later rulers added other groups,
notably the peasants of the church after the secularization of the church's
lands in 1764, and the peasants who lived on the manors owned by the tsar
and his close kinsmen. By 1858, on the eve of the emancipation, state peasants actually outnumbered the serfs; a contemporary estimate put the
population of state peasants at 27.4 millions and that of the serfs at 22.8
millions.

The state peasants lived on land that belonged to the government. That
covered almost half of European Russia and lay principally in the northern
provinces and along the Urals and the Volga River. The peasants were subject to the will of the government, which put them under the supervision of
bureaucrats. They had far more autonomy over their lives and activities
and far more personal freedom than serfs had. Their obligations to the state
were considerably less than the obligations that serfs had to pay their
owners, and the compulsory labor service that bore so heavily upon the
serfs did not figure among their obligations. However, theirs was an insecure status, for the tsar could give them and their land to private persons,
whose serfs they then became. That happened to many thousands of state
peasants. The government also assigned them to full or part-time employment in state-owned and privately owned industrial enterprises, especially
in mining and metallurgy.

After the state peasants, the appanage peasants were the most numerous
category of non-seigniorial peasants in Russia. They lived on the estates
owned by the imperial court. The income from these properties supported
those members of the imperial family who stood outside the line of succession to the throne prescribed by Tsar Paul in 1797. By 1860 there were over
800,000 male appanage peasants and nine million desiatins (38,000 square
miles) of appanage land, five millions of it in forest. Like the state peasants,
the appanage peasants paid only a money fee and did not have other obligations in kind or labor. In 1805 only 5 imperial relatives had drawn income
from the appanage properties. They received a total of 385,000 rubles. By
1860 the number had risen to 23 who drew 3,324,000 rubles from the appanage.[37]

[37] Blum (1961), 475-503.

[43]

The gypsy slaves of the Danubian Principalities were the last true thralls in Christian Europe. In the mid-nineteenth century there were about 200,000 of them, or between 5 and 6 per cent of the estimated population of the Principalities. They were the property of monasteries and private persons who used them principally as domestics, though monasteries sometimes assigned them to work in the fields. Others, in return for payments to their owners, were allowed to go off and earn their livings as nomads, or as sedentary artisans in towns and villages. Being slaves, they had no legal personality and so possessed no civil rights. They therefore had no claim to the protection of the courts or of the police, nor did they have any civil obligations, such as paying taxes or performing labor services for the government. They were bought and sold like beasts of the field, and because they were poor workers they usually did not command good prices. And, like a beast, they could never acquire freedom or a legal personality because it was not possible to enfranchise them any more than it was possible to enfranchise a beast. If their owner did release them, another person could claim ownership, just as he could of an ownerless animal or object.

There was also a smaller group of gypsies who theoretically belonged to the sovereign (initially all the gypsies had belonged to the ruler who had alienated them to monasteries and private persons). These gypsies, numbering around 37,000 in 1837, had nearly complete personal freedom, paid only a small fee to the ruler, lived the traditional tribal nomadic life of the gypsy, and earned their living in traditional gypsy fashion as artisans, bear trainers, musicians, beggars, and thieves.

Bukovina, populated chiefly by Romanians, had only about 2,400 gypsy slaves out of a population of around 75,000 when the Hapsburgs annexed it in 1775. The new rulers decided to free these bondsmen—probably because they wanted to be able to tax them. However, they also wanted to keep the good will of the slaveowners, most of whom were monasteries, and so they proceeded slowly with the plans for emancipation—so slowly, indeed, that most slaves were freed not through an act of emancipation, but indirectly when in 1785 Emperor Joseph II ordered the secularization of the land of the monasteries. The gypsy slaves of the monasteries thereby acquired the same status as other peasants. Apparently, however, many of them found their new freedom less attractive than slavery and fled across the border into Moldavia, where slavery still persisted. After the liberation of the monasteries' slaves Bukovina still had 422 slaves who belonged to private owners. The government could not make up its mind what to do about these people until, finally, the new civil law code of 1811 forbade the continued existence of slavery anywhere in the Austrian Monarchy.[38]

[38] Emerit (1937), 179-185; Grünberg (1901), 5-9, 11-17; Grünberg (1909), ii, 601.

IV

The subservience of the peasant and his dependence upon his lord were mirrored in the attitudes and opinions of the seigniors of east and west alike. They believed that the natural order of things had divided humankind into masters and servants, those who commanded and those who obeyed. They believed themselves to be naturally superior beings and looked upon those who they believed were destined to serve them as their natural inferiors. At best their attitude toward the peasantry was the condescension of paternalism. More often it was disdain and contempt. Contemporary expressions of opinion repeatedly stressed the ignorance, irresponsibility, laziness, and general worthlessness of the peasantry, and in the eastern lands the free use of the whip was recommended as the only way to get things done. The peasant was considered some lesser and sub-human form of life; "a hybrid between animal and human" was the way a Bavarian official put it in 1737.[39] An eyewitness of a rural rising in Provence in 1752 described the peasant as "an evil animal, cunning, a ferocious half-civilized beast; he has neither heart nor honesty. . . ."[40] In 1774 a progressive nobleman of Savoy and an "unreconstructed" Moldavian boyar made similar judgments of the peasants of their respective lands. The Savoyard Marquis Alexis Costa de Beauregard wrote of the peasants of his homeland that "in their order there is no courage, no vigor; all sorts of ills flow from this parlous state; laziness, slackness, negligence, work poorly done and done after the time that it should have been done. . . ."[41] The Moldavian Basil Balsch reported that the peasants of his land were "strangers to any discipline, order, economy or cleanliness . . . ; a thoroughly lazy, mendacious . . . people who are accustomed to do the little work that they do only under invectives or blows."[42] A counselor of the duke of Mecklenburg in an official statement in 1750 described the peasant there as a "head of cattle" and declared that he must be treated accordingly.[43] In debates in 1790 in the provincial diets and county assemblies of the Austrian Monarchy about the reforms of Joseph II and in their petitions to Joseph's successor, Leopold II, nobles described their peasants as lazy, drunken, irresponsible louts who would not know how to use freedom if they had it, and who were kept at work only by fear of the whip.[44]

A few were more understanding. Stanislaus Leszczyński (d. 1766), twice elected king of Poland and twice deposed, wrote that in that country "the

---

[39] Lütge (1949), 17.   [40] Valran (1899), 29.
[41] Bruchet (1908), xl.   [42] Grünberg (1901), 32.
[43] Mager (1955), 198.
[44] Palmer (1959), 394-396. For the view of the peasant in art and literature in central Europe see Frauendorfer (1957), I, 149-154, 316-318. For the attitude of the Russian nobility of the eighteenth century toward their peasants see Confino (1961), 51-63.

[45]

nobleman condemns his peasant to death without any legal ground and even more frequently without legal proceedings and without any ceremony. We look upon the peasant as a creature of an entirely different sort, and deny him even the air which we breathe with him, and make hardly any distinction between him and the animals who plow our fields. Often we value them even lower than the animals, and only too often sell them to cruel masters who compel them to pay for their new servitude by excessive toil. I shudder when I mention the law which imposes a fine of only 15 francs on the noble who murders a peasant."[45] Nearly a century later, another prince, Michael Sturza, hospodar of Moldavia from 1834 to 1849, wrote that the peasant there was "viewed as a being who ought not to exist except by the whim of others; reduced almost to the abject status of a beast; abandoned to the rapacity of all who use him, from the clergy, from the greatest official down to the smallest bureaucrat, squeezed by the large renter and by the proprietor, and after all this the poor peasant is accused of being lazy and idle."[46]

The conviction of their own superiority harbored by the seigniors was often compounded by ethnic and religious differences between lord and peasant. In many parts of central and eastern Europe the masters belonged to a conquering people who had established their domination over the native population. German seigniors ruled over Slavic peasants in Bohemia, Galicia, East Prussia and Silesia, and over Letts and Estonians in the Baltic lands; Polish lords were the masters of Ukrainian, Lithuanian, and White Russian peasants; Great Russians owned manors peopled by Ukrainians and Lithuanians and Poles; Magyars lorded it over Slovaks and Romanians and Slovenes—to list only some of the macro-ethnic differences. Few peoples of the rest of the world can match Europeans in their awareness of and, generally, contempt for or at least disdain for other ethnic and religious groups (even when to the uninitiated outsider the groups may seem indistinguishable). The dominant group, though greatly outnumbered, successfully maintained its cultural identity precisely because it considered the peasants over whom it ruled as lesser breeds of mankind, even pariahs. Count Sheremetev, victorious commander of Russian troops in Livonia in the Great Northern War, reported that "We have captured large numbers of cattle and Estonians; cows can now be bought for 3 *altyn*, sheep at 2 *den'gi*, little children for 1 *den'ga*, large ones for 1 *grivna*. . . ."[47]

Schooling for most peasants was, at best, pitifully inadequate and usually entirely absent, even where laws declared elementary education compulsory. When schools were established, their quarters and equipment

[45] Quoted in Sugenheim (1861), 401-402.
[46] Quoted in Evans (1924), 28.
[47] Transehe-Roseneck (1890), 111-112. There were 6 *den'gi* in an *altyn*; the *grivna* was equal to 20 *den'gi*.

were nearly always deficient and their teachers untrained and often un-
suited for the task assigned them. In some places reasonably adequate instruction was available, but by far the greatest part of Europe's peasantry
lived out their lives in darkest ignorance.[48]

The peasants themselves, oppressed, contemned, and kept in ignorance
by their social betters, accepted the stamp of inferiority pressed upon them.
"I am only a serf" the peasant would reply when asked to identify himself.[49] They seemed without pride or self-respect, dirty, lazy, crafty, and
always suspicious of their masters and of the world that lay outside their
village. Even friendly observers were put off by the way they looked and by
their behavior. One commentator complained in the 1760's that "one
would have more pity for them if their wild and brutish appearance did not
seem to justify their hard lot."[50] In 1763 the Danish publicist J. S.
Sneedorf, who favored reform, in reply to the arguments of conservatives
that education would spoil the peasants, said "They are probably right. . . .
[The peasants'] circumstances are so miserable that it is easy to believe that
a certain degree of stupidity and insensitiveness alone can render their condition supportable and that the happiness of the peasant, if he still enjoys
any, would cease as soon as he should begin to think and as soon as he
should be deprived of those two principal consolations, ignorance and
brandy."[51]

A few thoughtful people recognized that the responsibility for the misery
and ignorance of peasant existence lay not in the nature of the peasant himself, but in the nature of the social and economic order in which he lived.
J. C. Schubart (1734-1789) was a distinguished German agriculturist, ennobled as Edler von Kleefeld (Cloverfield) in recognition of his contributions. He explained that "the more industrious the poor peasant the more
miserable; for almost everyone wants to refresh himself from his sweat and
fatten himself from his blood; he is thereby beaten down, discouraged, and
in the end becomes slothful because he realizes that he is more tormented
and more ill-treated than a beast of burden."[52] Albrecht Thaer (1752-
1828), Germany's foremost agriculturist, wrote in 1806 of the serfs of
Brandenburg that "the evil lies deep in the present system under which the
peasant becomes ever poorer, lazier and more stupid."[53] An English diplomat, long resident in the Danubian Principalities, said much the same thing
of the peasants there. "Accustomed to the state of servitude," he wrote in
1820, "which to others might appear intolerable, they are unable to form
hopes for a better condition; the habitual depression of their minds has be-

---

[48] Sée (1939), 215-216; Babeau (1878), 143, 303-304; Friis (1905), 323; Fuchs (1888), 185;
Bruford (1935), 123; Feigl (1964), 270; Emerit (1937), 288; Mager (1955), 235-240; Hanssen
(1861), 27; Franz (1970a), 232-233, 242.

[49] Hanssen (1861), 28.   [50] J. M. von Loen quoted in Bruford (1935), 121.
[51] Quoted in Hovde (1948), i, 76.   [52] Goltz (1902), 482-483.
[53] Knapp (1887), i, 75.

come a sort of national stupor and apathy, which render them equally indifferent to the enjoyments of life, and insensible to happiness, as to the pangs of anguish and affliction."[54]

In their hopelessness, their desperation, and perhaps their self-hate, peasants everywhere, men and women and often children, drank heavily and even passionately. In many lands their addiction was encouraged by their seigniors, who had the monopoly on the manufacture and sale of spirits, who owned or leased out the village inn, and for whom these activities provided an important source of income. Some Polish seigniors even paid their hired labor in scrip redeemable only at the village tavern for drinks.[55] Contemporaries frequently commented on the endless drinking and on its destructive effects. An account in an official publication in Silesia in 1790 that told of the crushing poverty and misery of the Polish peasants of Upper Silesia, reported that "Brandy or the mere thought of it transports these people from laziness, sluggishness and slackness to lightheartedness, happiness and exuberance. . . . They consume it with a frenzy. . . . Brandy is everything to these people; the infant, the senile, the maiden and the wife, everyone, all drink it; they drink in the morning, the evening, at noon and at midnight; they drink whenever they can get it. . . . The consequences of their intemperance are to be expected, the destruction of their health, disorder, neglect, need, confusion, discord, and sometimes murder."[56] In the canton of Zurich, heavy drinking was reportedly most common among the workers in cottage industry. Almost always poor and landless or nearly landless, they depended for each day's bread upon their employers and upon the vagaries of the market for their wares.[57] A knowledgeable contemporary estimated that in mid-nineteenth-century Poland annual per capita consumption of distilled liquor amounted at a minimum to 1 *vedro*, or 3.25 gallons. That was about six times the annual per capita consumption of mid-twentieth-century Poland.[58] In the German and Slav crownlands of the Austrian Monarchy, official data for 1841 showed an annual per capita consumption of 2.4 gallons. In the first half of the 1960's per capita annual consumption of 100 proof distilled liquor in Austria was between 2 and 2.5 quarts; in Czechoslovakia it was about 1 quart.[59]

In light of their subservience and of their lowly condition, it could be expected that the peasantry would be politically powerless. Unlike the other orders of the traditional society, most peasants did not have in-

[54] Wilkinson (1971), 155.

[55] Transehe-Roseneck (1890), 184-185; Babeau (1878), 228-229; Link (1949), 21; Jacob (1826), 65; Valran (1899), 25.

[56] Ziekursch (1927), 144-145.   [57] Bollinger (1941), 29-30.

[58] Tegoborski (1852), III, 210. Per capita consumption in Poland of 100 proof distilled liquors in the first half of the 1960's was about 2 to 2.5 quarts per year. *Produktschap voor gedistilleerde Dranken* (1968), 47.

[59] *Tafeln zur Statistik* (1841), table 2, table 40, sect. xv; *Produktschap voor edistilleerde Dranken* (1968), 44, 54.

stitutionalized instruments, specifically representation in assemblies and estates, by which they could express their interests and voice their demands. Peasants were represented as an order in the diets of some of the lesser German principalities, especially those along the frontiers close to Switzerland and the United Provinces, and in the Austrian provinces of Tyrol and Vorarlberg, where the peasants were free. In tiny Vorarlberg there were only two estates, that of the burghers and that of the peasants. In some assemblies, peasants were represented, at least theoretically, by urban delegates who sat for their towns and the surrounding countryside. In the rural cantons of Switzerland, the free peasantry dominated the cantonal assemblies; in other cantons, urban oligarchs ruled over townspeople and country people alike. In some parts of France, peasants had sometimes been allowed to participate in the choice of delegates to the Estates General, the national assembly, which had last met in 1614. When the Estates General were summoned on the eve of the Revolution, representatives of the third estate were chosen by the system of indirect elections in which all heads of peasant families were allowed to participate.[60]

Peasants did have scope for political activity and for some degree of self-government at the village level. Nearly everywhere seigniors had allowed their peasants much autonomy in the management of their village communities. In the eighteenth and nineteenth centuries, however, communal autonomy declined significantly as seigniors, for their own private reasons, intervened increasingly in the internal operations of the peasant community.[61] In Russia the government in 1797 established district organizations for self-government by the state peasantry. Each *volost*, as these organizations were called, had about 3,000 adult male peasants and was headed by an administrator chosen by the *volost* assembly. However, the constant intervention and supervision by government officials reduced the self-government to a formality and a facade.[62]

[60] Carsten (1959), 424-425; Lütge (1967), 193; Stolz (1940), 24; Springer (1840), I, 256; Marion (1968), 218; Franz (1940a), 229.
[61] Blum (1971b), 566-567.
[62] Zaionchkovskii (1968), 29.

CHAPTER 3

The Obligations of the Peasantry

I

OVER the centuries a seemingly infinite variety of dues and services owed by peasants to their seigniors had evolved in the lands of servile Europe. In the petty princedom of Hildesheim in northwest Germany, for example, there were 138 different obligations, each with its own name. A Swiss official in 1798 said of the obligations of the peasants there that "to demand a complete listing is to demand the impossible." The emancipation operation in Moravia revealed 246 different types of money payments alone.[1] No individual peasant, of course, owed all the different types of obligations. The amounts they did owe to their lords differed widely, not only among countries and regions of a country, but also within an individual region, and even within a single manor. Some owed more, some owed less, some paid their obligations in one form, some in another, most in several forms. Frequently the origins of the differences lay in much earlier times, when the obligations had first been imposed and when lords had succeeded in reducing some peasants to a greater degree of subservience than others. Often, too, seigniors had allowed certain peasants to redeem or commute specific obligations, or had freed them voluntarily from the performance of certain dues and services required of others. The location of the peasant's cottage could have an effect. Those who lived at a distance from the lord's demesne might be likely to have a lesser labor obligation than those who lived nearby. Many manors or parts of manors were fused with other estates through purchase, inheritance, exchange, or gift, with the peasants on each manor retaining their traditional obligations. And, of course, the differing needs of the seigniors themselves sometimes explained why the demands they made upon their peasants differed.

Nonetheless, despite the extreme diversity in the nomenclature of dues and services and in seigniorial requirements, there was much similarity and even congruity among the levies imposed upon the peasantry in all of the servile lands. Labor services were perhaps the most common of all obligations, though in western Europe they were a relatively unimportant part of the total burden of the peasant. Seigniors in western Europe, with some notable exceptions, especially in northwestern Germany, were as a rule not as active in agricultural production as were the lords of eastern Europe, so that they had at most a moderate need for labor services. Many of them allowed their peasants to commute their labor dues into money payments.

[1] Henning (1969b), 99; Rappard (1912), 145; Schiff (1898), 16.

Others used the labor service for such non-agricultural tasks as building and repair, nightwatchmen, guards, messengers, and the like. Seigniors frequently used part or all of the labor dues for hunting, a pastime of enormous popularity with the nobility and which required the services of the villagers as beaters, dog-handlers, gun bearers, net setters, and carriers of dead game. Almost always the peasant owed his labor services to the seignior from whom he held his land. In some places, however, including Lorraine, Hannover, southern Lower Saxony, and Württemberg, there were peasants who paid all or part of their labor obligation to their *Gerichtsherr*, the lord who had court jurisdiction over them. In contrast, in eastern Europe many lords engaged extensively in direct production and depended upon the labor dues of their peasants to work their fields. And so for most of the peasants of eastern Europe the compulsory labor obligation was by far their most onerous obligation.

Usually the labor service was set as a fixed number of work days per year. Often, however, the peasant was required to perform a given task, or accomplish a certain amount of work such as plowing so much land. Supposedly, the assigned tasks could be accomplished within the total number of labor days the peasant had to provide the seignior. If the peasant completed his assigned task before the day ended, he could leave; if he did not meet his production norm, he had to spend additional time that was not deducted from the total number of days of his annual labor obligation. Presumably, some seigniors employed the task system as an incentive to greater efficiency on the part of the peasant, who could shorten his work day by his diligence. (When the labor service was measured by the day, the peasant was inclined to loaf.) Often, however, by establishing unrealistic norms the task system served to extort more labor from the peasant than custom or law sanctioned.[2]

Whether measured by task or by work day, the work rules of the labor obligation were set in precise terms by custom, or by agreement, or in some lands by statute. Nearly everywhere peasant and seignior knew what kind of work the peasant had to do, how long the work day lasted, how many rest periods it included, how many animals and what implements the peasant had to provide, whether or not the seignior provided meals for the workers, what the meals would include or how much money the peasant received in lieu of meals, and so on. Customarily, the work day went from sunup to sundown, with appropriate rest periods. Sometimes, though, it began and ended at specified times, as in places in Schleswig-Holstein, where it lasted from 8 a.m. to 6 p.m. in summer and 8 or 9 a.m. to 4 p.m.

[2] Knapp (1902), 29-32; Wittich (1896), 168-169, 207; Jordan-Rozwadowski (1900), 349, 392; Darmstaedter (1897), 151; Lütge (1957), 119-121; Riemann (1953), 100; Zaionchkovskii (1968), 17; Blum (1961), 444-448; Hanssen (1861), 19n., Rutkowski (1927), 86; Transehe-Roseneck (1890), 119-120; Mager (1955), 192; Scharling (1909), 578.

in winter, with a two-hour lunch period in both summer and winter. Time spent going to and coming from the work site sometimes counted as part of the work day and sometimes did not. In Hungary, for example, from February to October the work day included up to 1½ hours for travel, but no travel time was included in the work day from November through January when the days were short. In neighboring Bohemia, however, statute specified that travel time had to be counted as part of the work day in both summer and winter. To reduce the time lost in travel, lords in Livonia and in Hungary (and doubtless elsewhere) sometimes required peasants to remain at the work site for several days at a time and even a week, rather than return home each evening.

In winter, when the need for labor fell off, seigniors might not demand any labor services for two or three months. Often, however, they used the labor obligations for such activities as threshing grain, cutting and hauling timber, building and repair, transport, and so on. In eastern lands some seigniors required labor services during winter in factories owned by the lord that produced beet sugar or whiskey or cloth or metallurgical wares. In Poland and White Russia serfowners who could not use all of the labor services owed them by their serfs sold the labor by leasing out the peasants to other seigniors, or to factories or mines and other enterprises, sometimes far from the peasants' home village.

In some manors the head of the peasant household himself had to appear to work for the seignior. Generally, however, he could send members of his household, including hired hands if he had them, to perform the labor services. As could be expected, the workers he sent and the animals and implements that they brought with them were the ones that could be most easily spared, though seigniors would not accept obviously unfit workers such as the aged or the infirm.[3]

There was great diversity in the amount of labor services required. In France those peasants who were burdened with this obligation did as little as 2 or 3 or even 1 day a year. More often the obligation called for up to 12, and in a few places as much as 15 days annually. Obviously the obligation was not overly burdensome, but sometimes seigniors demanded it at times that were highly inconvenient for the peasant. In *cahiers* drawn up in 1789 in Champagne, Artois, and Maine for the delegates to the Estates-General, villagers complained that their seigniors demanded 3 to 5 days a week with

[3] Germany: Lütge (1957), 120; Knapp (1902), 33; Wittich (1896), 202; Riemann (1953), 97; Jordan-Rozwadowski (1900), 356; Henning (1969b) 118; Müller (1967), 32-33; Stein (1918), I, 363, 369. Lorraine: Darmstaedter (1897), 151. France: La Monneraye (1922), 59. Schleswig-Holstein: Hanssen (1861), 19. Austria: Grüll (1952), 242; Grünberg (1893), II, 262; Grünberg (1901), 41, 42; Hlubek (1860), 114; Stark (1952), 365, 370; Feigl (1964), 94. Hungary: Mailath (1838), 28, 192-193. Livonia: Transehe-Roseneck (1890), 120. Poland: Leslie (1956), 58. Danubian Principalities: Emerit (1937), 41, 272. Russia: Chepko (1959), 176-177; Blum (1961), 318-319, 444, 447.

team at plowing and harvest times, thereby making it difficult and costly for the peasants to work their own fields at these critical periods. In Switzerland the labor service was even lighter than it was in France. In southwest Germany, too, it did not amount to much more than a token payment, except in Baden, where it averaged out at 14⅓ days a year for the peasant who had no work team, and 16 days for the peasant with a team. In central Germany, where seigniors were more active in agricultural production, some lords required 52 days per year, but most demanded less than that.[4]

When seigniors demanded heavy labor services, they scaled the amount required to the size of the peasant's holding, whether he had work animals and how many, and the age and sex of the people in the household. In northwest Germany, where many proprietors engaged in large-scale farm production, peasants who had full holdings often did 104 days, and in a few places 156 days a year with a team. That averaged out to 2 and 3 days a week. On some manors in Lüneburg in eastern Hannover, peasants with full holdings did 156 days a year with a team, or 300 to 312 days, namely 6 days a week, without a team. In Poland many serf households with full holdings had to furnish their master with two workers with draft animals for 4 to 6 days every week, those with half-holdings did 3 to 4 days per week, and so on down to those with one-eighth of a holding who were responsible for half a day each week. On manors of the crown and of the church, and on some privately owned estates, too, the lords demanded not quite as much. In Lithuania full holdings had all but disappeared. Those peasants who had land rarely held more than a quarter-holding. Though there were many variations, a common pattern was for the household to provide two workers, a man and a woman, each for 3 days per week. The man worked with draft animals and the woman did manual labor. On thoses manors where the peasant also paid a quitrent the man did 2 days and the woman 1 day a week. In Russia Tsar Paul, in a decree in 1797 that forbade seigniors to require labor services on Sunday, observed that serfowners in general demanded 3 days of labor services per week. The tsar did not order, nor did he even recommend, that seigniors not ask for more than 3 days. In later years, however, his observation was interpreted as the establishment of a norm for the labor service. Most lords observed the norm, but labor services of 5, 6, and even 7 days a week were not unknown, especially at harvest and other times of heavy labor demand.[5]

In East Prussia there were lords who demanded as much as 6 days a

[4] Lizerand (1942), 98-99; Soboul (1960), 123; Darmstaedter (1897), 146-148, 150-151; Sée (1906), 103; Kowalewsky (1909), I, 262; Rappard (1912), 140, 144; Riemann (1953), 98-100; Liebel (1965), 43n.; Lütge (1967), 188-189.

[5] Wittich (1896), 206, 208; Rutkowski (1927), 128; Revesz (1964), 245; Henning (1969b), 66; Rusinski (1960), 418; Conze (1940), 180; Zaionchkovskii (1968), 61; Blum (1961), 444-445; Chepko (1959), 175.

week with two people and four horses from serfs who had full holdings. Other proprietors there asked for less. In the Ermeland district, near Königsberg, peasants on private estates did three days a week with two people and four horses. Those peasants on manors of the crown who had to perform labor services did only between 9 and 60 days a year. In contrast, some peasant households in Swedish Pomerania in the 1760's had to provide two people and four horses every day. In Mecklenburg, too, lords made inordinately heavy demands. On many privately owned manors there peasant households with full holdings (there were not many in this category) had to work 6 days a week for the lord with three people and six animals. Only a little less was required of peasants who lived on the estates of the sovereign. In comparison, the seigniors of Brandenburg seemed almost moderate in their demands for labor services. Peasant households with holdings had to do 3 days a week with a team. Cotters, the peasants who had only a house and yard, were responsible for 3 days of manual labor, except in the Uckermark district, where they had to do 4 to 6 days a week. In Lower Silesia peasants with holdings did only 1 or 2 days weekly with a team. However, the Polish peasants who made up most of the population of Upper Silesia had to provide their seigniors with 5 to 6 days a week during the summer months and three to four days in winter. In Saxony, where the labor obligation was often determined by task, it ran between 30 and 80 days a year, and was concentrated in spring, when the fields had to be prepared and sown, and at harvest.[6]

The labor obligations of peasants in the Danish realm, and especially in Holstein, were possibly the heaviest in all Europe. In Denmark a medium-sized holding had to furnish the seignior with 200 or more days a year, much of it with animals. Most of the work had to be done at sowing and harvest times, precisely the busiest periods of the year for the peasant on his own holding. In eastern Holstein, peasant households with full holdings had to provide eight horses with five workers every day in summer, and eight horses with four workers every day in winter. Those with half holdings had to furnish four horses and three people daily, and so on. Even the landless peasant who earned his meager living as a hired hand, and who in other lands paid no labor service or a very small one, was not overlooked here. His wife had to do 60 to 70 days a year of work for the lord, spin several pounds of flax for him, and had to do additional days if her husband was allowed to keep a cow on the village green or collect firewood in the lord's forest.[7]

In the Austrian Monarchy the government in the 1760's and 1770's had

[6] Stein (1918), I, 363, 368; Henning (1969b), 61; Riemann (1953), 96-98; Eggert (1965), 26-27; Mager (1955), 192; Müller (1967), 32; Dessmann (1904), 65; Stulz and Oppitz (1956), 25, 25n.
[7] Skrubbeltrang (1953), 18; Hanssen (1861), 19-20, 30.

issued provincial codes to protect the seigniorial peasantry from excessive exploitation. These codes fixed the amount of the obligations of the peasant, with special attention to the labor service and the conditions under which it was to be performed. In general, the codes reduced, sometimes substantially, the labor services hitherto demanded, though in some cases seigniors who had asked for fewer days raised their demands to the new norms. In the German and Slav crown lands the obligation now ranged from 156 days a year, that is, 3 days a week, with four animals, for the peasant household with a full holding in Bohemia, Moravia, Silesia, and Galicia, down to 14 days a year in Upper Austria, where most seigniors were not engaged in large-scale agricultural activity. In the provinces, where heavy labor services were the rule, peasants with smaller holdings sometimes did the same number of days as those with full holdings. Thus, in Bohemia households with three-quarter or half holdings did 156 days a year, but with three and two work animals, respectively, rather than the four animals that the peasant with a full holding had to provide. Those with less than a half holding did from 26 to 156 days of manual labor, that is, without a team, depending upon the size of their holding, and landless laborers had to do 13 days annually. In Hungary the code, or *Urbarium* as it was called there, issued in 1767, set the labor obligation of the peasant with a full holding at 104 days of manual labor, or 52 days with work animals; the *Urbarium* did not prescribe the number of animals. Occupants of smaller holdings had to do proportionately less, and a maximum of 12 days was set for landless laborers.[8]

In the Danubian Principalities, too, princes in the eighteenth century issued laws that fixed the obligations of the peasants, particularly the labor dues. In the Principalities, however, unlike the Austrian Monarchy, the actions of the government served not to protect the peasants but rather to satisfy the demands of the seigniors for increases in the labor obligation. In Wallachia, legislation in 1746 set the obligation at 6 days a year, in 1775 at 12 days, and in 1818 a minimum of 12 days. In Moldavia, legislation in 1749 set it at 24 days, in 1766 at 30 days, and in 1805 at 43 days. Moreover, the "work day" in the Principalities involved the completion of tasks that could take as much as 3 days, so that the peasant actually worked as much as three times more than the legislation prescribed. Then in 1831 the so-called Organic Statutes, imposed by the Russians who had occupied the Principalities (which were under the suzerainty of the Porte), established new norms that resulted in a reduction in the amount of labor time that many lords had been demanding.[9]

The heavy labor obligation, so prevalent in eastern Europe, obviously cut

[8] Stark (1952), 364-365, 370; Blum (1948), 48-50, 72-73, 183.
[9] Evans (1924), 21-27, 31; *Règlement organique* (1834), art. 118e.

severely into the time and labor available to the peasants to work their own land. Those households who had to use most or even all of their workers and animals for their labor dues had to till their own fields on Sunday and on moonlit nights. More fortunate households still were handicapped by not being able to use all their resources on their own holdings, and by having to maintain additional animals for use in the service of the seignior.

The unpaid labor obligation was not the only labor service the lord could demand. He could compel his peasants to work additional days for him. In most lands law or custom required the seignior to pay for these extra days, in some lands at the going wage for hired labor, but often at a lower rate. In places in central Germany peasants who had to provide additional days as harvesters and threshers were paid one-eighth to one-twelfth of the grain they harvested or threshed. In contrast to this reasonable payment, peasants in Congress Poland in the first half of the nineteenth century received the equivalent of 3 to 3½ kopecks for each compulsory extra labor day. That was about one-fifth to one-fifteenth of the daily wage paid hired labor. In Hungary the law required extra days to be paid for in cash and at a fair wage. In Bohemia, Moravia, and Silesia peasants whose labor obligation was less than 3 days a week could be compelled to work up to 3 days at a fixed wage that varied according to the season. In Russia seigniors sometimes paid wages for extra days or deducted them for the peasant's labor dues, but sometimes they neither paid nor deducted. In Austria seigniors demanded unpaid labor services above the legal limit. And though the laws there provided for appeals from such seigniorial extortions, the peasants' inferior status and their fear of the consequences apparently kept them from appealing to the courts.[10]

Peasants also had to provide transport services for their seigniors. They used their own animals and carts—and their backs if they lacked other means—to carry the goods the lord sent to market, the dues in kind and the tithes that he collected from them, the supplies he needed for his own use, and any other need he had for transportation. Sometimes the service counted as part of the labor obligation. That was often the case in Russia, where an estimate made in 1851 reckoned that the carting obligation accounted for 30 per cent of all labor services performed during the winter and 8 per cent in summer. More often it was a separate obligation demanded in addition to the labor dues. It could take the peasant away from his village for days, and in eastern Europe for weeks at a time, often during the cruel winter weather. Generally, the peasant had to meet all of the expenses of the journey, though in a few lands lords paid part or all of the costs. In some places the lord could demand as much carting service as he

[10] Kostiushko (1954), 199, 201; Blaschke (1956), 266; Blum (1948), 184-187; Rutkowski (1927), 129; Koroliuk (1956), ı, 346; Redaktsionnye komissii (1859), ı, ch. 6, 38-41; Haxthausen (1866), 118n.

wished. In other lands custom or statute set limits on the amount that the peasant had to furnish.[11]

In eastern Europe many seigniors, in addition to labor dues and carting services, made still further demands upon their peasants. They drafted peasant children to work for them. They usually paid wages to the children, or to their parents, at a rate always less, and frequently much less, than the local scale for hired labor. Sometimes the children received only food and clothing, and these in sparse amounts and of the poorest quality. Each year on a certain day the peasant children of the village were assembled and the seignior or his bailiff selected the ones best suited for their purposes. In Schleswig-Holstein they took children as young as six or seven to serve as gooseherds or shepherds; as the child grew older he was given more difficult tasks. Sometimes the seignior assigned drafted children to work for those of his peasants who needed additional labor. In Brandenburg the children of free peasants were liable for the draft of child labor for the estates of the crown. In some lands custom or law restricted the choices of the seigniors; thus, in Anhalt, Saxony, Silesia, and East Prussia they could take only children who were not needed to work on their parents' holding.

Sometimes, too, law or custom fixed the length of time the child had to serve. Usually it was between 2 and 4 years. In parts of Brandenburg, however, the service continued until the peasant married. In Livonia and in Schleswig-Holstein the period of service was undetermined and could last a lifetime. Even in lands with a fixed period of service, lords sometimes compelled the peasant to remain in their employ as a hired laborer. In East Prussia a royal decree of 1763 abolished the child labor draft on manors of the crown but not on other properties. Another decree in 1767 ordered seigniors to pay the drafted workers the prevailing local wage, and an edict in 1773 set the length of service, hitherto unfixed, at 5 years. Meanwhile population growth brought an increase in the number of adults available for hire. This, plus the increase in the wage that had to be paid to drafted child labor, persuaded most proprietors to abandon the draft. By the end of the eighteenth century it survived in only a few East Prussian villages. In the Austrian Monarchy until 1781 seigniors could require compulsory labor service of 3 years of 14-year-old peasant children who were not needed at home. In 1781 Emperor Joseph II abolished the obligation, except for orphans who had lost both parents. The rationale here was that these children became wards of the seignior, and paid for their upkeep by working for him. Up to the age of 14 they received lodging, board, and clothing. At 14 the law required the seignior to pay them the local going wage for their work, and placed a limit of 3 years on their compulsory service. Despite the

[11] Scheibert (1973), 9; Grünberg (1893), II, 264-265; Conze (1940), 183; Ziekursch (1927), 88; Stein (1918), I, 369; Darmstaedter (1897), 148; Wittich (1896), 10, 203-204; Henning (1969b), 107; Knapp (1902), 54; *Règlement organique* (1834), art. 120c.

legislation, seigniors in Moravia were reported to have continued to demand labor services from all the children in their villages. In 1785 Joseph ordered the end of the obligation in Hungary. The Diet, however, did not give its required approval to this particular reform, and Hungarian lords continued to draft child labor.

The labor draft of peasant children as a separate obligation, with its own rules, was unknown or all but unknown in Mecklenburg, Swedish Pomerania, Poland, and Russia. The reason for this was a simple one. The lords in those lands had so much authority over their peasants that it went without saying that if the lord wished, the children of his peasants had to work for him. In Russia the seignior could remove peasants of any age from the land and use them for his personal service, as household serfs. In the Danubian Principalities the Organic Statutes of 1831 authorized the seignior to draft one person out of every 10 families and use them "in the interest of his rural economy." Those proprietors who had 200 or less peasants on their properties could take two persons out of every 10 families.[12]

In western Europe, with few exceptions, the compulsory labor of peasant children was either not demanded or at most only traces of it persisted. In Bavaria it had been banned in the sixteenth and again in the seventeenth century. However, the law code of 1756 permitted the practice until it was again outlawed in 1801. In the Saar region of Lorraine, seigniors with sizable agricultural operations of their own required the children of their serfs to work for them for a year, at an annual wage of 10 florins for the boys and 6 florins for the girls. Children needed on their parents' holding did not have to serve, and families in which one child served for a year were exempt for the next 3 years. The family could commute the obligation by a payment equal to the wage the child would have received.[13]

Though the labor service was a widely demanded obligation, there were many peasants in all of the servile lands who were not called upon to pay it. In some places the seigniors had never required labor dues. More often, they had permitted their peasants to commute all or part of their labor obligations, including carting services and the compulsory labor of peasant children, into periodic payments in cash or kind. As could be expected, this happened most frequently in lands and regions where typically seigniors did not operate large-scale farming operations. These lands included France, Switzerland, western and parts of central Germany, the Alpine

[12] Germany: Dessmann (1904), 77-80; Eggert (1965), 28; Blaschke (1965), 267; Stein (1918), I, 326, 329; Jordan-Rozwadowski (1900), 354-355; Schönebaum (1917), 514; Aubin (1910), 169. Schleswig-Holstein: Hanssen (1861), 21-22. Poland: Rutkowski (1926), 49. Austria: Stark (1952), 287; Grüll (1952), 35-37, 185; Blum (1948), 78-79, 186. Russia: Blum (1961), 455-460. Danubian Principalities: *Règlement organique* (1834), art. 72.

[13] Brentano (1899), 244; Lütge (1949), 164-166; Knapp (1902), 34; Darmstaedter (1897), 168-169.

provinces of Austria, parts of Slavonia and the Banat in southern Hungary, and parts of Wallachia.[14] In lands in which seigniors engaged actively in agricultural production, commutation of the labor obligation was infrequent; in White Russia in the 1850's, for example, 92.7 per cent of the serf population performed labor services. However, in other lands where labor dues were commonly required, a surprisingly large number of peasants did not have to pay them. An estimated 30 per cent of peasant households in Poland at the end of the eighteenth century, and nearly the same ratio in Russia in the late 1850's, paid quitrents instead of labor dues. Some of the greatest Russian proprietors, including the Sheremetevs, the Iusupovs, and the Vorontsovs, had all or nearly all of their serfs on quitrents. Presumably these magnates wanted to avoid the heavy administrative costs involved in assigning and supervising the labors of the tens and even hundreds of thousands of peasants who belonged to them. Also, in the years that immediately preceded the emancipations of the peasantry, commutations increased in some regions, such as East Prussia. Proprietors there preferred the increasingly abundant and more efficient hired labor to the forced, unpaid labor of their peasants. So they commuted the labor dues of their peasants and used the money to hire workers.[15]

Most peasants understandably preferred quitrents to labor services. The payment liberated them from the surveillance and supervision and discipline that necessarily accompanied a forced labor system, allowed them to use all their working time and resources for themselves, saved them from the expense of maintaining additional draft animals for use in the seignior's service, and gave them freedom to seek work elsewhere. In Russia and in Poland thousands of these quitrent peasants, with their lords' consent, left their villages to earn their livings as artisans, peddlers, factory and service workers, and paid a fixed sum or a portion of their earnings to their seigniors as quitrent. Under certain conditions, however, labor services offered an advantage over quitrent. The smallholder sometimes had more labor in his household than he needed for his own operation. Opportunities for outside employment or cottage manufacturing for sale did not always present themselves. The smallholder therefore lacked cash for a quitrent in money, and payments in kind took away food he needed to feed his family. So he preferred to make his payment in labor, the one commodity of which he had an adequate supply.[16]

[14] Louchitsky (1911), 27-28; La Monneraye (1922), 59; Rappard (1912), 142; Knapp (1902), 78; Wittich (1896), 8-9; Lütge (1957), 113-115; Turnbull (1840), II, 51; Hlubek (1860), 114, 119; Preyer (1838), 101-102; Mitrany (1930), 31.

[15] Koval'chenko (1967), 61, table 6; Chepko (1959), 175; Koroliuk (1956), I, 348; Sivkov (1951), 121; Stark (1952), 366; Pokhilevich (1966), 392; Loone (1959), 210; Kieniewicz (1969), 9-10; Corfus (1969), 32-33; Stein (1918), I, 361; Hanssen (1961), 23; Conze (1940), 183.

[16] Koroliuk (1956), I, 348-350, 351; Henning (1969b), 114.

II

As earlier shown, labor dues were not a major obligation of most peasants in western Europe. The principal charges for them were the payment commonly called the *cens* in French-speaking lands and *Gült* or *Grundzins* by speakers of German, the fees demanded on the transfer of holdings, and tithes. All three of these obligations were either unknown or of minor importance in the servile lands of eastern Europe.

The *cens* was owed by those peasants who held their land by hereditary tenure. They paid it to the seignior who had the *dominium directum* of their land as recognition of his superior ownership. Depending upon custom or agreement, the payment was made in cash or kind or in both forms. (In France when paid in kind it was called variously *champart, terrage, tasque,* or *tierce.*) When paid in money the charge was usually—though not always—a negligible one. It had been fixed long ago as a perpetual and unchangeable fee when money had a greater purchasing power than it had in the last century of the old order. When demanded in kind, however, it could be a heavy and even crippling obligation if the peasant had to pay, as he did in places in France and in northwest Germany, one-third to one-fourth of his crop. Usually, however, the payment amounted to around one-twelfth of the peasant's produce.[17]

The fee levied on the transfer of holdings was, like the *cens*, demanded of those peasants who had hereditary tenure of their land, and could sell, exchange or bequeath it as they pleased. Like the *cens* it represented acknowledgment of the superior property right of the seignior. Sometimes the fee remained the same whether the property was transferred by sale (when, to name a few of the fee's names, it was called *laudemium, Lehngeld, Handlohn,* or *lods et ventes*) or by inheritance (when the fee was called *mortuarium, Besthaupt, Hauptrecht, rachat* or *relief*). In some places the peasant paid the fee for one kind of transfer and not another. Sometimes the fee was lessened or not demanded at all when a direct heir took over the holding. In other places the seignior on the death of the peasant occupant and the transfer of the holding asked for only a token payment, such as a fowl, or a few jugs of wine, or a pair of gloves, or a few small coins, simply as a recognition of his superior ownership. And there were villages in Saxony and in Thuringia, and doubtless in other places, where the peasants did not have to pay any fee.

Far more frequently, however, the seigniors imposed large charges when hereditary holdings changed hands. If the transfer came as the result of the death of the occupant, the seignior took the best of the deceased peasant's work animals and demanded a cash settlement that varied with local cus-

[17] Millot (1937), 100; Marion (1902), 223-230; Sheppard (1971), 133; Goubert (1966), 29; La Monneraye (1922), 53-56; Wahlen and Jaggi (1952), 109-110; Schremmer (1963), 43-46, 85, 191; Darmstaedter (1897), 16, 155-156; Lütge (1957), 169-176.

tom. Sometimes it was a year's income from the holding, or one-half or twice the annual income, or a percentage of the property's value, which ranged from as little as 1.25 to 10 per cent, and exceptionally as much as 20 per cent. The fee on transfer of holdings by sale tended to run even higher. In much of France peasants had to pay one-eighth, in some places one-quarter or one-third, and in parts of Lorraine and Auvergne, one-half of the purchase price. On the other hand, in Württemberg seigniors asked for only 2 per cent of the purchase price.[18]

It was not unknown, particularly in southwest Germany, for more than one seignior to have a claim to a fee on the transfer of a holding. The new occupant had to pay fees to the lord who had the *dominium directum* of the land, the lord who had judicial authority, and, if the peasant was a serf, he paid a fee to the lord whose serf he was. When one individual held more than one of their seigniorial roles, he received the appropriate fee for each of his roles. In Switzerland the cantonal governments through conquest or purchase had acquired the right to the fees on property transfers. They provided an important source of state revenue; for example, at the end of the eighteenth century the fees made up one-eighth of the receipts of the Republic of Geneva, and Geneva was essentially an urban canton. In the shift from private to governmental control the nature of the fees themselves shifted from a private and servile obligation to a public tax. When the government of the short-lived Helvetic Republic emancipated Swiss peasants in 1798, it called the fee a registration tax, set it at a uniform figure of 2 per cent, and from then on it became part of the state's fiscal system.

French seigniors, in addition to levying heavy fees on transfers, required the peasant who took over an hereditary holding to make a statement in which he formally acknowledged the superior ownership of the seignior. The *aveu*, or avowal, as it was called, included a detailed description of the holding and the obligations for which the peasant was now responsible. The preparation of this document could sometimes be expensive. In addition, seigniors, especially in the second half of the eighteenth century, often ordered a revision of the manor rolls, or *terriers*, at intervals of 10, 20, or 30 years. This meant a new *aveu*, prepared usually at the peasant's expense, though sometimes seigniors helped out. Generally, the revision was made by a professional *commissaire à terrier*, who often received a premium from the seignior scaled to the amount of additional revenue he could add to the seignior's income.[19]

In most of eastern Europe, with the exception of the Austrian Monarchy,

[18] Knapp (1919), 112; Darmstaedter (1897), 157-158; Haun (1892), 170, 173; Engels (1957), 22-23; Sée (1906), 113-114; Schremmer (1963), 46, 56-57; Millot (1937), 102; Herbert (1969), 22, 24; La Monneraye (1922), 68-69.

[19] Knapp (1902), 131-132; Rappard (1912), 162-164; Sée (1906), 78-81; Herbert (1969), 18-22; La Monneraye (1922), 129-131.

hereditary peasant tenure was uncommon and fees on property transfers were not usually demanded. In the Austrian Monarchy, reforms of Joseph II in the 1780's had transformed insecure tenures into hereditary ones. Legislation in the German crown lands of the Monarchy sanctioned the payment of fees on property transfers and set the maxima that could be charged in each province. These ranged from 3 to 10 per cent of the value of the holdings. In the Slav provinces, legislation did not authorize the imposition of the fees, though some seigniors there did collect them. In Lower Silesia and in Denmark, seigniors exacted fees when hereditary holdings passed from one peasant to another.[20]

The tithe was the third and by all odds the most ubiquitous of the major obligations demanded of the peasants in western Europe. Every peasant with land, no matter how insecure his tenure, had to pay the tithe. In fact, all land, including the demesne land of noblemen, the church, and burghers, had a tithe levied upon it, though in France nobles and churchmen often paid at a lower rate and a few of the older religious orders had acquired exemptions for their land. Originally intended for the support of the church and of the needy, the tithe had become a caricature of what it was supposed to be. Now governments, laymen, nobles, burghers, and even peasants, through purchase, conquest, or secularization, had become owners of tithes. In France the church still owned most of the tithes and drew an estimated 100 to 120 million livres from them. Privately owned tithes produced about 10 million livres. Most of the church-owned tithes, however, belonged to wealthy prelates and monasteries; perhaps one in ten parish priests received all the tithes in his parish. French laws of 1695 and 1768 had ordered recipients of the tithes to give one-third to the poor, maintain and repair the parish church, and provide an adequate living for its priest, but most tithe owners paid no heed to these prescripts. Some of them did support the parish church, but all too often they gave so little and so reluctantly that the local peasants had to lay out additional moneys to keep their church going. There were places where the peasants could not afford to do this or chose not to, and so the parish went without church and curé. In some parts of Switzerland the tithe was all but unknown. In most of that country, however, local governments had supplanted clerical and lay tithe owners to such an extent that by the latter part of the eighteenth century the tithe was sometimes regarded as a land tax. In 1798 a contemporary estimated that the tithe's value averaged out to about 8.5 million Swiss livres a year, of which 6.6 million went to the state and 1.9 million to institutions, clerics, and private persons.[21]

[20] Ziekursch (1927), 79; Feigl (1964), 74-75; Skrubbeltrang (1953), 16; Blum (1948), 54, 77-78.
[21] Henning (1969b), 101; Borcke-Stargordt (1960), 183; Rappard (1912), 150-152, 154-156; Knapp (1902), 53; Engels (1957), 24-25; Schremmer (1963), 60; Millot (1937), 210; Babeau (1878), 151, 153-154; Goubert (1969), 87, 120-121; Herbert (1969), 39-40; Wahlen and Jaggi (1952), 111.

The products on which the tithe was paid depended upon local custom and upon the ability of the tithe owner to impose his demands. It was always levied on the major products, such as grain, wine, or the natural increase in livestock. This was known as the "great tithe." Then there was the "lesser tithe" on other goods such as, perhaps, fruit, vegetables, and in some places bees. Often several recipients divided the tithes of a parish among themselves, with each entitled to a specific tithe. Frequently the great tithe belonged to a lay seignior, while the lesser tithe, which was smaller in value and harder to collect, went to the parish priest. Which products were liable to tithes and which were exempt sparked constant disputes between tithe owner and tithe payer, especially with the introduction of new crops such as potatoes, clover, and maize, or with the conversion of hitherto untilled land into arable. The tithe payer, using tradition as his defense, argued that since the new crops and the new arable had (obviously) never been tithed, they should not now be; the tithe owner, of course, disagreed.[22]

Sometimes the tithe actually amounted to the tenth that its name implied. More frequently it fluctuated in amount, not only between villages but even from one field to another in a single parish. There were places where it was only one-twentieth or one-thirtieth or even one-thirty-sixth of the tithed products. In many places in France it was around one-eleventh to one-thirteenth of the grain crop, or between 7.7 and 9 per cent. However, the tithe came out of the gross yield. It represented a much larger share of the net—that is, what was left after the grower had taken out his costs and the seed for next year's sowing. At the prevailing low level of productivity in which yields often averaged as low as three to four bushels to one bushel of seed, the tithe could amount to one-seventh of the net harvest on good soil, one-fifth on medium, and one-third of the net on poor soil. In short, it could be an inordinately heavy obligation and was often the heaviest burden the peasant had to bear.

The tithe was sometimes commuted into a fixed annual cash payment, but typically it remained a payment in kind. Sometimes the producer delivered his tithe to the tithe owner. Far more often, however, he had to leave the crop standing in the field (sometimes to its detriment) until the tithingman arrived and collected the tithe out of the field. This was to prevent the payer from cheating or from giving the poorest grain as his tithe.[23]

The tithe was much less common in eastern Europe than it was in the west. In many regions it was unknown and in others it was not widely demanded. When it was levied, as it was in Poland, Denmark, and the Aus-

[22] Knapp (1902), 54-55; Goubert (1969), 120-121; Sée (1906), 175; Marion (1902), 216-218; Rappard (1912), 149-150; Babeau (1878), 152; Lefebvre (1972), 105-107.
[23] Soboul (1960), 63; Sée (1906), 162-163, 165, 167-168; Lefebvre (1972), 109-111; Chevallez (1960), 213; Rappard (1912), 146-147; Sée (1921), 28; Borcke-Stargordt (1960), 183; Schremmer (1963), 66-67; Henning (1969b), 139; Knapp (1902), 54.

trian Monarchy, the products liable to the tithe varied according to local law or custom and the amount demanded was not always a tenth. Sometimes, too, the payers had commuted all or part of the obligation into an annual cash payment. As in the west, laymen now often owned the tithe, and frequently it was split among several owners. Generally, too, the crops had to remain in the field until the tithe collector arrived. Whether or not the peasants tithed, they were responsible almost everywhere for small payments in cash and kind and often had to provide a few days of labor services for the support of the local priest and church. The Hungarian peasant had to pay two tithes, one to his lord and one to the church. He paid the church one-tenth of his cereal crops and of his lambs, goats, and bees. He had to pay his lord one-ninth of everything he produced except for the products of his garden and his meadow. If the lord happened to be a prelate, he received both tithes. The *nona*, as the one-ninth payment to the seignior was called, had been introduced by King Louis the Great in 1351 and continued to be collected up to the emancipation in 1848. In practice the obligation varied, with some lords taking a ninth, some a tenth, and some requiring the peasant to make the payment in cash. In the Danubian Principalities the peasants had to give their lords one-tenth of their produce except that which they grew in their gardens for their own use. Here, too, the amount actually taken by the seignior was sometimes more and sometimes less than the prescribed share.[24]

Besides their principal obligations, peasants everywhere had a host of minor dues in cash and in kind. Some were fixed in amount, some fluctuated, some recurred at regular intervals, and some irregularly. They included such things as supplying a certain amount of eggs, or fowl, or vegetables, or nuts, or mushrooms and the like, and spinning and weaving a specified quantity of thread and cloth. Then there were small cash payments for all manner of things, such as a fee to let their swine root in the lord's forest, or a payment in kind when they used the lord's oven or his winepress. These obligations were rarely overly burdensome and often peasants commuted part or all of them into a single annual cash payment to the seignior. Sometimes, though, these lesser dues could be oppressive. There were seigniors in Brittany who, according to the *cahiers* of peasants there in 1789, imposed a chimney tax payable in kind that equalled 18 livres for a house that rented for only 3 livres a year. In some villages in Champagne lords charged each peasant household, including landless ones, 3 livres 7 sols merely for the right to reside in the seigniory.[25]

[24] Poland: Rutkowski (1927), 96; Revesz (1964), 251. Austrian Monarchy: Feigl (1964), 31, 229, 231-236; Grüll (1952), 19, 44-45; Brunner (1949), 268-269; Blum (1948), 80; Revesz (1964), 265. Germany: Lütge (1957), 192-194. Denmark: Skrubbeltrang (1953), 21; Scharling (1909), ii, 578. Russia: Drakokhrust (1938), 125; Indova (1955), 96-97. Danubian Principalities: Corfus (1969), 17, 20-24, 78-82; Oṭetea (1960), 340-341; *Règlement organique* (1834), art. 120f.
[25] Herbert (1969), 11, 14; Knapp (1902), 61; Wittich (1896), 34; Lizerand (1942), 88-89;

In most of eastern Europe peasants could not leave their villages without the consent of their seigniors. In Russia the serf who received permission to depart had to make regular payments to his seignior no matter how long he stayed away, and he always remained the property of his master. In Lower Silesia a peasant could buy the right to leave, though, as in Russia, he remained the serf of his seignior. A decree of 1748 set the price he had to pay for himself and for each member of his family who left with him. He could not take a holding in his new village, for that would make him the serf of the seignior there, and so he had to earn his living as a hired laborer or as an artisan. Moreover, he had to pay dues and services to the proprietor of the new village for permission to live there. These and other restrictions made departure unattractive. Only extreme deprivation in their native village, or the desire to escape the rigors of compulsory military service (to promote the linen industry residents in certain specified linen-producing districts of Silesia were exempted from conscription) could persuade peasants to leave their homes. Departure was much easier in the Austrian Monarchy. The reforms of Joseph II had given the peasant the right to leave the manor if he met all of his obligations to his lord and to the state, and if the peasant to whom he turned over his holding was acceptable to the seignior. In certain manors in Saxony and in some other German states the peasant who wanted to leave had to pay an exit fee to the lord. In Saxony the fee was sometimes a fixed sum, and sometimes a percentage of the value of the peasant's property, usually between 2 and 5 per cent, but on occasion 10, 20, and even 25 per cent. In the Danubian Principalities the peasant who wanted to leave permanently had to give notice to the proprietor and the local government office six months before St. George's Day (23 April), pay his seignior all the obligations he owed for the current year, pay his taxes for each year up to the next census (the census was supposed to be taken every seventh year), and turn over his house and land to the proprietor without receiving any indemnification for them.[26]

III

The peasants' obligations did not end with the dues and services they paid to their lords. They were by far the chief source of the state's fiscal income. Their number, the relative unimportance of the bourgeoisie and the tax exemptions or favors its members sometimes won for themselves, and the full or partial exemption of the nobility and the church, saw to that. To

---

Stein (1918), I, 362; Helfert (1904), 71, 73; Revesz (1964), 250; Drakokhrust (1938), 125; Shchepetov (1947), 80-85; Rutkowski (1927), 129-130; Indova (1955), 95-96.

[26] Silesia: Ziekursch (1927), 101-112. Austria: *Handbuch aller unter der Regierung . . . Joseph des II . . . Verordnungen und Gesetze*, IX, 399-400; Mailath (1838), 49-50. Germany: Lütge (1957), 190-191; Blaschke (1965), 269-270. Danubian Principalities: *Règlement organique* (1834), art. 124.

make matters even more unjust, the taxes the peasants paid were usually assessed inequitably. In most of France the *taille* was based upon an arbitrary assessment by officials of all of the peasant's possessions. In the rest of the country it was levied on the value of the land held by the peasant. The two methods of assessment led to considerable differences in the tax. These differences occurred not only between the two systems. Even neighboring communities showed wide disparities. Compiègne, northeast of Paris, with 1,700 homesteads, paid a *taille* of 8,000 livres, or an average of 4.7 livres per hearth. The neighboring village of Conly, with only 150 homesteads, had to pay 4,500 livres, an average of 30 livres per homestead. Prosperous peasants who were best able to pay taxes managed, through bribery of corrupt officials or through use of loopholes in the law, to evade their fair share of the levies, so that the burden fell heaviest on those least able to afford it.[27]

To aggrandize their revenues and to correct inequities, some of the governments of the servile lands introduced new methods of assessment or new kinds of taxes. In Russia the use of the peasant household as the unit of assessment had proved unsatisfactory, in large part because peasants evaded the tax by living together in a single homestead. Peter I scrapped that system and, instead, in 1722 ordered that every adult male, or "soul," must pay the same head tax. Noblemen, clergy, and officials were exempted. The government made periodic censuses, starting in 1719, and the tax had to be paid for every "soul" entered in the census lists until the next revision (as the subsequent censuses were called). That meant that the village had to pay the soul tax for those who died in the interval between revisions—these were the "dead souls" of Gogol's great novel. The Danubian Principalities also had a capitation tax, levied with only a few exceptions on all male peasants above the age of 15. A head tax had been imposed in Poland in medieval times and after a lapse of 150 years it was revived in 1662. The list of eligible taxpayers provided by each manor was not revised regularly, so that over time the tax burden fell unequally as the numbers of taxpayers in each village changed. In 1775 a more equitable assessment was introduced, but within a few years independent Poland disintegrated and the tax systems of Russia, Austria, and Prussia were introduced into the respective parts of Poland that each had taken in the partitions. In France, too, the regime introduced new taxes, but, as mentioned previously, members of the upper orders managed to avoid paying their fair share. In Germany governments made the *Hufe*, the conventional unit for full-sized peasant holdings (see pp. 95-96), the unit of tax assessment and thereby facilitated the introduction of more systematic and equitable taxation. In Savoy a cadastre that registered the quantity and value of the land was

[27] Gromas (1947), 124-125; Marion (1968), 528-529; St. Jacob (1960), 124-126; Behrens (1963), 465.

drawn up at ducal command between 1728 and 1738. As mentioned earlier, it served as the basis for a more just distribution of taxes, which included the taxation of land owned by nobles and by the church. A half century later Joseph II of Austria ordered a cadastral survey of his German and Slav crownlands. Made hurriedly, it contained many deficiencies and so a more accurate survey got underway in 1817. It went on for decades; meanwhile the government used the Josephine cadastre with corrections to levy its land tax.[28]

In some of the servile lands the state levied its imposts upon the village as a whole, so that the villagers had joint responsibility for the tax bill. The proprietor was charged with the responsibility of collecting the taxes. It was left to the villagers or to the seignior or his employees to decide how to divide the tax among the villagers, and, where the lord paid land taxes, how much he should pay. Some seigniors took advantage of their position and authority to reduce their share and pass on most of the burden to the peasants. Sometimes, though, the lord paid the largest part or even all of the taxes. That could happen when the lord had responsibility for the taxes and could not get the money out of his impoverished serfs. In France seigniors did not have this responsibility, yet they often paid part or all of the *taille*. They paid it indirectly when tenant farmers bargained with them about rents and took into account the *taille* they would have to pay on the leasehold. They paid it directly when they had sharecroppers who were usually so poor they could not pay the tax, and the proprietor had to pay part or all of it for them.[29]

Governments also imposed a myriad of other levies, such as taxes on the consumption of certain goods, sales taxes, internal tariffs, and so on. These imposts, of course, were not demanded exclusively from the peasantry. There were, however, other obligations that the state required only of peasants. Nearly everywhere peasants had to perform labor services for the state, almost always for no pay. Usually the peasants had to build and maintain roads and bridges in their vicinity, and they were called upon for other work, too, such as the construction, repair, and maintenance of public buildings or the residence of the sovereign. As with other obligations, this one, too, was imposed inequitably. In France, for example (where the government did not demand labor services, or the *corvée* as it was called there, until around the 1730's), only peasants who lived not more than 4 leagues from a road repair site or from construction had to perform the service. It was never introduced into Languedoc and rarely if ever required in the Paris and Valenciennes administrative districts. In the places where it

[28] Blum (1961), 463-464; Wilkinson (1971), 60-61; Rutkowski (1927), 95-96; Lütge (1967), 173-174; Bruchet (1908), xiii; Blum (1948), 254-255.
[29] Feigl (1964), 100-102; Revesz (1964), 251; Raeff (1960), 96; Hanssen (1861), 20; Behrens (1963), 458-459; Andrews (1774), ii, 368-369.

was demanded, all males up to the age of 70 and women up to 60 had to do the work. If not enough men were available to do the needed work, two women had to replace one man.

In many places the peasants did not have to work for the state for more than 3 or 4 days a year. In Switzerland they often received wages for the work. Many peasants commuted the service into an annual cash payment. In France commutation became so general in the last decades of the old order that by 1789 the actual performance of the state labor service had all but disappeared. In some lands, however, the labor obligation could cut deeply into the peasants' time. In France the law did not put a ceiling on the number of days of labor required of the peasant, and before commutation became general officials demanded from 6 to 40 days a year. In Denmark an ambitious state road-building program compelled peasants in many places to work 3 days a week during the summer on this construction. In the Danubian Principalities there was much road building during the first half of the nineteenth century, most if not all of it done by peasants. The Organic Statutes of 1831 had reduced the peasants' labor obligation to the state to 6 days a year, and ordered that the peasant was to do this work only in his own district. The latter provision was not observed, and peasants sometimes had to leave their own districts to work in labor-short districts. Their travel time did not count against the 6 day limit, and it was claimed that a peasant could spend as much as a month in performing the legally sanctioned 6 days.[30]

Other services that the state required of the peasants included quartering of troops, furnishing transport for the military, and providing relays of fresh horses and conveyances for official messengers and vehicles. These obligations recurred irregularly and years could pass without the state demanding any of them. Often, too, the peasants were allowed to commute one or more of these services into cash payments. They could be oppressive, however, as in time of war, when the government had urgent and heavy needs for transport or billeting. The peasants who lived along major routes found the posting service an onerous obligation. They received a set fee for much of this work, but the fee was too small to cover the expenses and the loss of time and animal power they incurred in carrying out their duties.[31]

There was one last claim that the state made upon the peasantry: liability for conscription for peace-time military service. In the modern world, conscription, universal in application, reflects the civic equality of modern so-

[30] Marion (1968), 153-154; Babeau (1878), 265-266; Feigl (1964), 136; Revesz (1964), 254; Lütge (1957), 166-167; Rappard (1912), 143-144; Grüll (1952), 185-186; Scharling (1909), 578; Emerit (1937), 202-203; Knapp (1919), 17; Storch (1848), 89-92, 114-117.
[31] Feigl (1964), 96-97; Hovde (1948), 67; Henning (1969b), 56; Revesz (1964), 65-66; Nielsen (1933), 173-174; Storch (1848), 89-92, 114-117.

ciety. Conscription in the traditional society was based upon civic inequality. In Prussia, where systematic conscription began in 1732-1733, and in the German and Slav crownlands of the Austrian Monarchy, where it was introduced in 1771, legislation had defined conscription as a universal obligation. In fact, so many non-peasants had received exemptions that the burden rested upon the sons of the peasantry just as it did in other servile lands. In Prussia the country was divided into conscription districts, called cantons, with each canton responsible for the recruits for a specific regiment. Actually, the cantonists, as the conscripts were called, were trained reserves rather than regulars. After their first year of service they went on active duty for two months each year and remained at home for the rest of the year; only men who had enlisted served all year around. In Denmark, where only peasants were drafted, the recruiting districts were much smaller than the Prussian cantons. Each district had to provide one conscript at each draft call. Villagers were liable for conscription up to the age of 36 and served for 10 years. However, most of the conscripts were on active duty for only a few months each summer.[32]

The German and Slav crown lands of the Austrian Monarchy were divided into 37 recruiting districts, each assigned a quota of conscripts to be drawn from men between the ages of 17 and 40. The term of service lasted for 10 to 14 years, depending upon the branch of service. Local authorities often filled their quotas by sending off vagabonds, criminals, and other undesirable types. Conscription did not apply to Tyrol, where the peasants were free. Instead, all able-bodied peasants there were supposed to take up arms whenever the sovereign proclaimed a *levée en masse* in time of national emergency. In Hungary military service was theoretically voluntary. However, "volunteers" were often shanghaied, or were persuaded to enlist by being paid a bounty by villagers. If no one volunteered, the county or the local community had to draft recruits. In 1830 the Hungarian Diet ordered the drawing up of lists from which recruits would be drawn. Prosperous peasants managed to have their sons' names kept off the lists, and those who were drafted could avoid service by the purchase of substitutes.[33]

Peter I introduced systematic conscription in the Russian empire early in the eighteenth century. Draft calls came at irregular but frequent intervals. There were 94 of them between 1724 and 1830, with the numbers conscripted fluctuating according to need. Until 1793 the recruit served for life. In that year the term of service was reduced to 25 years, in 1834 to 20 years plus 5 years in the reserve, and in 1855 to 12 years on active duty and 3 years in the reserve. Each village was assigned a quota at each draft call, and the villagers or the seignior chose the recruits from men between 20 and 35

[32] Speier (1936), 312-313; Macartney (1969), 15-18; Hintze (1915), 285; Dorn (1940), 94-95; Drake (1969), 34-35.
[33] Macartney (1969), 15-18, 158-159; Revesz (1964), 62-63.

(in the 1850's the upper limit was lowered to 30). Service could be avoided by hiring a substitute, or by purchase of a recruit quittance from the state or from a seignior who had received credit from the government for recruits he had provided above his quota. Unlike some of the other servile lands, where the numbers taken into the army were relatively few and where active duty was for a limited period, the military obligation in Russia was a cruel and heavy burden. The soldier was on active duty for long years, far from home and under harsh and even barbaric discipline. The draft calls placed a heavy drain on the villagers. For example, in an estate in the province of Tver between 1800 and 1855, out of a total male population of 8,000-8,500, 2,442 men were drafted and in addition the villagers paid out 101,132 assignat rubles to purchase recruit quittances. Another manor in that province between 1800 and 1853 sent 76 recruits out of a total male population of between 500 and 550, and spent 32,649 assignat rubles for quittances.[34]

In France obligatory service in the militia, introduced during the reign of Louis XIV, had at first been required only of peasants. It was later extended to townsmen, though in a lesser proportion than in the country. The militiaman served for 2 to 4 and later 6 years, remaining in his home village and responsible only for periodic drills and reviews of short duration. His village had to outfit him, pay his wage, and help support the battalion to which he was assigned. Only about 10,000 men were drafted each year, and to minimize disruptions of family life the army took only bachelors and childless widowers between the ages of 20 and 40. The military obligation, then, bore lightly upon the French peasant in comparison with other lands. Yet it seemed to attract greater loathing than more onerous demands made of the peasantry by seigniors and by the state.[35]

Acute distaste for military service was not unique to French peasants. Villagers everywhere resorted to all manner of shifts and ruses to avoid it. Sometimes they even maimed themselves, or parents maimed their infant sons, so that they would be declared unfit for duty. Usually, single men were drafted first, and so youths often married at an early age—sometimes at 14 or 15—and their parents provided them with small plots of land. The proliferation of small holdings in Denmark has been attributed in part to this practice. Nor were the efforts at evasion limited to peasants. In Russia seigniors did not want to lose their serfs to the army and so they, too, practiced various deceits to reduce the number of conscripts from their villages.[36]

[34] Koval'chenko (1967), 178-179; Blum (1961), 465-467. The assignat (paper) ruble was worth around one-fourth of a silver ruble.
[35] Babeau (1878), 288-295; Marion (1902), 213-215; Dupaquier (1956), 220; Carré (1920), 314.
[36] Drake (1969), 34; Revesz (1964), 64; Semevskii (1881), 303-306; Drakokhrust (1938), 124-125; Shchepetov (1947), 142-143.

Besides his payments in cash, kind, and labor to seignior and state the peasant had to contribute to the support of his village communal organization. He also had to support the local church, the school if there was one, and sometimes he had to give a small amount of money or part of his crop for relief for the poor and for storage of foodstuffs against times of famine.[37]

IV

In servile lands of both east and west the obligations demanded of peasants reached new peaks during the last century of the old order. In France seigniorial dues began their ascent after 1690. They took on new momentum in the so-called "feudal reaction" of the second half of the eighteenth century, when many seigniors (or the bourgeois or prosperous peasant renters to whom they had leased their seigniorial privileges) collected dues more vigorously, insisted upon the payment of arrears, and revived and enforced old and forgotten claims.[38] In other lands there was a sharp rise in the amount of labor services demanded by seigniors. In Little Russia in the eighteenth century, lords had usually required two days a week from their peasants. By 1850 three days had become the rule. In White Russia and Lithuania the labor service increased 1½ to 2 times over in the second half of the eighteenth century. In Upper Lusatia in Saxony after the Seven Years' War, lords demanded additional labor dues, and compelled their peasants to work out their arrearages in cash dues that they owed to the seignior. In Bohemia and other provinces of the Austrian Monarchy, seigniors in the course of the eighteenth century raised the labor dues of smallholders to 2 and 3 days a week, and on at least one manor, to the entire week. In the Danubian Principalities, as explained earlier in this chapter, seigniors set impossible norms for a day's work and thereby could as much as triple the number of work days prescribed by statute. Lords everywhere took advantage of the parcelling of holdings that accompanied the rise in population, to increase their demands for unpaid labor. Thus, in Congress Poland during the first half of the nineteenth century, the labor obligation went from 3 days a week for a holding of 15 *morgi* to 3 days a week for holdings of 6 to 10 *morgi*. The lords of Great Russia seem to have been the exception to this stepped-up seigniorial demand for labor. Many of them shifted peasants from labor services to quitrents during the last half century of serfdom in that land. Though the proprietors sometimes sharply increased the amount of quitrent, it appears that the real value of the obligations of most Russian serfs declined in the last decades of the eighteenth

[37] Blum (1971b), 545-547; Henning (1969b), 102; Andrews (1774), ii, 373.
[38] Davies (1964), 35-36; La Monneraye (1922), 49, 126-127, 131-134; Cobban (1971), 48-49; Forster (1960), 49-51; Forster (1971), 92-102.

century and remained at this lower level until the time of the emancipation.[39]

The price rise of the second half of the eighteenth century[40] and the opening of new and of expanded markets in the eighteenth and first half of the nineteenth centuries help to explain the increased demands of the seignoirs. They needed more money to maintain their scale of living in an era of rising prices and of more luxurious tastes. The heightened exploitation of their peasants presented itself as an obvious way to increase their income.

In some lands the state, too, increased its demands to hitherto unknown proportions. The people of Savoy had been relatively well-off until their rulers began to levy always heavier taxes to finance their grandiose ambitions in northern Italy, where, in 1720, the House of Savoy took over the kingdom of Sardinia. The fiscal burden, on top of their obligations to their seigniors, impoverished most of the peasantry, forced thousands of them to seek employment as migrant workers in neighboring lands, and reduced many of them to beggars. Similarly, the introduction of French taxation into Lorraine brought ruin to many peasants there. In 1737, when Lorraine was given to Stanislaus Leszczyński as compensation for his loss of the Polish throne, 76,629 peasants had paid a total of 1,162,936 livres in taxes, for an average of 15 livres per peasant. Then French taxation had been introduced. By 1762, 84,346 peasants paid 2,011,258 livres in taxes, or an average of almost 24 livres per peasant, an increase of 60 per cent. In France the experience of the Consulat of Lampaut, a small district of about 3,000 acres in southern France, illustrates the proportions of the increase in taxes over several centuries. In 1600 the people there paid 572 livres in taxes; in 1789 their tax bill amounted to 7,500 livres, an increase far in excess of the decline in the value of money.[41]

The increased economic pressure upon the peasant was accompanied in a number of the servile lands by a deterioration in their legal status and in their personal rights. In Mecklenburg, Pomerania, Holstein, and elsewhere, jurists steadily reduced the peasants' right of freedom of movement, allowed lords to raise their demands for labor services beyond long-accepted norms, and weakened and even did away with the security that attached to some peasant tenures. For example, a law of 1616 in Mecklenburg had provided that a peasant family whose land had been appropriated by the seignior had to be set free. In a decision of 17 November 1797, the law faculty of the University of Greifswald decided that this "previous custom" (which had, in fact, been long disregarded) was no longer applica-

---

[39] Pokhilevich (1966), 394; Boelcke (1957), 190-193; Stark (1952), 370-371; Blum (1961), 451, 470-471; Kostiushko (1954), 198-199; Koval'chenko (1967), 162; Sozin (1959), 146-148.

[40] Between the 1730's and the first decades of the nineteenth century grain prices rose by 210 per cent in Germany, 163 per cent in France, 283 per cent in Denmark, and 259 per cent in Austria. Abel (1966), 183.

[41] Bruchet (1908), xxiv-xxv; Darmstaedter (1897), 240-241; Falguerolles (1941), 145.

ble.[42] In the Russian empire the government by the last quarter of the eighteenth century had all but withdrawn from the lord-peasant relationship and left the serf to the mercy of his owner. The master could raise dues and services, convert peasants into household servants, sell serfs apart from their families, sentence them to severe penalties that included beatings with the knout, exile them to Siberia, or send them off into the army. The right of legal redress for seigniorial mistreatment was taken away from the peasant, and those who dared to complain to the authorities were subject to severe punishment by the government. And the oppressive and degrading status of serfdom was extended to multitudes of people who had been in possession of a large measure of freedom. Legislation by Peter I made serfs out of thousands who had till then lived as free men. Later in the eighteenth century, rulers ordered the extension of serfdom into Little Russia, New Russia, and the Caucasus, and (as mentioned earlier) tsars and tsaritsas gave hundreds of thousands of state peasants to their favorites and thereby transformed these peasants into serfs.[43]

In the Danubian Principalities seigniorial demands upon the peasantry mounted steadily from the mid-eighteenth century, and especially in the nineteenth century, in the last few decades before the emancipation there. The labor obligation doubled and tripled for many villagers, their rights in forest, pasture, meadow, and pond were frequently curtailed, and often they had to pay a fee for their restricted use of these resources. Lords demanded heavy cash dues when they did not use all of the labor services owed them by their peasants and, though it was supposed to be illegal, required labor services from women, children and landless peasants.[44]

The Austrian Monarchy was an important exception to the general deterioration in the status of the servile peasantry of Europe. There had been a decline in the condition of the peasantry in the German and Slav crownlands after the Thirty Years' War and in Hungary after the expulsion of the Turks at the end of the seventeenth century. Half-hearted efforts by the government to stem the deterioration had proved ineffective.[45] Then in the 1770's and 1780's legislation of Empress Maria Theresa and of her son Joseph II reversed the downtrend and made the Austrian peasant's status superior to that of any of the other servile peasants of eastern Europe (pp. 222-225).

V

When the attempt is made to add up the charges that rested upon the peasants of the servile lands, the totals reach seemingly incredible proportions.

[42] Mottek (1964), I, 350-351; Mager (1955), 168-169.
[43] Blum (1961), 355-358, 414-415, 418, 422-424; 428-441; Transehe-Roseneck (1890), 156, 159-160.
[44] Emerit (1937), 272-273; Mitrany (1930), 40.
[45] Grüll (1952), 20-21; Stark (1937), 417-419; Eszlary (1960), 387.

In 1786 a Livonian household with eight able-bodied members of both sexes and a quarter holding had to furnish its seignior with two workers for 3 days a week, one with team throughout the year, the other without a team for 22 weeks from St. George's Day (24 April) to Michaelmas (29 September). It also had to provide 10 to 12 days of labor a year in rotation with other households of the village for miscellaneous tasks, four carting trips for the seignior that amounted to 56 work days, postal and relay services that added up to about 42 work days, and spinning flax that took up 24 work days. All told, the household's labor obligation added up to 356 work days a year. Then there were the obligations in kind. Each year the household had to give the seignior about 6 bushels of grain, 53 pounds of hops, one-quarter of a sheep, a sack of wool, 1 hen, and 3 eggs. These payments had an estimated value of 6.26 rubles. The household also paid cash dues of 1.80 rubles. Payments of grain for the pastor and the poll tax of 70 kopecks for each adult male added 6.36 rubles. All together, then, this household paid 14.42 rubles in cash and kind to lord, state and church, or the price of about 15 bushels of grain—this in addition to 356 days of unpaid labor services.[46]

A family in Austrian Silesia in the 1840's who had about 42 acres of land had to give its lord each year 108 to 144 days of labor service with a two-animal team, 28 days of hand labor, 2 days of herding, and 3 days of hunting services. The household also had to cut 36 cubic yards of wood, spin a set amount of yarn for the seignior, give him 1 goose, 6 hens, 60 eggs, 7 1/5 kreuzers as commutation for a spinning obligation, and 1.44 silver florins as quitrent. The land tax on the holding amounted to 23.24 florins. In addition, the family had to supply workers for road maintenance, quarter soldiers, support the village priest and the local school, and pay a tax to the village commune. These payments added up to about 13 florins a year. Altogether, the household's annual cash obligations ran to around 38 silver florins. Hired hands in Silesia at this time were paid 14 to 16 kreuzers a day without board, so that the household's 28 days of hand labor were worth about 7 silver florins (there were 60 kreuzers in a florin). Wages of workers with teams are not available, but, assuming that they were double those of handworkers, the 144 days of labor service with team were worth 72 silver florins. The total cash value, then, of this household's obligations added up to 117 silver florins (not including the value of the woodcutting and of the goose, hens, eggs, and yarn).[47]

One warm July day in 1787 in eastern Champagne, Arthur Young walked up a long hill to give his horse a rest. He fell in with a peasant woman who looked to Young as if she were 60 or 70 years old, but who, it turned out, was only 28. In the course of this often-cited encounter she told Young that she had 7 children and that her husband had "but a morsel of

---

[46] Transehe-Roseneck (1890), 181-182.
[47] Zenker (1897), 250-252; wages from Blum (1948), 188-189.

land, one cow and a poor little horse." Yet he had to pay 42 pounds of wheat to one seignior as quitrent and 168 pounds of oats, one chicken, and one sou to another seignior. In addition, he had to pay taxes. "Les tailles et les droits nous écrasent," she sighed.[48] In the 1780's in the village of Hyemondans in Franche-Comté each of its 33 households, all of whom were *mainmortable*, paid an average of 155 livres a year in taxes and in dues in cash and kind. Apparently theirs was an unusually heavy burden. In a neighboring village of *mainmortables* with 120 hearths the average annual obligation amounted to 62 livres, in another village of 35 households 25 livres. In Marlenheim, a village of Alsace, the charges on each household averaged out at 31 livres a year.[49]

Disparities such as these among villages and a lack of complete coverage allow only estimates of the impact of obligations upon rural incomes. In 1755 Richard Cantillon calculated that it cost the French peasant 33 per cent of his agricultural production to meet his payments to lord, state, and church. In 1766 Dr. Quesnay in his analysis of his *Tableau économique* set the figure at 40 per cent.[50] Marcel Marion estimated that the obligations of a peasant in the *généralité* of Bordeaux took 60 per cent of his income.[51] In the small corner of northwestern France called the Beauvaisis, villagers with not more than 8 hectares, and usually with only 4 or 5, paid out an estimated 52 per cent of their gross income to meet their obligations.[52] In the 1780's the 33 households of Hyemondans had to give up 5,100 livres, or 75 per cent of their combined annual income of 6,800 livres, for seigniorial dues, taxes, and tithes.[53]

In Switzerland a *tableau économique* drawn up in 1772 for 157 communities in the canton of Zurich indicated that it took 29 per cent of the gross product of the villagers to meet their obligations. In Reinach, a community of the canton of Aargau, data for 1758-1769 showed that obligations absorbed 27 per cent of the gross product.[54] Estimates for Germany hold that the peasants there paid from 22 to 40 per cent of their gross agricultural product to meet their obligations. These average figures conceal wide variations. For example, in Lower Saxony in 1760 dues and taxes accounted for 53.2 per cent of the gross farm product of one village, 20.7 per cent in another, 29.7 per cent in a third in 1770, 39.9 per cent in 1774 in a fourth, and a mere 8 per cent in a fifth village in 1819. Peasants on royal manors in East Prussia had to give up about 20 per cent of their gross product to meet their obligations. In contrast, free peasants there (the *Kölmer*) had to pay only about 7 per cent.[55]

In Austria in the 1840's contemporaries estimated that obligations to

[48] Young (1970), I, 148.
[49] Millot (1937), 114-115; Juillard (1953), 77.
[50] Henning (1969b), 1-2; Quesnay (1958), II, 793-795.
[51] Cited in Knowles (1919), 18.   [52] Goubert (1960), 180-181.
[53] Millot (1937), 112-115.
[55] Henning (1969b), 156, 158; Abel (1966), 193, 210, 254.

lord, state, and church took about one-third of peasant income.[56] Some peasants paid much more. In 1848 a Lower Austrian peasant who had 24.3 acres of land, assessed as producing an annual net income of 83.28 silver florins, reported that his obligations, at current prices, totalled 57.51 silver florins, or nearly 70 per cent of his assessed net annual income. At that he was more fortunate than a Silesian peasant who had over 40 acres and who, after paying his obligations, was left with only 17 per cent of his net income to meet his other expenses and support his family.[57] The dues and taxes of Bohemian peasants in the eighteenth century are said to have amounted to about 73 per cent of their gross incomes.[58] A study of 100 villages in Galicia in the 1780's showed both the weight of the obligations and how unevenly the burden was distributed. The 2,012 peasants in these villages who had full, half, and quarter-holdings paid the equivalent of 42.8 per cent of their gross product for dues and services. The 3,329 who had less than a quarter-holding had to give up 37 per cent of their gross product, while the 1,236 cotters and landless peasants used 85.9 per cent of their gross product to meet their obligations. Finally, there were 380 peasants in these villages who, unlike the other peasants, did not have to provide any labor services and paid all of their dues in cash and kind. Their obligations amounted only to 27.7 per cent of their gross product.[59] In the Danubian Principalities, under the arrangements introduced by the Organic Statutes, peasants had to spend more than half of their productive efforts to meet their obligations to lord and state.[60]

Sparse data on individual peasant households reflect the impact of this heavy burden of obligations upon peasant budgets. Information collected in Saxony at the government's request in 1769 for 19 peasant households on manors of the sovereign showed that only in 4 did income exceed expenditures. The margins were 1, 5, 45, and 49 thaler, respectively. In one other household income equalled expenditures. The remaining 14 had deficits of 16, 17, 20, 23, 27, 36, 37, 40, 48, 50, 75, 95, 97, and 225 thalers. (The 225 thaler deficit was in a large-scale peasant farm whose income was 345 thaler.)[61] The peasants on a manor in Poland in 1825 had holdings of 15 *morgi*, or about 21 acres. Their fields gave them yields of 3.5-4 to 1, so that the grain crop of each household ran around 50 *korce* (181.5 bushels). The tithe took one-tenth of the crop and each household kept 13.5 *korce* for seed. Taxes amounted to 5.55 rubles. To raise this money, the peasant had to sell at least 3 *korce* of wheat, the cash crop. That left him with 28.5 *korce* (103.5 bushels) to feed his family for a year. In addition, he owed his seignior 156 days of labor with a team and 164 days of hand labor, and lesser obligations in labor and kind. To meet his cost of living, the peasant and his family had to find part-time outside employment. The wages for this work

[56] Zenker (1897), 252; Tebeldi (1847), 217.   [57] Zenker (1897), 249-252.
[58] Kerner (1932), 240.   [59] Rosdolsky (1951), 262-263.
[60] Emerit (1937), 258.   [61] Wuttke (1893), 170-171.

was so low that a family of parents and three grown and one small child earned only 15 rubles in a year. At 1825 prices that could buy about 14 *korce* (51 bushels) of rye, the chief peasant foodstuff.[62]

Besides the annual payments there were the obligations that recurred irregularly. Of these the most expensive in western Europe and in Austria were the fees on the transfer of hereditary holdings. Generally, the new occupant amortized the fee with interest over a period of years. Finally, in addition to all the authorized regular and irregular payments, the peasant often had to put up with venal tax officials and manorial employees who demanded extra payments, and who could be bribed to shift levies from those best able to pay them to those who were least able.[63]

There were striking differences in the relative weight of taxes and of seigniorial dues in the total obligation of peasants, for, like the demands of the seigniors, the levies of the state often fluctuated from place to place. This seemed especially true in France. In the *généralité* of Bordeaux an estimated 36 per cent of the peasants' income went for taxes, compared with 11-12 per cent in seigniorial dues and 14 per cent for tithes.[64] In the village of Loumarin in Provence direct taxes in 1788 took 16 per cent of the villagers' income. With indirect taxes the tax burden probably ran around 20 per cent of their income.[65] In 1766 Turgot, then intendant of Limousin in south-central France, made a study of taxes in two districts of the province. He concluded that landholding peasants there paid 50 to 60 per cent of their gross income in taxes.[66] A study of 2,834 homesteads in 28 communities in the southeast corner of Ile-de-France showed that seigniorial demands, including fees for property transfers and for use of seigniorial monopolies, amounted to about one livre per hectare. Direct taxes averaged out to about 4 livres 4 sous per hectare, and indirect taxes increased the burden.[67] In other places dues took a much larger share of income than did taxes, as in *mainmortable* villages in Franche-Comté. In one village there 62 per cent of the obligations went to the lord and only 33 per cent to the state. In another village seigniorial dues were three times larger than taxes and so on.[68] In his analysis of his *Tableau économique* Quesnay estimated that of the 40 per cent of the peasant's agricultural product that was used to meet obligations, over half (57 per cent) went to the seigniors, 29 per cent went to the state, and 14 per cent was used for tithes.[69] Whatever the proportion of taxes was in their total obligation French peasants found them a heavy and hateful burden, as a verse from a peasant song of Auvergne in central France related:[70]

[62] Rostworowski (1896), 16-17, 88. The *korzec* (pl. *korce*) equalled 3.63 bushels.
[63] Marion (1902), 115-121; Druzhinin (1946), I, 346-353; Schiemann (1904), 393; Stark (1952), 282; Confino (1963a), 70-71; Tebeldi (1847), 217.
[64] Knowles (1919), 18.   [65] Sheppard (1971), 106-108, 108n.
[66] Behrens (1967), 32.   [67] Dupaquier (1956), 218-219.
[68] Millot (1937), 115-116.   [69] Quesnay (1958), II, 797.
[70] Babeau (1878), 336.

Le pauvre laboreur
Est toujours tourmenté,
Payant à la gabelle
Et les deniers au roi ;
Toujours devant sa porte
Garnison et sergent,
Qui crieront sans cesse
'Apportez de l'argent!'

In central and eastern Europe taxes usually took much less of the peasant's product than did seigniorial dues. An estimate made in the 1840's figured that the average peasant in the German and Slav crownlands of the Austrian Monarchy turned over about 17 per cent of his income to the state for taxes and services, and 24 per cent to his seignior.[71] Some, of course, paid more and some less. A peasant of Lower Austria reported that in 1848 payments to the state took about the same bite (25 per cent) of his assessed net income as did his payments to his lord. In contrast, in Austrian Silesia smallholders with 4 to 7.5 acres paid the equivalent of 44.36 silver florins for seigniorial obligations and 6 florins for taxes.[72] In northern and eastern Germany taxes and services required by the government was the biggest obligation for some peasants.[73] In the middle third of the nineteenth century, Romanian peasants spent an estimated one-fifth of their working time to meet state levies in cash and services, and one-third for seigniorial dues. A calculation made in the 1840's indicated that the Russian serf paid the equivalent of 10 rubles a year to his seignior and 1.85 rubles to the government. In White Russia and Lithuania in the second half of the eighteenth century, the typical obligation owed to the seignior for a half-holding (about 25 acres) had a cash value of between 95 and 120 *zloty*. Taxes were only 5 to 7 *zloty*.[74]

This sampling of the scattered, disparate, and inadequate data indicates that generalizations about the actual size of peasants' obligations and of the proportion of these obligations to their income can be made only with many reservations and with much imprecision. It is clear, however, that for the great majority of the peasantry the burden was a very heavy one. For out of the amount left to the peasant after he had met his obligations had to come the costs of the operation of his holding and the support of his household. Yields of only three or four times the seed that prevailed in most of the servile lands meant that seed for the next year's sowing could take as much as a quarter to a third of the peasant's crop. Other charges included such expenses as the care and feeding of his animals, cost of farm equipment and of manufactured goods, payments to the communal organization

[71] Tebeldi (1847), 217.   [72] Zenker (1897), 249-251.
[73] Henning (1969b), 101; Wuttke (1893), 172-173.
[74] Emerit (1937), 258; Storch (1848), 123; Pokhilevich (1966), 394.

of the village, wages to hired hands, and interest on loans. Estimates of these outlays, plus the costs of supporting his household, indicate that they absorbed from 40 to as much as 90 per cent of the peasant's income, and often took more than 100 per cent. These estimates assumed average crops. In the many years in which harvests were poor, expenses took an even greater share of income. To stay alive many peasants had to seek out other sources of income, such as day labor or cottage industry. And they borrowed. Their lords advanced them cash or produce or seed. They borrowed, too, from fellow peasants, who often charged them usurious rates of interest. Frequently the seignior and the state became involuntary creditors. That happened when peasants could not meet their obligations so that arrearages accumulated, sometimes reaching staggering proportions.[75]

An official report to the Prussian Ministry of the Interior in 1809 observed that when all the payments demanded of the Pomeranian peasant were added up he turned out to be nothing more than a servant whose master allowed him a paltry allowance.[76] That could have been said of nearly every peasant in all of the servile lands.

[75] Arnim (1957), 99; Meyer (1965), 50-51; Falguerolles (1941), 144-145; Blum (1961), 464-465; Louchitsky (1911), 96-97; Fridman (1958), 28.
[76] Quoted in Knapp (1887), I, 75-76.

CHAPTER 4
The Privileges of the Seigniors

I

THE authority of the seignior over his peasants extended beyond his right to the dues and services they had to pay him. He also had control over many aspects of the lives and activities of his peasants. That control was greatest in the eastern lands, but western seigniors had privileges and public powers of the same nature, if not always of the same intensity, as those exercised by the lords of the east.

One of the most effective and most widely employed instruments of seigniorial control was the monopolies that they possessed. These exclusive privileges were in areas of critical importance to the everyday life of the peasants. In some lands the villagers could buy certain wares only from his seignior at prices that were often inflated for merchandise that was often of inferior quality. These goods included such staples as salt, tobacco, and herring in Poland and White Russia, grain and other foodstuffs and wool in Silesia, and meat and groceries in the Danubian Principalities and in the south Slav provinces of Hungary. Some lords in White Russia, Poland, Russia, Bohemia, and Silesia compelled their peasants to offer products they had for sale to their seigniors, or to persons to whom the seigniors had rented the right, before they could sell them to others. In some places the seigniors were supposed to pay the market price, but that regulation was not always observed; in other places the seigniors set the price themselves.[1]

Nearly everywhere, in east and west alike, the seigniors had a monopoly on milling. The peasants had to bring their grain to the lord's mill. They could not mill it themselves or take it to some other miller. The lord's mill, the only one allowed in the seigniory, was almost always leased out. The miller, everywhere a notoriously dishonest folk figure, apparently usually deserved that reputation by charging high fees for his services, payable by a share of the grain or the flour, and by cheating his customers in one way or another during the milling process. In western Europe seigniors often required their peasants to bake their bread in the seignior's ovens and to use his press for their grapes and oil seeds—all for a fee, of course.[2]

[1] Koroliuk et al. (1956), I, 346; Shlossberg (1958), 121-122; Dessmann (1904), 86-87; Oţetea (1955), 306; Leshchilovskaia (1961), 320; Gitermann (1945), 449; Stark (1952), 441-442; Semevskii (1888), 483.

[2] Koroliuk et al. (1956), I, 346; Dessmann (1904), 86; Grüll (1952), 235; Feigl (1964), 99, 172; Knapp (1902), 29; Henning (1969b), 27; Carsten (1959), 419; Evans (1924), 28; La Monneraye (1922), 79-80, 88-89; Herbert (1960), 25-26; Darmstaedter (1897), 11, 138; Tobien (1899), I, 5; St. Jacob (1960), 120-122, 420-422.

Another widespread seigniorial monopoly concerned the manufacture and sale of alcoholic beverages. In most of the servile lands only seigniors or persons to whom they leased the privilege could engage in these activities, though sometimes special exemptions were allowed, as in Livonia, where parish clergymen were allowed to distill spirits for their own use. Severe punishments were visited on those who violated this monopoly. Often, too, especially though not exclusively in the eastern lands, the seigniors had the sole right to operate taverns on their manors. They always turned over the operation of these enterprises to lessees. They encouraged patronage of the village tavern because the beverages sold there were their products, and because the more business the tavern did the more rent the lord could charge. In Poland, as mentioned earlier, some lords paid their hired laborers with vouchers that the worker traded in at the tavern for whiskey. In Lower Austria lords required their peasants to have all of their celebrations in the village tavern and forbade them to frequent any other tavern.[3] In wine-producing regions of France and of the Danubian Principalities seigniors had the sole right to sell wine produced on their properties for a specified period after the vintage. In France the period usually lasted for 30 to 40 days. Only after the specified interval had elapsed could peasants offer their wine for sale to outside buyers. In Moldavia after 1775 peasants could not plant vines without special consent from their seigniors.[4]

Seigniorial monopolies persisted up to the end of the old order and, indeed, new ones were introduced and old ones expanded. In Russia, during the eighteenth century, the government gave proprietors in most of the empire the monopoly on the manufacture of spirits. The exclusive right of the Polish nobility to the manufacture and sale of spirits on their manors, first granted in 1496, was confirmed in 1768, and continued after the partitions in both Russian and Prussian Poland. In the Danubian Principalities the seigniors received legal sanction for their monopolies in the last third of the eighteenth century and had them confirmed by native rulers in the 1820's and by the Organic Statutes of 1831. In France the seigniorial monopolies were vigorously enforced and in some places were expanded down to the outbreak of the Revolution.[5]

There were other special privileges that weighed heavily upon the peasantry. One of the most common and certainly one of the most resented was

[3] Austria: Grüll (1952), 235; Leshchilovskaia (1961), 320; Feigl (1964), 99; Grünberg (1901), 25. Danubian Principalities: Oţetea (1955), 306; *Règlement organique* (1834), art. 129. Russian empire: Transehe-Roseneck (1890), 130; Shlossberg (1959), 121; Conze (1940), 17; Kahan (1966), 58-59. Poland: Leslie (1956), 62-63; Koroliuk *et al.* (1956), I, 346. Germany: Dessmann (1904), 86; Henning (1969b), 28; Wittich (1896), 188; Knapp (1902), 29.

[4] Tocqueville (1955), 292-293; Emerit (1937), 46; Evans (1924), 28.

[5] Struve (1913), 46-47; Pazhitnov (1940), 240-241; Leslie (1956), 62; Kieniewicz (1969), 91, 117; Emerit (1937), 46-47; Grünberg (1909), II, 599; La Monneraye (1922), 82-84; Soboul (1960), 124.

the exclusive right of the seigniors to hunt. For centuries the chase had been a passion of princes and lords. It was also a symbol of their status and so they determinedly restricted it to their order. They even established strata within their own caste. Thus, in the French province of Maine, customary law reserved large game to the great nobles. In the bishopric of Osnabrück in northern Germany only princes and nobles of the highest rank could go after large game. In Lower Austria ownership of a forest did not automatically give the right to hunt in it; often that privilege belonged to some important nobleman, and sometimes one lord had the right to kill large game in a forest and another small animals.[6]

The restriction of the right to hunt to the nobility not only deprived the peasants of a source of food, hides, and fur. More important, the nobility's monopoly upon, and fascination with, hunting could bring much damage to the crops of the peasantry. Laws sometimes forbade hunting over sown fields and over vineyards. Huntsmen paid no regard to these restrictions and there was no one to call them to task, for the hunters themselves sat as judges in the local courts that were charged with the enforcement of this legislation. The damage they did to the growing crops was compounded by the depredations of the game animals, who fed in the peasants' fields without fear of retribution from the powerless peasants. In many places in France, and doubtless elsewhere, peasants were forbidden to weed their fields or mow hay in their meadows at certain times, lest they disturb nesting partridges or destroy their eggs. When French peasants tried to protect their seedlings from wild animals by setting up fences, the seigniors made the peasants take them down. In Lower Austria peasants could fence their fields against wild game, but the fence could not have pointed pales lest the game injure itself in leaping over it. Peasants there had to keep their dogs tied up to prevent them from chasing game. To add insult to injury, peasants in most lands, as part of their labor obligation had to serve as hunting attendants, and sometimes had to keep and feed the seignior's hunting dogs.[7]

In a few districts, including the valleys of the southern Vosges in Lorraine, places in Brittany and in the Vendée, peasants were allowed to hunt. Elsewhere villagers who killed game or snared birds risked severe punishment for poaching. In Brittany the *parlement* forbade (without much success) the possession of firearms by peasants, and Maria Theresa outlawed ownership of firearms by the peasants of her realm. The empress wanted to

[6] La Monneraye (1922), 113; Jacob (1820), 98; Feigl (1964), 166-167.
In Weimar burghers who purchased noble properties (knight's tenures) sometimes had the right to hunt on the property. Jacob (1820), 340.
[7] Kareev (1899), 61-64; Bauer (1907), 62; Stark (1952), 29; Feigl (1964), 167-168; Babeau (1878), 202-204; La Monneraye (1922), 115-116; Sée (1906), 152-153; Tobien (1899) i, 5; Stulz and Oppitz (1956), 26-27; Darmstaedter (1897), 149; Lütge (1967), 192; Knapp (1902), 32; Hovde (1948), i, 393, n. 25; Andrews (1774), ii, 357.

deprive the peasants of weapons they might use in risings against their lords or against the regime, but it seems likely that, as was clearly the case in Brittany, the law was also designed to keep the peasants from killing game.[8]

Often seigniors also had the sole right to fish in the ponds and non-navigable streams of their manors. In eighteenth-century Brittany lords extended their monopoly to navigable streams, too, despite legislation that forbade this. The fishing privilege could be commercially rewarding and seigniors frequently leased it.[9] In France only seigniors could have a pigeon cote; indeed, the presence of a cote served to identify the house of a seignior. Apparently French seigniors had a special appetite for pigeon pie, or in the case of impoverished nobles increased their incomes by selling pigeons. The birds, protected from being shot or snared by peasants, fed in the fields, where they did much harm. Peasants of one district in 1789 blamed their seignior's pigeons for the loss of one-fifth of their crops. In German Austria a law of 1678 allowed peasants with full holdings to have a dovecote whose diameter could not exceed that of a wagon wheel. Peasants with smaller holdings could keep the birds but could not have a cote for them.[10]

Seigniorial authority extended to the personal lives of their peasants, too. In Mecklenburg, in Poland, and in Russia the peasant could not freely choose his occupation. It was assumed that he would follow his father's calling. If he wanted to earn his living in some other way he had to get his lord's permission, especially if he had to leave the manor in order to learn his new trade or to pursue it. Peasants in the Austrian Monarchy had suffered the same restrictions until 1781, when Joseph II freed them to learn any trade they wished and to go wherever their work took them. In Prussia the law code of 1794 ordered that a peasant could not enter a bourgeois occupation, nor have his children follow such a calling, unless he had permission from the government.[11]

In medieval western Europe one of the distinctive features of serfdom had been that the serf needed permission from his lord before he could marry someone from outside the manor. He frequently had to pay a fee for the permission. Traces of this requirement, called *forismaritagium* or *formariage*, persisted in parts of western Europe among those peasants who

[8] Darmstaedter (1897), 138; Babeau (1878), 202-204; Feigl (1964), 166-167; Sée (1906), 149-150; Link (1949), 70.

[9] Soboul (1960), 125; La Monneraye (1922), 116-117; Sée (1906), 154-156; Leshchilovskaia (1961), 320; Mailath (1838), 47; Bernardt (1848), 149; Emerit (1937), 46-47.

[10] Calonne (1920), 109-110; Meyer (1966), I, 469 and 469n.; Herbert (1969), 29-30; Buchinger (1952), 334.

[11] Mager (1955), 171; Rutkowski (1926), 485; Stark (1952), 360; Joseph II's patent of 1 November 1781 in Grünberg (1893), II, 390; *Allgemeines Landrecht für die Preussischen Staaten von 1794* (1970), pt. II, title 7, sect. 1, art. 2 (p. 433).

were still legally serfs.[12] In eastern Europe, except for the Danubian Principalities, peasants had to have their lord's permission to wed and often had
to pay him a fee that, for wealthy peasants, could be extortionate. In the
Austrian Monarchy after a reform of Joseph II in 1781, the lord could refuse permission to marry only for special reasons. In Prussia, too, the lord
could not refuse permission except for specified causes, including a criminal
record, obstinancy, laziness, and dissipation. Usually seigniors did not
allow their peasant girls to wed outsiders, for that could mean the loss of
the girl since wife followed husband. Sometimes lords compelled two of
their people to marry without regard to the wishes of the couple, in order to
provide the proprietor with a natural increase in his labor force. Sometimes
they acted in what they thought was the best interest of the peasant. A
great Danish proprietor, Count A. G. Bernstorff, refused to permit one of
his peasant girls to marry the father of her twins because Bernstorff claimed
that the gallant was a drunkard and the girl and her progeny would be better off if they remained in the home of her father, a well-to-do peasant.[13]

II

The amplitude of the seignior's authority went beyond his intervention in
the private lives and economic activities of his peasants. He also served as
the representative of public authority out in the countryside. In some lands
the seignior or his representative were the only public authorities with
whom villagers, free and unfree, had any dealings. Even in the western
lands, where the peasant was the direct subject of the sovereign (rather
than the "hereditary subject" of his lord who stood between him and the
sovereign as was the case in the east), the local seignior was, for nearly all
purposes, the government. The most widespread and most important of the
public functions provided by seigniors was the conduct of a court of law,
and the supervision of police authority in his seigniory or manor. In addition, to give a sampling of the public administrative functions of seigniors
in one or the other of the servile lands, they checked weights and measures,
enforced standards of quality in artisan production, had responsibility for
the care of orphaned and abandoned children, supervised the observance of
the Sabbath, issued letters of safe conduct, gave permits for new construction, provided emergency relief for vagabonds, dealt with problems of public health, proclaimed and enforced the laws of the land, and, as mentioned

[12] Darmstaedter (1897), 71, 165, 170; Millot (1937), 41; Wittich (1896), 224; Herbert
(1969), 10.
[13] Oțetea (1955), 303; *Allgemeines Landrecht für die Preussischen Staaten von 1794*
(1970), pt. II, title 7, sect. 3, art. 161-164 (p. 438); Mager (1955), 170; Stark (1952), 361;
Transehe-Roseneck (1890), 161, 193; Rutkowski (1926), 485; Albert (1969), 74-77; Revesz
(1964), 116; Semevskii (1881), 270-284; Friis (1905), 322-323.

earlier, frequently had overall responsibility for the imposition and collection of taxes.

The compass of the public powers of the seignior varied inversely with the amount of local authority exercised by the central government. The less able or the less willing the central government was to provide adequate and appropriate services, the broader the spectrum of public services provided by the seigniors. In providing these services the seigniors made an important—and often overlooked—contribution to the establishment and maintenance of public and private order in their societies. At the same time, their public powers, and especially their judicial role, provided them with a valuable instrument for the preservation and the expansion of their own private interests. They could and did use their public powers to compel peasants to accede to their demands.

Usually the area in which the seignior had jurisdiction and drew income from fines and fees coincided with the boundaries of his seigniory. That meant, of course, that there was a vast number of separate jurisdictions. In France, Brittany alone had 2,326 in 1766. On the eve of the Revolution there was an average of two seigniorial courts in each Breton parish, and some had 10, 16, and even 30 courts. In Marche and Limousin there were 800. In all France there was an estimated 80,000 manorial courts in 1789. A *cahier* in 1789 from a village of the Dordogne complained that "there are in this province more small jurisdictions than there are seigniors; one often counts ten of them within a circumference of two leagues."[14]

Often, and particularly though not exclusively in central and western Germany, a seignior's jurisdiction did not coincide with the boundaries of the seigniory. As pointed out earlier, there were seigniories with several seigniors, each of whom filled a different seigniorial role. Through inheritance, purchase, gift, or exchange, each of these roles, including that of jurisdiction, sometimes belonged to a number of owners. That could lead to ridiculous situations. One of the owners of a jurisdiction in Württemberg owned 1/108th of the jurisdiction. Another jurisdiction there had four owners in 1700, namely, the Archbishop of Mainz, who owned 2/21sts; the Bishop of Würzburg, with 1/21st plus 1/28th; Count von Hohenlohe, who had 3/7ths plus 13/70ths; and one Herr von Stellen, who had 6/35ths plus 1/28th.[15] The seigniorial jurisdiction over the 15 homesteads that made up the tiny village of Rogeville à Pont-a-Mousson in Lorraine belonged to 6 people, each entitled to a different-sized share that ranged from 0.5 to 43 per cent of the income from the jurisdiction.[16] Often the seignior did not

[14] Marion (1968), 321; Sée (1906), 119; Ducros (1926), 287-288; Soboul (1960), 122; Lütge (1957), 104; Schremmer (1963), 6; Jordan-Rozwadowski (1900), 479.

[15] Knapp (1902), 24; *cf.* St. Jacob (1960), 71-72

[16] Darmstaedter (1897), 125.

have jurisdiction over a discrete geographical area but rather over scattered individual homesteads, like one German imperial knight who had jurisdiction over 11 peasants and 1 Jew.[17]

To complicate matters still further, the servile lands of western and central Europe recognized different levels of seignioral jurisdiction. In France and in Savoy there were three jurisdictions, the high, the middle, and the low. The other lands of western and central Europe had only the high and the low. High justice theoretically meant competence to hear civil and criminal cases, except in France *lèse majesté* and counterfeiting, and competence to sentence offenders to corporal punishment or to execution. Only great lords had the right of high justice, and in practice limits had been put upon the fullness of their powers. In France the death sentence had to be confirmed by the provincial *parlement* or by a royal court. Other restrictions, too, had been imposed, as in Maine, where the seigniorial court could hold the first examination in criminal cases but then had to bind over the accused to a royal court. Middle justice (which in France and Savoy always accompanied high justice) gave the right to hear cases that, in France, could involve a fine up to 3 livres. Low justice encompassed lesser offenses, and in practice dealt chiefly with the enforcement of the privileges of the seignior and the obligations of the peasant. In some jurisdictions one or more lords owned the high and the middle justice, and others owned the low. In central and western Germany few lords had the right of high justice, and some of those who did turned serious offenders over to the courts of the sovereign. Most seigniors had only the low justice, and even this had restrictions placed upon it by the central government. In most of Lower Saxony officials of the state provided local justice or else supervised the activities of the seigniorial courts. In Saxony the lords' courts served to determine the facts; only royal, city, or university courts could pass sentence. In Switzerland nothing more than vestiges remained of seigniorial jurisdiction, and in the four duchies of the lower Rhine, Cleve, Mark, Jülich, and Berg, it was entirely absent.[18]

In central and western Europe seigniors proudly exhibited a gallows near their manor house or in a public place in the seigniory. They wanted to let the world know that they had the right of justice and the gallows announced that to all who passed. In France the number of uprights that supported the gallows told the passerby of the rank and dignity of the seignior. A simple lord had two or three uprights in his gallows, barons four, counts six, and dukes up to ten. In Saxony the erection of a gallows by a seignior

[17] Wittich (1896), 156; Knapp (1902), 23, 26.
[18] Marion (1968), 320-321; Soboul (1960), 122; La Monneraye (1922), 27; Link (1949), 18; Darmstaedter (1897), 154; Knapp (1902), 22; Wittich (1896), 147-152, 180; Carsten (1959), 259, 350; Meyer (1965), 22; Lütge (1957), 104-105; Blaschke (1965), 245-246; Rappard (1912), 132.

was a symbol of his rank and power was an occasion for celebration, with music and merrymaking for everyone.[19]

The fragmentation of public authority, and with it the judicial competency of the seignior, was greatest in those lands where the peasants were most dependent upon their seigniors—trans-Elbian Germany, Denmark, the Baltic lands, Poland, and Russia. Even in these lands, however, the state imposed limitations, with greater or lesser success, on the powers of the lord's court. Until 1768 Polish seigniors had the right to sentence to death peasants, whether serf or free, who lived on their manors. A decree of that year ordered that henceforth all criminal offenses punishable by death had to be tried in royal or city courts. Actually, most lords had regularly transferred capital cases to the nearest royal court, so the new law did not change anything.[20] In the duchy of Lauenburg on the lower Elbe all seigniorial courts had criminal jurisdiction, but, in practice, they bound over the most serious cases to the sovereign's court. In Prussia seigniorial courts had to call in justices from a neighboring city to pronounce sentence in criminal cases, the sentence had to be approved by the royal high court, and sentences of exile or execution had to have the approval of the king.[21]

In Russia, Peter I early in the eighteenth century gave legal recognition to the long-standing judicial authority of the seigniors, and later decrees of rulers during the eighteenth century extended that authority. In the nineteenth century the government made gestures in the direction of limitations on the punitive powers of the seigniorial courts. In 1809 lords lost their right, granted to them in 1765 by Catherine II, to sentence serfs to hard labor at the Admiralty. Reportedly, the government decided to rescind this power after a serfowner in 1807 condemned peasants to hard labor there for 20 years "in order to moderate the impudence of their behavior." In succeeding years, and especially in the 1830's and 1840's, statutes defined the maximum sentences seigniorial courts could pronounce, and required the seignior to hand over to government officials those whom he sentenced to punishments heavier than those now allowed him. After Russia's annexation of Livonia the new rulers charged the proprietors there with the responsibility for the maintenance of public order and gave them the same judicial and punitive powers possessed by the seigniors of Russia. In the duchy of Courland prior to its annexation by Russia in 1795, the lord's punitive power over his serfs had extended up to, but had not included, the death penalty. The *Statuta Curlandica* of 1617 order that the seignior could not execute his serf on his own authority but had to convene a special criminal court that included peasants. If the lord disregarded this

[19] Haun (1892), 158-159; Link (1949), 18; Darmstaedter (1897), 128; Babeau (1878), 211-212.
[20] Rutkowski (1926), 492; Kieniewicz (1969), 20.
[21] Meyer (1965), 22; Knapp (1882), II, 30.

2. Punishment in an Hungarian village of the 18th century. (E. Tárkány Szücs, *Vásárhelyi Testamentumok*, Budapest, 1961.)

provision and executed the accused serf, he could be fined all of 30 silver rubbles or 100 florins.[22]

In the Austrian Monarchy almost all seigniors once had possessed the right to administer civil justice, and most of the great lords criminal justice as well, including the right to impose the death sentence. Then during the reigns of Maria Theresa and of Joseph II the government intervened and reduced these powers. The patent of 22 December 1769 ordered that seigniorial courts could not jail offenders without the prior consent of the provincial government. Joseph II's Law Concerning Subjects of 1 September 1781 established the procedure, which included the free services of a government attorney, by which a peasant could lodge a complaint against his lord. Joseph's Penal Patent, also issued on 1 September 1781, reduced all seigniorial judicial competence to courts of first instance, severely reduced the cases they could hear, abolished money fines, and required approval of the local governmental bureau for prison sentences of more than 8 days. During the Napoleonic era the French had occupied Tyrol, Vorarlberg, Istria, Dalmatia, and much of Carinthia and Upper Austria, and had abolished seigniorial jurisdiction. When the Austrians regained these territories in 1814, they did not reestablish the system of seigniorial courts.[23]

In the Danubian Principalities the law did not recognize seigniorial jurisdiction. All justice was supposedly in the hands of the law courts of the

[22] Blum (1961), 428-431; Tobien (1899), i, 101; Creutzburg (1910), 3.
[23] Link (1949), 18, 46-47, 120-121; Comité des k. k. Ackerbauministeriums (1899), i, 5.

rulers of Moldavia and Wallachia. In fact, however, the peasants of those semi-anarchic principalities were at the mercy of their lords, who freely imposed their wills upon the people who lived on their land.[24]

In some lands, including Schleswig-Holstein, Livonia, and northern Germany, seigniors sometimes sat as judges in their own courts. As a general rule, however, lords hired someone, or appointed one of their estate officials or a village elder, to serve in this capacity.[25] In certain sovereignties the law specifically forbade the seignior to preside in his court, or required the judge to have a certain amount of formal legal training that seigniors rarely possessed. Great lords could afford to employ full-time judges and legal staffs for their courts; some French magnates sold their judicial posts as heritable offices at sometimes remarkably high prices.[26] Lesser lords could not afford, nor did they need, full-time judges, and so one judge often worked for a number of seigniors. Thus, in 1778 a certain Goeury, a lawyer of Lorraine, served as judge in 28 seigniories of that province. Sometimes these hired judges received adequate salaries. Mostly they were paid modest wages but were allowed to keep part of the court fees and fines, and some of them drew all of their pay from their share of the fees and fines.[27]

Their dependence upon the seigniors for their employment, and upon fines and fees for part or all of their salaries, must have lessened the objectivity and fairness of the judges and increased their venality. This apart from the fact that many of them lacked qualifications for their posts, for seigniors often disregarded the statutes, which required legal training for the persons they employed as judges. Given these circumstances, peasants could scarcely hope to get a fair hearing in their lord's court in disputes between themselves and the seignior.[28] A few years before the outbreak of the French Revolution, a French diplomat in America, struck by the large immigration of Alsatian peasants, inquired of them as to why they had left their homeland. He was told that they had fled because justice was administered there with "a shocking partiality" so that "a peasant was not able to enjoy his property in peace, and was ceaselessly the prey to the greed of court officials and lawyers."[29]

[24] Emerit (1937), 47.
[25] Hanssen (1861), 28; Transehe-Roseneck (1890), 192; Knapp (1902), 26; Jordan-Rozwadowski (1900), 480; Babeau (1878), 212; Sée (1906), 53-54; Brusatti (1958), 510.
[26] La Monneraye (1922), 30, 32-33; Wittich (1896), 157; Darmstaedter (1897), 12, 129; Blaschke (1965), 245; Marion (1968), 319-320; Hanssen (1861), 3; Lütge (1957), 106; Link (1949), 120-121; Sée (1906), 55, 55n.; Andrews (1774), ii, 366.
[27] Babeau (1878), 213, 227; Darmstaedter (1897), 13, 130; La Monneraye (1922), 32; Haun (1892), 155-156, 158; Hanssen (1861), 3n.; Meyer (1965), 22; Ziekursch (1927), 122; Link (1949), 121; Jordan-Rozwadowski (1900), 480.
[28] Marion (1968), 319; Ducros (1926), 288; Sée (1906), 121-122, 125-126; Brusatti (1958), 510; Hanssen (1861), 28; Mottek (1964), i, 325, 327; Király (1969), 88-89; Soboul (1960), i, 122; Ziekursch (1927), 123; Jordan-Rozwadowski (1900), 484.
[29] Quoted in Marion (1968), 320; *cf.* Sée (1906), 128-129.

Peasants in France, Germany, and, as mentioned earlier, Austria, could appeal decisions of the seigniorial court to higher jurisdictions, and could appear in these courts as plaintiffs in actions against their seigniors. The process, however, was costly and time-consuming, and the members of the higher courts and bureaus to which they could appeal usually belonged to the seigniorial order and were disinclined to side with peasants against their fellow lords. For many peasants, then, the right of complaint and appeal must have seemed illusory, though some were undaunted, for appeals and complaints were frequently made. In Russia, the Baltic lands, and Poland peasants did not possess these rights. For these unfortunates the lord's tribunal served as the court of first and last instance. The law ordered that those who dared to enter complaints with the authorities against their seigniors were to be beaten and even sentenced to imprisonment at hard labor.[30] These rules did not apply to the province of Bessarabia, annexed by Russia in 1812, where the peasants, albeit dependent upon their seigniors, were not serfs. An imperial ukase of 1834 included the right for Bessarabian peasants to take complaints against their seigniors to higher jurisdictions. However, the venality of these courts was such that the peasants could not expect fair treatment. For, as a rich proprietor explained to a French traveler in the 1840's, "How can you expect the peasant to obtain justice when he only gives [the judge] an egg, while we give a silver ruble."[31]

Statutes of the central government set limits on the type and amount of punishment the lord's court could impose without referral to a higher authority. The restrictions ranged from small fines, or a session in a pillory, or a few days in jail in western and central Europe, to the power of the Russian lord to sentence his serfs to as much as forty blows with the rod, six months' imprisonment, or life-long exile to Siberia. These limitations seemed to have had little effect upon many seigniors, particularly in eastern Europe, where lash, rod, and knout were favored and frequently applied instruments of punishment. The enforcement of the statutory restrictions rested with the lord himself. If a seignior or his agent exceeded the statutory punishment—and evidence indicates that they often did—there was little likelihood that the authorities would hear of it, especially when the law forbade peasants to enter official complaints against their master. The governor-general of Livland, in an address to the diet in 1765, spoke of the excessive punishments meted out to peasants. The least offense, he said, brought on beatings so severe that "only the stump of the rod is left and skin and flesh are stripped off."[32] Statements of this kind by officials were a

[30] Germany: Knapp (1902), 7; Jordan-Rozwadowski (1900), 487; Blaschke (1965), 246; Ziekursch (1927), 125-129. France: Babeau (1878), 217-218; La Monneraye (1922), 351; Forster (1960), 29-30. Austria: Feigl (1964), 48-50, 209; Stark (1952), 373; Wright (1966), 18. Russia: Zaionchkovskii (1968), 25. Poland: Rutkowski (1926), 493; Warszawski (1914), 111-112.

[31] Hommaire (1845), II, 577.

[32] Tobien (1899), I, 104; Mager (1955), 200-201; Emerit (1937), 270-271.

rarity. Seigniorial brutality and abuses of their judicial function went nearly always unchallenged by the central government. On rare occasion the authorities could not overlook especially flagrant abuses, and fined and even imprisoned nobles who were guilty of these excesses.[33]

The fines and the legal fees levied by the seigniorial courts provided lords with a source of revenue that for some of them was an important part of their incomes. But there were expenses involved, too. The seignior had to pay the costs of maintaining the court, police investigations, and a jail. That could run into a fair amount of money. In criminal cases in which the sentence was imprisonment rather than a fine, the court received no income. Some lords tried to hold down expenses by not prosecuting criminal offenses, especially minor ones, by not conducting investigations, and by hiring unqualified persons to whom they could pay low wages for court positions. Appeals by disgruntled defendants to higher courts cost seigniors money, too, especially when as in France an obstinate and determined pleader could take his case to five or six appellate levels. The costs, the bother, the restrictions put upon their jurisdiction, and, for some, the insignificant revenues, persuaded a number of French seigniors to relinquish their judicial privileges to the royal courts. In Austria after Joseph II severely clipped the authority of manorial courts, many lords favored the abolition of their judicial privileges. This attitude was so widespread that Joseph, faced with the problem and expense of establishing and staffing a comprehensive network of state courts, insisted in a decree of 16 August 1786 that for the time being seigniors must retain and exercise their judicial role. The emperor also ordered that the seigniors had to appoint certificated judges to preside in their courts. These regulations persuaded many smaller proprietors to turn over their jurisdictions to larger landowners. In 1833 the estates of Lower Austria declared themselves ready to give up seigniorial judicial rights to the state, in 1845 the government assumed jurisdiction in all criminal matters, and three years later seigniorial jurisdiction was officially abolished.[34] Most seigniors of the servile lands, however, held on tightly to their judicial powers, along with all their other privileges and prerogatives.

III

As the preceding pages and chapters have made clear, the flow of services and obligations ran overwhelmingly from peasants to seigniors. Lords,

[33] *Cf.* Eggert (1965), 30n.; Babeau (1878), 188-189; Blum (1961), 438-441; Creutzburg (1910), 6; Oţetea (1960), 339, 342-343.

[34] Germany: Knapp (1902), 26, 28-29; Mottek (1964), I, 327; Lütge (1957), 109; Ziekursch (1927), 122. Austria: Feigl (1964), 207; Grüll (1952), 216-217; Brusatti (1958), 507, 512; Vilfran (1973), 26-27. France: Tocqueville (1955), 27-28; La Monneraye (1922), 28-29, 35-37; Bois (1960), 402-403, Sée (1906), 123. Savoy: Darmstaedter (1897), 142-143. Schleswig-Holstein: Hanssen (1861), 24, 24n.

however, did have certain responsibilities toward their peasants. The nature and the amount of these obligations were fixed by custom or statute. They were most extensive in those lands in which the peasants were most dependent upon their seigniors. The lords there had the responsibility to provide food, shelter, seeds, tools, animals, and whatever else their peasants needed to stay alive in time of crop failure, famine, or other natural disasters. Generally, too, the seignior's duties included provision for the care of the aged, the infirm, and homeless orphans. In some lands the state instructed seigniors to have their peasants build granaries and to store grain against emergencies, or, as in mid-nineteenth-century Lithuania, required the seigniors to build the granaries themselves. In Lithuania, too, the government ordered the seigniors to have their peasants establish funds to lend money to needy fellow villagers at low or no interest. In the Danubian Principalities the Organic Statutes ordered proprietors to provide every ten peasant families with one hectare of land on which they were to plant maize and store the crop as a reserve in time of need. In Württemberg legislation required seigniors to provide care for the sick and the infirm among those peasants who were their serfs. In central Germany the seignior who had jurisdictional authority had the responsibility for the care of the poor, the infirm, and the feebleminded who had no one else to look out for them.[35]

Generally in central and western Europe the seignior furnished meals to his peasants and fodder for their animals when they performed their obligatory labor services for him. Custom or agreement often defined the amount of food the lord had to provide each worker, and apparently sometimes sizable quantities were required. At Haraucourt in Lorraine, for example, the seignior had to supply each worker with a jug of wine, or of beer if wine was scarce, about two pounds of bread, and a piece of cheese. In central Germany warm meals were served, and in places there workers reportedly received so much they had food left over to take home to their families. Some seigniors found it more economical to pay their peasants a cash sum and let them supply their own food, or gave them a limited amount of food and a cash supplement.[36]

Everywhere officials of the central government had the responsibility to exercise a greater or lesser amount of supervision to ensure the performance of seigniorial obligations to their peasants. Given the hierarchical nature of the traditional society, it seems likely that laxity and inattention characterized their supervisory activities. Doubtless, the extent and the

[35] Austria: Feigl (1964), 44, 105-106; Wright (1966), 18; Grünberg (1901), 36-37. Schleswig-Holstein: Hanssen (1861), 23-24. Germany: Mager (1955), 165; Ford (1922), 195; Schremmer (1963), 17; Lütge (1957), 110; Ziekursch (1927), 121. Poland: Rusiński (1960), 420. Russia: Sivkov (1959), 31; Haxthausen (1866), 120-121. Lithuania: Strazdunaite (1961), 186-187, 189. Danubian Principalities: Oțetea (1960), 341.

[36] Haun (1892), 202; Lütge (1957), 159-162; Feigl (1964), 95; Wittich (1896), 202; Knapp (1902), 33; Darmstaedter (1897), 151; Hlubek (1860), 114.

spirit with which seigniors carried out their obligations depended upon the personal character and outlook of the lord himself. Most seigniors probably took some interest in the welfare of their peasants, if only because it was to their own advantage.[37] Peasants who did not feel maltreated or neglected were less likely to strike, or to run away, or to riot, loot, and burn. Seigniors, however, all too often did not meet all the obligations they owed, and not infrequently they exhibited a callous and even brutal disregard for the welfare of their peasants. Complaints from peasants and reports of contemporary observers make that clear.

Finally, just about everywhere in the servile lands, custom or statute, or both, guaranteed peasants certain rights in the property of their seigniors. These rights, called servitudes in the civil law, correspond closely to the easements of the common law. They were privileges that persons other than the owner had in the use of his property. They therefore limited freedom of ownership in that the property "served" others, regardless of the wishes of the owner of the property. There were many kinds of servitudes, each with its own distinctive name and each carefully defined by law or tradition. They were of much, and sometimes of critical, importance to the peasant economy. The right to use pastures and harvested fields of the seignior provided villagers with additional and often sorely needed grazing land for their animals. In heavily forested regions, or where lords had no interest in the exploitation of their timber, peasants could freely, or for a small fee, cut as much wood as they needed for fuel, construction, or even for sale. Often, though, the servitude allowed the peasant only to gather wood in the lord's forest, with specific restriction on the purposes for which the wood could be used. Pigs could root and cows could graze in the lord's forest, and sometimes the peasants could take fish from the manor's streams and ponds, and cut peat for fuel.[38]

The servitudes enjoyed by the peasant had their counterpoise in rights possessed by the seignior to the use of peasant land and common. Usually the lord's livestock were part of the village herd, and usually lords did not own many animals. Their peasants provided them with work animals and with animal products as part of their servile obligations. Sometimes, however, they owned large numbers of animals, especially of sheep, which they kept apart from the village's animals. The seignior had the right to pasture his livestock on the harvested fields and other common pastures of the village. Law and custom demanded that he had to see to it that his animals left enough on the pasture for the animals of the peasants. The requirement was, however, unenforceable for, unlike the peasants, who each could keep

[37] *Cf.* Kahk (1969), 21-22.
[38] Schönebaum (1917), 524; Semevskii (1881), 35-36; Le Play (1877), ii, 57-58; St. Jacob (1960), 146-147, 156; Lefebvre (1972), 100-101; Katus (1961), 131; Feigl (1964), 162-163; Corfus (1969), 24; Sée (1939), 189-190.

only a certain number of animals on common pasture, there was no limit on the number of animals the lord could put on the common.[39]

The absence of a limit on the flocks of the seignior vis-à-vis his peasants was typical of the relationship between lord and peasant and indicative of the status and privileges of the lords. They had much latitude—indeed, in some lands an all but free hand—in their dealings with the people who lived on their manors. True, as preceding pages have shown, statute and custom placed restrictions on what they could do and what they could demand. This chapter has shown that during the last century of the old order the central government trimmed its judicial authority to a greater or less degree, and later pages will discuss other aspects of the intervention of the government in the lord-peasant relationship. Nonetheless, despite the restrictions, the seigniors enjoyed a remarkable degree of freedom of action, with all manner of privileges and with much power over the millions of peasants who depended upon them and who supported them. Long ago Adam Smith observed that all men love to reap where they never sowed. Few have been as successful at this as were the seigniors of the servile lands of Europe during the last century of the old order.

[39] Barth-Barthenheim (1818), I, pt. 2, p. 43; Feigl (1964), 142; Bauer (1907), 61-62; Meyer (1965), 48-49; Bloch (1930), 514, 516; Riemann (1953), 102-103; Kieniewicz (1969), 90; Müller (1965a), 120; Jacob (1820), 82, 119.

CHAPTER 5

Peasants, Large, Middling and Small

I

I N the eyes and minds of the upper orders and in the legislation of princes, all peasants were alike in belonging to the lowest order of the traditional society, and all bore the responsibilities and obligations that rested upon that order. But, of course, the village world was not monolithic. Like the nobility, the clergy, and the bourgeoisie, the peasantry had its hierarchy of wealth, power, and privilege.

In most places the rank ordering in the village depended upon the size of the peasant's holding.[1] That size was expressed often not in terms of quantitative measurements of area but as a proportion of what was called a "full" holding. In many parts of Europe custom, legislation, and sometimes fiat had established a conventional holding or unit of exploitation, made up of house, house lot, garden, plowland, and servitudes. This conventional unit had many names, among them *Hufe* in German-speaking lands, *bol* in Scandinavia, *włoka* or *lan* in Poland, *adramaa* in Estonia and Latvia, *voloka* in White Russia and Lithuania, *Haken* in Livonia, *session* in Hungary, *mansus* or *meix* in France, and hide in England. In the early centuries of settled agriculture in Europe such a unit had probably been the amount of land necessary to support a family—presumably the extended family of several generations living together. But the conventional unit, where it still persisted, had long since lost its significance as the holding necessary for the maintenance of a family. Instead, it served as the unit for the assessment of obligations owed to the seignior and to the state. The dues, services, and taxes that the peasant household paid were proportionate to the amount of the conventional unit it held. Usually, the conventional unit coincided with what was considered a full-sized peasant holding, that is to say, the holding that carried with it the maximum in obligations. There were exceptions, however, as in Lower Saxony, the duchy of Wernigerode in north-central Germany, and on royal manors in Brandenburg and East Prussia, where the full-sized holding often contained two conventional units, or *Hufen*. On certain princely manors in Anhalt in central Germany the full peasant holding was fixed in 1687 at 4 *Hufen*. In a village in the bishopric of Halberstadt it had between four and one-half and seven and one-half *Hufen* and the peasant who had what was called a half-holding had between one and one-half and two and one-half *Hufen*.[2]

---

[1] There were a few peasant communities where wealth and its accompanying prestige depended upon other than agricultural activities. *Cf.* Kellenbenz (1962); Kulischer (1931).

[2] Wittich (1896), 86; Lütge (1957), 51.

There was much diversity in the size of the conventional unit not only between regions but even within a single community. In one place in Württemberg the amount of land in the *Hufe* ranged from 4 to 389 *morgen*, or 6 to 584 acres.[3] That was an extreme instance, but data from other areas show large if not as extreme disparities. In Lower Austria full-sized holdings went from 24 to 89 yokes (34 to 126 acres). In Hungary the average size of a full *session* was a little over 34 acres, but could vary from 17 to 57 acres. In Bohemia the conventional unit contained about 61 acres.[4] In the duchy of Lauenberg in Hannover some *Hufen* had as many as 135 to 163 acres. In Brandenburg the *Hufe* as a rule had 30 Prussian *morgen* (19 acres) but in some places measured as much as 200 *morgen* (126 acres).[5] In Saxony it was often between 32 and 41 acres and in mountain districts 60 acres.[6] In White Russia the conventional unit had about 52 acres of arable, pasture and homestead. In Poland it had something over 40 acres.[7] In the plainland of the Mühlviertel of Upper Austria the full peasant holding had about 57 acres, while in the wooded or mountainous districts it often contained over 280 acres.[8]

By the last century of the old order, most villagers who had land held only a part of a full holding, and the numbers of those who were entirely landless, or at best had only a scrap of land, had greatly increased. Economic fluctuations, differences in initiative, and efficiency among peasants and consequent upward and downward mobility, expansion of seigniorial demesne at the expense of peasant land, and, above all else, the rise in population, brought ever greater pressure for the subdivision and parcelling of holdings. Lord, peasant, and prince all recognized the perils to their respective interests if they yielded to this pressure. The lords knew that it would reduce holdings to proportions too small to provide the peasants with sufficient income to meet their obligations to the seigniors. The peasants knew that repeated subdivision of their holdings went hand-in-hand with poverty and, ultimately, pauperization. They knew, too, that as the ranks of the smallholders and the landless swelled, the burdens of seigniorial obligations, and of taxes that the state often levied on the village as a whole, would fall more heavily on those who still had holdings. The princes, for their part, wanted a peasantry able to pay taxes and to provide the civil and military services demanded of it.

And so lords, peasants, and princes all tried to prevent the subdivision of holdings, or at least to impede it. By command, by tradition, and by statute they forbade the division of a holding at the death of its occupant, and in-

[3] Knapp (1902), 67. The *morgen* in Württemberg was equal to 1.5 acres or .607 hectares.
[4] Tebeldi (1947), 200; Barany (1968), 192; Varga (1965), 12; Stark (1952), 363. The Austrian yoke (*joch*), containing 1,600 square *klafter*, equalled 1.42 acres or .574 hectares.
[5] Müller (1967), 31-32.   [6] Blaschke (1965), 275.
[7] Fridman (1958), 23; Kieniewicz (1969), 53.   [8] Hoffmann (1952), 277.

sisted that it had to descend undivided to a single heir. That rule of impartible inheritance prevailed in Denmark, in four-fifths of Germany (where, as one authority put it, "the notion of undivided transfer was so firmly fixed in the peasant mentality . . . that only in certain regions was the custom sanctioned by law"),[9] in central Switzerland, in the German crownlands of the Austrian Monarchy, in much of northern and central France, and in Little Poland, that is, southern and southwestern Poland. Partible inheritance, the practice of dividing holdings among heirs, prevailed in southern France, southern and western Switzerland, and in southwest and parts of northwest Germany. In much of Poland and in Bohemia and Moravia limited division into sections no smaller than one-fourth of a full holdings was permitted if seignior and government consented. In Lower Austria division among heirs was not uncommon, especially in the event of an intestate succession.

When single inheritance was the rule, the heir was sometimes the youngest son and sometimes the eldest son. In a number of regions there was no fixed rule of succession. In some places the seignior designated the heir. In certain districts custom or statute required the single heir of the holding to pay a certain amount of money, if it was available to him, to his siblings, and to divide the personal property of the decedent with them.[10]

The fact that subdivisions of holdings occurred, and at an increasing rate, makes it obvious that the prohibitions were not entirely effective. However, they were far from ineffective. There were many peasants with full, three-quarter, and half holdings. Those with full holdings made up the topmost stratum of village society. Then came in descending order those with three-quarter, half, and quarter-holdings, followed by smallholders who had less than a quarter-holding, next cotters who had a house and yard and perhaps a small vegetable garden, then the landless laborer who worked for the seignior or for a landholding peasant and who lived as a renter in another peasant's hut, and, finally, the servant or hired hand who was a member of the household of a more prosperous peasant. Each category had its own name, often a local or regional one. Some communities made fewer distinctions among its people than did others. For example, in Haute-Maine in northwestern France there was a tripartite division into *laboreurs*, who lived comfortably from their holdings; the more numerous *bordagers*, who had 5 to 10 hectares and just about made ends meet; and the *journaliers*, who had to work for others to earn their living. In Lower Saxony there were five subdivisions within the smallholder category alone.[11]

[9] Tcherkinsky (1941), 175.

[10] *Ibid.*, 167, 175-176, 177; Abel (1967a), 169; Chevallez (1949), 57; Revesz (1964), 206-208; Scharling (1894), 398; Mottek (1964), I, 325; Stark (1952), 350; Wittich (1896), 3, 46, 48-49; Schremmer (1963), 34; Skovgaard (1950), 12-13; Ziekursch (1927), 81; Hodgksin (1820), I, 260-261.

[11] Bois (1960), 436-439; Sering (1908), 233.

Sometimes the rank order depended upon the number of work animals owned by the peasant. In the canton of Zurich, for instance, the villager with a team, and who therefore could perform his labor obligation with his own animals, was known as a *Bauer*, a peasant. The number of work animals he needed for this status differed in different places; in one village a man needed only two animals while in another he had to have four or five oxen and one or two horses. The man with less than the prescribed number was known as a "half-peasant," *Halbbauer*. He combined with another *Halbbauer* to furnish a team of work animals. The man who had no animals and paid his labor obligation by his own manual labor was called a *Tauner*, a day laborer.[12] In Ukrainian villages peasants fell into five categories: those with at least one team of work animals, those who had only one horse or one ox, those with no animals and a small holding, those with a house and garden, and, finally, the landless peasants who earned their livings as hired laborers.[13] In the Danubian Principalities the Organic Statutes of 1831 divided the peasantry into three strata: the *fruntaşi*, who owned four or more oxen, the *mijlocaşi*, who had two oxen, and the *codaşi* who owned one ox or none at all.[14]

II

Peasants held their land by a variety of tenures, each with its own attributes and often with its own local name and special features. Many of the characteristics of these tenures shaded into one another so that distinctions among them were often blurred. All of them, however, can be separated into two categories that can be simply termed as "good" tenures and "bad" tenures. The "good" tenures included all those manners of landholding by which the peasant occupant had a permanent and often heritable right to the use of his holding. "Bad" tenures were those by which the peasants held for a limited period, or at the will of the proprietor. Different tenures coexisted within a region or a locality or even within an individual manor. Typically, however, one or another form predominated in a given area. In general, "good" tenures were most common in the lands of the west, while "bad" tenures were the rule in the eastern lands.

The best of the good tenures was that of the free peasant proprietors who were scattered through all of the servile lands. These people had full ownership of their land. However, they made up only a small part of the peasantry. By far the most common of the good tenures was the hereditary right of occupation. Many peasants held their land by this tenure in France, particularly in the northern half of that country, in Germany west of the Elbe, and in the Austrian Monarchy after the implementation of reforms of

[12] Bollinger (1941), 36.   [13] Zaionchkovskii (1941), 22-23.
[14] Emerit (1937), 285.

Joseph II. Poland and eastern Germany, especially Lower Silesia and Brandenburg, also had peasants who held by hereditary tenure, but they formed
a minority in those lands.

Hereditary tenure gave the peasant a lifelong right to the use of his holding and allowed him to bequeath, alienate, or mortgage it. Indeed, hereditary tenure often seemed indistinguishable from ownership. But, as earlier pages explained (pp. 20, 93), the hereditary occupant owned only the
right to the use of the land and its accompanying servitudes in forest,
pasture, meadow, and waste. It was this right of use that the occupant could
bequeath, sell, or hypothecate. The superior ownership, the *dominium directum*, belonged to a seignior who had rights and powers over the use and
disposition of the holding that could severely limit the occupants' freedom
of action. The fee that had to be paid to the seignior whenever and however
the holding changed hands has already been discussed. The persons eligible
to inherit were almost everywhere restricted to the direct line of descent.
Failing eligible heirs, the holding reverted to the seignior. In many places,
however, the seignior was required to turn over the holding to another
peasant rather than add it to his own demesne. In central and western Germany the seignior had to give his approval before the peasant occupant
could take a loan against the holding, and he could limit the amount of debt
the peasant could incur. In Burgundy the seignior had to give his approval
before the peasant could alter crop rotations or introduce new crops or make
changes in techniques, and he exercised constant supervision of the agricultural activities of the peasants in his seigniory to protect his own interests.

Usually, if the peasant occupant wanted to sell his right to the use of his
holding, he first had to get the permission of his seignior. In most of
France, in many parts of Germany, and in places in Switzerland, seigniors
had the right to buy for themselves a hereditary peasant holding in their
seigniory that the peasant occupant had already sold to someone else. This
privilege was known as *retrait féodal*, *prélation*, or *clameur* in French-
speaking lands, and *Losungsrecht*, *Vorkaufsrecht*, or *Einstandsrecht* by
German speakers. The seignior paid the purchaser the price that he had
paid, though in many places in Germany the seignior paid a lower fixed
price. In some places the seignior was allowed from as little as 40 days to as
much as 30 years in which he could exercise the right. The seignior could
also refuse permission to a peasant to sell his holding to another peasant
and could buy the holding himself. In Brittany when a holding passed from
a decedent to his heir the seignior could, if he wished, buy the holding for
himself. In the Rhine Province of Prussia the seignior had the first option
when a peasant wanted to sell his holding.

Finally, seigniors had the right to evict the occupant of an hereditary
holding for reasons generally, though not universally, defined by statute.
Among the frequently specified grounds were neglect of the holding, ar-

rearages of two to three years in payments of obligations owed to the seignior, excessive debt, and alienation of all or part of the holding without the lord's prior consent. In Lower Saxony and in the German and Slav crownlands of the Austrian Monarchy the seignior could dispossess the hereditary tenant only after he had received permission from a court or from the district bureau of the central government.[15]

Leaseholds, widespread in the west and fairly common in some of the eastern lands, held third place among the good tenures, after ownership and hereditary tenancy. Many leaseholds were for the life of the tenant, and though the seignior could rent it to whomever he wished on the death of the tenant, it usually went to an heir of the decedent. Sometimes the tenant had tenure for several lives, as for example his own life, that of his widow, and that of his son. This kind of secure tenure approximated hereditary tenure, and in some lands it gradually mutated into that category. Despite its seeming advantages, however, large turnovers occurred in life tenancies, judging at least from Danish experience. An analysis made of the eighteenth-century records of some 70 Danish manors and a sampling of a number of others showed that barely 45 per cent of the tenants kept their holdings until death. After a life tenant's death his widow had the right to continue in occupancy, but even if her tenancy is included, the average period of occupancy was not much over twenty years. Many gave up their holdings voluntarily, but a large minority, reaching 25 to 30 per cent in the island of Zealand, were evicted for non-payment of their rent. These people generally joined the ranks of the landless laborers.

The most common form of leasehold was the term lease. Peasants in all of the servile countries rented land for a specified period at a fixed rent, though the frequency of use of this tenure varied considerably among regions. In Germany it had an unimportant role except west of the Rhine in the Rhine Province, where over one-third of the land was farmed by term lessees. It was employed extensively in some parts of France, particularly in Flanders, where it was just about the only tenure available to peasants. Elsewhere in France it was relatively uncommon.

Many peasants rented all of the land they farmed, but often peasants who held land by some other tenure rented additional land from seigniors or from other peasants. Nearly always they leased land because the holding

---

[15] Austrian Monarchy: Grünberg (1894), I, 270-272, 364-365; Feigl (1964), 23, 67, 75; Wright (1966), 16; Blum (1948), 82-84; Revesz (1964), 206; Mésáros (1961), 70. France: Forster (1963), 685; La Monneraye (1922), 77; Marion (1968), 488; St. Jacob (1960), 68-69; Sée (1906), 110-111. Germany: Blaschke (1965), 257; Engels (1957), 23; Jordan-Rozwadowski (1900), 501, 504; Knapp (1887), I, 16; Haun (1892), 162-163; Hodgskin (1820), II, 83-84; Knapp (1902), 63; Knapp (1964), 398-399; Ludwig (1896), 53; Lütge (1949), 47-51, 81, 86-94; Lütge (1967), 176-177, 189; Schremmer (1963), 23; Wittich (1896), 3, 57-59; Müller (1967), 28-30; Ziekursch (1927), 78-80. Poland: Revesz (1964), 206; Rutkowski (1926), 490-491. Savoy: Darmstaedter (1897), 154. Switzerland: Chevallez (1949), 177-178; Wahlen and Jaggi (1952), 110.

they had did not suffice to meet their needs, and nearly always they could afford to rent only small pieces. There were instances when individual wealthy peasants, or groups of peasants, rented large blocks of land, which they usually divided into smaller pieces and sublet to fellow peasants. Typically, however, lessees on this scale were burghers and professional men, and, in some cases, as in White Russia and Lithuania, nobles who saw an opportunity to profit by subletting or by farming part or all of the rented land on their own account. Peasant lessees paid their rents in a variety of forms. Some paid it all in cash; some in cash and produce; some, as in the Hungarian county of Pest, in Brittany, and in the Danubian Principalities, paid a combination of cash, produce, and labor; some, as in Hainault and Cambrésis in northern France, paid in produce and labor. Leases usually were for three years, or a multiple of three, to accommodate the lease to the three-year rotation that was the most commonly used field system of the old order. Sometimes the lease was for as long as 18 or 24 years, but apparently most of them were for 3, 6, and, especially in parts of France, 9 years. In Poland peasants often rented for only a year but subject to annual renewal so that the arrangement amounted to a long-term lease.[16]

The yearly leases in Poland were made orally with brief entries inserted in the manorial records.[17] Elsewhere the terms of the lease were usually written down, and they spelled out in precise language the conditions the lessee had to observe. These included such items as the requirement that the peasant keep the holding and its buildings in a good state of repair; that he follow the crop rotations indicated by the proprietor, which nearly always meant the traditional three-field rotation; that he pay the taxes on the holding; that he had to take his grain to the seigniorial mill; and so on.[18] In other words, as is still the rule with leases, the lessor set the terms of the contract and rented his land to those who agreed to accept his terms— except in parts of northern France. Peasant renters there claimed that an ancient right which they called *droit de marché* gave them perpetual leases; they denied the right of the proprietor to evict them or to rent the land to someone else, or even to sell it to someone of whom they did not approve. If the landlord refused to accept these unwritten laws, the peasants resorted

[16] Austria: Grünberg (1894), I, 54. Danubian Principalities: Corfus (1969), 117-118. Denmark: Skrubbeltrang (1953), 167, 169-172; Steensberg (1951), 187-188. France: Lizerand (1942), 89-91; Juillard (1953), 86; Lefebvre (1972), 261-264; Venard (1957), 70-71; Calonne (1920), 189; St. Jacob (1960), 41-42; Forster (1960), 37, 59; Forster (1970), 1606-1607; Sée (1906), 73-75, 242-243, 247, 249, 250, 255; Louchitsky (1911), 84-85. Germany: Engels (1957), 22, 24; Lütge (1949), 81-82, 85; Lütge (1967), 79; Schremmer (1963), 23; Knapp (1919), I, 109; Knapp (1964), 396-398; Müller (1964a), 642; Müller (1967), 31; Wittich (1896), 447-448. Hungary: Spira (1968), 357-358. Poland: Rutkowski (1926), 491; Revesz (1964), 203. White Russia and Lithuania: Pokhilevich (1966), 391.

[17] Rutkowski (1926), 491.

[18] Knapp (1887), 18-19; Grünberg (1894), I, 54; Sée (1906), 245-247, 248; Wittich (1896), 28; Venard (1957), 83; Louchitsky (1911), 78; St. Jacob (1960), 41-42.

to a practice fittingly known as *mauvais gré*, "ill will," in which they made the new renter or owner the object of vilification and violence and sabotage to force him to give up the land.[19]

Upon the expiration of his lease the renter had no claim to the holding, though his toil or the improvements he introduced may have increased its value. Indeed, the expiration of the lease gave the proprietor the opportunity to increase the rent. That happened frequently during the price rise of the second half of the eighteenth century, and especially after 1770. Landlords raised rents with each successive lease; in Toulouse cash rents more than doubled between the 1740's and the 1780's, and in addition the lessors demanded supplementary rents in kind.[20]

To continue on the descending scale of peasant tenures: sharecropping comes next. It seems to have been employed most extensively in western, central, and southern France. An estimated three-quarters of all leased land in these regions was held by sharecroppers. It was rarely found north of the Loire River except in Lorraine. It was also common in the Rhine Province of Prussia, in Savoy, and in a few localities in Switzerland.

With sharecropping the line was crossed from "good" to "bad" tenures. Some peasants who had holdings too small to support their families took additional land on shares. Most sharecroppers, however, were little more than rural proletarians, almost always in debt to their landlords, and barely able to earn their living. They could not afford to lease land, and in any event they lacked the tools and animals needed to work a holding. They had no choice but to accept the terms offered by the proprietor. He usually provided half or more of the working capital, including animals and seed, needed to work the holding. In return the peasant turned over a share of the produce of the holding to the proprietor. The amount of the share depended upon the agreement made between peasant and proprietor. Generally, both parties received equal shares. Sometimes the sharing applied only to field crops, sometimes to everything produced on the holding in field, garden, orchard, pasture, and barnyard. Sometimes, as in Brittany, the sharecropper made a cash payment in lieu of the proprietor's share of products other than field crops. Actually, the peasant usually wound up with less than the agreed-upon share because, generally, he had to make payments to the proprietor in addition to the shares of his produce. These supplementary payments included such obligations as transport and other labor services for the proprietor, payment of part of the taxes, providing all of the seed for the next year's crop, and reimbursement to the landlord for the use of the work animals he supplied.[21]

[19] Lefebvre (1972), 103-110; Calonne (1920), 192-194.
[20] Abel (1966), 198-199; Forster (1960), 59; Sée (1906), 257-260; Eggert (1965), 9.
[21] Forster (1970), 1605; Lefebvre (1955), 92; Soboul (1970), 123; Vermale (1911), 145-147; Sée (1906), 251-253; Falguerolles (1941), 146, 148; Merle (1958), 91-92, 116-118, 184, 203-204; Forster (1963), 686; Engels (1957), 22.

The demands of the proprietors tended to go up during the course of the eighteenth century. Still, some peasants managed to escape the progressive pauperization that seemed the fate of the sharecropper. Presumably a bit of the new prosperity of the second half of the eighteenth century rubbed off on some of them. They accumulated enough working capital to free themselves from their dependence upon their landlords, and to step up from sharecroppers to cash renters on term leases. A study of the Gâtine district of the French province of Poitou showed that 80 per cent of the rural tenants there in 1700 had been sharecroppers and only 20 per cent cash renters on term leases. Thereafter the ratio of sharecroppers declined, at first gradually and then from the 1740's precipitously, until in 1790 only 38 per cent of all tenants rented on shares and 62 per cent were cash renters with term leases.[22]

With all of its shortcomings, sharecropping was still preferable to the tenure that prevailed in Europe east of the Elbe. At least the sharecropper had an agreement with his landlord that afforded him a degree of security. He knew for how long he could occupy the holding, and he knew that he could harvest the crops he had planted and so benefit from the labor he had put into raising them. He had a time horizon. Most of the peasants in the servile lands of eastern Europe held their land at the will of their seignior. He could evict the occupant of a holding whenever he wished, for any cause or for no cause. He could turn over the holding to another peasant, or add it to his demesne, or allow it to lie empty. In some regions the lord did have to allow the evicted peasant a grace period, usually of six months (one year in the Danubian Principalities) before the peasant had to leave the holding. The lord did not have to compensate the evicted peasant for any additions he might have made to the value of the holding, such as drainage, breaking new land, or construction of farm buildings. The lord could move the evicted peasant to another holding, or he could withhold land from them and thereby reduce the household to landless laborers or cotters. In Russia, eastern Galicia, Bukovina, Moldavia, and Hungary, where many peasants held their land communally, the tenure was still at the will of the seignior. He could take away part or all of the land of the commune and could move the villagers from one place to another as a group or as individuals.

In practice, tenure at will had a certain security attached to it. Apparently, seigniors rarely used their authority to evict a peasant except for suitable cause, such as neglect of the holding. The occupant could expect to keep his holding for life and have his heir take it over after him. However, he had no legally recognized right to the use of the holding, much less hereditary use, and, of course, he could not alienate the holding nor borrow against it. And the danger of eviction was never absent.[23]

[22] Merle (1952), chart 3, p. 179; Roupnel (1922), 280 ff; Engels (1957), 22; Forster (1960), 57-58; Sée (1906), 259-260.
[23] Kuhn (1955), 162; Koetzschke (1953), 126; Hötzsch (1902), 263; Watters (1968), 134-

In Poland and in the German and Slav crownlands of the Austrian Monarchy peasants, with their lords' consent, had long been allowed to buy hereditary tenure of their holdings, with all the powers of disposition over the holdings that accompanied this tenure. During the reign of Maria Theresa the Austrian government encouraged this practice, and after the first partition of Poland in 1772 promoted it also in the newly annexed Polish territories. The government pursued this policy because it believed that hereditary tenures would provide the peasant with the incentive to work harder and to improve his farming, and thereby promote the economic growth of the state. The authorities did not use compulsion, preferring to keep the procedure on a voluntary basis. Their efforts proved largely futile. Most peasants lacked the money needed to buy the better tenure, and most lords showed no willingness to cooperate. Then Joseph II, in typically direct manner, solved the dilemma when in 1785 and 1789 he issued decrees that by fiat transformed tenants at will into hereditary occupants. In Upper Lusatia, in northeastern Saxony, nobles in the late eighteenth century voluntarily shifted most of their peasants who held at will to hereditary tenures. They did this because peasants with insecure tenures did not take care of their holdings, and the lords had to spend their own money to maintain them. The seigniors charged their peasants for the improvement in their tenures. Those who could not afford to pay the price, or who for whatever reason did not want to make the change, were evicted from their holdings.[24]

III

The kind of tenure by which the peasant held his land was only one of the variables of peasant life. Another was the amount of land he held, whatever the tenure. In the discussion of the relative size of holdings, custom and language dictate the use of the adjectives large, middling and small. But as J. H. Clapham (among many others) asked long ago, "there is the constantly recurring question, what, after all, is a small, moderate, or large holding? . . . The economic answer should not be in acres but in net product. . . . On a couple of well-watered acres in the country by Avignon [Clapham was using French data for 1908-1909] a family can live in reasonable comfort. A small holding there, for a peasant who tries to live by it, is an acre and a quarter. In the rather infertile corn lands of *la triste Sologne*, 125 acres is reckoned a small holding. In Burgundy, a man is counted a

---

135; Blum (1971a), 171-172; Müller (1967), 30-31; Knapp (1887), I, 16-17; Ziekursch (1927), 77; Mager (1955), 180; Grünberg (1894), I, 54-55; Grünberg (1901), 49-51, 58, 78; Mésáros (1961), 70; Vaillant (1844), III, 68; Rutkowski (1926), 492; Andrews (1774), II, 359-360.

[24] Grünberg (1894), I, 260-262, 270-272, 364-365; Kieniewicz (1969), 16-17; Boelcke (1957), 255.

small holder who has less than about seven acres of vines, or less than 50 acres of corn land."[25]

The want of data, aside from a few estimates, make it impossible to find the "economic answer" that Clapham suggested, that is, the net product for large, middling, and small holdings of the servile lands. Some obvious distinctions can be made. It seems warranted to assume from domestic architecture, general living style, and comments of contemporary observers, that peasants with what were considered large holdings were prosperous, and, indeed, sometimes wealthy. This, however, was not always a valid correlation. In Congress Poland and in Little Russia some peasants preferred smaller holdings because the obligations demanded by their seigniors from the occupants of full holdings were too oppressive. In Russia, where the household's share of the communal tax burden was proportionate to the size of its holding, peasants in the infertile soil of northern Russia tried to get as little land as they could in the periodic redistributions of the village plowland.[26] It seems clear, too, that peasants whose holdings were just about large enough or productive enough to support the household were considered of middling size. Peasants with so little land that they had to find other sources of support belonged to the category of smallholders.

The number of these smallholders, and of entirely landless peasants, grew prodigiously in the great demographic upsurge that began in the eighteenth century. In Saxony peasants with full holdings had made up 49.5 per cent of the population in 1550. By 1750 their number had risen by 3 per cent from 214,800 to 221,500. But their proportion in the total population had fallen to 25 per cent, and by 1843 it was only 14 per cent. Meanwhile, the ratio of cotters and landless peasants rose from 18 per cent of the total population in 1550 to 38 per cent in 1750 and 52 per cent in 1843.[27] Data for other regions show the same pattern of development. Over half of the peasants who had any land at all in that part of Brandenburg called Kurmark (over 60 per cent of the province) were smallholders and cotters. Early in the eighteenth century most peasants in Farther Pomerania had middle-sized or large holdings. By 1805 smallholders and cotters were in the majority among the landholding peasants there.[28] In addition, these and the other eastern provinces of Prussia had many thousands of landless people who earned their livings as farm laborers. Their numbers grew with astonishing speed in the second half of the eighteenth century. Between 1770 and 1880 in Kurmark landless peasants who took lodings in a peasant household increased by 44 per cent. The

[25] Clapham (1951), 165.
[26] Leslie (1956), 58-59; Semevskii (1881), 123; Wallace (1912), 136-137.
[27] Blaschke (1956), 149-150; Blaschke (1965), 280.
[28] Goldschmidt (1910), 107, 108; Henning (1969b), 58. *Cf.* Korth (1953), 163-164 and Muhlen (1951), 352 for other parts of western Germany.

category of male and female farm servants, who lived with their employers, grew by 29 per cent and 16 per cent, respectively. At the end of the eighteenth century there were three times as many landless peasants in Kurmark as there were peasants with holdings. In East Prussia as early as 1700 landless farm laborers had outnumbered peasants with holdings (72,611 laborers and 69,231 peasants with holdings), and the gap widened as the century wore on. Between 1750 and 1802 farm labor families increased from around 18,000 to 48,000, or more than two and a half times over, while the number of peasants with holdings grew only by about 40 per cent. In central and western Germany, too, the number of landless and nearly landless rose steadily. As an example, in the Hochberg district of Baden in southeastern Germany around the 1780's, of 2,897 peasant families:[29]

    1,303 (45%) were landless or had less than 1.8 acres
    1,140 (39%) had between 1.8 and 7.2 acres
      307 (11%) had between 7.2 and 14.4 acres
      147 (5%) had over 18 acres.

In Denmark between 1688 and 1800 the number of cotters increased 6 to 7 times over in Zealand, 4 times over in Fyn, and 2 times over in Jutland and in the islands of Lolland and Falster. Meanwhile, the number of peasants with full holdings showed a small decline. In the 1840's of over 490,000 peasants who had holdings in the Austrian provinces of Lower Austria, Styria and Moravia, 58 per cent (285,897) had less than one-fourth of a full holding, and in addition there was a large number of landless peasants. In Bohemia by 1848 over half of the villagers had dwarf holdings or were landless. In 1850 in Galicia 15.4 per cent of the peasants with holdings had less than .5 hectares and 42.47 per cent had from .5 to 5 hectares. When at the beginning of the eighteenth century the Hapsburgs reestablished their rule over all of Hungary, peasants with less than a quarter-holding, cotters, and landless peasant lodgers were practically unknown in many parts of the country. By 1828 nearly half (47.2 per cent) and by 1848 nearly two-thirds (60.4 per cent) of Hungary's greatly increased peasant population were in these categories. In the county of Pest the number of full holdings increased by 4.8 per cent between 1770 and 1828. During these same years the number of peasant families doubled from 23,985 to 47,955. In 1770 42 per cent of the serfs of Pest county were cotters and landless lodgers (called *inquilini* and *subinquilini* in the Latin that was Hungary's official language). By 1846 that ratio had risen to 72.2 per cent. In Poland an average-sized peasant household could about meet its expenses in a good year with a holding of around 17 acres. In the second

[29] Kurmark: Müller (1964b), 238-239. East Prussia: Korth (1953), 164; Ipsen (1954), 32n. Baden: Liebel (1965), 98; Berthold (1962), 85-86.

half of the eighteenth century an estimated 16 per cent of the peasant population had no land, about 33 per cent had less than 10 acres, about 30 per
cent had 10 to 20 acres, and around 21 per cent had over 20 acres. In 1859
official statistics for Congress Poland showed that the landless made up 41
per cent of the peasant population. Of 324,809 peasants with holdings, 27.1
per cent had less than 12.4 acres, 46.1 per cent had 12.4 to 29 acres, 15.2
per cent had 29 to 41 acres, and 11.6 per cent had over 41 acres.[30]

In Russia the peasants periodically redistributed their plowland to
achieve some measure of equality in holdings. Nonetheless, scattered data
from the last part of the eighteenth century indicate the presence of a considerable number of cotters and landless peasants among the state peasantry. In the mid-1830's the newly established Ministry of State Domain,
charged with the supervision of the state peasantry, reported that over 7
per cent of the adult male state peasants had less than 5½ acres, including
63,000 who had no land at all. By the middle of the century the ministry,
under the dynamic leadership of Count P. D. Kiselev, had reduced much of
this inequality by the resettlement of state peasants and by distribution of
state-owned land. The few studies of villages of seigniorial peasants or of
privately owned land complexes also indicate stratification in the serf community in the amount of land held by each household.[31]

In general, Russian state peasants had holdings larger than those of serfs,
serfs who paid no labor dues had holdings larger than those of serfs who
did, and holdings in the black earth provinces of the steppe tended to be
slightly smaller than those in the less fertile non-black earth regions. The
Russian peasant in the late eighteenth and early nineteenth century is estimated to have needed 5.4 to 6.75 acres (2-2½ desiatins) per adult male
soul to support himself at the subsistence level.[32] Apparently most peasants
were in this category. Data collected in the 1850's by an official agency indicated that the average holding in the 43 provinces covered by the survey
amounted to 8.64 acres (3.2 desiatins) per adult male serf. The average
holding of state peasants (who, it will be recalled, made up over half of the
Russian peasantry by the mid-nineteenth century), was over 16 acres (6
desiatins). The average for state peasant holdings was much inflated by the
large size of their holdings in the infertile provinces of northern Russia—in
Olonets, for example, the average was 50 acres—and in the fertile but
sparsely settled frontier provinces of eastern and southern Russia. The av-

[30] Denmark: Steensberg (1951), 187-188. Austria: Blum (1948), 171-172. Bohemia: Klima
(1961), 21. Galicia: Ballerstedt (1939), 20. Hungary: Revesz (1964), 302; Varga (1965), 131-
132; Spira (1968), 357. Poland: Leskiewicz (1962), 243; Koroliuk *et al.* (1956), I, 345; Kostiushko (1954), 175, 209-210, 237. The accuracy of the mid-nineteenth-century figure for
landless peasants in Poland has been challenged on the ground that it included many smallholders. Kieniewicz (1969), 145-146.
[31] Blum (1961), 533; Zaionchkovskii (1968), 20-21; Koval'chenko (1965), *passim*; Sivkov
(1962), 264-276; Bibikov (1938), 108-111.
[32] Koval'chenko (1967) 263-264. The desiatin equalled 2.7 acres or 1.09 hectares.

erages were much smaller in other provinces, but, with few exceptions, were still significantly larger than the average size for the holdings of serfs. Partial and not entirely comparable data for earlier years indicate that the average size of serf holdings declined during the first half of the nineteenth century. There are data, too, that show that many peasants fell below the subsistence level, as, for example, in the northwestern and infertile province of Pskov. A study made there in the 1830's showed that not more than 30 per cent of the state peasant households there had enough land to support them even under optimal conditions.[33]

There was also a considerable number of landless peasants, though proportionately much less in Russia than in the other servile lands. These were the "household serfs," the people whose masters had taken them off the land and converted them into domestic servants. In 1858 in the last census before the emancipation in 1861 they totalled nearly 1.5 million males and females, or 6.8 per cent of the total serf population of the empire. Sometimes, too, lords made full-time field hands of their serfs, giving them a monthly allowance of food, clothing, and cash. Their number seems not to have been large, and apparently most of them had small holdings. In the Ukrainian provinces of Kharkov, Poltava, and Chernigov, where the peasants did not hold their land by communal tenure, 15 per cent to 24 per cent of the serf population had no land on the eve of the emancipation.[34]

Communal tenure and periodic repartitions of the land were employed by the peasants of eastern Galicia. Despite this, inequalities in holdings were a common phenomenon there. Data from the eighteenth and the first part of the nineteenth century revealed that some peasants managed to get more land than their fellows. Others received no plowland at all, and lived as cotters or else took lodgings in the homes of fellow peasants.[35]

In France in the decades before the outbreak of the Revolution most of the peasants who had land had very small holdings. In Limousin in south central France out of 5,314 peasant households with land 58 per cent had less than 5 acres; in the Laonnais in the northeast corner of Ile de France 76 per cent of those with holdings had less than 5 acres. In the department of Nord, on the Belgian border, 75 to 80 per cent of the peasants had less than 2½ acres or were entirely landless. Of the 5,186 peasants with holdings in 28 parishes in Brittany 623 (12 per cent) had less than 1.2 acres, 2,402 (46 per cent) had from 1.2 to 6 acres, and 1,179 (23 per cent) had between 6 and 12 acres.[36] There were many landless peasants who were distributed unevenly through the kingdom. In some areas they formed only 1 to 2 per cent of the peasant population. In others they were far more numerous. In

---

[33] Blum (1961), 529, 534; Druzhinin (1946), I, 387; *cf.* Kusheva (1951), 50n.
[34] Troinitskii (1861), 57; Blum (1961), 532-533.
[35] Rosdolski (1954), 109, 113-114.
[36] Lefebvre (1929), 510; Lefebvre (1972), 31-34; Soboul (1960), 106; Sée (1906), 66-67.

Picardy 86 per cent of the heads of peasant households, 75 per cent in the maritime plain of French Flanders, 70 per cent in villages around Versailles, and 30 to 40 per cent in Lower Normandy had no land. In parts of Brittany landless and nearly landless peasants made up one-fourth to one-fifth of the population, and as much as two-thirds in some places.[37] In villages in Switzerland that were near cities, or whose residents were active in cottage industry, most peasants had between 1.5 and 5 acres, and many had no land at all.[38]

IV

Villagers whose holdings were too small to support their families, and those who had no land, had to find outside employment. Usually they found work in their own villages as hired farm laborers, employed by the seignior or by a fellow peasant who needed help to run his holding or to meet his labor obligation to the lord. Others, unable to find work at home moved to another village, if they could, in search of employment, or became migrant workers. Some turned to cottage industry, some found work in mining and metallurgy and in transport, some felled and hauled timber, or went out with packs to peddle small wares, or became wandering artisans.

These rural proletarians had many names, some of them unusually descriptive, such as *Brinksitzer* in Lower Saxony for those with scraps of land on the edges of the village. In many places the smallholders, the cotters, and the landless did not have a vote in the communal assembly that governed the village, were excluded from active participation in the management of the community, and from the privileges that accompanied active participation. Generally, they were allowed to keep a cow or a goat or some geese on the village common. The obligations demanded of them were nearly always considerably less than those required of peasants with holdings. In some places, as in northwest Germany, they paid only a small fee to the seignior. Often, however, they had to do labor services that ranged from as little as 6 days a year in Galicia and Bukovina for both cotters and landless peasants to as much as 3 days a week in Bohemia for some cotters, and even 4 to 6 days a week in places in Brandenburg.[39]

The land of the smallholders sometimes lay within the open fields of the village. Frequently, however, their holdings were outside the open fields,

[37] Lefebvre (1929), 510; Louchitsky (1911), 18; Louchitsky (1933), 120-124; Sée (1906), 306-307.
[38] Walter (1966), 84-85, 87; Bernhard (1915), 8-9; Chevallez (1949), 57; *cf.* Durst (1951), 63.
[39] Schremmer (1963), 13; Dessmann (1904), 75; Sée (1921), 75, 153; Nielsen (1933), 191; Blum (1948), 72-73; Blum (1971b), 549-550; Müller (1967), 32.

perhaps in unused common land, or on the edge of the village, or even between the subdivisions—the shots—of the open fields. These holdings were not included in the communal regulation of the village plowland. Those who were cotters had only a house and yard. Landless peasants who had families sometimes rented a hut and a scrap of garden from a landholding villager. Others rented lodgings, living often as a member of the household of the peasant who employed them, sleeping in barns, or stables, or other outbuildings, or in Livonia in the saunas. Many of these farm hands were young and unmarried. Often they spent their entire lives as farm hands. Sometimes their employers allowed them to marry, but oftentimes this was not permitted. Since male and female farm hands frequently shared the same sleeping quarters in barn or stable many of the women had illegitimate children. Farm hands who did marry were sometimes given a small piece of land by the seignior, in return, of course, for dues or labor services to the seignior. Sometimes well-to-do peasant employers provided a small piece of land and a hut for their laborers as part of their wages.[40]

In many places a hiring fair was held one day a year—in Lower Austria, for example, it was on Candelmas, 2 February—at which employers engaged farm hands. The period of employment usually lasted for a year until the next fair. During that time the employer could not discharge the worker, nor could the worker quit, without serious cause. Apparently, these provisions were not always observed, at least not in northern France. A sixteenth-century decree had forbidden farm hands hired for a set term to leave without the written permission of the employer, and had ordered a heavy fine for those employers who hired workers who had left their previous employer without his permission. The ordinance had long since fallen into disuse, and employers of the late eighteenth century complained ceaselessly about faithless farm hands who deserted them before the expiration of their contracts.[41]

The growth of population increased the supply of rural labor, sometimes to superfluity, as in Toulouse, where a contemporary told of crowds of unemployed workers from the countryside seeking alms in the city in the 1760's and 1770's. In Bavaria in 1794 out of an estimated population of 122,000 adult male peasants over 21, over 50,000 were farm hands who lived with their employers. Yet, despite the great increase in the rural proletariat, there were complaints of labor shortages in the 1780's in parts of France, and in the first half of the nineteenth century in Lower Austria, in

[40] Blaschke (1956), 145; Wittich (1896), 102, 108, 115; Engelbrecht (1913), 33-34; Stark (1952), 370-371; Revesz (1964), 71-72; Schremmer (1963), 12; Mühlen (1951), 352; Sering (1908), 232; Feigl (1964), 104; Dessmann (1904), 75; Transehe-Roseneck (1890), 176; Pokhilevich (1966), 390; Rutkowski (1927), 81; Sée (1906), 310-311; Knapp (1964), 166 n.2; Kieniewicz (1969), 54; Ziekursch (1927), 73.
[41] Buchinger (1952), 101-102; Calonne (1920), 260, 262.

many parts of Congress Poland, and in the still sparsely populated plains of Hungary and of southern Russia.[42]

The seasonal demand for farm labor was met often by migratory workers. Each spring the roads of Europe came alive as peasants streamed out of their villages and fell in with the bands from other villages to seek work in distant places, and the roads teemed again in late autumn when the workers began their homeward trek. In France peasants of Burgundy travelled to Brie, east of Paris, to harvest grain and then returned home for the grape harvest; bands of hill people came down into the Languedoc plain to work in the vintage; Bretons each year went to the region around Paris to work in the grain harvests, and so on.[43] Lower Austrian proprietors depended upon the annual migration of thousands of workers from other provinces. Most came from Moravia and Silesia, and many from Styria; an observer in 1848 estimated that 10,000 migrants came annually from that province. A seasonal influx into the Hungarian plain came each year from the hill people of Slovakia and from Croatia.[44] Landowners in Poland organized agencies to enlist people from the Tatra mountains of Galicia to work at haying and harvest, and even paid them double to get in the crop speedily. In Wallachia peasants came down from the hills to find work in the fertile plain. In Russia in the mid-nineteenth century an estimated 300,000 migrant workers from the central provinces descended on the thinly peopled provinces of New Russia to work in the fields there.[45]

Not all peasant migrant workers found employment in agriculture. Many thousands left their homes to engage in other pursuits. Not infrequently all of the migrants from a village or from a region followed the same trade. All the migratory workers from the valley of the Giffre in Savoy were masons and carpenters, those from the lower basin of the Arve were mercers. In Russia migrants from the Rostov district of the province of Iaroslavl worked as gardeners, migrants from other sections of Iaroslavl and Vladimir were masons and carpenters, and many of the peddlers who travelled the roads of the empire also came from sections of these two provinces. The departure of the migrants sometimes stripped their home villages of all the able-bodied men. A report of 1776 from Savoy told of 299 migrants from a village of 475, 105 out of 205 residents of another village, 43 out of 141 in a third settlement, and so on. In the 1850's in villages owned by Count Sheremetev in the less fertile parts of Russia, over half of the adults left home annually to seek work. The modest earnings that the migrants brought back with them give eloquent testimony of the poverty of

[42] Forster (1960), 48; Lütge (1949), 162-163, 172; Kostiushko (1954), 174; Festy (1947), 21-22; Louchitsky (1911), 36; Blum (1948), 175-182; Haxthausen (1847), ii, 24, 97; Kulischer (1932), 47-48.

[43] Davies (1964), 27; Hufton (1974), 73-91.   [44] Blum (1948), 176-178, 184.

[45] Kieniewicz (1969), 146; Corfus (1969), 58; Blum (1961), 401.

the peasantry. In 1758 the construction workers from the Giffre valley of Savoy returned home after 8 months' employment with an average of 21 livres per worker in one village, 40 livres in two others, and a maximum of 50 livres in still another village. Travelling mercers from the Arve valley reported earnings of 100 livres. At that time a cow cost 50 livres.[46]

The rules set by custom, statute, or mutual agreement that defined the working conditions for peasants on their obligatory labor services did not apply to hired labor. In Bohemia and in much of Germany the work day for these people during spring and summer—in Bohemia that was from Easter to Michaelmas (29 September)—started at 3 or 3:30 in the morning and ended at dusk. In the long daylight hours of summer in northern Europe that could mean as late as 10 p.m., or a work day of 19 hours. In the other six months work for the hired laborer began at 4 or 4:30 a.m. and ended at nightfall. And convinced that their hired workers, who were the lowest and poorest stratum of the village, were lazy, crafty, and thieving, employers insisted on constant activity, and inflicted quick and heavy punishments for any infractions of their work rules.[47]

Most of the rural proletariat knew only poverty and deprivation. In slack seasons and when they grew old they often had to beg for their daily bread. Many of them, defeated in their efforts to survive in their home villages, joined the bands of vagabonds who swarmed across the rural landscape of Europe, finding work when they could, and begging and stealing to keep themselves alive. Others went to the towns and cities in search of employment and of alms.[48] Not all of them, however, lived at or below the margins of subsistence. In labor-short regions of Denmark where wages were relatively high, there were farm laborers who accumulated cash and lent money to peasant landholders. In Prussia some of the peasants whose land lay outside the open fields of the village had more acreage than did their fellows with quarter- and even half-holdings. In regions where unused land lay close at hand, peasants with little or no land cleared forest and brush and reclaimed wastelands.[49]

The peasants who had holdings thought of themselves as the "owners" of the village and the superiors of the cotters and the landless. They sometimes looked upon the rural proletarians as dangerous people who robbed and stole whenever they had the opportunity. They resented the fact that they had to allow these people to graze their animals on the commons and thereby reduce the amount of food available for their own livestock. Though they lived cheek by jowl in their villages, they rigorously main-

[46] Bruchet (1908), xxxvii-xxxix; Blum (1961), 452-453; Hufton (1974), 73-74.
[47] Haushofer (1963), 135; Stark (1952), 288.
[48] Soboul (1960), 107; Sée (1906), 310; Brentano (1899), 247; Lütge (1949), 163; Feigl (1964), 126; Nielsen (1933), 192; Forster (1960), 48; Krzhivoblotskii (1861), 301; Ziekursch (1927), 72.
[49] Feigl (1964), 62; Nielsen (1933), 191; Knapp (1887), i, 12; Spira (1968), 356-357.

tained their superior social status so that, for example, in many places the children of landholding peasants did not marry into families of small-holders or landless peasants.[50]

The disparities in economic status among the villagers enabled the more prosperous peasant to gain a large measure of economic and social control over his poorer neighbors. He rented land to them. He employed them as day laborers and as full-time farm hands and live-in servants. He rented them work animals and implements they needed to till their small hold-ings, he carted their produce to market for them at a fee, he lent them money against their crop, he advanced or sold them grain in times of short-age, he often served as the representative of the seignior or of the govern-ment, and, of course, he could withhold the jobs and the loans and the serv-ices he provided from those villagers who fell out of his favor. He was, indeed, the *coq du village*, as the French called him.[51]

The economic power within the village of the more prosperous peasants had its inevitable consequence—their domination of the community. They formed the village oligarchy in which each oligarch's authority and influ-ence varied directly with the size of his holding and the amount of his in-come. Their will usually prevailed in the village assemblies even when all of the villagers could vote, and in many places they managed to exclude the poorer elements from active participation in the governance of the commu-nity. They used their power to get additional land for themselves, to en-large their rights to the use of common resources and even to expropriate common land for their private use, to pay less than their share of the obli-gations due lord and state, to avoid military service, and to influence village officials to show them special favor.[52] The plain fact was that there was not much egalitarianism or popular democracy in the village community. The poorer people in the village were second-class citizens.

The domination of the community by its richer members did not find easy acceptance. Conflicts went on endlessly between the village oligarchs, who wanted to preserve and extend their privileges, and the other villagers, who resented the restrictions imposed upon them in such things as the use of the commons or inequities in the distribution of land and obligations. Most of the time the quarrels and difficulties were handled within the vil-lage itself by its officials or its assembly, or by the seignior, which meant that most of the time conditions remained essentially unchanged. Some-

[50] Brentano (1899), 247; Feigl (1964), 127; Schremmer (1963), 12; Bloch (1930), 521-523; Goubert (1956), 75; Winkler (1941), 55; Lefebvre (1929), 510; Franz (1970a), 229; Brüngger (1962), 168.

[51] Raveau (1926), 249-252; Lefebvre (1972), 307-310; Winkler (1941), 53; Quirin (1953), 73-74; Maçzak (1958), 49-50; Davies (1964), 25-26.

[52] Wyss (1952), I, pt. 2, 5-6; Rostworowski (1896), 81; Goubert (1966), 30; St. Jacob (1960), 124; Andrews (1935), 221; Revesz (1964), 281; Druzhinin (1946), I, 346-353; Katus (1961), 127-128; Behrend (1964), 18-20.

3. Meeting place of a village assembly in Schleswig. The elders sat on the bank around the linden tree. The small rocks in the circle around the tree served as seats for the heads of the village's households. (R. Mejborg, *Das Bauernhaus im Herzogthum Schleswig und das Leben des schleswigischen Bauernstandes im 16., 17., und 18. Jahrhundert*, Schleswig, 1896.)

times, though, the peasants turned to the courts of the sovereign for adjudication of their disputes over such matters as the claims by well-off peasants to the exclusive use of the common pasture, or the number of sheep the wealthier peasants pastured on the common land.[53]

Despite the discontents and quarrels of village life, the villagers apparently adjusted to and accepted the situation in which they found themselves. When in 1789 the peasants of France were given the opportunity to unburden themselves of their grievances in the *cahiers de doléance*, they did not complain about the domination of their villages by their rich neighbors, or of their own exclusion from decision making. A survey of the records for the eighteenth and early nineteenth century of villages in eastern Galicia showed that the villagers there rarely entered formal complaints with their seigniors or with the district government office about unfair treatment accorded them by their more prosperous fellows.[54]

This apparent acquiescence to their inferior status may not necessarily have reflected contentment on the part of the poorer villagers. Complaints to authorities might well have cost them dearly when, as mentioned above,

[53] Lefebvre (1929), 510; Rosdolsky (1954), 114; Lütge (1957), 80; Frauendorfer (1957), I, 196-197; Knapp (1919), 93; Brüngger (1962), 168.
[54] Babeau (1878), 39; Bois (1960), 439-440, 442; Rosdolsky (1954), 115.

they had to depend upon the more prosperous peasants for loans and employment. It seems reasonable to assume that the well-to-do peasant would not continue to employ or to help the man who complained about him or his fellow prosperous peasants to the seignior or to the state, nor would he be likely to make him loans of cash, seed, or grain. The record shows that wealthy peasants sometimes took cruel revenge on those who complained to the authorities about them. The vice-governor of the Russian province of Viatka reported in 1807 that in villages there that belonged to the crown and the imperial court, dishonest commune officials, with the connivance of local government officials, sent off peasants, who brought complaints against them to the army as recruits or even had them exiled to Siberia.[55]

Social pressures, too, may have restrained villagers from carrying their quarrels with their fellows to outsiders. They lived in close proximity and saw one another constantly; they were often related by blood or marriage; and rich and poor alike shared the same concerns about weather and crops, and the demands of lord and state and church. Tradition had accustomed them to bring their grievances to the village officials and the assembly. Perhaps, too, many of them had learned from experience that formal complaints to outside authorities were more likely to annoy and anger those authorities than to bring the desired result. They also had learned that the less they called in lord and state to settle their disputes, the better off they all were.

[55] Schiemann (1904), I, 393.

CHAPTER 6

The Retardation of Agriculture:
Techniques and Implements

I

THE preceding chapters have dealt with the people of the rural world, the lords and peasants who were the *dramatis personae* of the old order, and with the relationships between them. It is time now to consider the ways in which they went about earning their livings, above all the agriculture upon which their way of life depended.

The economy of the servile lands of eighteenth- and nineteenth-century Europe resembled that of the underdeveloped countries of the second half of the twentieth century. As in these countries of today, the people of the servile lands devoted by far the largest share of their resources to agriculture. They employed crude implements and extensive systems of tillage. They lived in a seemingly permanent condition of underemployment, or disguised unemployment. Most of them existed at the margin of subsistence most of the time. In good years they raised enough to keep themselves at the level of survival. In the years of drought and crop failure and famine that came with frightening frequency, survival itself was threatened. In this marginal way of life, people could not afford to postpone any substantial part of their current expenditures in favor of savings and capital formation. That meant that they lacked the wherewithal needed to introduce the improved techniques and intensive cultivation that would have raised their output per man hour, and thereby would have raised their standard of living above the subsistence level. As in the underdeveloped countries of the modern world, they were trapped in the vicious cycle of poverty, in which poverty itself is the major barrier to economic growth.

The servile society did produce a surplus, squeezed out of the peasantry, that supported the small groups who formed the upper strata of the traditional order. This elite, composed in largest part—and in some lands almost exclusively—of landowners, owed its primacy to inherited status and to family connections rather than to talent and ability. If it had been so inclined, the elite could have invested some of the surplus that came to it from the peasantry in the economy and thereby have provided the capital that was so badly needed. Instead, except for a small number of progressive landowners, the elite chose to spend the surplus for creature comforts.

There were other perplexities that fettered the enterprise and innovation needed to break out of the cycle of poverty. The obligations in cash, kind, and labor demanded from the peasant took away resources he could have used to better advantage on his own account. Still worse, these obligations drained the peasants of interest and initiative. They knew that their increased efficiency would only benefit the seignior, and they knew that as forced laborers they could not be discharged. So they idled as much as they could in the performance of their labor services and they wasted time going to and coming from the work site. Contemporaries estimated that hired laborers, who, of course, could be dismissed for poor performance, were two to four times more efficient than forced laborers (pp. 316-317). The poor quality of the labor obligation not only severely affected the productivity of the lord's demesne; it also hobbled the productivity of the peasants' own fields. It reduced the amount of labor and of time available to him to till his own holding; contemporary reports from eastern Europe, where the labor obligation was notoriously heavy, told of peasants who had only moonlit nights and Sundays to till their own fields.[1] Everywhere they had to provide the work animals and the implements they used in their performance of their labor service, and the cost of maintaining the animals and furnishing and repairing the implements put a further drain on their meager resources.

Similarly, the church tithes and other payments in kind of a fixed proportion of the peasant's output—such as the *champart* in France, the *Zehent* in Austria, or the *nona* in Hungary—had a damaging effect upon the peasant's economy, quite apart from what these obligations cost him. Custom or law often ordained the imposition of these levies only upon certain crops, and especially upon the staples. New crops were either clearly not titheable, or the right of the lord to the payment was an unsettled or disputed question. To avoid disputes and to prevent reduction in their incomes, seigniors opposed, and if they were able forbade, the introduction of new products, and thereby retarded and even stifled improvements in peasant farming. In any event, the tithe diminished the initiative and the interest in improvements of the peasants, who reasoned that efforts to increase their output would reward the titheowner at the expense of the peasant.[2]

The fees demanded by seigniors on transfers of hereditary holdings could act to curb interest in improvements. "Why should I build a better house," a Bavarian peasant asked a state official on an inspection tour, "so that my seignior can line his pockets by taking a bigger *laudemium* from my children."[3] The transfer fees also discouraged the efforts of peasants to consolidate their holdings by sale or exchange of their scattered parcels, because of the fees they would have to pay for each individual transaction.[4]

Too few animals and the poor quality of the ones the peasants did have

[1] Radishchev (1958), 46-47; Ford (1919), 372; Rosdolski (1951), 254; Hanssen (1861), 25.
[2] St. Jacob (1960), 402; Schremmer (1963), 65; Walter (1966), 25; Grüll (1952), 19; Rappard (1912), 147, 147n.
[3] Quoted in Lütge (1949), 15.   [4] *Cf.* Rappard (1912), 163.

contributed to the backwardness of agriculture. The peasants lacked the resources to buy more livestock, and the low productivity of their agriculture compelled them to use most of their land to raise foodstuffs instead of using it for forage and pasture. The insufficiency of cattle meant less manure and therefore less ability to restore fertility and increase yields. The general practice of herding all of the village livestock together, with resulting indiscriminate breeding, and the inadequate supply of forage and pasture, produced small and weak animals. That meant that the peasant did not have enough draft power for efficient field work and carting, and that his cattle produced minimal amounts of milk and meat.

Tenures, too, sometimes acted as hindrances to agricultural improvement. Neither sharecropping nor short-term leases provided the tenant with the incentive to increase his efficiency. The sharecropper and the short-term lessee saw little or no benefit for themselves in making improvements to the holding because of their brief tenures. In any event, the terms of the leases often forbade the lessees to introduce new rotations or crops, and thereby effectively barred innovations the tenant might have been inclined to make. In 1787 Thomas Jefferson, then American minister to France, in a letter to his friend the Marquis de Lafayette, called attention to the retardative effects of short leases upon French farming. "I suppose" he wrote, "that could the practice of leasing for three lives be introduced in the whole kingdom, it would, within the term of your life, increase agricultural production fifty per cent; or were any proprietor to do it with his own lands, it would increase his rents fifty per cent, in the course of twenty-five years."[5] In eastern Europe, where so many peasants held their land at the will of the seignior, the villager could never be certain of his continued occupancy of his holding, or whether his children would hold it after him. Why, then, spend the time and labor and money to improve the holding when someone else might enjoy the fruits of his efforts?

Exogenous circumstances reinforced the barriers to growth produced from within the rural social and economic structure. The inadequacy or the complete absence of transportation facilities made it difficult or impossible to reach markets, and so cooled possible interest in producing a surplus by the use of more efficient methods. Government restrictions on domestic and foreign commerce in farm goods also hampered the development of trade and markets and therefore of a more efficient and profitable agriculture. The fiscal demands of the state aggravated the retardative effects upon agricultural efficiency of the impositions levied by the seigniors; indeed, as we saw earlier, the demands of the state sometimes exceeded those of the seigniors.

[5] Jefferson to Lafayette, Nice, 11 April 1787, *Papers of Thomas Jefferson* (1955), XI, 284. Jefferson travelled extensively in France, explaining to Lafayette, "I am never satisfied with rambling through the fields and farms, examining the culture and cultivators, with a degree of curiosity which makes some take me to be a fool, and others to be much wiser than I am." *Ibid.*, 283.

The realities of rural life in the servile lands undermined the initiative and enterprise of the peasant. There were a scant few among the men of the upper orders who tried to help him, but they had no real success. Chained to a treadmill from which there seemed no escape, powerless, ignorant, scorned by those above him in the social hierarchy who for centuries had gulled and exploited him, the peasant was naturally suspicious of those who sought to persuade him to adopt more efficient methods and to plant new crops. It was not only that he was a "prisoner of tradition" (as one historian has called him).[6] Harsh experience had taught him that the seignior and the state were the principal beneficiaries of increased efforts on his part. When the peasant could keep most of the rewards of his greater efforts, the traditional image of peasant indolence and of resistance to change has to be tempered. The intensive and careful cultivation and even experimentation in the gardens that adjoined the cottages and huts of many French peasants, and that were free of tithe and *champart*, the successful peasant entrepreneurs in transport, trade, and manufacturing, and prosperous and even wealthy peasant farmers and large-scale renters scattered through all of the servile lands proved that enterprise, initiative, and willingness to work were not foreign to the peasant character.

Still, the peasantry did bear part of the responsibility for the retardation of agriculture. They hung onto the old inefficient ways long after the emancipations did away with the pressures and demands of the seigniorial system. They did not invest the additional income now available in agricultural improvement; they continued to splinter their holdings; and most of them remained for many years outside the market nexus as producers.[7] Their continued opposition, long after the emancipations, to the consolidation of the scattered parcels that made up their holdings revealed most clearly their traditionalism and their opposition to change. It took repeated legislative acts, governmental intervention, and pressure to get them to establish unified farms that were easier to operate and that were more productive, and even so many still held out. In the middle of the twentieth century, excessive parcelling prevailed on about half (6 million hectares) of the agricultural area of West Germany, and on about one-third (10 million hectares) of the farmland of France. In southern Germany over half of the farms were broken into over 10 separate pieces, and holdings with over 100 individual parcels were not uncommon. In France the individual parcels averaged about .86 acres (.35 hectares) in size—which meant, of course, that many were even smaller.[8]

Whatever the responsibility of the peasants for the backwardness of ag-

---

[6] Festy (1947), 35.

[7] E.g., in the 1890's 85 per cent of all peasant farms in France were less than 10 hectares (*ca.* 25 acres); 39 per cent were less than 1 hectare. Farms able to produce grain for the market would rarely be less than 5 hectares. International Institute of Agriculture (1939a), 15.

[8] Dovring (1956), 40; Abel (1964), 76-78; Bergmann (1952), 25.

riculture, the greater part of the blame belonged to the men who owned the land, and to the government. The landowners failed to provide the leadership and the initiative expected of those who occupy the dominant role in society. Those among them who engaged directly in agriculture followed the same wasteful and inefficient techniques used by their peasants. Often their demesne lay parcelled into strips in the same fields with the strips of the peasants. Many of them eschewed all direct contact with the land and drew their incomes from seigniorial dues and from rents. They had no interest in agriculture, much less in its improvement. If they wanted more income from their properties, they tightened the screws on the peasants rather than seeking to rationalize the economy of their manors. Instead of investing some of their income in improvements, they chose to spend their money on luxuries and services and sterile expenditures and, typically, wound up with debts that sometimes reached spectacular proportions. When they kept records of their operations, they usually failed to take account of costs, and considered gross revenue from their properties as profit. They made no effort to determine the relative profitability of capital inputs, and sought to aggrandize their gross income by minimizing expenditures on improvements and reinvestments.[9] The state, nearly everywhere the largest of all landowners, was not different from other proprietors. It, too, failed to provide the stimulus for, and the leadership in, the adoption of agricultural innovations.

The stagnation ended, as later chapters will show, when in the second half of the eighteenth and first half of the nineteenth century a new interest in efficient and profitable agriculture appeared among a small but influential group of noble landowners. Only then did the agriculture of the servile lands begin to escape very slowly from the low-level equilibrium in which for so long it had been trapped. The critical role of these "improving landlords" in effecting change gives witness to the importance of the ruling elite as innovator and exemplar. Equally significant, central governments employed their power and their resources to introduce innovations on their own properties in the hope that others would follow their example.

II

The techniques of tillage used by the peasants, along with the constraints imposed by climate and geography, the amount and nature of the obligations they had to pay, the patterns of their settlement, the way in which they decided how to till their land and what crops to raise and how to regulate the pastures, meadows, woods, and wasteland that lay outside the plowed fields, all were part of an indivisible ensemble. The most widespread agrarian regime in the servile lands was that associated with open field

[9] *Cf.* Confino (1963a), 170-176, 183; Forster (1970), 1611-1612.

country—the champion, as the English called the open fields. That regime prevailed throughout the Great European Plain that reached from the English Midlands across France north of the Loire, through Denmark, southern Sweden, and the northern half of Germany, broadening out into the Polish plains and hills of the basin of the Vistula, and then into the vast Russian tableland that reached from the Arctic to the Black Sea. The soils in most of the Plain were fertile, easy to work, retained moisture, and were especially well suited for the growing of cereals. There were open fields, too, outside the great lowland plain, as in the valleys and plateaus of Switzerland.

The plowland of the champion lay unbroken by hedge or permanent fence or even by trees; the trees clustered around the village or stood in clumps away from the fields. The land of each village was divided into several large fields that were rotated between crops and fallow at predetermined time intervals. The size and shape of the field varied according to the confines and dictates of topography and sometimes according to the quality of the soil. That is, the field with less fertile soil was made larger than the ones with better soil so that their total production would be about the same. The fields were divided into rectangular plots, called in English "shots" or "furlongs." Their size and shape were determined by relief, drainage, and distance from the village. The furlongs were themselves split into long and narrow strips. These strips were distributed among the villagers according to the amount of land in their holding. Nearly always the peasants of each village had all their strips in the fields attached to their village. Sometimes, though, as in the fertile Danish island of Lolland, peasants of neighboring villages had strips in fields that they worked in common. And often, as mentioned earlier, the demesne land of the lord lay scattered in strips in the open fields along with the strips of the peasants.[10]

The problems of plowing have usually served to explain both the shape of the strips and their use as the units of cultivation. The land was tilled with a heavy wooden plow pulled by as many as six to eight draft animals. The plowman found it difficult to turn with this clumsy and hard-to-manage implement and team. So presumably the strips were made long and narrow to reduce to the minimum the need to turn. The actual operation of turning at the end of each strip gave the strips their slight reverse "S" shape. This explanation seems plausible enough but, as one writer has observed, "the association of long, narrow strips with the use of the heavy plow is by no means an exact one"; in many places in central France and in Sweden land divided into long, narrow strips was worked by a light plow.[11] The dimensions of the strips depended upon local conditions, such as the contours of the field, the quality of the soil, and the pressure of population. Scattered

[10] Berthold (1962), 90; Henning (1969a), 10; Schröder-Lembke (1954), 127; Ivanova (1966), 166; Skovgaard (1950), 9-10; Roupnel (1922), 262-265.
[11] Smith (1967), 200.

data indicate that commonly they were around 200 to 300 yards in length. Longer stretches of uninterrupted plowing were too hard on the animals without the break that came when the plow was turned. There were reports, however, of strips that ran for a kilometer (nearly 1,100 yards) and in Bohemia there were actually strips that were 4 kilometers long and only 7 meters wide. Width varied, too, but it seems likely that the favored width for convenience in sowing was 5 to 6 yards. A single cast by the arm of the sower could distribute seed evenly across this width.[12]

Because of plowing and throwing the furrow slice the same way decade after decade, the strips became raised in the center and depressed along their edges, so that the champion was an endless procession of undulating ridges and valleys. The plowman kept the ridge at the desired height, or raised or lowered it, by altering his plowing pattern. For example, if he wanted to lower a ridge he started to one side of it and plowed counter-clockwise around it, throwing the soil down into the valleys. The valleys served as drainage ditches (much needed in the heavy clays of northern Europe), so that the ridges dried out more quickly than did level land. However, in wet years the slopes were waterlogged and only the raised middle portion bore good crops, while in dry years the grain on the raised part suffered from drought. The arched ridges had another disadvantage in that they made it more difficult to harrow the fields and to harvest them. The ridges and valleys served to mark off the individual strips from one another. Sometimes, though, grass-covered untilled strips, or balks, separated the arable strips of one peasant from those of his neighbors. (Tethered animals often grazed on the balks.) In much of the limestone country of northern France stones were used to mark the boundaries.

Each household had strips in each of the fields of the village. The number of strips the household had depended upon the total size of its holding and upon the number of strips into which the field had been divided. This latter number grew as population growth increased the pressure for land and as holdings became subdivided. A middling peasant might have 30 to 60 separate strips scattered through the fields of his village, and many had more. In eighteenth-century Holstein full holdings had 100 to 150 separate parcels of plowland, and an official document of 1792 reported that in Burgundy a typical peasant holding of 30 *arpents* (ca. 25-35 acres) was broken into 200 to 300 pieces.[13]

The splintering of the holding of the individual peasant, and often of the lord's demesne, into strips scattered through the open fields of the manor, demanded continuous cooperation to regulate such matters as access to in-

[12] Houston (1963), 56; Lizerand (1942), 130; Confino (1969), 109; Stark (1957), 21; Smith (1967), 197; Wallace (1912), 140.

[13] Smith (1967), 197-198; Bloch (1966), 37; Thorpe (1951), 119-120; Hanssen (1861), 70-71; Blum (1948), 150; Scharling (1909), 578; Herbert (1969), 21.

dividual strips, sowing, harrowing and harvesting, pasturing of cattle on the fallows and on the stubble of the harvested fields, protection of the sown fields from trespass by cattle, and water rights. In short, it required the communal regulation of husbandry. Usually this evolved into compulsory communal tillage, in which the villagers all grew the same crops and performed the same field operations at the same time. The origins of this practice (which began in the Middle Ages) have been attributed to a shortage of pasture. The increased demand for cropland hastened the conversion of much grassland into arable, and simultaneously created a need for animals for draft, and thus a demand for pasturage. The villagers met this problem by pasturing their animals on the open fields after harvest when the fields lay fallow. This required the coordination of the farming operations of all of the villagers, so that when the animals entered the field it had been cleared of all of the crop. Similarly, the time of plowing had to be coordinated so that all would know when the livestock had to be driven from the fallow field. Some villages of the champion managed without ever adopting this system. Presumably, they had enough grassland and so did not need stubble and fallow as supplementary pasture. Or, perhaps, they tethered their animals to graze on their own unplanted strips, the tether preventing the animal from wandering into the possibly planted strips of other villagers.

Communal regulation of husbandry extended beyond the management of the plowland to the control of the other resources of the village, whether pasture, meadows, marshes, bogs and other wastes. The community decided how and when they could be used, who could use them, and how much use could be made of them. Sometimes neighboring villages agreed to allow mutual use of their common lands or a contiguous common waste, though this "intercommoning" tended to decline as population increased and as village boundaries became more firmly fixed.[14]

Communal control reached the extreme of collective restraint in agrarian communism. Here the village commune held all of the land of the village; the member households had permanent possession only of their dwellings and house lot. Each member household had a right to an allotment of plowland and the right to the use of common pasture, meadow, and forest. The commune decided how much land each household should have; it could subdivide holdings, order their periodic redistribution, lease additional land, or rent out some of its own land. The seignior could overrule any action of the commune, but usually he allowed it much autonomy. By the nineteenth century communal landholding was nearly universal in Great Russia, and was also used in many parts of Hungary, in eastern Galicia, in a number of places in Poland, in the plainland of Bukovina, and in Mol-

---

[14] Pettitpierre (1871), 161-162, 172; Confino (1969), 123-124; Bloch (1930), 330-331; Blum (1971a), 161.

4. A village near St. Petersburg. (R. Johnston, *Travels through Parts of the Russian Empire and the Country of Poland*, London, 1815.)

davia. Nor was it unknown in western Europe; villages in districts along the Moselle River in western Germany practiced communal landholding into the nineteenth century.[15]

The structure of the open field system, with holdings scattered through the fields and with communal controls and coordinated activities, almost inevitably dictated the agglomeration of the peasants in a village. Throughout the region of the champion, then, villages were by far the most common form of settlement, though isolated farmsteads and hamlets were not incompatible with open fields, even if they were less convenient.

Fields often lay open, too, south of the zone of the champion. But there the land was divided into small, irregularly shaped plots, instead of the long, narrow strips of the champion. A number of hypotheses have been suggested to explain this phenomenon. Though none of them seems entirely satisfactory, it is likely that one significant factor was the variety of the topography and of the soils of that region, in contrast to the relatively homogeneous soils and configurations of the Great Plain. This required selective planting of crops, with the appropriate crop grown in the patch of soil best suited for it.[16]

Finally, many peasants lived in the midst of their own fields in isolated farmsteads or in tiny hamlets. Here the landscape was broken by trees and

[15] Blum (1971a), 168-169.
[16] *Cf.* Lizerand (1942), 125-127; Bloch (1966), 48-56; Forster (1960), 41; Houston (1963), 60.

hedges, or by low stone walls or earthen embankments, which enclosed the holding of each homestead. This was the dominant pattern of settlement in mountainous and forested regions. It prevailed, too, in the maritime fringes of western Europe, in Poitou, Brittany, and in parts of Normandy and Flanders. Other regions, among them Lower Saxony, Westphalia, Bavaria, Schleswig, the Baltic lands, parts of Brandenburg and Posen, and the Great Hungarian Plain, contained many isolated farmsteads in addition to villages.[17] In the principality of Wallachia, peasants of both hill and plain lived in isolated farmsteads until the 1830's. At that time the government decided that it would best serve its own interests to compel its rural subjects to live in villages. Despite strong objection from the peasants, who were understandably reluctant to abandon their old homes, the government persisted and the process of agglomeration was well on its way to completion by mid-century.[18]

Usually pasture was more plentiful and more important than arable in regions of isolated farmsteads and hamlets. This was especially true in hill and mountain country, where topography favored animal husbandry over tillage. Unlike the arable, which was held in severalty, that is, by individual right, pastureland was most often held by the communal organization to which the peasants belonged, or by several neighboring communal organizations. In general, these organizations exercised much less authority over their members than did the communes of the champion. Land divided into individual farms obviously did not need the constant supervision and the constraints demanded where the holdings of the peasants lay scattered in strips through the open fields. Instead, these communes concerned themselves chiefly with the regulation of common lands. To ensure that all shared equitably in the use and the benefits of these resources, the commune imposed regulations that limited the number of animals each member could pasture on the common grassland, the amount of timber he could take from the forest, and the amount of meadow he could mow.[19]

III

Tradition, soil, and climate all helped to determine the system of tillage that seigniors and peasants chose to work the land. In the champion the three-field rotation was by far the most widely employed method. The arable of the manor was divided into three large fields, or into several units each with three fields. Each field was planted in a different cereal for two

---

[17] Demangeon (1927), 2-8; Dion (1934), 94; Merle (1958), 76-77; Behrend (1964), 13; Tsentral'nyi statisticheskii komitet (1863), 71; Sée (1906), 405; Müller (1967), 146-147; Druzhinin (1946), I, 384-385; den Hollander (1960), 75; Lütge (1949), 64; Creutzburg (1910), 9-10.

[18] Corfus (1969), 180-189.   [19] Blum (1971a), 167-168.

years out of every three, and then to regain its fertility was fallowed for a year and fertilized by the droppings of the livestock pastured on it. The villagers planted one field in early autumn with a winter cereal—rye, wheat, or maslin, a mixture of rye and wheat. When spring came, they sowed the second field with a spring cereal such as barley, oats, or other small grains, or perhaps field peas or vetch, or in more northerly climes flax or hemp. Meanwhile the third field lay fallow. Often the peasants put up temporary wattle fences around the two sowed fields to keep out the cattle. They harvested the winter grain in early or mid-summer, the spring grain in late summer, and then in early autumn they planted the fallow field with a winter cereal and began the cycle all over again. Thus, the entire thrust of the three-field rotation was directed toward the production of grain; "animals," wrote the French scientist Antoine Lavoisier in a memorandum of 1787, "are only instruments used to till and to manure."[20]

The three-year cycle was by all accounts the most commonly used rotation. On some manors, however, the peasants had discovered that cycles of two or four to six or seven years better served their purpose. In a number of localities in Germany and Bohemia in the eighteenth century, and in White Russia and Lithuania by the mid-nineteenth century, fields were fallowed every fourth or fifth year.[21] In the infertile soil of northern Russia, the land of many villages was divided into four to six fields of which each year two to four lay fallow and were used as pasture, while the others were planted in winter and then spring cereals.[22] In parts of Alsace and in nearby areas of Germany, the villagers shifted from the three-field to the two-field cycle when they replaced rye with wheat as their principal cash crop. They found that they could get two good wheat crops out of a field every three years and still have a higher income than they could with the three-field rotation (even though this had yielded a larger volume of cereals), because wheat prices were so much higher than the barley and oats they used to raise in the three field rotation.[23] Similarly, in 1769, when grain prices were high, the peasants of Saint-Seine-en-Bâche in Burgundy decided to shift from triennial to biennial rotation. Conversely, in 1783, when grain prices were down, the communal assembly of Glanon, another village of Burgundy, decided to abandon the two-field rotation in favor of three fields.[24] And sometimes different rotations were employed in the same neighborhood and even on the same manor. There were peasants in Brandenburg who used the two-field rotation on poor, sandy soils, the three-field rotation on better land, sowed some of the best land every year, and

[20] Quoted in Festy (1947), 15.
[21] Riemann (1953), 26; Stark (1957), 21-22; Ulashchik (1961), 179; Abel (1967), 217; Widding (1949), 270.
[22] Tooke (1799), III, 259-260.   [23] Juillard (1952), 34ff.; Schröder-Lembke (1959), 29.
[24] St. Jacob (1962), 119-123.

employed shifting cultivation with long fallow (soon to be discussed) on land that lay outside the regular fields of the village.[25]

In short, the open fields of the champion allowed more flexibility than is sometimes realized. The shots or furlongs could be regrouped to allow changes in patterns of rotation, and new crops could be introduced, especially in the fallow fields. Innovations however, required the consent of all who had strips in the fields, and that often proved an arduous and long-drawn out proceeding. Usually the villagers resisted innovations, and persisted in their traditional—and inefficient—methods. It has been suggested that this resistance had its own rationale. The retention of the traditional ways kept alive the awareness of community, and of the individual's responsibility to the whole. They preserved the cohesive spirit that made the villagers recognize their common interests and band together against the outside world. The old ways, too, fostered social and political stability, and cushioned the impact of new and disturbing influences.[26]

The far more apparent defects of the open field system, however, outweighed whatever merits it possessed. As much as one-third or more of the plowland was always out of production. In France in 1789 an estimated 40 per cent of the arable lay fallow each year. In Germany at the beginning of the nineteenth century around 25 per cent of the arable was in bare fallow; in Bohemia in 1848 the ration was 21.6 per cent, and in Russia in the 1870's it was over 30 per cent. In Poland immediately after the end of the Napoleonic wars half of the arable was said to have been in bare fallow. By 1863 that figure had dropped to 27 per cent.[27] The emphasis on grain, and the accompanying inattention to animal husbandry meant a shortage of manure for use as fertilizer. Much time and effort was lost in going to and from the multitude of strips that made up the holdings of each household. A study made early in the twentieth century in Russia (where the open fields still persisted) found that one peasant travelled 1,266 miles in a single season in going to and from his strips.[28] All of the peasants with strips in a field were at the mercy of a slovenly or uncooperative strip holder. If he plowed late, he did much damage by driving his animals across the already sown strips of his neighbors. If he did not take care of his strips, weeds sprung up and spread quickly to adjacent strips. If he drained improperly, other strips were damaged, and if he left his grain standing when others had harvested, he kept his fellows from turning their cattle into the stubble

[25] Müller (1965a), 94. For the use of two or more tillage systems in other lands *v.* Spira (1968), 361; Stark (1957), 21-22; Vil'son (1869), 57-63; Gay (1958), 403; Festy (1950), 10-11.

[26] Zink (1969), 221; Blaschke (1965), 275; Wiessner (1946), 62-63.

[27] France: Toutain (1961), I, 53. Germany: Bittermann (1956), 24. Bohemia: Kodedova (1967), 140. Russia: Ermolov (1878), 76. Poland: Kieniewicz (1969), 93. In Bohemia at the end of the nineteenth century 1.5 per cent of the arable, in Germany in 1913 2.6 per cent, was in fallow.

[28] Cited in Borders (1927), 44.

field. It is easy to imagine the frustrations and bitterness this kind of behavior engendered. Quarrels and feuds were brought on, too, by the not uncommon practice of encroachment on neighboring strips, either by plowing into the balks, or moving the boundary stones between strips, or when no visible boundaries existed by edging bit by bit over the years into neighboring strips.[29] And surely the most harmful effect of the open field system was the shackles it imposed upon the efforts of individuals to introduce improvements. The need for communal approval and cooperation for change, and the rigidity and inertia of tradition, served nearly always as insuperable barriers to the more efficient use of the human, animal, and natural resources of the manor. As Albrecht Thaer, the leading German agronomist of the late eighteenth and early nineteenth century, explained, "Custom long ruled with irresistible power over arts and sciences, and the least doubt about the conformity [of the open fields and the three-field system] with Nature's laws was regarded as heresy."[30]

In a few places especially favored by natural conditions, fields were cropped continuously. That happened on some fertile bottom land in Brandenburg, where spring grain followed winter grain in unbroken succession in well-dunged fields. In places in northwest Germany and in Switzerland, too, fields were always in crops, with turf and muck from nearby marshes used to maintain the fertility of the soil.[31]

South of the region of the champion, summers were too hot and too dry to produce a satisfactory crop of a cereal planted in spring. So the peasant there usually employed a two-field rotation, planting half of his holding and fallowing the other half. However, as in the champion, other systems were used, too. Thus, in Provence, and in Auvergne in the Massif Central, some peasants used both the two- and the three-field systems, depending upon the quality of the soil and the accessibility to markets for the products they raised. Other peasants, either because of the compulsion of necessity or because of indifference, used methods that they knew exhausted the soil. That happened with sharecroppers in Lempart in Languedoc, who cropped their fields almost continuously, and as a result produced paltry yields and weed-infested grain.[32]

What of the peasants who lived in isolated farmsteads on their enclosed farms? It could be expected that these people, free of most of the communal restraints that prevailed in the open field country, would have used more efficient methods. Certainly Arthur Young expected to discover this when

[29] Confino (1969), 109; Tegoborski (1852), I, 335; Bloch (1966), 37-38; Seebohm (1883), 15-16; Gonner (1912), 314.

[30] Thaer (1809), I, 302.

[31] Müller (1965a), 96; Riemann (1953), 25; *Handwörterbuch der schweizerischen Volkswirtschaft* (1903), I, 953-954.

[32] Faucher (1961), 10; Soboul (1958), 60; Sclafert (1941), 473-474; Rigaudière (1965), 36-37; Falguerolles (1941), 163-164.

on his journey through France on the eve of the great Revolution he rode through the regions of enclosures in Anjou, Maine, Brittany, and Normandy. His disappointment has been reported so often that it has become a standard piece of historical literature. "The marvelous folly," he wrote, "is, that in nine-tenths of all the enclosures of France, the system of management is precisely the same as in the open fields: that is to say fallows as regularly prevail."[33] Young would have found the same folly in regions of enclosures in other lands, too, such as Upper Austria, eastern Bavaria, Silesia, and in parts of the canton of Zurich.[34]

On the other hand, enclosures in Schleswig-Holstein and in neighboring Mecklenburg would have delighted Mr. Young had he journeyed to those regions. There, in the southwest corner of the Baltic littoral, farmers used a superior system of cultivation. They called it *Koppelwirtschaft* because in Low German a field permanently enclosed by a hedge or a fence was called a *Koppel*. It was a form of convertible husbandry, or improved field-grass husbandry. The essence of the system lay in the regular rotation of grain and grass on the enclosed fields. The manor was divided into between 7 and 14 separate fields; by the mid-eighteenth century the favored number had become 11 in Mecklenburg, 12 in Schleswig, and 10 in eastern Holstein. A rotation frequently used in Schleswig kept the field in grain for 6 years, with buckwheat the first year, rye or sometimes wheat the second year, barley the third year, and oats for 3 years. Then the field was put into grass and used for pasture for the next 6 years.[35]

Convertible husbandry appeared in Holstein and then in Schleswig in the sixteenth and early seventeenth centuries, displacing the three-field and other even more extensive tillage systems. In 1697 a Mecklenburg nobleman, Joachim Friedrich von der Lühe (1675-1742), introduced the method on his manor near Wismar. From there it spread into other parts of Mecklenburg. In contrast to the three-field rotation, *Koppelwirtschaft* emphasized the rearing of cattle for dairy products and meat. The relatively even temperatures of the littoral, the high humidity and the fertile soil favored the growth of nutritious grass, and the proximity of Amsterdam, Hamburg, Bremen, and other large urban markets explained the emphasis on cattle. The system also produced excellent yields of cereals of good quality, for the fields were well fertilized by animal droppings during the years in which they served as pasture.[36]

In contrast to this productive technique of cultivation, other far less efficient and antiquated methods of land utilization persisted in many parts of Europe. Shifting cultivation with long fallows, named field-grass hus-

[33] Young (1970), I, 398.

[34] Haushofer (1963), 44; Bernhardt (1915), 5; Ziekursch (1927), 35n.

[35] Thaer (1809), I, 317, 330; Mager (1955), 268; Schröder-Lembke (1956), 50; Arnim (1957), 90.

[36] Schröder-Lembke (1956), 49-50, 52-55; Behrend (1964), 36; Abel (1967), 174-176.

bandry by Georg Hanssen in the last century, was employed by many in mountainous regions of France and Germany, in Alpine fields of Switzerland and Austria, in Jutland, in White Russia, in Great Russia and particularly in the steppes of southwest Russia, in much of Moldavia and Wallachia, in eastern Galicia, and in many parts of Hungary. The system was simple enough. The peasants cleared and cropped a piece of land for several years, then abandoned it and allowed it to go back to brush, while they shifted to another piece of land. When that piece became exhausted, they returned to the first piece and cleared and plowed it, or moved to still another unworked plot. Obviously peasants could use this method on a large scale only where land was plentiful and population pressure low, or where the soil was poor, as in mountain country, and cattle raising or some other rural occupation provided the chief source of income. When the man-land ratio increased, the peasants adopted the more intensive two- or three-field system.

The time interval during which the plot lay fallow ranged from as little as 2 to 3 years to as much as 20 years. Sometimes a regular rhythm developed, with the field planted for a set number of years and then fallowed for a set number of years. Usually each household had its own patches of land scattered through the field and could grow whatever it wanted on them. The only communal compulsion required the individual household to plant and till in that part of the village lands designated as the arable, and to aid in certain communal tasks, such as fencing the arable field to keep out cattle. The land that lay fallow was used in common for pasture.[37]

In some regions the peasants used what in Britain was called variously the infield-outfield or runrig or rundale system of tillage. The infield, located near the village and in the best soil, was the most intensively cultivated part of the village's land. It was an open field, divided into strips that were held by the households of the village. It was carefully tended and dunged and often was planted every year, though sometimes the less intensive three-field system was used. Fences or hedges separated the infield from the rest of the arable, called the outfield. There the peasants used shifting cultivation, first planting one part of the outfield for a period of years, then another, and with each household having its own plots and farming them as they pleased. Cattle grazed on those parts of the outfield not in crops, and the peasants brought in the dung from these pastures to spread on the infield.

The infield-outfield system found special favor in upland country, where rainfall was heavy and where land suitable for plowland was relatively

[37] Austria: Grünberg (1901), 54; Rosdolski (1954), 106-107; Strakosch (1917), 33; Zailer (1903), 56-57. Denmark: MacDonald (1809), I, 90-91. France: Zolla (1893), 202; Rigaudière (1965), 36-37; Bloch (1966), 27. Germany: Hanssen (1880), I, 132-135, 137. Danubian Principalities: Corfus (1969), 56-57. Russia: Vil'son (1869), 52-57; Redaktsionnye komissii (1859), XIV, 9-10. Switzerland: Bernhard (1915), 5-7. White Russia and Lithuania: Ulashchik (1961), 179.

scarce in comparison to the abundant natural pastures. It was not restricted, however, to such regions. In sparsely populated places, where natural conditions provided much arable land, it offered a selective use of the best soil. It was widely used in the interior of Brittany, in Maine, Poitou, parts of the Massif Central, in Alpine and Pyrenean areas, in the thin soils of the Rhineland Massif, in Alsace and Lorraine, and in Brandenburg in eastern Germany.[38]

Finally, in isolated, forested, and thinly populated regions peasants used slash-burn tillage. They made a clearing in the forest with axe and fire, left the ashes on the ground to serve as fertilizer, scratched the litter with a primitive hoe or a hooked stick, broadcast the seed, and then waited for harvest. They cropped the field continuously, getting high yields at first and having them diminish steadily until the field was exhausted. Then they moved to another forest clearing that they had prepared beforehand. This technique was used in places in White Russia and Lithuania at the end of the eighteenth century, but had apparently vanished by the second half of the nineteenth century as the pressure of population on the land rose. It was still employed in the first half of the nineteenth century in mountainous districts of Germany and Austria, and in the forested and infertile land of the provinces of northern Russia.[39]

IV

The implements that the peasants used to work the fields contributed significantly to the inefficiency of their operations. Everywhere they employed tools whose design had changed little if at all over the course of the centuries and that were often ill-suited for the task for which they were used. The high cost of iron was responsible in part for this retardation; manufacture of improved tools in volume became possible only with the development of cheap iron in the nineteenth century. However, tradition and resistance to change bore most of the responsibility, for even with the limited technology available to them peasants could have made improvements in their implements. Most were made locally so that there was much variety in their designs, particularly in the plow. But soil and climate dictated a general similarity among the implements in a given region. In most of the open-field country of the Great Plain, the peasants used a heavy wheeled plow drawn by several pairs of draft animals, and with both a plowman and a driver to guide the animals in a straight direction. The plow had a coulter mounted in front of the share to cut through the turf, and a moldboard to turn the furrow slice to one side. South of the Great Plain,

[38] Müller (1965a), 87, 90; Smith (1967), 212-214; Flatrès (1957), 609; East (1950), 104; Houston (1963), 54-55.
[39] Stamm (1856), 109; Zailer (1903), 56-57; Haushofer (1963), 48; Vil'son (1869), 47-52; Ulashchik (1961), 179.

the peasants favored a light, wheelless plow that was without coulter or moldboard. It really was little more than a hoe that was pulled by a single animal (or by a human). The soil there was light, dry, and stony, rainfall was scant, and the plowman did little more than scratch the earth in a criss-cross pattern to make a mulch, or cap, which would hold the moisture in the ground.[40]

There were many exceptions to these generalizations, notably in Mecklenburg and northern Brandenburg, in parts of Scandinavia, in the Baltic lands, and in Russia. In these regions many peasants used wheelless plows that were essentially nothing more than a crooked stick with one end shod with iron. In Russia this primitive instrument (called a *sokha* there) suited the thin soils of the north. But the Russian peasant carried it with him into the heavy and deep soil of the fertile black earth. This seemingly contrary behavior was not entirely without its rationale. The *sokha* cost far less than did a true plow, it took little skill to make, it could be easily repaired, it was so light that the plowman could carry it on his shoulder, and, most important, it needed only one animal to pull it. Still, it was at best a poor tool.[41]

Not that the true plow was an efficient implement. It was heavy, badly constructed of wood with at most only the plowshare of iron—and sometimes not even that—it was hard to manage, and it cut a shallow furrow at the cost of much human and animal labor. Most households did not own a plow nor the six or eight animals often needed to pull it through the heavy soil. A group of households had to pool their resources to get their land plowed.[42] Other implements, too, were poorly made. In the Toulouse region, for example, hoe handles were so short that the peasant had to work at a back-breaking angle, and handles of shovels were fixed straight to the blade so that digging required extra effort.[43] Harrows usually had wooden rather than iron teeth and in many places peasants used the so-called brush harrow—a small tree or a large limb, weighted down with heavy objects—to smooth the topsoil and cover the seed. In the Mediterranean littoral of France and in places in central France the peasants did not harrow. Instead, they used their plows to cover the seeds.[44]

In harvesting, the scythe was a demonstrably more efficient tool than the sickle. Data gathered by Albrecht Thaer in the late eighteenth and early nineteenth century indicated a labor saving of 25 to 30 per cent if it was used. Yet in many regions harvesters used the sickle, even though this re-

[40] Bratianu (1952), 53-54; Faucher (1954), 27-29; Merle (1958), 122-123; Rigaudière (1965), 32-34.
[41] Mager (1955), 272; Bratianu (1952), 54; Transehe-Roseneck (1890), 123-124; Kahk (1969), 50; Confino (1963a), 118-119; Confino (1969), 112, 309.
[42] Spira (1968), 362; Corfus (1969), 55; Jacob (1826), 47; Festy (1947), 19; Hoffmann (1952), 278; Chevallez (1949), 96-98.
[43] Forster (1960), 45.
[44] Jacob (1826), 47; Hovde (1948), i, 69; Corfus (1969), 135; Müller (1967), 86; Leroy-Ladurie (1966), i, 79; Rigaudière (1965), 34; Pallas (1794), i, 4; Tooke (1799), iii, 243-244.

quired more workers. Adherents of the sickle argued that it had advantages that outweighed the superior efficiency of the scythe. The heavier blows of the scythe damaged the ears and resulted in excessive spillage of the grain. (For that reason in some localities the scythe was used for cheaper cereals, such as oats and barley, while wheat and rye were cut with the sickle.) The sickle cut higher on the stalk so that the villagers could gather more straw from the stubble for roof thatches, stable litter, mats, and a myriad of other uses. When the animals were turned into the harvested field, they had more on which to feed, and when the stalk rotted it enriched the soil. Still another advantage of the sickle was that its light weight and ease of handling enabled women to work as harvesters.[45]

Fertilizers were used scantily, if they were used at all. Animal manure was in short supply because of the relative unimportance of animal husbandry in most of servile Europe. In addition, for much of the year animals grazed in pastures, woods, and waste, where their manure was lost, and because of slovenly farming habits peasants often neglected to store barnyard manure. Instead, they allowed it to lie in the farmyard, where rain leached it of much of its chemical nutrients. In a few places peasants compensated for the shortage of manure by using lime, pond mud, tree ashes, and if natural deposits were close at hand they applied gypsum (hydrous sulphate of calcium) or marl (a mixture of clay and calcium carbonate).[46] They did not always make extensive use of these often readily available materials, and sometimes they took no advantage of them. For example, in Haut-Poitou in western France, the fields generally lacked lime. The region had many deposits of marl and, centuries before, Pliny had reported that the people there spread it on their fields. Then the practice had been abandoned, perhaps as long ago as Merovingian times. In the eighteenth century the marl still was not used so that the land was much less productive than it might have been. Only in the 1820's did farmers once again marl, and as a result the agriculture of the area was transformed.[47]

The inadequacies in the supply of fertilizers and the farming habits of the peasants affected the frequency with which fields received fertilizers. In some localities, such as in the Swiss canton of Vaud, in parts of Brandenburg, and in places in the duchy of Brunswick in central Germany, all or part of the fallow was fertilized every three years. Far more often, the period between manurings ran from 6 to 12 or even more years—when the fields were fertilized at all. In many places in the important Danish grain-producing region of Zealand, fields received manure only every 12 to 14

[45] Veit (1841), 140; Chatelain (1956), 495-499; Collins (1969), 83; Stark (1957), 30; Festy (1947), 17-21; Weber-Kellermann (1966), 47-49.
[46] Berthold (1962), 117; Sée (1906), 384; Stark (1957), 26; Calonne (1920), 204; Riemann (1953), 35-36; Saalfeld (1960), 93; Vil'son (1869), 69; Tooke (1799), III, 256; Liashchenko (1945), 108-109.
[47] Raveau (1926), 135-136.

years. In the rich black earth of the Russian steppes fields were, with rare exception, never fertilized. In those treeless prairies the peasants dried cattle dung into briquettes and used it as fuel, when they did not throw it away. An economist on a data-gathering trip through the steppeland in 1850 reported that he saw hundreds of cartloads of manure thrown on the roads.[48] In sheep-raising regions shepherds were sometimes required to fold their sheep for a certain time—in Bohemia, for example, for a night and the following morning—in an arable field to manure it, and then moved on to another field.[49]

The peasants seeded their fields by hand. They carried the seed in an apron or in a sack slung across a shoulder, and broadcast handfuls at regular intervals as they strode across the land. The seeds came from the preceding year's crop so that the fields received the same genetic strain year after year. They were rarely washed and so included much foreign material, especially seeds of other grains and of weeds. To make matters worse, the peasants had a tendency to oversow in the hope of increasing output. Not surprisingly, these pernicious practices resulted in low yields and grain of poor quality. The methods used to thresh and store the harvested grain added still more impurities. Threshing, a winter-time occupation, was done either by peasants with the flail (in eighteenth-century Russia often just with long, crooked sticks), or it was trodden out by horses or oxen driven back and forth across the grain stalks. In either case the threshing floor was the ground itself, so that much soil was mixed in with the grain. When animals did the threshing, their droppings were mixed in. Winnowing removed some of the foreign matter but much remained. Young, in his travels through France, noted that "no miller can grind corn as he receives it from the farmer, without further cleaning." At the beginning of the nineteenth century bread grain shipped from Denmark into Norway was reported to have been about one-third rye; the other two-thirds were a mix of other cereals, weeds, and rubbish of one sort or another.[50] Grain often was stored in pits dug into the ground, where it frequently became moldy, infested with insects, or rotted. When stored above ground, the storage bins were poorly suited for granaries so that the grain often deteriorated.[51]

Scattered data from some of the servile lands afford an insight into the productivity of the farm labor force. In plowing, topography and the friability of the soil had a determining influence on the amount of land that could

[48] Köppen (1852), 122.

[49] Berthold (1962), 117; Chevallez (1949), 96; Müller (1965a), 89; Henning (1969a), 21, 24; Nielsen (1933), 188; Saalfeld (1960), 93; Zenker (1897), 23; Stark (1957), 26; Haxthausen (1847), II, 15.

[50] Young (1970), I, 354-355, II, 121; Nielsen (1933), 398n.; Jacob (1828), 46; Jacob (1826), 66, 105; Transehe-Roseneck (1890), 124; Forster (1960), 44; Paget (1839), I, 259; Skene (1854), I, 419; Tooke (1799), III, 245, 256; Weber (1740), 120 Druzhinin (1946), 417.

[51] Corfus (1969), 151; Jacob (1826), 105; Braudel and Labrousse (1970), II, 155; Skene (1854), I, 120; Meyer (1966), I, 505, 505n.

5. Threshing grain. (*L'Encyclopédie: Receuil des planches sur les sciences* . . . I, Paris, 1762.)

be plowed in a day. Also the first plowing of a fallowed field in preparation for a crop was more difficult and time-consuming than were later plowings (if, indeed, there were later plowings). In the first decades of the nineteenth century it took 4 to 5 pairs of oxen from 2 to 3 days to plow 1.2 acres (half a hectare) in the hill country of Wallachia, while in the light soil of the maritime provinces of Prussia a man could plow an acre or more in a day with two small oxen or even with a single ox. In general, the central European plowman, given reasonably favorable conditions, could plow about .9 to 1.4 acres in his long work day.[52] In late-eighteenth-century England a plowman using an improved Norfolk plow could do approximately 1.5 to 2 acres a day. In the United States in the first half of the nineteenth century the rate of plowing with a wooden plow was "more nearly one acre than two acres per day."[53]

Data from East Prussia for the eighteenth century, and for Mecklenburg and Holstein in the 1820's, show that a mower with a scythe could cut between .9 and 1.5 acres of a hayfield in a day. Mowing, however, was but the first step. The hay had to be raked and spread to dry and then brought in. In East Prussia a worker in a day could rake and spread the mowed hay on about .6 of an acre in a day, or could bring in the hay from 1.2 to 1.5 acres.[54] Harvesting was an especially labor-intensive operation and done

[52] Corfus (1969), 56; Jacob (1826), 46; Henning (1969a), 143; Blum (1948), 190; Jacob (1828), 185, 236, 290; Müller (1967), 95.

[53] Slicher van Bath (1960), 16; Rogin (1931), 16. In the 1970's farmers in the United States plowed an average of 12.8 acres in an eight-hour day (computed by the National Tillage Machinery Laboratory, U.S. Agricultural Research Service, U.S. Department of Agriculture, Auburn, Alabama).

[54] Henning (1969a), 144; Jacob (1826), 186-187, 236, 239.

under great pressure of time. Grain has to be harvested within 10 days or two weeks after its maturation or it will spoil, and inclement weather during that period can do much damage to the ripe grain. The harvesters worked in teams to reap, rake, bind, and shock and then bring in the crop. Tests conducted in 1836 in Styria showed that a team composed of a man with a scythe and two followers could reap, bind, and shock about an acre of grain in a 10-hour work day; in other words, three man-days per acre. When a sickle was used, only about .6 of an acre could be harvested. A contemporary agricultural expert reported that the requirement of three man-days per acre was in close agreement with the experience on manors in other provinces of Austria. In East Prussia and in the duchy of Brunswick in central Germany harvesters in the eighteenth century were slightly more productive. In Lower Alsace, however, until the second half of the nineteenth century it took almost five man-days to harvest an acre. In contrast, in the United States in 1800 an acre was harvested in 1.3 man-days with the reaper using the scythe.[55] Threshers sometimes spent only part of the day in that task. Perhaps that is why threshers in Austria reportedly flailed out only 2.5 to 3.5 bushels of winter cereal and 3.5 to 5.2 bushels of the lighter summer grain in a day. Landowners in Holstein reported that a worker there could thresh 5 to 6 bushels of winter grain and from 6 to 10 bushels of summer grain. In New England and the Middle States in the early decades of the nineteenth century, threshers averaged 7-8 bushels a day from grain that yielded 20 bushels per acre, and 5-6 bushels in regions with lower yields.[56]

The retardative effects of inefficient and wasteful techniques and inadequate implements were compounded by other factors. Peasants knew that their land should be plowed and harrowed several times to prepare it for planting, but plowing was the most demanding and time-consuming of all field work. As mentioned earlier, few peasants owned the six to eight animals needed to pull the plow in heavy soil and not everyone owned a

[55] Blum (1948), 190-191; Henning (1969a), 144; Saalfeld (1960), 92; Juillard (1953), 377; Slicher van Bath (1960), 16.

[56] Blum (1948), 191; Jacob (1826) 239; Rogin (1931), 179. Data on the increase over time in the productivity of farm labor could illustrate the backwardness of agricultural operations in the first half of the nineteenth century, and the advances made since then. I was unable to find this information for the servile lands. However, the above paragraphs indicate that the productivity of farm labor in the United States in the early part of the nineteenth century was comparable to that in the servile lands. Thus the data for our country can serve as an indicator of the advances made in productivity, though, in general, progress in Europe was not as remarkable as it was in the United States. In 1830 it took the American farmer 57.7 hours to produce an acre of wheat, yielding 20 bushels, using walking plow, hand seeding, brush harrow, sickle, and flail. In 1896 it took him 8.8 hours to produce the same acre of wheat of 20 bushels, using improved implements, such as gang plow, seeder, harrow, binder, and machine harvester, with horses as prime movers. In 1971-1973, using machinery with gasoline engines as prime movers, it took 2.9 man hours to produce an acre of wheat yielding 32.7 bushels. Hurst and Church (1933), 1-3; U.S. Department of Agriculture (1974), table 637, p. 446.

plow, and so the villagers had to pool their resources. That meant that they had to wait their turn to plow their strips, and the delays made it difficult, if not impossible, to have later plowings, since that would have carried plowing into the growing season. That happened anyway where population was thin and labor in short supply. In Brittany, for example, because of the labor shortage rye, which should have been sown in October, was not put in until mid-November.[57] In some of the servile lands the brevity of the growing season forced the peasants to compress their field operations into a relatively short period, and often the work carried out under pressure was done poorly. And, finally, and most important of all, the forced labor demanded of peasants, which was the principal source of labor for seigniorial demesnes, was performed so negligently that it offered an insuperable barrier to increased productivity. "When no advantage is gained by care in the work," William Jacob observed in his report of 1825 to the British Privy Council for Trade, "it will naturally be very imperfectly executed."[58]

There were a few shining exceptions to the agricultural inefficiency that prevailed in the servile lands. The convertible husbandry used in Schleswig-Holstein and in Mecklenburg was one of these exceptions. And farming in French Flanders (and in neighboring Belgium) was a model of what could be done. Fallows had disappeared there long ago, root crops enriched the soil and provided food for man and beast, fields were skillfully and thoroughly plowed, seeds carefully selected and cleaned, cattle were stalled, and natural fertilizers of all sorts, including night soil and road droppings, were liberally applied to the fields.

Even that stuffiest of Englishmen, Arthur Young, had to admit, albeit grudgingly, that husbandry in Flanders, and in a few other places in France, "is to be ranked very high amongst the best in Europe." "These are provinces," he wrote, "which even an English farmer might visit with advantage." (Young may not have known that many of the improvements in English agriculture had been introduced from Flanders; if he did know it, he was not likely to admit it.) He was impressed especially by the Alsatian plain, which he called "one of the richest scenes of soil and cultivation to be met with in France, and rivalled only by Flanders, which, however, exceeds it." Alsace did disappoint Young in one respect. He complained that he saw no pretty country girls there.[60]

[57] Sée (1906), 383.
[58] Jacob (1826), 66.
[59] Lefebvre (1972), 191-216.
[60] Young (1970), I, 153, 364.

CHAPTER 7

The Retardation of Agriculture: Crops and Livestock

I

IN 1758 the author of a treatise on French agriculture wrote that "all of the farmers have a kind of mania that compels them to think that they cannot raise too much grain, and some of them consider themselves disgraced if they do not plant their two fields in grain. . . ." A few decades later Antoine Lavoisier called French agriculture "a gigantic grain factory."[1] The section on the economy in a statistical work published in Bavaria in 1806 began with the words "Grain is Germany's most important product."[2] These statements could have been made about all of the servile lands. Of the estimated 23.9 million hectares of arable in France in 1789, about 54 per cent (13 million hectares) was in cereals, 40 per cent (9.5 million hectares) lay fallow, and only 6 per cent (1.4 million hectares) was given over to other crops. In Germany at the outset of the nineteenth century 61 per cent of all of the arable there had grain planted on it, and around 25 per cent was bare fallow. In 1848 two-thirds of the plowland of Bohemia was planted in cereals and 21.6 per cent lay fallow. In Wallachia data collected in 1831 showed that over 99 per cent of the arable was used for cereals. In Russia in the 1860's, grain and fallow took up 96 per cent of the arable.[3]

The reason, of course, for this overwhelming emphasis on grain was that it was by far the chief human foodstuff. And as population increased, the demand for grain increased. Farmers responded by planting more and more of it to feed their own growing numbers and to supply the expanding urban markets. Contemporary estimates in France indicate that production of cereals there went from 94.5 million hectolitres in 1760 to 115.8 million hectolitres in 1788. An official estimate set the average annual grain harvest in Russia between 1800 and 1813 at about 155 million chetverts. By 1857-1863 it had increased to 220 million chetverts. In Poland between 1822 and 1864 wheat production rose from .6 million bushels to 3 million bushels, barley from 1.1 million to 10 million bushels, and the production of rye and oats increased three times over.[4]

The inefficiency and low productivity of agriculture, and the poverty of the great mass of the population, explained the extreme dependence on

---

[1] Festy (1947), 15.　　　　　　　　　　　[2] Kuczynski (1961), I, 10n.

[3] Toutain (1961), I, 52; Bittermann (1956), 24; Kodedová (1967), 140; Corfus (1969), 133-134; Liashchenko (1949), 324.

[4] Razous (1944), 360; Khromov (1950), 18-19; Kieniewicz (1969), 92-93. The hectolitre is equal to 2.837 bushels. The chetvert was equal to 5.95 bushels or 2.1 hectolitres.

grain. One or another of the cereals will grow almost everywhere, they are easy to store and transport, and they contain no toxic materials. Most important, they are cheaper per thousand calories of energy than almost any other food. They are concentrated storehouses of the carbohydrates that fuel most of the energy that men need to move about and to work. Proteins, necessary for the building and maintenance of the body, form the second largest constituent of cereals, though not all of the essential amino acids are present in adequate quantities. Nor do cereals meet all of the vitamin and mineral requirements for the human diet, and they are generally low in calcium. Certain root crops, such as yams, plantains, breadfruit, taros and cassava, staples of the diets of some non-European peoples, furnish calories more cheaply than do the cereals, but they do not provide enough protein.[5]

As societies grow wealthier, their people can afford a more varied and expensive diet, and the role of grain diminishes, though it still retains much importance. A large part of the cereal crop in these societies is used for animal food, to produce the meat and dairy products that wealthier societies consume in increasing quantities. The servile societies of Europe were poor, their people ate very little meat or other non-cereal products, and they could not afford to feed large amounts of grain to their animals.

Governments, fearful of the unrest that often followed shortages of grain, placed all manner of regulations and restrictions on the culture and trade in grain. Experience had taught them to expect extreme fluctuations in the annual harvests and they wanted to make as certain as they could that some grain would always be available for their subjects. Sometimes they took extreme measures in pursuit of this goal. The French revolutionary government of the Year II guillotined a 55-year-old widow, the marquise de Marbeuf, and her steward, named Payen, because the marquise, who was a progressive agriculturist, had planted forage crops on some of her land that hitherto had been used for cereals. The Revolutionary Tribunal called her action part of "a conspiracy against the safety of the French people."[6]

Grain entered the human diet principally in the form of porridge, beverages, and bread. Porridge was made of whatever cereal was available, boiled with water or milk. Rye and wheat made sticky and soggy porridges; they were, however, the best suited among the grains for baking leavened bread. Because of the inadequate supply of these two cereals, however, other grains and sometimes peas, beans, chestnuts, and vetches went into the preparation of the loaf. In Lower Alsace, for example, many peasants ate bread made of barley, while those who could afford it used a mixture of one-fourth to one-third wheat flour and the rest barley meal. In Picardy

[5] Harper (1959), 88; Majors (1951), 336; Clark and Haswell (1970), 7.
[6] Festy (1947), 134-144.

bread was made of rye and barley; in northern Burgundy the more prosperous peasants ate bread made of a mixture of wheat and rye while the
poorer families had to content themselves with bread made of oats and barley.[7]

All grains are rather similar in their nutritive value, but each is preferred
for certain specific purposes. Usually, however, the growers in the servile
lands had to compromise between their preferences on the one hand, and
the quality of the soil, the climate, and the resources at their command on
the other. That was why less wheat was grown than other cereals, though
wheat was the most desired grain. Wheat bread has a better texture than
does rye bread, tastes better, is more easily digested, and its dough rises to
a greater volume.[8] But wheat is the most demanding grain in terms of soil
and climate. It will not grow on sandy soil, is more sensitive to soil acidity
than other grains, supports low temperatures poorly, is more rapidly affected by humidity or dryness, and reacts more quickly to soil exhaustion
than do other grains. Wheat does respond to good farming practices, including fertilizing, more satisfactorily than does rye, its chief rival as a
bread grain. But, as preceding pages have shown, good farming practices
were very much the exception in the servile lands. And so wheat production lagged far behind that of other grains. An estimate made in 1794 in
France for the decade 1781-1790 maintained that of the total amount of arable planted in cereals 16 per cent was in wheat, 32 per cent in rye, 14 per
cent in barley, and 38 per cent in oats. An estimate for Germany drawn
from data of around 1800 found that of 22 million hectares in cereals at that
time only 7.5 per cent was planted in wheat, 41 per cent in rye, 19 per cent
in barley, 25.5 per cent in oats, 4 per cent in spelt, and 3 per cent in
buckwheat. In 1831 in Wallachia wheat grew on 10.26 per cent of the arable, millet on 10.22 per cent, oats and barley on 9.19 per cent, and maize
on 70.3 per cent.[9]

These data, though they show the relative unimportance of wheat, actually reflect a very large increase in wheat production in comparison with
earlier years. During the last decades of the old order wheat production rose
significantly in response variously to rising prices, rising living standards in
the towns, and increased exports to more economically advanced lands.
Contemporaries estimated that French wheat production went up from 31.5
million hectolitres in 1760 to 40 million hectolitres in 1784, or from 150
litres per inhabitant to 167. This increase was at the expense of other
grains, as in Lower Alsace, where wheat displaced rye from its premier position and where the culture of spelt disappeared between 1760 and 1790. In

[7] Jasny (1940), 35-37, 40-41; Juillard (1953), 37; Calonne (1920), 453; St. Jacob (1960),
539; Babeau (1878), 91-92; Falguerolles (1941), 156.
[8] Commercial "rye" bread in the United States contains between 60 and 85 per cent of
wheat flour and only 40 to 15 per cent of rye flour. Pyler (1973), II, 791.
[9] Toutain (1961), I, 61; Berthold (1962), 98; Corfus (1969), 133-134; Jasny (1940), 41-44,
470.

Mecklenburg, farmers grew little wheat until the widespread adoption there of convertible husbandry. Then wheat acreage began to grow, while buckwheat, formerly much more widely raised there than wheat, and millet, spelt, and lentils were pushed into the background. Wheat production tripled in the duchy of Brunswick in the last decades of the eighteenth century. In the Kurmark district of Brandenburg the acreage in wheat increased by 90.6 per cent between 1778 and 1805. In eighteenth-century Russia wheat had been grown only in a few regions and not in significant quantities. Then in the first half of the nineteenth century the center of agricultural production moved southward into the black earth of the steppeland. Though lack of rain often curtailed yields, wheat and especially spring wheat could be grown there successfully, and it assumed first place among the grains produced south of 50°-52° of latitude. North of that line, rye retained its leadership. Russian grain exports rose 15 times over from about 2.38 million bushels at the end of the eighteenth century to 35.7 million bushels in 1850. That amounted only to a small part of Russia's total grain crop—about 3.5 to 5 per cent in the 1850's. But wheat made up by far the largest part of the exported grain, totalling 61.4 per cent of all grain exported in 1850, while rye made up 19.9 per cent of exported grain, oats 7.8 per cent, and barley 4.2 per cent.[10]

Despite the increase in the area sown in wheat, rye easily retained first place as the single most important crop in most of the servile lands. When William Jacob travelled through Saxony, Prussia, Poland, Austria, Bavaria, and Württemberg in 1825, he reported that he never saw "either in the bakers' shops, or in private houses, a loaf of wheaten bread." He found that he could buy rolls of white bread in large towns, but smaller places had only rye bread for sale. "Travelers," he explained, "commonly take in their carriages sufficient wheaten rolls to supply them from one large town to the next." Rye continued to be the leading bread grain in Germany throughout the nineteenth century. Wheat flour was considered a luxury to be used only for special occasions.[11]

Rye owed its preeminence to its field qualities. It is the least demanding of the major cereals in its soil requirements, so that it does not suffer as much from lack of fertilizer as does wheat. Its extensive root development provides greater absorptive capacity and a greater ability than other cereals to grow in unfavorable soil conditions. It requires less sunshine than does wheat, can survive lower winter temperatures, can endure alternate freezes and thaws, tolerates more excessive conditions of soil moistness, and equals wheat in its resistance to drought. It produces more straw than does wheat and so helped fill out the always inadequate supplies of forage, and its

[10] France: Razous (1944), 60; Juillard (1953), 254. Germany: Mager (1955), 135, Saalfeld (1960), 89; Müller (1964b), 218. Russia: Gille (1949), 156-157; Blum (1961), 288, 331.
[11] Jacob (1826), 36; Riemann (1953), 12; Ashley (1928), 20-21.

quicker early growth made it easier to get rid of weeds. In short, rye requires less labor and less application of capital and still gives yields superior to those which wheat would give under the same circumstances. On the other hand, rye, unlike wheat, responds poorly to good cultivation practices such as the use of fertilizer. It shares with wheat the lowest ranking in yield among the major cereals, and it is usually more expensive to produce than barley and oats, the other two chief grains.[12]

Oats was second only to rye in popularity. In the dominant three-field system oats was by far the most popular spring cereal. It often held first place, too, in regions where farmers used convertible husbandry; in a popular rotation used in Schleswig-Holstein oats was planted for 3 or 4 years in succession, and more was raised there than of any other cereal. Oats uses nutrients in the soil that are not accessible to spring wheat or barley, so that it yields well with little preparation of the field. It grows on poor or exhausted soils, withstands heat, cold, dry or humid conditions, and is less affected by weeds and by inferior tillage than are other cereals. It provides food for man and beast. As forage oats has twice the nutritional value of good hay and all animals like it. Usually, however, when oats was used for forage in the servile lands it was fed only to horses. With the replacement in some regions of oxen by horses as work animals, oat culture increased. In Kurmark, for example, where the number of horses went up by 21 per cent between 1779 and 1803 (from 142,777 to 173,327), the area sown in oats increased by nearly 40 per cent.[13]

Barley, the other principal spring cereal, was much less widely planted than oats. Barley grows in a great variety of climactic conditions and has a short growing season, so that it could be raised successfully in the cold of northern Russia and at an elevation of 2,000 meters in the Swiss Alps. But it is to oats as wheat is to rye, in that it is more sensitive to soil quality and tillage practices, and without proper cultivation is easily overrun by weeds. With less labor, then, the peasant had larger yields per acre with oats than he did with barley, and so preferred to grow oats.[14]

Buckwheat was raised in many places; in parts of Russia and in eighteenth-century Brittany it was a major crop. First planted on an important scale in Europe in the late fifteenth and early sixteenth centuries, its chief advantages were that it could produce a crop, albeit a meager one, on the poorest soils and with the most primitive tillage, and that it matured in a short time. In Germany the area in buckwheat declined in the last decades of the eighteenth century. Millet, like buckwheat able to grow under the poorest conditions, lost favor, too, so that by 1800 its culture in Germany

[12] Jasny (1940), 235, 504-506; Nuttenson (1958), 8-9; Riemann (1953), 12-13.
[13] Hanssen (1880), i, 309; Jasny (1940), 533; Müller (1964b), 221; Riemann (1953), 13; Faucher (1949), 175-177.
[14] Jasny (1940), 521; Walter (1966), 46; Müller (1964b), 218.

was largely limited to Upper Lusatia and Silesia. In France it was raised in parts of Brittany, and in the southern Russia millet was still an important crop in the mid-nineteenth century.[15]

In France (and in England) wheat and rye were often sown together in a mixture called *meteil* in France and maslin in England. Since wheat was less frost-resistant than was rye, the mixed sowing reduced the danger of a total crop failure if wheat alone was planted. Maslin seems to have been used little, if at all, in central and eastern Europe in the eighteenth and first half of the nineteenth centuries; it was sown in the seventeenth century in Lower Austria (where it was called *Halbgetreide*). Other grains, however, were sown together, such as barley and oats, spelt and rye, barley, spring wheat and oats, and so on.[16]

Though the people of the servile lands lived largely by grain alone, they did raise other foodstuffs. They grew vegetables and a few fruits in their gardens, and they sometimes planted vegetables, usually legumes, in the fallow fields. Often they sowed a mixture of a grain and a vegetable, as in southern France, where maize and field beans were planted together, or in Brandenburg, where summer rye was sown with peas and vetch. Data for Germany and Bohemia reflect the unimportance of vegetables as a field crop. In Germany in 1800 only an estimated 3.9 per cent of the arable was in legumes and 2.3 per cent in root crops. In Bohemia in 1848 legumes took up 2.8 per cent of the arable and root crops 4.5 per cent.[17] Peasants raised industrial crops, too, in their gardens and sometimes on the fallow. These included such plants as flax, whose fiber was used for linen and its seed for linseed oil, hemp, dye plants, and rape for oil. In most places peasants raised only small amounts of these products to meet their own needs for cloth, cordage, and fats. In Russia and in the Baltic lands, however, flax and hemp were major cash crops; up to the mid-1840's the value of flax and hemp exports from Russia exceeded that of grain. Flax was also an important crop in places in northern and eastern Germany into the first half of the nineteenth century.[18] Many parts of the servile lands once had vineyards, but from the sixteenth and seventeenth centuries on viniculture had increasingly concentrated in regions best suited by nature for grapes. Hops, too, became concentrated in naturally suited areas such as in Franconia, Bavaria, and Bohemia.

In the last decades of the old order new crops, and notably potatoes, maize, and forage plants, gained increasing attention in the servile lands. Because of their late appearance and because of their part in the transformation of the traditional society they will be discussed in a later chapter.

[15] Sée (1906), 390-392; Confino (1969), 71; Vil'son (1869), 120; Dieck (1954), 26-27; Jasny (1940), 5; Berthold (1962), 97; Mager (1955), 270; Meyer (1966), I, 451.
[16] Slicher van Bath (1963), 263-264; Buchinger (1952), 342.
[17] Berthold (1962), 98; Kodedová (1967), 140.
[18] Strazdunaite (1961), 189; Vil'son (1869), 228, 261-263; Haushofer (1963), 206.

6. Winemaking. (F. Rozier, *Cours complet d'agriculture . . . ou dictionnaire universel d'agriculture*, IX, Paris, 1796.)

II

The inadequacies and inefficiencies of agriculture in the servile lands resulted, as could be expected, in abysmally low yields. From the end of the Middle Ages the ratio between harvest and amount of seed planted oscillated within a narrow band, indicating the static level of agricultural efficiency.[19] Yields were down in the seventeenth and first half of the eighteenth centuries (in Germany the decline seems to have started in the latter part of the sixteenth century). Then in the second half of the eighteenth century the available data indicate that yields moved upward to about where they had been in the sixteenth century, and in many places somewhat higher than they had been at that time. Poland seemed to have been an exception: yields there remained at the lower level.[20]

Figures for average grain yields for an entire country mask wide differences among and within individual regions and localities. To cite but one illustration of this, yields per acre in Flanders were just about double those for France as a whole, while in a district in Tarn in southern France, or in Brittany in the west, yields were half or less of the national average.[21] Contemporary and later estimates of yields in eighteenth-century France for rye and wheat are between 5 and 6 times the amount of seed planted. The

[19] Experiments conducted at the agricultural research station at Rothamstead, England, between 1839 and 1905 showed that under conditions of continuous cropping without fertilizers yields declined annually, and then after a certain term (30 years in the case of Rothamstead) reached a stationary level of productivity, with yields averaging 13.7 bushels of wheat per acre. Yields on manured land averaged 34.5 bushels per acre. Lennard (1922), 27; Marshall (1929), 46n.

[20] Slicher van Bath (1965a), 138, 144-145; Slicher van Bath (1969), 175; Wyczański (1960), 586.

[21] Lefebvre (1972), 198-199; Falguerolles (1941), 155; Sée (1906), 385-387.

peasants are said to have used about 2 hectolitres (5.7 bushels) of seed per hectare. That would have given yields of 10 to 12 hectolitres (28.4 to 34 bushels) per hectare, or from 11.5 to 13.8 bushels per acre.[22] In Denmark and Schleswig-Holstein, yields of the major grains in the mid-eighteenth century were between 3 and 4 times the seed. In Germany, average yields ran around 4 to 1. In White Russia, in the first half of the nineteenth century, yields moved between 2.5 and 3.5 to 1. In Livonia, they were 3 and 4 to 1. Data for Russia indicate that yields for the principal grains averaged around 3 to 1 in the last decades of the eighteenth century and around 3.5-4 to 1 during the first half of the nineteenth century. A mid-nineteenth-century governmental study estimated an average yield of 6 hectolitres per hectare, or about 7 bushels per acre. In Poland grain yields in the second half of the eighteenth century averaged between 3 and 3.5 to 1.[23]

Comparisons with some modern yields afford a measure of the low productivity of the agriculture of the old order. In Germany, the yield of rye around the beginning of the nineteenth century was estimated to have been around 8 to 9 quintals per hectare, and about 10.3 quintals for wheat. In 1971 these grains yielded 35.1 and 46.2 quintals per hectare, respectively, in West Germany, and 22.5 and 36.7 quintals in the German Democratic Republic. In France, wheat yields before 1789 had been somewhat less than 10 quintals per hectare. In 1971 they averaged 38.6 quintals. In communist eastern Europe, modern yields are strikingly smaller than they are in free western Europe, but they are still much larger than they were in the days of serfdom. In 1971 average yields in Poland were 20 quintals per hectare for rye and 24.4 quintals for wheat. In the Soviet Union, yields were 12 quintals for rye and 14.1 quintals for wheat.[24]

A glance at the charges against the peasants' harvest before they could consume any part of it reveals the narrow margin afforded by the prevalent yields of the traditional agriculture. A yield of 4 to 1 (considered very satisfactory in most places) meant that 25 per cent of the harvest had to be put aside for seed for the next planting. Obligations in kind to the seignior and tithes took a sizable share of the crop—sometimes perhaps as much as 15 per cent. A part of the harvest had to be stored against possible crop failures in the next season, some had to be fed to the animals, and some had to be sold to raise the money the peasants needed to meet their obligations in

[22] Toutain (1961), 74-75; Morineau (1971), 24, 77; Zolla (1893), 201; Sheppard (1971), 11, 11n.
[23] Denmark and Schleswig-Holstein: Nielsen (1933), 189; Meyer (1965), 28; Beyer (1957), 54-57. Germany: Bittermann (1956), 33; Henning (1969b), 123-124. Livonia: Transehe-Roseneck (1890), 123. Russia: Köppen (1845), 526-527; Razgon (1959), 203-204; Vil'son (1869), 115. White Russia: Fridman (1958), 9-10. Poland: Wyczański (1910), 586; Topolski (1962), 36.
[24] Earlier yields for Germany: Lütge (1967), 273; Riemann (1953), 36; Franz (1963), 449; for France: Morineau (1971), 24; Braudel and Labrousse (1970), 99. Modern yields from FAO (1971), 37, 38, 43, 44. The metric quintal is equal to 220.46 pounds.

7. Grinding grain with a quern. Painting by J.-P. Norblin, 1745-1830. (J. S. Bystron, *Dzieje obyczajów w dawnej Polsce*, Warsaw, 1960.)

cash they owed to lord, state, church, and community, and to buy the wares they did not produce themselves. The wonder is that, given the demands against their meager crops, they were able to stay alive and even to increase their numbers.

The wonder grows in light of the frequency of crop failures and famines. Even in years of "good" harvests, hunger was an accepted part of village life, especially in the weeks before the new crop was ready for harvesting, when the grain left from the last harvest was running out.[25] Imagine, then, the peasants' plight when, as happened all too often, harvests fell short of expectations or failed completely. France during the eighteenth century knew sixteen years of general famine, or about one year out of every six. Russia had several universal crop failures and over thirty partial ones during the eighteenth century. Contemporary statisticians at the beginning of the nineteenth century calculated that Russia had a general crop failure and famine and two partial famines every ten years. In the province of Volynia in southwest Russia, known as one of the empire's best farming regions, poor harvests and partial famines in one out of every three years was considered normal. The governor of Livonia in his annual report for 1805 wrote that "not a year goes by without a partial crop failure in some part of the province." The White Russian provinces of Vitebsk and Mogilev experienced ten crop failures between 1820 and 1850 and Grodno had eight just between 1844 and 1857.[26]

Crop failures sometimes had shattering consequences. In his journal, the marquis d'Argenson referred time and again to the great suffering when crops failed in France in 1739 and 1740. He claimed that more people had died of want in those two years than had been killed in all of the wars of Louis XIV.[27] In 1770 and again in 1771, when heavy rains ruined most of the grain crop in Bohemia, 250,000 people, or about 14 per cent of the population, are said to have died. In Saxony, where crops failed, too, in these same years, comparison of average annual births and deaths for the years 1767 to 1770 with those for 1771 to 1773 showed that there were about 60,000 more deaths in 1771 and 1772, and 36,000 fewer births in 1772 and 1773, resulting in a net population decrease of 6 per cent.[28]

III

The essential feature of plow agriculture, as one authority has pointed out, is "the integration of animal husbandry with plant production. It involves

[25] *Cf.* Leskiewicz (1965), 243.

[26] Toutain (1961), I, 6-7; Augé-Laribé (1955), 43; Confino (1969), 134; Chepko (1964), 177; Kahan (1968), 358; Liashchenko (1945), 116-117; Liashchenko (1913), I, 120.

[27] Argenson (1861), III, 76, 92, 96, 102, 125-126, etc.

[28] Weinzerl-Fischer (1954), 478-481; Grünberg (1894), I, 200-202; Blaschke (1962), 126-129.

not merely a juxtaposition . . . but a genuine wedding whereby one branch supports the other. The animals are not only an object *of* production but also an important factor *in* production; the cultivated land serves not only for direct human use but also for the maintenance of livestock."[29] Unfortunately, in the servile lands the marriage was not that successful; indeed, nearly everywhere animal husbandry was always the neglected and sometimes the well-nigh forgotten partner.

The neglect had a simple explanation. When population increases while technology remains the same or changes only to a negligible degree, land is used to raise foodstuffs that will give high yields in calories per unit of land and labor. A kilogram of grain yields between 750 and 900 grams of flour (the coarser the milling, the greater the yield), and provides 350 calories per 100 grams. Beef provides only between 160 and 225 calories per 100 grams.[30] In terms of land utilization, an acre in grain produces at least five times as many calories as the acre does when it is used to pasture animals. Similarly, it is much more efficient to use grain for human consumption than it is to feed animals. It takes about 12 pounds of grain to produce 1 pound of beef on the hoof, 1.3 pounds to produce 1 pound of milk, and about 6 pounds for 1 pound of pork on the hoof.[31] In other words, a vegetable diet can support more people than can a diet of animal products. So, as population grew, and as the price of cereals began to rise more rapidly than did other farm products, pasture was converted into plowland. The tillers of the soil could not get along without animals, but they kept their number to a minimum. They fed them as little grain as possible, and instead turned out the animals to fend for themselves on the stubble in the harvested fields, on wastes, and, to the extent that the seignior allowed, in the lord's forests. This inattention produced half-starved, small, and weak animals, but it held down costs. Modern studies made in a number of Indian states show that when bullocks there were fed on common grazings the computed costs of bullock labor used for one crop could account for less than 10 per cent of the total cost of the crop. When fed on fodder grown for them, the computed cost of bullock labor sometimes exceeded 50 per cent.[32]

Special seigniorial privileges in common land, fallows, and forest set up still further obstacles to peasant animal husbandry. In France seigniors had the right to claim as their own one-third and sometimes two-thirds of the commons, and even to seize all of it if the villagers' rights were based only on prescription and long usage instead of a specific title. Privileges such as these reduced the grazing resources available to the livestock of the peasantry. In France many seigniors who did not have their own herds rented

[29] Pfeiffer (1956), 249.
[30] Chatfield (1949), 9, 17. The beef is assumed to be comparable to U.S. utility and commercial grades.
[31] Fourastié (1960), 42.   [32] Boserup (1965), 37n.

out their special grazing privileges, often to cattle dealers who ran large operations. These dealers in their cattle drives to the market grazed their animals on the fallows and commons whose use they had leased from seigniors. Sometimes, too, French lords leased the common land they had taken from the peasants to a few large renters. It is easy to imagine the outrage of villagers when strangers grazed their animals on land which the peasants considered as their own, or when they saw the land turned over to a few renters.[33]

Pastures, fallows, woods, brush-covered wastes, marshland, and even roadside ditches served as animal feeding grounds for much of the year. The livestock were turned out to graze in the damp weather of late winter or early spring. Their hooves trampled down the grass before it was fairly grown; it was "more trodden down than eaten up" was the way one Austrian observer put it early in the nineteenth century. Rooting swine dug up the turf (though in some places laws ordered that pigs had to wear nose rings to prevent that). By mid-summer the pastures had become mats of dry, dust-covered straw. In time of drought and crop failure, the animals were the first to feel the effects. In 1785 a drought in Brittany compelled the peasants there to sell half of their cattle. In White Russia during the famine years from 1844 to 1858 about half of the livestock died of starvation.[34]

The animals were kept out as long as there was a scrap of grass or brush for them to eat; in Lower Alsace, for example, that meant nine to ten months of the year. During the remaining months the peasants stalled their livestock in filthy stables or sheds, or took them into their huts. Meadows supplied the hay the animals consumed during this period. Often the hay ran out, and the animals lived on straw left after the grain had been threshed, bean stalks, leaves, ferns, corn husks in the maize-growing threshed, bean stalks, leaves, ferns, corn husks in the maize-growing Danubian Principalities, and even old straw roof thatches. By the time spring arrived the beasts were often too weak to get up to their feet and move out to the fields under their own power. The peasants had to put them on sleds and pulled them by their tails out to the fresh air and sunshine and pasture.[35] If the livestock was fed any grain, it was in small amounts and then only to certain animals. Data from the eighteenth century for East Prussia and for the bishopric of Paderborn in northwest Germany indicate that from around 5 to 7 per cent of the grain was used to feed horses, swine, and calves. Swine were sometimes fed barley and oat groats to fatten them just before slaughter. Calves were taken from their mothers

[33] Bloch (1930), 517-518; Herbert (1969), 50-51.
[34] Sée (1921), 49; Chepko (1959), 177.
[35] Buchinger (1952), 319; Transehe-Roseneck (1890), 60; Ziekursch (1927), 33-34; Tooke (1799), III, 188; Wallace (1877), 96; Juillard (1953), 51.

at birth, fed milk for a week and then a mix of milk and barley groats with water gradually substituted for the milk, until by the fifth week water had completely replaced the milk. In winter the calf was fed hay and then the following spring the yearling was put out on the common pastures with the older animals.[36]

In most places the care of the village cattle was entrusted to a herdsman, who was paid by the village community. Each morning at the sound of the herdsman's horn the villagers led their cattle into the village street and the herdsman drove them to the place then in use as pasture. That could be uncultivated land, a fallow or newly harvested field, or a meadow from which the first crop of hay had been mowed—or, as became increasingly common in France in consequence of special legislation, after the second cutting. Custom often set the day on which a field could be used for pasture. The meadows in the Swiss canton of Vaud were open for grazing on St. Mary Magdalene's day, 22 July. In northern France in Picardy three days had to elapse before cattle could be led into a newly harvested field, to allow gleaners time to go through the field.[37] In many places the peasant community placed a limit on the number of animals each household could turn out to graze on common pastures. This was to ensure that there would be enough pasture for all of the households of the village. The stint for each household depended upon the size of its holding. In Lower Austria, for example, the peasant with a full holding could put four animals on the common pasture. Landless peasants presumably did not have the right of common, but long usage had sanctioned the non-observance of this (and other) restrictions on the use of the common resources of the village by its poorest inhabitants. In mountainous regions the peasants led their animals to upland pastures when spring came. In Scandinavia, in Switzerland, in the Carpathians, and in other regions with cold winters, the animals wintered in stalls. In southwestern Europe the milder climate allowed the cattle to spend the winter on pastures in the valleys and plainland.[38]

Except for sheep, most of the livestock belonged to the peasants. They needed the animals to meet their own demands for draught power, food, leather, and wool, and to perform the labor obligation they owed to the seigniors. The labor obligation required peasants to keep far more draft animals than they needed for their own operation. In some places in Schleswig-Holstein the peasant with a full holding had to provide his lord with 8 horses in summer and 4 in winter. These peasants usually had 12 horses, 8 for the daily labor obligations and 4 for their own use.[39] The excessive number of draft animals reduced the ability of the peasants to take proper care of their animals, and also reduced their ability to keep other

---

[36] Henning (1969a), 67-68, 73-74; Henning (1969b), 124; *cf.* Juillard (1953), 55.
[37] Bloch (1930), 340-341; Chevallez (1949), 67; Lizerand (1942), 112.
[38] Bull (1930), 61; Rigaudière (1965), 13; Walter (1966), 49.
[39] Hanssen (1861), 24.

animals. In the Danish islands, for example, peasants who had 8 to 10 horses, most of them for use in the labor service, could afford to keep only a calf or two and a few sheep and swine, to meet their own needs.[40] Peasants sent to market few, and in most cases none, of their animals, and little or none of their animal products. They needed the animals and their products for their own purposes, and to make payments in kind to their seigniors.

Nearly always animal breeding was left to chance. Only rarely was there an effort to improve the breed by selective mating, and then it was done almost exclusively by those exceptional seigniors who interested themselves in agricultural improvements, and who kept their animals apart from the village herd. The combination of inadequate food, poor maintenance, and haphazard breeding produced weak, scrawny, undersized, and poorly formed beasts. Their deficient diets delayed their maturity. In Germany horned cattle could not be bred until their fourth or fifth year and sheep in their third or fourth year (heifers now calve as 2 year olds and ewes lamb at approximately 24 months).[41] Livestock suffered all manner of debilitating ailments and fell easy prey to the epizoötics that periodically swept through the countryside. Sometimes animal mortality in these plagues reached catastrophic proportions. In Denmark a murrain that erupted in 1745 killed almost 270,000 animals. The disease lingered on for seven years, during which time 2 million animals in Denmark and Schleswig-Holstein sickened and died. In Livland and Estonia thousands of animals perished in six major epizoötics between 1826 and 1850. The outbreak in 1844 in Livland, which was made worse by a severe shortage of forage, was especially devastating, claiming, according to official figures, 20,110 horses, 64,084 horned cattle, and 196,063 sheep.[42]

Scattered data on milk and meat production reflect the inferiority of the animals of the servile lands. In 1780 in Zurich canton cows produced 1,075 to 1,650 liters of milk a year. Average annual milk production per cow in Germany in the eighteenth and early nineteenth centuries ran around 1,000 liters. In 1971 milk yields in Switzerland averaged 3,447 liters and in West Germany 3,679 liters per cow per year.[43] Animal weights, too, were much less than those of modern times. In Germany in 1800 live weight of cattle averaged around 200 kg. In 1938 average live weight was 500 kg. Slaughter weight (or carcass weight) rose from an average of 113 kg. in 1800 to 238 kg. in 1949-1951. Slaughter weight of swine increased from 50 kg. to 103 kg. over these same years, and that of sheep from 15 kg. to 23.8 kg.[44]

[40] Nielsen (1933), 189.
[41] Riemann (1954), 64; Ensminger (1969), 400, 684.
[42] Nielsen (1933), 184; Kahk (1961), 160-161. For epizootics elsewhere *v.* Mager (1955), 287; *Festschrift zur Säcularfeier* . . . (1865), II, 9; Calonne (1920), 334, 345-346; Rigaudiére (1965), 17-18.
[43] Hausser (1965), 143; Franz (1963), 449; Mager (1955), 286; FAO (1971), 396.
[44] Bittermann (1956), 50.

Draft power, supplied by horse or ox, was the primary interest of most peasants in animal husbandry. Contemporary experts heatedly debated the relative merits of these two beasts as work animals. Horses could work at a faster pace in light soil and with a light plow, they were more agile, and they had the advantage over oxen in such operations as harrowing and hauling. In heavy soil with a heavy plow, oxen, with their sustained strong pull, were steadier, did not jerk the plow and start it out of the ground when it met with an obstruction, and would pull longer at more draft. Horses cost more, and were more expensive to feed and shoe. Oxen could be fattened and eaten at the end of their work careers.[45]

In a few places both horses and oxen were used for field work, sometimes in western France working in a team, or each was used for the operations for which it was best suited. In general, however, one or the other seems to have been the preferred draft animal. In most of France, oxen provided the draft power, though in Picardy and Flanders horses dominated by far. In Denmark and Schleswig-Holstein horses were preferred. The peasants of northern and eastern Germany usually used horses, too, while those in Bavaria and the southwest and in Lower Saxony used oxen. Oxen provided nearly all of the draft power in Poland, White Russia, and the Danubian Principalities. In Russia horses provided most of the draft power, though oxen were sometimes employed.[46]

Besides horned cattle and horses, peasants usually had some small animals. Pigs kept by city people met much of the urban demand for pork products, so when peasants raised swine it was generally for their own consumption. Goats, the poor man's cow, and fowl helped fill out the peasants' meager diet, though often they had to use their fowl for payments in kind. Fowl fed on grain and so competed with humans for food, and that served to hold down their number. Most of the sheep belonged to the seigniors. Lords sometimes had huge flocks, especially in central and eastern Europe when sheep-raising boomed to meet new domestic and foreign demand for wool. These flocks often included improved breeds. When peasants had sheep they were almost without exception inferior native breeds. The peasants used their sheep to meet their own needs for wool, tallow for candles, and meat.

There were a few exceptions to the general neglect of animal husbandry in the servile lands. French Flanders was one notable variation from the norm (as it was in nearly every aspect of agriculture). To the Flemish farmer the chief advantage of livestock was the production of the manure that the peasants there applied so liberally to their fields. They did not keep

---

[45] *Cf.* Thaer (1809), I, 113-117.

[46] France: Sée (1939), I, 196; Gay (1958), 403; Calonne (1920), 209. Denmark and Schleswig-Holstein: Nielsen (1933), 189; Hanssen (1861), 24. Germany: Abel (1967), 224; Mager (1955), 273-276; Saalfeld (1960), 118. Poland: Rutkowski (1927), 97-98. White Russia: Shlossberg (1959), 110. Danubian Principalities: Emerit (1937), 199. Russia: Koval'chenko (1960), 176; Confino (1969), 111.

many animals, but they took good care of the ones they had. They stalled them so that their droppings were not lost on pastures and wastes, and they fed them forage crops, oil cakes, and brewery and other industrial residues. They bred strong horses, excellent sheep with heavy fleeces, fat pigs, and cows that gave much more milk than those in neighboring French provinces. Animal husbandry remained of secondary importance to tillage, but it provided a valuable source of income to the Flemish peasants.[47]

In regions where population was thin and land plentiful, or where topography made tillage difficult, animal husbandry was the leading sector of agricultural production. In the sparsely peopled plains and hills of the Danubian Principalities, and in the Great Plain of Hungary, grassland stretched out for great distances. The animals often stayed out on the range throughout the year. Costs were low, for the animals received scant attention or care, and when the time came to sell them they were driven to market by a few herdsmen.[48] In much of Switzerland the terrain dictated an emphasis upon cattle-raising rather than tillage. The Swiss did not grow enough grain to meet their needs and depended increasingly upon imports. By the second half of the eighteenth century only the two neighboring cantons of Solothurn and Aargau in the plateauland between the Juras and the Alps produced grain surpluses. Contemporaries estimated that Switzerland had to import one-third or more of the grain it consumed. In return, the Swiss exported cattle and dairy products.[49]

Proximity of large markets sometimes served to encourage concentration on animal husbandry. The demand from nearby Dutch and German port cities stimulated the production of meat and dairy goods in Jutland and the Danish islands, and in Schleswig-Holstein. In Schleswig-Holstein proprietors since early in the seventeenth century had leased their herds to men called "Hollanders" (though often they did not come from Holland) who specialized in butter production for export. With the advances of convertible husbandry, with its alternation between grain and grass, dairy production took on increased importance in the two duchies.[50] In France the Paris market was provisioned with cattle from nearby northern and western provinces, and especially Normandy. In many parts of these provinces pasture predominated over plowland.[51]

Starting in the fifteenth century, great numbers of cattle had been driven into central and western Europe from the continental borderlands— Denmark, Poland, Bohemia, Hungary, and parts of Russia and the Danubian Principalities. These drives reached their zenith in the second half of the sixteenth and the first two decades of the seventeenth century. Between 1600 and 1620 customs returns showed an average of 55,000 to 60,000

[47] Lefebvre (1972), 192-193, 199-200.
[48] Corfus (1969), 49; Marczali (1910), 47-48; den Hollander (1960), 156-157.
[49] Walter (1966), 47-48; Hausser (1961), 135, 144; Rappard (1912), 76-80, 82-83.
[50] Arnim (1957), 87-89; Wiese (1966), 126-127; Riemann (1953), 163, 167.
[51] Vidalenc (1952), 116-132; Razous (1944), 64.

horned cattle exported each year from Denmark alone, and uncounted thousands of head were smuggled out. Fattening cattle for export was a valued monopolistic privilege of the Danish nobility. Then war and the long secular downward trend of the European economy sharply reduced demand. Exports rose somewhat with the economic revival after the middle of the eighteenth century. Still, at the end of the eighteenth century Danish cattle exports were only about half of what they had been two hundred years earlier. The climb in grain prices in the second half of the eighteenth century was one reason why cattle exports lagged. The price rise apparently persuaded Danish farmers to convert pasture into arable and plant grain. Surely, too, the cattle pestilence that erupted in 1745 and killed so many Danish cattle had much to do with the retardation of Danish animal husbandry.[52]

Cattle exports from the east declined even more than the Danish trade. Presumably the importing lands now were better able to meet their needs from their own production. More important, the demand for meat declined as grain became more expensive.[53] Cattle and animal products, such as wool and hides, continued to be the principal and almost the only export of the Danubian Principalities until 1829. That was when the Treaty of Adrianople, which ended the Russo-Turkish war of 1828-1829, opened the Black Sea to international trade. The Principalities began to export on an increasingly large scale, particularly grain. Still, animal husbandry retained its preeminence (as it did in neighboring Hungary) until the second half of the nineteenth century.[54]

The almost unrelieved picture of an inefficient and wasteful agriculture presented in this and the preceding chapter persisted in the servile land up to—and beyond—the end of the old order. The plain fact was that, despite the advances in so many sectors of European civilization, the foundation upon which most everything else rested lagged far behind. Georges Duby, in his study of the rural economy in medieval western Europe, found that agricultural techniques at the end of the thirteenth century fell short of meeting "the needs of a teeming population which lay at the mercy of a shortage of food as cruel perhaps as it had ever been in Carolingian times."[55] Five hundred years later that was still true of the agricultural techniques of the servile lands. The methods and implements of tillage had changed amazingly little in the course of half a millennium. The face of rural Europe looked much as it had in the Middle Ages, the farm animals were not of better quality, and the yields from the fields were, at best, not significantly higher. The great mass of the people of the servile lands lived at the narrow margin of subsistence, as much at the mercy of a shortage of food as their forebears had been in the thirteenth century.

[52] Slicher van Bath (1963a), 286, 286n.; Abel (1966), 196; Wiese (1966), 128.
[53] Abel (1966), 197.
[54] Corfus (1969), 54-55; Mitrany (1930), 25; Eddie (1967), 305-306.
[55] Duby (1968), 125.

CHAPTER 8

The Rural Economy

I

THE organization and internal structure of the rural economy reflected the disinterest of seigniors in the advancement of agriculture. Most of them showed no concern about improvements in the operations of their manors, even though the manors were usually their chief or only source of income. They did not think of their properties as investments whose returns could be increased by careful management and by innovation. When they engaged in agricultural production they used the same methods that were used on peasant land, and they grew the same crops. Often their land was scattered in strips in the open fields along with the strips of the peasants. Many of them had no direct connection with agriculture. They drew all of their income from their properties in rents and in payments in cash and kind.

Seigniorial abstention from direct production was most frequent among the lords of the western lands. In France in the 1780's, out of 112 noble proprietors in Limousin who had a total of about 40,000 *arpents* in their *réserves*, only 13 had their own demesnes. The combined area of these demesnes amounted to 2.9 per cent of their total *réserves*. Less than 2 per cent of the noble landowners of Berry, 4 per cent in Quercy, and 3 per cent in Picardy and in Artois had demesnes. Bourgeois proprietors were even less likely to engage in direct agricultural production. Proprietors often rented their land in small pieces to cash renters or sharecroppers, or they leased their entire estate to a "farmer-general." The farmer-general took over the manor and ran it as if it were his own property, receiving the dues and services owed by the peasants, renting out land, and sometimes farming on his own account. The farmers-general came usually from the bourgeoisie, though sometimes a wealthy peasant joined their ranks. Apparently it was a profitable calling, for the farmers-general prospered. They bought land for themselves from impoverished noblemen, and during the revolutionary era were among the principal purchasers of land confiscated from the church and nobles by the government.[1]

In western Germany and in Switzerland, too, relatively few proprietors engaged in direct farm production. In western Germany those who did nearly always had small demesnes. The largest rarely exceeded 150 to 300 acres, and often they lay scattered among the strips of the peasants. Landowners did take advantage of their special grazing privileges to keep flocks

[1] Louchitsky (1911), 57-59, 69-70; Louchitsky (1933), 131-136; Roupnel (1922), 262-265; Soboul (1957), 296; Bourde (1953), 34n.

of sheep. They also drew considerable income from the woodlands, which (as in France) covered a large part of their properties and which became increasingly valuable as wood prices rose.[2]

Though many more seigniors in central and eastern Germany engaged in direct agricultural production, there was a large number who did not. In Silesia, for example, one out of every three villages had no demesne and many others had only a small amount. Nor did the existence of a demesne necessarily imply that the proprietor himself engaged in farming. Often the owner leased out his demesne, preferring rental income to the uncertainties of direct production. The typical lease in Brandenburg was for six years and typically the lessees were men of the middle class.[3]

In the Austrian Monarchy demesne farming was most common in Bohemia, Moravia, and Austrian Silesia. In the 1840's an estimated one-fifth of all the arable in these provinces, a bit over 30 per cent of all meadows and gardens, and about a third of all the pastures was demesne land. Most of it was consolidated, though sometimes it lay intermingled among the land of the peasants. In the German provinces, the mountainous terrain, and the competition from the Slavic crownlands, which were more favored by nature for farming, limited demesne operations. However, many seigniors there had demesnes, and their number increased through the years as opportunities presented themselves for profitable market production.[4]

In eighteenth-century Denmark demesne occupied about 15 per cent of the tilled land. Only a small part of it was mixed in with peasant land; most of it was consolidated. In Poland involvement of estate owners in farming varied directly with the accessibility of markets. Demesnes were rare in the Carpathians and in eastern Poland. They had been exceptional, too, in southeastern Poland until the construction of canals in the late eighteenth century, and the signing of the treaty of Kuchuk Kainarji in 1774 between Russia and Turkey, which opened Turkish waters to Russian shipping. Grain from southeast Poland could now reach the Black Sea ports, especially the new city of Odessa. Many of the lords of southeast Poland turned to production for the market, and by the late eighteenth century demesnes there occupied an estimated one-third or more of the tilled land. The size of the demesnes varied, but the average ran around 500 acres per manor. Many lords in all parts of Poland rented out their manors and the lessee operated it as if he were the proprietor, with the peasants paying him the obligations they owed to the seignior. These rented estates usually had demesnes.[5]

[2] Lütge (1967), 162-166, 191; Meyer (1965), 38; Hodgskin (1820), II, 79-80; Schmitt (1932), 28; Brentano (1899), 253.

[3] Ziekursch (1927), 63-64; Müller (1967), 117-122.

[4] Blum (1948), 95-96, 150-152.

[5] Skovgaard (1950), 9-10; Nielsen (1933), 150-151, 180; Christensen (1960), 184; Rutkowski (1926), 504; Rutkowski (1927), 69-70; Kostiushko (1954), 178; Zytkowicz (1968), 155.

Nearly every manor in White Russia and Lithuania had a demesne, which usually was separate from the land of the peasants. In the eighteenth century the demesnes had not been extensive: data from the 1750's to 1780's show that they took up between 7 and 13 per cent of the tilled land. Then during the first half of the nineteenth century demesnes expanded rapidly as seigniors became increasingly engaged in production for market. By the 1840's demesnes occupied more than 50 per cent of the arable in more than one-third of the estates of the region, in another third they took up between 30 and 35 per cent, and in one-fifth of the manors between 15 and 30 per cent of the arable. Most of the increase came from land taken under the plow for the first time, rather than from land hitherto held by peasants.[6]

In mid-nineteenth-century Russia most proprietors in the non-black earth provinces, the less fertile zone that lay north of the 55th parallel, drew their revenues from their manors in the form of quitrents and other dues in cash and kind. In the fertile black earth, and especially in the central black earth region and in the Ukraine, most proprietors had demesnes and engaged in direct agricultural production. Generally, the demesne was interspersed among the strips of the peasants, though it was not subject to periodic redistribution as were the strips of the peasants. The available evidence indicates that direct seigniorial production was of less importance, relatively, on manors with over one hundred adult male serfs than it was on smaller properties. Income from the obligations in cash and kind paid by the peasants apparently satisfied many of the larger proprietors and saved them the overhead expenses involved in the operation of demesne. This seemed especially true of the greatest proprietors. For example, in 1838 nearly 75 per cent of the income of Count D. N. Sheremetev came from the payments of the 300,000 serfs who belonged to him. The sale of agricultural produce accounted for only 9 per cent of his income.[7]

In the Danubian Principalities seigniorial agricultural production and demesnes had been unimportant until well into the nineteenth century. Many proprietors leased their estates to large renters, who often were members of the lesser nobility, or rented their land in small pieces to peasants. Because few seigniors engaged in farming on their own account, most peasants could commute their labor services. When lords did demand the obligation, they frequently used it for work other than tillage. In 1831 in Wallachia the peasants in only 156 out of 3,556 villages, or 4.4 per cent, performed labor services on seigniorial demesnes. The unshackling of foreign trade by the Treaty of Adrianople in 1829, the growing demand for grain from the west, and the rising prices drew the attention of proprietors to production for sale. Demesnes grew rapidly as proprietors took over land

[6] Chepko (1964), 390; Pokhilevich (1966), 388.
[7] Koval'chenko (1961), 194, 200; Blum (1961), 395-400.

that they had rented to others and added new land, and peasants were required to perform the labor services they had hitherto commuted.[8]

As could be expected, many of the proprietors who did not engage in direct farm production spent little or no time on their manors. In France most large and medium-sized landowners, whether noble or bourgeois, were absentee owners who, if they resided on their estates at all, did not stay for more than three or four months at a time. Absenteeism, however, was not a universal phenomenon among French proprietors (as Arthur Young discovered on his first arrival in France in 1787). Significantly, in northern France, the best-farmed part of the kingdom, most proprietors lived on their properties and engaged in agricultural activities. Rural residence, however, did not necessarily involve direct seigniorial participation in farming. In Brittany, for example, many nobles lived on their manors but showed no interest in its operations, and contented themselves with the revenues paid them by their peasants and by renters.[9]

Absenteeism was a common phenomenon, too, in central and eastern Europe, even though seigniors there were much more likely to be engaged in agricultural production on their own account. In Bohemia and Hungary the great magnates who owned so much of the land there rarely visited, much less resided on, their many properties. Lesser proprietors, too, were often absentees, as data from the eastern provinces of Prussia indicate. In Poland absenteeism was reportedly relatively uncommon. In the Danubian Principalities, too, most lords lived on their properties, although from the outset of the nineteenth century an increasing number of large proprietors moved into the towns. In Russia absenteeism was widespread, though lesser proprietors were likely to live on their properties.[10]

Involvement in the court, the army, government service, or social life provided the chief reasons for absenteeism. Nobles sought and found the preferments, the power, the honor, and the income, which distinguished them from other men, in careers as courtiers, officers, and bureaucrats. Service in bureaucracy or army kept many Prussian, Russian, and Austrian noblemen away from their properties for years, and even for life. Still others preferred the social and cultural attractions of city residence, whether in the capital or in a provincial town, to living on their estates. Others could not abide absence from the court of the sovereign. Arthur Young told of the duke d'Aiguillon, who had been exiled to his estate in the Garonne for eight years. To occupy himself he engaged in building projects. As soon as the king ended his banishment, Aiguillon hurried back to Versailles and the construction ended, unfinished. "It is thus," wrote

[8] Emerit (1937), 232, 266-268; Corfus (1969), 41-47, 109, 113-115, 190-191; Jonescu (1909), 26.
[9] Roupnel (1922), 280-281; La Monneraye (1922), 41; Avenel (1922), 186-188; Calonne (1920), 157; Young (1970), I, 4; Sée (1906), 49-50.
[10] Conze (1948), 25; Király (1969), 131; Martiny (1938), 37-38; Ziekursch (1927), 47; Kieniewicz (1969), 100; Jonescu (1909), 28; Emerit (1937), 241-242; Blum (1961), 387-388.

Young, "that banishment alone will force the French nobility to execute what the English do for pleasure—reside upon and adorn their estates."[11]

Residence of the proprietor on his manor did not guarantee efficient management or fair treatment of the peasants, any more than absenteeism necessarily produced bad management and excessive exploitation. Absenteeism, however, obviously prevented the establishment of personal relationships and understanding between seignior and peasant, and injustices and inefficiencies that might have been corrected by the proprietor persisted in his absence. Absentee owners entrusted their properties to hired managers. All too often these men abused the trust placed in them. Proprietors who lived on their estates often hired managers, too, but presumably they were in a position to exercise constant supervision of the activities of their stewards.

Although seigniors sometimes appointed one of their own peasants as their steward, they apparently preferred outsiders. They hired men of the lesser nobility or of the bourgeoisie. In Russia and in the Danubian Principalities, proprietors sometimes employed foreigners to manage their estates for them. In France and in Austria, and probably in other lands, too, estate managers formed a special caste and enjoyed a relatively high social status. They married into one another's families and son followed father in the managerial profession. When William Jacob traveled in Poland in 1825, he found that the managers of the estates of the wealthier nobility were usually men of good education, most of them former army officers, who were well acquainted with the writings of central and western European agronomists.[12] Stewards of lesser proprietors, however, were often poorly equipped to handle the tasks assigned to them.[13] Great proprietors who owned many manors sometimes had elaborate administrative organizations, directed from a central office headed by a general director. Each individual estate had its own manager and staff who reported regularly to the central office.[14]

The manager was a salaried employee who received his pay in cash and kind, sometimes supplemented by prerequisites that allowed him to levy fees on the peasants for certain specified activities. Apparently, many managers did not content themselves with the wages paid them—which were sometimes very small. Instead, they used their position to cheat their employers and to steal as much as they could. It was claimed that many of them became wealthy and bought property for themselves with the money they had embezzled.[15] In 1768 a delegate to the Legislative Commission convened by Catherine II to draw up a new law code for Russia blamed the

[11] Young (1970), I, 59.   [12] Jacob (1826), 73.
[13] Brusatti (1958), 513; Emerit (1937), 264; Confino (1969), 74-77.
[14] Stark (1952), 273-274, 277-281; Feigl (1964), 275-276; Rutkowski (1927), 71-72; Blum (1961), 388; Emerit (1937), 264.
[15] Stark (1952), 281; Confino (1969), 44, 70-71; La Monneraye (1922), 44; Roupnel (1922); 281; Paget (1839), II, 314-316; Wilkinson (1971), 132.

low state of Russian agriculture on the lords' passion for luxury and the cupidity of the stewards. It has even been suggested that the revision of the land registers in France in the second half of the eighteenth century was not always evidence of a "feudal reaction." It could also have been an effort to restore orderly management to a long-mismanaged and plundered estate.[16]

Reduction in the income of the proprietor was not the sole ill that resulted from managerial mismanagement and peculation. The peasants suffered even more from managers who exploited them and enriched themselves at their expense. That was why stewards became a special target of peasant hatred. The villagers saw the proprietor infrequently, if at all, and when he did appear it was likely to be in the guise of a Lord Bountiful, giving away small coins and free beer and wine at some feast day. Even the honest steward who acted in his employer's best interest encountered the hatred of the peasants, because he was the highly visible agent of the authority that demanded so much of them. They complained frequently to their seigniors about harsh or unfair treatment they had received at the hands of stewards, and peasant unrest was often directly attributable to managerial exactions and oppression. Prince D. A. Golitsin in a letter of 1765 observed that the Russian peasants who were not under the supervision of a steward were a hundred times better off than those who were. Little or nothing seems to have been done to improve the situation. Yet in France at least, peasant hostility toward stewards was not so excessive as to prevent the election of a number of stewards by peasants to serve as their representatives to the Estates General in 1789.[17]

II

Whether directly involved in agricultural production or whether the receiver of rents and seigniorial dues, the usual noble of the servile lands did not look upon his property as an enterprise to be run for profit. He considered its primary function to be the support of his household—his family and domestic staff. Only the surplus left after meeting his needs went to the market. That included the surplus from his payments in kind, as well as the surplus from his own production. He used the money he received from the sale of his surplus for consumption. If high prices increased his cash income, he spent the additional revenue on luxury wares, or added a new wing to his house. For lesser lords the additional income perhaps paid for a visit with his family to a fashionable spa, or a month's stay in the provincial capital, or even a visit to court. Conspicuous consumption and ostentatious display were matters of great moment to a nobleman. They could determine his social and political status among his peers and affect his own and

[16] Confino (1963a), 72; St. Jacob (1960), 73.
[17] Brusatti (1958), 508-509; Feigl (1964), 290; Confino (1969), 70-71, 73-74, 80; La Monneraye (1922), 44.

his family's fortunes. And so the usual noble showed scant interest in investment in improvements to increase the productivity of his property. That would postpone present consumption, and most nobles did not think in those terms. In any event, the many petty seigniors who in the best of times barely managed to make ends meet, and who lived always in fear of ruin, could not afford to invest for future gains. It did not follow from this attitude of nobles that they were less exploitive of their peasants. Rather, it intensified their demands. Their disinterest in (or ignorance of) investment as the roundabout method to increase their revenues left increased exploitation of their peasants as the way to gain larger incomes.

There were, of course, proprietors who were market-oriented and who wanted to make a profit from their estates. Nobles invested in business enterprises, too; some of the great families of France had money in Flemish mines, forges and iron works, and in the colonial trade. Many proprietors in Schleswig-Holstein, in the Baltic lands, in Prussia and Silesia and in Bohemia were active producers of grain and other commodities for the domestic market and for export to western Europe. The provincial nobility of Bordeaux, Rennes, and Toulouse had long been actively engaged in production for market and were shrewd, profit-oriented businessmen. And there was a small, but as history was to prove, a very influential group of noble proprietors scattered through the servile lands who led in the introduction of innovations designed to increase the productivity of agriculture as well as the revenues of the proprietors.[18]

Whatever their interest or lack of it in commercial agriculture, the fact was that in every land nobles or large renters were by far the chief suppliers of farm goods to the market. The peasants, overburdened by their obligations, were barely able to support themselves from their labors, and usually had little left over for sale. In mid-nineteenth-century Russia, where the nobility was notoriously uninterested in agricultural improvement, only about 15 per cent of the grain crop went to the market. Of that amount an estimated 90 per cent was supplied by noble landowners. Only 10 per cent came from the peasants. In eastern Germany at the end of the eighteenth century most peasants sent less than 20 per cent of their gross yield of animal and plant products to the market, while proprietors sold over half of their output. In France most of the grain and meat on the market was produced by the large renters of seignorial demesne.[19]

Not all of the blame for their lack of enterprise lay with the seigniors themselves. The shortcomings of transportation contributed importantly to the retardation of the market economy. Poor roads that became impassable in bad weather or no roads at all, rivers that inconveniently ran the wrong

[18] McManners (1953), 30; Kellenbenz (1960), 496; Korth (1953), 169; Grünberg (1894), I, 39; Forster (1961), 19-20, 33; Forster (1963), 687.
[19] Liashchenko (1913), 124-125; Nikishin (1953), 178-181; Henning (1969b), 144; Labrousse (1933), I, xxiv.

way or were not navigable for parts of the year, or had shallow or rock-strewn stretches so that cargoes had to be off-loaded and reloaded, weak draft animals and poorly built wagons, and a myriad of tolls, made it difficult, time-consuming, and expensive to transport goods. J. H. von Thünen (1783-1850), German economist and agriculturist, estimated that the cost of shipping a bushel of rye in the early nineteenth century equalled the cost of the rye in 375 kilometers or 233 miles. A sack of rye that sold for 6 to 8 rubles in the provinces of south-central Russia in 1835 sold for as much as 30 rubles in the northwestern province of Pskov. A beef carcass that sold for 15 to 20 rubles in the southern steppes in the mid-nineteenth century cost 50 to 60 rubles in St. Petersburg.[20]

The partial self-sufficiency of urban settlements also served to discourage production for market by rural producers. The townspeople of servile Europe raised much of their own food in gardens and stables in the town, and on fields and pastures in the surrounding countryside.[21] In 1805 in the kingdom of Prussia 9 per cent of the swine, 8 per cent of the cows, 4 per cent of the sheep, 3 per cent of the oxen and bulls, and 3 per cent of the calves were kept in towns and cities. Indeed, the "town" was often that in name and legal status only; in other respects many of them were indistinguishable from a village. Of the 1,106 cities in the kingdom of Prussia in 1800, 118 had fewer than 500 civilian inhabitants (the smallest "city" had 59 people), 276 had between 500 and 1,000, 378 had 1,000 to 2,000, 189 had 2,000 to 5,000, 37 had 5,000 to 10,000, and 18 had over 10,000 civilian inhabitants.[22] Data for 678 cities in Russia in 1856 show that 119 had fewer than 2,000 people, 236 had 2,000 to 5,000, 56 had 5,000 to 15,000. Fifty-seven had 15,000 to 50,000, 7 had 50,000 to 100,000, and three had over 100,000.[23]

III

Earlier pages spoke of the stratification of wealth among the nobles of the servile lands, from men of vast riches to poverty-stricken squireens who were not much better off than their peasants. He who was a lord could not always afford to live like one. The sources of the income of nobles included the revenue from their own farm and forest operations, rental income, dues from their peasants, income from their monopolies, salaries from posts at court, service in the bureaucracy or the military, and pensions granted by the sovereign.

It could be expected that the inefficiency so prevalent in agriculture and

[20] Abel (1967), 169; Tegoborskii (1854), III, 277; Kulischer (1932), 60.
[21] Cf. Bernhard (1915), 7-8; Kulischer (1931), 329, 329n.; Skalweit (1942), 6-9; Buschen (1862), 68; Hodgskin (1820), II, 80-81; Kaplow (1972), 9-11.
[22] Riemann (1953), 62; Krug (1970), II, 62-90. Berlin, the largest city in the Prussian kingdom, had 153,128 inhabitants in 1803.
[23] Tsentral'nyi statisticheskii komitet (1858), 222-224.

in estate management would have severely affected the rate of return received by nobles from the capital investment represented by their manors. The available data are far too exiguous to permit any generalizations. In the Kurmark district of Brandenburg there were in 1800 about 500 nobles who owned rural properties. Around one-seventh of these proprietors had net incomes of 5,000 to 50,000 talers from their land; two-thirds netted between, 1,000 and 5,000 talers (the equivalent of the salary range of high Prussian state officials); 17 per cent received between 500 and 1,000 talers; and about 3 per cent drew less than 500 talers. These figures amounted to a return to the nobles of about 5 per cent on the value of their estates. An analysis made in the 1840's of the net income earned by 3 small, 5 middle-sized, and 2 large estates in the Baltic provinces of Russia showed that 5 of the properties netted from 2.5 to 5 per cent, 2 made between 5 and 5.74 per cent, 2 returned 6.26 and 7.0 per cent, respectively, and one, a small property, returned 13 per cent.[24]

The rise in prices that started in the 1740's and continued on into the early years of the next century increased the cash income of lords who sent goods to market. And, since prices of farm products rose more than did the prices of manufactured wares, the seigniors profited. The price rise also affected forest products, and that benefitted the seigniors, too. Most of the privately owned forests in the servile lands belonged to them. Timber and other forest products became valuable sources of income, especially since forests cost so little to maintain. Usually, the seigniors did not cut and sell their own wood; instead they sold or rented out the right to log in their forests.[25]

Rents went up, too, often even more than prices of farm products, to the benefit of those seigniors who drew much or all of their income from renting out their lands. In France rents doubled, and sometimes rose even more in the course of the second half of the eighteenth century. In Germany they tripled between the 1730's and 1800, with an especially steep climb in the last two decades of the century.[26] The price rise also brought about an increase in the value of the payments in kind made by the peasants. In France, for example, the tithes paid to the church approximately doubled in value in the course of the eighteenth century.[27] On the other hand, the real value of cash dues, whose amount had been fixed long ago, fell as the purchasing power of money declined. In Bohemia customary cash dues lost an estimated 70 per cent in value between the twelfth and seventeenth centuries. The lords of Bohemia, however, were more fortunate than their peers in other lands, who relied more heavily than did the Bohemian seigniors on cash dues. The imposition in Bohemia of labor dues and their

[24] Martiny (1938), 9-10; Kahk (1969), 107-109.
[25] Sée (1906), 42-43; Karpachev (1964), 285; Katus (1961), 151; Schremmer (1963), 90.
[26] Abel (1966), 198; Sée (1939), 179; Gay (1958), 409.   [27] Soboul (1960), 63.

increase from the fifteenth century onward more than compensated the seigniors there for the losses they sustained from the devaluation of money.[28]

Seigniorial monopolies sometimes proved to be valuable sources of income for their proprietors. Data from the second half of the eighteenth century for a number of manors in White Russia and in Bohemia show that between 25 and 40 per cent of the revenues produced by these properties came from monopolies, and especially from the brewing and distilling monopolies. The latter took on increasing importance in the eastern lands during the first half of the nineteenth century as principal sources of seigniorial income.[29] The monopolies on inns and mills, nearly always rented out by the seigniors, proved remunerative, too. Rents from the lessees of inns provided as much as one-half of the gross cash income of many Polish manors in the first half of the nineteenth century.[30] In France the monopoly on mills was an important income producer for seigniors, especially when, as in Brittany, their rentals sometimes rose two and three times over in the course of the eighteenth century. The fines and fees that lords levied in their courts were another and sometimes significant source of seigniorial income, as were the tolls they charged at roads and bridges on their properties, and the taxes they levied upon goods brought in to the markets and fairs in their seigniories.[31] The fees levied by lords when peasants transferred holdings could bring in sizable revenues to large proprietors. Between 1790 and 1804 these payments made up 8.2 per cent of the revenues from manors owned by the Hohenlohes' in their south German principality.[32]

In addition to the revenues generated by their landed possessions and by their seigniorial prerogatives, many nobles received salaries or pensions, and outright gifts of money, land, and, in Russia, of peasants, from their sovereigns. Undoubtedly, many of these people earned their wages for their services as bureaucrats and army officers. But many others did little or nothing for the rewards they received. The courts of kings and princes pullulated with high court officials and counselors, all of whom were well-paid, and many—perhaps most—of whom occupied sinecures. Had they not had these incomes, many noblemen would not have been able to keep up appearances suitable to their station, either because their properties were too small to provide them with an income sufficient for their needs, or because their prodigality exceeded the revenues from their properties, or because they had no land at all. A random listing of 1,700 nobles of Kurmark and

[28] Rosdolski (1951), 260; *cf.* Bloch (1966), 119-120.

[29] Pokhilevich (1966), 391; Stark (1952), 273; Pazhitnov (1940), 240-242; Transehe-Roseneck (1890), 173; Chepko (1964), 395; Kostiushko (1954), 149-150; Blum (1948), 166.

[30] Kieniewicz (1969), 92.

[31] Sée (1906), 134-136; Herbert (1969), 28; La Monneraye (1922), 82-84; Soboul (1960), 124-125.

[32] Schremmer (1963), 89; *cf.* Sée (1906), 114; La Monneraye (1922), 72.

Pomerania in 1767 showed that 1,300 of them depended upon employment by the state for their livelihood, 960 serving as army officers, and 340 in the bureaucracy. Of the 8,000 nobles in Silesia at the end of the eighteenth century, 2,700 had to seek employment because their estates were too small to support them or because they were landless. A study of 2,952 Russian officeholders who served between 1846 and 1854 showed that many of these men had no serfs (as mentioned earlier, landed wealth in Russia was measured in serfs, not acres), including 42 per cent of those who were in the highest grades of the bureaucracy.[33]

The contribution of the different sources of revenue to the total seigniorial income varied, of course, with circumstances. In 1702 the Abbey of St. Denis had an income of 90,000 *livres tournois* (the equivalent of about one million new francs in 1960), of which only 3,300 livres came from its own direct agricultural production. A study of 20 estates near Toulouse showed that seigniorial dues made up only 8 per cent of the average gross annual revenue per estate of 5,750 livres. The sale of grain accounted for 62 per cent, the sale of wood, hay, and wine 25 per cent, and seigniorial monopolies contributed 5 per cent. In 1755 among 68 noble landowning families in the Bordelais, seigniorial dues contributed 5 per cent to the average family income of 12,691 livres; 73 per cent of the aggregate income of the 68 families came from the sale of wine produced by the landowners or by their sharecroppers. In contrast, in the nearby provinces of Aunis and Saintonge seigniorial dues comprised 63 per cent of the income of a group of nobles there. An analysis of 28 estates in Bohemia in 1756-1757 whose combined area covered nearly one-tenth of the province showed that brewing accounted for 40.8 per cent of the aggregate seigniorial income from the properties. Rents provided 22.3 per cent, payments from peasants 13.8 per cent, labor services 13.3 per cent, forest products 5.5 per cent, and fisheries 4.1 per cent. In White Russia in the 1840's as much as 60 to 70 per cent of seigniorial income from their properties came from the sale of their own production, including distilling.[34]

Whatever the sources of their income, most nobles used their income for consumption rather than for investment in their properties. They did not alter that pattern when the rise in farm prices and in rents during the second half of the eighteenth century increased their revenues. The more they made, the more they spent, for as their incomes increased so, too, did the standard of living expected of a nobleman. Lords in Silesia and Saxony and Prussia and Poland and Russia and Hungary and the Danubian Principalities built luxurious manor houses and palaces with rich furnishings, often with gardens and parks in the English style. Over 200 palaces were

[33] Dorn (1932), 263-264; Pintner (1970), 436-440.
[34] Meuvret (1960), 344; Forster (1960), 38; Forster (1961), 23; Forster (1967), 72; Stark (1952), 273; Chepko (1964), 391, 394.

8. Country residence of a grandee. Kuskov, built by Count P. B. Sheremetev, 1713-1787. (L. V. Antonova, *Krepostnye talanty v usad'be Sheremetevykh*, Leningrad, 1964.)

built in Hungary just during the 40 years of Maria Theresa's reign (1740-1780), besides many manor houses and town residences. One of the Esterhazy palaces had 200 rooms and stables for 200 horses. It cost 12 million gulden to build. The palace of the Branickis' in Bialystok, Poland—one of the several they owned—also had space in its stables for 200 horses (and had only 170 books in its library). Noblemen spent vast sums, too, on less durable luxuries, and on all manner of high living, and for the maintenance of swarms of servants.[35] The richer the noble, the more profligate he was likely to be. The income of Count Henry-Charles de Saulx, military governor of Burgundy, amounted to 1,239,953 livres in 1763; his expenditures totalled 1,287,456 livres.[36] In 1838 Count D. N. Sheremetev, probably the richest nobleman in all of Russia, had an income of 2.2 million rubles, and spent 3.4 millions.[37] In 1847 Prince Alois Liechtenstein, one of Austria's greatest proprietors, already heavily in debt, borrowed one million florins. He used most of the loan to pay for renovations of his palace on the Bankgasse in Vienna. The total cost of that renovation reached 3 million florins.[38] Less affluent noblemen spent proportionately less, but they, too, often spent more than their incomes. And so they, together with the great lords, fell into ever deeper debt.

In fairness to the nobility, not all of them were spendthrifts, and reasons other than self-indulgence and conspicuous consumption compelled them to go into debt. A son who inherited an estate frequently had to borrow to

[35] Ziekursch (1927), 43-44; *Cambridge History of Poland* (1941), II, 74-75; Emerit (1937), 33, 242; Blaschke (1965), 266; Király (1969), 29-30.
[36] Roupnel (1922), 285. For other examples of the improvidence of French noblemen see Carré (1920), 80-82; Forster (1971), 119-128.
[37] Blum (1961), 379.   [38] Stekl (1973), 27.

9. The orangery and parterre at Kuskov. (L. V. Antonova, *Krepostnye talanty v usad'be Sheremetevykh*, Leningrad, 1964.)

pay the legacies of the decedent to kinsmen. The need to provide dowries for daughters was often responsible for indebtedness. So were the inadequate salaries paid to many bureaucrats and army officers. Proprietors impoverished by war's devastation and faced with the costs of reconstruction at war's end had no alternative save to borrow. War losses sometimes reached astonishing proportions. After French and Russian armies had passed through the provinces of Grodno and Vilna in Napoleon's invasion of Russia in 1812, incomplete (and possibly inflated) returns showed losses of 131,814 horses and 399,952 head of cattle and draft oxen.[39] The sharp drop in prices at the end of the Napoleonic wars brought heavy debts and ruin to many seigniors. And the small number of proprietors who wanted to introduce improvements on their properties in the hope of increasing their revenues sometimes had to borrow, too, to get the capital they needed for their innovations.

Excessive borrowing by noblemen was an old story. It had gone on for centuries. But in the last decades of the traditional order it reached proportions that helped undermine the continued existence of the nobility as a special and privileged caste. Their burden of debt became so great that many of them lost their properties. In Silesia, for instance, at the end of the 1760's over 400 estates were put up for forced sale to satisfy unpaid debtors.[40] Princes and their counselors recognized the threat presented to the established order by the impoverishment of the nobility and the loss of their manors. So they instituted programs to keep the nobility solvent, and to rescue them from the private money lenders, who charged exorbitant

[39] Leslie (1956), 86.   [40] Ziekursch (1927), 7.

[167]

rates of interest. In Germany already in the seventeenth century, rulers had declared periodic moratoriums on debts, mandated reductions in rates of interest and even in the size of debts, or made special funds available for loans or subsidies. In 1765 Frederick II of Prussia ordered a moratorium of three years on the repayment of loans by Silesian noblemen. It is doubtful that Frederick's decree helped; many Silesian nobles used the grace period to borrow still more.[41]

Starting in the second half of the eighteenth century, rulers took more positive measures. In Russia the government established a Nobles' Bank in 1754, in subsequent years broadened credit sources available to the nobility, and in the Charter of the Nobility of 1785 granted permission to the newly authorized assemblies of the nobility of each province to organize provincial banks to lend to nobles. The nobles borrowed not against their land but against their adult male serfs, or "souls." At the outset the maximum loan per soul from a state lending institution could not exceed 10 rubles. By 1804 the limit had gone up to 60 rubles. The first lending institution for nobles in Germany was founded in Silesia in 1770, as part of the effort to help the nobility there recover from the setbacks it had suffered in the Seven Years War. Frederick II authorized the Silesian provincial estates to establish a land mortgage bank that would lend up to two-thirds of the assessed value of a nobleman's estate. The bank issued transferable mortgage bonds bearing 5 per cent interest. The bonds were backed by the property of all of the noble members of the Silesian estates. The advantages and security of the new organization attracted capital, and the interest rate the bank charged dropped from 6 per cent in 1769 to 4 per cent in 1791. The Silesian land bank proved so successful that it served as a model for the creation of similar institutions in succeeding decades in most of the other provinces of Prussia. In 1825 a bank of the Silesian type opened in Poland, and by 1853 three-quarters of all the estates in the Kingdom of Poland owed money to it. In 1830 the tsar gave his permission for the establishment of a credit union in Courland that began activity in 1832. Noble estates in the German and Slav provinces of the Austrian Monarchy repeatedly petitioned the throne in the years after 1815 to allow them to organize mortgage banks on the Silesian model. The government refused all but one of these requests. It feared that the issuance of the bonds of these banks would attract investors who might otherwise purchase the government's own securities. The one exception was the approval given in 1841, after long years of hesitation, to the establishment by the Galician estates of a mortgage bank.[42]

The new banks doubtless proved of economic value to noblemen who

[41] Abel (1964), 56; Ziekursch (1927), 7; Borovoi (1948), 73-76; Marczali (1910), 125-126.
[42] Russia: Blum (1961), 382-384. Silesia: Ziekursch (1927), 8; Frauendorfer (1957), ɪ, 188. Poland: Kostiushko (1954), 177. Courland: Creutzburg (1910), 42-49. Austria: Blum (1948), 116-124.

borrowed to introduce improvements in the operation of their properties. For most seigniors, however, the lenient lending policies adopted by the banks and the low interest rates acted as incentives to incur still more debts. And since the purpose of these banks was to save their estates for the nobles, they were loathe to foreclose. Instead, they readily gave extensions so that delinquents could remain in possession. The consequence of such a policy could be expected: the indebtedness of the nobility climbed at a dizzying pace. Of 156 estates scattered through Silesia, 73 had been free of debt in 1750, and the total indebtedness of the other 83 amounted to 449,000 *Reichstaler*, or an average of 5,410 *Reichstaler* per estate. By 1800 only 18 of the 156 properties were free of mortgages, and the aggregate debt of the other 138 amounted to 1,764,500 *Reichstaler*, or an average of 12,786 *Reichstaler* per property. In the Hungarian county of Pest, mortgages on land owned by nobles increased from 964,229 *forints* in 1780-1789 to 2,282,386 *forints* in 1830-1839. In Russia by 1820 1.8 million, or 20 per cent of all adult male serfs were mortgaged with credit institutions of the state for a total of 110 million assignat rubles. By 1859 7.1 million or 66 per cent of all adult male serfs were mortgaged with these institutions, and the total debt had climbed to 425 million credit rubles. (The assignat ruble, the paper money first issued in 1769, was replaced by credit rubles, also paper money, in 1843.) The increase in debt was even greater than these figures indicate since the assignat ruble was equal to about one-fourth of a silver ruble, while the credit ruble in 1859 equalled about nine-tenths of a silver ruble. In addition, nobles owed great amounts of money to nongovernmental sources; official data for Russia for 1842 showed that nobles there had mortgaged 2.1 million of their serfs with private lenders.[43]

As the mortgage debt piled up, its relation to the value of the mortgaged property climbed. In 1750 in Silesia 62 estates in the Lüben district had no mortgages; by 1800 mortgages on these properties amounted to 58 per cent of their value, and by 1825 the ratio had climbed to 92 per cent. By 1806 the noble-owned manors in the Neumark district of Brandenburg were mortgaged up to 72 per cent of their purchase prices and 106 per cent of their assessed value. In Poland in 1824 mortgages on noble properties amounted to 62 per cent of their value. Only 7 per cent of the manors had no mortgage, 28 per cent were mortgaged up to one-fourth of their value, 20 per cent up to one-half, 18 per cent up to three-quarters, 11 per cent were mortgaged up to their full value, and 16 per cent had mortgages greater than the value of the property.[44]

Debt became so general among the nobility that it became a way of life for many of them. It seemed as if the chief value to them of a property was

[43] Ziekursch (1927), 54; Ivanyi (1960), 284-285n; Blum (1961), 380; Koval'chenko (1961), 201.
[44] Ziekursch (1927), 56; Abel (1966), 204; Kostiushko (1954), 176.

that money could be borrowed against it. English and American observers were appalled by the calm acceptance among the elite of living beyond one's means. William Jacob in his report to Parliament in 1825 reported that Polish landowners spoke about their debts "with as much coolness as an English farmer would speak of his rent, tithe and taxes." John Quincy Adams, American minister to St. Petersburg from 1809 to 1814, in a letter to his mother in 1810 wrote that "The tone of society among us is almost universally marked by an excess of expenses over income." He explained that many officials were notorious for never paying their debts and "for preserving the balance by means which in our country would be deemed dishonorable, but which are here much less disreputable than economy."[45]

The sharp rise in the price of land and the accompanying acceleration in turnover of ownership introduced another factor that served to destabilize the privileged position of the nobility. Between 1740-1760 and 1801-1805 the average price of manors went up by 225 per cent in Silesia, 310 per cent in Schleswig-Holstein, and 394 per cent in Brandenburg. In Livonia land prices increased by over 150 per cent between 1761-1770 and 1806-1810. In France land prices nearly doubled between the early years and the last part of the eighteenth century.[46] In some individual instances the price rise far exceeded the average increase. An estate in Upper Silesia changed owners ten times between 1761 and 1797, with the sale price increased at each transaction, going from 13,667 *Reichstaler* in 1761 to 79,500 *Reichstaler* in 1797. A property in Kurmark sold for 6,900 *Reichstaler* in 1706, 17,800 *Reichstaler* in 1779, and 32,300 in 1794. The price of an East Prussian estate that had eight different owners between 1754 and 1804 increased from 23,300 to 140,000 *Reichstaler*.[47]

The price rise in land tempted debt-ridden proprietors to sell, and thereby rid themselves of their oppressive burden of debt. The availability of easy credit tempted others to speculate by buying estates with borrowed money and depend on a quick turnover to make a profit. Estates changed owners so frequently that a Silesian observed in 1788 that the commerce in manors was "almost like horse-trading." Estates that had been in the same family for two and three centuries were sold and resold two, three, and even six times in little more than a decade, with a higher sale price at each transaction. In the Mecklenburg 49 manors were sold in the decade 1770-1779. In 1790-1799, 327 were sold. In Livonia only 8 estates were sold in the years 1765-1770. Eighty-four were sold between 1796 and 1800. In Kurmark between 1801 and 1825, one out of every six estate owners was involved in the sale of land. One manor there had five owners between 1800 and 1804, with the purchase price going up from 12,000 talers in 1800 to 22,000 talers in 1804.[48]

[45] Jacob (1826), 81; Ford (1914), III, 396; *cf.* Forster (1971), 114-116.
[46] Abel (1967), 331; Transehe-Roseneck (1890), 175; Avenel (1927), 259.
[47] Ziekursch (1927), 58; Krug (1970), I, 408.
[48] Abel (1966), 203; Schwabe (1928), 288; Martiny (1938), 32-33; *cf.* Richter (1964), 60.

The seigniors, as earlier pages pointed out, were by far the principal suppliers of farm goods to the market. The great mass of the peasantry were outside of the market nexus, or at most were involved in a highly localized market system. They lived in small villages that had only rudimentary commercial machinery. Theirs was an economy that lived almost completely off its own resources. They had a traditional skill in making use of these resources, which included materials that seemed of trifling value to others. They had little use for money, aside from that which they needed to pay cash dues to their seigniors and taxes to the sovereign. The primary, and indeed, often the sole purpose of their holdings was to meet their own needs. The small size of so many holdings, the burden of dues and taxes, and the low level of productivity gave them no other choice. In France an estimated 600,000 peasants, at the most, out of about 4 million with holdings, produced for the market in the 1780's.[49] In Germany at the beginning of the nineteenth century only between 20 per cent and 30 per cent of the peasants with land produced for the market. In years of normal yields they offered about 25 per cent of their crops for sale. Crop failures, however, came so frequently that over the years the average amount they sent to the market was much less than 25 per cent.[50] Peasants who brought goods to market often offered pathetically small amounts for sale. "I was in Frankfurt on market day," wrote William Jacob in 1820, "and observed there, as I had done in many other parts of Germany, how much it was crowded with the peasants offering their commodities for sale in very small quantities. Some had a few apples, plums, pears, or grapes, the whole value of which could not be more than three-pence or four-pence. I remarked many with not more than half a peck of peas or beans, or a peck of oats. Several women were sitting in the market with small bundles of hay before them of ten pounds weight each, a few with more than five or six of them."[51] Peasants who had goods to sell did not always carry them to market. They sold them to their seigniors or to large renters who sent the wares to market. They sold produce, too, to middlemen who travelled through the countryside to buy goods from lords and peasants alike.[52]

There were exceptions to the general unimportance of peasants in the market place. In some regions, among them southwest Germany, Switzerland, parts of Wallachia, French Flanders, the district around Königsberg in East Prussia, and around Moscow, peasants were major suppliers of foodstuffs to the nearby towns. Nor was peasant market activity restricted to local markets. For example, peasants in Mecklenburg raised fruit for ex-

---

[49] Forster (1970), 1604.
[50] Henning (1969a), 40; Henning (1969b), 143-145, 173; Müller (1967), 148-154.
[51] Jacob (1820), 402.
[52] Corfus (1969), 55; Forster (1970), 1604, Transehe-Roseneck (1908), 130.

port, much of it going to St. Petersburg, prosperous peasants in Haders-leben in Schleswig shipped as many as fifty heads of cattle at a time to Holland, Swiss peasants drove their cattle to distant fairs, some Wallachian peasants sold their sheep to foreign buyers, and in Russia by the mid-nineteenth century peasant output of flax, hemp, and potatoes helped meet the demand for those commodities of both the domestic and the foreign market.[53]

The overall unimportance of peasants as producers of farm goods for the market was to some degree counterbalanced by their activity in rural industry. In the last century of the old order, more and more of them turned to that branch of production to help piece out their livelihoods. Peasants had always manufactured wares in their own homes to meet their own needs or to sell or barter to their neighbors, some had worked in forges and mines and other rural industries, and in some regions manufacture for sale beyond the village borders had a long history. But now the numbers of those who involved themselves in home manufacture of goods for sale swelled. The increase in population, and the resulting pressure on the limited resources of land, meant that now there was a surplus of workers who could not earn their livings from agriculture alone. At the same time the expansion of the market for manufactured goods, and in some lands the abolition or dilution of gild restrictions and of limitations upon freedom of entry into trades, encouraged the growth of rural industry. Peasants who lived on the margins of village society—day laborers, charcoal burners, widows, and orphans—turned to industrial occupations. More prosperous peasants, too, were attracted to manufacturing as full-time or part-time workers. In Saxony spinners, weavers, miners, and other industrial workers made up 18 per cent of the rural population in 1550, 38 per cent in 1750, and 52 per cent by 1843. In Silesia 19,810 looms were in use in 1748. By 1790 their number had increased to 28,704, with more than 50,000 peasants employed in weaving. Of the 170,000 inhabitants of the canton of Zurich in 1787, over one-fourth were engaged, many of them full-time, in the manufacture of cotton and silk wares. Rural industry in France, especially textile manufacture, expanded rapidly in the last two decades of the old regime there. At the beginning of the nineteenth century an estimated 70,000 peasants in Bohemia and 50,000-60,000 in Upper Austria worked in their cottages, spinning yarn for wool cloth manufacturers. In Russia peasant manufacturing had a spectacular growth from the second half of the eighteenth century.[54]

Rural industry flourished especially in regions of marginal and sub-

[53] Lütge (1967), 192; Rappard (1912), 206-207; Corfus (1969), 55; Henning (1969a), 75; Lefebvre (1972), 244; Blum (1961), 391-392; Mager (1955), 293-294; Arnim (1957), 65.
[54] Saxony: Blaschke (1967), 233-234. Silesia: Kisch (1959), 546. Zurich: Bollinger (1951), 48-49. France: Tarlé (1910), 8-12; Hufton (1974), 38-42. Bohemia and Upper Austria: Brusatti (1965), 279; Hoffmann (1952), 323. Russia: Tugan-Baranovsky (1970), 171-214.

marginal agriculture, such as the mountain districts of Silesia, Bohemia, Upper Austria, the Swiss Alps, Haute-Loire in south central France, and in the non-black earth provinces of Russia. It took root, too, in more fertile areas with heavy populations where peasants had too little land to support themselves from farming alone, and where the numbers of those without any land steadily increased. In the rich farm country of French Flanders, Hainault, Artois, Cambresis, and Picardy, the manufacture of textiles gave employment in 1795 to 1.5 million cottage workers, and others worked in rural industries such as tanneries, forges, and glassworks.[55] In other regions, rural manufacture for sale was all but unknown. Data assembled in 1769 by the Prussian Commission-General of Commerce showed that, excluding Silesia, rural industrial workers made up only 10 per cent of the total number of persons occupied in manufacturing in the entire kingdom. Ninety-two per cent of this rural work force were concentrated in three small districts in the western part of the kingdom, two of them in Westphalia and one in the Rhine Province.[56]

As time went on, cottage industry sometimes came to dominate certain branches of production, and even became the most important sector in the entire manufacturing industry of a country. That happened in Russia. Though exact data are lacking, it is clear that the number of people engaged there in cottage industry, and the value of their output, far exceeded both number and value of production of the factory and urban artisan work force. The predominance continued until well into the second half of the nineteenth century. The manufacture of linen, exclusively a cottage industry, became the most important part of Prussian textile manufacture after the annexation of Silesia in 1740. Linen held first place among Prussia's chief manufactured exports on into the nineteenth century. In France, peasant industry assumed major importance after governmental edicts of the 1760's and 1770's freed peasant manufacturing from restrictions that had fettered it. Cottage industry now took over leadership in the cloth industry, to the detriment of the towns in which the industry had centered. For example, in 1766 Valenciennes in northern France, long a major producer of woolens, turned out 48,228 pieces of fine wool cloth. Then merchants began to put out work to peasants in the surrounding countryside, and by 1789 the town's output had plummeted to 5,448 pieces. In 1788 the cloth industry of Elbeuf, center of woolens manufacture in Normandy, employed 15,300 workers, of whom at least two-thirds were peasants of the surrounding countryside. The Swiss textile industry, one of the most important in eighteenth-century Europe, was overwhelmingly rural; for example, in the canton of Basel, center of ribbon manufacture, 2,246 out of the 2,268 ribbon looms in the canton were in the cottages of peasants.[57]

[55] Lefebvre (1972), 281-288; Tarlé (1910), 43.   [56] Hoffmann (1969), 34-35.
[57] Russia: Blum (1961), 301-303. Prussia: Henderson (1963), 138-139. France: Kulischer

Spinning and weaving held undisputed first place among rural industries. Both could be done at odd times during the entire year and all members of the family could participate in the manufacturing process. Wool was the usual raw material, but linen, made often from flax grown and prepared by the peasant himself, was in many places the principal textile produced by countrymen. In Russia cotton weaving took on increased importance as a cottage industry from the end of the eighteenth century, and by the mid-nineteenth century its output far exceeded factory production of cotton cloth. A few regions specialized in silks or in lace. Other rural industries included most other branches of manufacturing and metallurgy, including such specialized products as clocks, toys, gloves, and needles.

Most peasants engaged in cottage industry to supplement their incomes from agriculture. For these people manufacturing was a spare-time or winter occupation; often it provided work for the women, the children, and the elderly of the household. As rural industry grew in importance, however, and as the numbers of landless or nearly landless villagers increased, a growing number of peasants became full-time industrial workers. They either abandoned agriculture, or relegated it to a secondary or subsidiary occupation.

Some peasants produced their manufactured goods directly for the market. They sold their wares themselves to customers in their home village or nearby market, or they sold them to merchants who travelled through the countryside buying up the products made by the villagers. Most peasants, however, worked for an entrepreneur under the domestic or putting-out system. The entrepreneur, usually a townsman but sometimes another peasant, provided the cottage workers with raw materials or semi-processed goods, and paid them a wage for the work they did. The scale was nearly always less than that paid to town labor. Peasants, and especially those for whom cottage industry was a supplementary source of income, were willing to work for less pay. That, of course, encouraged the entrepreneurs to use rural cottage workers.[58]

Townsmen were well aware of the threat of rural competition. For a long time, through the requirement of membership in gilds and other restrictive legislation, they succeeded in hobbling cottage industry. In the second half

(1971), II, 122-123; Lefebvre (1972), 284; Kaplow (1964), 291; Sion (1909), 181-186. Switzerland: Kulischer (1971), II, 125; Schmitt (1932), 73-74.

[58] France: Lefebvre (1972), 288-290; Kaplow (1964), 29-32; Tarlé (1910), 12, 15-16; Sée (1906), 71; Goubert (1956), 60; Sheppard (1971), 27. Germany: Henderson (1963), 138-139, 146-147; Henning (1969b), 160; Hodgskin (1820), II, 155, 157; Kellenbenz (1962), 22-25; Blaschke (1967), 231-234. Switzerland: Bollinger (1941), 49-51; Braun (1960), 55; Walter (1966), 93. Poland: Revesz (1964), 284. Danubian Principalities: Corfus (1969), 57; Emerit (1937), 260-261. Austria: Klíma (1974), 50-51; Hoffmann (1952), 313; Zenker (1897), 25-26. Russia: Tugan-Baranovsky (1970), 40, 174-175, 178-180, 187-191; Razgon (1959), 213-215, 239-240; Meshalin (1950), 27-28; Ministerstvo Gosudarstvennykh Imuchestv (1858), I, 31-34, II, 75.

of the eighteenth century, however, legislative action either lessened or abolished the restrictions, or peasants simply evaded them. In France, as mentioned earlier, legislation in the 1760's and 1770's ended limitations on peasant cottage industry. Now peasants could manufacture goods without having to join the gild corporations to which town artisans had to belong. The villagers were supposed to abide by the rules that regulated production in each branch of manufacturing. Rural industry, however, was so dispersed that surveillance was impossible, and peasants freely disregarded the regulations. Their avoidance of the rules struck a fatal blow at the whole elaborate structure of corporations, and reduced their regulations to dead letters even in the towns, by the end of the *ancien régime*. In the Rhine Province of Prussia, entrepreneurs in Aachen, major woolens center of the region, in defiance of city authorities and gild rules put out work with villagers. In Silesia gilds tried and failed to limit the manufacture of linen in the countryside. In the central and eastern provinces of Prussia the gilds met with more success. With the cooperation of the government they were able to restrict manufacture for sale largely to the towns (which helps to explain the unimportance, noted earlier, of rural industry in those regions). Peasants who engaged in cottage industry in these provinces were expected to join the gild in the nearest town. Actually, many of these people did not become gild members and the government did not exert itself to compel compliance with the law. In Denmark the law code of Christian V in 1683 forbad industry outside the towns, except for certain specified and typically rural occupations. As time wore on, however, the ban was not rigidly enforced. In the Hapsburg Monarchy reforms that began in the 1770's and that were intensified during the reign of Joseph II in the 1780's progressively weakened gild restrictions and monopolies. In Russia gilds never became important. However, special privileges and monopolies had so restricted manufacturing and commerce that cottage industry was actually illegal, though peasants engaged in it. Then in the 1760's and 1770's a series of legislative acts freed manufacturing (as well as domestic commerce) from all restrictions. The establishment of free entry into manufacturing and trade sparked the great expansion in cottage industry in Russia referred to earlier.[59]

The involvement of peasants in industrial activity depended often upon the nature and quantity of the obligations they owed to their seigniors. If the lords engaged extensively in farm production, and so demanded excessive labor services, the peasants did not have the time to manufacture goods for sale. They had to use the time they could call their own to grow the food

[59] France: Tarlé (1910), 4-7, 63, 80; Sion (1909), 178-180. Rhineland: Kisch (1964), 523-525. Silesia: Kisch (1959), 543. Prussia: Hoffmann (1969), 32, 36-37, 84 n.30; 89 n.100; Skalweit (1942), 41-50. Denmark: Kellenbenz (1962), 21. Austria: Pribram (1907), i, 362-374. Russia: Tugan-Baranovsky (1970), 33-35; Blum (1961), 288-290, 302.

they needed for their sustenance. If, however, the seigniors, such as those of the non-black earth provinces of Russia, were relatively inactive in farm production on their own account and commuted the heavy labor obligations of their peasants into quitrents, the peasants were free to work in industry and commerce. In Silesia, too, seigniors commuted all or part of the heavy labor obligation. The peasants there paid their dues in money, or in yarn or linen that the seigniors sold. It is not surprising that these Russian and Silesian lords strongly supported the abolition of restrictions on manufacturing and commerce.[60]

Proprietors adopted a quite different attitude in regions where the labor obligation, when it existed, was only a few days a year, and where the proprietors, or those who rented from them, engaged in agricultural production. They had to depend upon hired workers to fill their needs for labor. Cottage industry interfered with this labor supply because the peasant could earn more in manufacturing than he could as a hired farm hand. In Picardy agricultural labor was paid 12 to 15 sous a day, while cottage workers earned 15 to 25 sous, and some specially skilled workers could make as much as 40 sous a day. Similar differentials in other parts of France explain why seigniors sought to impose restrictions on cottage industry. The *parlement* of Rouen in Normandy in 1749 forbad the putting out of work to peasants from the opening day of harvest until 15 September, and ordered the excessively heavy fines of 500 livres for entrepreneurs who disregarded the prohibition, and 100 livres for the peasant who accepted the work. The central government in Paris, however, worked at cross-purposes to the seigniors. It supported cottage industry in order to give the peasants the opportunity to increase their incomes (and so be able to pay more taxes). The government not only liberalized the corporate restrictions but actively encouraged peasants to enter cottage industry. Thus, it supported the growth of the silk industry among peasants, and distributed spinning wheels to promote the manufacture of hemp, flax, and cotton yarn; between 1760 and 1775 it gave out over 1,500 spinning wheels just in Limousin.[61]

The impact of rural industry on the labor supply was only one of its effects upon rural society. In districts where a large proportion of the population earned their living from rural industry, severe tensions developed between these people and those who depended primarily upon agriculture. The industrial peasants had little or no reason to concern themselves with the problems and the operations of communal agriculture, or with the preservation of the village communal organization and its communal agricul-

[60] Pokhilevich (1966), 396-397; Henderson (1963), 139-140; Kisch (1959), 543; Kahan (1966), 55; Tugan-Baranovsky (1970), 33-34.
[61] McCloy (1946), 270-271; Tarlé (1910), 21, 34-36; Sion (1909), 186-189; Kuczynski (1967), xxxii, 75, 75n.

tural resources.[62] Sometimes, though, cottage industry served to advance agriculture. That happened in villages in Zurich, where peasants used revenues from their manufacturing to introduce improvements in farming that raised productivity, and thereby increased their overall income.[63]

The peasant who took goods to market nearly always sold wares he had made himself, and when he disposed of his goods he returned home. A few peasants, however, became full-time traders, dealing in goods they bought from other peasants. They were peddlers who came to villages and isolated farmsteads with their wares in a backpack or in a pannier hanging from their shoulders. Some of these itinerant merchants travelled long distances, spending most of the year away from their home villages. Town merchants and their gilds complained about this competition, but their protests were in vain. The peasant trader filled a need that the town merchant could not meet. A few among these peddlers, specially gifted with business acumen, built up large trading enterprises.[64]

[62] Blum (1971a), 175.   [63] Braun (1960), 53, 176.
[64] Babeau (1878), 71-83; Zopfi (1947), 50; Redlich (1955), 69-70; Bruchet (1908), xxxviii-xxxix; Blum (1961), 288-291.

CHAPTER 9

The Condition of the Peasantry

I

THE low yields and frequent crop failures, the increased pressure of population on the land, the encroachments of seigniors on peasant land, and the burden of obligations to lord and state, all conspired to make peasant life an unceasing struggle to survive. For many villagers the struggle must have become more difficult in the last century of the old order than it had ever before been because of the mounting demands made of them, the simultaneous decrease in the amount of land available to most households, and the prodigious growth in the number of cotters and landless peasants.

Lack of data makes it impossible to measure the extent of deterioration in the condition of the peasantry, but a sampling of contemporary observers reflects the poverty, misery, and deprivation that was the lot of most of them. In 1692 Robert Molesworth, then English ambassador to the court of Denmark, reported that the peasants in the province of Zealand "are all as absolute slaves as the Negroes in the Barbadoes, but with this difference, that their Fare is not so good." In the mid-eighteenth century Auroux des Despommiers wrote of the peasants of Haut-Poitou that "misery appears in a thousand forms; the laborers, broken under the weight of their misfortunes, seem to be a different species than ordinary men; competition and the ambition to work are stifled by the impossibility of reaching any comfort; they see about them nothing but distress. . . ." A report by an Imperial commission on Bohemia in the famine year of 1771 told of poverty so extreme that people went about half-naked, of widespread disease, of children stunted and deformed by illness and inadequate diet, and of the filth and stench of the peasants' huts. Nearly eighty years later a writer declared that the want and misery of the peasants who lived in the mountains of Bohemia was beyond description. Time and again as Arthur Young traveled through France on the eve of the Revolution, he noted the extreme poverty in which so many peasants lived. An account in 1792 of life among the Wends, the Slavic people of Upper Lusatia in Saxony, reported that hordes of these people were reduced to begging, and that their huts were not much better than cattle sheds. Another account, this one in 1818, told of children of six and eight who went barefoot even in the snows of winter, and who slept on straw or on the ground. As soon as they could stand alone, children there were put to work, in a work day that lasted from four in the morning until eight at night.[1]

[1] Denmark: Molesworth (1694), 79. Bohemia: Stark (1937), 417; Violand (1850), 36. France: Debien (1945), 133; Young (1970), I, 12, 18, 98, 148, 402. Saxony: Boelcke (1957), 200-201.

The peasants of Switzerland had the reputation among contemporaries of being well off. A German traveler in the 1780's wrote that "It is known that in all Europe with the exception of England and Holland, there is no more fortunate peasant than in Switzerland." Actually, many Swiss peasants lived in great want. In a modern study of the canton of Zurich in the eighteenth century, the author, after presenting data that showed the appallingly large number of paupers among the peasants there, observed that "the numbers alone do not tell the need, the misery and the hopelessness of these wretchedly poor people."[2] Masterly surveys of three regions of France in the eighteenth century—Brittany, the department of Nord (in which lay some of France's richest farmland), and northern Burgundy—found that the largest part of the peasantry in each of these regions lived in deepest poverty and misery. Worst of all, peasants despaired of being able to improve their condition. A *cahier* of a community of the Nord department pointed out that nine-tenths of its land belonged to the seignior and then declared that "the rest of the community is condemned to remain eternally miserable." Another peasant *cahier* concluded bitterly that "It seems that it is a settled matter that the poor will remain poor."[3]

The dwellings of the peasants reflected their poverty—and often their apathy and sloth. Many lived in houses of earth or of wattle and daub, that is, clay mixed with straw and pressed into a matting of reeds or willow twigs. An official survey in Romania showed that as late as 1906, 31 per cent (257,457) of the rural dwellings there were wattle and daub, and another 29 per cent (242,537), were made of earth alone. John Quincy Adams, then American minister to Prussia, described the peasant huts he saw in 1800 as he traveled through Brandenburg from Berlin to Frankfurt-on-Oder as a "meagre composition of mud and thatch . . . in which a ragged and pallid race of beggars reside." Arthur Young saw some earthen houses in lower Brittany and called them "miserable heaps of dirt." But earthen houses did not have to be hovels. When Young rode through the Cotentin peninsula of Normandy his attention was caught by "the best mud houses I ever saw, excellent habitations, even of three stories." Earth well kneaded with straw was cut into 9-inch squares that were laid atop one another to build walls that were about 2 feet thick.[4] In the plainland of Hungary and the Danubian Principalities peasants hollowed out underground burrows for their homes. A traveler in Hungary in the 1840's saw dugouts on the shores of Lake Balaton that were entered by a sloping path. Straw roofs covered the burrows, which frequently had no opening save doorway and chimney, and were, he wrote, "as filthy and miserable as can well be imagined."[5] In Romania in 1912 there were still 32,367 of these dwellings.[6]

[2] Hauser (1965), 137; Braun (1960), 229-230; see also Walter (1960), 90-91.
[3] Sée (1906), 491; Lefebvre (1972), 292-298; St. Jacob (1960), 553.
[4] Mitrany (1930), 484; Adams (1804), 3; Young (1970), 96-97, 99.
[5] Paget (1839), I, 256-257.   [6] Mitrany (1930), 484.

10. Underground peasant dwellings in Hungary. (J. Paget, *Hungary and Transylvania*, London, 1839.)

In the forested regions that covered so much of Europe, wood served as the primary building material. In hardwood zones the houses often were half-timbered. The spaces between the wood framework were filled with wattle and daub or other locally available materials, including stone or brick. In the great coniferous forest belt of northern Europe, the dwellings were nearly always entirely of wood. The chinks between the log walls were filled with mud and clay, and even manure, and in winter the house was banked around with branches to keep out the cold. In northern Russia roofs sometimes extended beyond the sides of the house to protect its residents from the summer's sun and the winter's cold.[7] Roofs were covered with thatch made of straw or reeds, and sometimes with tiles or wooden shingles. In eastern Germany (and doubtless elsewhere) the wandering thatch maker and mender was a familiar figure. Windows, nearly always small and few in number, were usually covered with paper or other materials, some of them of curious nature, such as bull bladders in southern Russia.[8]

House design often followed regional patterns in external appearance and in floor plan. A study of German peasant houses in the nineteenth century showed five major types of house design, each extending over a large area of central Europe, and with clear geographical lines of demarcation between each style. In European Russia, too, geographical areas had their own distinctive house design. Colonists sometimes brought their old house styles with them to the new regions into which they settled. The Germans who migrated east of the Elbe into Mecklenburg built houses of Saxon design. When Baron von Haxthausen visited German colonies in southern Russia in 1843, the dwellings (and everything else) looked so familiar that he felt as if he were back in his native Germany.[9]

[7] Houston (1963), 116-122; Malthus (1966), 30; Hodgskin (1820), II, 143; Porter (1809), 177-178; Sion (1909), 466-469; *Village of Viriatino* (1970), 58; Ziekursch (1927), 142.

[8] Young (1970), 449, 450; *Village of Viriatino* (1970), 59; Sée (1939), 208; Zelenin (1926), 264-265; Knapp (1887), I, 251; Sombart (1928), II, pt. 2, 666.

[9] Henning (1882), *passim*; Mager (1955), 52-53, 331-332; *Russkie istoriko-etnograficheskii atlas* (1967), 152-156; Matosian (1968), 4-8; Haxthausen (1847), II, 172.

Well-to-do peasants built comfortable homes for themselves, often of stone and brick and sometimes with elaborate decorations and expensive furnishings. But well-to-do peasants were very much the exception. Most peasants lived in huts that were small, low, uncomfortable, and unhealthy. Many had only one room, or one room used as living quarters and a second room that served for storage or as a stable. Not infrequently the floor was dirt. The hut held a few pieces of crude furniture that included a table, benches along the wall, a shelf or two and perhaps a cupboard, and, especially in eastern Europe, a large stove that took up much space in the crowded room. A traveler in Wallachia saw wooden troughs in the cabins he visited, which served variously as cradle, washtub, kneading trough, and, when not otherwise in use, receptacle for provisions. Frequently there was no chimney, and the walls were blackened by smoke that could escape only through a hole poked in the roof or in a wall. The small windows let in little light, so that the hut's interior was dark, damp, and gloomy. Lighting often was provided by burning pine sticks or, in regions without pine, laths of birch and aspen.

The shortcomings of design and of furnishings were only parts of the discomforts of rural home life. Many peasants shared their one or two room huts with their animals. Pigs, ducks, chickens, and calves lived together with their owners. Larger animals usually were in nearby sheds or lean-tos. A mid-nineteenth century correspondent of the Russian Geographical Society reported that during the winter a peasant in Tambov in south-central Russia might keep 10 to 15 lambs with their mothers in his hut, 2 or 3 pigs and their progeny, 2 or 3 calves, sometimes a young colt, and would lead his cows into the hut to be milked. "In the evening," wrote the correspondent in a gem of an understatement, "the air in the hut was not too bad, but in the morning before the oven was lit and the door opened, it was stifling." The peasants slept on benches around the wall, or on the floor, or on planks set between oven and roof. In summer they often slept out of doors, and to keep warm in cold winter nights they might curl up beside the cow or the horse in the straw of the animal shed.[10]

In light of this style of living it is scarcely surprising that contemporary observers were overwhelmed by the filth, stench, vermin, and general wretchedness that they encountered. An official of the French government, after visiting peasant houses in Normandy in 1805, reported that they "resembled more foul dungeons than houses inhabited by useful and honest citizens." John Quincy Adams could not contain his disgust with what he

[10] Denmark: Malthus (1966), 43; Arnim (1957), 65. Switzerland: Winkler (1941), 55. Danubian Principalities: Noyes (1858), 99, 162. Germany: Franz (1970a), 228-229; Lengerke (1847), 91; Ziekursch (1927), 142; Adams (1804), 94; Hodgskin (1820), 143; Knapp (1887), I, 251. France: Calonne (1920), 440-441; Babeau (1883), 12; Sée (1906), 459-460; Hufton (1974), 50; Sion (1909), 474-475. Austria: Stark (1937), 417; Stark (1957), 37. Poland: Jacob (1826), 65. Russia: Johnston (1970), 164-165; Zelenin (1926), 263-264, 280; *Village of Viriatino* (1970), 58-60; Lyall (1970), 61.

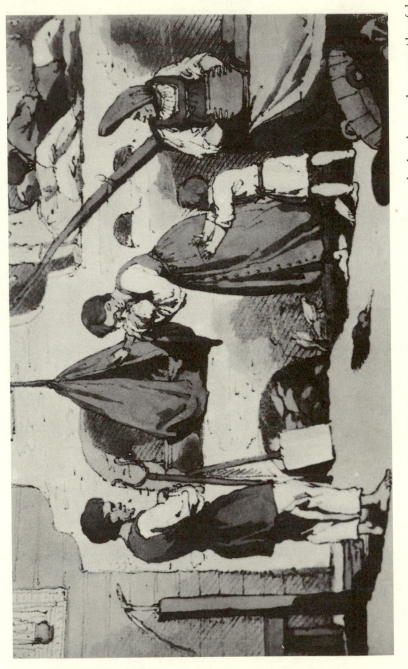

11. Interior of a Russian peasant dwelling. "All the family . . . live together in one room. A wooden bench runs along two sides of the room . . . in the angle of which stands a large wooden table for the family. The opposite corner of the room is occupied by a large oven in which they cook their victuals; the top of it is flat and serves in lieu of a bedstead for the family." (J. A. Atkinson, *A Picturesque*

saw of peasant life in a journey of Silesia. In a letter to his brother on 6 August 1800 he wrote: "Of their persons they appear to take no concern at all, and are, of course, as dirty as any other peasant in the most wretched hovels of Europe. The houses are generally full of children, clad in no other garb than a coarse shirt; oftentimes stark naked, and loaded with vermin like the land of Egypt at the last of its plagues. Such is the condition of these venerable and blissful beings, whom we have heard extolled as the genuine children of nature—the true samples of mankind in the golden age. Their manners . . . all are coarse, most of them disgusting, and some rude and insolent."[11]

II

The specific data available on peasant diets, together with observations by travelers and others, make it clear that meals for most peasants were dreary repetitions of a few items. Foods prepared from grain dominated their cuisines. Every meal centered around a grain dish. In many regions it was porridge. Known by many names, it was eaten two and three times a day in peasant cottages from one end of Europe to the other. Sometimes the peasants ate bread, but bread was relatively expensive compared with the easily prepared porridge. In the uplands of Zurich, bread was served only after the diners had satisfied their hunger with other foods. In 1755 a government official reported that some peasants in Silesia went without bread for as long as six months at a time, and in Posen bread was a holiday treat.[12]

Modern estimates of grain consumption in the eighteenth century reflect the overwhelming importance of grain in the human diet in the servile lands. In Germany per capita grain consumption in the eighteenth century is estimated to have been 300 kilograms (660 pounds) per year. Assuming an average family size of five or six persons of whom one-third were younger than twelve, about 16.5 quintals (3,638 pounds) of grain were needed to feed a peasant family for a year. One estimate of grain consumption in eighteenth-century France holds that peasants there used as much grain as their German counterparts. Another appraisal sets French annual per capita grain consumption at between 212 and 240 kilograms in 1700, 220 and 276 kilograms in 1750-1760, and 216 to 275 kilograms in 1790. An estimate made in Russia at the beginning of the nineteenth century set the minimum per capita grain consumption there at 262 kilograms (16 poods) per annum.[13] Data collected by the Food and Agricultural Organization of

[11] Sion (1909), 474-475; Adams (1804), 96-97.

[12] Calonne (1920), 453, 455; Babeau (1883), 88-89; 91-92; Hufton (1974), 44; Hauser (1971), 46, 174-175; Ziekursch (1927), 143, 143n.; Weidmann (1968), 33; Knapp (1887), I, 251; Stark (1952), 289; Hanssen (1861), 27; Arion (1895), 16; *Village of Viriatino* (1970), 98.

[13] Henning (1969b), 126; Goubert (1956), 66; Toutain (1961), I, 82; Sivkov (1958), 26.

the United Nations show to what extent the role of grain in the human diet has waned since the days of the old order. In 1969-1970 in France 80 kilograms of cereal per capita were available for human consumption; in the German Federal Republic 69 kilograms; and in eastern Germany 99 kilograms in 1964-1966 (the last years for which this information for East Germany is available).[14]

Among vegetables, peas and beans were especially popular. These two foods are equalled by few vegetables in the calories and proteins they supply per 100 grams, and the amount of edible matter they contain.[15] In central and eastern Europe cabbage, often in the form of sauerkraut, or, as in Russia, in soup, held first place among vegetables, though in Russia it apparently shared preeminence with cucumbers. Potatoes began to appear in peasant diets only in the last decades of the old order. Until then country people (and city people, too) had spurned potatoes as unfit for human consumption.[16]

In regions where animal husbandry was a major activity, dairy products figured importantly in rural cuisines. In French Flanders peasants reportedly had butter at every meal, and milk dishes and cheese appeared frequently in their menus. In Brittany, too, villagers ate much butter. Dairy dishes were staples in the diets of cattle-raising peasants in Switzerland, though they usually sold their butter; it was too expensive for them to consume it themselves. John Quincy Adams, journeying in the mountains of the border between Silesia and Bohemia, found that milk, butter, and "tolerable" cheese were available everywhere "even when you can get nothing else." In Bohemia, cheese, or more generally curds of cow and sheep milk, were next to bread the most important part of the board furnished to farm hands. In western Germany in the Palatinate, milk was a standard part of the diet of rich and poor alike.[17]

Day in and day out, meals were nearly always the same. The Swiss peasant in the uplands of Zurich in the eighteenth century lived on milk soup, porridge, dried fruits, and a few vegetables. An account from the Boulonnais, in northern France, related that for breakfast the peasants there had a soup of flour mixed with skimmed milk and diluted with water, and bread

[14] FAO (1970), table 135, pp. 435-441. None of the countries listed in the FAO yearbook equalled the estimated per capita grain consumption in France, Germany, and Russia in the eighteenth century. The Republic of Korea in 1969 with 209 kilograms, Yugoslavia in 1968 with 182, and Romania in 1964-1966 also with 182 kilograms of cereal available for human consumption, came closest. In the United States in 1970, 64 kilograms of cereal per capita were available for human consumption.

[15] McCance and Widdowson (1947), 84-91.

[16] Hauser (1971), 173; Braun (1960), 92; Ilzhofer (1942), 165; Knapp (1887), i, 251; Ziekursch (1927), 143; Abel (1938), 434; Goubert (1956), 68; Falguerolles (1941), 156; Zubrzycki (1953), 253; Jacob (1826), 65; *Village of Viriatino* (1970), 98; Swinton (1792), 442-443; Bremner (1830), i, 151-152.

[17] Calonne (1920), 455-456; Meyer (1966), i, 456; Hauser (1962), 38-40; Adams (1804), 81; Weidmann (1968), 34.

and salt; in winter a baked apple was included. At mid-day they had a soup made of bread, butter, and vegetables or potherbs of the season, and a thin slice of bread with a little butter. Supper was a repetition of the mid-day repast, plus raw or cooked fruits of the season. Prosperous peasants had a bit of salt pork in their soup, and a few had a piece of boiled beef on Sundays and holidays. The meal was usually washed down with water; beer, cider, and wine were too expensive. There were local fermented beverages, one made with raisins and another concocted of hops, honey, and grain. An old village priest of Picardy, writing around 1761, said that he was certain that nine-tenths of his parishioners had never tasted wine. In Brittany the peasant lived on rye bread, soup and dairy products, and drank water with his meals; he had cider and brandy only in years of abundance. The peasants of Schleswig-Holstein had grits and milk in the morning and evening with bread and small amounts of butter and bacon. At mid-day in the field they often had only a pot of sour milk and at harvest time thin beer. The daily meals served to farm hands on several manors in central and northwestern Germany included soup, often made with milk, and vegetables at

12. Peasant houses in Transylvania. "The houses of the Wallacks generally consist of one small room. . . . The material of the building is usually the unhewn stems of trees lined inside with mud and covered with a very high roof, composed of straw, thrown carelessly on, and frequently retained in its place by branches of trees hung across it." (J. Paget, *Hungary and Transylvania*, London, 1839.)

[185]

most meals, sometimes bread, butter and cheese, and meat in some places
as often as twice a week, but in other manors only on holidays. An English
traveler in Silesia in 1780 found that the daily diet of the peasants there
consisted of sauerkraut, groats, and milk. William Jacob in Poland in 1825
learned that the usual food of the peasants was "cabbage, potatoes sometimes, but not generally, peas, black bread, and soup, or rather gruel,
without the addition of butter or meat. Their chief drink is water, or the
cheap whiskey of the country, which is the only luxury of the peasants;
and is drunk whenever they can obtain it, in enormous quantities." Rye
bread, potatoes, cabbage, and, if the family owned a cow, milk, was the
standard diet of Galician peasants in the nineteenth and early twentieth
centuries. In Russia peasant meals consisted mainly of black bread, dishes
made of cabbages or cucumbers, gruel, and kvas, a thin, sour beer made
from rye or barley or from dried black bread.[18]

The most conspicuous gap in peasant diets everywhere was the absence,
or near absence, of meat. A well-to-do household might have meat every
Sunday, but for most peasants weeks and even months intervened between
meals at which meat was served, and then only in small portions. It was a
very special treat that marked a holiday, and, for many, holidays with meat
came only twice a year. When meat was part of the meal it was often salted
or ground into sausage. Even in Hamburg, chief port of entry of animals
from Denmark, which was a major supplier of meat, only 20 per cent of
the meat consumed was fresh. In most households pork was the usual
meat. Beef and mutton appeared much less frequently, and the beef often
came from sick or half-dead beasts who could no longer function as work
animals.[19]

Estimates of annual per capita meat consumption in Germany at the end
of the eighteenth century differ widely. Some run from 13 kilograms (28.6
pounds) to 29 kilograms (63.8 pounds). After surveying some of the data,
one scholar has suggested that per capita meat consumption of German
peasants was anywhere between 18 and 90 kilograms (39.6 to 198 pounds) a
year.[20] Five estimates made in France in 1789 and 1790 of annual meat consumption there ranged from 16.8 to 22 kilograms (37 to 48 pounds).[21] It
seems most probable that the low estimates are much closer to the mark

[18] Braun (1960), 92-93; Calonne (1920), 455-467; Sée (1906), 466-467; Labrousse (1933),
II, 575-577; Hanssen (1861), 27; Neumann (1911), 378, 384; *Deutsches Museum* (1780), I,
214; Jacob (1826), 65; Zubrzycki (1953), 253; *Village of Viriatino* (1970), 98; Bremner
(1839), I, 151-152; Le Play (1877), II, 177-178, 191.
[19] Hauser (1962), 43-44; Hauser (1971), 173-174; Braun (1960), 92-93; Babeau (1878),
97-98; Calonne (1920), 461; St. Jacob (1960), 540; Abel (1938), 434; Braudel (1967), I, 142;
Leskiewicz (1962), 243; Violand (1850), 36; Stark (1953), 289; Knapp (1887), I, 251; Riemann
(1953), 126-128; Ziekursch (1927), 143n.; Abel (1938), 434-435, 444; Arion (1895), 17-18.
[20] Abel (1938), 444; Franz (1963), 449; Riemann (1953), 129; Saalfeld (1964), 28, table 1;
Henning (1969b), 137.
[21] Toutain (1961), I, 160.

than are the higher ones. Indeed, there is reason to believe that meat consumption in Germany (and presumably elsewhere) started to decline in the sixteenth century and reached its low point in the last years of the traditional order. Scholars who maintain this view call the period the era of "depecoration"—a term first used by Gustav Schmoller in the last century.[22] As earlier pages have pointed out, the increased pressure on the land as population increased, combined with the retention of inefficient agricultural techniques, brought about a greater emphasis upon cereals and a deemphasis of animal husbandry. In any event, it is difficult to believe that the people of the servile lands, given the conditions in which they lived, ate as much meat as did their descendants in the second half of the twentieth century. Estimates of annual per capita meat consumption of 50, 60, and even 90 kilograms (110, 132, and 198 pounds respectively) in the eighteenth century nearly equal or exceed the rate of meat consumption in 1975. In that year annual per capita consumption of meat was 67 kilograms (147.4 lbs.) in France and 68 kilograms (149.6 lbs.) in the German Federal Republic.[23]

Other foodstuffs included the wild foods that peasants gathered in the woods and fields and ditches. Fish, often dried or salted, sometimes figured in their diets. Colonial goods began to gain in popular use. A curé in northern France wrote in 1761 that sugar was still regarded as part of the stock of the apothecary rather than as a foodstuff, and he also reported that only the bourgeoisie drank coffee. In Switzerland, however, by the end of the eighteenth century many peasants drank coffee every morning, and there was a rise in the consumption of sugar and chocolate. In the duchy of Hohenstein in Saxony by the turn of the nineteenth century farm hands were served coffee every morning. These foods, however, had a very limited role in peasant diets. "To eat," as Braudel wrote, "was to eat bread, and more bread, or porridge, all life long."[24]

When food was available in sufficient quantity, peasants' diets, though severely limited in their variety, seem to have been reasonably healthy and satisfactory in terms of their nutritional value. The cereals that were their chief foods contain most of the elements needed for human nutrition. They are rich in calories and proteins. They do not contain vitamins and minerals in sufficient quantities, but shortages in these items were unlikely to occur in rural societies. Peasants ate their food in comparatively unprocessed

[22] Abel (1939), *passim*. But see Mandrou (1961), 966-972.

[23] U.S. Department of Agriculture, Foreign Agricultural Service (May 1977), 20. Annual per capita meat consumption in the United States in 1975 was 82 kilograms (180.4 lbs.) Uruguay, with 104 kilograms (228.8 lbs.) had the world's highest per capita meat consumption in 1975.

[24] Hauser (1962), 42; Goubert (1956), 68; Zelenin (1926), 117; Le Play (1877), II, 91; Stark (1952), 289; Ilzhofer (1942), 164; Matosian (1968), 13-14; Calonne (1920), 465; Chevallaz (1949), 226; Riemann (1953), 128; Braudel (1967), I, 97.

form, and, as just pointed out, supplemented their diets with wild foods obtained directly from natural sources, such as berries, nuts, and fungi, greens, and fruit, which provided them with other nutritional essentials.

Estimates of the food value of peasant diets, however, are tenuous because of the inadequacy of the information about actual food intake, and because the nutritional content of any food may vary considerably.[25] As mentioned earlier, per capita consumption of grain in the eighteenth century is estimated to have been about 300 kilograms a year in Germany, and between 200 and 300 kilograms in France. Assuming a flour yield of 80 per cent and a caloric content of 350 calories per 100 grams of flour, one kilogram of grain provided 2,800 calories. The protein content of the grain varieties produced in the servile lands ranged from around 7 to 13 per cent, depending upon the cereal and the milling. Thus, an annual per capita consumption of 300 kilograms of grain provided a daily ration of 2,300 calories, and an average of about 80 grams of protein. If per capita consumption is set at 250 kilograms for France, daily intake amounted to about 1,900 calories and 75 grams of protein.[26]

These calculations are, of course, for grain consumption alone. They do not include the calories and proteins derived from other foods eaten by peasants. The estimates also include the grain consumed by children up to 12 years old, and by adults over 50. Nutritional needs in these age groups are considerably less than those for persons between the ages of 13 and 50. Also, caloric requirements of adult women are 25 to 30 per cent less than those of men in the same age group. When these qualifications are kept in mind, the caloric intake per capita in eighteenth-century France and Germany is not out of line with requirements suggested by a committee appointed by the Food and Agricultural Organization of the United Nations in 1957. At a mean annual environmental temperature of 10° Centigrade (50° Fahrenheit), these suggested requirements go from 1,300 calories for infants of 1 to 3 years, 2,500 calories for children of 10 to 12 years, 3,100 for boys and 2,600 for girls aged 13 to 15, and 3,600 for males and 2,400 for females aged 16 to 19. For adults, assuming a workday of 8 hours spent mostly standing, and an average weight of 65 kilograms (143 pounds) for males and 55 kilograms (121 pounds) for females, the requirements are from 3,200 calories for males and 2,300 calories for females in the 20 to 30 age group, down to 2,210 for males and 1,590 for females over 70. The estimated daily intake of 70 to 80 grams of protein exceeds the recommended minimum requirement of 41 grams for adult women and 55 grams for adult men.[27]

---

[25] For estimates of daily caloric intake in the canton of Zurich, in Paris, and in Germany, respectively, see Hauser (1971), 174; Philippe (1961), 565; Saalfeld (1964), 28.

[26] Caloric and protein contents from Chatfield (1949), table 1, p. 9.

[27] Davison and Passmore (1966), 27-34, 85.

The estimated daily caloric value of these eighteenth-century diets is considerably higher than the caloric intake in most of the less developed countries of the modern world[28] (though caloric requirements in these lands are not as great as in Europe, since minimal needs vary with climate, body weight, and, most important, physical activity). The European diet was also healthier than the rice, maize, or starchy roots such as yams, cassava, taro, or sweet potatoes that are the mainstay of diet in many underdeveloped lands. These foods lack certain essential nutritional substances, so that their use as staples tends to lead to beriberi, pellagra, or multiple-deficiency diseases.

Although monotonous, the European peasant diet, then, had the compensation of being nutritious—providing that enough food was available. All too often, as earlier pages pointed out, crops failed and food was in short supply. Then hunger, malnutrition, starvation, and death swept through the countryside.

III

Perhaps nothing spoke more of the poverty and misery of peasant life than the large number of vagabonds, beggars, and runaways in all of the servile lands. Some spent their lives as vagrants and mendicants. Others took up the beggar's staff to tide themselves over a season when crops failed. Many were landless day laborers and cottage workers who had nothing to fall back on when hard times came and work grew scarce. Old people, and the infirm, and others not competent to earn a living, often had no alternative save to beg for their bread. Some were peasants who had run away from their home village to escape seigniorial obligations and oppressions. And some were reckless people who preferred the chancey and irresponsible life of the open road to the routine and responsibilities of village life. The people about whom noble proprietors of Lower Austria complained in 1844 must have been of this last-named variety. The Austrian law required the proprietors to feed, house, and clothe vagabonds who wandered onto their manors, until the vagrant could be returned home. The nobles' complaint was that, once home, the erstwhile vagabond sold his clothes for brandy, then set off again for another stay at the manor that had taken care of him.[29]

Quantitative data about these people, and, in fact, any data about them are scant. It seems probable, however, that their numbers swelled in the last decades of the servile society.[30] Certainly alarmed contemporaries thought so. Governments issued sometimes draconic legislation to control

[28] FAO (1970), table 136, pp. 444-447.   [29] Bibl (1911), 253.
[30] Zenker (1897), 80; Braun (1960), 239-240, 242; Nielsen (1933), 192; Lefebvre (1972), 313-320; McCloy (1946), 260-261; Revesz (1967), 161-163; Schorer (1904), 176-177; Sée (1906), 484-485.

the phenomenon, but found it impossible to enforce. "The highways are inundated with unhappy citizens who have become mendicants and robbers," wrote J. J. Rousseau in the early 1750's.[31] Thirty years later, Thomas Jefferson, traveling along the Rhine in April 1788, found the road "strung with beggars." Later in that year a youthful Bostonian touring through southern France, in a letter to Jefferson, said that he had but one complaint: "it appears to me astonishing," he wrote, "that the policy of France . . . should suffer such herds of beggars to croud [sic] the roads and fill the Cities . . . ; indeed it is a sight we are not used to in America and to me a most melancholy spectacle."[32]

Themselves products of the malfunctions of the social order, the vagrants and mendicants created serious social problems. Thousands of them poured into the cities, where alms were easier to come by, and where perhaps there were more favorable opportunities for pilferage. In March 1792 Paris was said to have 100,000 beggars in a population of half to three-quarters of a million people. A report of 1790 claimed that 20,000 of the 50,000 people in Cologne were beggars. The estates of Lower Austria complained in the 1840's of the hordes of vagrants and beggars who descended upon Vienna.[33] The problem was sometimes even more severe in the villages. In June 1786 a parish priest in Pas-de-Calais wrote, "I have been a parish priest for thirty-three years; I have never yet seen so much misery and poverty as we have now. How can I and five or six households support thirty-three other ménages that are in need."[34] Scattered reports from other parts of France and from other lands revealed similar if not equally parlous conditions. Thus, of the 1,500 inhabitants in a parish in Normandy, 400 lived by begging. In a village near Douai with 332 dwellings half the households were beggars. The *cahier* of the parish of Marboeuf in 1789 complained that of the 500 people there half were supported by alms. No social opprobrium seemed attached to vagrancy, perhaps because it was so common. In France the tax rolls often listed "beggar" as a person's occupation.[35] Vagabonds roamed the countryside or lived in or on the edge of forests. Without roots and beyond the reach of the law, they were charcoal burners, smugglers, poachers, collectors of wild honey, and the like. They resorted often to violence and crime. Some of them organized into bands with their own chieftains and with a special name for the band. Everywhere they were recognized as menaces to public and private security, and everywhere they inspired terror. They robbed travelers, plundered villages, and spread disease. Peasants, cowed by the threats of brigands to burn their villages, set fire to their crops, or kill their animals, gave the

[31] Quoted in Gay (1959), 88.　　[32] *Papers of Thomas Jefferson* (1956), XIII, 26, 616.
[33] McCloy (1946), 274; Sombart (1928), I, pt. 2, 793; Bibl (1911), 253.
[34] Quoted in Sombart (1928), I, pt. 2, 790.
[35] Kareev (1899), 237; Davies (1964), 28; cf. Skrubbeltrang (1953), 27.

robber bands whatever they demanded. A writer in 1787 asserted that the "alms" given by German villagers to beggars sometimes equalled the amounts the peasants spent on their own families.[36]

The efforts of the public authorities to control begging and vagrancy and to curb the crimes associated with them, were at best palliatives and usually complete failures. Local authorities, upon whom the burden fell, were unequal to the task assigned them, and unhappy about it because it cost them time and money. They tried to avoid the obligation, like the seigniors in Maine who, to keep down the costs of court hearings and imprisonment, often paid no mind to vagabonds and acted as if they were not there.[37] Private alms and welfare, police measures, and compulsory work programs, all had little effect. About the only thing that the authorities could do was to move the vagabonds along. The name used for them in Austrian legislation, *Schubpersonen*, "push people," revealed the attitude of the government. Vagrants were people to be pushed from one place to another.[38]

IV

Not every peasant, of course, lived in grinding poverty. There were prosperous villagers, and a few who were truly rich. But these people were exceptions. William Jacob's comment in 1825 about well-to-do Polish peasants can serve for all of the servile lands. "Such cases as these occur so rarely," he wrote, "that though they produce individual comfort and wealth, they have no perceptible influence on the general mass of society, or on the surplus quantity of agricultural productions." The peasant counted as prosperous was nearly always wealthy only in comparison with his fellow villagers. In the Beauvaisis a man who owned a plow and two horses was thought of as well-to-do. Indeed, French peasants who could support themselves and their families from their own holdings were a sort of peasant aristocracy. There were, however, pockets of truly wealthy peasants scattered through the servile lands, and sometimes the leading peasants of a village were men of means.[39]

In general, rich peasants were likely to be those who were personally free and who had secure tenures, or who had light obligations to the seigniors that were payable entirely in cash and kind. They were likely, too, to live in regions where undivided inheritance of land was the rule, or where there were unusual opportunities for trade or manufacture. Most of them earned their livings from the land, as could be expected. A few ran large operations

[36] Valran (1899), 40; McCloy (1946), 261; Link (1949), 21; Balazs (1956), 302-303; Emerit (1937), 51; Hufton (1972), 117-120; Gagliardo (1969), 46; Schorer (1904), 183-184; Zenker (1897), 81.

[37] La Monneraye (1922), 28.   [38] Link (1949), 21.

[39] Jacob (1826), 66; Young (1970), I, 402; Goubert (1956), 64; St. Jacob (1960), 186-187; Walter (1966), 85.

that approached or equalled the proportions of a medium-sized noble estate.[40] A very small number gained fortunes through trade, manufacturing, and shipping. They seemed to have been among the wealthiest. Peasants in Silesia and in Upper Austria became rich by engaging in the overland transport of goods. Peasants in Hadersleben in Schleswig prospered as shippers of cattle. Other peasants of the Baltic and North Sea littorals were wealthy traders and shipowners. In Russia there were serfs who became millionaires through manufacturing and trading.[41]

Rich peasants adopted living styles suitable to their affluence, and that sometimes equalled or exceeded that of middling nobles. An English traveler in the fertile Elbe lowlands of Hannover in 1817-1818 told of peasant homes "surrounded by lofty trees and handsomely laid out gardens, the floors carpeted and the windows of plate glass."[42] Contemporaries on occasion made it clear that they considered it unseemly for peasants to live so well. "It is unbelievable to see how the peasant here knows luxury, gluttony, and all the artful stratagems," wrote an observer in Silesia in 1806. "He knows how to drink his coffee, his wine, his punch; he doesn't drink some inferior wine, the best is not too good for him."[43] Others told of peasants having silver table services and faience and porcelain and wearing expensive clothes.[44] At the wedding banquet in 1763 of the daughter of a rich serf who lived near Magdeburg, the 300 guests consumed 1,500 talers worth of carp, 150 talers worth of brandy, 14 calves, and 42 capons that were used for bouillon. The bridal furnishings cost 300 talers, and a dowry of 14,000 talers went with the bride.[45] In Russia rich serfs bought serfs for their own use; since the law allowed only nobles to own people, the serfs made their purchases in the name of their seignior.[46]

These prosperous peasants aside, the evidence affirms the conclusion that most peasants in all of the servile lands had a thin time of it. Their payments in cash, kind, and labor took away much of what they produced. They lived often in animal-like squalor and filth. Their limited and monotonous diets apparently satisfied nutritional needs, but the threat, and the all too often reality, of famine was never far away. Many of them could stay alive only by becoming vagabonds and beggars living from alms, thefts, and extortions.

The lack of adequate quantitative information makes it impossible to distinguish gradations among nations in the material condition of the peas-

[40] Revesz (1964), 281, 300; Heitz (1960), 1369-1371; Hanssen (1961), 30; Lütge (1967), 185; Müller (1965a), 96; Schremmer (1966), 67-68.

[41] Ziekursch (1927), 154, 154n.; Hoffmann (1952), 95; Arnim (1957), 64-65; Kellenbenz (1962), 6ff.; Blum (1961), 472-474.

[42] Hodgskin (1820), i, 255; see also Blackwell (1968), 207-208; Hoffmann (1952), 269; Calonne (1920), 443-446.

[43] Quoted in Ziekursch (1927), 154-155.

[44] Franz (1963), 270-271, 330-331; Hodgskin (1820), i, 255; Abel (1969a), 201-202.

[45] Ford (1919), 370n.   [46] Blum (1961), 361.

antry. A brief sampling of comparisons made by contemporaries and by later writers illustrates the futility of attempts to establish such rankings, and also suggests that national pride may have influenced some judgments. A French historian stated that "if one compares France to England and to eastern Europe the first characteristic which emerges . . . is the much better condition of the peasantry."[47] However, another modern historian, this one an Englishwoman, pointed out that nothing has yet appeared to invalidate Arthur Young's repeated insistence that the French standard of living was lower than that of England in all classes except the top.[48] Travel accounts suggested that the Polish peasants were the worst off in all Europe. An English visitor there in 1831 said of the Polish peasant that "of all the living creatures I have met in this world, or seen described in books of natural history, he is the most wretched."[49] But an outstanding Polish historian maintained that the Polish peasant was no worse off than peasants in other lands, and, indeed, may have been better off than the peasants of eastern Germany.[50] A French scientist traveling in Hungary in 1818 found that "the peasant's lot in Hungary is often superior to that of the same class in countries that have more freedom," and decided that "on the whole, the condition of the peasant is not inferior to that of many farmers in France."[51] A modern historian concluded that the Romanian peasants who lived in Transylvania, then part of Hungary, were better off than their fellows in neighboring Moldavia, and a traveler in 1820 insisted that no people were more oppressed by lord and state than the peasants of the Danubian Principalities.[52] Yet in 1818 concerned Hungarian authorities reported a mass emigration of peasants from Transylvania into Moldavia, caused, to quote from an official statement, by the "oppressive and inhuman treatment" suffered by the peasants at the hands of the seigniors. Five years later there were still reports of mass flight of Transylvania peasants into Moldavia.[53]

The contradictions in these efforts at comparison deprive them of significance. In any event, distinctions among the servile lands in the condition of their peasants would be only gradations in a scale of poverty and misery. The fact is that the traditional society, with its hierarchical structure of orders and its inefficient agriculture, failed to provide even a minimally satisfactory standard of living for most of its people.

[47] Lefebvre (1929), 508.
[48] Behrens (1963), 470.
[49] Quoted in Leslie (1956), 51.
[50] Rutkowski (1926), 494-496.
[51] Beaudant (1823), 26, 27.
[52] Matl (1965), 165; Wilkinson (1971), 155.
[53] Barany (1968), 190.

Part Two
Transition

CHAPTER 10

Absolute Monarchy and the Nobility

I

MONARCHS who laid claim to absolute power held sway in nearly all of the servile lands. The coexistence of these royal absolutists and of an hierarchical society in which a person's status and rights depended upon the order to which be belonged, and not upon the will of the absolute sovereign, was an internal contradiction of the traditional society. That was true above all of the status and rights of the nobility. The monarchs had managed to divest the nobility of many of its functions and of much of its political power as a corporate entity. Yet the nobles not only continued but were strengthened in their social position and in their claim to special privilege, and they retained and broadened their claim to the land, labor, dues, and subservience of the peasantry. Paradoxically enough, the "age of absolutism" encapsulated the "era of the feudal reaction."

Inevitably, the aims and the ambitions of absolutists and nobles clashed. Theirs was an unceasing, usually polite, but nonetheless deadly serious struggle for power. The nobility stood in the way of the monarch. True supremacy was his only if he could reduce the authority of the nobility. The nobility, for its part, was determined to preserve and to extend its prerogatives. One of the most significant facets of the struggle concerned the monarch's policies dealing with the peasantry, the ways in which it held its land, and the relationship between lord and peasant. The throne saw its interests best served by a landed peasantry with secure tenures, with greater personal freedom, and with regulation by the state of the obligations owed to the seigniors. The seigniors resisted these princely assaults upon the existing order of things, maintaining that they were infringements of their inalienable rights as members of the nobility, and fearing loss of prestige and of income if the will of the sovereign prevailed.

The struggle for predominance between throne and nobility had gone on for a long time. It reached its apogee in the last century of the old order, when monarchs, more secure in their power than they had ever been before, decided to intervene directly in the relationship between lord and peasant. In some lands their programs had little direct effect; in others they were more successful. Everywhere, however, their efforts prepared the way for the great reforms that ultimately freed the peasants and swept away the traditional society of orders. Those epochal reforms owed a great debt to the policies of the absolute monarchs, policies inspired not by humane concern for the peasantry, nor by ideas of freedom and equality, but by self-seeking ambitions that are sometimes conveniently concealed by the grave and seemingly impersonal catch-phrase, *raison d'état*.

The special brand of absolutism called enlightened despotism that flourished in the second half of the eighteenth century added a new dimension to the struggle for power between throne and nobility. The ranks of the enlightened despots included Frederick II of Prussia and Joseph II of Austria, and lesser princes such as Karl Eugen of Württemberg, Margrave Karl Friedrich of Baden, Duke Charles Emmanuel III of Savoy, and Elector Frederick Christian of Saxony. These sovereigns conceived of themselves as rulers whose absolute power provided the best instrument for bettering the welfare of their subjects—and thereby aggrandizing their own power and authority. Their policies seemed infused with the rationalism and humanitarianism that figured so importantly in the intellectual life of the era, and they had close relations with leading figures of the Enlightenment. Some knowledgeable skeptics, however, have questioned whether the ideology of the Enlightenment actually influenced these sovereigns. They dismiss the rationalistic and humanitarian declarations of the enlightened despots (Lefebvre called them *jeux d'esprit*) and suggest that the rulers used those new ideas which served their own interests and forgot those which did not. Like absolutists of the unenlightened variety, they were interested not so much in justice and the rule of law, as they were in the augmentation of their own power.[1]

Whatever their motivation, and whether they were "enlightened" or "unenlightened," the princes, in their efforts to promote agrarian reform, ran counter to the interests of the landowning nobility. The opposition of the nobles was so determined, and their influence so considerable, that they were able to hold back change for many decades. But some of the responsibility for the retardation of reform lay with the rulers themselves. Though they wanted to reduce seigniorial authority, they were not ready to give peasants their complete freedom, nor to violate what they considered to be the property rights of the seigniors. Empress Maria Theresa of Austria expressed the sentiments of her fellow rulers when, early in her long reign, she wrote "to abolish hereditary subjection is not possible . . ., to free the peasant from his obligation to his seignior would make the peasant unruly and the lord dissatisfied, and in any case would violate justice."[2]

The resurgence of the nobility in the eighteenth century seems to have been a nearly pan-European phenomenon. A new cohesiveness and consciousness of their caste appeared among nobles in many lands. They revived old privileges and demanded new ones, they reaffirmed their claim to a special position in society, and they gained a monopoly or near monopoly of the important posts in the central government. Monarchs, even those who seemed most secure in their power, had to bend before these pres-

---

[1] Lefebvre (1949), 103, 109, 113; Wangermann (1959), 1-4.
[2] Quoted in Mayer (1909), II, 452.

sures. Neither throne nor nobility triumphed. Instead, an uneasy compromise between *étatisme* and administrative centralization, on the one
hand, and seigniorial privilege and private proprietary rule, on the other,
worked itself out. It was a compromise in which sometimes king, and sometimes noble, seemed to have had the better of it.

The resurgence of the nobility appears all the more remarkable in view of
the obsolesence of its traditional military and administrative functions. The
current of events had swept away the need for these services—services that
had provided the justification for the privileges of the nobility. In central
Germany the military service required of knights was last demanded in
1656. In the Kingdom of Prussia a decree of 1717 converted the estates of
nobles from fiefs held in return for military service (which had not been
demanded in living memory) into the free property of their occupants. In
Russia Tsar Peter III in 1762 abolished the requirement that every noble
had to serve the state as an army officer or a bureaucrat throughout his
adult life. In the German and Slav crownlands of the Austrian Monarchy
the state, during the second half of the eighteenth century, assumed many
of the fiscal, judicial, and police functions that had been the special preserve
of the nobility. In France by the middle of the eighteenth century, officials
of the central government replaced the seignior in large part in the political
and fiscal administration of the village community. These officials checked
the village accounts; any proposed sizable expenditure had to receive their
approval; in some provinces they prescribed the procedures for the election
of village officers, and sometimes they even appointed or dismissed these
officers.[3]

The traditional role atrophied, yet the privileges remained and, indeed,
increased. The persistence of the privileges summoned forth criticisms and
complaints that grew in volume as the years went by, and that were inspired by the ideas of equality that were winning favor, particularly among
the increasingly self-confident bourgeoisie. A few nobles conceded the justice of these criticisms. Most of them met the attacks with defiance, and
with renewed efforts to aggrandize their power so that they could more
adequately defend their privileges. Writers among them lauded the merits
of an hierarchical society, attacked autocracy and its centralization of
power, and demanded increased and more effective participation of the nobility in government. Some flatly declared that nobles were a superior
breed of mankind who inherited their special qualities through birth, and
vigorously defended their privileged status and their authority over their
peasants as both natural and beneficial to the society as a whole.[4]

[3] Ipsen (1954), 30; Lütge (1967), 175; Romanovich-Slavatinskii (1870), 181-194; Brusatti
(1958), 506-507; Babeau (1878), 64-66, 87-92, 100-101, 110.
[4] Shcherbatov (1969), 26-27, 34-35, 43-47; Andrian-Werburg (1843), I, 26-38, II, 14-15;
Epstein (1966), 188-200; Diedrichs (1870), 41; Reinhard (1956), 5-6; Soboul (1970), 199,
241-242; Brunner (1949), 329.

In France the *parlements*, the regional high courts of the realm, provided a potent medium through which the nobility could express and organize its resistance to the authority of the central government. These bodies, whose political revival had begun after the death of Louis XIV in 1715, were made up of the so-called nobility of the robe. In earlier times members of the *parlements* had bourgeois origins. Now noble birth or direct descent from a member of a *parlement* became requirements for admission. By the mid-eighteenth century the *parlements* had taken over the leadership of the French nobility. The *parlement* of Paris, the most prestigious of these bodies, and the other *parlements* used their judicial powers to enforce seigniorial claims, and to combat even insignificant attempts at reform that affected the rights of property. If they deemed it necessary, the *parlements* could refuse to register royal decrees and thereby prevent their promulgation as law. Nor did noble influence end here. The nobility made the top reaches of the bureaucracy their private preserve. Of the thirty-six ministers who served Louis XVI (1774-1792) all but one were of noble birth, and nearly all of them were of the nobility of the robe. The scions of the old feudal nobility, the nobility of the sword, were passed over. Louis' *intendants*, too, the men who ruled for him in the provinces, were recruited from the inner circles of the robe nobility. The corps of army officers became a near-monopoly of the nobility. In 1751 a new academy to train officers was founded in which youths of four generations of inherited nobility received a free education at public expense. In 1781 pressure from the nobility persuaded the government to publish an ordinance that in effect limited commissions as army officers to men with four quarterings of nobility. High ecclesiastical offices, too, became completely albeit not formally restricted to men of noble birth.[5]

The nobility of Prussia swelled in numbers in the last decades of the old order. At the end of the eighteenth century there were twice as many nobles as there had been in the first half of the century. French nobles who fled the Revolution, and Polish nobles who found themselves subjects of the King of Prussia as a result of the partitions of their homeland, contributed to the increase. In 1806 the Prussian army officers corps of over 7,000 included 1,059 men with French and Polish names. Most of the increase in the nobility, however, came through the new creations of nobles, above all by King Frederick William II (1786-1797). In his brief reign he created five times as many nobles as had his predecessor Frederick II in his reign of 46 years.[6]

Frederick William of Brandenburg, the Great Elector (1640-1688), and his grandson, King Frederick William I of Prussia (1713-1740), had established the sovereignty of the throne over the nobility. King Frederick William said that his goal was to make the nobility "acknowledge no master

[5] Cobban (1950), 64-72; Carré (1912), 20-21; McManners (1953), 28-29, 35, 38-39.
[6] Martiny (1938), 75-80.

but God and the King in Prussia." Frederick II (1740-1786), instead of continuing in this policy, restored much of its lost prestige and authority to the seigniors. "The great age of the Prussian nobility," wrote Otto Hintze, "began only with the reign of Frederick II." He propitiated the nobility because he needed internal support and domestic peace so that he could pursue his dream to establish Prussia as a great power by force of arms. Most important, Frederick was convinced of the moral superiority of men of noble birth. He believed that they were motivated by a sense of honor that gave them the resolution to face danger, hardship, and death without flinching and without thought of reward. Their qualities gave them a natural claim to leadership and social precedence. Frederick showed his bias in many ways that included the establishment of land mortgage banks to lend money to nobles, encouragement of the creation of entails to protect noble families from impoverishment through testamentary division of family property, cessation of the purchase of noble land for estates of the crown, and, most significantly, failure to intervene meaningfully in the relationship between lord and peasant except for an effort to restrain seigniors from conversion of peasant land into demesne (according to Hintze the only issue in which Frederick acted against the interests of the nobility). "The race is so good," he once said, "that it deserves to be preserved by every means." To Frederick the preservation included the right to hold the highest posts in the bureaucracy, and a monopoly of commissions in the army. Nobles multiplied in the rank and file of the bureaucracy, too, where they were given preference over men of bourgeois origin. The overwhelming influence of the nobility moved Christian Jakob Kraus, Professor of Practical Philosophy and Cameralistic Studies at the University of Königsberg, to write in 1799 that "the Prussian state, far from being an unlimited monarchy is but a thinly veiled aristocracy [which] rules the country in undisguised form as a bureaucracy."[7]

A few decades later two highly placed Austrian bureaucrats, both of them of common birth, independently used almost the same words as Professor Kraus to describe the government of the German and Slav crownlands of the Hapsburg realm.[8] During the reigns of Maria Theresa and of her son Joseph II the central government had made deep inroads into the powers and privileges of the nobility. Then during the long tenure of Francis I (1792-1835), whose reign was an unceasing campaign to turn back the clock, the nobility made a spectactular comeback from the lean years of the eighteenth century. The recovery was furthered by Francis' policy of deliberate postponement of decisions in the hope that the problem would ultimately solve itself or vanish. Winston Churchill's indictment of Stanley Baldwin's government could be applied to Francis; that he was "decided

[7] Rosenberg (1958), 44-45, 135-136, 201; Goodwin (1953), 94-98; Ritter (1936), 198; Hintze (1915), 53, 56.

[8] Beidtel (1898), II, 45; Kübeck (1909), I, pt. ii, 378-379.

only to be undecided, resolved to be irresolute, adamant for drift, solid for fluidity, all-powerful to be impotent."[9] The indecision at the center gave the nobility the opportunity to take over the running of the state. The emperor, for his part, identified the reactionary interests of the great nobility with those of the throne, and so he deemed it wise, and in keeping with old tradition, to fill the highest posts in the bureaucracy, the army, and the church with grandees. Nobles of lesser lineage filled other posts. Commoners were not excluded, but since they owed their offices and their continued tenure in them to the favor of some great lord, they allied themselves with the noble interest.[10]

In Denmark royal absolutism had established itself in 1665. Strong rulers managed to keep control of the administration for the next sixty-five years, though always hard pressed by the old nobility. Then, with the accession of Christian VI in 1730, a series of weak monarchs allowed the great proprietors to take over the direction of the state. The trappings of absolutism remained, but power rested in the hands of the magnates, who ran the privy council and headed the ministries. Their domination experienced a brief hiatus of sixteen months in 1770 and 1771, when Count Johann Friedrich Struensee, acting in the name of the mentally unbalanced Christian VII, reestablished absolute rule. In January 1772 a palace revolution drove Struensee from power, and restored control to the great nobles.[11]

In the unique service state that the rulers of old Muscovy had created, every subject, from the mightiest to the least, was assigned a role determined by the interests of the state. Peter I was in that tradition when in 1722 he drew up the Table of Ranks as part of his program to provide structure to Russian society. The goal of the program was to enroll each of his subjects in a legally defined order, each order with its own privileges and obligations. The Table of Ranks provided that a non-noble servitor of the crown, whether in the bureaucracy or in the armed forces, automatically acquired hereditary nobility when he was promoted to a specified grade or rank. That produced a steady stream of new accessions to the nobility, especially when in later years the military and the bureaucracy swelled in size. The accretions, however, were not as great as they might have been, because men of noble birth received preferred treatment in promotions and in appointments to high offices.

By making the acquisition of nobility dependent upon service to the throne, and by his legal definition of the orders of society, Peter welded the nobility into a corporate body, held together by common interests and sharing common corporate privileges. An awareness of their special status as a privileged order and of their common interests quickly evidenced itself. Men whose fathers and grandfathers had referred to themselves as "slaves

---

[9] Churchill (1938), 326-327.   [10] Blum (1948), 28-32.
[11] Commager (1928), 40-43.

of the tsar," now spoke of themselves (at the Legislative Commission convened by Catherine II in 1767) as "the corps of the nobility which includes within itself its own prerogatives and invulnerability." Already in the mid-eighteenth century spokesmen of the nobility urged that entry into the nobility through promotion in the Table of Ranks be abolished, or at least restricted, claiming that such men lacked the qualities of mind and character that only hereditary nobles possessed.[12]

The rulers who followed Peter had to depend upon the support of the nobility to win and to hold the throne. To gain that support, they made a series of concessions to the nobility. The most spectacular concession came in 1762, when Peter III abolished the requirement of compulsory service. Peter's wife and successor Catherine II showered the nobility with her unending favor, among other things allowing them even greater power than they already possessed over their serfs. In 1785 she granted the nobility a charter that confirmed old privileges and bestowed new ones. During Paul's brief reign of five years, the tide of imperial favor turned against the nobility, until a band of noblemen brutally murdered the tsar in 1801. Paul's assassination ended the threat to the supremacy of the nobility. His sons and successors, Alexander I (1800-1825) and Nicholas I (1825-1855), were supporters of the prerogatives of the nobility—though they recognized the need for some measure of reform in the lord-peasant relationship. Noblemen continued to dominate the bureaucracy and the army. A study of 2,952 officials who served in the years from 1846 to 1855 showed that 70 to 80 per cent of the highest posts were held by men of noble birth. Nearly a fifth (18 per cent) of these high officials belonged to the wealthiest families of the empire. And as the mechanism of the state grew more complicated, the power and the authority of the bureaucracy grew at the expense of the monarch.[13]

In Hungary, in Poland until the end of its independent existence, and in the Danubian Principalities, the central power was weaker than in any of the other servile lands. That left the nobles with far more authority than their peers in lands whose rulers laid claim to absolute power. Hungary was a limited monarchy in which the nobility governed in concert with the throne, held by the house of Hapsburg since 1526. Only nobles participated in government, for in Hungary only the nobility was considered to be the nation. Nobles, who in the mid-1820's made up about 4 per cent of the population, alone could hold office, and only nobles could own land. Members of the great landowning families monopolized the highest posts in government, church, and army. In Poland before the partitions nobles elected the king. He was subject to the advisory authority of the senate and his actions could be nullified by the house of deputies. All of the seats in

[12] Romanovich-Slavatinskii (1870), 58-61; Ruffmann (1961), 167.
[13] Pintner (1970), 437-438; Torke (1967), 297, 297n.; Blum (1961), 351-355.

both senate and house were held by noblemen. The final authority and the real power in the kingdom lay with a few great families. The rest of the nobility nearly always followed the lead of the magnates. Noblemen sat as judges in the law courts, and held all the higher offices in the church. As could be expected in such circumstances, the central government did nothing to protect the peasants from excessive exploitation by their seigniors. Protective measures came only after Poland had been dismembered, and the Polish peasant became a subject of Prussia, or Russia, or Austria.

In the Danubian Principalities the domination of the boyars, and more specifically of the great boyars, was all but uncontested. During the eighteenth century the office of hospodar, or ruler, of each principality was sold and resold by the sultan. The brief terms of the hospodars, who rarely served more than three years, and the venality that stigmatized the administration of the Principalities, enabled the boyars to do pretty much as they pleased, especially in matters concerning the peasantry. Their domination became even more pronounced when in 1831 the Organic Statutes, which they had drawn up, were imposed by the Russians on the Principalities. The Statutes established assemblies in each principality that were heavily weighted in favor of the great boyars, authorized the assemblies to elect one of their number as hospodar for life, and gave the assemblies power to limit the hospodar's authority. The Statutes also placed still further restrictions and burdens upon the peasantry, to the benefit of the boyars.

The near-envelopment of the state apparatus in the servile lands by the nobility, and the natural alliance between noble bureaucrats and their fellow nobles, created what Hans Rosenberg, in his study of the Prussian bureaucracy, described as a "united front against the arbitrary power of the throne."[14] Even in autocratic Russia the *chinovniki*, the bureaucrats, had become so central in the operations of the state by the mid-nineteenth century that some contemporaries declared that the autocracy had become the prisoner of the bureaucracy. Tsar Nicholas I himself (who by nature and choice was a pluperfect bureaucrat) once remarked that Russia was ruled not by the emperor but by chief clerks.[15] The bureaucrats employed their mastery of detail, their expertise, their local influence, and sometimes their inefficiency and venality,[16] to frustrate proposals of the monarch for improvements in the condition of the peasantry or for limitations on the authority of the seigniors. They were especially effective in Bavaria and in Prussia, where during the eighteenth century they thwarted most of the efforts of the throne to protect the peasantry. They had less success in the Austrian Monarchy. The alliance there of bureaucracy and landed proprietors failed to block implementation of reforms introduced by Maria Theresa

[14] Rosenberg (1958), 196.   [15] Kliuchevskii (1937), v, 344.
[16] *Cf.* Raeff (1957), 77ff.; Bosher (1970), 279-280.

and by Joseph II until the last months of Joseph's reign, when his last and greatest reform foundered on the opposition of the nobility.[17]

Not all bureaucrats, of course, arrayed themselves against the authority of the monarch, or sought to obstruct his efforts at reform. The first loyalty of many officials was to the sovereign, and they devoted themselves to carrying out his program. There were nobles who held high office who called the ruler's attention to the need for reforms, and planned them and helped carry them out. To cite but a few examples, Prince Kaunitz, scion of an important and wealthy Bohemian family, and chancellor and foreign minister of the Austrian government from 1753 to 1792, spoke openly of the need to limit the power of the nobility over the peasantry, in the interests of the general welfare. Franz Anton von Blanc, born to a family of the minor nobility in Breisgau, counselor of Empress Maria Theresa, and devotee of the Enlightenment, was chiefly responsible for initiating and drafting legislation that effectively limited seigniorial authority over their peasants in Bohemia and Austrian Silesia.[18] The principal officials of the dukes of Savoy in their reports repeatedly drew their sovereign's attention to the need for reform of the lord-peasant relationship there. They warned that the prevalent system of *mainmorte* was harmful to the peasant, and to the state as well, because the seigniorial demands upon their peasants deprived the state of additional revenues. One official in 1731 observed that the authority enjoyed by the seigniors over their peasants created in the minds of the seigniors a chimera of petty sovereignty which made them forget that they were as much subjects of the prince as were their peasants.[19] In eighteenth-century Denmark, too, and in mid-nineteenth-century Russia, nobles in high office urged the need for reform on their sovereigns, and prepared the way for it.[20]

II

The power and the pretensions of the nobility, and their stubborn resistance to the extension of the authority of the sovereign, did not sit well with the absolutists of the eighteenth and nineteenth centuries. They thought that they should be independent of any other authority, and that their power should be so great that no one would dare to disobey them. They looked with special disfavor upon the authority of the seignior over the peasants who lived on his land. So long as that authority persisted, the monarch was not truly the sovereign of all who lived in his realm. The seignior had first claim upon the labor of his peasants, and upon their pay-

---

[17] Dorn (1932), 266; Knapp (1887), I, 88-89; Hausmann (1892), 89.
[18] Mayer (1909), II, 452; Grünberg (1921), 23-44.
[19] Bruchet (1908), lix-lx; Memoire of Secretary of State Bruel, October 1761, *ibid.*, 1-5.
[20] Commager (1928), 88-90, 95-98; Lincoln (1971), 411-421.

ments in cash and kind. The peasants were dependent upon him, and because of that dependence the prestige and the income of the throne suffered.

As early as the late fifteenth century some princes had recognized that, from their point of view, it was the better part of wisdom to protect the peasantry from the exactions and the oppressions of their seigniors. They and later rulers had attempted to limit aspects of seigniorial authority, but their legislation had been sporadic and piecemeal, and usually had not been rigorously enforced. The Tudors of England had been among the first princes to take the offensive. They tried to curb the engrossment of peasant-held land by lords. Francis Bacon explained the policy with these words: "When enclosures began to be more frequent, whereby . . . tenancies for years, lives, and at will, whereupon much of the yeomanry lived, were turned into demesnes . . . the king knew full well . . . that there ensued withal upon this a decay and diminution of subsidies and taxes." The efforts of the government did not end enclosures nor the "letting down of houses of husbandry," but it did serve as a partial check. The policy continued on into the seventeenth century. However, as opposition to absolutism waxed, the zeal of the government in enforcement of its laws against engrossment waned. Significantly, the last serious attempt to restrict seigniorial expropriations came during the years from 1629 to 1640, when Charles I governed England without Parliament.[21]

In contrast to the failed effort at absolutism in England, the absolutists of the Continent established and magnified their power. Their endeavors to protect the peasants took on new vigor from the second half of the seventeenth century. Greater seigniorial pressures on the peasant, and particularly on his land, acted as the goad that spurred rulers into action. Lords, in their effort to maintain their incomes in hard times and to increase them in good times, often took over peasant land and demanded more dues from the peasants. In the bad times of the seventeenth and early eighteenth centuries, peasant holdings were emptied by the devastations of war, famine, plague, and the stagnation or decline of population in some parts of servile Europe. Seigniors added the vacant holdings to their demesnes, and when they could, they increased the labor obligations of their peasants to get the labor they needed for their enlarged operations.[22] Then, around the middle of the eighteenth century, the secular trend in economic life turned upward, prices went up, and demand increased. Seigniors, motivated now by the rise in both the scale and the cost of living, continued to absorb peasant land, but now it was populated land. By expropriation,

[21] Ashley (1913), 177; see also Thirsk (1967), 213-238.
[22] Eggert (1965), 3-4; Boelcke (1957), 186; Franz (1970a), 178; Hanssen (1861), 8-10; St. Jacob (1960), 66-67; Sering (1908), 222; Knapp (1887), I, 49-50; *Mittheilungen der k. k. mähr.—schles. Gesellschaft* . . . (1863), 305.

foreclosure, or purchase, they converted peasant land into demesne, dispossessing the occupants and reducing them to smallholders or to landless laborers. And at the same time they squeezed more payments in cash, kind, and labor out of the peasants by reasserting old and forgotten dues and privileges, or by arbitrarily adding to the obligations they demanded of their peasants. Their acts of engrossment—in central Europe it was called *Bauernlegen*—continued on into the nineteenth century in many places in central and eastern Europe.[23]

These actions of the seigniors threatened, and indeed damaged, the interests of the monarch. Lords usually paid reduced taxes or no taxes on their demesne land, so that when they took over peasant holdings the state lost revenue. The dispossession of peasants from their land, like the imposition of excessive dues and services, impoverished the peasantry and thereby reduced the amount of taxes and services it could afford to render to the state. Princes feared, too, that an impoverished and landless peasantry would hold back the growth in population that was one of the principal aims of their policies. They wanted more subjects because more subjects meant more taxpayers, more workers and consumers to stimulate economic life, and more recruits for their armies. Often, too, rulers depended upon the peasantry to provide important public services that included the quartering of soldiers, the maintenance of roads and bridges, and posting services. They knew that a people reduced to pauperdom by seigniorial exactions could not afford to continue these valuable functions.

Law, tradition, and the power of the nobility limited the range of options available to rulers in their efforts to protect the peasantry from expropriation and excessive seigniorial exploitation. One thing they could do was to issue legislation that limited or forbad seigniorial appropriation of peasant land, and that provided for the preservation of peasant land in peasant hands. Their legislation, though not without effect, failed to end the practice. In the Kingdom of Prussia seigniors evaded the laws promulgated during the eighteenth century, especially by Frederick II. In East Prussia, where Frederick's edicts against expropriations did not apply, the conversion of peasant land reached its peak during the second half of the eighteenth century. In Mecklenburg and in Swedish Pomerania, where the central power was weak, no legislation was issued to forbid the practice. Nobles took peasant land at will. In the course of the eighteenth century between 4,000 and 6,000 peasant holdings in Mecklenburg, and an equally large number in Swedish Pomerania, were swallowed up by seigniors. Among these grasping proprietors were the University of Greifswald, and cities that owned rural land. Legislation in Saxony had long outlawed engross-

[23] Lizerand (1942), 57-64; Lütge (1967), 150; Fuchs (1888), 132-138; Sering (1908), 222; Benda (1958), 224; Ivanyi (1960), 280; Rosdolsky (1954), 125-127; Kostiushko (1954), 170; Chepko (1959), 176.

ment of peasant land by seigniors, but proprietors, and even the sovereign himself, paid no heed to the prohibition. However, expropriations were relatively uncommon there. Between the sixteenth and the mid-eighteenth centuries Saxon peasants lost only an estimated 4 to 5 per cent of their land to engrossers. In western and southwestern Germany, where most lords had little or no demesne, there was neither seigniorial appropriation of peasant land nor legislation to prevent it.[24]

French seigniors during the eighteenth century, and especially in the second half, took back land on which dues were unpaid or in arrears, claimed common land for their own exclusive use, foreclosed on loans which they had made to peasants, and, by the right called *retrait féodal*, exercised their privilege of buying recently alienated peasant holding within the legally specified period. In Denmark the number of manors remained about the same—between 700 and 800—from the sixteenth to the eighteenth centuries. The total area of their demesnes, however, nearly doubled between 1525 and 1744, despite royal decrees of 1682 and 1725 that forbad the conversion of peasant land into demesne. Some of the additional demesne was newly cleared land. Most of it, though, came from the annexation of over 2,500 peasant holdings, including 264 entire villages. Not until 1769 did the throne issue a decree that succeeded in calling a halt to seigniorial expropriations.

In the Austrian Monarchy legislation to protect peasant land from engrossment appeared in the seventeenth century, inspired by seigniorial appropriation of emptied peasant holdings after the Thirty Years' War. Annexation of peasant land was relatively unusual in the German crownlands. It was more prevalent in the Slavic provinces, Bohemia, Moravia, Silesia, and Galicia. Peasants in two districts of eastern Galicia lost 14 per cent of their holdings to their lords between 1789 and 1820. For all of Galicia, however, the aggregate loss of peasant land between 1789 and 1847 amounted to less than 6 per cent (from 6,028,096 yokes in 1789 to 5,685,437 yokes in 1847). Though overall data are lacking, it seems probably that seigniorial engrossing was more common in Hungary and Transylvania than in other parts of the Monarchy. The colonization of these lands after their reconquest by the Hapsburgs, and their growing importance as suppliers of agricultural products, prompted seigniors to expand their demesnes. They began this in the eighteenth century and continued on into the first half of the next century, despite legislation aimed against the practice.

In Livonia, starting in the last part of the eighteenth century, and in White Russia in the first half of the nineteenth century, lords converted

[24] Prussia: Korth (1953), 157, 161-162; Brentano (1899), 231-233; Goldschmidt (1910), 107. Mecklenburg and Swedish Pomerania: Mager (1955), 144-160; Berthold (1962), 85; Saxony: Blaschke (1955), 102-107, 111-116. Western Germany: Hötzsch (1902), 242-244; Brentano (1899), 233.

peasant land into demesne at an accelerated rate. In one large estate in White Russia peasants had 30,000 desiatins taken from them between 1834 and 1846. In another manor, this one owned by Prince Lubomirski, the lord's demesne increased 3.5 times over at the expense of peasant land. Expropriations of this type, though not always of this scale, were common occurrences in White Russia. In Poland, legislation of the grand duchy of Warsaw, created by Napoleon in 1807, had given seigniors the right to evict peasants from their holdings after giving them six months' notice. When Russia annexed the duchy after Napoleon's fall, this provision was retained until 1846 when it was repealed. In 1810-1820 sowed land in peasant hands amounted to an estimated 58 per cent of all the sowed land. By 1846 the peasants' share of sowed land had fallen to 32.5 per cent. And, despite the ban issued in 1846, seigniorial expropriations continued, though not as intensively as before. In Russia private landowners sometimes appropriated land that belonged to state peasants. Legal action to recover the land was costly, long drawn out, and usually was settled in favor of the expropriator. In the Danubian Principalities the peasants had a traditional right, confirmed by princely decrees, to have as much land as they wanted. Then in 1803 the ruler of Moldavia ordered that proprietors could reserve one-quarter of the meadowland for their own use, and could limit the number of cattle the peasants could graze. In 1828 a new decree provided that one third of arable, meadow, and pasture could be reserved by the proprietor, and the Organic Statute of 1831 ratified this arrangement.[25]

III

Unsuccessful, or at best only partially successful, in their efforts to confine seigniorial expropriation of peasant land, princes decided upon another tactic. They would introduce reforms in the status and tenures of the peasants who lived on lands that belonged to the state or the crown. In some of the servile lands these peasants made up a significant portion of the rural population. In European Russia nearly 55 per cent of the 50 million peasants there in the mid-nineteenth century were state peasants. The Prussian throne had extensive holdings in all of its provinces except for Silesia and Westphalia. The largest concentrations of royal property were in East Prussia and Brandenburg: 55 and 33 per cent, respectively, of all the peasants in these provinces lived on royal manors. Most of the crownlands were rented

[25] France: Lizerand (1951), 57-64; Forster (1960), 51-53, 65, 77. Denmark: Christensen (1960), 181; Scharling (1894), 369-370; Albert (1969), 44-45. Austria: Link (1949), 15; Feigl (1964), 102; Hoffmann (1952), 93; Rosdolsky (1954), 127-131; Grünberg (1894), I, 123-126. Hungary: Spira (1968), 355-356; Benda (1948), 224; Király (1969), 132-135. Transylvania: Georgescu-Buzău (1965), 12-13. Livonia: Transehe-Roseneck (1890), 157-158. White Russia: Chepko (1959), 176. Poland: Kostiushko (1954), 170, 237; Revesz (1964), 279. Russia: Druzhinin (1946), I, 85-86, 323-325. Danubian Principalities: Mitrany (1930), 21-22; Jelavich (1939), 4-5; *Règlement organique*, (1834), art. 123.

out to non-noble lessees who worked the properties with labor provided by the crown peasants. In Bavaria in the second half of the eighteenth century about 20 per cent of all the estates belonged to the sovereign.[26] Properties of state and crown were of similar, if not equal, proportions in other of the servile lands. Reforms introduced on such large tracts of land would presumably have much impact upon the entire society. That hoped-for impact was a principal motive that inspired the reforms. Their success would persuade private landowners to adopt them, and thereby amelioration in the status and tenure of the peasantry would be achieved without compulsion, or invasion of the property right of the seigniors.

The first effort at this kind of reform came in the duchy of Lorraine. In 1697 the Treaty of Ryswick restored Leopold of the house of Lorraine as absolute ruler. He found the duchy devastated by war, and devoted himself to its economic rehabilitation. He opposed *mainmorte* as a hindrance to economic growth, and, in addition, as a status unfitting the dignity of man. High circles in his realm supported him in these views, and in a decision of 1701 the *parlement* called *mainmorte* "the hated sign of slavery that degraded the person and the property." In 1711 Leopold decreed the abolition of *mainmorte*, with indemnification to be paid by the peasants to their seigniors. In the preamble to the decree he declared that "nothing is more worthy of our attention than to save the liberty of the people whom God has put under our dominion, and to make them equal to each other by suppressing their most odious servitude." Instead of being greeted by huzzas, as Leopold expected, the decree aroused so much opposition, including that of the peasants, who objected to the size of the indemnity, that Leopold had to suspend it in 1713. An effort at amendment of the law, including halving the indemnification, still met with strong resistance so that it, too, was dropped. Finally, on 31 December 1719 Leopold ordered the abolition of *mainmorte* without indemnification on his own properties, and hoped that other proprietors would follow suit. "My income will be reduced," he said, "but I can afford it, for Lorraine will be enriched with many new citizens from whom I can only profit." Apparently, the other serfowners of Lorraine did not think that they could afford it. Their peasants remained in the *mainmorte* status until the French Revolution, when they, and all the other *mainmorte* peasants of France (which had annexed Lorraine in 1766), were freed of their bonds by governmental fiat.[27]

In Prussia the flight of peasants from crown estates occasioned concern about the need for reform. In 1709 Frederick I declared that efforts should be made to improve peasant tenures on his manors that bordered Poland, the country to which many of his peasants fled. Apparently, very little was

[26] Tsentral'nyi statisticheskii komitet (1863), 306; Ford (1922), 197; Lütge (1967), 227; Müller (1965), 153-154, 165-171, 176-178; Lütge (1949), 28.
[27] Darmstaedter (1897), 117-118, 191, 199-203.

accomplished. His successor, Frederick William I, in 1718, 1719, and 1723 ordered the introduction of hereditary tenure on the royal domain in East Prussia, Lithuania, and Pomerania. Again the royal mandate was without effect, primarily because of the foot-dragging and outright opposition of the bureaucrats charged with the implementation of the legislation. Frederick II was more successful. In 1763 he forbad the lessees of royal properties to demand the compulsory labor of peasant youths. In 1777 he ordered the establishment of hereditary tenure on crown estates in all provinces. Then in the reign of his next two successors, and particularly of Frederick William III (1797-1840), a series of decrees had by 1807 allowed the crown peasant to redeem his obligations, end his servile status, and become a free, hereditary tenant and in some instances the full proprietor of his holding. In Mecklenburg, peasants on estates of the sovereigns were allowed to commute their labor services into cash payments. In Bavaria, Elector Karl Theodore decreed in 1779 that peasants on his properties could change their insecure tenures into hereditary ones, and could convert the fee payable to him upon transfer of a holding into a fixed annual sum. The measure met with resistance and even sabotage from the bureaucrats who were supposed to administer it, and with suspicion and mistrust from the peasants, whom it was supposed to help. As a result, it was almost entirely without result.[28]

In Austria the efforts of the ruler had a limited success. In 1775 Franz Anton von Raab presented Empress Maria Theresa with a detailed plan of reform for manors of the crown. Raab (1722-1783), member of the Imperial Commerce Commission, made his reputation as an agricultural expert and had been appointed director of the crown estates in Bohemia. He proposed to free the peasants on these estates from their serfdom without indemnification to the crown, and to convert them into hereditary tenants. The crown would give up all of its demesne land and divide it into peasant holdings. Buildings and equipment would be sold to the peasants at reasonable prices, to be paid over a period of 10 years. The annual rent for each holding would be based upon the average net income from the holding over the preceding 10 years. The empress and her advisors expressed interest in the plan and turned over two manors to Raab for a test of his proposal. The quick success of the system on these two properties, and particularly the increased income the crown now drew from them, persuaded the government to extend the system to other manors of the crown in Bohemia and in other provinces. Despite its success, private landowners, aside from such corporate proprietors as the royal cities of Bohemia and certain welfare and religious foundations with whom the government had special influence, avowed little enthusiasm for the reform, and only a few of them adopted it.[29]

[28] Knapp (1887), I, 81-89; Knapp (1909), 543-544; Mager (1955), 341; Brentano (1899), 258-259; Lütge (1949), 31-32.

[29] Wright (1960), chs. 4, 7, 8.

Tentative efforts at reform on royal estates in Denmark began in the 1760's, when peasants there were allowed to commute their obligations into an annual cash payment, and were given hereditary tenure. The state also sold some of its properties to raise money, and gave peasants the opportunity to purchase land. The sales began in 1764 on Fyn, second largest of the Danish islands, and on the mainland in south Jutland. Most of the royal land in these regions was, indeed, bought by peasants. Elsewhere, however, peasants either lacked the money or found the terms of sale too difficult. As a result, instead of many peasant-owned holdings, about fifty new privately owned manors were created between 1764 and 1774 out of these former crown estates. Positive reforms came only in 1784, when Crown Prince Frederick assumed the regency. He ordered the conversion of about 1,300 peasant holdings on crown manors in north Zealand into hereditary tenancies at a fixed annual rental. He also mandated the consolidation of the open fields shared by these holdings into individual farmsteads. The crown bore the cost of the operation, which was completed by 1790. Meanwhile, serfdom had been abolished between 1765 and the mid-1780's on nearly all of the sovereign's estates in Schleswig-Holstein, and hereditary tenure introduced.[30]

In France *mainmorte* was widely criticized in enlightened circles as a vestigial form of serfdom, and therefore an offense against natural liberty and human dignity. In response to these protests, and prodded by Jacques Necker, the minister of finances, King Louis XVI decided to take action. In a decree of 8 August 1779 he ordered the end of *mainmorte* on manors of the crown, with the peasants to pay an indemnification of 1 sou for each *arpent* of land they held (the *arpent* of Paris equalled .34 hectares). The decree also abolished the *droit de suite* for all owners of *mainmorte* peasants. The text of the law condemned serfdom, declared that the king wished to see it ended everywhere in France, but explained that his regard for the right of private property constrained him from ordering a general abolition. Instead, he hoped that other serfowners would follow his example and voluntarily free their *mainmorte* peasants. Louis' pious wish was destined to disappointment. Some seigniors, especially in Haute-Saône in Franche-Comté, did release their peasants in response to the king's plea. Other would-be emancipators ran afoul of bureaucratic inefficiency and opposition. The abbot of Luxeuil wanted to free the serfs of his abbey but was unable to secure the needed governmental approval from the bureaucrats, so that the peasants were still serfs when the Revolution came. Most owners of *mainmorte* peasants, however, not only refused to follow the precedent set by the throne, but actively opposed it. One cogent reason for their opposition was expressed by the bishop of St. Claude, whose chapter

[30] Nielsen (1933), 318-319, 319n.; Scharling (1909), 579; Sugenheim (1961), 519; Hvitfeld (1963), 498.

owned 12,000 *mainmorte* peasants. His Grace explained that emancipation would cost the chapter 25,000 livres in annual income. Nearly half of France's serfs lived in Franche-Comté and the *parlement* there, most of whose members owned serfs, bitterly opposed the royal decree of 8 August 1779 and refused to register it. That prevented it from becoming law and being put into effect in Franche-Comté. Finally, in 1787 the king compelled the *parlement* to register the decree, along with other of his ordinances that it had refused to register during the preceding ten years. Even after this, the government did not immediately proceed to carry out the reform on all of its properties. Peasants of a village of the crown in Franche-Comté complained in their *cahier* in 1789 that they were still in the *mainmorte* status.[31]

As in most everything else that affected the common welfare, the sovereigns of Russia lagged behind other rulers in concern about the condition of the peasantry on state land. Indeed, while other monarchs of the eighteenth century sought to improve the lot of the people who lived on their properties, the tsars went in the opposite direction, imposing new restrictions on the state peasantry. Now, like the serfs, peasants had to obtain official approval before they could make a trip away from their home village, and the passport given them was valid only for a limited period. They were forbidden to operate factories and workshops, to be parties to leases and contracts, or to draw and accept bills of exchange. Government officials were set over them to supervise their activities. Worst of all, state peasants were always in danger of being reduced to serfdom. Between 1740 and 1801 tsars and tsaritsas gave 1,304,000 adult male serfs to private individuals, most of them court favorites. The practice continued on into the nineteenth century but on a much reduced scale.

In 1764 Catherine II, in a directive that concerned two manors that belonged to the court, called attention to the need to improve the farming practices of the peasants who lived on these properties, and of their need for larger holdings so that they could support themselves from their land. A small number of peasants were moved to larger holdings on other manors. Catherine's son, Paul, while still heir to the throne, decided in the 1780's to convert the peasants on his personal estate at Gatchina, near St. Petersburg, to hereditary tenants. He reduced their obligations, advanced loans to them, provided instruction in improved farming methods, and supplied them with new implements. His experiment proved to be a failure. If a contemporary English traveler can be believed, the blame lay with the peasants, who, according to the Englishman, "made shift to sell their new property, and drink the value in two years; they failed to pay even the stipulated rent, and petitioned to be put under the old establishment."

[31] Millot (1973), 132-137, 141-142, 147-168; Soboul (1960), I, 112; Aulard (1919), 13-18.

After Paul became tsar he created a new agency, the Department of the Appanage, to administer certain properties of the crown that he assigned for the support of members of the royal family not in the direct line of succession. (Those in the direct line were supported by the regular fiscal revenues of the state.) By 1861 over 800,000 adult male peasants and their families lived on Appanage land. They found themselves worse off than they had been before they were put under the supervision of the new department. Nearly all of them now paid larger quitrents, they had to put up with bureaucratic meddling and inefficiency, and most of the efforts of the department to advance their economic wellbeing proved unsuccessful.[32]

In contrast to the Appanage peasantry, the lot of the Russian state peasants did improve, beginning with the last years of the eighteenth century. The restraints on their activities in trade and industry (which actually had been largely disregarded) were lifted, restrictions on their freedom of movement were eased, and they gained the right to own uninhabited land in their own name. By 1858 state peasants were the proprietors of about ten million acres in European Russia. The most significant and far-reaching reform came during the reign of Nicholas I. From the outset of his reign in 1825 Nicholas had concerned himself with considerations of improvements in the status of the peasantry. Like monarchs elsewhere who confronted this problem, Nicholas' respect for the right of private property and for the prerogatives of the nobility dissuaded him from introducing reforms that would affect the peasants of private landowners. He feared, too, that if he freed these people without giving them land that now belonged to their seigniors he would call into being a rabble of landless rural proletarians who would be a threat to civil order. So Nicholas, like rulers of the eighteenth century in other servile lands, decided to restrict his reforms to the peasants of the state. In 1837 he transferred the state peasantry from the jurisdiction of Count E. F. Kankrin, Minister of Finance, who had obstructed the introduction of changes Nicholas wanted to make, to a newly established agency, the Ministry of State Domain. He chose Count P. D. Kiselev, member of an old, well-placed, and moderately wealthy landowning family, to head the new ministry. Kiselev had distinguished himself as governor of the Danubian Principalities during the Russian occupation in 1829-1834, and as director of a new bureau created in 1835 to reorganize the administration of state lands in the province of St. Petersburg. Both Nicholas and Kiselev calculated that successful regulation and reform of the state peasantry would persuade private serfowners of the benefits to the serfowner of improvements in the status of their peasants, and would gradually persuade them to free their serfs voluntarily. Kiselev, with the full support of the tsar, set out with his accustomed vigor and imagination to

[32] Semevskii (1901), ii, 146-147; Swinton (1792), 448; Blum (1961), 355-358, 488-489, 493-499.

improve the lot of the state peasantry. Among his innovations was a cadastral survey of state land that led to a more equitable distribution of the obligations paid to the government by the state peasants. The survey also put an end, or certainly made more difficult, the expropriation or the illegal use by private proprietors of the land of state peasants. Other improvements sponsored by Kiselev's ministry included programs in general and agricultural education, publication of agricultural manuals, the distribution of land to peasants with small holdings, and encouragement of new crops and better farm techniques. Instead of inspiring imitators, however, Kiselev's labors on behalf of the state peasantry gained him the enmity of many seigniors, who recognized his activities as the entering wedge of the tsar's program to end serfdom.[33]

Well over a million peasants lived on state-owned land in nine provinces in White Russia, Little Russia, and Lithuania that Russia had annexed in the partitions of Poland (or reunited with Russia, as the tsarist government preferred to put it). The government leased most of these properties to the highest bidder. The peasants who lived on the rented properties had to pay obligations to the lessee, or arrendator as he was called. The amount of these obligations was set in the inventories that were drawn up for each property. There was little or no supervision of these arrangements so that the arrendators were free to exploit and mistreat the peasants. The complaints of the peasants about their mistreatment went unheeded until the 1830's. Then investigations were ordered and their findings caused the government to declare in 1853 that it would no longer rent out populated state land.[34]

Tsar Nicholas and earlier rulers in other servile lands were disappointed in their hopes that the success of their reforms on lands of the state and the crown would persuade private proprietors to follow their example. The record shows that few proprietors did. But the record also shows that the movement that ended with the emancipation of the peasantry began with the reforms on the properties of the state and the crown. The emancipation, wrote Otto Hintze in a study of the Prussian experience, was like a play in two acts, with the reforms on the manors of the crown the first act.[35] Those reforms were the first major assault on the old hierarchical order. That this assault was made at the command of the sovereign must have proved unsettling to many seigniors. They must have been shaken, too, when they learned that the reforms not only benefited the peasants, but could also produce an increase in the revenues the state drew from these peasants.

[33] Pintner (1967), 153-155, 157-160; *Krest'ianskoe dvizhenie . . . 1826-1849* (1961), 15-16; Blum (1961), 485-493.
[34] Blum (1961), 480-481.   [35] Hintze (1967), 508.

CHAPTER 11

First Attempts at Reform

I

THOUGH daunted by the opposition of nobles and bureaucrats, and though reluctant to interfere with the rights of property, monarchs did not restrict their efforts at reform to their own peasants. They proclaimed laws and directives that they hoped would reduce the privileges of the seigniors and diminish their authority over their peasants. Generally, only small successes at best, and often failure, attended upon their attempts at reform. In a few instances, however, sovereigns did effect significant changes, and in one small land the decrees of the ruler brought about the dismantling of the entire traditional agrarian structure. That small land was the duchy of Savoy.

The 4,131 square miles of Savoy were wedged between the Rhone River and Lake Geneva. In 1760 it had a population of about 400,000. The Savoyards had been able to support themselves adequately until their duke became king of Sardinia in 1720. Thereafter, their rulers imposed always heavier taxes to get the money they needed to support their grandiose ambitions in northern Italy. These levies, on top of the obligations owed by the peasants to the seigniors, impoverished the villagers, forced thousands of them to become migrant workers who sought employment in neighboring lands, and reduced many to beggars. The duke was one of Europe's most absolute rulers. The States-General had been suppressed late in the sixteenth century. Neither nobles nor clergy nor commons were united into corporate bodies, so that there was no vehicle, as there was in other lands, for organized opposition to the will of the sovereign. In any event, most of the nobles were of recent creation. They had purchased their patents of nobility from the kings of Sardinia, who raised large sums from these sales to bourgeois lawyers and merchants who had social ambitions. Apparently, these jumped-up Savoyards used up most of their wealth to buy their titles: a memorandum of 1774 declared that "there is no land that has more poor nobles than Savoy."[1]

The rulers of the duchy appreciated their position and took full advantage of it. "Our authority is despotic," wrote Victor Amadeus II in 1721 in his instruction to the governor of Savoy, "and does not need consent from any corporate body. . . . The first estate, the clergy, cannot assemble without our permission and the other two estates cannot form themselves into corporate bodies."[2] Victor Amadeus' son and successor, Charles Emmanuel III

---

[1] Bruchet (1908), xxi-xxii, xxiv-xxv.   [2] *Ibid.*, xiii.

(1730-1773), used that despotic authority to reform the lord-peasant relationship. Charles Emmanuel was a high-minded, honorable, and humane man, of whom Frederick II of Prussia remarked that "without the king of Sardinia it would be disreputable to be a king." He was also precise to the point of pedantry and possessed of extreme caution. However, once all of his doubts had been resolved, he settled upon a course of action to which he held fast. For many years there had been discussion of reforms and concrete proposals, but Charles Emmanuel did not take positive measures until late in his long reign. The humanitarian and rational ideals of the Enlightenment, to which he subscribed, helped persuade him to order reform. Other considerations may have been more influential. The flight of peasants from the duchy reduced the fiscal income of the duke. The abolition of servility and of obligations to the seignior would keep others from leaving, and perhaps lure back many of those who had already left. Emancipation would also banish forever the endless friction and the costly legal actions between lords and peasants over the exact terms of tenures and of obligations, whose origins and justification lay far in the past and so were uncertain. Cancellation of obligations to the seigniors would allow the state to increase its taxes, and it was hoped that the peasants would have enough left to invest in capital improvements to their holdings.

After three separate commissions appointed by Charles Emmanuel had studied the problem of emancipation, the duke issued a decree dated 20 January 1762. It freed his own peasants from *mainmorte*, and ordered that peasants of private seigniors could demand their freedom from their lords, with indemnification to the lord. The peasants could not afford to pay the sizable sums needed for indemnification, and so the decree had small results. Charles Emmanuel then ordered the Procurator-General of Savoy, Count Tonengo, to draft more effective legislation. Tonengo's proposals, after study by three more commissions, became the law of 19 December 1771. The decree, published in May 1772, arranged for voluntary emancipation, but ordered that, if lord and peasant could not reach agreement within a specified period, government officials would set the terms. The indemnification fee was fixed at a low level. To raise the needed money the peasant community (the entire operation was on a communal basis) could sell part of its communal land. To provide the seigniors with a secure investment for the indemnification money they received from their peasants, the state offered drafts on the land tax that were transferable and similar to state bonds, and that paid 3.5 per cent. Once the redemption agreement was concluded, the peasants would become the free owners of their holdings and the direct subjects of the duke. Simultaneously, all the ties that seigniors had with the land and with their peasants would be severed. Since few seigniors operated demesnes, the emancipation completely divorced the nobility from the land.

The peasants greeted the new law with enthusiastic approval. Noble and church proprietors met it with gloomy forebodings. It would reduce their already low incomes, and they regarded it as a violation of the right of property. Charles Emmanuel died just as the law went into effect. His successor, Victor Amadeus III, a weaker and more pliable man, acceded to the plaints and persuasions of the proprietors. In 1775 he ordered the suspension of the emancipation decree, and appointed a commission to study it. The commission recommended amendments but did not alter the basic principles of the legislation. On 2 January 1778 the amended decree was issued. After that the redemption proceeded smoothly though slowly until 1790. Then peasants, inflamed by the revolutionary happenings in neighboring France, demanded immediate completion of the emancipation, and emphasized their demand by pillaging chateaus and burning their archives. The regime tried to appease the peasants by speeding up the operation. In 1792 the French invaded and annexed Savoy, and by a decree of 27 October 1792 ordered the immediate emancipation of all peasants without indemnification, and cancelled the redemption payments that were still owed by peasants.[3]

The proclamation of emancipation by the rulers of Savoy had aroused admiration in neighboring France. *Philosophes* like Voltaire invoked the example of Savoy as a model for France. So did obscure rural communes in their *cahiers* to the Estates General in 1789. Conservatives, too, admired the Savoyard emancipation. Joseph de Maistre, himself a native of Savoy, in arguing against the French intervention in his homeland, pointed out that the House of Savoy enfranchised men and land "without injustice and without discord, but wisely and tranquilly."[4] Yet, despite the attention attracted by the emancipation in Savoy and, more significantly, despite the importance of France as the center of the Enlightenment, the French government of the *ancien régime* did nothing to forward the emancipation of the French peasantry. The rulers of France, alone among the major sovereigns of servile Europe, did not make even a limited or half-hearted sustained effort to persuade seigniors to agree to reforms in the status and obligations of their peasants.

In those Swiss cantons where peasants were in a servile status, oligarchies of patricians and burghers controlled the government. In Berne, and in Zurich, initiative for reform came from societies organized to promote progressive measures in the economy and the society of their respective cantons. The members of these societies recognized the retardative effects of the existing system upon agricultural advancement. But much of their own incomes and much of the cantonal revenues came from the dues and services paid by the servile peasants. So plans for reform were discussed but

[3] *Ibid.*, doc. no. 1-18, 29-31; Darmstaedter (1896), 33-42, 52-59.
[4] Bruchet (1908), 320-322.

little was actually accomplished. The merchant-oligarchs of Basel in 1764 ordered the commutation of the labor services demanded of the peasants there, but they did not see fit to free the *mainmortable* peasants. In June 1785 a special commission in the canton of Solothurn arrived at the conclusion that it was unseemly for serfdom to exist in a "free republic." A few months later the government emancipated without indemnification all *mainmortable* peasants within its borders. The act of emancipation, issued on 9 August 1785, resounded with such phrases as "equality and natural dignity" and "the precious joy of liberty."[5]

In Denmark nobles had blocked the efforts made by the throne during the first half of the seventeenth century to improve the condition of the peasantry. Then in the second half of that century the monarchs seized absolute power and successfully maintained and asserted it. In a decree of 21 February 1702, Frederick IV ordered the abolition of serfdom in all Denmark. Actually it existed only in the islands of Zealand and Fyn. Many of the freed peasants gave up their holdings and became hired laborers, or migrated to the towns. Their departure apparently put an intolerable burden upon the seigniors. The state held the seigniors responsible for the taxes it levied upon peasant holdings, and the state expected its taxes, whether the holdings were occupied or vacant. The seigniors also depended upon the labor obligation of their peasants to work their demesnes.

Though dismayed by the decree, the nobles lacked the power to force its repeal or to obstruct its implementation. But the throne itself supplied them with the way to frustrate the law's intent. A royal decree of 22 February 1701, the first in a series of decrees that dealt with compulsory service in the militia, placed the obligation of service exclusively upon the peasantry. The draft call went to the manor owner, who had to produce the required number of recruits. To make sure that the proprietor had a pool big enough to meet the draft calls, the 1701 law required all male peasants to remain on the manor until they had completed the six years of military service required of the conscripts. The seignior decided who would serve. It was a simple matter for the seignior to arrange that, instead of a service of six consecutive years, the term of each peasant draftee was split up, so that the peasant did not complete his six years until he was in his forties or even fifties. So, for all practical purposes, the emancipation decree of 1702 was without effect. Even worse, the militia legislation not only allowed serfdom to stay on in the islands; it provided the vehicle for the introduction of serfdom into those parts of the kingdom where it had not before been known.

In 1730 Frederick's successor, Christian VI (someone once remarked that Danish history was a dreary procession of Fredericks and Christians), recognizing that serfdom had been reintroduced through the back door, so to

[5] Frauendorfer (1957), I, 196-197; Nabholz (1938), 167; Darmstaedter (1897), 72; Rappard (1912), 138.

speak, abolished the militia. That meant freedom for the peasant. The damaging impact this apparently had upon the welfare of the nobility persuaded Christian to change his mind. On 4 February 1733 he reestablished compulsory service in the militia, and directed that all male peasants at age fourteen had to register as potential recruits, and remain on the register until they turned thirty-five. During the years from fourteen to thirty-five the peasant could not move from his home village without the permission of the seignior. In 1746 a new law ordered that after completion of his militia service the peasant, if his lord so commanded, had to continue to live in his home village and take over a holding. Now the peasant was bound to the manor of the seignior for the rest of his life. In 1764 the process was completed when the king decreed that male peasants had to be registered as potential recruits at the age of four. That prevented children between four and fourteen from leaving their home villages. These, and other decrees in the succeeding years, provided the nobility with greater authority over their peasants than they had ever before possessed.[6]

Meanwhile, in mid-century Denmark—as in other European lands of that era—the upper reaches of the social order developed a keen interest in agriculture. Publications appeared that stressed the need for improvements, and in 1757 the government appointed a committee to determine the causes of agricultural retardation in Denmark. The committee's recommendations on such matters as the consolidation of scattered strips, the division of common lands, and improvement in the network of roads, were enacted into law. Proposals affecting the relationship between lord and peasant, however, were treated with much caution until 1770, when Johann Friedrich Struensee became chief minister of state. German physician to the king and inamorato of the queen, Struensee had quickly made himself master of his weak-minded patient. He dismissed from office all those hostile to him and became the dictator of Denmark. Between March 1771 and January 1772 he issued over a thousand cabinet orders, for an average of more than three a day, that affected every sector of Danish life. His agrarian legislation would have transformed rural society. His tenure of power, however, was shortlived. Early in 1772 he was overthrown and executed by nobles who were outraged by his political acts, his disregard for Danish national culture (for instance, all his decrees and regulations were in German), and by his personal behavior—particularly, his relationship with the queen. A group of conservatives, headed by Oeve Höegh-Guldberg, and supported by the king's stepmother, Queen-Dowager Juliana Maria, and her son, the king's half-brother, took over control of the state. The new government, which held on to power until 1784, scrapped Struensee's reforms, but did advocate measures to improve farm production and to facilitate the consolidation of scattered parcels into compact farms.[7]

[6] Sugenheim (1861), 513, 514-515; Jensen (1937), 43-45; Commager (1928), 76-77; Ashley (1924), 245-246.

[7] Nielsen (1933), 316-318, 324-325; Commager (1928), 38.

II

In the Hapsburg monarchy determined autocrats carried through more reforms in the lord-peasant relationship than did the rulers of any other of
the major servile lands. In the second half of the seventeenth century peasant unrest had erupted in Bohemia, where seigniors had imposed heavy
demands upon their serfs and had appropriated much of their land. Emperor Leopold I was fearful lest the risings spill over into other sections of
his crown lands. He was concerned, too, about the loss of tax income that
followed from the flight of oppressed peasants, and from the conversion of
peasant land into demesne on which no taxes were paid. He decided that
action was necessary. In 1680 he issued a decree that set limits to the demands that seigniors could make of their peasants, and he forbad unfair
treatment of the peasants. However, the law contained no provisions for its
enforcement, and so was a dead letter from the moment of its appearance.
If anything, it worsened the condition of some peasants, whose seigniors
had demanded fewer days of labor services than the 1680 law fixed as a
maximum, and who now increased their demands to the legal limit. Later
legislation in 1717 and 1738 proved no more effective than the law of 1680.
Meaningful reform came only during the reigns of Empress Maria Theresa
and of her son Joseph II.

The first years of the empress' long reign did not augur well for substantive change. Her accession in 1740 provided the signal for an expensive war
that ended with grievous territorial losses. Her early efforts to strengthen
the central administration brought confrontation with the still powerful
provincial estates. She herself, in interests and in intellect, seemed scarcely
suited to preside over the reconstruction of her empire and, as one historian
has put it, to "overcome the storm that threatened the existence of the
House of Austria."[8] Events were to show that she accomplished that difficult task. They also showed that she was far more effective in peacefully
bringing about changes in the condition of the peasantry than any of her
more glamorous and more intellectual contemporaries among the crowned
heads of Europe.

The empress realized or, perhaps more accurately, the able advisors she
so wisely chose convinced her, that the welfare of the peasantry, the prime
source of tax revenue and of recruits, was of paramount importance to the
well-being and the power of the state. "The sheep should be well-fed," she
once said, "in order to make it yield more wool and more milk." In a
memorandum of 1770 she wrote, "The peasantry, who are the most
numerous class of the citizenry and who are the foundation and greatest
strength of the state, should be maintained in such a condition that they
can support themselves and their families and in addition be able to pay
their taxes in times of both war and peace. The rights of the seignior must
give way before these considerations."[9] She never abandoned these opin-

[8] F. Walter in Hantsch (1962), 235.   [9] Király (1969), 56; Grüll (1963), 375.

ions. Nor did she abandon her resolve to strengthen the central power and impose uniformity throughout her realm by regulations, legal codifications, and an expanded bureaucracy.

In the reorganization of local governments ordered by Maria Theresa in the 1750's, imperial bureaucrats replaced the officials of the provincial diets. That introduced a greater impartiality in the assessment of taxes, and in the dispensation of justice and the right of appeal. All of this added up to increased protection for the peasant from extortionate demands and unjust treatment by his seignior. Indeed, the new bureaucracy was specifically charged with the responsibility of looking after the welfare of the peasants, so that they could afford to pay their taxes. The fees paid on the transfer of holdings were regulated. Restrictions on the sale of agricultural goods by peasants were repealed, and peasants could now trade freely in the farm goods they produced. Ordinances made excessive subdivision of holdings more difficult. A law of 1769 limited the authority of the lord's court, and another decree in 1772 prescribed the manner by which peasants could lodge complaints against their masters. Special efforts were made to stop further seigniorial annexation of peasant land, and consequent reduction in land tax revenues. An attempt to restore previously annexed land to peasants failed, but the drive to prevent further engrossment met with success in parts, if not all, of the empire.[10]

Serious peasant unrest in Silesia in 1766, in Bohemia and Moravia in 1770 and 1775, famine in these provinces in 1770, 1771, and 1775, and the resistance to change of the nobility, stirred up debate in Vienna and proposals for further reform. The empress and her advisors decided that the times called for more positive and direct action. Beginning in 1771 a series of codes were promulgated that established norms to which lords and peasants had to adhere. The codes set maxima on the obligations the seigniors could demand, especially the number of days of labor services. The first of these codes was for Silesia. It was followed by similar codes for Lower Austria in 1772, Bohemia and Moravia in 1775, Styria and Carinthia in 1778, Carniola in 1782, and Galicia in 1781 and 1786. The codes were apparently not rigorously enforced, and the establishment of maximum obligations brought no benefits to the many peasants whose lords demanded less than the maximums set by the codes. Their issuance, however, marked an important advance in the intervention of the state in the lord-peasant relationship.[11]

The central government had concerned itself with the lord-peasant relationship in the kingdom of Hungary even before it had put out codes for the German and Slav crown lands. In 1756, after a peasant rising in Slavonia,

[10] Wright (1966), 36-37; Grüll (1952), 174-175; Link (1949), 47, 61-62, 66; Hoffmann (1952), I, 285-286.
[11] Vilfran (1973), 8-9; Feigl (1964), 92-93; Wright (1966), 51-52.

in southwestern Hungary, Maria Theresa ordered the introduction of legislation there that set the size of holdings and the amount of obligations that seigniors could demand. Then in 1765-1766 peasants in the Great Hungarian Plain revolted against increased seigniorial obligations and seigniorial expropriations of their land. Troops had to be sent in to put down the disturbances. That gave the empress the opportunity to impose a code in 1767 that regulated the lord-peasant relationship. The code, called the *Urbarium*, was a long and detailed document. It set the size of peasant holdings according to the quality of the land, spelled out the obligations the lord could require, and forbad seigniors to remove peasants, without special permission, from land designated as urbarial, that is, held by villein tenure, or to decrease the amount of this land. Peasants and their lords could agree to conditions that differed from those prescribed in the *Urbarium* so long as they were not disadvantageous to the peasant.[12]

The Hungarian Diet refused for years to give its endorsement to the *Urbarium*. Legally that made it an extra-constitutional regulation. Not until the session of 1790-1791 did the Diet agree to accept it. To make certain that the code would be enforced despite the obduracy of the Diet, Maria Theresa ordered that special commissioners were to handle all matters concerning its application. Actually, though the provisions of the code benefitted peasants in western Hungary, they were detrimental to those who lived in the far larger part of Hungary that had been ruled by the Turks, for the obligations set by the code exceeded those which the peasants there had hitherto paid. Perhaps this may have softened the opposition of the nobility to the forced application of a law to which they had not given their approval. In 1780 the government extended the *Urbarium* to Croatia and the Banat. It was never applied to semi-autonomous Transylvania, so that peasants of that province were more harshly exploited than their fellows in the rest of the Hungarian kingdom.[13]   During the last fifteen years of her reign Maria Theresa had her eldest son, Joseph, as her co-ruler. Mother and son had frequent and sometimes bitter clashes over policies, but the empress was very much the senior and deciding partner. In 1780 the mother died and now the son had free reign. Joseph had no taste for compromise and possessed neither tolerance nor understanding of those who disagreed with him. He wanted to make over his empire and he thought he could do that by use of his despotic power. The motivations for his revolutionary program have been attributed variously to ideology, politics, fiscal and military considerations, and humanitarian regard for his subjects. Whatever the compulsions that drove him, his agrarian program lay at the heart of his overall plan. He wanted to transform the agrarian structure of his em-

[12] Eszlary (1960), 392; Mailath (1838), *passim*.
[13] Marczali (1910), 193; Wellmann (1968), 1194; Paget (1839), II, 311-314; Király (1967), 142n., 156.

pire. The measures he introduced were the most radical reform program of any of the servile lands up to that time.

He took his first major step in September 1781. He limited seigniorial jurisdiction over their peasants, and provided procedure by which peasants could lodge complaints against their masters with local officials of the central government. A few days later, on 1 November 1781, he promulgated a short decree that bestowed important new freedoms upon the peasants. Now the peasant could move away from his home village at will, needing only a certificate from his seignior attesting that he had met all of his obligations. He could learn any trade or skill that he wished, and he could freely go wherever his work took him. He no longer needed his lord's permission to wed. The compulsory labor service required of peasant children was abolished except for parentless orphans. Finally, the law forbad the imposition of obligations beyond those already demanded. When first issued, the decree applied only to Bohemia, Moravia, and Silesia. In the immediately succeeding years it was extended to other crown lands, and in 1785 the emperor signed a similar edict for Hungary.[14] In a patent of 1 November 1781 Joseph inaugurated his drive to improve rural tenures. This initial act provided greater security for peasants with hereditary tenure. In later legislation of 1785 and 1789 he converted the tenures of those who held at the will of their masters—and most of the empire's peasants held by this most insecure of tenures—into hereditary occupants of their holdings. By the terms of this single most successful of Joseph's reforms the seignior could evict the peasant only for causes specified in the legislation.[15]

The commutation of labor dues into cash payments was another facet of Joseph's agrarian program. Convinced that peasant farming was more advantageous than large-scale farming both to the economy of the empire and to the peasant himself, he wanted the peasant to use all of his labor on his own holding.[16] He was convinced, too, of the need to erase the legal and fiscal distinction between noble and peasant land, and to tax them both at the same rate. In 1785, to prepare the way, he ordered a survey of the area and yield of all productive land in the German and Slav crown lands, to serve as the basis for tax assessments. The cadastre, made hurriedly by inexperienced workers and containing many errors, was completed in 1789. Joseph now had the foundation for his most revolutionary—and final—reform. On 10 February 1789 a patent appeared that was to become effective on 1 November of that year. The patent ordered that all populated land, whether held by seignior or peasant, had to pay an annual tax of $12^2/9$ per cent of its assessed value. The law also decreed that the dues and services

---

[14] Text of 1 November 1781 decree in Grünberg (1893), II, 390-391; Balazs (1956), 298; Grünberg (1901), 37.
[15] Grünberg (1894), I, 55, 260-272, 364-365.   [16] Lütge (1967a), *passim*.

the peasant had to pay his seignior were to be commuted into a cash rental not to exceed 17⁷/₉ per cent of the peasant's annual gross income from his holding. Peasants who paid less than 2 florins in land tax, and those who held land on which the seignior paid the land tax, were excluded from the operation of the law.[17] That last provision meant that smallholders and cotters and landless laborers, all of whom paid servile obligations to their seigniors, would not benefit from the legislation. These people made up a large and always increasing proportion of the rural population, and in some places were already a large majority of the peasantry. In Bohemia, for example, in 1790 about 122,000 peasant taxpayers paid a land tax of 2 florins or more, while about 442,000 paid less than 2 florins.[18] In reality, then, Joseph's famed reform would have affected only a part, and often only a minority, of the peasantry.

Whatever its shortcomings, the new law never was put into effect. In February 1790, less than four months after it was supposed to become operative, Joseph died. He left behind an empire in confusion. War had broken out with the Ottomans and was going badly. The Austrian Netherlands had successfully revolted. At home the crown lands were seething with discontent, and Hungary and Galicia teetered on the edge of open rebellion. In his efforts to reshape his realm Joseph had overreached himself. His reforms, capped by the decree of 10 February 1789, brought about a groundswell of opposition that threatened to tear apart the realm. The last decree not only would have done away with the privileged status of demesne land; the limit set on the cash rental paid by the peasant in lieu of his dues and services would have severely reduced seigniorial incomes, in a few cases by as much as two-thirds. Nor did the February decree satisfy the peasants. Those who were excluded from its benefits had the most cause for dissatisfaction. And those who did come under its terms were unhappy because it did not go far enough for their tastes.

Joseph realized that he had to yield ground. In the last weeks of his life the saddened reformer repealed all of his reforms in Hungary (where unrest was most threatening) except the patent of 1785, which had removed many of the restraints upon the freedom of the Hungarian peasant. His brother and successor, Leopold II (1790-1792), revoked the decree of 10 February 1789, but he retained the earlier reforms, despite insistent demands from the estates of every province for their repeal.

The widespread and deep-seated dissatisfaction, and the real danger of the dissolution of the state engendered by Joseph's policies, persuaded Leopold, and after him Francis I, to abandon the program of agrarian reform. Their conviction of the perils of such a program was strengthened and confirmed by the events of the French Revolution. Now any and all

[17] Patent of 10 February 1789 in Grünberg (1893), II, 442-445.
[18] Wright (1966), 147n.

reforms were identified as the work of revolutionaries who conspired to spread the "fever of freedom" and "the poison of Jacobinism." And so, instead of accelerating change in the Austrian Monarchy, the French Revolution helped to retard it. Over a half century passed before the rulers of the Monarchy once again faced up to the problem of agrarian reform. Rather than regarding servility as undesirable, inhumane, and harmful to state and peasant alike, the men who ran the Monarchy during these years feared that lessening the peasant's burdens and granting him freedom would encourage idleness and breed public disorder. To their way of thinking, the labor service was a "school of obedience and humility." The only reform of any significance came in 1836, and then at the insistence of the nobles of the Hungarian Diet. A new *Urbarium* appeared in that year, superseding the code of 1767, with provisions that introduced some improvements in the status of the Hungarian peasantry.[19]

In contrast to the achievements in agrarian reform of the Austrian sovereigns of the eighteenth century, the rulers of Prussia accomplished remarkably little. They talked a good deal about the need to improve the condition of the peasantry, and to limit the authority of the seigniors. Frederick William I, who came to the throne in 1713, spoke of improving the tenure of peasants on private estates, and even of granting freedom to the peasants of Pomerania, but nothing came of these discussions.[20] The record of his son, Frederick II, was not much better. This seems to embarrass some German historians, for Frederick, of course, is a great national hero. He was renowned as a devotee of the Enlightenment, an intimate of *philosophes*, and as something of a minor *philosophe* himself, who could produce statements that had the proper humanitarian resonance. "Surely no human being is born to be like a slave," he once said. "Reason is offended by such an abuse," and he referred to serfdom as a *"coutume barbare."*[21] Certainly a man of these sensibilities could not be responsible for the failure to initiate reforms. So German historians usually put the blame upon the bureaucrats and the provincial estates, who stoutly, and nearly always successfully, thwarted proposed reforms, or dragged their feet in applying the reforms they could not repress. The exigencies of *raison d'état* are used, too. Humanitarian and philosophical considerations had to give way to Frederick's need to provide for, and hold the loyalty of, the nobility, who staffed the army he needed to make Prussia a great power. These and similar explanations doubtless possess some merit. One wonders, however, why Empress Maria Theresa, whom no one would ever consider a disciple of the Enlightenment, who was not given to homilies about Reason and humanitarianism, who faced problems at least as difficult as those which

[19] Bibl (1911), 65-66; Wangermann (1959), 3-4; Blum (1948), 56-61, 87-88.
[20] Franz (1963), 195-197; Lütge (1967), 227; Knapp (1887), II, 27-28.
[21] Quoted in Eggert (1965), 50.

confronted Frederick, and who leaned heavily upon her bureaucracy, was able to accomplish so very much more than Frederick.

In 1748 Frederick ordered the conversion of the labor dues of the Pomeranian peasants from the task system to a fixed number of days per week. That reduced an obligation that had amounted to as much as six days a week to three, or at most four days. In 1763 he made two failed efforts at reform. He decided to abolish what he called "slavery" in Pomerania. The Pomeranian seigniors promptly and correctly pointed out to their sovereign that slavery did not exist in Pomerania, and so could not be abolished. He also tried to convert non-hereditary into hereditary tenure and even full ownership in Upper Silesia. Despite the low redemption price provided for in the legislation, few peasants took advantage of the opportunity. Doubtless the extreme poverty among the Polish peasants who peopled Upper Silesia explained this seeming reluctance to improve their position. They simply lacked the money needed to gain the better tenure. In 1763, too, Frederick abolished the compulsory labor services of peasant children on royal manors in East Prussia; the ban was extended to royal properties in the rest of the kingdom only between 1799 and 1805. In 1773 an edict set a limit to the number of years of labor service private proprietors could demand of the children of their peasants.[22]

Princes of small states in southern and western Germany, unlike the sovereigns of Austria and Prussia, encountered little opposition in their introduction of agrarian reform in their realms. The servile bonds of the peasantry were lighter than those which prevailed in Austria and Prussia, and the seigniors in the small states generally did not engage in large-scale demesne production. Most important, in many of these states a large majority, and even all of the dependent peasants had the prince himself as their seignior as well as their sovereign. In Baden, for example, the margrave owned all of the manors, except for those which belonged to members of his family and to monasteries. In fact, many of his high officials were his *mainmortable* serfs until 1764, when he decided to emancipate them. The elector of Bavaria was the seignior of about one-fifth of the peasants of that land, and possessed judicial rights as *Gerichtsherr* (see p. 34) over approximately half of all peasants in Bavaria. In the princedom of Hohenlohe the ruler was the seignior of all the dependent peasants in his realm. When sovereigns of such principalities decided upon agrarian reform, they had little more to do than to change the status of their own peasants. In fact, in Hohenlohe the princes discovered that it cost them more to collect the dues owed them by their serfs than the income from the dues. So they readily freed their peasants for a small fee of one or two gulden, and often for no fee at all. As a result, the number of serfs there stead-

[22] Eggert (1965), 44; Knapp (1909), 545; Epstein (1966), 211-212; Henning (1969b), 25-26; Gagliardo (1969), 15.

ily declined during the eighteenth century, until by 1803 serfdom had disappeared in the princedom.[23]

Margrave Karl Friedrich of Baden followed a more usual pattern, and was impelled by a motive quite different from that of the rulers of Hohenlohe. Karl Friedrich had the reputation of an ardent disciple of the Enlightenment. He evidenced much interest and enthusiasm for the new ideology, and he chose men who championed the principles of the Age of Reason as his advisors. Yet he long rejected their counsels to free the peasants. He acted only after Joseph II in nearby Austria issued his patent of 1 November 1781, which freed peasants there from galling restrictions on their personal freedom. Karl Friedrich feared that word of this reform would sow discontent among his peasants. So in 1781 he commissioned a study of the possibility of the abolition of serfdom in Baden. On 23 July 1783 he issued a decree that freed the dependent peasant. The emancipation cost the margrave somewhere between 19,000 and 40,000 florins in revenues from the dues his peasants had paid him, a sizable sum, but not large enough to affect significantly the state budget. In Bavaria the electors sponsored the introduction of improvements in peasant tenures, but they stopped well short of emancipation.[24]

III

Until the reign of Alexander II (1855-1881), the sovereigns of Russia scrupulously avoided the use of their great power to compel, or even to persuade, the serfowners of Great Russia to adopt reforms that would improve the condition of the peasantry. They did not show the same caution and consideration for the seigniors in the other parts of their empire. Instead, the throne supported or dictated reforms whose purpose was not so much to benefit the peasants as it was to clip the powers of the noble proprietors. In the view from St. Petersburg, these noblemen, most of them Polish or German, were threats to the hegemony of the tsars (events were to prove that St. Petersburg was not wrong so far as the Polish lords were concerned). By forcing reform, the Russian overlords hoped to alienate the peasants from the proprietors, and win their loyalty for the tsar.

In the Baltic provinces this represented a turnabout from the policy first followed by Russia, after it took Livonia from the Swedes early in the eighteenth century. The Russians had cancelled the restrictions upon seigniorial authority, and had given the Livonian serfowners the same powers over their peasants that Russian seigniors had. The first signs of change appeared during the reign of Catherine II. Her attention may have been brought to thoughts of reform in Livonia by a book on serfdom there, writ-

[23] Liebel (1965), 42; Franz (1970a), 227; Lütge (1967), 172; Schremmer (1963), 20-22.
[24] Liebel (1965), 52-53; Schlögl (1954), 15, 515. For the text of the Baden decree of 23 July 1783 see Franz (1963), 292-294.

ten by J. G. Eisen, a Lutheran pastor in Livonia, and published in 1764 by the Russian Academy of Sciences. Possibly, too, reports from some Livonian noblemen may have influenced her. In any event, she visited her Baltic provinces in 1764 and decided that something had to be done to help the peasantry there. She instructed the governor-general of Livonia, Count George Browne (an Irish-born adventurer who had entered Russian military service in 1730), to present reform proposals to the Livonian diet in 1765. The reforms, to which the diet gave its grudging approval, turned out to be of minor and even trifling importance, and even then were not often applied.[25] Then in the 1780's and 1790's heightened rural unrest, economic difficulties that beset many noblemen, and the influence of western liberal ideas, persuaded some noblemen of the need for change. In 1795 the diet approved a proposal advanced by Count F. W. Sievers, marshal of the provincial nobility and liberal leader. It went forward to Tsar Paul for his approval. He pigeonholed it. When Alexander I succeeded Paul, the proposal was resubmitted, and after amendment it received the imperial assent in a ukase of 20 February 1804.

The legislation provided the peasants with hereditary tenure, and fixed their obligations according to the quantity and quality of the land they occupied. Its terms satisfied neither lord nor peasant. The serfs were aggrieved because they had not been set free. Liberal nobles, too, were disappointed because the ukase had not abolished serfdom. In addition, they objected to the grant of hereditary tenure to the peasants, for as proper liberals they maintained that this violated the property rights of the seigniors. And serfowners in general complained about the costs and the inconveniences of the surveys needed to establish accurate norms for the obligations of the peasants.

Meanwhile, the Estonian diet had accepted much the same plan of reform, and Tsar Alexander had given his approval by a decree of 27 August 1804. But when the Estonian nobles saw the troubles that their neighbors in Livonia were having with the reform, they had a change of heart. They decided that the best course would be to free their peasants, but without giving them any land. A serious peasant rising in 1805 in which troops had to be used to restore order undoubtedly helped persuade the Estonian seigniors to free their serfs. So, too, did severe crop failures and famines in 1807 and 1808, when serfowners found themselves burdened with the costs of supporting their starving peasants. Freedom for the serfs meant freedom for the lords from their obligation to care for their peasants in times of need. Alexander approved the Estonian diet's proposal of emancipation in 1811, but did not proclaim the ukase until 23 March 1816. The decree contained the declaration that the freed peasants, when in need, had to depend upon the reserve grain stores of their own communities. In Courland, the

[25] Schwabe (1928), 271-272; Transehe-Roseneck (1890), 165-166; Löning (1880), 112-113.

third of the Baltic provinces, formally annexed by Russia in 1795, the tsar took the initiative. In 1814 he ordered the establishment of a commission to draw up a proposal for reform. When the commission submitted its draft, which was modelled after the Livonian law of 1804, Alexander presented it to the Courland diet, and directed the diet to choose between this plan and a landless emancipation. The diet, by an overwhelming majority, opted for a landless emancipation, and, by a decree of 25 August 1817, the tsar freed the peasants of Courland without land. The course of events came full circle when the diet of Livonia decided to scrap the law of 1804 in favor of a landless emancipation. The tsar endorsed their action by a decree of 26 March 1819.[26]

Despite the laws that freed them from their serfdom, the Baltic peasants were, in fact, still bound to their former owners. The legislation had not given them full freedom of movement nor the right freely to choose their occupation. Worst of all, the legislation had taken away their land. Now the peasant had to rent a holding from his former master, or work for him as a hired hand. Formerly he had been an unfree and servile dependent of his master. Now he was free, but economically dependent upon the landowner. He had merely exchanged one form of dependence for another, and in the process had lost both his land and the right to support by his seignior in times of need. When he rented land the proprietor dictated the terms of the rental and usually demanded all or part of the rent in the form of labor services on the proprietor's demesne. In the 1840's over 90 per cent of all peasant renters in Livonia, and 50 to 60 per cent in Estonia, paid part or all of their rent in labor. The proprietors engaged increasingly in production for market, and so had a growing need for labor. They often demanded more labor from the peasant renters than they had required of these same peasants in the days of serfdom. In some cases the amount of labor the peasants had to provide as rent was twice as much as the labor services they had rendered as serfs.[27]

In short, the emancipations had turned out to be a disaster for the Baltic peasantry. Reports to St. Petersburg of the misery to which the peasantry had been reduced, and fresh waves of rural unrest, awakened fears of social upheaval and drew attention to the need for remedial measures. Years passed, however, before the government took positive action. An imperial order of 1845 limited the amount of labor rent that Livonian and Estonian landlords could demand. Decrees in 1846 and 1849 established regulations designed to assure peasants a permanent right to the use of a holding on equitable terms, to promote and protect peasant ownership, and to reduce

[26] Löning (1880), 112-113, 126-127; Kahk (1961), 164, 172; Schwabe (1928), 271-272; Transehe-Roseneck (1890), 165-166, 214-226; Tobien (1880), 276-298. For a summary of the 1817 decree for Courland see Creutzberg (1910), 6-35.
[27] Loone (1959), 202-204; Schwabe (1928), 252-253; Creutzberg (1910), 35-38.

and ultimately abolish the use of labor rents. Labor rents, however, continued to be demanded until, finally, an edict of 23 April 1868 ordered their commutation into cash payments in all of the Baltic provinces.[28]

In Poland, too, governmental policies of reform, instead of benefitting the peasants, aggravated their misery. In the era before the partitions, the nearly powerless central government lacked the authority, and the will, to intervene in the relationship between lord and peasant. Reform was discussed at the diet in 1768 but no action was taken, other than to forbid seigniors to sentence their peasants to death. In 1770 the government did issue a decree to require court action by a seignior who wanted to reclaim a runaway serf. In 1778 Andreas Zamoyski presented the diet with a proposal for limited reforms. The assembly not only unanimously rejected the proposal but voted to prohibit it from being presented again. In the last days of Polish independence, however, the Polish nobility began to change its tune. The diet, in its frantic efforts to save the state from extinction, adopted a constitution in 1791. Article 4 of the document paid tribute to the peasants as the nation's most vital force. But the constitution did not free the peasants from serfdom, nor did it reduce their obligations. The new government established by the constitution endured for only fifteen months. It was driven out of office by Russian intervention, supported by conservative Polish nobles. Soon thereafter Poland suffered its second partition. In a last desperate gamble to save the remnant of their state, patriots led by Tadeusz Kosciuszko rose against the powers who threatened to wipe out the rest of Poland. In the hope of winning the support of the peasant masses Kosciuszko issued a manifesto on 6 May 1794 in which he promised (among other things) to free the serfs, reduce their labor obligation, and abolish it for those who fought with him. The insurrection lasted less than seven months, and Kosciuszko's promises could not be kept. In 1795 the last part of independent Poland disappeared in the third partition.

From then until 1918 the people of Poland were the subjects of either Austria, Russia, or Prussia, except for a few brief years during the Napoleonic era. In 1807 the victorious Bonaparte created the grand duchy of Warsaw out of part of Prussian Poland, and in 1809 added some of the territory Austria had taken from Poland and that had now fallen to Napoleon. The new state had a population of 2.3 million, most of them, of course, peasants. In July 1807 Napoleon granted a constitution to the duchy. Article 4 of that document announced that "Slavery is abolished; all citizens are equal before the law; the estate of the peasantry is under the protection of the courts."[29]

Napoleon fancied himself as the liberator of the Polish peasantry, and history has often joined him in that conceit. In truth, the freedom he so

[28] Semevskii (1888), II, 618, 618n.; Simkhowitsch (1899), 615, 618.
[29] Quoted in Laubert (1934), 12.

grandly bestowed was more rhetorical than real. The constitution did, indeed, give the peasant his personal freedom. But it did not give him the right to a piece of land. It gave him freedom of movement, but if he left his home village he departed empty-handed. For the proprietor kept not only the holding and its buildings but also the inventory, without any compensation to the departing peasant. A decree of 21 December 1807 gave the proprietor the authority to evict peasants from their holdings at will; the only condition required of the proprietor was that he had to give the peasant six months' notice. The Napoleonic legislation said nothing about the abolition or commutation of the obligations the lords had required of their peasants before the emancipation. So lords continued to demand these payments in return for allowing the peasants to occupy holdings, or to live in the villages on the lord's property. And, despite his legal freedom of movement, the peasant could not leave his village until he had met all the obligations he owed the proprietor. Since apparently most villagers were in arrears in their obligations, or owed money on loans from the proprietor, they were actually still bound. The so-called free Polish peasant was almost as dependent upon the will of the seignior as he had been when he was a serf. True, he could no longer be bought and sold. But that, too, turned out to be a legal illusion. William Jacob discovered in 1825 that when landed property changed hands, either by testament or by conveyance, "the persons of the peasantry are not indeed expressly conveyed, but their services are, and in many instances are the most valuable part of the property."[30] And, of course, since the peasant was now "free," the seignior no longer had the obligation to provide relief for the peasant in times of disaster and famine, and to take care of the aged and the infirm. Now peasants had to fend for themselves.

Matters were worsened by the introduction of the Napoleonic Code in January 1808. Drafted for France, it did not take cognizance of conditions special to Poland. Thus, the code recognized only absolute ownership and tenancy. It did not recognize the hereditary claims that peasants had to their holdings, or to the use of common land. Instead, by the terms of the code the seigniors became the absolute and sole owners of their properties, and the peasants lost whatever hereditary rights of use that they had formerly possessed.[31]

The grand duchy vanished in the collapse of the Napoleonic empire. In 1815 the Congress of Vienna turned over most of it to Russia, and it became the Kingdom of Poland (or Congress Poland as it was called), with Alexander I as its monarch. Because he wanted to placate the Polish nobility, and because he liked the centralized Napoleonic system, Alexander or-

---

[30] Jacob (1826), 64.

[31] Jacob (1826), 45, 63; Rostworowski (1896), 12-15; Leslie (1956), 69-70; Kieniewicz (1969), 47.

dered the retention of the Napoleonic Code. It became the law of Congress Poland. Nor did he repeal the emancipation of the peasantry. In view of the dependent position of the freed peasantry there was no compelling reason to do this. Nor did the seigniors want serfdom to be reintroduced. The Napoleonic legislation had provided them with all of the benefits of serfdom, relieved them of the obligations they owed to their peasants, and allowed them to appropriate peasant land without hindrance. Understandably, they welcomed the retention of this legislation by their new sovereign.

Revolt in the neighboring Austrian (and formerly Polish) province of Galicia abruptly ended the imperial indifference to the plight of the peasants of Congress Poland. A bloody rural uprising broke out in Galicia in 1846, and raged with special virulence in the western part of the province, where the peasants were Polish (in eastern Galicia they were mainly Ruthenians). The Galician peasants rose against their lords, and not against the Austrian government. Nonetheless, fear gripped the rulers of Russia lest the revolt spill across the border into Poland. The viceroy of the Kingdom of Poland, General Paskevich, advised Tsar Nicholas to forestall this possibility by introducing reforms. Nicholas, after a visit to Poland, ordered certain changes in a ukase of 7 June 1846. The edict specified that peasant tenants with holdings of three *morgi* (about four acres) or more could not be evicted at the will of the proprietor, if they had met their obligations to him. The law did not protect peasants with smaller holdings from eviction. It forbad seigniors to increase the obligations they required of their peasants, prohibited them from reducing the size of the peasants' holdings, and, as mentioned in the preceding chapter, it forbad the conversion of peasant-held land into demesne. A vacated holding had to be assigned to another peasant within two years. Another edict on 26 November 1846 ended all those peasant obligations whose exact amount was not specified.

These reforms were scarcely earth-shaking. However, they represented the first significant intervention of the state in the lord-peasant relationship in Congress Poland since the era of the grand duchy of Warsaw. Indeed, that may have been their chief significance. For the landowners of Congress Poland thwarted the intent of the decrees by evasions, or by simply disregarding them. Still, no matter how inadequate the enforcement, the legislation represented a forward step in imperial concern about the lot of the Polish peasantry, for whom even the smallest favors were great boons.[32]

Other parts of Poland that Russia had acquired in the partitions had become provinces of the empire. The peasants in these nine provinces, which lay on Russia's western frontier, were still serfs. Most of the lords were Polish and Catholic. Their serfs were White Russian, Lithuanian, or Ukrain-

---

[32] Leslie (1963), 68; Rostworowski (1896), 21-38. For the Galician revolt see p. 340 below.

ian. In the White Russian and Ukrainian, or Little Russian, provinces they were almost exclusively of the Orthodox faith. The proprietors had long been required by the terms of the old law code, the so-called Lithuanian Statute, to draw up inventories that defined the mutual obligations of the lord and his peasants. The weak central power could not enforce the law and seigniors evaded or disregarded the terms of the inventories. When these regions became part of the Russian empire, the tsar commanded that the seigniors were to have all the rights and privileges possessed by the landowners of Great Russia. However, the inventories were not abolished, even though they were not known in Great Russia, and even though they set limits on the powers of the seignior. They persisted until 1840, though the proprietors continued to disregard their provisions. In 1840 the new Russian law code, first published in 1833, was introduced into the nine western provinces. It supplanted the Lithuanian Statute, which had provided the legal authorization for the inventories. Now the law no longer required them.[33]

Two years later the government reintroduced the requirement of inventories in the western provinces, and insisted, though not always successfully, on their enforcement. The explanation for this rapid volte-face had its roots in the failed Polish insurrection of 1830, when nobles tried to win independence for their nation. Tsar Nicholas, infuriated by the rising and convinced that it was part of an international conspiracy against the entire social and political order, imposed harsh repression, including the maintenance of martial law for the next twenty-four years. Some of his punitive measures worked to the benefit of the peasants. He turned over manors confiscated from rebellious Polish noblemen to 138 Russian high army officers, with the understanding that they had to introduce major changes in the situation of the peasantry. Within six years peasant land was to be clearly demarcated from demesne; the peasants could pay their dues in cash, kind, or labor, as they chose, with commutation rates set by law; and the labor obligation was not to exceed three days a week.

The purpose of these reforms on the confiscated estates was to win the loyalty of the peasants for their new Russian lords, and to make peasants who lived on Polish-owned manors envious, and discontented with their Polish masters. Meanwhile, counselors of the tsar recommended that Russia's position in Poland would be strengthened by an improvement in the status of all the peasants in the nine western provinces. They reasoned that the cruel oppression of the peasants by their Polish seigniors offered the opportunity to win the loyalty of the peasants for the tsar by giving them protection against the excesses of their masters. As Count Kiselev explained in a memorandum in 1835 to the tsar about the political situation in Little Russia, the possibility to win over the peasantry rose not from any devo-

[33] Engelmann (1884), 232; Schnitzler (1866), I, 364; Conze (1940), 67-70.

tion to Russia, but out of the peasants' hatred for their Catholic lords. As part of this unsavory policy, Kiselev and others convinced Nicholas that inventories which precisely specified the obligations of the peasants should be enforced in the western provinces. In a ukase of 6 December 1842 the tsar ordered the reintroduction of inventories, to begin in 1844.

The task of preparing the inventories was assigned to the seigniors themselves. That quickly proved unsatisfactory. The government then decided that it would promulgate a general inventory for each region that would regulate the lord-peasant relationship in the region. In December 1848 a general inventory was published for the Little Russian provinces of Kiev, Podolia, and Volynia. Though the seigniors there protested against its terms, and though complaints about infractions poured in, the introduction of the inventory clearly proved beneficial to the peasants. It was a different story in the White Russian and Lithuanian provinces, where the government promulgated a general inventory in 1852. The nobles in these provinces protested so vehemently that the government kept postponing enforcement of the inventory. Finally, the project was abandoned in 1857, when Tsar Alexander II appointed a commission to prepare legislation that would emancipate all of the serfs in his empire.[34]

In Great Russia itself the government did almost nothing to improve the condition of the serfs, or to protect them from excessive demands and maltreatment at the hands of their masters. The only restrictions the law placed upon the serfowner were that the peasant "must not suffer ruin" because of the lord's demands, and the serfowner had to give the peasant some free time to get his own work done. Catherine II had encouraged discussions and publications that dealt with the need for change. Yet, instead of an era of reform, her reign saw serfdom become more oppressive than it had ever before been. In contrast, her successor Paul in his brief reign made it clear that he had no interest in reform, and banned publication of anything that dealt with the peasant problem. Yet this strange and troubled man was responsible for the first positive restriction imposed by the government upon the serfowners. He outlawed labor services on Sundays and holidays, and prohibited the sale of serfs without land in Little Russia. In the edict in which he dealt with labor service on Sundays, the tsar mentioned that the other six days of the week were "as a rule split into equal parts and divided" between work for the lord and work on the serf's own account. This arrangement, he said, provided enough time to meet the needs of both lord and peasant. The ukase did not command, nor even recommend, that the labor service not exceed this amount. In later years, however, these words were interpreted as establishing three days per week as the legal norm for the labor obligation.

[34] Leslie (1963), 61; Semevskii (1888), 484-488, 494-500; Haxthausen (1847), 492-493; Dodge (1950), 371-376; Engelmann (1884), 234-235.

Seigniors often disregarded the restrictions Paul had imposed, and the government took no action against them. Nonetheless, Paul's edicts proved to be the turning point in the history of Russian serfdom. From the onset of serfdom in that land in the fifteenth century until Paul's reign, the sovereign's decrees had always deepened the dependence of the peasant upon the will of his seignior. Paul had reversed that centuries-old trend. His next two successors did little to improve the condition of the serfs but at least did not worsen it. Alexander I did issue a ukase in 1803 that allowed serfs to purchase their freedom from their owners and enter into a new status called "free farmers." The hopes that the tsar and some of his advisors held for the results of this decree were destined to quick disappointment. Few peasants had the money, and few lords were willing to sell freedom and land to their serfs. More than a half-century later there were only 151,895 adult male "free farmers," or about 1.4 per cent of the total adult male serf population. Similar efforts by Tsar Nicholas were even less successful.

One might have thought that Alexander would have shown his gratitude to the peasants for their heroic resistance to the invading armies of Napoleon, by some gesture that would have loosened their bonds, however lightly. In his victory manifesto on 30 August 1814 he granted privileges to the other orders of society as a reward for their services against the French. The only recognition the peasants received was one sentence in the manifesto. The sentence said, "The peasantry, our loyal people, will receive their reward from God."[35]

In the earlier part of his reign Alexander had the reputation of being something of a liberal. No one ever mistook his brother and successor, Nicholas I, for anything but what he was, namely the archetypal unreconstructed reactionary among the crowned heads of nineteenth century Europe. It seems surprising, then, that during his thirty years on the throne he appointed ten separate commissions to work out plans for the improvement of the status of the peasantry. The fact was that from the outset of his reign Nicholas, haunted by the fear of mass peasant revolt, believed that the preservation of his realm demanded agrarian reform. But he could not bring himself to the point of introducing changes that would substantially alter the status quo, and so only trifling measures emerged from the deliberations of the committees. Despite this failure to take decisive action, Nicholas's concern with the need for reform created an awareness of the urgency of the problem in high governmental circles, and helped to prepare the way for the emancipation that came so soon after his death in 1855. That was his greatest legacy to his son, Alexander II, who was to win fame as the Tsar-Liberator.[36]

35 Tarlé (1943), 233.   36 Blum (1961), 107, 445-446, 538-551.

IV

The Danubian Principalities of Moldavia and Wallachia had long been part of the Ottoman Empire, though they managed to avoid direct rule from Constantinople. Instead, each principality had its own ruler, called the hospodar or voivode. Until the early eighteenth century the hospodar had been elected by the native great nobles, the boyars, of each principality from among their own number. In 1716 the Ottomans introduced a new system. They sold the office of hospodar to the highest bidder. To increase their income from these sales they rarely allowed the purchaser to remain in office for more than three years, though they were perfectly willing to sell it to the incumbent if he wanted to continue as hospodar. The purchasers were usually Greeks from the Phanar, the chief Greek quarter of Constantinople, and so their rule was known as that of the Phanariots. Early in the 1770's the Turks introduced a uniform system of administration for Moldavia and Wallachia. Thereafter their history became much more of a unified narrative than it had been, though they maintained their separate identities until 1862, when they were united as the principality of Romania. It was the fate of the two principalities (as it was of Romania) to find themselves between hammer and anvil. The powers that surrounded them warred with one another, and hostile armies ravaged and plundered the luckless principalities. The treaty of Kuchuk Kainarji, which in 1774 ended the Russo-Turkish war that had started in 1768, accorded Russia a virtual protectorate over both Moldavia and Wallachia, although the Ottomans retained nominal suzerainty. The Hapsburgs, who had a jealous eye on the region, and who were never ones to miss the opportunity to pick up territory, in 1775 seized the northern tip of Moldavia, till then without a name of its own, but henceforth called Bukovina.

Men who buy office usually expect to be more than repaid by the rewards of the office, and the Phanariotes were anything but exceptions to that generalization. Theirs was an oppressive and grasping regime, made worse by the Greeks who came with them from Constantinople to grow rich at the expense of the indigenes. The rapacity of the rulers and their entourage, the excessive demands of the native boyars, and the near-slavery into which the peasants had fallen, were more than many peasants could stand. Tens of thousands ran away into neighboring lands, or became vagabonds or brigands. Censuses made in Wallachia showed a decline in the number of families from 147,000 in 1741 to 70,000 in 1746, and 35,000 in 1757.

The flight of so many taxpayers convinced Hospodar Constantine Mavrocordato of the urgent need for reform. Mavrocordato, best-known of the Phanariote rulers, was three times hospodar of Wallachia, and twice hospodar of Moldavia. In 1746, as ruler in Wallachia, he decreed the abolition of serfdom, fixed the labor service at six days per year, limited payments in kind to one-tenth of the peasant's produce, gave peasants the right to redeem their obligations at a fixed fee, promised them freedom of movement, and to lure back the runaways promised them exemption from taxation for six months. In 1749 Mavrocordato, now hospodar of Moldavia, freed the serfs there, too, and set their labor service as twelve days a year. Unlike the Wallachian decree, the Moldavian law did not promise freedom of movement, nor the right of the peasant to redeem his obligations. It did allow the peasant to move away from his home village if the seignior gave his consent.

As a result of Mavrocordato's decrees the generic name for the peasant changed from *vecini* in Moldavia and *rumiñi* in Wallachia when they were serfs, to *clăcaşi* in both princedoms, *clăca* being the voluntary labor rent the peasant was to provide to the seignior. Actually, that change in nomenclature was about the extent of the practical effects of the reforms. The stubborn resistance of the boyars and their open evasion of the legislation nullified the intent of the decrees. In later years legislation increased the legal number of work days, but these edicts were essentially meaningless since the work quota for a day could not be met in that time. An edict of 1770 required the Moldavian seigniors to provide holdings for their peasants, and in 1790 the law ordered that these holdings had to occupy at least two-thirds of the area of the manor. In Wallachia, during the reign of Alexander Ypsilanti (1774-1782), the government accorded peasants hereditary rights to their holdings, and forbad lords to dispossess them or to appropriate land cleared by peasants. The seigniors showed scant respect for these regulations and seigniorial encroachments on peasant land continued all but unabated.[37]

Meanwhile the principalities continued in their role of passive objects of the thrusts for power and territory of their Christian neighbors, and of the exactions of their Ottoman suzerains. The Treaty of Adrianople in 1829, which ended another in the seemingly interminable series of Russo-Turkish wars, formally made the principalities a Russian protectorate. The treaty also provided for Russian forces to occupy the principalities until the defeated Ottomans met all the conditions prescribed by the treaty. One of these conditions required the redrafting of the fundamental laws. Under the direction of Count Kiselev, the Russian governor of the protectorate, a committee of boyars in each principality drew up a constitution. They were approved by the Russian government and accepted in 1831 by assemblies of the boyars in each principality. The document was called the Organic Statute for each principality, rather than a constitution, because the word "constitution" symbolized all the things that Tsar Nicholas and his counselors despised and feared. The Porte ratified the Statutes in 1834, whereupon Russia withdrew its troops but remained the dominant power.

[37] Grünberg (1909), 597; Grünberg (1901), 28-30; Oţetea (1960), 302, 304-306; Constantiniu (1973), 56-59; Economo (1911), 116-131.

Section VII of Chapter III in each statute dealt with the agrarian problem. Count Kiselev tried to persuade the boyars who drafted the statutes to make the provisions of Chapter VII more equitable for the peasants, but save for a few ameliorations they disregarded his counsels. St. Petersburg, too, over-ruled his objections. The statutes guaranteed the same amount of land for each peasant family, and then ordered an additional amount for each pair of oxen, up to two pair. The Moldavian peasant without oxen was supposed to have 3.2 hectares, with one ox team 4.41 hectares, and with two pair, 7.68 hectares. The range set by the Wallachian statute was considerably less, going from 2.21 hectares to 3.20 hectares. In light of the plentitude of land in the principalities, the unimportance of seigniorial production, and the readiness of proprietors to rent land on easy terms, it is difficult to explain the refusal of the drafters of the statutes to provide larger holdings, except to attribute it to their greed and their lack of concern about the welfare of the peasantry. The labor services specified in the statutes, including farm work, carting, and construction and repair, amounted to at least 23 days a year. However, the unrealistic quotas set for each day stretched the obligation to about 36 days. In addition, each 10 families had to furnish one of its members to work for the seignior, or 2 per 10 families if the seignior had 200 or less peasants on his land. The peasants had to continue to pay one-tenth of their produce to the proprietors. The statutes allowed them to move away, but they had to give notice of their intention to the district government office and to their seignior 6 months before St. George's Day. Before they could leave they had to pay the seignior the equivalent of a full year's obligations, and pay a full year's taxes or their equivalent into the communal treasury.[38]

The net effect of the statutes was probably to worsen the condition of the peasantry, though it apparently did reduce their labor obligation (p. 55). The size of their holdings as set by the law was too small to support a family, so that they had to rent additional land. The provisions about freedom to leave were interpreted to mean that each year not more than two families could move away from the village. The landowners retained their exemption from taxation and they retained their monopolies. The inequities of the Statutes were compounded by the attitude and activities of the proprietors. They were notorious for their immorality, corruption, extravagance, and their total lack of sympathy and understanding for the woes of the peasantry.

In the 1840's a liberal nationalist movement surfaced, led by young boyar sons who had studied in western Europe. The movement climaxed in revolution in 1848. After brief triumphs a joint Russian and Turkish occupation put down the rising. The two powers agreed by the Convention of Balta Liman of 1 May 1849 on the need to revise the Statutes. They turned

[38] Grünberg (1909), 598-599; Grünberg (1901), 29; Mitrany (1930), 31-32; *Règlement organique* (1834), arts. 72, 118-129.

over the task to commissions of boyars. In 1851 the commission for each principality submitted its proposals. The principal changes increased the arable of peasant holdings, doubled the amount of pasturage allotted for each peasant-owned animal, and regularized the village communal organizations. A commission of the European Powers in 1857-1858 (appointed after the Treaty of Paris in 1856 ended the Russian protectorate) determined that these changes had not brought about any enduring improvement in the condition of the peasantry. It found that corrupt officials of the government blocked action needed to protect the peasants, and left them to the mercies of the proprietors.[39]

The failure of the reform efforts in the Danubian Principalities was of a piece with the fate of the efforts to reform the lord-peasant relationship in other of the servile lands. The successes in a few states, such as Savoy, Baden, and the Austrian Monarchy, were exceptional departures from the norm. The original intent of the sovereigns to make improvements in the condition of the peasantry, for reasons that served the sovereigns' own interests, was nearly everywhere subverted, so that the peasants found themselves no better off, and sometimes worse off, than they had been before the introduction of the reforms. But, as the preceding pages have several times noted, these attempts at change, though they accomplished little, had much significance because they were the precursors of the acts that finally freed the peasants. They were imposed from above at the will of authoritarian rulers, who thereby let their societies know that the existing relationship between lord and peasant was unacceptable to them. Their insistence upon change began, and, indeed, nearly everywhere was the principal moving force, in the process that led to the emancipations. That process was a difficult one, too difficult for the monarchs to carry through unaided. The assistance they received, from both men and events, is the subject of the next four chapters.

[39] Emerit (1937), 322-338; Mitrany (1930), 44.

CHAPTER 12

New Directions in Agriculture

I

THE efforts of princes to reduce the power of the seigniors and, in fact, the entire movement that led ultimately to the emancipation of the peasants of the servile lands, coincided with a new era in European economic life that began around the middle of the eighteenth century. Perhaps the most striking feature of this new era was the rapid increase (for reasons that are still not clear) in Europe's population after a long period of stagnation and in some places even decline. By 1750 Europe had an estimated population of 139.6 million. By 1800 that figure had gone up by 34 per cent to 186.8 million, and by 1850 it was 267 million, or 91 per cent more than the population of a century earlier. The servile lands not only shared in the increase; some of them were responsible for a disproportionate share of it.

Population[1]
(in millions)

	1750	1800	% increase 1750-1800	1850	% increase 1750-1850
Germany	18.9	24.3	28.6	35.4	87.3
France	22.0	27.3	24.0	34.9	58.6
Denmark	0.8	0.9	12.5	1.5	87.5
Austrian Monarchy	18.3	24.3	32.8	32.6	78.1
Russia	24.0	39.9	66.3	61.6	156.7
Danubian Principalities	—	1.5	—	3.7	146.7

Annexation of new territories accounted for part of the spectacular growth in Russia's population, but natural increase in the older parts of the country accounted for most of it. The increase in some of the recently added parts of the Austrian Monarchy was equally remarkable. Hungary's population doubled, or may even have tripled, in the century after the Hapsburg's reconquest of that kingdom. Population in Bukovina, annexed by the Hapsburgs in 1775, rose from about 75,000 in 1775 to 208,498 in 1807, and 370,673 in 1846, or nearly five times over in seventy-one years. Immigration from other parts of the Monarchy and from foreign lands was responsible for much of these increases.[2]

Greater population, growth of cities, and the beginnings of industrializa-

[1] Population estimates from Urlanis (1941), 414-415, except for Danubian Principalities from Haufe (1939), 57.

[2] Liashchenko (1949), 272-273; Revesz (1964), 9; Grünberg (1901), 74.

tion in some lands in the first half of the nineteenth century expanded the market for farm products. Improvements in transportation facilitated their movement. Rivers were cleared and deepened, canals were built to link major streams, roads were laid down, and, in the second quarter of the nineteenth century, railroads and steamships made their debut. Large increases in the shipment of goods followed soon after these improvements. For example, improved and new canals in Languedoc and an active road-building program opened up new markets for the farmers there within the province and outside its borders. The value of grain shipped from Languedoc rose from 6 to 16 million livres between 1745 and 1768. Regular steamship service on the Danube started in 1831, with one vessel plying between Vienna and Pest. In 1847 the line had 41 ships and 101 tugs, and covered most of the Danube. It was of much importance to the trade between Hungary and the rest of the Austrian Monarchy. That trade rose by over 80 per cent between 1831 and 1847. And by 1847 the Monarchy had over a thousand miles of steam railroad, heavily used as a carrier of farm goods. Even in Russia, where progress in transportation (as in everything else) lagged, the construction of canals connecting major streams enhanced the usefulness of the river system. The amount of grain shipped to Moscow rose by more than 400 per cent between the end of the 1780's and 1861, from about 3.3 to 17 million bushels (Moscow's population increased by 150 per cent during this period). Most of the grain came by way of the rivers and canals; waterborne shipments into Moscow went up by 1,500 per cent.[3]

The upswing in economic life that began in the second quarter of the eighteenth century ended a long period of secular stagnation and regression that reached back in some lands to the 1620's. In one land after another economic activity took on new vigor, and continued to move forward until the second decade of the next century. Manufactures and commerce thrived. New markets opened up and old ones expanded. Only a few regions seem to have been unaffected, most notably Poland. The economic decline that started there at the end of the sixteenth century continued unrelieved until the end of the eighteenth century. At that time, Poland's production of grain and cattle is estimated to have been only two-thirds of what it had been in the sixteenth century.[4]

A rise in prices accompanied the resurgence of economic activity. The increase remained gradual until the 1780's, when prices moved sharply upward. The inflation was most pronounced in bread-grains. Between the 1730's and the first decade of the nineteenth century, cereal prices went up by 283 per cent in Denmark, 259 per cent in Austria, 210 per cent in Germany, and 163 per cent in France.[5] In Russia the much scantier data indi-

[3] Forster (1960), 67-70; Blum (1943), 29-32; Koval'chenko (1964), 475.
[4] Topolski (1962), 37-38.   [5] Abel (1966), 182-183.

cate an even steeper rise, with agricultural prices going up on the average by an estimated 580 per cent during the eighteenth century.[6] Other prices went up, too, but everywhere they rose less than the price of cereals.[7]

Expansion of the money supply accounted for part of the price rise. The production of precious metals increased in the second half of the eighteenth century. In addition, some of the servile lands introduced paper money into their economies. In Russia the government began to print paper rubles, called assignats, in 1769. At first the authorities showed restraint, but soon their resolve faded and a flood of notes poured from the presses. By 1817 the assignat ruble was worth only one-fourth of a silver ruble. In Denmark paper money first appeared in 1713 but was withdrawn in 1728. Then in 1737 the government allowed a privately owned bank to issue notes, and these soon became an increasingly important part of the currency. In addition, from the 1760's to 1787 the government reduced the amount of silver in the coinage (gold and copper coins made up only a negligible part of the Danish currency).[8]

Increased foreign demand for grain, particularly from the Low Countries and from England, also helped to push up prices. In the mid-eighteenth century England had exported enough grain to feed a million people. At the end of the century England had become a net importer of grain. Most of the grain imported by the western lands came from central and eastern Europe. By 1800 Polish and German grain shipped to western Europe just from the three eastern German ports of Danzig, Königsberg, and Elbing amounted to nearly one-third of the volume of the entire international grain trade.[9] Poor harvests, and then the outbreak of war, helped boost prices in the last years of the eighteenth century. And, most important of all, as population increased, the growth in domestic demand pushed up prices for foodstuffs, and especially for grain, the staple of European diets.

Mounting farm prices, in their turn, created a heightened demand for farm land. Rents and the prices of land climbed, on occasion going up even more than the prices of the commodities produced on the land.[10] In some places the price of peasant land went up even more than did that of manors. In Denmark in 1801-1810 peasant holdings sold for 300 per cent more than they had brought in 1751-1760, and almost 900 per cent more than the price asked in the crisis years at the beginning of the eighteenth century. Data for peasant holdings in a few districts of Lower Saxony show a similar though not as precipitous rise. Information for Bohemia indicates that it was an exception to the general rise in land prices. Presumably, the reforms

[6] Mironov (1973), 327-330; *cf.* Markina (1964), 338, 340.

[7] *Cf.* Arnim (1957), 71, 72; Labrousse (1933), II, 362-363; Riemann (1953), 155; Markina (1964), 345; Eggert (1965), 7.

[8] Abel (1966), 186; Blum (1961), 304-305; Friis and Glamann (1958), 7-14.

[9] Abel (1966), 196; Abel (1955), 8.

[10] Labrousse (1933), II, 379-383; Arnim (1957), 77-80; Abel (1966), 198-199; Chevallez (1949), 157.

of Joseph II, which reduced seigniorial incomes and introduced uncertainties about the future, and the state's decision to sell some of its Bohemian properties, drove down land prices there.[11]

The rise in the prices of farm goods and of land outpaced the rise in the price of manufactured goods. That brought increases in the income of landowners. Only a small part of this new money was returned to the land. Most proprietors used their increased incomes for consumption. The landowners profited, too, from the nearly universal disparity between the increase in the prices they received for farm goods, and the wages they paid their farm laborers. Unlike most other rural prices, farm wages, particularly in the lands where peasants were most dependent upon their seigniors, responded only partially to economic fluctuations. These farm workers were not selling their labor on a free market. In many lands the seignior could require his peasants to work for him for wages, in addition to their unpaid labor services. The authority of the seignior and the subservience of the peasant made wage bargaining one-sided, if not impossible. In Schleswig-Holstein, for example, farmhands on the free labor market could command 8 schillings a day plus maintenance. Those who had to work for their seigniors were paid only 5 to 6 schillings.[12]

Despite their stickiness, farm wages were not uninfluenced by supply and demand. Data from the early eighteenth century showed that employers whose properties lay close to Prague, with its competing job opportunities, paid higher wages than did those whose manors lay at a distance from the metropolis. Wages were higher, too, where labor was in short supply. In the first half of the nineteenth century farm workers were paid more in the Alpine provinces of Austria than they were in Bohemia and Moravia, where labor was more plentiful. In Russia wages were higher in the sparsely peopled regions of the lower Volga and New Russia than they were in the populous provinces of central Russia.[13]

In France, Ernest Labrousse, using 1726-1741 as the base period, found that the cost of living in 1785-1789 had risen by 62 per cent, while wages had gone up by only 22 per cent. In the base period a farm laborer's family of five, in which only the father worked for wages, would have spent 45 per cent of his yearly wage just on bread. In 1785-1789 this proportion had risen to 58 per cent, and in 1789, alone, to 88 per cent. In Denmark the prices of major farm products nearly doubled in the last three decades of the eighteenth century, while wages went up by only 50 to 60 per cent.[14]

There is, however, reason to question the generalizations about the decline in the real wages of hired farm labor. Some workers were paid all of

[11] Nielsen (1933), 342; Achilles (1965), 10-11; Wright (1966), 162.
[12] Abel (1966), 184, 186; Hanssen (1961), 26n.
[13] Blum (1948), 178-189; Haxthausen (1847), II, 24, 97; Krzhivoblotskii (1861), 306.
[14] Labrousse (1933), II, 598-603; Nielsen (1933), 340; *cf.* Razous (1944), 80; Arnim (1957), 74-75; Slicher van Bath (1963a), 317.

their wages in cash, and the real wages of these people certainly fell. But many hired workers, and in some regions probably the great majority, received part or all of their pay in kind. In addition to foodstuffs, their wages often included a house (or more accurately, a hut), garden, and a small patch of arable for married employees, and even the right to keep an animal or two with those of the employer. Unmarried hired hands often received lodging and board, and, generally, clothing. Wages in kind were widely used for hired labor engaged in harvesting, and, especially, threshing. These workers received a share of the grain they harvested or threshed. The share varied with local custom. In Lorraine threshers kept 1/18th to 1/19th of the threshed grain, or a little better than 5 per cent. In Hainault and Cambrésis in French Flanders, reapers kept from 6 to 8 per cent of the grain they harvested as their pay. In Bohemia the thresher's share was usually 1/17th, or nearly 6 per cent, in Carinthia it was 10 per cent, in lower Styria 8 per cent, and in the Marchfeld as much as 13 per cent. Hired workers on a manor in Ermland in East Prussia kept 9 per cent of the grain they threshed during the winter months. From Easter to St. Martin's (11 November) these Ermland peasants and their wives worked in the fields. They were paid a cash wage of 8 florins, and in addition were given 4 florins 10 groschen to purchase meat, 8 *Scheffel* of breadgrain, 2 *Scheffel* of barley, 3/4 *Scheffel* of peas, 1 *Scheffel* of oats, 2 *Stof* of butter, 10 *Stof* of salt, and one cartload of hay.[15] Farmworkers who received part or all of their wages in kind benefitted from the price rise, so that their real wages increased. It is, of course, possible that as prices rose the amount of the payments in kind were reduced, and it seems reasonable to assume that the quality, and perhaps the quantity, of the board provided "live-in" farm workers declined. Scant data rule out generalizations. However, a comparison for the manor in Ermland mentioned above showed that between 1636 and 1766 nominal cash wages changed little, while wages in kind changed not at all.[16]

In any event, many peasants, and in the eastern lands probably the great majority, were scarcely affected by the cash nexus. They lived in largely self-contained local economies, in which money transactions had a minor, even insignificant, role. "To him who pays his rent in labor, or in produce, or who consumes the rest of his growth," wrote William Jacob in 1820 of the peasants of Westphalia, "it is of small consequence what price commodities yield in a market to which he has little to carry."[17] In the canton

---

[15] Germany: Engelbrecht (1913), 125, 127, 128; Stein (1918), I, 327-329; Ahrens (1960), 93; Finck von Finckenstein (1960), 197; Ziekursch (1927), 91-92. France: Young (1970), I, 443-446; Lefebvre (1972), 279. Schleswig-Holstein: Hanssen (1861), 25-26; White Russia and Lithuania: Pokhilevich (1966), 390; Ulashchik (1961), 183. Poland: Kostiushko (1954), 206, 229. Russia: Krzhivoblotskii (1861), 304-305, 306. Austria: Blum (1948), 187.

The size of the *Scheffel* in East Prussia varied. I have used the *Scheffel* that contained 57.1 liters (1.62 bushels). Each *Scheffel* contained 40 *Stof*. Each *Stof* equalled 1.43 liters. Henning (1969a), 237.

[16] Riemann (1953), 126-127; Engelbrecht (1913), 131.   [17] Jacob (1820), 105.

of Zurich, a relatively economically advanced region, and certainly not an isolated one, a village vicar in 1771 said of his parishioners, "Almost everyone has a cow, harvests enough grain to feed his family, pays his *cens* from his vines, and clothes himself with the hemp which he grows. With this style of life they always have enough food in the village, but no money. . . . No one pays anyone else with money; they only barter." A few years later, in 1783, another rural pastor of Zurich observed that "Even the wealthiest [peasants] often have absolutely no cash money. Money everywhere is a rarity."[18]

Prices remained high until the middle years of the second decade of the nineteenth century. Then they broke sharply, with grain prices the most severely affected. Wheat prices fell by 75 per cent in Denmark between 1817 and 1825, and in France by 50 per cent between 1817 and 1822. In the grain-exporting ports of Germany prices of bread-grains in 1825 were 28 percent of the average price in 1817, and in the interior of Germany they were 23 per cent of the 1817 average.[19] Some proprietors managed to counteract the impact of falling grain prices by raising sheep and sugar beets, and by increasing the output of their distilleries. Many others could not adjust, and were forced into bankruptcy and lost their properties. Hundreds of manors came on the market, and land prices plummeted. In the 1820's manors in Schleswig-Holstein sold for as little as one-fourth of their price of twenty years earlier. A contemporary estimated that over half of the proprietors in East Frisia on the North Sea coast were bankrupt. In East Prussia, of 594 large properties indebted to the Estates mortgage bank, 98 were sold at forced sale between 1815 and 1826. In the following years the bank foreclosed on over 140 more manors. In West Prussia, in 1824 alone, 74 of 195 large properties mortgaged with the Estates bank there were put up for auction. Prices of manors in many parts of Prussia did not get back to the level of the 1790's until the 1880's.[20] The already excessive borrowing by nobles mounted spectacularly. Between 1805 and 1845 the total debt of the Prussian nobility doubled, going from 162 million to 325 million marks. Data from Russia, Poland, and Hungary also show a strong increase in the debt burden of the nobility.[21]

Price movements in the Danubian Principalities and in New Russia were exceptions to the general decline. Until 1829 the Porte had allowed the Romanians to export their grain only to Turkey. The opening of the Straits and of the Danubian ports by the Treaty of Adrianople in 1829 created new

[18] Bollinger (1941), 28-29, 45; see also Meuvret (1947), 20-21.

[19] Abel (1966), 211; *cf.* Nielsen (1933), 383-384; Kahk (1969), 88-89; Körösi (1873), 20-25; Creutzburg (1910), 40.

[20] Abel (1966), 216, 221; Abel (1964), 106; Finck von Finckenstein (1960), 119, 133-135; Engel-Janosi (1924), 100-101; Creutzburg (1910), 40.

[21] Hamerow (1958), 51; Koval'chenko (1961), 201; Kostiushko (1954), 176-177; Ivanyi (1960), 284-285n.

markets for the Principalities. Grain prices shot upward as a result. Before 1829 wheat sold at 15 piastres and maize at 5 piastres. In 1834, after a series of poor harvests, the price of wheat had gone up to 70 and maize to 50 piastres. After a sharp break in 1836 the prices stabilized around 50 piastres for wheat and 15 for maize. As could be expected, land prices went up, too, doubling and even tripling between 1828 and 1849. The proprietors, given to profligacy, used their increased incomes to live even more luxuriously. Unconcerned about balancing income and outgo they lived beyond their means, and to cover the deficit they borrowed at usurious rates of 10 to 24 per cent per annum, and in times of pressing need they paid 4 to 6 per cent per month. The colonization of New Russia, the southwest corner of the Russian empire, and its emergence as a major agricultural area, pushed up land prices there. At the end of the eighteenth century land sold at about 1.5 silver rubles per desiatin (2.7 acres). By the early 1850's the price had gone up to 15-20 silver rubles, and was even higher at the end of that decade after the Crimean War (which was fought in that region) had ended.[22]

II

Not unexpectedly, the price rise of the second half of the eighteenth century served to arouse a new interest in agriculture, and in its improvement. By the same token, the decline in the first half of the nineteenth century stimulated proprietors to introduce innovations in order to find shelter from the drop in farm prices. Until the middle of the eighteenth century the techniques of husbandry in the servile lands (and with a few notable exceptions in all of Europe) had over a long period of time undergone strikingly few changes. Innovations had not been entirely absent during these centuries. A host of new food plants were introduced from the New World. Improved field systems were adopted in Schleswig-Holstein and in Mecklenburg (p. 129). Texts on improved agriculture appeared in the late fifteenth and in the sixteenth centuries. Some of them were new editions or translations of classical works. Others were newly written, though they drew much of their material from the ancient authors. They combined traditional and often inaccurate farming information, instructions for the management of a farming operation, and a guide to rural living that included such things as recipes and the treatments for illnesses. In central Europe the second half of the seventeenth and first half of the eighteenth centuries saw the efflorescence of the so-called *Hausvater* literature. These manuals treated agriculture as an operation of a manorial household that included servants and dependent peasants, in which the proprietor was the *Hausvater*, the *pater familias* charged with the supervision and care of all

[22] Oțetea (1965), 331, 333; Emerit (1937), 227-229, 412; Borovoi and Kopievskii (1966), 477.

who lived on his property.[23] The net effect of the innovations in crops and techniques and of the agricultural writings were, as earlier chapters showed, remarkably limited. The use of new techniques and the cultivation of new crops were very much the exception. The retardation of agriculture persisted, and so did the lack of interest of seigniors, peasants, and governments in its improvement.

Then, around the middle of the eighteenth century, the indifference of the upper orders of society transformed itself into an intense and widespread enthusiasm for everything connected with the land. The passion for agriculture reached such proportions that the French, who yielded to no one in their ardor for the latest fad, gave it the name of *agromanie*. A German talked about the *Wut des Ackerbaues*.[24] The marquis de Mirabeau (father of the revolutionist), who won fame as an economist when in 1756 he published *L'Ami des hommes*, could barely control his prose when he counselled his readers to cherish agriculture because it was "not only the most admirable of all arts . . . the most necessary, the most useful, the most innocent." It was also "the most profitable and the most productive . . . and of all arts the most sociable. What nobility, what generous hospitality dwells in the manners of those who spend their lives at the head of their harvesters and at the head of their flocks! . . . Enter the garden of a poor man and he will freely and without ostentation offer you that which the artisan displays and dresses up for sale. . . ."[25] The new craze did not escape the pen of Voltaire, whose genius included the ability to put things into proper perspective. In the article on grain in his *Dictionnaire philosophique* he made such delightful mockery of the fad that later writers have rarely been able to resist quoting at least part of what he wrote. "Around 1750," he declared, "the nation, surfeited with poems, tragedies, comedies, operas, novels, romantic histories, even more romantic moral reflections, and theological arguments about grace and convulsions, began at last to think about grain. People even forgot to talk about vineyards and spoke only of wheat and rye. Useful books were written about farming: everyone read them except the farmers."[26]

The rage for agriculture reached up to the throne. Crowned heads gave it the supreme cachet of their approval. Joseph II of Austria had himself painted guiding a plow, albeit costumed in his customary satins and silks and laces, and wearing a powdered wig. King Louis XVI turned over some land to Antoine Parmentier, noted French agronomist, to grow potatoes. When the first blossoms appeared, Louis, to propagandize potato culture, wore them in his buttonhole. That evening Queen Marie Antoinette wore

[23] Fussell (1969), 538-551; Brunner (1949), 265-270; Rutkowski (1927), 99-100; Frauendorfer (1951), I, 116-126; Krzymowski (1961), 243; Meuvret (1953), 353-355.
[24] Ahrens (1969), 31.   [25] Mirabeau (1970), I, 32-34.
[26] Voltaire (1816), III, 91.

the flowers in her hair. That was all it took for Parmentier to be besieged by princes, dukes, and the like, for potato flowers. Marie Antoinette amused herself in a Disneyland version of a farm at Petit Trianon. George III of England was celebrated as Farmer George, and royal sprigs farmed plots at Kew, west of London, where Farmer George had a palace. Frederick II of Prussia, echoing the physiocrats, intoned with his customary ponderosity that "agriculture is the first of all arts; without it there can be no merchants, no poets, no philosophers. Only that which the earth brings forth is true wealth." Towards the end of the 1760's, Empress Catherine II invited J. C. Schubart, the noted central European agronomist and practical farmer, to move to Russia and spread the word about improved agriculture. She offered him an enormous amount of land, plus an advance of 50,000 rubles and a like sum at the end of ten years, but Schubart turned down the invitation.[27]

Art, literature, and philosophy exalted agriculture and the rural life. So, too, did the writings of the French physiocrats. This short-lived school of economic thought, established in the 1750's, numbered among its followers prominent people in France and abroad, among them high officers of state and royal advisers. Physiocracy was a reaction against the mercantilist doctrines that made manufacturing and commerce of primary importance to the strengthening of the nation's economy, and therefore of its military and naval prowess. The physiocrats held that agriculture was of supreme importance in economic development. They maintained that the land alone produced the disposable surplus after costs, or the net product, as they called it, that was necessary for economic growth.

The fancies of monarchs, the fads of the moment, and the teachings of physiocrats, were not the only reasons why things rural won the attention of men of the upper orders. The rise in farm prices, and the fact that the price scissors operated in favor of the landed proprietor, awakened many to the attractions of agriculture. (Auroux Des Pommiers addressed himself directly to these people in the blunt title he gave to his manual published in Paris in 1772. He called it *The Art of Getting Rich Quickly through Agriculture*.) Concern for the national interest made some recognize the need to raise the productivity of agriculture in order to strengthen the resources of the nation. Many were affected by the romantic appeal to nature and the glorification of the simple rustic virtues, associated principally with the teachings of Rousseau. A few wanted to help the peasant. "I am a friend of humanity," wrote J. C. Schubart, "and there is nothing I want more eagerly than to improve the wretched circumstances of the poor peasant through my own knowledge."[28]

[27] Krichauff (1895), 226-227; Abel (1967), 277; Khoroshailov (1956), 478-479.
[28] Quoted in Frauendorfer (1957), I, 144; *cf.* Van Regemorter (1968), 5-19; Brocard (1970), 88-91; Confino (1969), 133.

A more relaxed attitude of governments toward open discussion of the shortcomings of agriculture, and of the need for reforms, aided in creating and nurturing the interest in rural matters. In Denmark, Count Adam Gottlob Moltke persuaded King Frederick V to invite contributions on agricultural improvement to a new journal. That freed advocates of innovation and reform of the fear of offending their sovereign by publishing their views. The appearance of the new journal *Denmarks og Norges Oeconomiske Magazin* in 1757 was followed by other publications that dealt with agricultural and general economic affairs. In Russia the relative official tolerance that marked the earlier years of the reign of Catherine II allowed public discussion of controversial questions about agriculture and the lord-peasant relationship. Journals and books appeared that dealt with these problems, and proposals for reform were freely discussed.[29]

Finally, an interest in and admiration of things foreign, and above all others for things English, had much to do with the new enthusiasm for agriculture. Anglomania had become the rage among fashionable continentals, who seemed to find everything English irresistible. English agriculture was the object of special interest, and for good reason. In a gradual evolution that reached back into the seventeenth century, English farming had become one of the most intensive in Europe, rivalled only by that of the Low Countries. The accumulation of land in the hands of large proprietors who were willing to make large capital investments in their properties provided a favorable environment for agricultural progress that included the creation of enclosed and compact farms, suitable buildings, drainage, fertilizing, improved field systems, and the selective breeding of livestock.[30] Travelers and writers and translators spread the word of the high yields and prosperity of English farming, of the transformation of backward regions into flourishing farmlands, and of what seemed to be the high standard of living of the English peasantry. The first French treatise on what came to be called the "new husbandry" was a greatly expanded translation by Duhamel du Monceau of Jethro Tull's *Horse-Hoeing Husbandry*, published in six volumes between 1750 and 1756. (Tull's book, which appeared in England in 1733, advocated drilling seeds—that is, planting them in rows rather than broadcasting them—and systematic and frequent cultivation to improve the quality of the soil and keep down weeds.) There was a steady flow of agricultural experts back and forth across the Channel, and a number of Britons settled in France and made valuable contributions there.[31] In Germany the electorate of Hannover, bound to Great Britain by a common sovereign, served as the port of entry for the English influence. Starting in the 1750's Germans published translations of English agricultural treatises soon after their appearance in England. In succeeding decades

---

[29] Hovde (1949), I, 75; Nielsen (1933), 314-315; Sivkov (1952), 553-560.
[30] Mingay (1963), 123-133. [31] Bourde (1953), 15-23, 41-52, 179-199.

the translations continued to pour from German presses to that Arthur Young, in a letter in 1790, commented that, "The Germans, by translating every work of merit in whatever language, gain considerably by appropriating all the literary merit of other enlightened nations, whilst these remain ignorant of the daily increasing treasures of German erudition."[32] Leading German cameralists called attention in their lectures and publications to the superiority of English agriculture. Frederick II imported experts from England to apply their expertise to royal manors, and he and Margrave Karl Friedrich of Baden both sent young men to England to study the new agriculture. Acquaintance with English and French writings helped stir interest in agricultural improvement among Danish lords. In Poland and Hungary, translations of French, English, and German treatises introduced the new agriculture in those lands. "Enlightened" proprietors in Russia and in the Baltic lands made frequent references in their writings to German authorities.[33]

The devotees of the new husbandry did not restrict their activities to translations. They wrote treatises of their own, and they turned out hundreds of articles for the agricultural and economic journals that appeared in nearly all of the servile lands. A French bibliography published in 1810 counted 26 titles on agricultural topics published in France in the fifteenth century, 108 in the sixteenth, 130 in the seventeenth, and 1,214 in the eighteenth century, most of them appearing after 1750. A modern bibliography of Danish agricultural writing published before 1814 lists 6,225 entries. Of these only 54 appeared before 1740, and 100 were published in the 1740's. All the rest appeared between 1750 and 1814. In Poland 32 treatises on agriculture were published between 1700 and 1772. In the remaining 28 years of the century, 109 appeared. In Russia only one book on agriculture was published between the 1730's and the 1750's. A few more were put out in the 1760's, then in the succeeding decades their number increased. All told, 117 books on agriculture appeared between the 1770's and the 1790's; 57 were published in the 1790's alone. In addition, many articles appeared in the six journals dealing with rural economy which were founded during these years.[34]

Education, too, was used to spread the gospel of more intensive husbandry. In central European universities, professors of cameralism devoted their attentions to agriculture, along with fiscal and juristic studies. Agricultural schools were founded by landowners and by agricultural experts to teach the principles of improved agriculture. The best known of these

---

[32] Ahrens (1969), 33. For a list of German translations in the eighteenth century of English books on agriculture see Müller (1969), 129-135.

[33] Ahrens (1969), 38-39; Schröder-Lembke (1964), 29-33; Hovde (1948), I, 75-76; Leskiewicz (1962), 238; Wellmann (1968), 1197-1198; Confino (1969), 144-145, 146.

[34] Morineau (1971), 7; Pedersen (1958); Koroliuk (1956), I, 352; Sivkov (1959), 22; Sivkov (1961), 153.

schools, and the first one in Germany, opened in 1806 under the direction of Albrecht Thaer, the outstanding German agronomist of his time. The Berlin government had invited Thaer to leave his native Hannover and come to Prussia, to do research and establish a school. Thaer deliberately chose to locate the school and its experimental farm at Möglin, a 600-acre run-down estate in Brandenburg with poor soil, to demonstrate what good farming practices could accomplish. The students came from landowning and from wealthy bourgeois families and included foreigners who were drawn to Möglin by Thaer's international reputation. In its early years Möglin had around eighteen to twenty students and the course of instruction lasted for one year. Other noted agronomists who started schools included J.N.H. Schwerz, who opened an agricultural institute at Hohenheim in Württemberg, and Phillip Emmanuel von Fellenberg, who established a school on his estate of Hofwyl in the canton of Bern.[35]

In their writings, in their schools, and in their own farming operations, the advocates of improved agriculture spelled out the changes they supported. They urged the replacement of the three-field system by more intensive methods of cultivation. If farmers insisted upon retaining the three-field system, the improvers urged that restorative crops be planted in the fallow fields. They stressed the advantages of growing forage crops and stall-feeding cattle, and of the selective breeding of livestock to improve quality. They argued for the division of common land, and some of them recommended the consolidation of scattered strips into unitary holdings. They urged the adoption of new crops, especially clover, potatoes, and turnips. In short, they wanted to "modernize" the severely underdeveloped agriculture of the servile lands.

III

The great stretches of untilled, or intermittently tilled, land, some of it among Europe's most fertile soils, reflected the underdevelopment. There had been no appreciable increase in the farm land of western and central Europe since the great clearings of the Middle Ages. Indeed, during the difficult times of the seventeenth century much land had been abandoned. In some regions the number of deserted villages reached almost incredible proportions, as in Schleswig-Holstein, where, in 1700, one-third, and in some especially hard-stricken districts as many as one-half of all peasant holdings lay empty.[36]

The empty land was reoccupied only slowly, this despite the upward

[35] Király (1969), 145-146; Blum (1948), 127-132; Confino (1969), 206-207; Abel (1967), 281-282; Frauendorfer (1957), I, 224; Franz (1970), 86-89; Guggisberg (1970), 94.
[36] Arnim (1957), 57-58; *cf.* Lütge (1967), 146; Roupnel (1922), 19-74; Leroy-Ladurie (1966), 528-537; Nielsen (1933), 186.

surge of population. Some new land was also cleared or drained. The net addition, however, to the arable of the servile lands of western and central Europe was, on the whole, surprisingly small. In France the amount of land in crops, forage, and fallow increased by only 3.5 per cent, from an estimated 23.1 million hectares in 1700-1710 to 23.9 million in 1781-1790. These 23.9 million hectares took up 45 per cent of France's land area.[37] Thomas Jefferson, writing from France in 1785, was struck by the amount of untilled land he saw. He believed the land was kept idle so that it could serve as hunting preserves for the nobility. Most of the reclamation that was done in France was carried out in the last decades of the *ancien régime*, stimulated by tax exemptions offered by the government and by the rise in the price of farm land. Between 1766 and 1780 the government was said to have received declarations of intent to clear some 950,000 *arpents* (about 323,000 hectares), but it is not known how much was actually accomplished. Reportedly, more was done in Brittany than in any other province. Yet only about 45,000 hectares were reclaimed there, not all of this was taken under the plow, and much empty land remained. Moreover, the advance of sand dunes along the Breton coast took a considerable amount of land out of cultivation, thereby reducing the net gain from the clearings.[38]

Arthur Young reserved some of his sharpest reproofs for the failure of French proprietors to utilize their land resources. In late August of 1787, as he rode through southwestern France, he observed that "In these thirty-seven miles of country, lying between the great rivers Caronne, Dordonne, and Charente, and consequently in one of the best parts of France for markets, the quantity of waste land is surprising; it is indeed the predominant feature. Much of these lands belong to the Prince de Soubise, who would not sell any part of them. Thus it is whenever you stumble on a Grand Seigneur, even one who was worth millions, you are sure to find his property a desert. The Duke of Bouillon's and this Prince's are two of the greatest properties in France; and all the signs I have yet seen of their greatness, are wastes, *landes*, deserts, fern, ling.—Go to their residence, wherever it may be, and you would probably find them in the midst of a forest, very well peopled with deer, wild boar, and wolves. Oh! if I were the legislator of France for a day, I would make such great lords skip!"[39]

The disinterest of great proprietors was not the only reason why land reclamation projects did little more than "nibble at the edge of heathlands and sand dunes," as Marc Bloch put it. Clearing and draining were costly procedures that took much time, and only slowly paid back the money and labor invested in them. Furthermore, the attempts at reclamation ran into

[37] Toutain (1961), I, 36, 48.
[38] Jefferson to Madison, Fontainebleau, October 28, 1785, *Papers of Thomas Jefferson*, VIII, 681-682; Sée (1923), 64, 67-68; Meyer (1966), I, 563-564; Kareev (1899), 220-223.
[39] Young (1970), I, 62.

bitter and prolonged opposition from the local peasantry. They realized that their use of the wastelands to graze their cattle would end when the land was put under the plow. Their hostility surfaced in all parts of France and included formal protests to the government and occasional outbursts of sabotage and violence against the reclaimers and their work.[40]

In Germany rulers lent official encouragement and support to reclamation, and sometimes joined with private persons, or with companies specially formed for the purpose, to clear and drain land. In some places relatively large amounts were brought into cultivation. In the 1760's and 1770's in Farther Pomerania 480,000 *morgen*, equal to about 10 per cent of the total area of that region, were added to the arable. In Prussian Silesia the arable increased by about 15 per cent between 1721 and 1798.[41] Despite this activity, by 1800 only about one-third of the land surface of Germany was under cultivation.[42] An analysis of land use in the nine provinces that made up the kingdom of Prussia in 1815 showed that only 26.5 per cent of the total area of these provinces was used for field and garden crops, 19 per cent for meadows and pastures, 14.3 per cent was in forests, and the remaining 40.2 per cent was classified as "untilled, barren, roads, etc." The ratio of arable to total area ran from 11.9 per cent in Posen, in the east, to 41.4 per cent in the Rhine Province.[43]

In eighteenth-century Austria the government had engaged in land reclamation projects. In the first half of the nineteenth century private persons and especially great landowners carried on the work as individuals or in associations. Their efforts converted a considerable amount of swampland, moors, and ponds to agricultural use. In Bohemia, where proprietors seemed particularly active in reclamation, the successive cadastral surveys made by the government showed a growth of 19 per cent in plowland between the 1780's and the 1840's. Despite these additions to the cultivated land, much still lay untilled. In Bohemia in the 1840's, farm land occupied about 47 per cent of the area. In the 9 German-Slav provinces together (including Bohemia), farm land occupied just about one-third of the total surface.[44]

In contrast to western and central Europe, the area of farm land in regions of eastern Europe increased at a spectacular rate during the last century of the old order. The eastern lands contained the last European frontiers into which settlers came in increasing number. The population of

[40] Sée (1923), 75-80.

[41] Eggert (1965), 8; Abel (1966), 192; *cf.* Schlögl (1954), 207-212.

[42] Bittermann (1956), 13-17.

[43] Finck von Finckenstein (1934), 22. A half century later, in 1864, in these same nine provinces cropland occupied 51.4 per cent of the total area, the ratio of meadows and pastures remained nearly unchanged at 17.9 per cent, forests had increased to 24.6 per cent, while the "untilled, barren, roads, etc." category had fallen to 7.1 per cent. *Ibid.*

[44] Schnabel (1846), 71; *Tafeln zur Statistik*, 1845-1846, part I, table 1, p. 4; part II, table 1, p. 1.

Hungary had suffered a catastrophic decline during the one hundred and fifty years of Turkish rule over most of that kingdom. Much of the country lay desolate. After the restoration of Hapsburg rule at the outset of the eighteenth century the trend was reversed. Settlers poured into the Alföld, the Great Hungarian Plain. Besides people of Magyar stock, the newcomers included south Germans, Lorrainers, Slovaks, Serbs, Wallachians, Jews, and Greeks. Some of the colonists settled in towns, old and new, but by far the greatest number took holdings in the countryside. Between 1720 and the census of 1787 the estimated ratio of arable land to Hungary's total area rose from 5 per cent to 20 per cent.

Population continued its ascent on into the nineteenth century, so that by the mid-1840's Hungary had around 10 million people. Farm land grew, too, as demographic pressure brought more and more land under the plow. Large-scale reclamation projects added hundreds of thousands of acres. River regulation, and particularly that of the Theiss River, had special importance, for seasonal floods put vast stretches of potentially fertile land under water for long periods each year, caused great damage and sometimes heavy loss of life. By 1846 arable covered better than a third of the surface of Hungary (without Transylvania, Croatia, and the Military Frontier). That was about the same proportion that prevailed in the German and Slav parts of the Monarchy.[45]

Demographic pressure accounted for the increase in farm land in other eastern lands, too. Population densities in the east had been much lower than in the west: around 1770 France had an estimated 45 persons per square kilometer, Germany, 36.9, Poland, 19.1, and Russia only 5.5.[46] In the older regions of settlement in Russia, north of the 55th parallel of latitude, most of the land suitable for cultivation under the predominant methods of tillage may have been in use by the end of the eighteenth century. At least contemporaries thought so.[47] By the time that happened (if, indeed, it did), the area of Russia's farm land had already increased, as settlers pushed south of the 55th parallel of latitude into the chernozem, the fertile black earth of the steppe. Already by the turn of the century over 50 per cent of European Russia's sowed area lay in the black earth provinces. In the first half of the nineteenth century, colonists streamed into the provinces of New Russia, in the southwest corner of the empire, and into the rich lands along the middle and lower Volga. By mid-century, population density in some of these once nearly empty provinces was comparable to and even exceeded that of provinces in the old region of settlement. The sowed area in New Russia grew from about 800,000 desiatins at the beginning of the century to 6 million desiatins by the 1860's. In four Volga prov-

[45] den Hollander (1960), 154, 156-157, 159; Barany (1968), 147; Helleiner (1967), 58; Wellmann (1968), 1203; Blum (1948), 111-112.
[46] Gieysztorowa (1968), 9.   [47] Confino (1969), 135-142.

inces the increase was from 1 million to 4.6 million desiatins in the same time span. All told, between 1802 (the first year for which sufficient data are available) and the 1850's, the area planted in grain in all of European Russia—and well over 90 per cent of sown fields were in grain—rose from 38 to 58 million desiatins (102.6 million to 156.6 million acres).[48]

In White Russia and Lithuania, and on the right bank of the Ukraine, the wars and revolts and internal disorders of the seventeenth century, and in Livonia the Great Northern War that lasted from 1700 to 1721, left legacies of depopulation and desolation. When these times of troubles ended, the population curve turned upward, at first slowly and then with mounting speed, and more and more land came into cultivation. At the beginning of the nineteenth century the three provinces of Right Bank Ukraine, Volynia, Kiev, and Podolia already had about 1.5 million desiatins sown with grain. By the end of the 1850's that area had grown by 50 per cent, to 2.25 million desiatins.[49]

In the 1860's an estimated 20.9 per cent of European Russia, including the Baltic provinces, was reported to have been in use as plowland. As could be expected, particularly in a land as vast as Russia, this average figure concealed wide divergences. In 22 of the 49 provinces of European Russia, plowland occupied from 40 to 70 per cent of their surfaces, and in 16 others between 20 and 40 per cent. Only in 11 provinces did plowland occupy less than 20 per cent. These 11, however, included the largest and least fertile provinces of the empire, and so contributed a disproportionate weight to the national average. In semi-arid Astrakhan, on the Caspian Sea, for example, only 1.1 per cent of the land was in use as arable; in the provinces of Arkhangel and Vologda, in the tundra of the far north, arable occupied only 0.1 per cent and 2.2 per cent, respectively, of the land surface.[50]

In Poland the wars that raged for 55 of the 68 years between 1648 and 1716, and the epidemics and the barbarism that followed in war's train, brought devastation to many parts of that unfortunate land. Population fell by as much as 64 per cent in Masovia, the central region of the country, and by lesser but still frightening ratios in other parts of the realm. When some degree of internal order was finally established, it took long years to restore the great losses. At the end of the eighteenth century there was still less land under cultivation than there had been in the sixteenth century, and the total production of grain and the number of cattle were much less than they had been at that earlier time. In the nineteenth century population swelled, markets grew, and empty land was put into cultivation. In

---

[48] Liashchenko (1956), 520; Tsentral'nyi statisticheskii komitet (1863), 158-174; Borovoi and Kopievskii (1966), 476-477.

[49] Baraboi (1964), 341; Chepko (1964), 390; Loone (1959), 202; Shlossberg (1959), 117, 127.

[50] Ministerstvo Gosudarstvennykh Imuchestv (1869), 41-43.

1820 about one-third of Russian Poland had been used as farm land. By 1865 that ratio had increased to 50 per cent.[51]

Until well into the nineteenth century, population density in the Danubian Principalities was so low that most of the land there lay unbroken. As late as 1837 only an estimated 8 per cent was planted. Then heightened foreign demand and a reported population increase of astounding proportions combined to increase pressure on the land. The inadequate data indicate that population rose from somewhere between 1.8 and 2.2 million in 1834, to 3.7 million in 1859. Using the lower figure of 1.8 million for 1834, this represented an increase of over 100 per cent in 25 years, or an annual growth rate of over 3 per cent.[52]

IV

The proportion of arable to total area did not mean that this amount of land produced crops every year. As earlier pages pointed out, fallows were part of the field system used by farmers nearly everywhere in the servile lands, with as much as a third or more of the plowland unplanted each year. In the last decades of the old order, however, a small band, almost exclusively of seigniors, adopted what was known as the "improved" three-field system, or "green fallowing," by planting forage crops on the hitherto bare fallows. A few abandoned traditional field systems in favor of crop rotation.

Simple as it seems, sowing the fallow with forage plants was an advance of great moment. To recall what was said in an earlier chapter, the low grain yield of the traditional agriculture compelled farmers to use most of their land to produce food for humans rather than for livestock. That meant that they did not get manure in sufficient quantity to fertilize their fields, and this helped keep yields at abysmally low levels. The only recourse that the farmer had to restore some measure of fertility to his fields was to fallow them periodically. Planting forage crops in the fallow pried open the jaws of the vise that held the farmer prisoner of the traditional agriculture. Now he could keep more and better livestock because he had more forage for them, and the forage had a higher nutritional value than the dry stalks and parched grass and bushes and straw on which his animals used to feed. More animals, and more and better food for them, meant more manure to enrich the fields, and enabled the farmer to introduce new crops that needed heavy manuring. In addition, clover and other legumes planted for forage possessed chemical qualities that restored fertility to a field much better than fallowing could. If enough forage was raised, the cattle could be stall-

[51] Topolski (1962), 35-38, 41, 44-45; Rutkowski (1953), 258-259; Ivanova (1966), 171; Kieniewicz (1969), 93.
[52] Haufe (1939), 77-78, 84-85; Corfus (1969), 173-174.

fed. This released land hitherto needed for pasture for use as plowland. Usually, though, in green fallowing part of the fallow was left bare, because it was needed for pasture. Sometimes, however, clover was sown in the field when it was in grain, so that after harvest the cattle could graze on the clover.

Some farmers learned through experience that on their fields fallow crops did not succeed every third year, and so they planted them every sixth or even ninth year. These and similar considerations led to elaborations of the usual three-year cycle of spring grain, winter grain, and fallow. Around 1800 some German farmers, for example, used a six-year cycle of bare fallow, winter grain, spring grain, peas and clover, winter grain, spring grain. Albrecht Thaer, writing in 1809, said that few farmers who had green fallows adhered rigorously to fixed cycles. Most planted forage crops if the field was free of weeds and had a suitable texture, and put in the forage crops only in the cleanest part of the field.[53]

Among all forage crops clover held first place. It was truly "king of the green fallow," as someone called it. It had simple requirements for cultivation. It was rich in nutritive matter, and so was a valuable feed. It could be mowed at least twice during the growing season for hay to feed stalled cattle, and in autumn the livestock could be turned out to pasture on the regrowth. Its roots, which spread deep into the soil and in lateral directions, had nodules formed by the activity of bacteria that gathered nitrogen from the soil-air. When the clover was plowed under as "green manure," it decayed rapidly, and so released the nitrogen trapped in the nodules and thereby enriched the soil. Red clover, the most common variety, fared best in regions of good soil, abundant rainfall, and without extremes of summer and winter temperatures. Lucerne (known by its arabic name of alfalfa in Spain and in the United States) and sainfoin were legumes better suited than clover for dry climates and poor soils. Lucerne's exceptionally long roots reached deep into the earth for moisture. Like clover it produced several cuttings a season, and its regrowth served as pasture. Sainfoin flourished in soil too dry and barren even for lucerne. Sometimes vetch, another legume, was planted as a forage crop. Peas, beans, and lentils, too, were grown in the fallow for fodder, especially for horses, as well as for human consumption.[54]

Root crops, and notably turnips, were raised for their thickened roots, which provided first-rate feed for livestock. They could also serve as green forage, with the cattle eating the plant tops in the field. Root crops had to be hoed frequently and manured heavily to ensure worthwhile yields. This served to improve the physical condition of the field, so that succeeding grain crops gave higher yields. There was a price that had to be paid for

[53] Thaer (1809), I, 299-300; Henning (1969a), 20; Berthold (1962), 115.
[54] Hutcheson and Wolfe (1924), 411-413; Faucher (1949), 180-182; Bailey (1922), 564.

these advantages, namely, labor. Root crops demanded much more labor time, from the preparation of the field to the time when they were lifted from the field. In England, the admired model for continental improvers, turnips had great success. Despite the efforts of agronomists and governments, they did not catch on with the farmers of the servile lands.[55] Doubtless the labor requirement and the need for heavy manuring explained this rejection. Sugar beets were a minor exception to the general lack of interest in root crops. Raised for sugar production and not for forage (though the residue from the refineries was fed to livestock), their culture spread slowly and almost exclusively on demesne land during the first half of the nineteenth century. Plants other than legumes and root crops raised on the fallow included rape, grown for forage and for the oil that could be pressed from its seeds.

Green fallowing was not an invention of the improvers. Classical writers had known the value of forage crops, and they were raised in places in the servile lands long before the dawn of the new husbandry. Lucerne had come into southern France from Italy early in the sixteenth century, and reports from the middle of that century told of sainfoin being grown. In the seventeenth century farms in the southern environs of the Paris basin grew lucerne and sainfoin, and in the eighteenth century some farmers of the Midi rotated lucerne with maize. In Lower Alsace farmers had planted fallows with peas, beans, lentils, madder, and colza in the sixteenth and seventeenth centuries, and forage crops had long been raised in other parts of France. In Germany clover and lucerne were grown in the sixteenth century, and in Upper Austria and Bohemia in the seventeenth century. By the early nineteenth century green fallows had made their debut just about everywhere in the servile lands.[56] Yet, nearly everywhere bare fallows continued as the standard procedure. Indeed, when forage crops were raised, they were often planted not in the fallow but in small enclosures near the house, almost as if they were extensions of the kitchen garden. Planted fallows, as William Jacob pointed out in 1828, were in "the greater part of France, a still much greater portion of Germany, and nearly the whole of Prussia, Austria, Poland and Russia occasional and small deviations . . . minute exceptions to the generally established system."[57]

At the beginning of the eighteenth century about 4 per cent (900,000 hectares) of the 23.1 million hectares of cultivated land in France is thought to have been in forage crops; 7.7 million hectares, or 33 per cent, was in

[55] Iatsunskii (1966), 50; Festy (1950), 60-62; Meyer (1965), 101; Juillard (1953), 217-218; Lamartine Yates (1940), 30.
[56] France: Leroy-Ladurie (1966), I, 68-69; Venard (1957), 89; Juillard (1953), 41; Debien (1945), 133. Germany: Abel (1967), 167-168, 307. Austria: Hoffmann (1952), I, 302; Stark (1957), 21-23. *Cf.* Kostiushko (1954), 162; Kahk (1969), 43-50; Confino (1969), 193-202.
[57] Debien (1945), 133; Venard (1957), 89; Müller (1964b), 231; Bourde (1953), 33; Finck von Finckenstein (1934), 6, table 1; Jacob (1828), 140.

bare fallow. In 1789 an estimated 6 per cent (1.4 million hectares) was planted in forage crops. However, now about 40 per cent of the cultivated land was in bare fallow. Green fallowing apparently had a much wider acceptance in Germany. By 1800 an estimated 13.9 per cent (about 4 million hectares) of all the tilled land in Germany was in forage plants, vegetables, industrial crops (e.g., flax, hemp, hops, dye plants, rape, cole), root crops, or potatoes. An estimated 25 per cent of the arable was bare fallow. Green fallowing, with clover as the most common crop, was practiced most intensively in western Germany, and, in general, declined as one moved eastward. In Switzerland green fallowing made much progress during the last four decades of the eighteenth century. In contrast, in the Austrian Monarchy, despite the barrage of propaganda from agricultural societies and agronomists, bare fallows continued as the nearly universal norm. The official statistical publications of the government in the 1830's and 1840's did not even include a rubric for forage production. A modern study of Bohemia, the largest and most progressive agricultural producer among the German and Slav crown lands, found that in 1848 forage plants took up only 8 per cent of the cultivated area, while 21.6 per cent was in bare fallow. In the 1760's improvers in Russia first planted clover in their demesnes. More than a century later only 4.2 per cent of European Russia's farm land was in crops other than grain. Nearly 30 per cent was bare fallow. In 1881 a mere 0.9 per cent of the sown area was planted with clover. In the Baltic provinces of Russia, initial failures had discouraged green fallowing, but reports of the 1830's and 1840's told of a rising output of legumes and root crops. In neighboring White Russia and Lithuania, too, green fallowing apparently became fairly common by the middle of the nineteenth century. In Poland forage culture lagged. In 1840 only 0.5 per cent of the tilled land had clover planted on it; by 1863 the area had increased to 3 per cent. In the Danubian Principalities neither clover nor lucerne were reported to have been raised.[58]

Small as the number was of those who planted their fallows, far fewer jettisoned the three-field system in favor of crop rotation. The essential difference between the two methods was that in crop rotation a grain crop on a field was followed regularly by a root crop or a legume, while in the three-field system the field was planted in grain for two years in succession, and then fallowed. The difference had important consequences, whose end result was increased yields. Each plant, or family of plants, has certain typical

[58] France: Toutain (1961), I, 52. Germany: Bittermann (1956), 19; Riemann (1953), 17; Müller (1964b), 231-232. Switzerland: Bollinger (1941), 47; Bernhard (1915), 10, 11. Austria: Kodedová (1967), 140. Russia: Ermolov (1878), 76-77; Iatsunskii (1966), 48; Khoroshailov (1956), 468, 483-487. Baltic provinces: Strod (1959), 50, 58; Kahk (1969), 36-37. White Russia and Lithuania: Ulashchik (1961), 181. Poland: Kieniewicz (1969), 95. Danubian Principalities: Corfus (1960), 57.

insects and diseases associated with it. When one type of crop was grown continuously in a field, the harm done by these banes of plant life increased, and yields decreased. An alternation of crops checked the insects and diseases that affected a given species of plant. The frequent cultivation that non-cereal crops required cleaned the soil of weeds and improved its texture. In a properly chosen rotation each successive crop on a field used different chemicals in the soil. An alternation of deep-rooted plants like clover, and shallow-rooted ones such as wheat or rye, allowed utilization of different levels of the soil. In such a rotation, too, each crop returned to the soil some of what the preceding crop had taken from it. Cereals that used much of the nitrogen in the soil were rotated with clover, which returned nitrogen to the field. Rotations by themselves did not completely restore soil fertility. That required fertilizer. In the days before mineral fertilizers this meant manure, produced by the cattle fed on the forage raised in the rotation cycle, though sometimes, as mentioned earlier, farmers resorted to "green manuring," that is, they plowed under a forage crop. (Present-day farmers use mineral fertilizers and chemical weed and pest controls, and so do not need to employ regular crop rotations to restore fertility or clean the soil.)

Like green fallowing, crop rotation was not a new discovery. But, like other progressive farming techniques, it was part of the new husbandry that spread into the continent from eighteenth-century England. The famed four-course Norfolk rotation of wheat, turnips, barley, and clover became the admired model of European improvers. Observation and experience, however, taught them that the crops and their order of alternation were dependent upon local soil and climate, and they soon developed their own rotations. When they were used, rotations were nearly always limited to the demesne land of the seigniors.[59] So few seigniors used rotations, however, that the technique was of only minor importance up to the end of the old order, and well beyond it.[60]

Another system of improved husbandry did make appreciable progress in parts of northern Europe in the last decades of the old order. This was convertible husbandry, or *Koppelwirtschaft*, as it was known in northern and eastern Europe (see p. 129). Contemporary accounts told of increases in yields of two and three times over within a generation when convertible husbandry replaced the three-field system. Word of these successes spread and a growing number of seigniors adopted it. That is, they adopted it when, as Albrecht Thaer explained, "the free use of property is not re-

[59] Müller (1965a), 110; Debien (1945), 134; Kostiushko (1954), 102; Strod (1959), 58; Schnabel (1846), 84-86; Pokhilevich (1966), 388; Boelcke (1957), 171-176.
[60] Cf. Müller (1965a), 100-101, 110; Haushofer (1963), 45; Schnabel (1846), 86; Ulashchik (1961), 184; Strod (1959), 46; Ministerstvo Gosudarstvennykh Imuchestv (1869), 65-68; Industries of Russia (1893), 67-73.

stricted by hampers placed by old regulations and where the estates are large enough to afford this change, which can be made only with difficulties and the sacrifice of cash income during the first years."[61] The changeover to convertible husbandry meant the abandonment of permanent common pastures and open fields, and the consolidation of strips, and enclosure. In the last third of the eighteenth century a number of large proprietors in Brandenburg and in Pomerania adopted the system, working out rotations best suited to local conditions. In Denmark some proprietors had used convertible husbandry in the late seventeenth century. It became of major importance after the middle of the next century, and by the mid-nineteenth century it was used on most demesnes. A few Livonian proprietors tried the system at the beginning of the nineteenth century but apparently found that it did not suit their needs, and they turned to crop rotation. In neighboring Courland the method had more success, and by the mid-nineteenth century was used on many estates in the western part of that province.[62]

Earlier pages have discussed the constants that barred the way to the adoption of any and all innovations, namely, the devotion of peasants to traditional routines, their suspicion of suggestions for change that came from the seigniors, and the disinterest and even repugnance for change of most seigniors. These same obstacles help explain why many decades were to pass, and the servile system itself was to disappear, before green fallowing and crop rotations became generally accepted. The nexus of legal and traditional rights and obligations that characterized the traditional society presented a formidable barrier to the adoption of these two innovations. Planting the fallow ran directly counter to the right that peasants and seigniors had to pasture their livestock in the fallow fields. Keeping cattle in stalls and feeding and watering them there meant the end of common pastures and communal herds. Some owners of tithes opposed green fallows because they feared that their incomes would diminish if crops other than grain were planted. Other tithe owners demanded an appropriate share of the fallow crops, and thereby discouraged peasants from growing them. Leases often prescribed the field system that the renter had to use, and forbad any alteration or addition to the traditional system. In Brittany, for example, leases habitually contained a clause that ordered the renter "to farm according to the customs of the country," or "according to the old ways without innovations or changes."[63]

And then there was the matter of cost. Additional human and animal labor time had to be spent in field preparation, cultivation, and harvesting

---

[61] Thaer (1809), I, 332.

[62] Müller (1965a), 103, 110; Eggert (1965), 5; Schröder-Lembke (1956), 58-59; Nielsen (1933), 181-182; Ashley (1924), 252; Strod (1959), 54-55, 57; Strod (1962), 379.

[63] Meyer (1966), I, 501; *Mittheilungen der k. k. mähr.-schles. Gesellschaft . . .* 1852, 81-83; Festy (1950), 37-40; Abel (1967), 307-308; Confino (1969), 256-257.

of the forage crops. Money had to be spent to purchase feed for the live-stock during the period before the now planted fallow (on which the animals used to graze) once again provided forage. The planted fallows had to be fenced to keep out animals. The adoption of crop rotations brought a temporary fall in income. That happened because the reduction in the area sown in grain, the cash crop, at the outset would not be compensated for by increased yields. It was also possible that yields per acre of the cash crop would fall temporarily, because manure used on the root crops and legumes would have otherwise been used on the cash crops.

Finally, many would-be pioneers discovered, often at considerable cost, that the mere adoption of innovations did not guarantee success. All too often ignorance and inattention to proper procedures, and failure to take precautions, led to poor results that persuaded the pioneer and his neighbors that it was a waste of time to plant fallows or use crop rotations. Arthur Young, who encountered this reaction in France, explained that "the introduction of clover, wherever I have met with it, has been commonly effected in such a manner that very little benefit is to be expected from it." He pointed out that when the proper procedures were not used, clover "will do more mischief than good, and that a country is better cultivated without than with it."[64]

V

Important as the adoption of green fallowing and crop rotation was in shaping the future course of agriculture in servile Europe, the enclosure of commons and the consolidation of scattered strips into unified holdings had even greater significance. Enclosure and consolidation could lead to a more productive agriculture. They also brought about radical changes in the structure and *mentalité* of rural society. Enclosure and consolidation transformed land in which an entire community had rights of use into land in which only the individual occupant had the right of use. To employ legal language, land that had been held by right of common now was held in severalty. That metamorphosis was the single most important departure from the traditional agriculture, heralding as it did the transition from communalism, with its collective rights and collective controls, to individualism, with its private rights of property and its individual freedom of action. In the communal system the individual had to accede to the will of those who shared the land and its resources with him. Now, on his own consolidated holding, he could use whatever field system or rotation he wished, grow what he wanted, graze his cattle on his own land, and not have to share its resources with anyone else.

These gains, however, were possible only at costs so heavy that many

[64] Young (1970), II, 60; *cf.* Mayer (1966), I, 585; Confino (1969), 236-239.

lords and peasants were unable or unwilling to pay them. Consolidation and enclosure involved attacks upon long-observed property rights of the villagers. Each household had to give up land it held in exchange for other pieces of land, and had to relinquish its rights in the use of common resources. The effort to achieve equity for all parties in the exchange of parcels, and the division of common lands, offered enormously difficult problems. Land varied in quality and in its accessibility to roads and streams. To approximate fairness, the consolidated farms had to be of different sizes to compensate for the variations in the quality of the soil in each farm; each had to have a mix of soils of different qualities; and each had to have access to a road. It cost a lot of money to carry through the detailed survey and the other operations involved in these changes, and for many the costs did not seem to justify the outlay. And, inevitably, the new arrangements sparked bitter and protracted quarrels and lingering discontent among those who felt that they had lost out in the exchanges of land.

Enclosed fields and consolidated holdings were not new phenomena in the servile lands. Some seigniors whose land lay scattered in the open fields along with that of their peasants had exchanged their strips for those of peasants in order to create a consolidated demesne. And lords sometimes appropriated common lands for their own exclusive use.[65] Peasants had long lived on consolidated holdings in mountainous and forested regions, in the maritime provinces of western Europe, and scattered through other parts of the servile lands. In most of these regions the isolated farmstead has presumably been the original form of settlement. In a few places, however, peasants who had lived in villages with open fields had chosen to divide their land into enclosed farms. In eastern Schleswig that process began in the sixteenth century, or even earlier, among peasants with good tenures, and many of whom were freemen. It spread from there into other parts of the duchy. The law forbad peasants to enclose common lands because this interfered with the hunts of the nobles, but the peasants enclosed them anyway and the government rarely intervened to enforce the prohibition. In France and in Germany villages enclosed on their own initiative. In Germany peasants began to enclose in the sixteenth century in Allgäu, a district of Suabia in southwest Germany. The best known enclosures there were in Kempten, where they began in 1550, but were not completed until 1790, with over 200 individual farms.[66]

These enclosures had been sporadic or isolated phenomena. Then, late in the eighteenth century, as the currents of the new husbandry reached through Europe, loud and insistent voices demanded the abolition of open

[65] Szabo (1947), 189-190; Abel (1967), 267; Bloch (1930), 336, 537; Leroy-Ladurie (1966), 581.
[66] Steensberg (1951), 188-189; Parain (1952), 134-135; Dion (1934), 65-68; Gromas (1947), 95-101; Gamperl (1955), 55; Haushofer (1963), 54-55; Müller (1965a), 119.

fields and scattered strips, and what Arthur Young called "the pernicious rights of commage" on pastures and fallow fields. The voices were those of agricultural experts and improving landlords, who, as with other innovations, drew their inspiration from England.[67] They learned with admiration and envy of the extent of enclosures there, and they contrasted the English experience with what they called the "barbarous conditions" or the "primitive customs" of their own lands. Their admiration was not merely a reflection of the anglomania of the era. They wanted to maximize profits from agriculture, and they believed that enclosures would contribute importantly to that end. They also were firm believers in the economic superiority of individual ownership. They condemned communal rights and controls over the use of land as reactionary, and as inimical to the progress of agriculture.[68]

A few great seigniors introduced enclosures and consolidations on their own manors. Their example, and the insistence of agricultural experts, persuaded monarchs that their own and their subjects' economic interests would best be served by supplanting common rights in plowland and pasture with individual occupancy. The campaigns by governments to achieve this became almost a pan-European movement. It had its greatest success (outside of England) in Denmark. In other lands, governmental indecision, poor planning, bureaucratic bungling and obstructionism, the opposition of lords and peasants, and the weight of tradition held back the reforms.

The abolition of communal rights to the use of common lands, including fallow fields, was a special target of royal legislation. In 1768 Empress Maria Theresa ordered the division between lords and peasants of all land in her German and Slav provinces that was used solely for common pasture. The seigniors would get one half, and the other half was to be divided among the peasants who had used the land. The decree set a time limit of one year for compliance and ordered condign punishments for those who failed to obey the new law. Despite the stern language and the threats, the edict had little effect. The throne repeated its order to divide the common land six times during the following years with few results. Finally, in 1808 the government gave up, and contented itself with recommending, but not requiring, the division of the commons. In France a series of royal edicts and actions by *parlements* between 1769 and 1781 authorized the division of commons in certain designated provinces or in specific locations. The royal decrees allowed seigniors to appropriate one-third, or even one-half, of the commons in a parish, with the remainder to be divided among the

---

[67] Enclosures in England began early in the sixteenth century. By the turn of the eighteenth century, about half of England's arable was enclosed. The great new wave of enclosures that started in the 1760's completed the process.

[68] Bloch (1930), 332-333; Confino (1969), 286; Wittich (1896), 414; Haushofer (1963), 55.

peasants. In these same years rulings by provincial *parlements*, and then decrees of the central government, banned common pasturing on fallows in a number of regions. As in Austria, this legislative and judicial activity had small results.

In Germany the petty duchy of Lauenburg, which lay between Hannover and Holstein, was the first to take effective action. A decree of 1718 allowed seigniors there to move peasants from their holdings for purposes of consolidation. The evicted peasants had to receive land elsewhere of the same quality, the same number of peasant holdings had to be retained, and the government had to give its final approval before the consolidation could be carried out. The consolidation was accompanied by the division of common pastures and the end of common rights in the forests. By the latter part of the eighteenth century the process had been nearly completed and had proved itself to be a great success. In larger states princes tried to implement similar programs but did not meet with similar results. The rulers of Bavaria issued a series of legislative acts in the second half of the century that ordered the end of common pasturing and the consolidation of scattered strips. Little happened until the accession of Maximilian IV Joseph in 1799, when the government put new energy and determination into its efforts. Frederick II of Prussia moved cautiously in his drive to end common rights. He started out by giving his approval to individual requests for enclosure in which all parties were in accord. From 1763 on he issued orders that ended commons and promoted consolidation in the entire kingdom. The results of his legislation varied, with more being accomplished in some provinces, such as Brandenburg and Pomerania, and little in others, such as the Rhine Province or East Prussia. Everywhere the land that was consolidated was almost exclusively seigniorial demesne. The great mass of the peasantry still had their holdings scattered in many pieces through the open fields of their villages.[69]

The good results in Lauenburg, since 1705 part of the patrimony of the Elector of Hannover, excited the interest of George III, ruler of England and Hannover. George wanted especially to transform the great Lüneburg Heath, which lies between the Aller and the Elbe rivers, into a productive farming region. He thought he could do this by empowering his officials to carry out enclosures on an individual basis. The failure of this effort made it clear that a general decree to spell out the procedure was necessary. It was promulgated on 25 June 1802 and proved so successful that it became the model for later legislation ordering enclosures in other German states.

In several of the Swiss cantons there were lively discussions of the need

[69] Austria: Peyrer (1877), 1-3. France: Bloch (1966), 221-222; Lefebvre (1929), 512; Juillard (1953), 74; Forster (1960), 79. Lauenburg: Sering (1908), 231. Bavaria: Schlögl (1954), 164-165; Lütge (1949), 22, 65; Gamperl (1955), 53, 58-60. Prussia: Müller (1965a), 114, 115-116; Knapp (1887), I, 59-60; Engels (1957), 127-128; Henning (1969a), 46.

to end common pasture and to divide the allmends, the village common lands. In 1759 the government of Neuchâtel limited the right of pasture on fallows, in later decrees restricted it further, and finally abolished it in 1814. The Great Council of Bern in 1765 ordered the division of the allmends there, but left the execution of the order to the individual communities. Some complied; most did not. Not until well into the nineteenth century did enclosure of commons become general. In Russia an imperial ukase of 1766 allowed seigniors to carry out consolidation on their properties, after the manor had been surveyed for tax purposes in the general cadastre ordered by the government in 1754. In 1836 the government ordered the creation of a commission in each province to gather information about consolidation, and to prepare measures that would encourage it. Later decrees also sought to advance consolidation. All of these efforts had scarcely any effect. In Hungary the *Urbarium* of 1836 provided for the division of common land, if the seignior, or the majority of the peasants of the manor, demanded it. Apparently few, if any, of the lords and peasants took advantage of the legislation.[70]

The kingdom of Denmark was the only one of the servile lands, and, indeed, the only major state beside England, in which consolidation went swiftly and met with nearly universal compliance. In 1757 a special royal committee, established at the insistence of improving proprietors, addressed itself to a study of ways to correct deficiencies associated with open fields and common rights. Some of its recommendations were incorporated in a decree of 29 December 1758. A series of other laws followed during the next two decades. All of these edicts were consolidated and expanded by a decree of 26 July 1781. With that decree a comprehensive program of consolidation and enclosure got under way. The law provided that any individual landholder could demand consolidation of his holding into a single piece, or three pieces at most. The cost of the survey, mapping, and consolidation were prorated among all the landholders of the village, regardless of whether or not they favored consolidation. The decree fixed the pay scale for the surveyors and other technicians needed for the operation. In 1786 the government set up a fund to lend money to peasants to meet the costs of the reforms, and to convert their consolidated holdings into hereditary leaseholds or full ownership. Other decrees ordered the fencing of fields, required each landholder to clean and maintain streams that ran through his farm, share expenses of drainage with his neighbors, and provided for the construction of access roads for the new farms carved out of the open fields and the commons. Separate legislation for Schleswig-Holstein proved less successful than the Danish laws. Consolidation in the duchies proceeded rapidly, but was not carried out as efficiently, so that there many

[70] Hannover: Wittich (1896), 422-423. Switzerland: Petitpierre (1871), 161, 172; Wahlen and Jaggi (1952), 132-133. Russia: Confino (1969), 288-291. Hungary: Mailath (1838), 109-111.

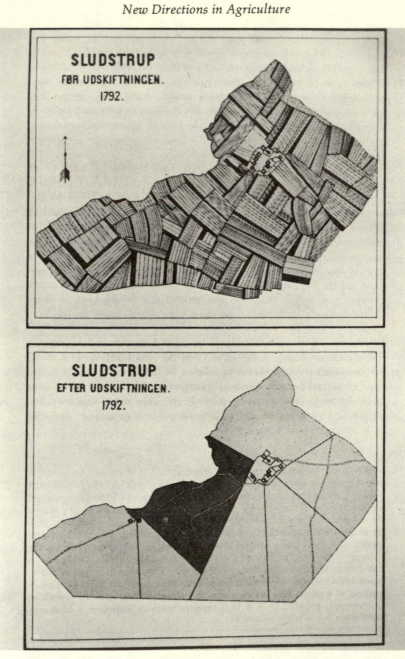

13. The village of Sludstrup, Denmark, before and after consolidation. Before consolidation in 1792 each of the seven households of the village had its land split into about 100 parcels. The shaded parcels in the upper map belonged to one household. The shaded block in the lower map is this household's now consolidated holding. After consolidation two households moved out of the village onto their holdings. (B. O. Binns, ed., *The Consolidation of Fragmented Agricultural Holdings*, Washington, 1950.)

small and badly shaped holdings, and the access roadnet was incomplete.[71]

The achievements of the Danish program gave witness to the need for decisive and firm governmental leadership, and for carefully drawn and comprehensive legislation. In the other major servile lands governments did not exhibit the necessary forcefulness of purpose. Perhaps they were not completely convinced of the value of the reforms. Perhaps most important, they feared that the widespread popular resistance to enclosure and consolidation would lead to serious discontent and civil disorders.

The roots of the resistance lay in the annulment of common rights that was the central feature of the reforms. These servitudes were much too valuable to most peasants for them to be relinquished without a struggle. Arthur Young, enthusiastic, indeed, heated advocate of enclosures, had grave doubts (borne out by events) that the revolutionary government of France would carry through a comprehensive program of reform. For, said he "as far as the present constitution can be understood, it is the will of *the people* (Young's italics) that is to govern; and I know of no country where the people are not against inclosures."[72] Above all, the peasants with small holdings or with no land at all, who in so many places formed the majority of the community, opposed enclosure. Pasture for their few animals was already at a premium. Many villages did not have enough pastureland to feed their animals, so that the right to pasture on newly harvested and on fallow fields was essential for survival. To extinguish these rights and other servitudes, such as the right to gather wood in the seignior's forests, would work great hardship on the many who now lived at the bare margin of subsistence. Those who had holdings feared that they would fare poorly in the exchange of strips that consolidation made necessary, and the costs involved in the operation repelled them.[73] They were unhappy, too, about the breakup of the village, for with consolidation each household would presumably live in its own isolated farmstead. In Denmark this problem took on serious proportions. Ninety per cent of Denmark's rural settlements had been nuclear villages. The peasants did not want to give up the close ties of village life. Many remained in their villages for years after consolidation, even though their farms lay at a distance.[74]

Members of the upper orders opposed consolidation, too. Some of these seigniors were as reluctant as the peasants to give up their right of common pasture. Some regarded the reforms as a violation of the property rights of the village community. Some feared that the reforms would create so much disorder, and stir up so much discontent among the peasantry, that their

[71] Nielsen (1933), 316; Gamperl (1955), 47; Hovde (1948), I, 278; Sering (1908), 231; Steensberg (1951), 189.
[72] Young (1970), I, 400.
[73] Bloch (1930), 523; Lefebvre (1929), 511; Babeau (1878), 84-85; Schröder-Lembke (1956), 58; Hovde (1948), 281.
[74] Thorpe (1951), 113; Nielsen (1933), 329; Skovgaard (1950), 42.

implementation would bring down the whole social structure. And there were those who, like their peers in England, opposed enclosures because they interfered with their hunting.[75]

The forces arrayed against the reforms did everything they could to hold them back, and to subvert them when they were carried out. Assemblies and courts of the nobility, and noble bureaucrats, protested strongly against the proposals for reform, dragged their feet in applying them, and, when they could, declared the enclosures illegal.[76] On manors in Austria that had enclosed in accordance with imperial decrees, the peasants sometimes threw their shares together and continued to use the land in common. When they could, peasants brought law suits to protect or to recover their old rights. *Cahiers* of grievances from many places in France in 1789 demanded the suppression of the enclosure legislation, and the end of the government-sponsored movement. The successive legislative assemblies of revolutionary France received many petitions of protest against enclosures, and demands for the retention of collective rights of common pasture. Sometimes, frustrated by the failure of their legal protests, peasants turned to violence to combat enclosures. They tore down fences and hedges, and drove their livestock into the enclosed fields.[77]

Not everyone, of course, opposed the reforms. *Cahiers* of some French seigniors urged enclosure as vital to the progress of agriculture.[78] Prosperous peasants who had many strips in the open fields were supporters, too. According to a Prussian adage of the era, "the division of the open fields makes a nobleman out of the big peasant and a beggar out of the cotter." And enclosure did seem to promise only greater poverty and increased misery for the poorer peasants of the village. "Progress in agriculture," wrote Georges Lefebvre, "could be achieved only at the expense of the poor," and Albert Babeau called the movement "sacrificing the present for the future."[79]

It did not have to be that, as the Danish experience showed. The legislation there ordered that those who suffered loss through the reforms—and that meant the smallholders and the landless peasants—had to be compensated with a leasehold of four to six acres. They did not get the best land and they still had to find other employment to make ends meet. But their government had not callously neglected them. On the contrary, many of the peasants, especially the landless ones, were better off now than they had been before enclosure. The government went even further in its protection of the small peasant. A decree of 1769 had forbidden the engrossment

[75] Stark (1937), 441; Bloch (1930), 512-513, 513n.
[76] Young (1970), I, 399-400; Behrend (1967), 174; Stark (1937), 441; Abel (1967), 290.
[77] Bloch (1930), 539-540; Young (1970), I, 400; Davies (1964), 34; St. Jacob (1960), 369-372; Abel (1967), 290; Confino (1969), 282.
[78] *Archives parlementaires*, I, 741, II, 429; Young (1970), I, 400n.
[79] Lefebvre (1929), 511; Babeau (1878), 84-85.

of peasant holdings (p. 208). The law's intent, and its effect, was to prevent the expropriation of peasant land by seigniors. Now the decree was used against voluntary amalgamations of peasant holdings. It allowed two farms to be owned by one person, but he could not join them into a single unit. That prevented the creation of large farms worked by landless hired laborers. Legislation also banned the division of a farm into pieces too small to support a peasant family.[80]

VI

Along with their concern for more intensive field systems, the progressive proprietors of the servile lands interested themselves in improved and new crops, more efficient implements, and better animal husbandry. The new crops, more often than not, were "Americans," introduced into Europe after the discovery of the New World. They had been grown in one place or other ever since their arrival on the Continent. Only now, however, in the last half-century or so of the old order, did they emerge as important crops in a few regions, and only now did their culture spread into lands where they had hitherto been ignored or unknown. By far the most important of these "Americans" were potatoes and maize—"poor man's crops and poor man's foods," as Doreen Warriner called them.[81]

Potatoes, a principal and indispensable part of European diets by the last third of the nineteenth century, were of minor significance in most places up to the end of the servile era. Yet Europeans had known the plant and been aware of many of its virtues ever since the sixteenth century, when the Spaniards had brought it into Europe from its native habitat in the Peruvian and Bolivian Andes. From Spain it was introduced into Italy and the Low Countries in 1587, into Lower Austria in 1588, into England sometime between 1581 and 1590, into France in 1600, and so on back and forth across the map of Europe. Disparate and sometimes unlikely types served as the transmitters of the plant. Returning students were said to have brought potatoes into Hungary from Germany in 1654. English and Irish soldiers are supposed to have introduced them into Flanders around 1659. A Swiss soldier named Jakob Straub, who campaigned in Ireland with William of Orange, is credited with bringing back potatoes to his native village of Schwanden in the canton of Glarus, from whence their culture spread to other parts of Switzerland. French Huguenots are reputed to have brought the potato into Denmark in 1719, and so on.[82]

---

[80] Thorpe (1951), 123-124; Ashley (1924), 245-246.

[81] Warringer (1953), 185. The other "Americans" included tobacco, sunflowers, cassava, sweet potatoes, peanuts, field beans (*phaseolus vulgaris*), cocoa, pineapples, tomatoes, red peppers, vanilla, and pimiento. Masefield (1967), 275-279.

[82] Lekhnovich (1956), 258-261; Gromas (1947), 146; Rappard (1912), 90-91; Commager (1928), 85.

Despite this long acquaintance, the plants were rarely grown in any quantity. When they were planted, it was usually as a garden vegetable rather than a field crop.[83] Efforts to popularize the plant, made sporadically by sovereigns and would-be improvers in the seventeenth and first seven decades of the eighteenth century, ran aground on the opposition of peasants. Perhaps nothing better illustrates the conservatism and suspicion of the peasants, and the injuries they inflicted upon themselves by their obduracy and ignorance, than their long resistance to planting and eating potatoes. Nearly everywhere they thought that the potato was fit only for animals—and they were not always sure of that. Even the poorest and hungriest of peasants rejected the tuber. When Frederick II of Prussia sent a load of potatoes in 1774 to the famine-stricken village of Kolberg, the peasants' reaction was, "The things have no smell nor taste and not even dogs will eat them. What is their use to us?"[84]

The attitude of Scandinavian peasants toward potatoes has been compared to Kipling's picture of nineteenth-century India, where "men would die at arm's length of plenty, sooner than touch food they did not know." In Denmark it was said that people would change their religion more easily than their food habits.[85]

In the Russian empire peasants not only disdained the potato; they looked upon it as a positive menace. In the Baltic provinces some people opposed the plant as a danger to health, and a writer in 1798 soberly reported that their consumption brought on asthmatic ailments. In Russia peasants, particularly among communicants of the sect of the Old Believers, called potatoes "apples of the Devil," refused (naturally) to eat them, and considered it a sin to grow them. The Old Believers claimed that the potato was the forbidden fruit of the Garden of Eden. Those who ate it disobeyed God's ban, and so lost their chance to enter Paradise. An ethnographic report of 1848 told of peasants who thought that the eyes of the potato made it resemble a human face, so that eating the potato was the same as eating a human soul. The suspicions of the peasants were so real, and their animus so strong, that efforts of the Ministry of State Domain in the 1830's and 1840's to require peasants to plant potatoes set off a train of resistance and violence known as the "potato revolts."[86]

Some Russian landowners and agricultural experts offered more rational objections to potato culture. They explained that in most of the central and northern provinces the soil, exhausted by grain, gave poor yields of potatoes. They pointed out, too, that potatoes sown in the fallow field ma-

---

[83] Thaer (1809), IV, 206-207; Müller (1969b), 224; Stark (1957), 36; Calonne (1920), 258; Iatsunskii (1966), 47; Kostiushko (1954), 163; Ulashchik (1962), 308; Strod (1959), 51.
[84] Bruford (1935), 117; Hauser (1971), 175; Young (1970), II, 78-79; Darmstaedter (1897), 115; Ilzhofer (1942), 161; Kahk (1969), 30; Berchtold (1942), 14-15; Marczali (1910), 55-56.
[85] Heckscher (1954), 151.   [86] Kahk (1969), 30; Confino (1969), 304-305.

tured toward the end of September. That prevented putting in the winter grain, rye, which should be planted in August. Potatoes required additional labor that had to be done during the 130 to 150 days available for work in the field. That entailed either an increase in the labor services demanded of the peasants, which, they said, would produce serious discontent, or the employment of hired labor, which would cost money that seigniors did not want to spend. In Germany, too, labor costs deterred landowners from potato production. "Harvesting of potatoes," wrote Albrecht Thaer, "has appeared to most large proprietors as the most difficult aspect of raising the crop, and explains why they have in large part held back from large-scale production." Thaer observed, however, that this concern had lessened through the employment of the cheap labor of women and children to harvest the potatoes.[87]

The turnabout in the acceptance of potatoes as human food came first in parts of Switzerland, Germany, and Austria during the years of grain crop failure and famine that engulfed these lands in the early 1770's. Hunger swept away the peasants' scorn for the vegetable. They had to eat potatoes or starve, and once they overcame their repugnance of this strange food they even found it palatable. In France as late as 1788, Arthur Young found that nearly everywhere people would not touch potatoes. Apparently a serious grain shortage in 1793 finally persuaded Frenchmen to abandon that prejudice. In Hungary the privations of the era of the French wars, and famine that immediately succeeded the peace in 1815, changed the attitude of the peasants there. In Poland, too, famine in 1816-1817 convinced peasants of the value of the potato as human food.[88] In short, crop failure and empty stomachs did far more to persuade people to grow and eat potatoes than all the commands and inducements of princes, the pronouncements of experts, and the propaganda of agricultural societies.

The acceptance of potatoes as human food did not mean that everyone now ate them. In some places it took years before they became a staple of diet. A report of 1844 stated that many peasants of Sologne, in north central France, "would consider themselves disgraced if they ate potatoes." Nor was the contempt for the plant restricted to the continent. In 1834 the irrascible William Cobbett called potatoes "this nasty, filthy, hog feed."[89] In other lands they quickly became a major field crop. In Zurich in 1842 an observer said that no one there could conceive of how people had lived without potatoes, and no one could believe that it had taken great effort to induce people to plant them. Two years later another commentator re-

---

[87] Confino (1969), 303-304; Thaer (1809), IV, 218-219.
[88] Braun (1960), 99; Durst (1951), 60; Thaer (1809), IV, 207; Schlögl (1954), 17; Mager (1955), 271; Weidmann (1968), 117; Otruba (1963), 117; Berchtold (1842), 15; Young (1970), II, 78-79; Toutain (1961), I, 94; Blum (1948), 108-109; Kostiushko (1954), 163.
[89] Bouchard (1972), 108; Connell (1950), 132.

ported that "the potato holds first place among all field crops. . . . There isn't a commune in all of the canton of Zurich in which it isn't grown."[90] In some regions of Germany, too, potato culture made rapid gains. In Kurmark, in Prussia, the potato harvest in 1765 amounted to an estimated 5,200 metric tons. By 1773 the harvest had increased to 19,000 metric tons, and to 103,000 metric tons in 1801.[91] Antoine Parmentier, famed as the propagandist of potato culture in France, first became familiar with the plant when, as a prisoner in Prussia during the Seven Years' War, he was for a time fed a diet made up almost exclusively of potatoes.[92] In Upper Lusatia, in Saxony, hardly any potatoes were grown until the 1790's. Then their culture expanded so rapidly that by 1800 the total volume of potato production exceeded that of the rye crop. In other parts of Germany the acceptance of the vegetable lagged. Thus, in Bavaria at the turn of the nineteenth century, potatoes were still used so sparingly that they did not even appear on the menus served in charitable institutions and hospitals of Munich. In East Prussia in the 1780's potatoes were grown only on estates of the crown, and only on those near the capital city of Königsberg.[93] For all of Germany the total area in potatoes in 1800 was still small, amounting to about 1.5 per cent of the cultivated area, or about 671,000 acres. At the end of the nineteenth century 7.6 million acres, or 13 per cent of the cultivated area in Germany, was planted with potatoes.[94]

France had about 50,000 acres planted in potatoes on the eve of the Revolution. By 1803-1812 that figure had risen to an estimated 765,000 acres, or nearly 1.3 per cent of the tilled area of the country. In the succeeding decades potato culture continued to expand, though at a considerably slower rate than in Germany. In Denmark, and in the Austrian Monarchy, production of potatoes was unimportant until the early decades of the nineteenth century. Then output climbed steadily, save for a temporary setback in the last half of the 1840's, when potato disease became a European-wide catastrophe. In the Austrian Monarchy potato cultivation assumed special importance in the Slav provinces of Bohemia, Moravia, Silesia, and Galicia. In the early 1840's these three crown lands raised nearly 78 per cent of the Monarchy's potato crop (without Hungary and Transylvania, for which data are not available). Galicia alone accounted for 36 per cent of the Monarchy's production.[95]

The Baltic, White Russian, and Lithuanian provinces held leadership in potato culture in the Russian empire, as they did in most other progressive agricultural activities. Until the 1820's proprietors in these provinces had

[90] Bernhard (1915), 11-12.
[91] Abel (1967), 313. The metric ton equals 1.102 short tons.
[92] Vandenbroeke (1971), 30.
[93] Boelcke (1957), 173; Ilzhofer (1942), 161; Henning (1969a), 17.
[94] Bittermann (1956), 24; Sutton (1896), 396.
[95] Toutain (1961), I, 48, 94; Sutton (1896), 396; Nielsen (1933), 397-398; Blum (1948), 107-110; *Tafeln zur Statistik*, 1842, table 37.

paid only desultory attention to new crops in general. Then they began to interest themselves in potatoes, in no small part because they had learned how to use them to make a fiery whiskey. That made potatoes an important source of seigniorial income. Potato acreage soared. In Estonia alone it reportedly increased twenty times over during the 1820's. By the 1840's a contemporary claimed that half of the manors in the three Baltic provinces (Estland, Livland, and Kurland) raised potatoes on a large scale. In the White Russian and Lithuanian provinces of Vitebsk, Mogilev, Minsk, and Grodno, lords and peasants had 557,550 acres, or nearly 30 per cent of their total plowland in potatoes at the beginning of the 1840's. In Congress Poland, too, potato production turned sharply upward starting in the 1820's; between 1822 and 1850 production increased from 11.3 million bushels to 60 million bushels.[96] In the rest—and by far the largest part—of European Russia potatoes had far less importance. In 1840 there was still very little land planted in that crop. Thereafter production grew, though very slowly in comparison with other European lands. A study published in 1878 by Alexis Ermolov, who in 1893 became Russia's first Minister of Agriculture, estimated that potatoes were planted on about 1 million desiatins (2.7 million acres). Official statistics that appeared in 1893 lent credence to Ermolov's estimate. These data showed that 1,375,176 desiatins were planted with potatoes, amounting to 2.1 per cent of the total sown area of European Russia.[97]

The remarkable expansion of potato culture was attributable to the many remarkable qualities of the plant. Potatoes grow in nearly any soil and they adjust to different climates, though they do best where weather is cool and moist. Once dug up they are ready for the pot; unlike cereals they do not require the additional labor and expense of processing to make them edible. They are easy to store, although they lose much of their nutirtional value in storage. They give a much greater yield per unit of land than do cereals, and thus provide much more food from a given area. Arthur Young in 1771 found that English farmers got 38 bushels of oats, 32 of barley, 23 of wheat, and 427 bushels of potatoes from an acre. A half-century later William Jacob reported that in Prussia an acre of land to which the same amount of labor and manure had been applied produced 300 bushels of potatoes at 38 lbs. per bushel, totalling 11,400 lbs., or 24 bushels of wheat, at 60 lbs. per bushel, or 1,440 lbs. The caloric content of a given quantity of potatoes was considerably less than that of the same amount of grain. However, the greater yield of potatoes more than made up for this. An acre in potatoes provides as much as three to five times as many calories as does an acre in grain. In addition, potatoes provide nearly all of the human nutritional requirements. Davidson and Passmore, in their standard work on

[96] Strod (1959), 51; Loone (1968), 254; Kahk (1969), 34; Chepko (1964), 392; Kostiushko (1954), 163.
[97] Lekhnovich (1956), 364; Ermolov (1878), 76-77; *Industries of Russia* (1893), III, 94.

nutrition, identify the potato as "the only single cheap food that can support life when fed as the *sole* (their italics) article of diet."[98]

In addition to its use as human food, potatoes provided a nourishing fodder for livestock. They also supplied the raw material for the manufacture of meal, of starch, and, most important of all of the potato's industrial uses, the distillation of whiskey. From around the 1830's potatoes began to displace rye as the principal ingredient in the manufacture of whiskey in central and eastern Europe.

Maize, the other most important of the "Americans," came into Spain from the New World around 1500. It was first grown in France around Bayonne, just across the Spanish frontier. It advanced from there at a snail's pace from village to village. It took about one hundred years for its culture to traverse the 250 miles from the Atlantic coast eastward to the Mediterranean, or about 2.5 miles a year. As with potatoes, the slow adoption of maize seems extraordinary in view of the many advantages of the crop. Its yield in pounds per acre is approximately twice that of wheat, and nearly twice that of other small grains. It provides a highly nutritious and palatable food for humans, and it is a first-rate feed for livestock and fowls. Its stalks made excellent stall litter, and its husks and cobs were used for fuel and for stuffing mattresses.[99] "Maize," wrote a French agronomist in 1785, "is one of the noblest gifts of the New World to the Old."[100] That seems an eminently fair judgment. Unfortunately, climate placed severe limits on the regions in which maize could be grown. It lacked the ability to withstand low temperatures, and it needed a great deal of warm but not too hot weather.

The Danubian Principalities led Europe in the acceptance of maize. Introduced there at the end of the seventeenth century, it had become the predominant cereal and the daily food of the peasant by the second half of the eighteenth century. Data for 1831 showed that it was sown on 70.3 per cent of the arable in Wallachia, and comprised over 81 per cent of all the grain harvested there. In neighboring eastern Hungary, too, it was widely grown by the second half of the eighteenth century. In the Principalities and in Hungary external circumstances helped promote the cultivation of maize. The Turkish suzerains of the Principalities requisitioned other grains, but excepted maize from their demands. In Hungary maize was not named in the old laws as among the products of which a tithe had to be paid by the peasants. It was grown in quantity in Bessarabia, the eastern section of Moldavia, annexed by Russia in 1812. From there it spread into the neighboring Ukrainian provinces of Kherson, Podolia, and Kiev. It was intro-

[98] Burton (1966), 180, 211-223; Davidson and Passmore (1966), 269-270; Jacob (1828), 169; *cf.* Vandenbroeke (1971), 37; Connell (1950), 156.
[99] Leroy Ladurie (1966), I, 71; Jasny (1940), 445-446; Faucher (1949), 106-107; Chombart (1946), 90; Corfus (1969), 51-52.
[100] Rozier (1785), VI, 359.

duced into Georgia early in the eighteenth century. In the late eighteenth and early nineteenth centuries it spread into the mountains of the northern Caucasus, where it gradually took over as the principal grain. It appeared in the plainland of the Caucasus during the first half of the nineteenth century. It was raised in the western half of the Austrian Monarchy in the second half of the seventeenth century. In the following decades increasing quantities were produced, but it never became a major cereal in the German and Slav crown lands. In 1857 it made up about 15.5 per cent in volume of the Monarchy's total grain production (without Hungary, Lombardy, and Venetia). In France maize had even less importance, though many grew it in southern France. Data from around 1820 showed that the maize crop made up scarcely 4 per cent of the national total of foodstuff production. That ratio was actually a little less than buckwheat.[101]

Among other "Americans," tomatoes, tobacco, and sunflowers appeared on an increasing, albeit still small, number of manors in the servile lands. Tomatoes, once suspected of being poisonous, spread in southern France in the last decades of the eighteenth century.[102] Tobacco culture made its appearance in a number of places from France across to the Ukraine in the sixteenth to eighteenth centuries. The European leaf could not compete in price and quality with American tobacco. In time of war, however, when importation became difficult or impossible, the area in tobacco expanded.[103] Sunflowers gained special importance in Russia. Introduced there in the eighteenth century as a decorative plant, it took on economic importance when in the 1830's people realized that its seeds were a rich source of oil. From then on its culture expanded, concentrated in the southern and southwestern regions of the central steppe, where it became one of the most profitable crops.[104]

Product innovation and improvement did not end with the "Americans." Some proprietors realized the risk of reduced yields when, year after year, they used the same strains of seeds for their cereal crops. They introduced new grain varieties on their demesnes, sometimes using seeds from faraway places.[105] Seigniors in regions as far apart as Brittany and Prussian Silesia were primarily responsible for a large increase in fruit trees. In Silesia the number of fruit trees rose by more than 150 per cent between

[101] Danubian Principalities: Corfus (1969), 133-134; Emerit (1937), 21. Hungary: Marczali (1910), 55. Russia: Ministerstvo Gosudarstvennykh Imuchestv (1869), 120; Tegoborskii (1852), II, 111-112; Iatsunskii (1966), 49. Austria: Buchinger (1952), 342-343; *Tafeln zur Statistik* , n.s., 1861, III, pt. 5, table 1, p. 4. France: Braudel and Labrousse (1970), II, 439.
[102] Gromas (1947), 150.
[103] Masefield (1967), 277-278; Grüll (1952), 135; Iatsunskii (1966), 50; Müller (1964b), 229; Mager (1955), 271-272; Marczali (1910), 56; Nielsen (1933), 183; Bickel (1947), 53; Jacob (1820), 239.
[104] Iatsunskii (1966), 50; *Industries of Russia* (1893), 150-151.
[105] Müller (1964a), 636; Pokhilevich (1966), 388; Kahk (1969), 29; Sivkov (1959), 24; Oṭetea (1965), 332.

1770 and the first years of the nineteenth century.[106] Progressive proprietors used calcareous earths, such as marl and gypsum, to fertilize their fields, and reported remarkable increases in yields.[107]

Attention was paid, too, by innovating proprietors to the improvement of farm tools. Often they imported British-made implements, and modified them to meet local needs. For a long time a lack of skilled artisans held back the fabrication of more efficient tools, and even of the traditional ones. In France a writer in 1786 complained that "It is astonishing that no workers in France occupy themselves with making scythes, and one is obliged to import them from Germany, or at least in largest part from there. . . . We are obliged to buy such as they send us from middlemen, and it is rare to find one good scythe in a dozen."[108] In the first half of the next century, however, manufacturers produced increasing numbers of improved implements. Farm machinery, too, especially threshers, made their appearance on a few manors.[109]

Progressive landowners also interested themselves in the improvement of livestock. The new agriculture stressed the advantages of mixed husbandry, in which cattle and field crops complemented one another. The animal produced manure for the arable, and the arable produced forage for the livestock, with greater yields in both animal products and in crops as the end result. Improvers imported blooded stock from abroad to build up their herds, and bred their own improved animals. Despite their efforts, the traditional neglect of this vital branch of production, and the poor quality of the animals, remained the norm. On the eve of the French Revolution, Arthur Young discovered that in nine-tenths of France "there would scarcely be any cattle at all, were it not for the practice of ploughing with them." Except for a few districts, he continued, "the management of cattle in France is a blank. On an average of the kingdom, there is not, perhaps, a tenth of what there ought to be."[110] Thirty years later another knowledgeable Englishman, who had traveled extensively on the continent, commented on the low state of animal husbandry there, and the retarding effect this had on yields. "The most productive branch of rural economy," wrote William Jacob, "next to the use of the plough, is that of breeding cattle; one, in which in every part of the continent, except the kingdom of the Netherlands, the practice is so much worse, and the extent so much smaller than in England, that no surprise is excited in those who remark it, that the quantity of corn grown on the arable bears so small a proportion to the extent that is sown."[111]

[106] Meyer (1966), I, 579; Ziekursch (1927), 41.

[107] Müller (1967), 98; Ziekursch (1927), 41; Eggert (1965), 8; Arnim (1957), 95; Hoffmann (1952), I, 272; Boelcke (1957), 174.

[108] Rozier (1786), IV, 444.

[109] Müller (1967), 88; Strod (1963), 297-300; Strod (1959), 49-50; Borovoi and Kopievskii (1966), 277; Blum (1948), 143, 164, 191-192; Skrubbeltrang (1953), 29.

[110] Young (1970), II, 52.   [111] Jacob (1820), 240.

Sheep, and more specifically the fine-wooled merinos, were the great exception to the continued backwardness of animal husbandry. As mentioned earlier, most of the sheep in the servile lands belonged to the seigniors; indeed, in some lands sheep approached a seigniorial monopoly because of the special rights held by lords to graze their flocks on the fields of the peasants. Until well into the eighteenth century the sheep in all of the servile lands were native, unimproved stock. The merinos, raised in Spain since the Middle Ages, were far superior to these animals. They had heavy fleeces of fine wool that was pure white when scoured. Thanks to the merino, Spain dominated the world market for wool from the mid-fifteenth to the mid-eighteenth centuries.[112] Determined to preserve their monopoly, the Spanish allowed merinos to leave the country only with the special permission of the monarch. Unauthorized exports invited severe punishments and even the death penalty. However, from 1723 to the close to the eighteenth century, foreign princes and important noblemen received permission to export small flocks for the improvement of the sheep of their own countries. In addition, merinos were smuggled across the Portuguese border, or shipped from Portuguese ports. Even royal personages are said to have engaged in this illegal activity: George III of England reportedly dispatched agents to Spain to smuggle out sheep for him. The first merinos to arrive in the United States—three of them—were smuggled out. Unfortunately, upon their arrival in this country they were eaten, instead of being used for breeding.[113] In 1748 merinos were introduced on royal manors in Brandenburg; in 1765 the first big flock of 92 rams and 128 ewes were brought into Electoral Saxony; in 1773 the Austrian government imported 325 head; Count von Hardenberg imported rams and ewes into Lower Saxony from 1783 to 1799; in 1786 Louis XVI installed 334 ewes and 42 rams on his estate at Rambouillet; in 1797 a mission sent by the king of Denmark to Spain to buy merinos purchased 314 of them; Baron Levenstern brought a flock into Livonia in 1798.[114] These first imports quickly became the progenitors of large flocks of pure-blooded sheep, and also were bred with the native animals to improve their quality. Some of the descendants, through skillful breeding, excelled the parent merino stock. These sheep, especially the breeds developed in Electoral Saxony and at Rambouillet, were themselves exported for breeding to other lands, and later to other continents. The Spanish, meanwhile, tried to reestablish their monopoly by a decree of 24 June 1798, which placed an absolute ban on the export of sheep. The ban was repeated in later years, but it had no effect, for now flocks of merinos or part-merinos were scattered across Europe.[115]

Native sheep continued to make up the largest part of the ovine popula-

[112] Lopez (1953), 161.   [113] Carman, Heath and Minto (1892), 132-133.
[114] Müller (1965), 163; Riemann (1953), 80; Saalfeld (1960), 124; Gromas (1947), 159; Feldborg (1824), 44, 46; Strod (1962), 379.
[115] Carman, Heath and Minto (1892), 133.

14. Folding sheep. A. Portable fencing. B. The shepherd's mobile hut. (J. Wiegand, *Des wohlerfahrenen Landwirths*, Leip-zig, 1763.)

tion of the servile lands. Their numbers grew, but the flocks of improved sheep grew at a far more rapid rate. In 1800 in the Ukraine there were around 9,000 fine-wooled sheep. By mid-century they had increased to 3.7 million. In all of European Russia in the early 1860's there were, according to an official report, 44,171,000 sheep, of which 11,655,000 were fine-wooled. In Hungary the number rose from about 4 million in 1800 to 8 million in 1840. Great magnates there owned vast flocks. There were 900,000 sheep in Poland in 1800, and 4 million by 1844. In 1816 Prussia had 8.3 million sheep. Nine per cent were merinos, 29 per cent part-blooded, and 63 per cent native sheep. In 1849 there were 16.3 million sheep in Prussia, of which 27 per cent were merinos, 49 per cent part-blooded, and only 24 per cent native stock.[116]

The stimulus for the interest of seigniors and sovereigns in improved sheep came from the expanding market for wool, and the higher price that quality wool commanded. John Quincy Adams in 1800 told of a Silesian proprietor who sold his fine wool at 50 per cent more than the prevailing price for common wool; in Brunswick around 1800 merino wool sold for four times the price of the wool from native sheep.[117] The market for wool had grown with the growth of population in the eighteenth century. Then the Napoleonic wars and the Continental Blockade gave a sharp upward thrust to demand. The end of the wars, and the reappearance of English wool on the continental market, proved only a temporary setback to the continental wool growers. Domestic demand held up, and, indeed, grew with the development of domestic woolen factory industry. Meanwhile, British manufacturers, to meet the greater demand for their product, had to import increased amounts of wool. They turned to the sheep raisers of the Continent, especially to those of central Europe. In 1816 the United Kingdom imported 2.8 million pounds of wool from Germany, excluding Prussia. In 1836 that figure reached 31.8 million pounds.[118]

Wool production continued to be of prime importance in many seigniorial economies until the middle decades of the nineteenth century. Then it began to falter. Rising grain prices made it more profitable to grow cereals on land used for sheep pasture. More important, the continental producers could not compete with wool from overseas, which began to arrive on the European market in the 1840's.[119]

[116] Zaionchkovskii (1968), 14; Ministerstvo Gosudarstvennykh Imuchestv (1869), 346; Ivanyi (1960), 279-280n.; Blum (1948), 101; Kieniewicz (1969), 90; Riemann (1953), table 23, p. 81.
[117] Adams (1804), 209-210; Saalfeld (1960), 124.
[118] Mitchell and Deane (1962), 192.
[119] Strod (1962), 384-385; Finck von Finckenstein (1960), 27.

CHAPTER 13

The Improvers

I

THE governments of the servile lands gave uncertain and indecisive responses to the plans and demands of the would-be reshapers of agriculture. The mercantilist policies followed by some of these countries to further their trade and manufacturing did not have their parallel in the agricultural sector of the economy. Instead, governments at irregular intervals gave their attention to some aspect of husbandry, then turned to other matters and seemed to forget the promotion of agriculture. Thus, in 1761 the French Royal Council formally offered the king's congratulations to the recently established Agricultural Society of Paris for its interest in agricultural improvement. But government aid to this and other new agricultural societies was intermittent and ineffective. In 1785 many cattle perished in a severe drought. This created so much unrest that the government felt that it had to make at least a gesture of concern. It issued instructions to promote the cultivation of forage crops, and to encourage the distribution of these crops to regions that suffered the greatest losses. It also requested the Royal Academy of Sciences in Paris to draw up detailed instructions on ways to alleviate the shortage of fodder. The Academy's report, which recommended thoroughgoing changes in the traditional agriculture, was published at government order, and sent to the *intendants* for distribution in the provinces. The government's consultation of the Academy led to the creation in 1785 of a permanent body, called the *Comité d'administration de l'agriculture*. Two years later Antoine Lavoisier, France's preeminent scientist and the most prominent member of the committee, complained of the total lack of attention paid by the government to the numerous and detailed memoranda and recommendations submitted by the committee. The government exhibited the same sporadic involvement, and then withdrawal, in its program to promote the enclosure of common lands, and to do away with the rights of pasture on fallow fields.[1]

After the end of the Seven Years' War—his last war—Frederick II of Prussia interested himself in the economic development of his realm, including the improvement of farming. In numerous ordinances, and in instructions to his bureaucrats, he ordered the introduction of new crops and more efficient techniques. The results of his efforts were neither general nor enduring. To instruct farmers and particularly the lessees of state lands in improved husbandry, in 1767 he converted Mühlenbeck, a royal manor in Kurmark, into a model and experimental farm. He imported a manager

[1] Sée (1923), 62, 64-66; Festy (1947), 52-54; Bloch (1966), 221-222.

from England to run the property, but the man soon proved incompetent and was dismissed. In 1769 Frederick hired another Englishman, Christopher Brown by name, who had been brought over a few years before to manage properties of Count Friedrich Paul von Kamecke. Brown, given a contract for six years by Frederick, ran a successful operation, and won the king's favor and continued support. Frederick ordered lessees of royal manors to visit Mühlenbeck to learn about the improved methods. Some came, while others said that they did not have the time, or could not afford the expenses of the trip. Brown himself ran into financial difficulties, was charged in 1775 with not having met all of his obligations, and fled from Prussia. He was arrested in Bohemia, brought back to Berlin, and jailed in debtors' prison for three years. Thus ended Mühlenbeck's use as a model farm, though the rental contract of the new lessee required him to continue the "English economy," which included the four-course Norfolk rotation Brown had introduced. In 1771 Frederick set aside 100,000 *taler* to lend to proprietors in Kurmark at 4 per cent interest, to promote the introduction of forage culture in that province. The government planned to use the interest payments to raise the pay of schoolmasters in Kurmark. The money was lent out quickly, but the loans had meager results in the advancement of forage culture—and the interest payments came in irregularly.[2]

In 1762 the Elector of Bavaria offered an exemption from taxes for ten years to encourage the cultivation of wastes and fallows in his realm. In following years he and his successors issued other decrees to stimulate the planting of fallow fields and of wastes, and the use of improved farming techniques. The government distributed seeds, gave prizes to promote animal husbandry, and in 1790 ordered that fallows must be planted with forage crops and cattle must be stall-fed. The efforts of the rulers, and even their direct commands, remained almost without effect. Rulers of other German states also sponsored occasional efforts to improve agriculture, without appreciable results.[3]   In Russia the government, from the reign of Peter I on, made statements at irregular intervals about the need to raise the efficiency of agriculture and to introduce improvements that had been developed in western Europe. A sustained government program appeared only with the establishment of the Ministry of State Domain in 1837. Under the aggressive leadership of Count P. D. Kiselev the Ministry promoted the introduction of new crops and improved techniques among the state peasants, organized model farms for purposes of instruction and demonstration, established training institutes in farming and forestry, and founded eight schools between 1841 and 1848, where state peasants and privately owned serfs received instruction in improved agriculture (four of these schools were closed between 1858 and 1862). These activities had lit-

[2] Habernoll (1900), 81-97; Müller (1969), 124-128.
[3] Schlögl (1954), 12-14, 51-52; Frauendorfer (1957), I, 195; Moericke (1905), 26-91.

tle impact on Russian agriculture as a whole, though they give witness that the government was aware of the need to raise the level of productivity out on the land.[4]

Kiselev had shown the same interest in agricultural improvement when he served as governor during the Russian occupation of the Danubian Principalities from 1829 to 1834. His administration recommended, among other things, that superior wheat seed be brought in from the west and distributed at cost to the peasants, and proposed the importation of blooded cattle, merinos, and stallions to improve the native livestock. These recommendations went to the boyar assembly, where they died. In 1841 the Administrative Council of Moldavia appointed four advisory commissions of prominent persons to promote agriculture through exhibitions and prizes. In that same year a decree of the Moldavian hospodar encouraged the planting of vegetable gardens, and especially of potatoes. As was the case in other lands, the actions of the government had remarkably little effect.[5]

The failure of governments to provide continued leadership and support to agriculture was compensated for, at least in part, by private landowners, who at their own initiative and expense introduced agricultural improvements on their properties. These men (their peers in eighteenth-century England were called "improving landlords"), acted as innovating entrepreneurs, who, as Joseph Schumpeter observed, "proceeding of their own accord or accepting the teaching of some advocate of improvement, went ahead to set up new production functions, the success of which induced others to follow—first few, then many."[6] As entrepreneurs, they seemed naive in comparison with their fellow innovaters in commerce and industry. Some of them apparently needed elementary instruction, like the Russian proprietors who were told in the pages of the journal of the Free Economic Society that "the object of animal husbandry is to make a profit," and so were advised to raise those cattle "which furnish the most profit to the proprietor." Indeed, Russian landowners needed even more basic instruction, for apparently most of them had no concept of costs, and so confused their gross cash revenue with profit.[7] Albrecht Thaer addressed himself to a more sophisticated audience of German landowners. Still, the opening words of his classic *Principles of Rational Agriculture* were, "The object of agriculture is to produce a profit or make money through the production (and sometimes through the further processing) of vegetable and animal matter. . . . The greater the retained profit the better is this object accomplished. The most perfect agriculture is therefore that which yields the highest possible retained profit. . . . Accordingly, the teachings of ra-

---

[4] Confino (1969), 207-208, 210; Pintner (1967), 178-179.
[5] Emerit (1937), 196-197.   [6] Schumpeter (1939), i, 238.
[7] Confino (1963), 135-147.

tional agriculture must demonstrate how the highest pure profit can be obtained from the enterprise under all conditions."[8]

The hope of profit, though certainly of much importance as the explanation for innovation, was not the only motive that inspirited the improvers. In central Europe, and in the Baltic lands, some of them had attended universities where the professors of cameralism had indoctrinated them with the importance of agriculture to the national well-being, and had impressed them with the need to raise its productivity. At the university, too, they learned about the new husbandry from the writings of the agronomists.[9] In Denmark Count A. P. Bernstorff, out of a sense of responsibility to his peasants, carried through a sweeping reorganization of the manors he had inherited from his uncle. His reforms included enclosures, the introduction of new crops and techniques, and the conversion of the peasants into hereditary proprietors of their holdings. Marquis Alexis Costa de Beauregard, owner of a great estate in Savoy, eschewed the high court offices guaranteed him by the distinction of his family, to live on his estate. There he engaged in experimentation and development that led to his publication of a book in 1774 on the improvement of agriculture in Savoy, with the purpose of increasing the numbers and wealth of his fellow countrymen. Some innovators, among them the French statesmen Choiseul, Maupeou, and Maurepas, had once occupied the seats of power. Now they found themselves out of favor. Still others had been banned from court by royal decree. These men retreated to their country seats, where they filled their empty days, and found consolation, by immersing themselves in the new agriculture. Some improvers were absentee owners, who spent their time as courtiers and high officers of state and army. They directed their properties through a central office, where a staff of hired managers carried out their orders.[10]

As with innovating entrepreneurs in other fields, the numbers of these "improving landlords" were strikingly small. Careful examination by Michael Confino found only seven instances in all of Russia of efforts to introduce improved agriculture in the last three decades of the eighteenth century. The number increased during the first half of the nineteenth century, but was still a tiny fraction of the many thousands of Russian proprietors. In Hungary in the first half of the nineteenth century, not more than twenty to twenty-five landowners employed progressive methods on their properties. A small number of French proprietors, principally from the highest levels of the nobility, applied the teachings of the new husbandry to their land.[11] Most landowners showed no interest in the innovations. Some

[8] Thaer (1809), I, 3.

[9] Martiny (1938), 11; Ahrens (1969), 42-55; Zopfi (1947), 62; Strod (1959), 51.

[10] Commager (1928), 100-101; Bruchet (1908), xl, 265; Bourde (1953), 205.

[11] Confino (1969), 186-187; Wellmann (1968), 1200; Bourde (1953), 202-209; Meyer (1966), I, 589; Forster (1963), 686; Andrews (1774), II, 358.

made sport of the innovators as dreamers and eccentrics, and pointed out that because something worked well in England that did not guarantee its success elsewhere.[12] Even if a proprietor wanted to introduce improvements, he was immediately confronted with the problem of cost. Most landowners lacked the money needed to reorganize their operations, to apply the new methods to their fields, and to buy improved implements and blooded stock. One had to have money, too, to stand the losses that always threatened when new methods were employed by people who had no experience with them. Baron József Lilien, one of the first Hungarian pioneers of the new husbandry, invested 500,000 florins in his property during the first fifteen years of his ownership of the estate he took over from his father-in-law in 1795. Caspar Voght said in 1801 that he had 618,000 *Courantmark* invested in his estate in Flottbeck near Hamburg, which he had purchased in 1785.[13]

Not all innovators, of course, laid out sums comparable to these great expenditures. A contemporary observed that Voght spent amounts "such as in all Germany no prince, much less a private person, had been able to sacrifice."[14] But almost always the leading innovators were men of wealth, and usually of great noble families. There were some wealthy proprietors of bourgeois origin among them, such as Caspar Voght. He made his fortune as a merchant in Hamburg, then turned his attention, and most of his money, to improved agriculture. The brothers Guerrir et de Lornay, scions of a wealthy merchant family, were pioneers of French animal husbandry. Karl Gottlob von Anton (1751-1818), a prosperous lawyer of Görlitz in Silesia, who was ennobled in 1802, distinguished himself as a practical agriculturist. He was also the author of treatises on the new husbandry, and of histories of German agriculture.[15] These men, and others of bourgeois background, were the exceptions among the innovating proprietors. One reason for this was that in some of the servile lands burghers were disqualified from the ownership of landed estates, or had only recently been able to purchase them. Still, the small number of bourgeois proprietors among the improvers seems surprising. Adam Smith maintained that "merchants are commonly ambitious of becoming country gentlemen, and when they do, they are generally the best of all improvers."[16] Smith, who, of course, was writing from his British experience, was not often wrong, but his words in this instance were at variance with the situation in the servile lands.

The lack of capital, or the unwillingness to invest it in agricultural improvement, though important, was not the only hindrance, nor perhaps even the most important one, to the general adoption of improved hus-

[12] Schröder-Lembke (1964), 32-33; Confino (1969), 248-249; Andrews (1774), II, 358-359.
[13] Király (1969), 143; Ahrens (1969), 99.   [14] Ahrens (1969), 99.
[15] *Ibid.*, 12-13; Bourde (1967), III, 1603-1608; Boelcke (1957), 163-165.
[16] Smith (1937), 384 (Book II, ch. 4).

bandry. The attitude of most seigniors was an even greater obstacle. As earlier pages pointed out, they did not think of their properties as commercial
enterprises from which to draw a profit. The manor's purpose, as they saw
it, was to support the seignior and his household. Finally, the persistence of
the traditional organization of agriculture provided an insuperable barrier
to the introduction of progressive innovations. So long as scattered strips,
compulsory communal tillage, common pastures and stints, the use of fallow fields as pasture, and the communal regulation of farming operations
remained the reality, the introduction of new crops and rotations and improved cattle and other innovations remained the pious hopes of well-
meaning idealists.

II

As part of their efforts to raise the level of agriculture the improvers took
leading roles in the societies for the advancement of agriculture, and in the
economic and scientific societies that from around 1750 were organized in
the servile lands. The agricultural societies had as their declared purpose
the improvement of husbandry in their respective lands through the use of
more productive methods. The economic and scientific societies directed
much of their attention to the same end. The marquis de Turbilly, an innovating landowner and a writer on agricultural improvement, could have
been speaking for all agricultural societies when, at the first meeting of the
Agricultural Society of Paris on 12 March 1761, he explained that agricultural societies had as their primary mission "to study by constant observation the best way to till the soil in each province and in each district; to
employ the different kinds of land for the uses to which they are best
suited; to let the public know their experiences, their findings, including
those made by other people, after the societies have confirmed them; to
stimulate in the country, principally by example, the liking for agriculture
and to spread some light through the nation on this important subject. The
second purpose of these societies is to propose to the government, each for
the province in which it is established, the favors and the help which they
believe will best contribute to the enthusiasm for agriculture and make it
prosper."[17]

Actually, among the least successful of the agricultural societies were
those founded in France during the *ancien régime*. The estates of Brittany
had established the first of these organizations in 1757, with 65 members.
In 1761 the then Controller-General of Finances, H.-L.-J.-B. Bertin, as
part of his campaign to increase farm productivity, ordered the formation
of agricultural societies. Shortly, 18 of them were organized in 22 *gén-
éralités*. They apparently did not have open memberships. Instead, the

[17] Sée (1924), 6-7.

local government named many of the members, and the societies served more as commissions of experts to advise the government on agricultural matters than as organizations of private landowners. They depended for their existence upon the superintendence and support of the government. When Bertin left office in 1763 the support vanished and the societies decayed. In 1785 the Agricultural Society of Paris was revived and attracted a number of distinguished names to its roster. In the next four years the government authorized the creation of two other agricultural societies, and even granted an annual subvention of 2,000 livres to one of these organizations.[18] The revived Paris society accomplished little, if anything, of practical value. Its sterile record doubtless helps to explain Arthur Young's sour comment after he attended a meeting of the society, of which he was an associate member, on 12 June 1789. There were nearly thirty members present, but only one, wrote Young, was a practical farmer. "I am never present at any societies of agriculture," he continued, "either in France or England, but I am much in doubt with myself whether, when best conducted, they do most good or mischief. . . . The only society that could be really useful would be that which, in the culture of a large farm, should exhibit a perfect example of good husbandry, for the use of such as would resort to it; consequently one that should consist solely of practical men; and then query whether many good cooks would not spoil a good dish."[19] In 1793 the revolutionary government suppressed the Paris society. Five years later the Agricultural Society of the department of the Seine was established. That was the turning point in the history of French agricultural societies. From then on they provided valuable guidance and encouragement to French agriculture.[20]

In the Austrian Monarchy, too, agricultural societies first came into being at the instance of the government. In a series of decrees in the 1760's Maria Theresa ordered the establishment of these societies in a number of her crownlands. By the end of that decade there were 10 provincial societies. As in France, they were quasi-governmental bodies. Then a shift in administrative policy abolished the bureaus that had dealt with economic matters in each province, and so had been concerned with the agricultural societies. As a consequence, six of the new societies vanished during the 1770's and the four that survived continued on in little more than name. During the last decade of the century new societies were founded in different parts of the Monarchy, but they either collapsed in short order or barely managed to cling to existence. In the second decade of the nineteenth century a few great proprietors and some outstanding agricultural experts joined together to revitalize the organizations. That happened first in Moravia and Silesia. The moribund societies there (in 1800 the Moravian society had 9 active members and the Silesian society had 5) combined in

[18] Sée (1924), 3-24.   [19] Young (1970), i, 120.   [20] Festy (1957), 288-290.

1811 and soon had a membership of 300 to 400. In 1812 landowners in Lower Austria revived the Agricultural Society at Vienna, and a few years later the Patriotic-Economic Society of Bohemia took a new lease on life. By the 1840's every province of the Monarchy had a general agricultural society. There were also a number of specialized organizations that concerned themselves with a single sector of agriculture, such as viticulture, animal husbandry, and the like. Most of the societies had several hundred members and a few had a thousand or more on their rolls.

In contrast to the poor performance in the eighteenth century of the French and Austrian societies, the Swiss societies had a record of achievement. In 1759 J. R. Tschiffeli (1716-1780), well-known both as a statesman and an agronomist, founded the Economic Society at Bern. The new organization quickly set up 14 branches scattered through the canton. Its accomplishments inspired an overenthusiastic, though still deserved, tribute in 1780 from a contemporary who, after listing the advances in Bern's agriculture, concluded by saying, "and this all in a period of twenty years, that is, since the establishment of the Economic Society." The model set by the Bernese was soon imitated by men in other cantons. All of these societies concerned themselves with the entire economy of their cantons but placed the improvement of agriculture in the forefront of their efforts.

Thuringia had the first agricultural society in Germany, established in 1762. Two years later, at the direct initiative of George III of England, who was also Elector of Hannover, an agricultural society was founded at Celle to transmit English farm expertise to Hannover. In that same year an economic society was organized at Leipzig. In the succeeding decades more of these associations were formed in most of the German states. The many academies of science, too, interested themselves in agricultural improvement. The Royal Danish Agricultural Society was launched in 1769. It was founded by individuals acting on their own initiative, but it soon formed close ties with the government. Fifteen charter members, most of them men of high rank in state service, established the Free Economic Society for the Encouragement in Russia of Agriculture and Household Management (to give it its sonorous full name). For the next three decades it was the only organization of its kind in the empire. It had branches in a number of provinces and by 1800 had 500 members. In 1796 landowners in Livonia, and in 1808 in Estonia, formed agricultural societies. In 1818 the Imperial Agricultural Society at Moscow grew out of meetings of a group of noblemen, most of them wealthy seigniors, at the palace of Prince S. I. Gagarin, one of Russia's greatest magnates. The new society, beginning with 45 members, expanded rapidly, and soon other agricultural societies were started. By mid-century there were 29 of these organizations in the empire, some of them provincial or regional associations, and others devoted to the advancement of a particular branch of husbandry. There was no society in the kingdom of Poland until 1857, when Moscow reluctantly allowed one to be established. The new organization quickly involved itself in Polish nationalistic politics and in plans for social reform. Its charter specifically forbad such activities, and in 1861 the central regime abolished the society. In 1834 the first agricultural society in the Danubian Principalities was founded in Wallachia, at the instance of Alexander Ghica, the hospodar.[21]

Everywhere the members of the societies came almost exclusively from the upper and upper middle levels of the social order—great proprietors, lesser landowners, wealthy members of the bourgeoisie, clergymen, and a few academic and professional types. The societies published journals and books and pamphlets about agriculture; established and supported model farms; sponsored the introduction of new crops, better techniques, agricultural industries, and improved breeds of livestock; conducted or cooperated in the conduct of agricultural schools, libraries, and museums; sponsored experiments and research; held exhibitions and fairs and awarded prizes; ran essay contests; and used whatever influence they had with their respective governments to gain legislation and action that would promote agriculture. Not every society did all of these things. Some did much more than others, but all of them engaged in some of these programs. Their overall effectiveness, as with the innovating proprietors, cannot be measured with any precision. In most instances years intervened between the sponsorship of innovations and improvements by the societies and their general adoption, and many of their activities and proposals proved abortive. Nonetheless, they made positive and important contributions as pioneers and propagators of improved husbandry.

Among those who worked to advance agriculture in the servile lands, Protestant parish clergymen earned themselves a high place. The improving landlords, the agronomists, and the agricultural societies addressed themselves primarily, and often exclusively, to the seigniors. The clergymen sought to bring the message of better farming to the peasantry. Usually of bourgeois origin, they were well educated, had higher living standards than the villagers among whom they lived, were often active members of agricultural societies, and were inspired by religious zeal to help their parishioners in every way they could. They had holdings, sometimes of fair size, from which they drew most of their livings. To teach the peasants and at the same time to increase their own incomes, and in some instances to satisfy their own scientific curiosity, parsons made model farms of their

[21] Austrian Monarchy: Dinklage (1965), 210-211; Blum (1948), 133-139. Switzerland: Wahler and Jaggi (1959), 130-132, 134; Muyden (1898), ii, 485; *cf*. Schmitt (1932), 101ff. Germany: Abel (1967), 277; Schröder-Lembke (1964), 29-30; Wuttke (1893), 174; Schönebaum (1917), 513. Denmark: Nielsen (1933), 321. Russian empire: Confino (1963), 24-25, 53; Sivkov (1961), 154-155; Trusova and Blumenfeld (1959), 280-285; Blum (1961), 405; Storch (1849), 420-432. Poland: *Polish Encyclopedia* (1922), iii, 392. Danubian Principalities: Oțetea (1965), 333.

land, introducing new crops and techniques. Many of these clerical improvers seemed to have been Pietists, adherents of the movement that began in seventeenth-century Germany as a reaction to the secularization and formalism of orthodox Lutheranism. It is tempting to associate their interest in better farming with Pietism's stress on the *praxis pietatis*, the substantiation of piety through the work of everyday life.

Innovating clergymen were especially active in Scandanavia. Their efforts there to persuade peasants to grow potatoes (among other new departures) won them the title of "potato priests." In Schleswig Phillip Ernst Lüders, a pastor in Glücksburg, founded the Danish Agricultural Academy to teach the peasantry improved agriculture. Lüders, who had studied at the universities of Wittenberg and Jena, wrote over fifty books and brochures. Of the 22 trustees of the Glücksburg academy whose names can be identified, 15 were clergymen. Among other preachers of Schleswig and Holstein who distinguished themselves by their agricultural and educational activities were Nic Oest (1719-1798) who served in Neukirchen for 54 years, and Georg Peter Petersen (1771-1846), who was pastor in Lensahn for 42 years.

In neighboring Hannover an English visitor observed in 1817 that, "The clergymen are also very often intelligent farmers, and spread by their influence, more knowledge, and better habits, among the people." J.A.F. Block, pastor of a villge in Anhalt-Zerbst, in central Germany, told in a farm manual that he published in 1774 of his transformation of a neglected holding into fruitful acres, and of the resistance of the peasants to his attempts to demonstrate to them the advantages of improved farming. J.G. Mayer (1719-1798), who had studied at the University of Jena, was a country pastor in Württemberg for 57 years. He was a prolific writer on agricultural subjects, was a member of a number of scientific academies, and corresponded with many of the leading scientists of his time. He dedicated himself with such fervor to the cultivation of clover, and its fertilization with gypsum, that he was known as the "Apostle of Gypsum." In Switzerland, too, and in the Baltic provinces of Russia, pastors concerned themselves with the improvement of agriculture, and tried to convince their parishioners to adopt them.[22]

One of the most remarkable of these clerical propagandists and innovators was Samuel Tessedik, the Lutheran pastor of the Hungarian village of Szarvas in the Great Hungarian plain. Tessedik founded an agricultural school at Szarvas that ran until 1806. There he trained peasant lads in farming, artisanry, and trade. In the early 1790's there were 991 students

[22] Scandanavia: Hovde (1948), 134; Drake (1969), 55. Schleswig-Holstein: Vollrath (1954), 133-134; Beyer (1957), 54, 55. Germany: Hodgskin (1820), II, 93; Abel (1967), 290; Schlögl (1954) 51-52, 871. Switzerland: Wahlen and Jaggi (1952), 131. Baltic lands: Kahk (1969), 26-29; Diederichs (1870), 43-44.

enrolled in the institution. Tessedik wrote a number of books and pamphlets in German and Hungarian, in which he urged the intensification and modernization of agriculture, and the emancipation of the peasantry with land. His skillful management of his own small farm proved the value of what he taught. To hold the shifting, sandy soil of his holding he planted acacias, a tree preeminently adapted to poor soil and dry climate. When he had arrived in Szarvas there was only one acacia in the entire parish. When he died there were 100,000 of them.[23]

III

The endeavors of parish priests, and of seigniors, agricultural societies, and governmental agencies to spread the practices of progressive farming met with even less success among the peasants than it did among the masters. Most seigniors met the recommendations with apathy. Peasants actively resisted them. Those who had insecure tenures, or who lived in villages that periodically redistributed holdings, saw no advantage in investing time and money to make improvements whose benefits they might not enjoy. Anyway, few of them, no matter what their tenure, had the available capital resources needed to make improvements. They reasoned, too, that most of the increased product that improvements might bring would be taken from them by increased demands from their seigniors. They were suspicious of the propagandists, who were all of the upper orders of society. Experience had taught them to be wary of those who for so long had exploited and scorned them, and who now suddenly assumed the guise of their benefactors. They realized that enclosure of common lands, and consolidation of scattered strips, would work severe hardships on the poorest villagers, who depended so much upon the right to pasture their few cattle on commons and fallow fields. Ignorance and superstition, and their constant companion, fear of anything new, also had much to do with their rejection of any and all improvements. An official of Zurich reported in 1787 that the peasant's "preconceived opinions bristle at everything which lies outside his obsolete way of thinking, and through hardheadedness, obstinacy, and uncooperative behavior, he often makes even the best arrangements ineffectual and useless."[24] The pressures of conformity had considerable influence, too. The adoption of a change, even a relatively minor one, involved abandonment of customs and traditions that formed part of the fabric of village life. It took a strong will to withstand the criticism, and even the opprobrium, of neighbors that an innovation would bring, and to survive their ridicule if the innovation did not succeed. In any event, the open-field system that prevailed in so much of Europe, with its scattered strips and compulsory tillage, and the consequent need to gain the approval

[23] Király (1969), 143-147.   [24] Bollinger (1941), 31.

of all concerned before a change could be made, acted as a forbidding obstacle that must have discouraged would-be innovators.

Sometimes peasants resorted to open resistance, and even to violence, in
their determination to thwart innovations. In Bavaria the authorities distributed clover seed to peasants in a village, and asked that they be planted.
To show their disdain for the new crop the peasants threw the seeds into
boiling water, dried them in their ovens, and then sowed them. Years later the
same thing happened in another village. This time the police were called in
to supervise proper planting and cultivation of the clover. In France villagers physically attacked proprietors who had enclosed land, tore down the
fences, and drove their cattle into the enclosed field. J.A.F. Bloch, the innovating pastor in Anhalt-Zerbst, had scarcely finished sowing a high
meadow when peasants drove their stock onto the field, and with shouts of
laughter watched the animals destroy his work. In Russia state peasants actually rose in revolt in the 1830's and 1840's, when the Ministry of State
Domain tried to persuade them to plant potatoes.[25]

Not every peasant shared in the opposition to innovation; as with every
generalization there were exceptions. Productivity increased significantly
on peasant holdings in part of Schleswig-Holstein, attributable, so it was
said, in no small measure to the work of Parson Lüders and his academy at
Glücksburg. In Silesia the German peasants often lived in street villages.
That is, their houses were lined up in a row along the village street, and
each household's land lay in a single piece directly behind its dwelling. That
made it simple for enterprising peasants to adopt improvements, such as
planting clover, or, according to a report of 1803, abandoning the three-
field system in favor of crop rotation. Most of the peasants who came at
royal invitation from other lands to settle as colonists in Brandenburg received their holdings on hereditary tenure, and were not burdened with the
heavy obligations borne by the serfs of private proprietors. Some of these
people had sizable holdings and presumably were relatively prosperous.
They adopted improved methods and planted new crops in the course of the
last four decades of the eighteenth century. In other parts of Germany, too,
there was a sprinkling of peasants with large holdings who, in the last decades of the eighteenth century, planted part of their fallow fields with restorative crops, and who made small beginnings in the cultivation of new
crops. In Lower Alsace peasants enjoyed good tenures, and many of them
applied improved methods and, as a result, received much larger returns
from their fields. Reports of the 1780's in Zurich told of improved cattle,
clover culture, and the use of purchased fertilizers by some of the peasants
there. An estimate made in the 1840's for Bohemia held that crop rotations
were used on 300,000 yokes (426,000 acres), or approximately 7 per cent of

[25] Schlögl (1954), 23; St. Jacob (1960), 369-371; Lefebvre (1929), 513; Abel (1967), 290;
Confino (1969), 304-305.

all the arable in that province. Forty thousand of the 300,000 yokes was land held by peasants; the rest was demesne.[26]

The story of a Swiss peasant named Jakob Gujer (1716-1785) illustrates the uncommonness of improving peasants. It is also revealing of the patronizing attitude of the upper orders toward rustics. Gujer, best known by his nickname Kleinjogg (Little Jake), had inherited a heavily indebted farm in the canton of Zurich. Undaunted by this handicap, he applied himself to the improvement of his holding with such diligence and intelligence that he transformed it into a profitable enterprise. When he was thirty-five he was "discovered" by J. K. Hirzel, a physician of Zurich and a disciple of the Enlightenment. Kleinjogg fitted perfectly with Hirzel's vision of the ideal peasant. He raised forage and vegetables, stalled his cattle, grew new crops, used compost, marl, and manure to enrich his soil, and so on. In other words, he ran his farm according to rational principles, and he made a profit. Hirzel spent much time with Kleinjogg and was so deeply impressed by his character, ideas, and achievements that in 1761 he published a small book about his peasant friend. In typical Enlightenment manner he called it *The Economy of a Philosophical Peasant* (*Die Wirtschaft eines philosophischen Bauer*). It quickly won attention, and within a year was translated into French, in 1770 into English, and into Italian in 1793. In 1800 the English version was printed anew in Hallowell, Maine, for the edification of the American market. The translators apparently did not care for the German title; the book appeared as *Le Socrate Rustique* in French, *Il Socrate Rustico* in Italian, and *The Rural Socrates* in the English version. Readers hailed the book. The economist Mirabeau called it a jewel of the century, and others gave it equally extravagant praise. In 1775 Hirzel, encouraged by such encomiums, wrote a second book about Kleinjogg and called it *New Investigations of the Philosophical Peasant*.

Hirzel's writings made Kleinjogg an international celebrity. Soon a pilgrimage to his farm, and ecstatic reports about the visit to all who would listen, became almost a required activity for those who would lay claim to enlightenment. Men of great eminence visited Gujer. They admired his combination of rationality and practicality, were enraptured by his achievements, and marvelled that they were the work of a simple peasant whom they always referred to as Kleinjogg, never as Herr Gujer. Goethe, who came to call in 1775, described Kleinjogg in a letter as "one of the most noble creatures that the earth, from which we also sprang, has produced." Angelo Quirini, a Venetian senator, had his portrait painted with Kleinjogg. He confided to his diary that the peasant "through his common sense had penetrated to many truths which others reached only after long study

---

[26] Schleswig-Holstein: Beyer (1957), 54. Germany: Ziekursch (1927), 35-36n., 155; Müller (1964a), 638-641; Müller (1965a), 98-99; Berthold (1962), 99-107. Lower Austria: Juillard (1953), 208-212. Bohemia: Schnabel (1846), 84-86. Zurich: Bollinger (1941), 47-48.

and fundamental reflection." Rousseau wanted to meet Kleinjogg, but never got around to it. That did not prevent him in a letter of 24 December 1761 from calling Kleinjogg "wiser, more virtuous, more judicious than all the philosophers of the universe." When Prince Ludwig Eugen of Württemberg made the pilgrimage in 1765, Kleinjogg told him that it was a wonderful thing when a great lord came down to a humble peasant. Whereupon, according to a witness of this touching encounter, the prince, with tears glistening in his eyes, replied, "I do not come down to you, I rise up to you, for you are better than I." Unflustered by this noble speech, Kleinjogg said, "We are both good if each of us does what he should. You lords and princes must order us peasants what to do, for you have the time to decide what is best for the state, and it is for us peasants to obey you and work with diligence and loyalty." Obviously, Kleinjogg, in addition to all of his other qualities, knew what princes wanted to hear.

That speech alone showed that Gujer was anything but the simple peasant that his wordly visitors made him out to be. His industry, his rationalism, and his singleness of purpose distinguished him from his fellows. It also made him a stubborn, opinionated, and difficult man. He openly criticized many of the time-honored customs and traditions of the peasantry, as the sources of laziness and therefore of economic backwardness. He refused to celebrate the holidays that ticked off the stages in the farmer's year, such as haying, harvest festivals, and parish fairs. Rational to a fault, he condemned eating meat on Sunday, because people should not get more food on a day of rest than they had on a work day. To prevent his children from becoming accustomed to the traditions that others found pleasant he refused to let them attend the village school, and forbad them to go to fairs and other local celebrations. He even opposed the traditional peasant dress, and himself wore a simple gray blouse, closed by an iron clamp. His bewigged and besatinned visitors from the upper orders often referred with praise to his dress as evidence of his rationalism and his simplicity.[27]

IV

Seigniors did not restrict their new interest in profitable agriculture to farming. A number of proprietors, especially in central and eastern Europe, established plants on their manors to process agricultural goods. Usually these were small operations, turning out such commodities as tar, potash, bricks, barrels, and the like. In some lands and in some industries, however, large-scale enterprises were common. This was particularly true of distilling.

[27] Hauser (1962a), 38-47; Ernst (1935), 96, 99-100, 104, 108. Denmark had a famed "learned peasant," too, named Hans Jensen Bjerregaard (1728-1781). *Dansk Biografisk Leksiko*, III, 177-179.

The manufacture of spirits became a major producer of income for many proprietors in central and eastern Europe. The seigniorial monopoly on distilling and the seemingly unquenchable thirst of the peasants made this a lucrative business. It also had the advantage of providing an alternate use of the seigniors' crops if the market price was too low, or if he had an unmarketable surplus. Grain had served as the raw material for the manufacture of spirits. Then the acceptance of the potato as a staple crop and its use to make whiskey sparked a spectacular expansion in seigniorial distilling. In White Russia the manufacture of spirits quadrupled between the 1820's and the 1840's. By that latter date there were over 3,000 distilleries in that region. They produced over 21 million gallons of whiskey a year. In Poland the number of distilleries doubled between 1830 and 1840. By 1844 Poland had 2,094 distilleries with an output of 13 million gallons. An estimated quarter of the annual potato crop there was used to make whiskey. In Russia, on the other hand, the number of distilleries fell off sharply during the first half of the nineteenth century, from 23,300 around 1800 to 6,080 in 1860. The explanation for the decline was that small operations were replaced by large and more efficient plants. Average annual production per distillery rose from around 2,600 gallons at the end of the eighteenth century to around 48,750 gallons in 1860. Between 70,000 and 100,000 people, 90 to 95 per cent of them serfs, are estimated to have been employed in the industry. In the Austrian province of Moravia the average annual production of potato whiskey increased more than 10 times over between the opening years of the nineteenth century and 1841, from 670,000 gallons to 6.8 million gallons. Contemporaries estimated that 25 per cent of the potato crop in Bohemia in 1846, and 40 per cent in Galicia (the two chief potato producing provinces of the Austrian Monarchy), went to distilleries. In 1841 the distilleries in all of the German and Slav crownlands of the Austrian Monarchy produced 32.4 million gallons of potato whiskey and 9.4 million gallons of grain whiskey.[28]

The manufacture of beet sugar was another industry in which noble proprietors took the leading role. A. S. Marggraf (1709-1782), German pioneer in analytical chemistry, in 1747 succeeded in separating sugar from a number of plants, and found that he extracted the most from beet roots. He urged the commercial application of his findings, but the method he used was expensive so that beet sugar could not compete with colonial sugar. In 1797 F. K. Achard (1753-1821), Marggraf's student and his successor as director of the physical section of the Berlin Academy of Sciences, announced a process that made production more efficient. The war era and the Continental Blockade drove up the price of colonial sugar and made beet

---

[28] White Russia: Chepko (1964), 395. Poland: Kostiushko (1954), 149-150; Kieniewicz (1969), 91. Russia: Pazhitnov (1940), 240-242. Austria: Elvert (1870), i, 324; Schnabel (1846), 80-81; *Oekonomische Neuigkeiten* (1847), 951; *Tafeln zur Statistik*, (1841), table 41, sect. xv.

sugar more attractive. Governments and scientific societies offered prizes and subsidies to encourage its manufacture, and refineries opened in several lands. The methods they employed were still inefficient and costly and their output was small. The beets they used had a sucrose content of only about 8 per cent, of which only half could be extracted. A hectare of beets produced scarcely more than 10 quintals (2,200 pounds) of sugar.[29] When peace returned in 1814 and colonial sugar reappeared in quantity and at lower prices, beet sugar could not compete, and nearly all of the refineries closed.

In the 1820's technical improvements in the refining process increased yields somewhat and the industry slowly revived, encouraged by governmental support that included tax exemption or reduced taxes and high tariffs on imported sugar. Up to the end of the servile order, however, and beyond, the industry remained of minor importance. In the mid-1840's the Austrian Monarchy had only about 9,500 acres in sugar beets. These fields produced the 2 million Viennese *Centner* (123,480 tons) used by the 89 refineries then in operation in the Monarchy. In all of the Russian empire there were only 7 beet sugar refineries in 1825. In 1830 there were 20, and by 1861 the number had risen to 448. By then sugar beets were planted on over 235,000 acres. The industry was scattered through 22 provinces, but both refineries and beet fields concentrated in the Ukraine, where natural conditions favored the plant. In 1860-1861 the refineries of the province of Kiev accounted for nearly half of Russia's beet sugar output, and an additional 25 per cent was produced in the neighboring provinces of Podolia, Chernigov, and Kharkov. In Poland, which had 49 refineries in 1860, barely one-fourth of one per cent of the tilled area was planted in beets. In every country nearly all of the beets were grown on demesne land, and most of the refineries belonged to the seigniors who raised the beets. There was a high mortality rate among the refineries because of poor planning, bad management, and the vagaries of the harvest. Thus, in Prussia where the industry revived in the 1830's, there were 105 refineries in 1839; six years later only 77 remained.[30]

A few nobles took an active interest in non-agricultural industries, too. Indeed, they pioneered in the establishment of major sectors of manufacturing in their homelands. During the eighteenth century nobles laid the foundations of modern factory industry in Bohemia, Moravia, and Austrian Silesia. They were especially active in the establishment of glass

[29] International Institute of Agriculture, doc. no. 5 (1939), 10. In the mid-1970's an acre of sugar beets in the United States produced about 5,000 lbs. of sugar (or 12,350 lbs. per hectare). Plant selection, better cultivation, and more efficient methods of extraction explain the increase. In the United States and in Europe sucrose content of beets averages about 16.5 per cent, of which 87 per cent is extracted. (Information from American Society of Sugar Beet Technologies, Fort Collins, Colorado.)

[30] Slokar (1914), 608-609; Iatsunskii (1966), 49; Vil'son (1869), 294-302; Baraboi (1962), 345-346; Kostiushko (1954), 148; Kieniewicz (1969), 93; Haushofer (1963), 94.

works, woolen and cotton mills, and mining enterprises. Indeed, in the early eighteenth century commoners rarely were involved in large manufacturing enterprises.[31] In the first half of the nineteenth century the role of the nobility in non-agricultural industry declined in favor of entrepreneurs of bourgeois origin. Still, it remained of importance in some sectors. Of the 48 iron works in Bohemia in 1846, 29 belonged to members of the nobility, among them such high personages as Prince Colloredo, Prince Metternich, and Prince Windischgrätz.[32]

In Prussian Silesia, too, noblemen, and particularly great magnates, organized a number of industrial enterprises during the eighteenth and first part of the nineteenth centuries. They involved themselves in many lines of production, but had special interest in mining. In contrast, noble industrialists seemed to have been a rarity in the rest of the kingdom of Prussia. A listing compiled in 1769 by the commissioner general of commerce included only five nobles among the hundreds of owners of manufacturing establishments. In Saxony the sovereign established factories and so did a number of his nobles, including men of the topmost ranks of the army and the bureaucracy. Most of the factories there, however, were founded by merchants. Nobles in the agglomeration of principalities that made up the Rhine Province, annexed by Prussia in 1815, were active participants in the establishment of mining and metallurgical enterprises.[33]

In seventeenth-century France Louis XIV's great minister, Jean Baptiste Colbert, had despaired of interesting the nobility in investment in business activity. A century later great nobles, and lesser ones too, were among France's leading industrialists. Some of them founded their own enterprises. Others participated in industrial stock companies, and thereby kept themselves free of the taint of commerce but shared in its rewards. The nobles concentrated in mining and metallurgy but also established factories that manufactured textiles, glass, faience, and other wares. In Poland the greatest magnates pioneered in the introduction of industry. In the eighteenth century Prince Joseph K. Czartoryski, Prince Anthony Potocki, and Prince Radziwill each established a number of industrial enterprises on their enormous properties. Anthony Tyzenhaus, an especially active entrepreneur, in 1789 had interests in 23 factories. Hyacinth Jezierski, Palatine of Lukov, organized foundries, ironworks, and a scythe factory, among other industrial undertakings. Prince F. X. Drucki-Lubecki (1778-1846), minister of finance and founder of the Bank of Poland, established important enterprises in mining and metallurgy during the first half of the nineteenth century, and Count Henry Lubienski was the founder of the

[31] Entrepreneurship of nobles in Austrian industry during the eighteenth century is discussed in Freudenberger (1960), Freudenberger (1963), Hassinger (1964), and Klima (1974).
[32] Slokar (1914), 451-452; Stékl (1973), 21-23.
[33] Schwerin (1957), I, 179; Hoffmann (1969), 61; Forberger (1958), 30, 36, 209-210; Winkel (1968), 33.

Polish beet sugar industry. In White Russia noble-owned factories swelled in number during the second half of the eighteenth century. Almost always these plants processed materials produced on the manor, and turned out such products as paper, potash, woolens, and linen. At the end of the eighteenth century there were about 9,000 of these enterprises, all save a few of them small operations. In Russia Peter I had introduced a program of industrialization early in the eighteenth century. Participation by nobles had been minimal so that they owned only an estimated 8 per cent of the manufacturing plants. Then, beginning in the 1760's, landowners in growing numbers organized factories on their properties. By 1813-1814 an official report on manufactures showed that 64 per cent of the mining enterprises, 78 per cent of wool cloth factories, 60 per cent of the paper mills, 66 per cent of crystal and glass plants, and 80 per cent of the potash works belonged to nobles.[34]

The desire to aggrandize their incomes provided the obvious motive for those nobles who engaged in manufacturing, whether of agricultural or non-agricultural products. They saw the opportunity to profit from the special advantages they enjoyed. They had a ready and cheap source of raw materials in the output of their own demesnes, in the payments in kind made to them by their peasants, and in the mineral deposits on their lands. The fuel for their factories and forges came from their forests. Their peasants provided them with transport services as part of the servile obligations owed by the villagers to their seigniors. In central and eastern Europe the peasants also provided an instant labor force that could be required to work in the plant, and that could be laid off without fear of losing the peasants to another employer. In many of the seigniorial factories in Russia, and in some of them in Austria, Poland, and Germany, the work of the peasants in the lord's factory counted as part of their labor obligation and so was unpaid. In other plants they received wages in cash, or in a combination of cash and kind. As might be expected, when noble factory owners paid wages to their dependent peasants they were less than those received by free, hired workers. There may have been some justification for this, for the peasants, fresh from the fields, lacked proficiency as factory workers. A few noble factory owners imported trained foreign workers to teach their peasants the skills they needed.[35]

There were other motives besides profit that persuaded seigniors to engage in industry. Some started factories because their sovereigns had entered upon programs of industrial development. These nobles felt obliged

[34] France: Richard (1962), 484-523; Soreau (1937), 26-32; Martin (1900), 215-216n. Poland: Leskiewicz (1962), 241; Kurnatowski (1933), 243; *Polish Encyclopedia* (1922), III, 385. White Russia: Karpachev (1964), 285; Shlossberg (1959), 123-124. Russia: Zlotnikov (1935), 59.

[35] Freudenberger (1963), 46-47; Leskiewicz (1965), 241; Blum (1961), 318-319.

to cooperate, and they also hoped to win royal favor by the establishment of manufactures. A few, infused with the humanitarian spirit of the eighteenth century, and concerned about the physical and moral well-being of their peasants, somehow persuaded themselves that factories on the manor would be a way to improve the work habits and the character of the peasants.[36]

Success, of course, did not always attend upon these noble-owned businesses. They often foundered, many of them soon after their establishment. Nor did ownership necessarily imply that seigniors actively engaged in the management of their plants. Some factory owners entrusted direction of the enterprise to a hired manager, or to estate stewards. (A number of Austrian industrial entrepreneurs began their careers in the capacity of steward, entering manufacturing on their own account after gaining experience through management of seigniorial factories.) Sometimes the noble owner leased the factory to a member of the bourgeoisie, or took in commoners as managing partners. In 1795 Count Heinrich von Haugwitz and a Viennese banker and industrialist started a woolen cloth factory on a Haugwitz estate in Moravia. Together with associates they made an initial capital investment of 100,000 florins. In the nineteenth century that factory became the largest single cloth producer in the Monarchy. In the 1770's Counts Johann and Franz Stadion and a Viennese wholesaler named Jakob Schmidt established a woolens mill on land owned by the Stadions in Bohemia. The business thrived and by 1825 employed over 6,000 workers, including those who worked in their own homes on goods put out to them by the mill.[37]

Some factories counted among those owned by noblemen actually belonged to men of bourgeois origin whose economic success had won them patents of nobility, and who, despite their new social eminence, continued to manage their businesses. The activities of these men cannot serve as evidence for the appearance of a new spirit of enterprise in the order of the nobility. There were nobles, however, some of them of old lineage, who actively engaged in their businesses, made the decisions, and who distinguished themselves as important innovating entrepreneurs and highly successful businessmen. Such a man was Count Detlev von Einsiedel (1737-1810), who held high office in the government of Saxony. In 1776 he inherited an estate on which there was an ironworks. Eleven years later he retired from government service and took over the management of the ironworks. He immediately set about improving and expanding the operation, acquired other plants, and introduced techniques that were new to the

[36] Salz (1913), 281; Freudenberger (1963), 7; Hassinger (1964), 118.
[37] Salz (1913), 281; Freudenberger (1960), 401; Freudenberger (1960a), 353; Brusatti (1949), 121, 121n.

Saxon iron industry.[38] Sergei Ivanovich Mal'tsev (1810-1893) was one of Russia's greatest serfowners. He had over 200,000 bondsmen on his estates in central Russia. Member of an important family with close ties to the uppermost stratum of Russian society, he spent his youth in court circles and in military service. He rose to the rank of major-general when in 1849 he decided to retire. From then on he devoted himself to industrial enterprise. He was enormously successful, owned over twenty factories, among them metallurgical, armaments and chemical plants, and employed thousands of workers. His factories produced the first rails, the first steamboats, and the first steam engines made in Russia. His grandnephew, destined to end his career as a lieutenant-general in the Red Army, remembered Mal'tsev as a man who lived alone, rose each morning at five and began work at seven. He left his entire fortune to his personal assistant, a commoner named Iurii Nechaev. He explained in his will that his factories were dearer to him than his kinsmen, and, since no one among his relatives had the ability to run the industrial empire which he had constructed, he left everything to a man who was capable of taking over.[39] Other noblemen, too, had successful, albeit less spectacular careers as entrepreneurs. Among them were seigniors of Bordeaux and Toulouse who produced wine and wheat, and who have been characterized as shrewd businessmen who may have been "more 'bourgeois' than noble at the end of the Old Regime."[40] Count Johann Josef von Waldenstein, a wealthy Bohemian landowner, set up a large woolen mill on his estate in 1715 that he managed himself, and was succeeded in the management for the next hundred years by four successive members of his family.[41]

Many—perhaps most—noblemen still regarded business activity as antithetical to the status and traditions of their caste, and they disdained the men of lesser orders who made their living from trade. Prince Alfred Windischgrätz reflected that attitude when he remarked that "Geschäfte macht kein Windischgrätz."[42] In point of fact, as the preceding pages have shown, proper nobles, including the haughty Windischgrätz, were not all that disdainful of industry and profit-making. Time and events had slowly eroded the old prejudices. The number of seigniors who engaged in manufacturing represented a small fraction of the nobility of the servile lands. However, in an era when industry was still in its swaddling clothes, noble-owned enterprise formed an important, and in some lands the predominant, part of the industrial sector.

[38] Redlich (1953), 72-96, 141-149.
[39] Article on S. I. Mal'tsev in Brockhaus and Efron; Ignatiev (1955), I, 9-10.
[40] Forster (1961), 33; Forster (1963), 687.
[41] Freudenberger (1963), 1-2, 42-43. For other examples of active participation by nobles in their businesses see Ziekursch (1927), 12-21; Schwerin (1957), I, 179-182.
[42] Zorn (1963), 242.

15. Romanian peasant woman spinning with a distaff. (T. Stratilesco, *From Carpathian to Pindus*, London, 1906.)

V

The preceding pages and chapters make it obvious that agriculture in the servile lands did not experience an "agricultural revolution." In any event, there is much disagreement as to exactly what the revolution was, when it happened, whether it was a revolution in any accustomed sense of that overworked word, and, in fact, whether anything happened in European agriculture generally that could be called revolutionary by any definition of that term. It is worth noting, too, that the phrase "agricultural revolution," when used, is restricted almost exclusively to the agricultural history of England and France. Clearly, agriculture in the servile lands, including France, remained remarkably unaltered from what it had long been, except for the expansion in some lands of the culture of potatoes and maize. The great majority of seigniors and peasants continued to follow the traditional routines, and to raise the traditional crops, up to the end of the servile order and well beyond it. It took a long time for the innovations even to begin to change the face of agriculture.

Much of the slow pace of change was certainly attributable to the inflexibility of seigniors, the attitude of peasants, and the indecision of governments. Not all of the blame lay with them, however. The nature of agriculture itself bore a large share of the responsibility. "Farming," as Mrs. Thirsk pointed out, "is not a highly flexible business which can twist and change directions at every trick and turn of the price curve. The land and its buildings impose severe limitations on most farmers. Moreover, within the framework of what is practicable, the successful farm business is a union of several interlocking enterprises. Complex problems arise for the man who makes a change in any one of them. Even if he can reorganize or rearrange them satisfactorily he may find a short-term benefit cancelled out by the long-term disadvantages. Understandably, then, the ordinary farmer is rarely a revolutionary, and often his knowledge of his land and his experience of the vagaries of the market, will make him a hardened conservative in agricultural matters."[43]

Whatever the reasons, the efforts of the first generation of improvers, when measured in quantitative terms, met with failure in their own time. When the measurer takes the historical view, however, very different conclusions present themselves. For the first time men in high places—the movers and the shapers of their day—recognized the retardation of agriculture and the need for its reform. Their recognition of these truths led to the intellectualization of agriculture, in the sense that it began to be considered a scientific discipline. The manuals, journals, experiments, model farms, agricultural societies, and the schools laid the foundations for agricultural

[43] Thirsk (1967), 212.

science, and for the increased efficiency and higher yields of improved husbandry. They were responsible, too, for the always growing number of seigniors who came to regard landowning from a rational economic point of view rather than as a traditional way of life, as a source of income rather than as a source of status and privilege.

CHAPTER 14

The Old Order Attacked and Defended

I

DURING the same years in which a small minority of the nobility developed an interest in a more efficient and profitable agriculture and in industry, ideologies emerged that levelled attacks upon the traditional order and, above all, upon the privileges of the nobility. As with the other forces of change of that era, at first only a few were influenced by the new currents of thought. But they included a disproportionate number of those who occupied high places in the social order, or who were leading intellectual and literary figures of their time.

The critics of the privileges of the nobility had a well-stocked arsenal of complaints. Depending upon the country, they deplored the tax exemptions enjoyed by the seigniors, their monopolies, their judicial powers, their special status before the law, their exclusive right to own populated land, the favor shown them in appointments and advancements in government service, and, not least, the powers and rights they possessed over their peasants. The questioning came from many quarters, and included philosophers, professors, jurists, bureaucrats, economists, and publicists. Whatever their order, whether noble or bourgeois, and whatever their metier, these critics reflected the concepts of freedom, human rights, and human dignity and equality loosed in Europe by the Enlightenment. When the Enlightenment gave way to a new era, the liberating ideology of the Age of Reason lived on under other names and other sponsors, and continued to inspire molders of opinion. Indeed, even more than their predecessors of the eighteenth century, the men of the post-Enlightenment era condemned the hierarchical structure of society, the inequality of privilege, and the bonds that held peasants in subjection to their seigniors. They knew that their demands for change meant the end of the old order. Only with its demise could their vision of freedom be realized. They had powerful forces arrayed against them, but they persisted and ultimately they saw their dream come true when in land after land decrees of emancipation gave the peasants their freedom and thereby abolished the traditional society of orders.

Remarkably enough, in France, home of the Enlightenment, discussion of the plight of the peasantry and criticism of seigniorial privilege were minor themes in the assault upon the old order. The literature of human freedom and equality that came from the presses dealt only occasionally with the peasants and their problems. The critics focussed upon what they called "feudalism." By that they meant the complex of privileges whose justification and military and political utility had long since vanished, which gave the nobility their special and elevated position in the social order. The privileges, of course, included the claim of the seigniors for dues, services, and submission from the peasantry. However, except for *mainmorte* and seigniorial justice, these seigniorial prerogatives were rarely singled out for censure. The same striking omission occurred in the writings of the agronomists, who urged the need for agricultural improvements. These experts scarcely mentioned seigniorial rights over the peasants, much less criticized them. Perhaps the philosophers and pamphleteers and agronomists assumed that their readers did not need to be told that freedom and equality could come only with abolition of the servile relationship of peasant to seignior, and that the nexus of seigniorial privilege held back the progress of agriculture. Or perhaps, as one historian suggests, the publicists who assailed feudalism lived mainly in Paris, and so, he claims, "lacked enough first hand knowledge to make their case convincing." A less charitable explanation, proposed by the Russian historian N. I. Kareev, suggests that many of the advocates of freedom and economic advance were themselves seigniors, and as beneficiaries of the system of privilege were reluctant to assail it.[1]

The offensive against *mainmorte*, the mild French version of serfdom, owed most of its impetus to Voltaire. In the last of his famed battles for freedom, this one inspired by lawsuits entered against their seignior by *mainmortable* peasants of the Abbey of St. Claude, the old *philosophe* agitated for the abolition of *mainmorte*. To Voltaire and the others who joined with him in the battle, *mainmorte* was a status that demeaned the human condition and so had to be abolished. Practical considerations, too, motivated would-be reformers. The abbot of Luxeuil petitioned the Royal Council in 1775 for permission to emancipate the *mainmortable* peasants of the abbey. The abbot explained that their lowly status humiliated the peasants and robbed them of hope. The apathy and indolence that resulted brought economic loss to the abbey, for its lands lay untilled or poorly cultivated. In addition, the abbot pointed out that *mainmorte* was a source of lawsuits that were "as burdensome, expensive and ruinous for the seigniors as for their subjects."[2]

Especially fierce attacks were reserved for the operations of seigniorial justice. Its opponents condemned it not on legal grounds, but because of its high costs, its inefficiencies, the multiplicity of courts, the great number of their officials, and the long delays in reaching decisions. Many of the severest critics were royal officials who may have been inspired by the rivalry between the courts of the king and of the seigniors.[3]

[1] Mackrell (1973), 13, 136-138; Kareev (1899), 266, 327-328.
[2] Herbert (1969), 8-9; Mackrell (1973), 107-122; Kareev (1899), 323.
[3] Mackrell (1973), 150-158.

Still another assault—this one on the grounds of social utility and enlightened economic self-interest—was levelled against the seigniorial system by the physiocrats and their associates. They argued that the continued existence of small-scale, capital-starved subsistence farms retarded agricultural progress. They maintained that large farms operated by agricultural entrepreneurs who were well supplied with capital, and who were profit-conscious and market-oriented, were necessary for the economic growth of the entire economy. And they pointed out that the seigniorial system had to go, not because they were concerned about the welfare of the peasants or the injustices of their status, but because the system helped to perpetuate the inefficiencies that plagued agriculture.

A pamphlet published in 1776, titled *Les inconvéniens des droits féodaux*, one of the very few direct treatments of the peasant question, reflected the utilitarian critique of the physiocrats. Its author, P. F. Boncerf, worked in the Ministry of Finances, whose head was Turgot, the famed physiocrat. Boncerf was apparently close to Turgot and possibly may have had his collaboration in writing the treatise. Boncerf said nothing new, and wrote in a moderate and conciliatory tone. He assailed neither the inequities of the seigniorial system, nor the hardships it inflicted upon the peasants. Rather, his point was to demonstrate that, as the title suggested, seigniorial privileges were not really profitable to their possessors, and he advocated cash redemption of the dues and services of the peasants. Notwithstanding the mildness of Boncerf's proposals and his non-revolutionary language, the *parlement* of Paris ordered the suppression of the pamphlet as "injurious to the laws and customs of France . . . and to the right of property." To emphasize its condemnation the pamphlet was burned by the executioner at the foot of the *parlement*'s grand stairs. Despite this repression, and perhaps because of it, the brochure gained much attention. Among those who read it was Voltaire, who described it as a wise and learned study that was "full of humanity"—the highest accolade of the Enlightenment. Voltaire declared himself "stupified with astonishment and sorrow" at the action of the *parlement*.[4]

Turgot himself is said to have had a plan for the gradual elimination of seigniorial dues, with some to be redeemed by money payments and others abolished without compensation. He was dismissed from office before he could implement such a scheme. After his fall in 1776, discussion of the peasant problem lagged until the eve of the Revolution. The king's decision to summon the Estates-General produced a new ferment. Jacques Necker, recalled in 1788 to the post of Minister of Finances, organized assemblies in several provinces to study ways to improve popular welfare. The assemblies established committees on begging, and they talked about the need for agricultural improvements. But they said or did nothing about reforming

---

[4] Kareev (1899), 325-326; Bruchet (1809), viii-ix.

seigniorial privilege or ending seigniorial dues. Meanwhile dissidents and proponents of reform put out a new spate of pamphlets. Nearly all of them passed over the peasant problem in silence.[5]

In contrast to the neglect of the plight of the peasantry in eighteenth-century France, the attacks upon the privileged position of the nobility in Germany were usually accompanied by denunciations of the traditional lord-peasant relationship there. The advocates of reform marshalled humanitarian, philosophical, and economic arguments to support their demands. The injustices, cruelties, and degradation that surrounded the servile status of the peasantry seemed to them to be unacceptable in what was supposed to be an enlightened age. Some of them pointed out, too, that the traditional order, with its forced labor, its tithes and other dues, and its outmoded farming techniques, retarded economic growth and prevented the introduction of a rational and more profitable agriculture.[6] Among those who pressed for reforms were famed philosophers such as Kant and Fichte, distinguished professors, outstanding agronomists, and the renowned Swiss educational reformer J. H. Pestalozzi, whose writings, well known in Germany, condemned the servile system as a barrier to self-development and self-fulfillment.[7]

The influence of the Enlightenment had much to do with the growth on German soil of the idea of freedom. But there were indigenous German sources, too, notably the teachings of the German philosophers of natural law. In the last decades of the eighteenth century these philosophers branded the servile status of the peasantry as contrary to natural law, and demanded emancipation for the peasants as a condition of human dignity.[8] The University of Königsberg, in East Prussia, whose greatest figure was Immanuel Kant, became the intellectual center for the reform movement. Kant himself bitterly opposed serfdom and in his lectures and writings struck out against privilege and inequality. Civil society, he wrote in 1793, was based *a priori* on freedom of all, equality of all, and individual independence. Since all are equal in civil society, every individual should be able to rise to the station to which his talents, diligence, and good fortune raise him, and no one should be able to stand in his way because of hereditary privilege.[9] Kant's opposition to the servile order was not restricted to this kind of cool, rational critique. He harbored a deep, emotional hatred of it, a hatred so intense that he once told his students that his insides turned over whenever he thought of serfdom.[10]

[5] Kareev (1899), 327-328, 341-346, 352-368.

[6] *Jahrbücher der preussischen Monarchie* (1800), 222-227, 230, 235-238; Epstein (1966), 201-203; Fuchs (1888), 194-197; Mager (1955), 339-340; Ziekursch (1927), 255.

[7] Schremmer (1963), 65-66; Gagliardo (1969), 155, 192-194; Frauendorfer (1957), I, 143-144, 252n.

[8] Rumler (1921), 184; Stolz (1940), 41-44.   [9] Kant (1968), VIII, 290-292.

[10] Rumler (1921), 190.

Kant's fellow professor, Christian Jakob Kraus (1753-1807), who had the chair of Practical Philosophy and Cameralistic Sciences at Königsberg, was an even more important academic figure than Kant in the offensive against the traditional order. One of Adam Smith's first German disciples, he made the Scotsman's doctrines the core of his lectures. He was an inspiring teacher who attracted students of practical bent, many of them nobles who went on to become men of affairs. Indeed, in 1800 a high Prussian bureaucrat ordered that no one could enter the administrative service of the government of East Prussia without a certificate of attendance at Professor Kraus's lectures. His advocacy of Smithian individualism and freedom led him to denounce the hierarchical order of privilege, and to call serfdom "the shame of humanity."[11] Professors at other universities, too, such as Ernst Ferdinand Klein and Johann Christoph Hoffbauer at Halle and, above all, the historian August Ludwig Schlözer (1735-1809), at Göttingen, denounced the traditional order and demanded its reform.[12]

Another current of reform, this one combining both theory and practice, came from the precepts of cameralism, the central European brand of mercantilism. Universities in Germany and Austria had courses and chairs of cameralism, and cameralists served as advisors of princes and of high officials. The paramount concern of cameralist doctrine was to raise the welfare of the state by proper management of and by increase in the revenues of the government. The very name, cameralism, came from *camera*, the chamber where in earlier times the royal treasure had been stored. In their lectures and their writings the cameralists dedicated themselves to the training of officials who would carry out their teachings. Cameralism assumed the subordination of individual interests to those of the state, and it emphasized the central role of the state in the promotion of economic growth. The cameralists directed much of their attention to agriculture as the most important sector of the economy and, as one cameralist put it, "the protector and foundation of the happiness of the state."[13] They insisted that the interests of national economic growth, and therefore of governmental revenues, were best served by reforms that protected the peasant from excessive seigniorial exploitation and expropriation, and that established the peasant as the owner of his own small farm. The fact that reforms that were introduced in the eighteenth century in central Europe on lands of the crown followed these lines was not coincidental.

The writings and teachings and counsel of cameralists, and particularly of J.H.G. von Justi (1705-1771) and of Joseph von Sonnenfels (1733-1817), both of whom repeatedly criticized the lord-peasant relationship,

[11] *Ibid.*, 189; Epstein (1966), 181.
[12] *Cf.* Schlözer (1793), 51, 61; Klein (1797), 228-229; Hoffbauer (1793), 179; Hoffbauer (1795), 244-249.
[13] J. F. Pfeiffer, quoted in Tautscher (1947), 15.

aroused sympathy and support in important circles in Austria for reform. Justi, in a book published in 1760 on the foundations of the power and well-being of the state, wrote: "The liberty of the citizen and of all members of a state is the first important quality of all civil constitutions. States where one order or one class of people is subjected to another, have as monstrous a constitution as those which existed in the most barbarous times. Moral and reasonable epochs like our own cannot allow such institutions to continue without ignominy."[14] In another study that appeared in 1761 Justi, like the physiocrats, appealed to the self-interest of the proprietor. He pointed out that the landowner drew small benefits from his seigniorial rights. The landowner could get more out of his property if the peasants became full proprietors or hereditary leaseholders, for the sale price or the rental income would exceed his present income. Forced labor was done unwillingly and therefore poorly. "If the peasant is not under the whip of the lessee or the overseer, which in a properly run state would not be permitted by the civil constitution, then the labor service, when viewed as a whole and in context, does more harm than good."[15] Sonnenfels, who was a trusted advisor of Empress Marie Theresa and of Joseph II, expressed his opposition to the servile status of the peasantry in essays, fiction, and in the lectures he gave as professor of cameralism at the Theresianum Ritterakademie, the school for noble youths established in Vienna.[16]

Support of reform evidenced itself in less exalted circles, too. By the early decades of the nineteenth century a considerable number of Austrians, especially though not exclusively among the bourgeoisie, looked upon the privileged status of the nobility and the servile status of the peasantry as a relic that had outlived its time and that could no longer be afforded.[17] However, the unrelenting conservatism of Emperor Francis, his tactic of purposeful procrastination, and the deeply rooted fear of change that was the legacy of the French Revolution, all conspired to inhibit reform. The excesses of the revolutionary era had cast a dark shadow over the faith the Enlightenment had in the beneficence of freedom and human rights. The spirit of Josephinism was only a memory. Now the rulers of Austria feared that reform of the hierarchical order of society would imperil the continued existence of the state.

Then in the 1840's a demand for changes surfaced in what seemed an unlikely source of discontent—the provincial estates of several of the Monarchy's crown lands. These assemblies, dominated by the nobility, in the eighteenth century had lost most of their authority to the centralizing forces of the throne. After many decades of acceptance of their emasculated role, restlessness manifested itself in the estates of Styria, Galicia, Carniola, Moravia, and especially Lower Austria and Bohemia. A new genera-

---

[14] Link (1949), 103.
[16] Kann (1960), 171, 180-181; Link (1949), 98-101.
[15] Franz (1963), 235-236.
[17] Brusatti (1958), 507.

tion of leaders had taken over. Some of them had liberal leanings, and many in the assemblies of the Slav provinces were caught in the rising tide of Polish and Czech nationalism. The estates demanded the right to debate the proposals of the central government and to suggest new legislation. When the government rejected these demands, the so-called "estates movement" took on the character of a loyal opposition. The assemblies proclaimed their dissatisfaction by the adoption of proposals for reform, and by a general attitude of recalcitrance. They concentrated on the need for a restructuring of the lord-peasant relationship, and especially on the need to abolish the labor service because of its inefficiency. The liberals contended that the existing relationship impeded agricultural progress and so damaged the interests of the proprietors and thus of the entire state. They pointed out, too, that the servility and submissiveness of the peasants to their seigniors conflicted with the spirit of the times. Nationalists took up the cause of peasant reform in order to win the support of the mass of the people for their nationalistic ambitions. Whatever the motives of the reformers in the estates, the proposals that they sent forward to Vienna were always rejected.[18]

In Hungary, where the national diet had a major voice in the conduct of the government, liberal nobles proposed a series of reforms to lighten the burdens of the peasants and to allow them greater personal freedom. Most of these recommendations were approved by the diet of 1832-1836 and were accepted by the throne. They were incorporated in the *Urbarium* of 1836, which revised the code regulating the lord-peasant relationship that had been issued in 1767. At later sessions in the 1830's and 1840's the diet continued to study the peasant question, and approved further reform legislation that the crown accepted. However, little use was apparently made of the most hotly debated section of these reforms. That was the right the peasant now had to buy his holding, and to redeem his obligations to his seignior by payments in cash or kind.[19]

In Denmark the abrogation in 1755 of the ban on the discussion of agrarian and economic questions in publications opened the way to the appearance of monographs and articles that counselled the need for changes in the social structure. Among these publications, a book by G. C. Oeder, a German physician and botanist who lived for a time in Copenhagen (where he directed the Botanical Garden), had a special and lasting influence. Oeder recommended that the peasants be freed from their servile status and that the seigniorial demesnes be divided among them. When his fellow German physician Johann Friedrich Struensee took over the reins of the government he made Oeder Commissioner of Agriculture to implement reforms. After the violent end of Struensee's brief tenure of power, Oeder left Den-

[18] Blum (1948), 204-205, 212-221; Kieniewicz (1969), 115.
[19] Leshchilovskaia (1961), 320, 323-324; Blum (1948), 206-207, 209-212.

mark for the nearby duchy of Oldenburg. He kept his ties with Denmark, and his book was studied and highly valued by Danish statesmen and by the young Crown Prince Frederick, during whose regency Denmark later carried out its successful reform program. The book was especially influential in Schleswig-Holstein, where the literary debate over serfdom began as a discussion of Oeder's monograph. Academics, too, had a part in the reform movement. Professors at the University of Kiel, in Holstein, were especially active in urging the abolition of serfdom, and many of them favored the division of large estates among the peasants, who would become hereditary tenants or proprietors.[20]

The books and articles, and the penetration into Denmark of the ideas of the Enlightenment, helped persuade noblemen of the need for reform. Most important, some of Denmark's greatest proprietors came to support change because they recognized the advantages it would bring to them, to the peasants, and to the state. During the reigns of the weak Christian VI (1730-1746) and Frederick V (1746-1766), and for much of the reign of the mentally unbalanced Christian VII (1766-1808), a small group of great landowners dominated the government. These men—the Moltkes, the Reventlows, the Rantzaus, and a few others—were responsible for most of the policies adopted by the government. Though factions often divided them, they agreed on the need for agrarian reform and they persuaded the monarchs to issue the legislation needed to carry it out.[21]

One of the earliest summons to reform in Poland appeared in 1749 when a book reputedly written about 1733 by King Stanislaus Leszczyński—who was driven from the throne that same year—was published anonymously. The royal author, if indeed it was Leszczyński, called for the abolition of serfdom and the commutation of labor dues into money payments. In the following decades pamphleteers and politicians advanced proposals for improvements in the condition of the peasantry. The advocates of reform increased in number after the first partition of Poland in 1772 revealed the weakness of the Polish state. Thoughtful men realized that changes had to be made if Poland was to survive. They appealed to the patriotism and the humanitarianism of the nobles, who were the rulers of the country, and whose irresponsibility and selfishness had brought it to the edge of ruin. They appealed to the self-interest of the nobles, too, claiming that progress in agriculture, and therefore increased incomes for the seigniors, depended upon ameliorations in the condition and status of the peasantry. Their proposals, however, were limited to palliatives that would lessen and regularize the obligations of the peasants and better their legal status. No one advocated the conversion of the peasant's holding into his own property, and no one wanted to end the hierarchical and noble-dominated structure of Polish society.[22]

[20] Hvidtfeldt (1963), 498; Sievers (1970), 154-155, 158-159, 171-172.
[21] Commager (1928), 88-89.   [22] Kieniewicz (1969), 18.

The first signs of a reform movement in the Baltic provinces of Russia appeared in the early 1760's, with leading parts taken by Schoultz von Ascheraden, a noble landowner, and J. G. Eisen von Schwarzenberg, a Lutheran pastor. Both were German, as were most of the proprietors and the pastors of the Baltic provinces. These German Balts had close ties to their ancestral homeland and were influenced strongly by the currents of enlightenment and reform that came from Germany. Schoultz von Ascheraden advocated that peasants be granted certain rights and privileges they did not then possess, and urged that their obligations be firmly fixed. Pastor Eisen (whose book of 1764, as mentioned in an earlier chapter, may have helped turn that attention of Catherine II to thoughts of reform) argued that the peasant should have hereditary ownership of his holding, and have the right to sell his grain wherever and whenever he wanted. In succeeding decades a number of critics pointed out that serfdom was wasteful, and harmed both lord and peasant because of its inefficiencies, its impoverishment of the peasantry, and its retardative effect upon innovation and agricultural progress.

The critics included members of the landowning nobility, but Lutheran pastors held a special place among the enemies of the old order, assailing serfdom in their books and undoubtedly in their sermons. Many of these clerical and noble critics had attended German universities, particularly Göttingen, then the premier center of learning in all Germany. Between 1770 and 1800, 277 young men from Livland, Estland, and Courland studied at Göttingen. Many of them had been students of August Ludwig Schlözer and had been influenced by his ideas. Before accepting a chair at Göttingen, Schlözer had lived in St. Petersburg from 1761 to 1770. There he had become interested in the history of eastern Europe and had been appointed professor of Russian history at the Academy of Sciences. In his voluminous writings, and in his lecures, he gave new dignity to the natives of the Baltic lands, and censured the German conquerors who in the late Middle Ages had invaded the region and enserfed its people. The students returned home burdened with a feeling of guilt for the sins of their forefathers, and resolute in their determination to make amends.

The most influential of the attacks upon the traditional order came from the pen of Garlieb Merkel (1769-1850). Son of a Lutheran pastor, Merkel from early youth had immersed himself in the writings of the *philosophes* and had become a passionate advocate of human rights and of the supremacy of reason. Employed as the tutor of noble youths, and living in the homes of his pupils, he learned at first hand of the degradation of peasant life. In 1796 he published a book that he called *Die Letten*, in which he argued for the freedom of the Lettish peasantry from their mainly German lords. His book contained nothing new, his data were often inaccurate or incomplete, he glossed over the economic aspects and consequences of his proposals, and he did not explain how to implement the reforms he wanted. But his fervor, his dedication, and his literary skill quickly won a wide audience for the book.[23]

There had been a few isolated expressions of opposition to serfdom from men of the upper orders in Russia during the first six decades of the eighteenth century. Then during the reign of Catherine II the liberal and humanitarian ideas of the Enlightenment reached Russia. That was when the criticism of serfdom began in earnest. The peasant question and the need for reform became the subject of frequent discussion in literary and scholarly circles. The best-known and the most enduring attack appeared in 1790 when A. N. Radishchev, member of a prominent noble family, published his *Journey from St. Petersburg to Moscow*. That book has been described as "the first in a long series of literary bombshells which the privileged aristocracy was to set off against the established order."[24] Its author's forthright condemnation of the cruelties and injustices of serfdom, and his criticism of some of the most revered institutions of Russian government and life, outraged Empress Catherine II. She sentenced Radishchev to death, then commuted the sentence to banishment to Siberia and deprivation of his status as a member of the nobility. But the book lived on, and helped arouse some among the landowning elite to continue the struggle against the status quo. Among them was Alexander Pushkin, who in 1836 wrote that he would be remembered "because, following in the footsteps of Radishchev, I sang the praises of liberty."[25]

Around the 1820's groups of young men, many of them university students and most of them from landowning families, began to meet together to discuss new philosophies that had come into Russia from the west, and to express their desires for changes in Russian society, especially the abolition of serfdom. These "circles," as they came to be called, dominated Russian intellectual life for the next three decades. During these same years Russia experienced a spectacular outburst of literary and scholarly genius. The poets, philosophers, essayists, and novelists of the Golden Age of Russian culture, almost to a man, were severe critics of the existing order, and singled out serfdom for their sharpest attacks. Many among the young army officers who revolted in December 1825, all of them nobles and some from great landowning families, included the abolition of serfdom in their program of reform. Other and less extreme advocates of reform included men in the highest levels of government service. Minister of Internal Affairs Count L. A. Perovsky in 1845 called serfdom a "mutually unprofitable" relationship, and saw its abolition as "extremely desirable." The governor of the White Russian province of Mogilev, in his report of 1859, called serfdom "the chief underlying reason for the unsatisfactory state of agriculture," and his fellow governor in neighboring Minsk reported that "serfdom stood in the way of new improvements."[26]

[23] Diederichs (1870), 41-48, 53-71; Kahk (1969), 8-9; Schwabe (1928), 271, 286-287.
[24] Billington (1966), 240.   [25] Radishchev (1958), 34-37.
[26] Skerpan (1964), 179; Fridman (1958), 10.

In the Danubian Principalities a few large proprietors who had been exposed to western ideas organized the Philharmonic Society in 1835. Ostensibly it was a literary association dedicated to the nurture and advancement of Romanian language and literature. Actually it had a strong political orientation, and has been called "the school of the great Romanian reformers of the nineteenth century." Among its founders were men who wanted to end the servile status of the peasantry, and who believed that the land held by the peasants should belong to them. In the 1840's youthful nobles, sent by their families to study in France, absorbed the democratic idealism that was so popular in the intellectual life of the Paris of that day. In 1848 they returned home, on fire with revolutionary ardor, determined to lead the way to a democratic republic founded upon the equality of all of its citizens. They had a ready-made program: abolition of the Russian protectorate, creation of an independent Romanian state with a democratic government based on universal suffrage, equal taxation, and the emancipation of the peasantry. The revolution began in April in Jassy, capital of Moldavia, with a protest meeting and a call to the people of town and country to rise. Within twenty-four hours the police had crushed the revolution and arrested its leaders or forced them to flee. The firebrands had better luck in Wallachia, where revolution broke out on 21 June. They gained control of the principality and held it for three months. Then Russian and Turkish troops marched in, easily routed the revolutionaries, and restored the pre-revolutionary government.

The revolution failed in large part because of the failure of its leaders. Like youthful zealots of other times and places, they knew little and understood less about the people whom they wanted to free. They talked endlessly about freedom and issued decrees "in the name of the people," but they ran the government as a dictatorship. The "people," who had helped in the overthrow of the old regime, waited in vain for the abolition of their servile obligations and the redistribution of land. For instead of taking direct action, the revolutionary government waited for the landowners to be inspired by the spirit of brotherhood, and voluntarily surrender their land and their privileges.

The revolution's failure did not end the movement for reform. People still spoke and wrote of the need for change. And the "men of '48" themselves matured and became more realistic. They returned to their homeland after the Crimean War had ended the Russian protectorate and took the lead in the creation of an independent Romania and in the emancipation of its peasants.[27]

II

To the foes of the old order, the hierarchy of privilege was an evil heritage that had to be expunged. There were others who desired changes, too, but

[27] Campbell (1944), 268-273; Campbell (1948), 181-189.

who were at the same time convinced partisans of privilege. These men, who not surprisingly were almost exclusively seigniors, wanted to get rid of the labor obligation of the peasants, but wanted to preserve the seigniorial domination of rural society. Altruistic humanitarianism or ideological commitment to freedom and equality did not concern them. Instead, self-interest persuaded them to advocate the end of the labor service because it was done so poorly and was so wasteful. They argued that they could draw greater revenues from their manors if they commuted the labor dues into cash and used the cash to hire workers.

The recognition of the inefficiencies of the labor obligation was not a new phenomenon. From early in the second half of the eighteenth century, however, it attracted far more attention than ever before. Market-oriented proprietors became restive because of the low quality and the administrative costs of forced labor, and economists provided them with theoretical and practical data that demonstrated the economic loss to proprietor and to nation brought about by the labor obligation.

From the outset the critics of the labor service stressed the advantages to the seignior that would follow from the end of the labor service, rather than its benefits to the peasants. For example, the first published criticism in Pomerania of the labor obligation, written in 1752 by F. D. von Behr, landowner and important political figure, recommended the reduction of peasant land to holdings too small to support a family. That would reduce or even wipe out the labor dues the peasants owed to the seignior since the dues were scaled to the size of the holding. To earn their livings the villagers would have to hire themselves out as farm laborers. Behr explained that because they would be working for hire and so could be dismissed for inefficiency, they would work harder than they did when performing their labor obligation, from which, of course, they could not be discharged. Other critics were sometimes more humane in their proposals, but essentially they all presented the same rationale—the gains to the seignior.[28]

In Denmark in the 1760's a few great proprietors experimented with commutation of labor services and found that it increased productivity. In the agricultural writings that started to be published in the 1750's the authors frequently observed that forced labor cost more than it was worth.[29] In eighteenth-century Austria the government of Maria Theresa had taken the lead in the movement to commute labor services, but had found few imitators among the landowning nobility (p. 211). In January 1783 Joseph II appointed Count Karl von Zinzendorff to head a special commission to promote commutation, and established similar commissions in the crown lands. Zinzendorff and the provincial commissioners pursued their task with much zeal but without much success. In his decree of 10 February 1789 Joseph made commutation compulsory, but, as was recounted on an

[28] Fuchs (1888), 190-192; *cf.* Meyer (1965), 48; Eggert (1965), 27-28; Stein (1918), I, 361, 369; Lütge (1957), 157; Boelcke (1957), 165-166.
[29] Scharling (1909), 578.

earlier page, the decree was repealed within a year and had no effect. In the spring of 1790 Joseph's successor, Leopold II, restored the pre-Josephine situation in which peasants could commute their obligations if their seigniors gave their consent. In the past, few had given the needed permission. Now, in those provinces where proprietors did not engage extensively in demesne production a surprisingly large number of seigniors allowed their peasants to commute their labor service. In crown lands in which nobles had large demesnes and were active in farm production seigniors continued to demand labor dues. However, in the early decades of the nineteenth century criticism of the inadequacies of the labor obligation began to be expressed in these provinces. Agricultural experts and some landowners were outspoken in their condemnation of the obligation as wasteful and therefore costly to the proprietor. The dissatisfaction grew with the years and, as was pointed out earlier in this chapter, the demand for abolition of the labor service was a central feature of the estates movement of the 1840's. Though other motives underlay some of their opposition, the estates made it abundantly clear that they wanted to abolish the labor service because they considered it to be the major barrier to the more profitable exploitation of their estates.[30]

The discussion in Russia followed a different course. For all save a small minority of landowners the choice there lay not between labor dues and hired hands to work the lord's demesne, but between labor dues as the major obligation, or quitrent as the major obligation, in which case the seignior abandoned all or most of his demesne operation. Many Russian landowners had long demanded only quitrents from their serfs, and many others required a mix of labor dues and quitrent. Questioning of the value of the labor obligation compared to quitrent occurred early in the reign of Catherine II. Then a hiatus intervened that lasted until the early part of the nineteenth century, when once again comparisons of the advantages of labor services versus quitrent were made in articles and books and discussions. The Free Agricultural Society sponsored essay contests that were concerned directly or indirectly with this topic. Meanwhile, scholarly writers developed the thesis, first advanced in Catherine's time, that serfdom itself was economically unprofitable, and that landowners would draw greater revenues from their properties if they ended serfdom and hired their freed serfs as wage workers. The censors, more lenient with scholarly publications than with other literature, consented to the publication of a number of treatises that favored emancipation. Until mid-century, however, the censorship did not permit discussion of the superiority of hired labor to appear in publications of general interest. Then the ban was lifted, and newspapers, journals, and books were allowed to examine and discuss the problem.[31]

[30] Lütge (1967a), 155-157, 162-167; Blum (1948), 56-57, 193-201, 243-244.
[31] Confino (1963), 201-217; Shlossberg (1959), 127; Kulischer (1932), 53.

By far the greatest number of Russian landowners, however, exhibited little or no interest in the debate. And of the small minority who involved themselves in the discussions, nearly all defended labor dues as more profitable to them than quitrents. In essays submitted to prize competitions, in articles, in letters to journals, and in replies to questionnaires, they explained their reasons for their preference. Peasants on quitrent, they said, sought endlessly to reduce or evade the payments, collecting the quitrent was difficult and expensive, arrearages piled up, peasants on quitrents often preferred non-agricultural employment and left farming to their women-folk who did it poorly, and manors tended to deteriorate and lose value unless they were under the direct operation of the owner. Data presented from actual experience showed that lords received more revenue from their serfs when they required labor dues. One of the winners in an essay contest of the Free Economic Society in 1809 computed that in Orel, a fertile agricultural province of central Russia, seigniors drew an annual revenue of 106 rubles from a serf couple on labor dues, and only 30 rubles annually from a couple on quitrent. Similar reports were still being made at mid-century. A proprietor in Tambov, another fertile province of the center, declared that he had doubled his income by shifting some of his peasants from quitrents to labor dues. In the province of Kostroma, in a much less fertile part of the country, where most seigniors demanded only quitrents, the claim was made that labor dues were three times more profitable to the proprietor than were quitrents.[32]

There were a few landowners, influenced by humanitarianism, by the interest shown by the tsar and by some of his high officials in reform, and most of all by self-interest, who believed that the best solution was to free the serfs. The first formal proposal of this nature came in 1819 from a group of proprietors of Vitebsk, a province of White Russia. In 1837-1838 some seigniors of Tula, and in the 1840's groups of proprietors in a number of other provinces, sponsored plans for reform. None of these proposals had the support of the majority of the proprietors in these provinces, and in any event the central government did not allow any of the proposals to go beyond the paper stage. The suggested reforms, like those proposed by seigniors in other lands, usually involved emancipation without land, or with very small holdings for which the peasants would have to indemnify the proprietor. The freed peasants, without land or without enough to support themselves, would have to work as hired hands for their erstwhile masters. The proprietors would thereby gain a more efficient labor force, would spare themselves the expenses and responsibilities that accompanied ownership of serfs, and could use the indemnification paid to them by the peasants to pay off their own mounting debts. In short, the seignior-reformers were looking out for themselves.[33]

[32] Struve (1913), 91-93; Kulischer (1932), 33; Picheta (1911), III, 119.
[33] Blum (1961), 571-573.

The explanation for the inefficiency of the labor obligation in all of the servile lands lay in the fact that it was compulsory and that the workers received no pay. The peasants knew that no matter how poorly they performed the labor service, the seignior had no recourse. There were no wages for him to reduce or withhold, nor could he discharge the workers, since then he would lose whatever labors they did accomplish for him. The peasants took no interest in the task assigned to them; they tried to do as little as they could; indeed, according to Albrecht Thaer, they considered it a point of honor to cheat the seignior in the performance of the obligation.[34] The lord's bailiff and his overseers could and did use the whip, but that seemed to make no difference in the amount of work that was done. Whenever it was possible the least able members of the peasant household were the ones sent to perform the labor service. In an article that appeared in 1847 a Russian serfowner described the work habits of his peasants when they did their labor dues for him. "The peasant," he wrote, "arrives on the job as late as possible, looks around and stares off frequently and for long periods, and works as little as possible. To him it is not a job to do but a day to kill. He drives zealous overseers to despair or anger. One disciplines unwillingly [he meant the use of the whip], but one is forced to this solution as the only possible way to get the work moving."[35] Nor was the seignior the only loser. The habits of sloth, neglect, and deceit carried over when the peasants worked their own holdings. Perceptive observers of that day were justified when, as an English traveller in Germany reported, they described the labor obligation as "a school to teach idleness."[36]

Poorly done work was not the only loss incurred by seigniors whose peasants did labor services for them. The peasants, fearful that work on something new would increase their burden, stubbornly maintained that they would do only the same kind of work their fathers had done before them. When they could, they refused to work on new crops or to use new techniques. When they were compelled to do this, they malingered even more than was usual. That made it difficult, and sometimes impossible, for seigniors to introduce innovations on their demesnes. Another source of loss rose out of the responsibilities owed by the seignior to his peasants when they rendered their labor dues to him. As mentioned in earlier pages, law or custom in many places required the lord to provide meals for the peasants and fodder for their animals. Generally, too, the seignior had to pay a small wage for the extra days of labor he could demand of his villagers, and give them a sizable fraction of the grain they harvested and threshed for him. These expenses could run into a considerable amount of money, which, given the inefficiency of compulsory labor, could exceed the cost of having the same work done by hired labor. In 1815 on a manor in

[34] Thaer (1809), I, 64. [35] Quoted in Khromov (1950), 23.
[36] Hodgskin (1820), II, 85; *cf.* Kulischer (1932), 43-44; Lütge (1967), 208-209; Király (1960), 142-143; Andrews (1774), II, 109-110.

the duchy of Wernigerode in north central Germany, the value of the share of the harvest given to workers doing obligatory labor amounted to 801 talers. Hired labor could have done the same work for 367 talers in wages. On another estate in Wernigerode the comparable figures were 395 talers in expenses against 220 talers in wages.[37] Data from the early 1840's for the province of Tula in central Russia showed that an adult serf couple who furnished their own work animals for their labor service, cost the proprietor 288 rubles a year, including the rental value of the holding he provided to the couple. The cost of a hired couple amounted to only 170 rubles a year, including 60 rubles for wages, 40 rubles for board, and 70 rubles for cost and maintenance of the work animals the seignior now provided.[38]

Some of the writings and reports about the inefficiencies and waste of the labor service in various of the servile lands included quantitative comparisons with hired labor. The ratios varied, but usually hovered between two and four to one. That is, the peasant as hired laborer was two to four times more productive in a given period than was the peasant doing his compulsory labor service. Sometimes the difference was much greater. Count Stephen Széchenyi, the Hungarian patriot and reformer, in a book published in 1827, reported that hired workers on a drainage project did thirteen times as much work in a given period as those who were doing compulsory labor.[39]

The transition from compulsory labor services to hired labor sometimes gave quick and spectacular results. Prince A. I. Vasil'chikov found that out of a large property that he owned in the Lithuanian province of Kovno. Each year his serfs provided him with 39,000 days of labor services, half of it with draft animals and half land labor. Of these 39,000 days the peasants spent 36,000 in work on the prince's demesne of 665 desiatins (ca. 1,800 acres), or an average of 54 days per desiatin. The remaining 3,000 days were given to other labors. In 1857 Vasil'chikov transferred his serfs from labor to cash dues, introduced improved field systems, hired labor, and purchased his own work animals and farm implements. In the first year of the new method of operation, gross income from the property (34,502 rubles) was nearly 2,300 rubles more than the average of the immediately preceding years, despite the outlay for animals and equipment. The hired workers (most if not all of whom were the same people who had paid labor dues to Vasil'chikov) spent a total of 20,000 days to do the work that had taken 39,000 days of compulsory labor dues. Instead of 36,000 days needed to work the prince's demesne, the hired hands needed only 18,000 days, or an average of 27 days per desiatin. Moreover, the work was done not only

[37] Lütge (1957), 164.   [38] Zablotskii-Desiatovskii (1882), IV, 281.
[39] Germany: Thaer (1809), I, 66; Boelcke (1957), 254-255; Stein (1918), I, 361; Meyer (1965), 48n. Austria: André (1846), 130-136; Kodedová (1967), 125. White Russia: Ulashchik (1961), 183; Fridman (1958), 17. Estonia: Loone (1959), 204. Denmark: Count Christian von Rantzau quoted in Conze (1957), Russia: Zablotskii-Desiatovskii (1882), IV, 283-284.

more rapidly, but also more effectively. Yields of winter and spring grain increased by nearly 20 per cent, hay and straw by 9.7 per cent, and the cash value of all products rose by 16.7 per cent.[40]

Despite such benefits, most proprietors who engaged in direct production continued to rely primarily on labor dues. However, the numbers of those who decided to commute part or all of the labor dues grew steadily. The increase in population helped to persuade them to make the change. The rise in the number of peasants with holdings too small to support a family and of entirely landless peasants provided a pool of cheap hired labor. Improvements in techniques also contributed to the greater use of hired labor. The level of productivity of hired workers had to exceed their wages by a substantial margin before a proprietor would be willing, or could afford, to hire them. Improved methods provided increased yields, but they demanded more care and greater efficiency than seigniors could expect from their compulsory laborers. That was why progressive landowners were among the leaders in the employment of wage labor. The different use made of forced and hired workers was illustrated by practices at Postelberg, an estate of over 28,000 acres in Bohemia owned by the Schwarzenberg family. In 1841 the manager of the property reported that demesne land still under the three-field system was worked by peasants doing their labor service. Those fields on which crop rotation had been introduced were tilled only by hired labors.[41]

Seigniors in East Prussia seemed to have been especially active in the commutation of labor dues and the employment of hired workers. As late as 1760 by far the greatest number of the Junker landowners there depended upon the labor obligation for all or nearly all of their labor requirements. The expansion of the market and the opportunity to profit from it, and the inefficiency of forced labor, persuaded proprietors to turn to hired labor. By 1806, on the eve of the first Prussian emancipation decree, nearly every Junker estate in East Prussia had gone far in the conversion of labor dues into money payments, and employed hired workers. In Upper Lusatia in Saxony commutation became general after 1800. In Brandenburg the bourgeois lessees of royal estates commuted labor services from the 1770's, and made increased use of hired workers, with resulting increases in productivity.[42]

In Russia the use of hired labor seems to have been much more a matter of compulsion than of choice. Landowners in New Russia, on the shores of the Black Sea, made the most extensive use of wage workers. The rapid development of that thinly populated region during the first half of the nineteenth century as a major grain producer created a demand for labor that the indigenous serf population could not satisfy. Nearly all of the adult

[40] Ulashchik (1961), 182-183.   [41] Blum (1948), 167-170.
[42] Stein (1918), I, 358-361; Boelcke (1957), 254-255; Müller (1965), 183-185.

male serfs there had to render labor dues, but their services met only an estimated one-half to one-third of the labor need of the seigniors. The proprietors had to hire wage workers, most of whom were migrants from the more densely populated central provinces of the empire. They came by the tens and hundreds of thousands, drawn by the relatively high wages and good food that the proprietors of New Russia had to supply to attract labor. Many came only for haying and harvest, but a large number arrived in early spring and worked throughout the growing season. In other parts of Russia merchants who owned land were employers of hired labor. An imperial decree of 1801 had allowed any free Russian subject to own land on which no serfs lived. Some merchants had taken advantage of the law to set up sizable farming operations. Since only nobles could own serfs, the merchants had to use hired labor, or sharecroppers, or rented serfs from other owners. The rented serfs performed the unpaid labor dues they owed to their lord on the land of the merchant, who paid the serfowner for the use of his peasants.

In a report to the government in 1849-1850, Iurii F. Samarin said that the introduction of sugar-beet cultivation in the Ukraine had created a need there for hired labor. This was because the speed required to process the beets (their sugar content declined the longer they remained out of the ground) demanded more labor than the serfs of the proprietors could furnish. Scattered reports from other parts of Russia indicated that a few progressive proprietors replaced labor services with hired workers. The Lithuanian province of Kovno seems to have been one region where hired labor was used extensively. Special circumstances helped to explain this. Kovno had an unusually large number of landless peasants, amounting to 22 per cent of the peasant population in the 1850's, and it also had a large number of progressive proprietors.[43]

The amount of money that seigniors agreed to accept in lieu of labor services provides telling witness to the low opinion proprietors had of this obligation. In provinces of Austria in the 1830's and 1840's the commutation rate paid by peasants for labor dues with a team often was less than the lowest wage paid to hired workers (who did not supply draft animals). The lowest wage paid hired labor was sometimes several times greater than the commutation rate charged by seigniors for labor services without a team. In Germany toward the end of the eighteenth century, labor services were commuted at half or less of their nominal value.[44]

The realization by seigniors of the inefficiency of the labor obligation was by far the principal reason for their willingness to commute the labor service. A contributing factor was the increase in the amount of money in circu-

[43] Semevskii (1888), II, 509; Pazhitnov (1940), 239-240; Blum (1961), 362, 401; Akademiia Nauk SSSR (1959), II, 34; Kulischer (1932), 49; Emmons (1968), 81; Ulashchik (1961), 173ff., 183-184.
[44] Blum (1948), 201; Henning (1969b), 168.

lation. World production of precious metals rose sharply during the course of the eighteenth century. For the first seven decades much of the new bullion came from the gold fields of Brazil. When that source began to taper off from 1764, the slack was taken up by a rise in the output of Mexican silver. Much of these new stocks of precious metals found their way to Europe. A contemporary German economist in 1805 calculated that the money supply had been growing by about 1.5 per cent per year. In addition, some governments issued paper currency, further swelling the circulating medium. The greater quantity of money and the economic expansion that began around the middle of the eighteenth century drew more and more peasants into the cash nexus. That enabled them to get the money needed to commute labor services into cash payments. And proprietors, whose own need for cash kept pace with the rise in the seigniorial standard of living, were quite willing to commute. Not only labor services were redeemed as money became more plentiful; dues in kind were also transformed into cash payments. Even in Russia many of the large proprietors in the central provinces, the principal agricultural region of the empire, where nearly half of the empire's serfs lived, drastically reduced or abandoned the labor obligation in favor of money quitrents. The expansion of the money economy made it easier for the serfs to accumulate cash, either through sale of their own produce, or through earnings as migrant workers or traveling artisans.[45]

Many peasants, however, and in eastern Europe probably the majority, lived out their lives barely touched by the money economy, so that cash payments would not have been possible for them. Even in lands where the money economy was relatively well developed, peasants were sometimes unable or reluctant to commute their obligations. Like poor people everywhere they had a chronic shortage of cash and a surplus of labor. It was much easier for them to supply the labor, whether their own or that of their children, than to pay dues in money. And they did not want to give up the meals and the forage and the wages and the shares of the crop that the seigniors had to provide when they paid their obligation in labor.[46]

The conversion of labor services into money payments did not necessarily imply that the seignior planned to use hired labor and continue his demesne operations. Proprietors often abandoned or reduced cultivation on their own account when they commuted the labor dues. They took this opportunity to turn over all or much of their demesnes to their peasants. They thereby saved themselves the expenses and troubles of direct production and, in some instances, found that they drew greater revenues from their properties than they had when they demanded labor dues.[47]

[45] Sombart (1928), I, pt. 2, 533-534; Abel (1966), 186; Blum (1961), 392-400.
[46] Lütge (1957), 159-166; Liebel (1965), 42; Rostworowski (1896), 15; Kieniewicz (1969), 99.
[47] Transehe-Roseneck (1890), 183-184n.; Müller (1964), 642-647; Kieniewicz (1969), 98;

III

The commutation of the labor obligation did not alter the structure of the lord-peasant relationship. It merely represented a shift in the obligations required of the affected peasants. There were, however, seigniors who of their own volition initiated reforms that altered to a greater or lesser degree the traditional order on their properties. Among these proprietors were a handful of French seigniors who renounced some of their privileges, either commuting them or giving them up without compensation. On occasion it was a minor concession, such as happened at Sablé, an estate in Maine, where the peasants were allowed to use the seignior's bake ovens without charge. In another seigniory the lord did not collect the *champart*, the payment in kind required of the peasants, from 1763 to 1787. The duchess of Beauvilliers abolished all of the seigniorial monopolies in her barony of Sonnois. Between 1770 and 1779, 13 seigniors in Franche-Comté voluntarily freed their *mainmortable* peasants.[48]

Proprietors in Schleswig-Holstein were particularly active in the introduction of major reforms in their manors. Indeed, the first known instance of the voluntary abolition of serfdom in north central Europe reputedly occurred in Holstein in 1688. That was when Count Christopher von Rantzau, member of one of the most prominent families of the region, freed all of the peasants on his estates. He did this, he said, because serfdom was not authorized in the Scriptures, and because it was contrary to God's command, as well as contrary to reason and nature, for a Christian to have so much power over his fellow Christians. The peasants were destined to enjoy their freedom for only a few years. In 1695 a new owner took over the properties and not too many years later the villagers were serfs once again. In 1704 another proprietor, one von Ahlfeld, emancipated his peasants. They remained free. In 1739 Count Hans von Rantzau freed the serfs at Ascheberg, his estate in Holstein. In 1766 he published a pamphlet in which he spelled out his motives for the reform and described its results. He explained that the poor living conditions and the low morale of the Ascheberg serfs had a damaging impact upon the productivity of the manor. After long consideration he decided to try to awaken the initiative of the peasants by giving them hereditary leaseholds at a fair rental, and cancelling all their servile obligations to him. He began the experiment on an inferior piece of land, and within five years met with such success that he decided to extend the experiment. Now, after twenty-seven years, the results had far exceeded his original hopes. Ascheberg's population had increased, and the attitude, welfare, and morale of the peasants had vastly

---

Leskiewicz (1959), 156-157; Paget (1839), I, 292-293n.; Hlubek (1860), 118-119; Indova (1955), 29-30; Sivkov (1951), 132-133.
[48] La Monneraye (1922), 128; Millot (1937), 128-132.

improved. And, despite his large capital outlay for new homes and other improvements, his income from the property had increased considerably and the property's value was much enhanced.[49]

Rantzau's pamphlet had a wide circulation (including a reprinting in Russia) and helped persuade other proprietors to follow his example. By 1797, when the Danish government announced that all serfs in Schleswig-Holstein would be freed in 1804, proprietors in Schleswig had voluntarily abolished serfdom on 27 estates. On 25 of these properties the freed peasants received land on hereditary leases or as their full property. Fewer lords in Holstein emancipated their serfs, but from 1791 on many of them abandoned labor dues in favor of quitrents. In contrast, in Denmark voluntary emancipations had been exceptional before the royal decree of 1788 freed all serfs there. The first among the few who did emancipate voluntarily was Count J.H.E. Bernstorff, great proprietor and long-time foreign minister. In 1767 he ended serfdom on an estate he owned near Copenhagen and leased the land to the freed peasants. In 1764 the manor had 77 serf households, and Bernstorff lost money on the operation. By 1783 there were 113 households, all free, whose rents provided the owner with 17,672 talers more per year than Bernstorff had received 19 years ealier. When Thomas Malthus was in Denmark in 1799 he was told that when Bernstorff informed his peasants that he intended to free them they begged to remain serfs. Bernstorff told them to try freedom for five years and if they still wanted to return to serfdom they would have their wish. When the five years elapsed, they gladly chose freedom. They said, according to the story, that they did not at first know the value of liberty, and that they were going to build a monument to Bernstorff to memorialize his wisdom and benevolence and their own gratitude. The monument, erected in 1783, was a pillar of marble, with suitable agricultural ornamentation and inscriptions.[50]

In other servile lands, too, a scant few proprietors freed their serfs. Sometimes they did this because their ownership of serfs clashed with their liberal principles. Thus Ion Câmpineanu, a founder of the Philharmonic Society in the Danubian Principalities, and a man who urged freedom for the peasants, decided in 1837 to practice what he preached, and freed his peasants from their servile obligations to him. When A. M. Unkovskii, leader of the liberal nobility in the Russian province of Tver, inherited his estate in 1852 his first act was to offer freedom to his household serfs. To his great surprise only a few accepted his offer. Other seigniors who freed their peasants were innovating proprietors like F.L.L. von Bredow. In 1797 von Bredow, who pioneered crop rotation in Brandenburg, made the peasants on three of his manors full owners of their holdings and worked

[49] Sugenheim (1861), 516-517.
[50] Hvidtfeldt (1963), 498; Sugenheim (1961), 520, 520n.; Malthus (1966), 63-64.

his own land entirely with hired labor. The much-travelled William Coxe, whose sycophantic manner did not dull the keenness of his observation, reported that in the last decades of the eighteenth century a few Polish magnates "of benevolent hearts and enlightened understanding" had freed their serfs to the profit of both lord and peasant. The freedom, however, was not hereditary, so that the lord or his heirs could return the descendants of the freed peasants to serfdom. In the 1820's Stanislav Staszic, a wealthy lord of eastern Poland, divided his properties among his peasants. His benefaction had been described as a "lonely act of philanthropy."[51]

IV

In all of the servile lands the foes of the traditional order, and even those who wanted only limited changes, had arrayed against them the great and certainly not silent majority of seigniors. These people expressed their opposition to reform clearly and firmly. In France the *parlements* were strong defenders of seigniorial privilege, and, indeed, of the entire hierarchic and corporate structure of French society. In 1776 the *parlement* of Paris drew up what has been called a kind of declaration of independence of the noble order. "The first rule of justice," the document declared, "is to preserve for everyone what is due him, a fundamental rule of natural right and of civil government, and one which consists not only in upholding rights of property but in safeguarding rights attached to the person and born of prerogatives of birth and estate." French seigniors rarely consented to give up their rights over their peasants, and the few who did nearly always charged heavy prices for their concessions.[52]

In Poland the diets of the 1760's, the 1770's, and 1780's rejected the mildest kind of reform proposals. "The generality of Polish nobles," wrote William Coxe in the 1780's, "are not inclined either to establish or give efficacy to any regulations in favor of the peasantry, whom they scarcely consider entitled to the common rights of humanity." When the French invaders created the grand duchy of Warsaw in 1807 the Polish lords had to accept Napoleon's abolition of serfdom. But they did not like it, even though the so-called free peasants were nearly as dependent upon the seigniors as they had been before the emancipation. They made their dissatisfaction clear soon after the Russian annexation of the grand duchy in 1815. Prince Adam Czartoryski, Tsar Alexander's chief advisor on Polish affairs, sent out a detailed questionnaire to local officials, all of whom were nobles, and to a number of proprietors, to find out how they felt about the Napoleonic emancipation. Almost to a man the respondents favored the

[51] Emerit (1937), 248; Emmons (1968), 79-80; Müller (1967), 129; Coxe (1802), I, 195-200; Kieniewicz (1969), 74.

[52] Palmer (1959), I, 450-452; Cobban (1950), 71-72; Roupnel (1922), 237-238; Aulard (1919), 17-36.

16.   Lesser Polish nobles with their patron, a magnate, late 18th century. Painting by J.-P. Norblin, 1745-1830. (*Sejmiki w rysunkach J.-P. Norblina*, Warsaw, 1958.)

withdrawal, or at least the limitation, of the personal liberty now possessed by the peasant, and they strongly supported the compulsory labor still required of the peasants. The few liberal respondents accepted the terms of the Napoleonic legislation, but wanted freedom from state interference in their relations with their peasants.[53]

In the Austrian Monarchy the displeasure of the nobility with the re-

[53] Coxe (1802), I, 195; Leslie (1956), 66-67; Kieniewicz (1969), 73.

forms of Maria Theresa and Joseph II reached its climax when Joseph issued his revolutionary decree of 10 February 1789. As earlier pages have pointed out, that law brought the empire to the brink of dissolution. Nobles everywhere in the Monarchy received the news of the decree with dismay, their assemblies issued statements expressing their outrage, and in Galicia and Hungary there was open talk of revolt. The protest was so powerful, and the threat to the continued existence of the state so real, that the decree had to be repealed soon after Joseph's death in February 1790.[54]

In Prussian Silesia a circular sent out by the government on 25 February 1799 provided a vehicle for the expression of seigniorial opinion there. The circular went to the forty-eight district commissioners (*Landräte*) in the province, with instructions to sound out the opinions of proprietors in their districts about the commutation of labor services. Silesia had only recently experienced serious peasant disturbances that had left a legacy of rural restlessness and uncertainty about the future of the lord-peasant relationship. Despite this, more than two-thirds of the commissioners in their reports, which mirrored the views of the proprietors in their respective districts, opposed the commutation of labor services. Even the minority of the reports that were not against the reform contained suggestions to restrict commutation to certain labor services, such as carting, or to allow commutation of part of the obligation, so that the peasant would work fewer days per week for his lord.[55]

The dimensions of the opposition of Russian proprietors to reform made themselves evident when Alexander II let it be known that he planned to free the serfs. In December 1857 Senator I. A. Solov'ev drew up a survey of the reaction of the nobility to a statement of the tsar's intentions that had been made public in November. Solov'ev gathered his data from reports sent in to St. Petersburg by marshals of the provincial nobility, and by governors of the provinces. Their reports made it eminently clear that the vast majority of Russian seigniors opposed the reform. From every side came expressions of dismay and dire warnings of the difficulties and dangers to the common weal and domestic tranquility if the reform was implemented. The only reaction that was not entirely unfavorable came from two provinces of Little Russia. The proprietors there declared their opposition to the reform but allowed that they understood the need for it. Nor was the virtually unanimous hostility restricted to the provincial nobility. Members of the highest circles of the court and the bureaucracy were against it, too, and expressed their fears for the future and their unhappiness with the ingratitude of the throne to the nobility, its strongest support.[56]

Proprietors in the Danubian Principalities exhibited a similar intransigence when confronted with the threat of reform of the lord-peasant rela-

---

[54] Blum (1948), 56-59.   [55] Ziekursch (1927), 255-259.
[56] Solov'ev (1881), xxx, 744-754; Starr (1972), 194; Kornilov (1905), 124.

tionship. The Treaty of Paris in 1856, which ended the Russian domination of the Principalities, had placed them under the joint guarantee of the contracting powers, with the understanding that their future status would be determined at a later date. In 1857, at the direction of the powers, the Turkish sultan, still the nominal sovereign of the Principalities, ordered the convocation of assemblies in each principality "representing the interests of all the social classes," to ascertain the wishes of the people themselves. The Moldavian assembly, which met at Jassy, included 70 boyar, 8 clerical, and 15 peasant delegates. The boyars refused even to consider the possibility of agrarian reform and would not allow it to be put on the agenda. When peasant delegates brought up the topic, the boyars and their clerical confederates denounced the proposals as "communistic." The Wallachian assembly did not discuss any internal reform.[57]

No matter what the country, the arguments of the defenders of the hierarchical society clustered around a few themes. They repeatedly stressed what they believed to be the natural superiority of noblemen to ordinary mortals. They portrayed their order as free of the vulgarity and materialism of the emerging plutocracy, and as the preserve of the true values of the society. They spoke of the patriarchal character of their relationship with their peasants and their concern for the well-being of the people who were dependent upon them, and they claimed that only under their aegis could the peasant be a useful member of society.[58] They emphasized the importance of the nobility as the guarantors of the continued existence of the state. Hue de Miromesnil, first president of the *parlement* of Paris and long-time minister of Louis XVI, explained that the French nation was "naturally bellicose," and that the nobility, who devoted themselves to the profession of arms, provided the state with that most vital and always necessary service. "Take away its distinctions from the nobility, and you will destroy the national character, and the nation, ceasing to be warlike will soon be the prey of neighboring nations." Others, too, dilated on the theme of France's dependence upon its armed forces, and therefore upon its nobility, for national survival.[59] The *parlement* of Paris, in its declaration of 1776, identified privilege with the will of God, explaining that the hierarchical order of society "takes its source in divine institutions; infinite and immutable wisdom in the plan of the Universe has made an unequal dispensation of powers and genius. . . ."[60]

Another constant was simply the fear of change—of almost any change. That fear clearly underlay much of the opposition to reform. It was fear of the unknown, or fear of a future in which nobles no longer had the protec-

[57] Mitrany (1930), 45-46.
[58] Karamzin (1959), 166-167; Andrian-Werburg (1843), pt. 1, 26-36 and *passim*; Fuchs (1888), 193; Epstein (1966), 188, 192, 204; Knapp (1887), II, 30; Ziekursch (1927), 258.
[59] Turgot (1923), v, 189, 190; Mackrell (1973), 85-90.
[60] Quoted in Palmer (1959), I, 451.

tion of privilege. That dread evidenced itself most frequently in the concern seigniors expressed about the threat that emancipation would present to the entire society. They believed, or professed to believe, that the very fabric of the social order would be imperiled if the peasants were given their freedom and full civil rights. Ove Höegh-Guldberg, leader of the coup against Struensee, prophesied that "the yoke of the peasant could not be removed without Denmark shaking and quivering to its foundations." Most of his peers in all of the servile lands would have said the same thing of their own lands. Armed with the conviction of the natural inferiority of the peasant, contemptuous of his sloth, of his lack of self-respect and motivation, and certain that he lacked the innate ability to improve himself, they foresaw certain catastrophe if the restraining hand of the seignior was removed. The freed peasant, they said, would spend his days drinking and loafing, or would leave the village for the more exciting life of the city, or would take to begging and vagabondage to escape work. The fields would lie untilled, the economy would stagnate, the state's revenues and its authority would shrink, and misery, disorder, and violence would stalk the land. Dreams of equality could bring only despair and disaster.[61]

Opponents of reform often charged that changes in the relationship between lord and peasant legislated by the government against the wishes of the seigniors was an invasion of the right of private property. In their view their privileges and their authority over their peasants constituted an integral part of their property. Lawyers and commentators on the law supported that position. They warned that a violation of seigniorial prerogatives by state action would serve as a precedent for the violation of other kinds of property.[62]

More immediate and pressing concerns also troubled defenders of the status quo. Seigniors who depended upon the labor dues of their peasants to till their demesnes were fearful that they would not be able to afford hired labor. This was especially true in less fertile regions, where the proprietors believed that hired workers would not produce enough to cover their costs. Seigniors claimed, too, that many of them lacked the capital to buy animals and equipment (provided by peasants as part of their labor obligation) and in addition pay wages. Another worry was that the available supply of wage workers in their neighborhoods would not meet their demands, especially if the freed peasants spent their time loafing or fled the land for the cities. Some recognized the economic advantages of hired labor, but supported the retention of labor dues as a way to discipline the peasants, to ensure that they would be productive, and to maintain domestic order.[63] Finally, there

[61] Solov'ev (1881), xxx, 752, 754; Karamzin (1959), 165-166; Knapp (1887), ii, 31; Ziekursch (1927), 258; Epstein (1966), 205-207.
[62] Carré (1912), 20; Epstein (1966), 206-207; Mackrell (1973), 56-59; Gitermann (1941), 366.
[63] Eggert (1965), 30; Lütge (1957), 158; Kulischer (1932), 46; Blum (1961), 573-574.

were those who were perfectly content with their way of life, and assumed that all was right with the world. They were of that large band of proprietors who lacked interest in, or understanding of, the rational operations of their properties. They were the men who shut their eyes to improvements that could increase their incomes. They could see neither rhyme nor reason for reforms or for innovations. They were like the proprietor of Tambov in central Russia, who in 1858 explained why he saw no point in purchasing a threshing machine. "If all the grain is threshed in autumn," he asked, "what will the peasant and his wife do in winter? Threshing machines cost money, need repairs, and require horses who have to be maintained, while the work of the peasant costs nothing."[64]

[64] Quoted in Zaionchkovskii (1968), 12.

CHAPTER 15

Peasant Unrest

I

RURAL unrest was as old as the servile order itself. Indeed, it was an integral part of that order, as inseparable from it as labor unrest is inseparable from the modern industrial order. Records of the ninth century tell of struggles of peasants with their seigniors over the right to use forest and pasture, and the thirteenth century churchman and historian, Jacques de Vitry, exclaimed "How many serfs have killed their lords and burned their castles!"[1] Actually, violence was nearly always the peasants' last resort. Refusal to perform labor services or to pay dues and taxes, purposefully neglectful fulfillment of their obligations, petitions to the sovereign, flight, and lawsuits, all were far more common ways by which they expressed their discontent.

Rural resistance to the impositions and demands of lord, state, and church in central and western Europe seemed to have peaked in the sixteenth and first half of the seventeenth centuries. The defeats suffered by the peasants in their risings in France, Germany, Austria, Switzerland, Bohemia, and Hungary, the sometimes barbarous punishments visited upon the vanquished rebels, and the strengthening of the alliance between throne and seignior to keep the peasant in subjection, all conspired to inhibit large-scale outbreaks in these lands in later years. This has led some to conclude that the spirit of the peasants had been broken, so that now they accepted their servility without protest.[2]

This passivity, this "dull resignation," as one writer called it, seems to have been a surface phenomenon. The peasants had not abandoned their struggle. They still resisted excessive exploitation and unfair treatment and injustices, though they resorted less frequently than in past centuries to mass rebellions. Indeed, men of the upper orders believed that rural unrest had intensified. Saxon nobles at meetings of the estates in the 1750's and 1760's remarked upon and deplored the increased intractability of their peasants. At the session in 1766 a memorandum presented by twenty-seven seigniors asserted that "although for some time there had been complaints about the disobedience and stubbornness of the peasants, the occasion for these complaints has never been so general and so important as is now. There are, indeed, few noblemen . . . who in recent years have not had to experience some of the effects of this, and right now many localities are in such distress that if this evil . . . is not remedied . . . the entire coun-

---

[1] Bloch (1966), 169; Bloch (1966a), 283.
[2] Cf. Holborn (1959), 63; Lütge (1967), 159; Link (1949), 13.

try stands in peril of indescribable damage and loss."[3] In a letter to a local newspaper in July 1806, a Silesian landowner wrote that "Only in the songs of our poets do we read the charming descriptions of peace, simplicity, diligence, love of order, and mutual trust among people who live out in the country. When we open the great book of real life we find entirely different descriptions."[4] Hippolyte Taine once hazarded the opinion that if one tried to count all the disturbances that took place in France during the eighteenth century the work would never end.[5] No one has attempted to test this hypothesis for France, but the investigations of Soviet historians seem to have proved its validity for Russia. They have been so indefatigable in their search for instances of rural unrest that one of their fellow-scholars has charged that they seek to turn up disturbances on the principle that the more the number of risings, the more the value of the research.[6] If we fully discount their zeal (which has led them to count even simple cases of trespass as disturbances), their work shows clearly the rise in the incidence of unrest in the first half of the nineteenth century. Between 1826 and 1849 Soviet scholars found 1,904 disturbances, with troops called out 381 times to restore order. Between 1857 and 1861 they counted 3,882 disturbances and 903 instances of the use of troops.[7] The demand for more detailed information made in the 1850's by the Ministry of the Interior explained part of the increase. Minor and hitherto unreported disturbances now appeared in the records. More important, the Crimean War precipitated a great new wave of unrest that swept across the empire. The actions of many proprietors also helped to swell the number. These seigniors, anticipating the emancipation and the accompanying partition of land between lord and peasant, converted serf-held land into demesne and moved serfs from good to inferior land, so that the lords could keep as much of the good land for themselves when emancipation came. Understandably, this angered the peasants and led to increased unrest.[8]

In every land the outbreaks were nearly always spontaneous and disorganized. A trivial incident or a rumor was enough to set off a disturbance. And as had been true of nearly all of the rural unrest in past centuries, the peasants continued to direct their protests against specific grievances, and not against the hierarchical society that held them in their condition of servility. Their risings, with only rare exceptions, did not embrace revolutionary goals, nor did the rebels ever offer a worked-out program of social and political reform. Whatever the reasons—whether it was the lowly status of the peasants, their self-deprecation, their ignorance, the weight of tradition, the conservative influence of religion (Otto Hintze called

---

[3] Stulz and Opitz (1956), 41.
[4] Ziekursch (1927), 277.
[5] Quoted in Kareev (1899), 242.
[6] Zaionchkovskii (1968), 41-42.
[7] *Krest'ianskoe dvizhenie* (1961), 817; *Krest'ianskoe dvizhenie* (1963), 731.
[8] Volin (1970), 27.

17. Peasant, pope, and emperor.

      Pope: "I with my teaching have converted many thousands."

Emperor: "And I with my power have acquired many provinces and people."

   Peasant: "O, God! If Thou wouldst not will it, and I would do naught, you two would have nothing to eat."

(K. Dinklage, *Geschichte der kärtner Landwirtschaft*, Klagenfurt, 1966.)

Lutheranism "a useful instrument for the domestication of the [German] peasant")[9]—peasant movements lacked ideological content.

The myth of the benevolent sovereign was another striking characteristic of peasant unrest. Time and again peasants by word and deed showed that they believed that the ruler was on their side against the seigniors and approved of their resistance. They were certain that the sovereign wanted to protect them, and even free them from their burdensome obligations. They were equally certain that his wishes were thwarted and his proclamations concealed by an unholy alliance of seigniors, bureaucrats, and lawyers.[10] This faith in the sovereign—a Polish historian has described it as "naive monarchism"[11]—must have proceeded, in part at least, from the need man has for hope. The peasants had no one else to whom they could appeal for aid and protection against their lords. Their trust must have been reinforced by the efforts of some rulers in the last century of the old order to improve the condition of the peasantry, though these rulers were adamantly opposed to the peasants' taking matters into their own hands. It has been suggested, too, that the faith in the prince was an aspect of the peasants' own reactionary *Weltanschaung*. They wanted him to turn back the clock to the "old law," the mythical good old days when lords and peasants had lived in amity and understanding.[12] They sent petitions to the monarch, even though in some lands the laws ordered severe penalties for those whose petitions were deemed "unfounded." When the sovereign journeyed through his realm, they lined the roads and pressed their petitions upon him as he rode by. Joseph II came back from a visit to Transylvania with nearly 19,000 of these documents. They sent delegations who sometimes walked hundreds of miles to the royal court to ask for an audience at which they could plead for redress against their oppressors. And when they resorted to disobedience or to violence they often insisted that their purpose was to force the seigniors to carry out the will of the monarch.[13]

The leadership in peasant disturbances came often, and not surprisingly, from the upper ranks of the social hierarchy of the village. They were the men who had the respect of their fellows. Generally, they were the wealthier people of the community. Village officials, too, or schoolmasters, or parish priests emerged as the commanding figures. Sometimes townsmen acted as the instigators and directors. And there were instances as in places in Hungary in 1790, when lesser nobles, burdened with many

---

[9] Quoted in Franz (1970a), 192; *cf.* Mousnier (1972), 343 on the repressive influence of Catholicism on the French peasant.

[10] Rozdolski (1961), 135-136; Czybulka (1949), 83; Lefebvre (1973), 38; Kieniewicz (1969), 125; Stulz and Opitz (1956), 74-75; Solov'ev (xxx) (1881), 747.

[11] Bobińska (1970), 155.   [12] Scheibert (1973), 116.

[13] Fridman (1958), 50, 54; Boelcke (1957), 230; Revesz (1964), 2; Grüll (1963), 10-11, 361-362; Hovde (1948), 204; Hitchens (1969), 35.

of the obligations demanded of their peasant neighbors, took over the leadership in rural protests.[14]

Specific misdeeds or injustices of a seignior, or his demand for increased or new obligations or services, provided the spark that kindled most instances of peasant unrest. Disputes often erupted, too, over pasturage. The new interest of nobles in wool production, and the rise in peasant population, which put increased pressure on land resources, aggravated this old source of trouble. To ensure maximum pasturage for their flocks, landowners in Saxony limited the number of sheep their peasants could own, and placed restrictions on plowing fallow fields, on use by peasants of commons and wastes, and even on their ownership of livestock other than sheep. These actions galled the peasants and led to unrest.[15] In 1834 villagers of four neighboring manors in Lower Austria decided that they had had enough, and forcibly drove the seigniorial flocks from their fallow fields and pastures. Troops had to be called in to restore order.[16]

The exactions and corruption of estate officials and their harsh treatment of villagers sometimes produced disorders.[17] The administration of seigniorial justice often roused hostilities, too. In 1789 in France many peasant *cahiers* complained of the inefficiencies and injustices of the lord's court (though a few actually asked for the retention of seigniorial courts because of their convenience, and their firsthand knowledge of the local situation.)[18]

Among the seigniorial monopolies none seemed to have aroused so much antipathy and active opposition as the hunting privilege. Peasants were angered by the damage game and hunters did to their crops, and by the inadequate compensation or lack of any compensation paid them for the damages. They resented, too, the restrictions sometimes imposed by seigniors on plowing and cultivating fields to protect nesting game birds, and they objected to the requirement to provide the hunters with labor services that included setting nets, serving as beaters, and carrying the game. Every once in a while the abuses became so unbearable that the peasants resorted to wholesale slaughter of the game in the fields and neighboring forests.[19] Attempts of seigniors to introduce new crops or new techniques could provoke serious unrest, too. In part this must have been the irrational reaction of people who suspected and resisted innovations because they had not been confirmed by tradition. In part, however, the opposition came from the

[14] Bobińska (1970), 150-153, 156; Leslie (1956), 177-178; Grünberg (1894), I, 216-217; Király (1967), 144-145; Rudé (1961), 325; Herbert (1969), 98; Lefebvre (1973), 95, 98-99; Stulz and Opitz (1956), 57-62, 85-86.

[15] Stulz and Opitz (1956), 25.   [16] Bibl (1911), 111-116.

[17] Brusatti (1958), 509; Confino (1963), 74.

[18] La Monneraye (1922), 34; Herbert (1969), 82-83; Marion (1968), 321.

[19] Knapp (1902), 31-32; Wuttke (1893), 177; Stulz and Opitz (1956), 39, 47-48; Franz (1970a), 183; Louchitsky (1931), 97-99; Lefebvre (1973), 44-45.

awareness derived from past experience that innovations often involved heavier obligations.

Nearly always these outbursts against the actions or demands of seigniors, limited as they were in scope and in the numbers involved, were easily contained. Every once in a while, however, there was an explosion of resentment and protest that engulfed large areas and that involved many thousands of peasants. These mass risings began usually on a small scale, and with the limited aim of restraining seigniorial exactions and impositions. Once in motion, the revolts often adopted wider goals that had social and political implications, and that made the rising a threat to the established order.

That happened in Bohemia in 1775. Long-simmering peasant unrest there had helped to convince the central government of the need to regulate the lord-peasant relationship. The government therefore entered into discussions with the Bohemian manor owners through the medium of their provincial estates. The negotiations dragged on for several years, until a few peasants decided to act on their own account. A revolt broke out on an estate near Königgrätz in January 1775. Instead of the usual quick subsidence, the rising spread rapidly and soon covered a large area. The rebels actually formed their own government, declared that an imperial decree had freed them from their labor obligation, and asserted that the nobles had suppressed the decree. They described themselves as soldiers of Empress Maria Theresa, and said that they fought for that which she had ordered for them. They swept through northern Bohemia, burning and looting, and picking up recruits, some of them by force, as they marched toward Prague. It took 40,000 infantrymen and 4 regiments of cavalry to rout the insurgents. Once the revolt ended, Joseph II, co-ruler with Maria Theresa, ordered leniency. In April the government offered amnesty to all who returned peacefully to their villages, and only a relatively small number received punishment.[20]

Another major rising that began as a protest against seigniorial exactions and privileges erupted in Saxony in 1790. Severe winters, drought, and poor harvests in 1789 and 1790 had brought much hardship and suffering to the villages. A few seigniors, who recognized that the inclement weather had reduced available forage, allowed peasants to graze their animals on land normally reserved for the seignior's livestock. Most proprietors, however, showed no compassion for the tribulations of their people. Indeed, peasants complained that some lords had actually increased their flocks, and so had further reduced the pasture available for the animals of the villagers. The peasants' anger was aggravated by damages inflicted on their already inadequate crops by game that was protected by the hunting monopoly of

[20] Grünberg (1894), I, 202-218.

the seigniors. These depredations served as the immediate cause of the rising. The people of ten communities joined together to demand a thinning out of the game animals, and compensation for the harm they had done. Once the peasants had decided on direct action, they quickly widened the target of their protest to include seigniorial restrictions on the number of animals they could own, the compulsory labor demanded of their children, and the judicial officers of the manor, who, according to the peasants, kept for themselves the fines they levied in the manorial courts.

The actual rising began on 3 August 1790 on a single manor in the most fertile and prosperous part of Saxony. The peasants there refused to perform their labor obligations, refused to appear in the lord's court, and drove his sheep out of their fields. The movement spread immediately to neighboring estates, and by the end of August it had extended to over 5,000 square kilometers in central Saxony, and paralyzed the normal operations of government throughout that region. Not all of the rebels were willing participants in the rising. Some were forced to join by threats of beatings or of having their cottages burned. Entire villages were reported to have confided to their seigniors that they dare not render their obligations for fear of reprisals from fellow peasants. Demands now surfaced among the rebels for the end of all obligations to the seignior, and for the return of land and fees the seigniors had taken from them. A rumor that the sovereign approved of the revolt and planned to abolish all obligations gained universal acceptance. The rebels invaded manor houses and compelled lords to renounce their claims to dues and services, they freed peasant youths who were compulsory laborers, and they sometimes destroyed the manorial documents that recorded their obligations. Events in revolutionary France may have helped feed this tide of social revolution; word of the great happenings there found an echo in some of the tracts and songs of the Saxon rebels.

The rising was put down with remarkably little bloodshed—and with no amelioration in the condition and status of the peasantry. The government exhibited a surprising leniency once its troops had restored order. That happened by early September. No one was sentenced to death, only 158 were imprisoned, and a number of others were pilloried. The rising, however, aroused much concern among the upper orders, not only in Saxony but in neighboring lands, too. They were already badly frightened by what was happening in France, and the Saxon rising intensified their fears. King Frederick William II of Prussia offered military assistance to the Elector of Saxony to help put down the peasants. After the end of the rising, Emperor Leopold II of Austria proposed to the Prussian monarch that they agree to support the Elector with troops "in order to suppress every new symptom of a democratic spirit in Saxony."[21]

[21] Wuttke (1893), 177-180; Haun (1892), 205, 208-212; Stulz and Opitz (1956), 44-48, 50-53, 65-69, 73-78, 86-88, 94-96; Franz (1963), 318-324.

In neighboring Prussian Silesia serious rural unrest persisted for half a century after the end of the Seven Years' War in 1763. The expansion in seigniorial farming operations placed greater demands for services upon the villagers, at the same time that the rise in population increased the number of smallholders and landless peasants. The resentment of German rule by many Polish peasants added an additional destabilizing factor. Small risings, and occasional large ones, became almost the order of the day, though even the largest risings never involved more than a few districts. Despite the use of military force to restore order, and the imposition of harsh punishments, the disturbances continued. They reached peaks in 1766-1768, 1784-1786, 1793-1795, and 1798-1799. The troubles in 1793-1795 proved especially threatening. Events in other lands—Joseph II's reforms, the rising in Saxony in 1790, and the news of the French Revolution—had added fuel to peasant discontent. The usual rumors that the seigniors had suppressed a royal decree that freed the peasants made the rounds of the villages. In addition, peasants now began to make menacing references to the events in France, such as the inhabitants of one village who in 1792 refused to pay their labor obligation, and warned that if troops were used against them "things will go with us as they have gone in France." Risings broke out at the end of 1792 in the southeastern corner of the province and spread rapidly. In the spring of 1793 rural weavers revolted. The War of the First Coalition against revolutionary France had brought restrictions on linen exports and hard times for the weavers. They were soon joined by urban artisans. By early April 1793 a high official reported that 20,000 people were in revolt, and in the following weeks the number grew. The unrest took the form of refusals to pay dues, work stoppages, manhandling of estate officials, threats to seigniors, illegal use of the lords' pastures, and destruction of the fences erected to enclose seigniorial land. Troops quelled the rebellion with relative ease. To avoid embitterment and more trouble, the authorities exhibited a relative leniency in the punishments they meted out. That tactic, however, did not succeed. The next year the promulgation of the new Prussian law code, which went into effect on 1 June 1794, triggered serious unrest in May and June in thirty-four villages in northern Silesia. Again troops were needed to end the disorders. The peasants, once more victim of their faith in the benevolence of the sovereign, confidently expected the new code to contain provisions that would curtail or end their obligations to their seigniors. The government sent copies of the new code to the seigniors for use in the administration of justice on their manors. The peasants believed that the lords conspired with the bureaucrats to conceal the provisions that ordered reform—provisions, of course, that existed only in the imagination of the peasants.[22]

[22] Ziekursch (1927), 229-238, 250; Czybulka (1949), 85; Boelcke (1957), 237-239; Bobińska (1970), 156-157.

The most serious of the revolts that owed their origin to peasant resentment of seigniorial exactions took place in Galicia in February 1846. Polish nationalists, among who were many Galician landowners, planned a revolt to break out on 21 February 1846 in all of what had once been Poland, with the aim of restoring an independent Polish state. To win the support of the peasantry the plotters made promises of rural reform when their cause triumphed. The secret of the revolt was poorly kept. In Russian and Prussian Poland the government crushed the rising even before it got started. Preventive arrests in Galicia almost aborted it there. Their hand forced, the rebel leaders had to give the signal for revolt prematurely. Armed insurrection broke out on 18 February in a dozen or so places and was put down almost immediately, save for Cracow, where the rebels held out for eleven days. Some peasants in upland regions where the villagers had light obligations gave support to the rising. Elsewhere, and especially in the Tarnow district of western Galicia, the peasants seized upon the revolt as the opportunity to even scores with their seigniors. They unleashed a cruel campaign of terror and pillage. They plundered well over 400 manors, and they murdered between 1,100 and 1,200 seigniors and their agents. They represented themselves as defenders of the Austrian emperor against those who had rebelled against him. They did this possibly because they wanted to avoid reprisals once order was restored. It seems more likely that they were indeed loyal to the throne, because they knew that their best hopes for protection against their lords' demands lay with the monarch. The jacquerie lasted until the first days of March, when troops ordered the rampaging peasants to return to their homes. They obeyed, convinced that their loyalty had won them freedom from the obligations they owed to their lords. Instead, military units marched from village to village to compel them to resume their labor services.[23]

II

Peasant unrest did not limit itself to protests against the seigniors. As in past centuries the actions and policies of the state aroused both active and passive discontent. Taxes sometimes brought about mass flight, and sometimes armed resistance.[24] Military conscription, always unpopular, on occasion sparked uprisings.[25] There was endemic unrest among the so-called assigned peasants in Russia. These were state peasants whom the government had assigned to compulsory full-time or seasonal employment in state-owned or privately owned enterprises. Most of these people worked for mining and metallurgical plants in the Urals. They received lower wages than those paid free hired labor, they worked under atrocious condi-

[23] Kieniewicz (1969), 117-123; Blum (1948), 225-227; Leslie (1963), 19-20.
[24] *Cf.* Bratianu (1933), 454; Oţetea (1960), 310; Bibl. (1911), 101.
[25] *Cf.* Schiff (1924), 199; Stulz and Opitz (1956), 36.

tions, their employers accorded them callous and even brutal treatment, and, most important of all, they were in the plants against their will. By the middle decades of the eighteenth century outbreaks and strikes reached serious proportions. Despite fierce reprisals by the authorities, the disturbances continued, and in 1773 many of the assigned peasants threw in with the great revolt led by Emilian Pugachev (discussed later in this chapter). After this frightening episode the government ordered reforms and wage increases. For the next two decades things seemed calm. Then serious troubles broke out again. The government, apparently recognizing that continuation of the existing situation meant inescapable strife, in 1807 freed all but 8 per cent of the assigned state peasants from the requirement to work for the plants in the Urals.

The establishment of military colonies by the Russian government early in the nineteenth century brought on a major rising. Initially, the government had planned to settle regular army units on state-owned land. The soldiers would support themselves, would continue their military training and so be ready for duty, would live with their families and follow the rural life to which they were accustomed, and would have a home and a source of livelihood when they became too old for active service. The project, interrupted by the war with Napoleon, was resumed after the peace. Now, however, in addition to settling regular army units in designated areas of state land, the government transformed all of the state peasants in these areas into military colonists. That meant that until they were forty-five they had to undergo military training and were considered members of the armed forces. Their sons were put into the same category as the sons of the regular soldiers, received military training from an early age, and became full-time soldiers when they reached eighteen. The government provided many benefits to the military colonists to improve their welfare. But these were accompanied by constant surveillance by army officers, harsh military discipline, and time-consuming military training. Discontent and resistance grew, and culminated in a mass rising in the province of Novgorod in the summer of 1831. The revolt was made more bitter by a cholera epidemic and a famine. The government had to employ much force to end the revolt, and inflicted barbarous and sometimes murderous punishments on over 3,000 of the rebels. But the government got the message, and, starting in October 1831, began a gradual liquidation of the military colonies, until by 1857 there were none left. Less serious risings of state peasants were brought on by such governmental actions as increases in obligations, efforts to reduce the size of peasant holdings, conversion of state properties into the manors of members of the royal family, and even (as mentioned earlier) attempts by an agency of the government to require peasants to grow potatoes.[26]

The repeal early in 1790 of Joseph II's decree of 10 February 1789, which

[26] Blum (1961), 308-314, 501-503; *Krest'ianskoe dvizhenie* (1961), 15.

had converted peasant dues and services into a money rental, stirred up serious unrest in many parts of the Monarchy. Prompt action by the government, which had anticipated disorders and made preparations for them, prevented serious trouble, though disturbances did occur in several provinces. In Bohemia the unrest began with the refusal of peasants in several localities to do their labor service. When officials punished the leaders by ordering them into the army, villagers armed with clubs and other primitive weapons stormed manor houses. Troops were called out to handle the rioters, and by late summer the troubles had subsided.[27]

In Hungary the peasants, disappointed in their hopes of immediate benefits from Joseph's reforms, grew increasingly disillusioned. The emperor's death and the repeal of his legislation intensified their dissatisfaction. Open unrest broke out in April 1790 in many parts of the kingdom. Statements that demanded radical reforms circulated through the countryside and stirred up the villagers. Worried by these developments, the central and local governments adopted preventive measures that included the dispatch of troops into some areas, placing other military units on alert, arrest of those suspected of incitement, and a system of passports and of searches of persons going from one village to another. Probably because of these and similar precautions, none of the disturbances grew into large-scale risings.[28]

In the Danubian Principalities the imposition by the Russian government of the Organic Statutes in 1831 worsened the condition of the peasants and aroused their open resistance. The first to rise were Hungarian colonists who had been induced to settle in Moldavia by promises of special privileges. Soon Romanian peasants joined them, and by the end of April there was said to have been 60,000 insurgents. The Russians dispatched Cossack regiments to crush the revolt. They carried out their mission in short order. The four principal rebel leaders were sentenced to the salt mines for ten years, and others received fifty blows of the cudgel.[29]

III

The frictions between peasant and seignior and peasant and state, engendered by the workings of the servile system, were not the only causes of peasant unrest. Exogenous events and circumstances often provided the flash-point. Grain shortages and high prices brought on many risings in France during the eighteenth century. To list only a sampling, there were at least 9 such risings in Normandy between 1725 and 1768. In 1752 peasants in Dauphiné and Auvergne laid siege to the warehouses in which grain was stored. Some years later in Arles, 2,000 armed peasants stormed the

[27] Wangermann (1959), 68-69; Kerner (1932), 284-290; Rozdolski (1961), 134.
[28] Király (1967), 140-156.   [29] Emerit (1937), 88-92; Corfus (1969), 43-44, 67.

town hall and demanded bread. In May 1775 depleted grain stocks, mounting prices, and the threat of famine incited peasants and townsmen alike to riots that convulsed Paris, Versailles, and the surrounding provinces. In other lands, too, hunger and famine goaded countrymen to unrest and violence.[30]

Epidemics sometimes provided another extrinsic cause of rural disturbances. In 1830 and 1831 cholera swept through the towns and villages of eastern Europe and took a frightful toll. In Russia in 1830 out of 68,091 reported cases in 33 provinces, 55 per cent (37,595) died. In 1831, in 48 provinces that reported cholera, 42 per cent (197,069) of 466,457 reported cases died. To check the spread of the epidemic the government imposed quarantines. This set off angry, and then violent, protests by the peasants, who were always suspicious and resentful of authority and innovation, and who, in addition, were badly frightened by the ravages of the disease. State officials were the primary targets of the villagers' opposition and violence, but they quickly added their seigniors, who, like the bureaucrats, represented the political order to the peasants. In some places, as in the south-central provinces of Kursk, Tambov, and Saratov, the disturbances became so serious that for a time the government lost control, and civil war threatened. In Hungary, too, the cholera brought risings in its train. In the summer of 1831 the disease struck down over 500,000 people, half of whom were said to have died. Fears aroused by the epidemic, and rumors that the walls had been poisoned by seigniors, doctors, Catholic priests, and Jews, ignited violent outbreaks. An estimated 45,000 peasants participated in these disturbances, in which they were often joined by petty nobles. The government had to dispatch troops to end the disturbances.[31]

Political happenings could act as the catalyst for peasant resistance to the established order. In Russia the accession of a monarch routinely inspired hope among the peasants that their new tsar would ease their burdens. When Nicholas I succeeded his brother in 1825, peasants, in expectation of the "tsar's mercy," refused to pay their obligations to lord and state. Widespread unrest and disturbances continued on into the next year. Finally, Nicholas had to issue a manifesto on 12 May 1826 in which he denounced as false the rumors that he had freed the villagers from their obligations. He commanded the peasants to cease their unrest and disobedience, and threatened with severe punishments those who did not obey his order.[32]

The reverberations of the French Revolution were felt in many places in rural Europe. However, knowledge of the successes of the French people in the establishment of the principles of freedom and equality did not kindle

[30] Kareev (1899), 242, 243; Rudé (1956), 140-143, 164-179; Rudé (1961), 325-326; Lefebvre (1973), 40; *cf.* Oţetea (1960), 310; *Krest'ianskoe dvizhenie* (1961), 14.
[31] McGrew (1965), 67-68, 98, 121, 154-155; Barany (1968), 228.
[32] *Krest'ianskoe dvizhenie* (1961), 13, 31-48.

widespread rural mass movements. There were outbreaks in Germany and the Austrian Monarchy that were partly influenced by the ideas of the Revolution. The linkage was at best a tenuous one, and the risings were with rare exception of minor significance.[33] The revolutionary ideology did manifest itself strongly in a revolt in the canton of Zurich in 1794-1795. The 10,000 inhabitants of Zurich city ruled over the 200,000 who lived out in the country, who had no political rights and who were not allowed to engage in commerce. The countrymen, of whom over a quarter earned part or all of their livelihoods as spinners and weavers, seized upon the egalitarian doctrines exported by the French. Many of them rose against their urban rulers, whose soldiers finally succeeded in putting down the rising.[34] In any event, the unrest inspired by the French Revolution had its antithesis in peasant risings in defense of the traditional order when the armies of the Revolution and of Napoleon invaded their homelands. That happened in a number of places in Germany and in Austria in the 1790's and 1800's. In Russia the peasants gave their loyal support to the regime's efforts to repulse the invading forces of Napoleon, and joined in the guerrilla campaign that harried the Corsican's troops in their calamitous retreat from Moscow. A sense of national identity among these peasants, and of loyalty to their sovereign, apparently prevailed over the hopes that a French conquest would bring freedom.[35]

Ethnic, national, and religious rivalries sometimes ignited rural unrest. One of the bloodiest of all peasant risings rose out of this kind of hatred. It took place in 1768 in the Ukrainian frontier of the still independent Polish Commonwealth. The Ukrainian peasants, who were of the Orthodox faith, bore a deep animosity against their Polish Catholic lords. They resented, too, the proselytising efforts of the Uniate rite which recognized the primacy of the Roman pope, and they harbored a centuries-old hatred of the Jews. The outbreak of civil war in 1768 between the Polish government and the Confederation of Bar gave the peasants the opportunity to revolt. The Confederation of Bar (a town in Podolia) was formed by Polish seigniors who opposed Russia's dominant influence in the Polish government. Stanislaus Poniatowski, one-time lover of Catherine II of Russia, who with her support had been elected king of Poland in 1764, called for Russian aid to crush the Confederation. When the Russian troops arrived in the Ukraine, the people believed that the soldiers, who were fellow Orthodox Christians, had come to free them from Catholic Poland. Rumors spread that Catherine had issued proclamations to this effect, and a bogus so-called "Golden Charter" appeared, ordering the extermination of Poles and Jews. Led by the Zaporozhian Cossacks who roamed the Ukrainian steppes, and joined by bandit groups, the rebels swept through town and country in the

[33] Franz (1970a), 242-243; Fuchs (1888), 189; Czybulka (1949), 85; Wangermann (1959), 32-33; Lütge (1957), 156.
[34] Franz (1970a), 244.   [35] Franz (1970a), 251-255; Tarlé (1942), 255-260, 267-268.

provinces of Podolia and Kiev. Their worst excesses took place in the town of Uman in Podolia, where many thousands had taken refuge. In their blood-lust the rebels killed a reported 30,000 people there—landowners and their families and employees, petty gentry, and Jews. Meanwhile the Confederation had gone down in defeat (though its remnants survived for several more years). The Poles now asked the Russians for help in the suppression of the Ukrainian peasants. Catherine issued a proclamation in which she denounced as forgeries the proclamations and the Golden Charter issued by the rebels. She ordered her troops to put down the rebellion, which they proceeded to do with little difficulty.[36] In White Russia, too, where most of the lords were Polish and Catholic and the peasants were White Russians and Orthodox, ethnic and religious intolerance underlay much of the rural unrest.[37]

Nationalism set off the largest peasant rising in the history of the Danubian Principalities, though the nationalist goals were quickly embellished with demands for social reform. The revolt's leader, Tudor (Theodore) Vladimirescu, the son of a prosperous free peasant, had risen to the status of a minor boyar. He fought for the Russians in their war against Turkey, which began in 1806, and had been awarded the Order of St. Vladimir— that was why his compatriots called him Vladimirescu. Tudor, who opposed the domination of Christians by Turks, associated himself with Greeks who wanted to overthrow Turkish rule in their Greek homeland. The Greeks, who dominated the political and cultural life in the principalities, planned to start their revolt for Greek independence there. They reasoned that a general insurrection in the principalities would attract Turkish forces, and so make it easier for the Greeks to rebel in Greece. Tudor agreed to start the insurrection, and on 18-19 January 1821 he began his revolt at the head of a troop of mercenaries. He issued a call to arms to the peasants, and promised rural reforms. Tudor, whose Greek backers included men who owned estates in the principalities, urged the peasants who rallied to his cause to destroy no property except those of the "tyrant boyars," by which he meant proprietors who did not support the rising. His followers, however, made no distinctions, and burned and looted indiscriminately. Meanwhile the Greek revolt, led by Alexander Ypsilanti, was foundering. Tudor decided to abandon the Greek cause, and to fight on for an independent Romania. To gain more support, he tried to reach an agreement with the very boyars whom he had only shortly before denounced as tyrants. That cost him the support of many of his followers. The boyars for their part preferred the rule of the Turks. The advance of Turkish troops forced Tudor to leave Bucharest, which he had entered in March. Soon thereafter his own officers betrayed him to the Greeks, who had him brutally murdered. The revolt, which had lasted for four months

---

[36] Hrushevsky (1941), 443-445; Kieniewicz (1969), 19.   [37] Fridman (1958), 50-51.

and had been confined almost entirely to Wallachia, came to an end. It was not without result; henceforth the Turks appointed native Romanian boyars as hospodars instead of Greeks, and the Greek influence waned. But the revolt accomplished nothing for the peasant.[38]

One further and frequent cause of unrest was rumor. Time and again disturbances traced back to some unfounded gossip, or to wishful thinking. To cite only a few examples: when in 1762 Tsar Peter III freed the nobility of its requirement to serve the state, rumors spread among the peasants that the tsar had abolished serfdom, too. When these rumors proved false, the disappointed peasants resorted to violence and terrorism. In one province alone they slew thirty proprietors between 1764 and 1769. In Livonia the introduction of the soul tax in 1783 inspired rumors that payment of the levy freed peasants from all of their obligations to their masters. When they found out that this was not true, unrest broke out in many places. The rumor that enlistment in the border guards brought freedom helped to ignite an explosion of violence in Transylvania in 1784. In 1847 a rumor spread through the White Russian province of Vitebsk that employment for three years on the construction of the Moscow-St. Petersburg railroad would free the worker from serfdom. Thousands fled into Russia in search of these liberating jobs. When they found that the rumor was false, they turned to violence, and troops had to be used against them. An estimated 10,000 peasants were involved. About 100 of them were sent into the army as punishment, and an estimated 4,000 were flogged. During the Crimean War Russian peasants believed that service with the army would free them from their servitude. They accused the lords of suppressing the tsar's manifesto, which had promised freedom for service in the war, and replacing it with a spurious document that specifically denied freedom to serf-soldiers. The latter, of course, was the genuine manifesto, issued by the tsar to scotch the rumor. Furious at this supposed deception, peasants turned against their seigniors. The risings became so serious that the government had to divert troops from the front to restore order. The disturbances continued after the war ended, when peasants who had served in the armed forces were demobilized and compelled to return to their previous condition of servitude.[39]

IV

As the preceding pages have shown, when peasants rose it was nearly always because of a specific grievance, whether rising out of the relationship between lord and peasant, or from other circumstances. They did not revolt

[38] Ştirbu (1955), 316ff.; Oţetea (1975), 316-323; Recordon (1821), 139-147.
[39] Semevskii (1881), i, 347, 356-357; Engelmann (1884), 225-226; Kovalevsky (1891), 226-227; Transehe-Roseneck (1890), 186-188; Fridman (1958), 52-53; *cf.* Lefebvre (1973), 94-95.

because they wanted to destroy the hierarchical order of privilege that held them in their servitude. Once the rising got underway, it sometimes took on a revolutionary aspect, but this did not become the dominating theme. At least three times, however, in the last century of the traditional society genuine attempts at revolution took place—revolts inspired from the outset by the determination to get rid of the existing order of privilege. These three instances were the Pugachev revolt in Russia in 1773-1774, the Horia-Cloşca rising in Transylvania in 1784, and the Great Fear in France in 1789.

For a few incredible weeks in the summer of 1774 it seemed possible that the revolt led by Emilian Pugachev might overthrow the established order in Russia. Pugachev, a Cossack of the Don, appeared among the Cossacks of the Iaik river on the Russian-Siberian frontier and declared himself to be Tsar Peter III, who had been deposed and murdered in 1762. Rumors had spread that Peter had miraculously escaped, and was in hiding awaiting the time when he could gain back his throne. Then he would carry through reforms that he had planned, and that his enemies at court had subverted.

In the ten years before Pugachev made his claim, at least ten other pretenders had declared themselves to be Tsar Peter III. (False tsars had been a familiar phenomenon in Russian history.) Pugachev found willing listeners among the Iaik Cossacks, who were angered by the intervention of the central government, which had reduced their autonomy and threatened their schismatic Old Believer religion. Pugachev promised to restore their freedoms, and they formed the core and provided much of the leadership of his army. He found recruits, too, among the Bashkirs. These semi-nomadic Islamic tribesmen of the southeastern frontier bitterly resented the conversions to Christianity forced upon them and the colonization by Russians of the empty borderland they called their home. When Pugachev moved northward into the industrial regions of the Urals, the assigned peasants there, long restive and riotous, flocked to his standard when he promised freedom for them. Many who belonged to an anachronistic group called the *odnodvortsy* threw in with him, too. They were petty nobles who in earlier centuries had been settled by the state as guards on the then frontiers. Now they had lost their status and were little different from state peasants. They thought Pugachev could win back for them their rights and privileges as noblemen. As his swelling army marched along the Volga, peasants on the recently secularized lands of the church, who had been unruly for years, joined his forces. Finally, in the late spring of 1774 when Pugachev led his troops across the Volga, he found willing recruits among the serfs in the provinces that bordered the great river. That was when the *Pugachev-shchina*, as the Russians call the rising, reached its climax.

The revolt clearly was not simply a peasant rising. Rather, it was a revolution of the discontented, joined in a common hatred of the upper orders,

[347]

and a common resolution to destroy the existing society and win self-determination for themselves. Some among Russia's leaders recognized this. General Alexander Bibikov, who commanded imperial troops against the rebels, told his fellow nobles that "this is a revolt of the poor against the rich, of the slaves against the masters." Pugachev's goal seemed to have been a society ruled by him as tsar, but with landowners and bureaucrats eliminated, with serfs converted into state peasants, and with local self-government in the Cossack manner. His pronouncements, however, were far more summons for savage revenge than visions of a future Russia. Excited by the bloodthirsty propaganda, and by offers of rewards for the murder of proprietors and the destruction of their properties, the rebels ran amok. They killed perhaps as many as 3,000 members of landowning families and did enormous damage to property. But Pugachev's odyssey was nearing its end. His army suffered several defeats at the hands of imperial troops, with the final one coming in August 1774. His forces melted away and Pugachev himself, betrayed by his own entourage, was captured, tortured, and executed. The government took a terrible retribution on the rebels, hanging, torturing, mutilating, and imprisoning those it accused of complicity in the rebellion.[40]

In Transylvania the burdens imposed by the state and by private landowners had become increasingly oppressive. Peasant discontent was deepened by the failure of the Hapsburg regime to introduce codes, as it had in other provinces, to regulate the lord-peasant relationship. Then early in 1784 the government ordered a conscription in the villages for border guard regiments. The rumor spread among the Romanian peasants who lived in the Maros River region that those who enlisted would gain freedom from serfdom. Their chagrin when they discovered the falseness of the rumor fueled their discontent. An incident at the end of October 1784 led to a local outbreak of violence. That provided the match for a general revolt that was already being planned by a peasant named Vasile Nicola, better known as Horia because of his skill in the *hora*, the native dance, and by his chief aides, Ion Cloşca and George Crişan. Horia and Cloşca (by whose names the revolt is known) were outstanding figures widely respected by their fellows. Both had been sent several times to Vienna—Horia four times and Cloşca three—by peasant communities to present their grievances to the emperor. Horia claimed that on his last journey to Vienna in 1784 he had a private audience with Emperor Joseph, and he insisted from the outset of the revolt that he acted in the name of the emperor. Crişan, the third member of the triumvirate, was a violent and ruthless man who had served in the imperial army and had gained some expertise in military tactics.

The rebellion quickly involved 20,000 to 30,000 peasants, Romanians,

[40] Avrich (1972), 180-254; Raeff (1970), 161-201.

Hungarians, and Saxons, in villages scattered over several thousand square kilometers. The rebels plundered and burned 232 manor houses, and visited terrible vengeance on those they called their enemies—landowners, stewards, government officials, money-lenders, priests, and townsmen. The leaders issued a list of demands that defined the dimensions of the social revolution they had in mind. They called for the abolition of the nobility, the distribution by the emperor of the land of the nobles among the peasants, equal taxation for all, and the conversion of the nobility, who were predominantly Hungarian Calvinists, to the Greek Orthodox faith. The demand for conversion alienated the Hungarian peasants, who had joined their Romanian brethren in the revolt, and brought on ethnic and religious clashes among the rebels themselves. By mid-November reports told of rebel attacks on non-noble Hungarians, and of rebel priests who forcibly converted captured Hungarians, including peasants, to Greek Orthodoxy. Meanwhile, government forces had come in and succeeded in the pacification of the province by the end of the year. Horia and Cloşca, who had gone into hiding in the hope of reviving the revolution when spring came, were betrayed and taken prisoners on 27 December. Crişan was caught a few days later. The first two were tortured to death on the rack. Crişan foiled his captors by committing suicide in prison. Their bodies were torn into pieces, and parts nailed to the gates of four towns as a warning. Thirty-seven others were condemned to death, but Joseph commuted their sentences to prison terms.[41]

The hunger and suffering that followed the poor harvest of 1788 provoked much unrest among French peasants during the winter of 1788-1789. In the spring of 1789 tensions heightened when the government asked the people of each parish to submit a declaration of their grievances, a *cahier de doléance*, and to elect delegates to the Estates General, convoked for the first time in 125 years. The peasants in their declarations did not ask for an end to the existing order. As Barrington Moore has pointed out, "To the extent that we can glimpse their demands through the refractions of the *cahiers*, we can see that they wanted mainly to eliminate the arbitrary aspects of the feudal system that had been increasing in the last years of the old order. In sharp contrast with the bourgeoisie, they did not attack the social position and special privileges of the nobility. Instead, they often expressly acknowledged them."[42] However, the villagers expected quick relief for the complaints they had so carefully listed in their *cahiers*, and they became angry when nothing happened. Then, with seeming inevitability, a rumor spread through the countryside that the king had given the order for peasants not to pay their seigniorial obligations, and that the seigniors had blocked the order. The truth was that a royal declaration of 23 June 1789

---

[41] Balazs (1956), 305-311; Király (1967), 143n.; Hitchins (1969), 37-40.
[42] Moore (1966), 73.

had stated that all property must be respected, and had explicitly declared that property included tithes, dues, obligation, and "all the rights and prerogatives, both political and honorific, that are attached to lands or to fiefs, or belong to individuals."[43] Meanwhile the dislocations brought on by the food shortage multiplied the number of beggars and vagabonds. That inspired new fears among villagers of still greater depredations than they already suffered at the hands of these people. Riots broke out here and there, peasants refused to pay their obligations, and in some places they systematically exterminated game as a protest against the seigniorial hunting monopoly.

Peasants, then, were already in movement when word came of the events in Paris on 14 July. The news served to intensify and spread the peasant revolt. Then, in the third week of July, a new and strange phenomenon appeared, known to history as the Great Fear. Somehow peasants became convinced that armed brigands were on the way to sack their villages and savage their fields. Wild rumors told of the great damage these marauders had done in other parts of France. Another rumor had it that these outlaw bands had been loosed on the countryside by the nobility, to crush the Third Estate and to preserve the traditional order. The panic first evidenced itself in six separate localities, and in an unbelievably short time spread from these places into most of France. The villagers armed themselves to repulse the imagined invaders. When none appeared, they turned against their lords, and demanded the end of the seigniorial order. They invaded chateaux, forced seigniors to renounce their rights, and often plundered and burned the manor house and destroyed the registers that recorded their servile status and their obligations to the seignior. They pulled down fences and hedges that enclosed fields, they restored common pastures where they had been eliminated, and they plundered seigniorial forests. They frequently claimed that the king had authorized their spoliations. Handbills that circulated in great number assured them of this. "In the name of the King," said one of these flyers, "all country people are permitted to enter all the chateaux of the Mâconnais to demand the manor rolls and, in the event that they are refused, they are allowed to ransack, burn and plunder, without any harm coming to them for this."

The rebels did great physical damage. In one district alone of Franche-Comté three out of every five manor houses were plundered. The government, severely shaken by the events in Paris, failed to contain the revolt at first. But soon it began a vigorous campaign against the rebels, aided often by town militias. In their work of repression the forces of the government spilled much more blood than did the rebels, who rarely used violence against persons and had apparently killed no one. Now many peasants met

[43] Quoted in Walter (1963), 349.

death at the hands of the military, many others were executed, and large numbers were arrested.[44]

V

Mass risings and violence, as observed earlier, were exceptional phenomena in the history of rural resistance. By far the most usual way in which peasants expressed their discontent was by work slowdown or by strike. Indeed, the former was the norm everywhere in the servile lands; the inefficiency and low productivity of compulsory labor compared with hired labor merely provided quantitative confirmation of what was common knowledge. In Poland and Russia the popular expression for loafing on the job was "to work as you work on the demesne."[45] Strikes, in which peasants refused to perform some or all of their dues and services, occurred frequently. When they persisted, troops sometimes had to be used to force the peasants to meet their obligations.[46]

Flight was another widespread form of protest. There were literally hundreds of thousands of runaways. Individuals, families, and sometimes even entire villages took off for other parts to escape from the exactions of lord and state. So many peasants ran away from Hither Pomerania and the island of Rügen, off the Pomeranian coast, that population there declined in the last decades of the eighteenth century. In pre-revolutionary France peasant flight from village to city to free themselves from the burdens of rural life led to complaints of rural depopulation and labor shortages. In the 1860's an estimated 300,000 Russian and Ukrainian runaway serfs were said to live in Bessarabia. A report of 1856 stated that since 1832 over 100,000 families of Romanian peasants had fled to Bulgaria, Serbia, and Transylvania.[47]

The never-ending stream of runaways sometimes swelled into a flood. That happened in the Danubian Principalities after the introduction there of the Organic Statutes in 1831. A rumor could trigger a mass exodus. In 1841 in just one district of Mogilev in White Russia, 1,178 peasants ran away to Chernigov in the Ukraine because of a rumor that settlement there carried with it freedom from serfdom.[48] When peasants decamped they usually took with them only what they could carry on their backs. But there were exceptions. In 1772 Count von Callenberg, an estate owner in Upper Lusatia, reported that between May 1771 and August 1772 two of his peas-

[44] Lefebvre (1973), *passim*; Walter (1963), 346-376; Herbert (1961), 89-100.

[45] Leslie (1956), 61-62.

[46] *Cf.* Czybulka (1949), 84; Buchinger (1952), 168-169; Corfus (1969), 40; Kieniewicz (1969), 142, 147-149; Zaionchkovskii (1968), 47-48; Fridman (1958), 53.

[47] Mager (1955), 233; Kareev (1899), 240, 240n.; Millot (1937), 145; Revesz (1964), 115; Mitrany (1930), 38.

[48] Mitrany (1930), 38; Fridman (1958), 52-53.

[351]

ant households fled with horses, oxen, cows, and a wagon. Another runaway took off with 2 horses, 4 oxen, 9 cows, 123 sheep, and some swine, and 2 cotters left with cows and oxen. Callenberg figured that his losses totalled 960 talers and 15 groschen. Other proprietors suffered material losses, too, even when the runaways took nothing with them, since they often were in arrears in payments of their obligations to the seignior, or owed him money they had borrowed from him.[49]

Princes and legislators, dismayed by the illegal departures, issued law after law that threatened harsh punishments to captured runaways and to those who harbored them. Their decrees were of little avail. Only a small minority of the fugitives were captured. Usually their seigniors could not locate them and, if they did find them, the process of recovery proved too difficult. That was especially true when peasants fled across frontiers. In 1771 the government of Mecklenburg complained that officials in neighboring Prussia refused to return runaways. In fact, Frederick II, as part of his program of colonization, settled 1,500 to 2,000 families of Mecklenburg peasants in his kingdom, and his successor continued to welcome runaways from Mecklenburg. Polish seigniors encouraged flight from East Prussia by offering the runaways holdings on good tenures and with light obligations. So many Russian serfs ran away to Astrakhan, New Russia, and Bessarabia that the government, anxious to colonize these frontier regions, decreed that after a certain term of residence fugitives, if apprehended, did not have to be returned to their owners. The owner was compensated with a recruit quittance; that is, he received credit for having provided a recruit to the army, or the seignior on whose land the runaway had settled made a payment to the owner. Officials in Siberia were supposed to return runaway serfs to their masters in European Russia. However, the need for colonists in Siberia outweighed the property rights of the serfowners. Instead, the authorities helped the fugitives get settled, regarded them as state peasants, and even went so far as to hide them when they were in danger of apprehension and return to their old homes.[50]

Some of the runaways became vagrants and beggars, some turned to brigandage, some went to the cities, and some enlisted in the army.[51] Most of them continued to live as peasants in their new homes. Some gained better tenures and lighter obligations, and even complete freedom. The great majority apparently drew little or no advantage from their flight. Settled on the land of another seignior, they had merely exchanged their old servitude for a new one.

Lawsuits provided another means by which peasants in some of the servile lands could ventilate their protests and their rancour. They seem to

[49] Boelcke (1957), 234; Albert (1969), 47.
[50] Mager (1955), 233; Henning (1969b), 65; Blum (1961), 553, 559.
[51] Grünberg (1901), 28; Kareev (1899), 240; Albert (1969), 47-48.

have been particularly favored by French peasants, whose communes brought frequent legal action against seigniors for alleged wrongs. During Louis XIV's reign the intendant of Burgundy, in an attempt to close out these cases, succeeded in ending the litigation brought by 2,400 communes in his province alone. Despite similar efforts by other governmental officials, the peasants continued to file suits, and the trial dockets continued to swell. In Germany, in Poland, Austria, and in the Danubian Principalities peasants resorted frequently to the courts to seek redress for their grievances. In Saxony, in 1792 alone, peasants entered 392 lawsuits against their lords. On one estate there, the villagers filed over 35 suits against their seignior between the end of the sixteenth and the middle of the eighteenth century.

One reason why there were so many cases in the courts was that the litigation often dragged on for years. It apparently was not unusual for a lawsuit to go on for twenty to thirty years. Sometimes they ran even longer; a village in the Neustadt district of Prussian Silesia had a case against its seignior in the courts for over forty years. Part of the responsibility for these interminable legal actions lay with the lawyers, who encouraged peasants to enter suits and to prolong them. Reputable attorneys were disinclined to take these cases, and so the peasants fell into the hands of pettifoggers, who were out to squeeze every penny they could out of their clients. As a result, the villagers spent much money which they could ill afford to pay lawyers' fees and court costs. And when the court finally returned its verdict it was often against the peasant plaintiffs. When the verdict was in their favor, the seignior sometimes chose to disregard it, or found some new ground on which to challenge it.[52]

The futility of so many of their lawsuits could not have surprised the peasants. With only rare exceptions their protests, whether large or small, whether violent or of a more passive nature, gained them little or nothing, except perhaps for the momentary exhilaration that their defiance of their seigniors must have given them. In the long run, however, the proportions of peasant unrest and its generality penetrated into the consciousness of the ruling orders. They became aware of the dangers to society if peasant disorders continued to grow, and the excesses of some of the rural rebellions made them fear for the personal safety of themselves, their families, and their properties. And so, in the last decades of the old order, peasant unrest helped to persuade nobles and princes, many of whom were already leaning toward reform, to "bite the bullet" and advocate freedom for the peasants and the end of the servile order.

[52] Babeau (1878), 102-107; Lütge (1957), 155-156; Franz (1970a), 192-193, 245; Stulz and Opitz (1956), 37, 108; Czybulka (1949), 82-83; Boelcke (1957), 222, 229; Ziekursch (1927), 242; Fuchs (1888), 188; Mises (1902), 98-99; Kieniewicz (1969), 114; Bobińska (1970), 144, 148; Oţetea (1960), 308.

Part Three

Emancipation

Initial Decrees of Emancipation

Savoy	19 December 1771
Baden	23 July 1783
Denmark	20 June 1788
France	3 November 1789
Switzerland	4 May 1798
Schleswig-Holstein	19 December 1804
Poland (Grand Duchy of Warsaw)	22 July 1807
Prussia	9 October 1807
Bavaria	31 August 1808
Nassau	1 September 1812
Estonia	23 March 1816
Courland	25 August 1817
Württemberg	18 November 1817
Livonia	26 March 1819
Mecklenburg	18 January 1820
Grand Duchy of Hesse	17 December 1820
Hannover	10 November 1831
Electoral Hesse	5 January 1831
Saxe-Altenburg	29 April 1831
Saxony	17 March 1832
Brunswick	12 October 1832
Schaumburg-Lippe	24 January 1845
Schwarzburg-Sondershausen	28 March 1848
Reuss, older line	25 April 1848
Saxe-Weimar	18 May 1848
Austria	7 September 1848
Saxe-Gotha	20 October 1848
Anhalt-Dessau-Köthen	29 October 1848
Saxe-Coburg-Gotha	25 January 1849
Oldenburg	18 February 1849
Schwarzburg-Rudolstadt	27 April 1849
Anhalt-Bernburg	29 August 1849
Lippe	20 November 1849
Saxe-Meiningen	5 May 1850
Reuss, younger line	14 April 1852
Hungary	2 March 1853
Russia	19 February 1861
Romania (the Danubian Principalities)	14 August 1864

CHAPTER 16

Background of the Emancipation

I

REFORMING princes, improving landlords, new crops and new techniques, new economic opportunities, noblemen interested in profitable enterprise, discontent with the economic inefficiencies of the servile order, new and disturbing ideas about the equality of man and the injustice of privilege, and restless and sometimes rebellious peasants, all formed the matrix out of which emerged the emancipation of the peasantry of the servile lands. The acts that freed the peasants and thereby ended the traditional order did not come as surprises. Their advent had been heralded long before they became realities. Yet as they drew nearer the opposition of most of the seigniors intensified. Their dire warnings reached a new crescendo—and near-hysteria—as they repeated their prophecies of earlier years that emancipation would fuel the democratic and revolutionary spirit that already endangered the established order, would bring on bloody and destructive rural rebellions, and would produce a drunken and indolent peasantry. Even when some among them acknowledged the possible advantages of reform, they argued that the instability it would introduce into the social order outweighed the supposed benefits. Nobles in Prussia, Pomerania, Mecklenburg, and Russia forecast that emancipation would guarantee economic ruin for the seigniors. The proprietors in a district of Farther Pomerania in a petition to the throne protested the decree of 14 September 1811, which allowed emancipated peasants to become the owners of their holdings. The peasants, they said, would no longer have to hire themselves out as laborers for the seigniors. "Our manors," they cried, "will become a hell for us if independent peasant proprietors are our neighbors."

The possible impact of emancipation upon agricultural production was not a matter of much concern to seigniors in the servile lands of the west. Many of them engaged little or not at all in the direct production of farm goods. Still, they stood as one with their peers of central and eastern Europe in their opposition to emancipation. Western and eastern lords alike were agitated by the loss they would suffer in privilege and prestige through emancipation. They were affronted by the thought that their peasants would approach the threshhold of civil equality with them. And they considered the forced abandonment of their seigniorial rights to be as much of an invasion of their property rights as the compulsion, imposed by emancipation decrees, to yield part of their land to the freed peasants.[1]

[1] Eggert (1965), 71-72; Frauendorfer (1957), I, 256-257n., 261, 268; Wiese (1935), 33-60;

The small minority among the nobility who favored reform, though not necessarily emancipation, included a few men who had long supported improvements in the status of the peasantry. Others, like the noblemen of the estates movement in the German and Slav provinces of Austria, came late to the cause of reform. So did those proprietors in Hungary who made agrarian reform a plank in the program of the Liberal Party to win support from the peasantry for their nationalistic aims. The arguments used by these supporters of reform in support of their demands included prophecies of economic benefits that would accrue to the seigniors once the peasantry gained its freedom. Some of them pointed to the injustices of the traditional order, and claimed that the abolition of the servile relationship would increase human happiness and welfare. The altruism and fellow-feeling of these men did have its limits. They were willing to make sacrifices, but they insisted that they must receive indemnification for most, if not of all, of what they were ready to give up.[2]

In some of the servile lands, seigniors who had opposed reform decided to support it when they saw that it was inevitable. In France the *cahiers* of the nobility and clergy made it clear that they had neither the desire nor the intention to relinquish any of their privileges or property, save for the exemptions from taxation. Their stand had the support of King Louis XVI, who on 5 April 1789 declared, "I will never consent to despoil my clergy and nobility . . . I will not give my sanction to decrees which would despoil them." But the resolution of the nobles, or at least of those nobles who sat as deputies in the National Assembly, dissolved before the rural unrest and violence that suddenly swept through the land in mid-July. Alarmed by these outbreaks, the noble deputies decided to introduce reform legislation in the Assembly to forestall more drastic measures that might be introduced there, and to pacify the countryside. On the night of 3 August about a hundred moderate delegates met in the Breton Club to discuss plans. The duke d'Aiguillon, the richest man in France after the king, announced that he would propose the abolition of seigniorial rights in return for suitable indemnification by the peasant. Vicomte de Noailles, landless and penniless scion of a famous house, heard of this. He decided to anticipate d'Aiguillon, and on the night of 4 August he rose in the Assembly to move the end of seigniorial privileges in taxation, the redemption by money payments of all seigniorial dues, and the abolition of *mainmorte* and other personal servitudes without indemnification to the seigniors. By this master stroke of one-upmanship he won undeserved but undying fame for himself.

Engels (1957), 53-54; Schönebaum (1917), 514; Laubert (1935), *passim*; Mager (1955), 346-347; Simon (1955), 11-12; Wittich (1896), 431-432; Knapp (1887), II, 273-274; Nielsen (1933), 323; Herbert (1969), 107-108, 156; Portal (1963), 73-76; Blum (1961), 580-581; Mitrany (1930), 47; Emerit (1937), 358-359, 362-363.

[2] Confino (1963), 64-70; Emmons (1968), 90-91; Philippot (1963), 241; Herbert (1969), 107; Carré (1920), 311; Finkenstein (1960), 127; Rostworowski (1896), 35-38; Kieniewicz (1969), 150-153.

Nobles of Schleswig-Holstein continued their resistance to emancipation after the serfs had been freed in 1788 in Denmark, whose king was also their sovereign. They knew, however, that they could not hold out indefinitely. They decided to accept the reform, but to introduce it gradually, and as much as possible on their own terms. In 1796, meeting in assembly, they agreed to emancipation, and the next year informed the Danish king of their readiness to end serfdom. They told him that the sacrifice they were prepared to make was done "more out of a feeling for human welfare and human happiness than out of necessity."

In late April of 1857 V. A. Nazimov, governor-general of the Lithuanian provinces of Vilna, Kovno, and Grodno, arrived in St. Petersburg bearing an unusual request to the tsar. The Lithuanian nobility petitioned its imperial master to free the peasants there without land. The explanation for this surprising proposal was easy to find. The seigniors of these provinces faced the reintroduction by the government of the so-called inventories (pp. 234-235). These inventories were to fix the amount of obligations the peasant paid, and required the seignior to provide holdings for his peasants. The Lithuanian lords decided that they preferred to keep all of their land for themselves, even if they had to free their serfs. Tsar Alexander II, remembering the failure of landless emancipation in the Baltic provinces, ruled against the request, although his committee on emancipation plans favored the proposal.

In Poland, whose nobility had earned the reputation of special insensitivity to the sufferings of the peasants, change came in the 1850's. Inspired in part by the desire to win the support of the peasantry for the cause of Polish independence, and doubtless, too, by the knowledge that the tsar had decided upon emancipation in Russia, many Polish seigniors now urged reform. The Agricultural Society of the Kingdom of Poland, founded in 1857, whose membership included nearly all of the great Polish landowners, devoted a number of its sessions to the peasant problem. Few among the proprietors seemed willing to defend the existing order. Instead, they directed their attentions to plans for reform which would best protect their interests, and would maximize the price and minimize the amount of land they would have to surrender to their peasants when the reforms were implemented.[3]

II

The calculated efforts of seigniors, once they recognized the certainty of reform, to save as much as they could from it stood in sharp contrast to the activities of the peasants. They, of course, welcomed any change that ben-

[3] France: Herbert (1969), 101-102, 107-108; Kareev (1899), 421; Mackrell (1973), 173-174. Schleswig-Holstein: Sievers (1970), 155. Lithuania: Blum (1961), 579-580. Poland: Rostworowski (1896), 35-38; Kieniewicz (1969), 150-153.

efitted them. However, they did not have a program of reform. They accepted the world as it was, albeit with many protests and with frequent unrest. Their resentment, their passive resistance, and their occasional acts of violence were almost always directed against specific grievances, and not the servile order itself. They were not revolutionaries. They seemed to lack an understanding, or even an interest, in the fundamental inequities and injustices of the traditional society. As the preceding chapter showed, only rarely in the last century of the old order did they make efforts to overthrow the system. The reforms and the emancipations came from above: the peasants were the objects of policies inaugurated and carried through by the state and the higher orders of society.

Nonetheless, though peasant discontent lacked ideological content, and though it was so rarely directed toward a reshaping of society, it had a major role in effecting reform, and ultimately in bringing about the abolition of the servile order. Harsh repressions were often imposed to convince the peasants of the futility of rebellion. Sometimes, however, piecemeal or partial reforms followed upon serious or prolonged disturbances. Monarchs, watchful for the chance to reduce the local power of the nobility, grasped the opportunity presented by these outbreaks to introduce reforms that increased their own authority, and that won and held the loyalty of the peasants to the throne. The Hapsburg rulers of the eighteenth century were especially adept at this strategy. Maria Theresa used peasant unrest as the excuse to impose legislation that regulated the lord-peasant relationship, and thereby provided direct state intervention in that relationship. After the suppression of the Horia-Cloşca rebellion in Transylvania in 1784, Joseph II extended his decree of 1 November 1781, which gave the peasants important new freedoms, to all of Hungary. Catherine II of Russia seized upon the revolt of church peasants in 1763 to secularize church property. She kept the land for the crown, and thereby converted the many hundreds of thousands of serfs who had belonged to the church into state peasants. They now paid their dues and services to the state, their status was superior to that of serfs, and their burdens were less.[4]

Sometimes the seigniors themselves reacted positively to peasant unrest. Rural troubles in the 1780's and 1790's helped to persuade seigniors in the Baltic lands of the need for reform. After the disturbances in Hungary in 1790, the diet there at last gave its approval to the *Urbarium* that Maria Theresa had introduced into that land in 1767, and appointed a committee of distinguished members of the diet to work out new reform projects.[5] Nor were sovereigns unresponsive when their own peasants revolted, as was evidenced in Russia by the reforms that followed the risings of the assigned peasants and of the military colonists.

[4] Hitchins (1969), 40-41; Miliukov (1932), ii, 548-550.   [5] Király (1967), 155-156.

Of greater significance, however, than the actual disturbances themselves in effecting reform, was the psychological impact of rural unrest
upon monarchs, upon their counselors, and upon seigniors. The spectre,
and the all-too-frequent reality, of peasant resistance and violence ultimately convinced many that some measure of reform was needed to fend
off future destruction and devastation. After the suppression of the Bohemian revolt in 1775, Empress Maria Theresa complained in a letter to
Count Mercy-Argentau, her ambassador to Paris, that "Not only in
Bohemia alone is the peasant to be feared; also in Moravia, Styria, Austria;
at our door, here at home, they dare to commit acts of the most extreme
insolence; the results of this for themselves and for many other and innocent people are to be feared. The most impudent and the worst now have an
easy time of it."[6] Following the death of Joseph II in 1790, the landowning
nobility exerted heavy pressures on the new emperor, Leopold II, to repeal
most of the reforms of Maria Theresa and Joseph. The rumor that Leopold
planned to do so spread through the countryside. Unrest shook the villages,
peasant delegations came to Vienna to plead with the new emperor, and
eruptions of violence had to be put down by the military. Leopold recognized the dangers of a general peasant rising and, defying the demands of
the nobility, refused to cancel the legislation.[7]

The serious outbreaks in Saxony and Silesia in the 1790's frightened
seigniors and officials, who were already shocked by the happenings in revolutionary France. In a letter of 23 April 1799 to Count Karl Hoym, provincial minister for Silesia, the Prussian chancellor Heinrich von Goldbeck
wrote that "many thoughtful proprietors in Silesia and other royal provinces at every opportunity say that it is better to give up something voluntarily than to be forced to sacrifice everything." He warned that "frightful
consequences will be unavoidable if the common man, driven by necessity,
and no longer able to hope for help from the state, so long and vainly expected, takes matters into his own hands. Since Your Excellency is well acquainted with all this, it is only necessary for me to repeat my request to
take the necessary measures as soon as possible, and thereby put the common man into a position in which despair will not compel him to resort to
violence." Others wrote to Hoym in the same vein. There were, of course,
hard-liners who counselled Hoym against any and all concessions, so long
as soldiers and guns were available to put down challenges to the established authorities. Adumbrating the modern theory of rising expectations,
they argued that indulgence would only serve to unleash revolution. More
thoughtful men, mindful of the fact that peasants' sons made up the rank
and file of the army, were not so confident about the use of force. They

[6] Quoted in Arneth (1879), ix, 360-361.
[7] Springer (1863), i, 29-30; Grünberg (1894), i, 346-357.

recognized, too, the dangers of reliance upon military power to maintain the status quo. "Woe unto us," wrote one of these men, "if it takes cannon to save us."[8]

The acceleration of unrest in Russia during the second quarter of the nineteenth century became a matter of deep concern to Tsar Nicholas I. His chief of police, Count Benckendorff, warned him of the dangers of peasant revolt. Serfdom, he said (in a time-worn analogy) was a powder keg that could blow up the state. It was all the more to be feared, continued Benckendorff, "because the army is made up of peasants, and is officered now by a huge mass of landless nobles who are driven by ambition, and since they have nothing else to do, rejoice over every disorder." Nicholas himself recognized the need for reforms, feared that if they were not made a new *Pugachevshchina* would sweep through his realm, yet (as noted earlier) could not bring himself to take the necessary decisive action. Rural unrest in the Baltic provinces, where the peasants had been freed without land, reached such proportions in the 1840's that Baron Karl M. von der Pahlen, governor-general of the region, warned Moscow that there was danger of disorders "on the scale of the Sicilian Vespers." In 1843 he appealed directly to the tsar for reforms. His efforts were to no avail, though Nicholas was well aware of the serious state of affairs in his Baltic possessions. In 1842 he instructed his Council of State not to consider a landless emancipation for Russia's serfs "in order," he explained, "to avoid the unsatisfactory situation that now exists in the Baltic provinces—a situation which has brought the peasants there to a most pitiable condition."[9]

In the very last years of the servile order, peasant unrest, or the fear of it, acted as a catalyst that precipitated the reforms that opponents of emancipation and hesitant princes had until now repressed. The Great Fear of 1789 persuaded French seigniors to surrender their privileges. In Savoy peasant violence in 1790 compelled the government to speed up the emancipation process that had begun twenty years before. When the French conquered Hannover in 1807, they abolished the servile system. In 1813 they were driven out. The restored regime, determined to wipe out every trace of the hated French rule, reestablished the old order. (That happened also in Electoral Hesse.) The peasants meekly accepted the reimposition of their servility. For the next few years the upper chamber of the estates, in which the nobility sat, successfully resisted liberal pressure for reform. Then in the 1820's economic downturn and hard times made it much more difficult for the peasants to meet their obligations. That stirred up their resentment against the servile order. News of the July Revolution in France in 1830 aggravated discontent in town and country alike. Riots erupted in two cities in 1831, and rural unrest became so threatening that it compelled

[8] Ziekursch (1927), 250-254; Czybulka (1949), 86.
[9] *Studia Historica . . . Kruus* (1971), 317-318; Korf (1896), 116.

18. Exploitation of the peasant by the landed proprietor. (1861 cartoon, re-printed in C. Corbu, *Tărănimea din România în perioada 1848-1864*, Bucharest, 1973.)

recognition by the seigniors of the need to make concessions or to lose all. The nobles in the upper chamber were able to put through reform legislation that was much more favorable to their interests than the bourgeois liberals of the lower chamber wanted it to be.[10]

The Galician revolt in 1846 had much to do with the emancipation of the peasants of the Austrian Monarchy in 1848. The government preened itself on the loyalty the Galician peasants had shown to the house of Hapsburg. The government realized that it had to act quickly to hold that loyalty by rewarding it, but it lacked the leadership, the vision, and the will to put through a genuine reform. The imperial decrees of 13 April 1846 for Galicia, and of 18 December 1846 for all of the German and Slav crown lands, did little more than repeat what the laws already allowed, such as commutation or redemption of obligations by mutual agreement between lord and peasant. The December law did contain an innovation that permitted the peasant to give up part of his holding to his seignior in lieu of cash, as payment for redemption of his obligations. The new law required that the peasant who did this was to keep enough land to support his household. Though little use was made of this provision, it effectively repealed the long-standing legislative prohibition against the enlargement of seigniorial demesne at the expense of peasant land.

The failure of the government to introduce meaningful reform stirred up new waves of discontent. Peasants in many parts of the Monarchy stopped rendering their obligations to their lords, and made no offer of indemnification to the seigniors. At the same time, the failure of the government to protect the nobles of Galicia from the vengeance of their peasants made nobles everywhere fear that they could not depend upon Vienna to defend their privileges, their properties, or even their lives. That made the nobles eager for agrarian reform that would appease the peasantry and provide the seigniors with indemnification for the land and the privileges they knew they would inevitably have to relinquish.

These currents of discontent and unrest set off by the Galician revolt grew increasingly threatening. Then in the spring of 1848 came the news of the March days in Vienna that had compelled the government to promise the convocation of a constitutional convention. All the competing factions realized that the peasants held the balance of power. The faction that won over the peasantry would emerge as the victor in the revolution that now gripped the Monarchy. The government quickly issued decrees for a number of crown lands that ended the peasants' servile obligations, with indemnification to the seigniors. These laws only aggravated peasant grievances, for they did not abolish the servile status of the peasants, and they required them to bear all of the costs of indemnification, except in Galicia. With remarkable ineptitude, the government promised that the state would

[10] Wittich (1896), 426-435; Franz (1959), 176.

pay the indemnification there. Peasants in the other crown lands naturally demanded the same consideration from the government. Meanwhile peasants everywhere refused to pay their dues and services, and in the prevailing anarchy the seigniors could not expect help from the state to compel the peasants to meet their obligations. The only possible solution to the impasse came on 7 September 1848, when the emperor signed the decree of emancipation.[11]

Even false rumors of peasant risings could convert already apprehensive seigniors into advocates of reform. On 14 March 1848 the Hungarian diet, in session at Pressburg, heard that 40,000 armed peasants, led by the poet Sandor Petöfi, had taken to the field near Pest, and were preparing to launch a great jacquerie. The rumor was untrue, but the members of the diet did not doubt it for an instant. The report frightened them so much that the very next day they voted the immediate abolition of serfdom.[12]

In Russia the tempo of rural unrest swelled alarmingly during and immediately after the Crimean War. Defeat in that conflict had revealed serious weaknesses in the administrative and military structure of the state. Alexander II, the newly crowned tsar, realized that great changes had to be made to preserve the internal order and the external power of his realm. In his manifesto of 19 March 1856, in which he announced the end of the war, he promised equality before the law for all of his subjects. Eleven days later he told representatives of the Moscow nobility who met with him that he planned to abolish the servile order. "It is better to begin to destroy serfdom from above," he said, "than to wait for that time when it begins to destroy itself from below." Those often-quoted words marked the beginning of five years of preparation and planning that finally produced the lengthy statute issued on 19 February 1861, which freed the serfs of Russia from their bondage. In the preamble to that law, Alexander explained that "the patriarchal relation founded upon sincere, just, and benevolent solicitude on the part of the lord and good-natured obedience on the part of the peasant" had degenerated, so that "the bonds of mutual good will have loosened to the extent that some seigniors were exclusively preoccupied with their own interests, and arbitrarily imposed excessive burdens on their peasants, and showed no concern for their welfare."[13]

Alexander's decree of 19 February did not apply to the kingdom of Poland, where the peasants were no longer serfs but were still in servile dependence upon their seigniors. Many Poles, including peasants, took the tsar's decree as a portent of imminent reform in their own land. This belief, and the news of nationalist agitation and street demonstrations in Warsaw, induced them to go on strike. Official reports claimed that 20 per cent of the villagers who owed labor obligations refused to pay them. Many refused to

---

[11] Blum (1948), 231-235; Leshchilovskaia (1961), 326.   [12] Spira (1968), 366.
[13] *Krest'ianskaia Reforma* (1954), 31-32; Blum (1961), 577-590.

pay rent for their land, and some would not pay their taxes. Fears of a jac-querie such as had convulsed Galicia in 1846 spread among the seigniors, and many nobles fled to the cities in search of refuge. The Russian govern-ment, most of whose local troop detachments were tied down in urban areas by nationalist disturbances, made only limited and sporadic efforts to put down the strikes by force. Instead, the government decided that the way to restore order in the countryside was to do away with the labor obli-gation. And so a decree of 16 March 1861 ordered the commutation of that obligation at the unilateral request of the peasant.[14]

III

Pressure for reform, or opposition to it, that came from peasants and sei-gniors produced tangible and overt phenomena. They rose from within the servile system, a product of the interaction between lord and peasant. Ex-trinsic pressures that bore in upon the rural world were often subtle and indirect and difficult to evaluate. That was especially true of the influence of the philosophies of freedom and equality that emerged during the last cen-tury of the old order. Those who were directly affected by these new ideologies were of the educated elite, who were everywhere few in number. Though there were noblemen who were members of that select company, most seigniors were, at best, barely aware of what was happening in the world of the intellect. The peasants, most of them illiterate, knew nothing of the writings of the philosophers and economists, and of the literary at-tacks upon the hierarchical society. Some of the new ideas, watered down for easy comprehension, did make their way into publications aimed at the peasantry, and gained some circulation by word of mouth.

Still, despite the limited circle of those who knew about and sympathized with the new currents of thought, these men helped prepare the way for the liberation of the peasantry. They stressed the incompatibility of the hierarchical society with the liberal ideas of individual freedom and equality before the law. They pointed out that personal freedom included the right of freedom of property. To be truly free, man must be able to do as he wished with his property. That meant full ownership by the peasant of his holding, without superior ownership by a seignior, and without the dues and obligations paid by the peasant in return for his holding. It also meant that these payments were part of the seignior's property for which he must be compensated. So the liberals, ever mindful of the sanctity of property, supported indemnification to the seigniors for the land and payments they had to relinquish.[15]

[14] Kieniewicz (1969), 155-158.
[15] *Cf.* Schremmer (1963), I, 101-102; Mager (1955), 339; Lütge (1943), 364, 367, 371; Wittich (1896), 430; Cobban (1971), 37-42.

The French Revolution, of course, had much to do with the propagation of the ideas of equality and of the rights of property. It was responsible for the implementation of these ideas first in France itself, and then in lands of western Germany and Switzerland. The Revolution, however, has often received more credit than it merits as the progenitor of the emancipations. Actually, it retarded the progress toward the liberation of the peasantry in much of Europe. It aroused deep-seated fears of change among the ruling elites of the servile lands. They believed that any concession to the demands of liberals and reformers would be interpreted as a sign of weakness, and would lead inevitably to further demands, and then to revolution. Thomas Malthus, in the journal of his stay in Denmark in 1799, noted that it was fortunate that the Danish emancipation in 1788 had come just before the outbreak of the French Revolution. "Had the measure been delayed a little longer," he wrote, "probably it would never have taken place; as the government would not have ventured upon it, after the popular commotion in France." In the Austrian Monarchy the shock of the Revolution dissipated the spirit of reform that had been inspired by Joseph II and that was already under heavy attack from within the realm. The events in France seemed to confirm the prophecies of the opponents of reform. Change became identified with revolution, and those who supported reform were branded as Jacobins. For the next twenty-five years the rulers of the Monarchy devoted all of their efforts and energies to combatting the Revolution and Napoleon. When victory finally came, it only intensified and justified the forces of conservatism and the repugnance and dread of change. It took thirty-three more years and another revolution before emancipation became a reality in the realm of the Hapsburgs. In Russia the Revolution summoned forth a reactionary chorus who warned that even moderate reforms would open the gates to the "French poison." Censorship grew tighter, foreign publications were banned, the government took action against Masonic lodges and secret societies, liberal writers were arrested, and rumors of a revolutionary plot to overthrow legitimate governments won wide acceptance. Empress Catherine, in a letter of 11 February 1794 to her long-time correspondent in France, Baron F. M. von Grimm, wrote: "Do you remember that the late king of Prussia [Frederick II] claimed that Helvetius confessed to him that the goal of the *philosophes* was to overthrow all thrones and that the *Encyclopédie* had been done with no other purpose than to destroy all kings and all religions." In Germany, too, the outbreak of the Revolution gave the signal for increased repression, and for the mounting of a campaign against egalitarianism and for the strengthening of the society of orders.[16]

[16] Malthus (1966), 59; Wangermann (1969), 173-191; Shtrange (1956), 89-95, 109-118, 140-150; *Sbornik Imperatorskago Russkago Istoricheskago Obshchestva*, XXIII (1878), 593; Valjavec (1951), 308-320.

Even in lands where the French had introduced emancipations, the outcome was not always successful. As mentioned earlier, French-imposed reforms in some western German lands were repealed when the French were ousted. The Napoleonic emancipation in the grand duchy of Warsaw had not improved the condition of peasant life there. In Switzerland the short-lived Helvetic Republic, created by French armies in 1798, ended some of the servile obligations of the peasantry, but final and complete abolition came only in 1846.

Agrarian reform in other lands sometimes served as a goad to action and as a model. In France the emancipation in Savoy was often invoked in *cahiers* of the Third Estate, in speeches, in publications, and in village discussions. In an address to the Constituent Assembly on the night of 4 August 1789, Abbé Sièyes told his fellow deputies that the method of emancipation in Savoy provided an example from which the assembly could profit and could perfect. "For it is beyond any doubt," said the Abbé, "that the spirit of justice, united with that of liberty, will add to the perfection of a task undertaken and achieved by an absolute ruler, just as it is not possible to believe that justice rendered to proprietors by a despotism can be refused by the representatives of a free nation." The first Prussian decree of emancipation, dated 9 October 1807, made a deep impression upon rulers of lesser German states. A number of them used the Prussian legislation as a model for their own decrees of emancipation. The Russian government showed much interest in the agrarian reforms in central Europe and collected relevant materials and data. In the Danubian Principalities the emancipations in the neighboring Austrian and Russian empires helped create a milieu favorable to reform.[17]

The interest in a more rational and profitable agriculture, though restricted to a minority of the seigniors, contributed significantly to the demise of the old order. Princes and their counselors, and national assemblies, responded to the argument that the persistence of the traditional lord-peasant relationship had severely damaging effects upon the welfare of the state. On the famed night of 4 August 1789, after (as mentioned earlier) the vicomte de Noailles had stolen his thunder, the duke d'Aiguillon presented the National Assembly with two motions designed to make the Noailles motion more precise and detailed. The second of the duke's motions demanded the abolition of seigniorial rights because "they harm agriculture and desolate the countryside." The official reporter noted that the motions were accepted "with an inexpressible transport of joy."[18] In their decrees of emancipation, rulers sometimes explicitly stated their concern about the economic effects of the traditional order as explanation for the

[17] Abbé Sièyes quoted in Bruchet (1908), x-xii; Lütge (1967), 223; *Studia historica . . . Kruus* (1971), 327; Emerit (1937), 433-440.
[18] *Archives parlementaires*, 1st series (1789-1799), viii, 344.

legislation. In the edict of 19 December 1804, which freed the peasants of Schleswig-Holstein, the sovereign explained that "with continuous consideration of the common welfare of lord and peasant" he issued his decree "so that the industrious peasant has more opportunity to support himself and his family through agriculture and to accumulate property."[19] Frederick William III of Prussia, in the preamble of the decree of 9 October 1807 that abolished serfdom in his realm, explained that after the conclusion of peace (with France) "attention to the depressed condition of Our loyal subjects," and the determination to improve it as speedily as possible, became his primary concern. "It is in accordance with the obligatory demands of justice," he continued, "as well as the principles of a well-ordered national economy, to remove everything which till now hindered the individual from achieving the prosperity which, according to his ability, he is capable of reaching. Further, We have considered that the existing restrictions, in part on the possession and use of landed property, in part on the condition of the rural laborer, works against Our benevolent purpose . . . the former by exercising a highly damaging influence upon the value of landed property and the credit of the proprietor, and the latter by lessening the value of labor."[20] King William I of Württemberg began his decree of 18 November 1817 with these words: "In the conviction that in a state whose chief wealth lies in landed property and in its appropriate use, the prosperity of the people must be based upon a freedom of the landowner and of the peasant that is in harmony with the laws and spirit of the time." Despite earlier remedial legislation, he continued, "an oppressive burden of manifold obligations still rests upon a large and especially the poorest part of Our subjects [and] . . . stands in the way of every aspiration to increase prosperity. . . . The obligations, presently disproportionate in themselves, through their nature, the time at which they are demanded, and the costs and oppression which accompany their collection, have deprived industry of self-confidence and the means to progress, have hindered cultivation, have increased poverty, and through this as well as through the diminished productivity and population of the state . . . must inflict ever deeper wounds."[21] William IV of Hannover declared that it was "appropriate for the advancement of agriculture" to abolish servile obligations and restrictions.[22] The preamble to the edict that ended the servile order in Saxony declared that "the establishment of the greatest possible freedom in the ownership of property is a pressing need of rural prosperity." The obligations upon the peasant "hinder the free development of agricultural activity and damage one of the chief sources of national wealth."[23]

---

[19] *Kong Christian . . . Forordninger . . . 1804*, 301.
[20] *Sammlung Preussischer Gesetze*, IX (1819), 85.
[21] *Regierungs-Blatt . . . Württemberg, 1817-1824*, II (1841), 98-99.
[22] Decree of 10 November 1831 in Conze (1957), 177.
[23] *Sammlung der Gesetze . . . für . . . Sachsen*, 1832, no. 17, 163.

Important as economic and other long-range considerations may have been, an event of catastrophic proportions, and particularly military defeat, sometimes was the most immediate cause of emancipation. Such an event revealed the anachronisms and the debility of the old order. The outbreak of revolution in France in 1789 and the Great Fear that inflamed so much of the countryside quickly persuaded the government to end the servile order there. During their brief hegemony in western Germany, the French annexed the German states on the left bank of the Rhine and made them departments of France, an act that made them subject to French national legislation. In 1798 the French government suppressed without indemnity all seigniorial rights in these German states over peasant land, and from 1804 sold off the land of princes, clergymen, and émigré noblemen. These and other revolutionary measures made it impossible to restore the old regime when at the end of the Napoleonic era the Rhenish provinces were incorporated into the Kingdom of Prussia. In the Hanseatic states, annexed by Napoleon, a decree of 1811 ended seigniorial rights. In the Kingdom of Westphalia, created by Bonaparte in 1807, legislation abolished some servile obligations without indemnification and ordered the redemption of others. The process had barely gotten underway, however, when, after the battle of Leipzig in October 1813, the Kingdom of Westphalia fell apart, and the old rulers were restored along with the old regime.[24]

Military disaster was the proximate cause of emancipation in Prussia. The Napoleonic legions inflicted crushing defeats on Prussia at Jena and Auerstädt in October 1806, and completed the destruction of the Prussian war machine in little more than a month. Then in July 1807 came the humiliation of the Peace of Tilsit, when Prussia lost nearly half of its territories. These calamities dispelled whatever hesitations and doubts that King Frederick William and his advisors harbored about the need for immediate reforms. "The abolition of serfdom has been my goal since the beginning of my reign," wrote the king in the order he gave to draft emancipation legislation. "I desired to attain it gradually," he continued, "but the disasters which have befallen the country now justify, and indeed require, speedier action."[25] Similarly, in Russia defeat in the Crimean War revealed grave weaknesses in the structure of the state and of society. It became clear even to the new tsar, Alexander II, who as heir to the throne had defended the servile order, that reform and, above all, the abolition of serfdom could no longer be avoided. And so, soon after the fighting ended, he gave the order for the preparation of plans for emancipation.[26]

The revolutions of 1848 often had a direct and immediate influence in bringing about emancipations in central Europe. Peasants seized the opportunity provided by the wave of revolutions. Those still in servile status, like the peasants of the Austrian Monarchy, the Danubian Principalities, and

[24] Sée (1921), 207-212.   [25] Simon (1955), 19.   [26] Blum (1961), 576-578.

some of the German states, wanted to be rid of the bonds that still held them. Others, like the peasants in Baden, Prussia, Württemberg, Denmark, Mecklenburg, Bavaria, and Hesse, sought to bring to its conclusion the emancipation process that had started in their lands decades earlier. So the peasants threw in with the bourgeois liberals and the democrats who had touched off the revolutions. The "bourgeois revolutions" of 1848 were also peasant revolutions. However, though allied in revolution, burghers and villagers each had their own cause. The enemies of the peasants were their seigniors, and not the absolute monarchs against whom the liberals and democrats rebelled. And the peasants had far more luck than did their bourgeois allies in reaching their goals. The hard-pressed governments of those lands where earlier legislation had started the process of emancipation adopted new laws that speeded up the tempo of reform. Thus, redemption of obligations, until now frequently voluntary, became obligatory; the capitalized value of the peasants' dues and services often was reduced, thereby decreasing the amount of the annual redemption payments the peasant had to make; the right to redeem obligations, or to acquire a freehold, until now restricted in some lands to certain categories of the peasantry, was extended to all peasants. In the Austrian Monarchy and in a few German states where the peasants were still the hereditary subjects of their seigniors, decrees freed them at one stroke from their servile dependence. When the peasants gained these concessions, they abandoned the revolutions. They had never been true revolutionaries (only in one minor rising did they even wear the revolutionary cockade), they made no significant political demands, and they remained monarchists and conservatives. And when they withdrew, the revolutionary movement foundered.[27]

The peasants of the Danubian Principalities were not as fortunate as their brethren of central Europe. They had joined in the revolution that broke out in Wallachia in June 1848 (p. 315). The youthful firebrands who led the revolution talked about egalitarianism, democracy, and republicanism. Unfortunately for the revolution, the leaders knew little about real conditions in Wallachia—"they knew the Napoleonic Code better than they knew the Organic Statues" was the way one historian put it. The peasants, for their part, did not understand the concepts about which the leaders talked. Still the peasants refused *en masse* to pay their obligations, occasionally engaged in violent action, and in August sent delegates to a constitutional convention at which there was much talk and little action. The bubble burst when Russian and Turkish troops came in and restored the old order.[28]

The emancipations have sometimes been attributed to the demands of a nascent capitalistic society dominated by the bourgeoisie. According to this view, the needs of burgeoning capitalistic production required the reorgani-

[27] *Cf.* Franz (1959), 176-193.   [28] Emerit (1937), 297-321.

zation of the rural sector. The purpose of the reorganization was to increase the productivity of agriculture in order to feed the growing industrial labor force, and to eliminate the restrictions on peasant mobility and on choice of occupation in order to provide industry with the workers it needed. This hypothesis does not take into account the actual conditions of the time. In none of the servile lands had bourgeois capitalism developed to the extent that its needs could dictate the reshaping of society. Indeed, in some of the servile lands the bourgeois capitalistic element barely existed. It is difficult to imagine, much less to document, the thesis that bourgeois capitalists in Russia or Romania or Hungary, or, in fact, any of the servile lands, had sufficient influence to persuade governments to end the servile order, or that governments freed the peasants out of their concern for the needs of bourgeois capitalism.

The ratio between land and labor has been suggested, most recently by Professor Evsey Domar and by Ester Boserup, as the root cause of both the origins and abolition of serfdom and slavery. Supposedly, when land is abundant and labor scarce, when farming does not demand much capital or skill, and when per capita income is relatively high (because of the ample supply of land), peasants can easily establish their own farms. Seigniors cannot command the labor they need to man their properties. Only governmental edicts and enforcement can tie down the peasants, and thereby enable the seigniors to be supported by the exploitation of their now dependent peasants. Conversely, when population increases and land becomes scarce, serfdom or slavery is no longer necessary. Land has replaced labor as the scarce, and therefore valuable, factor of production. The marginal product of labor falls to the subsistence level, and the wages of the free laborer amounts to little more than the cost of maintaining a serf or slave.[29]

Professor Domar himself has pointed out some of the inadequacies of this model. He recognizes that it does not explain the decline of serfdom in England (and, indeed, in all of western Europe) in the late Middle Ages, despite the sharp rise during these centuries in the ratio between land and labor. He acknowledges, too, that the role of government in the establishment of serfdom "makes the presence of free land by itself neither a necessary nor a sufficient condition for the existence of serfdom." He could have added that the absence (or presence) of free land is neither a necessary nor a sufficient condition for the abolition of serfdom. In Russia, Romania, and in Hungary there were still great stretches of empty or nearly empty land in the nineteenth century, and peasant flight into these empty lands was still a common phenomenon. Yet in all of these lands the government emancipated the peasants.

[29] Domar (1970), 18-32; Boserup (1965), 67.

IV

Peasant unrest, punctuated by outbursts of violence; the psychological impact of these disturbances upon the higher orders of society; seigniorial acceptance of the inevitable, new intellectual currents; the example of neighboring lands; economic considerations; catastrophes, wars, and revolutions—all contributed to bringing about the end of the old order. In different lands, and in the same land at different times, the influence of each of these elements varied. One factor, however, seems to have been of constant and crucial significance: the preservation, or the strengthening, of the power and authority of the sovereign. In nearly all of the servile lands, the efforts of the central power to ameliorate the condition, and elevate the status, of the peasantry had been a critically important facet of the struggle for supremacy between absolute monarchs and their nobility. The final reforms that freed the peasants from their servility, and accorded them civil equality with the other strata of society, were the last great triumph of royal absolutism over nobility—and, in truth, its last great achievement. At long last, the centuries-old struggle for supremacy between throne and nobility had ended. Now everyone in the state, down to the humblest and poorest peasant, owed his allegiance directly to the throne. No longer was anyone the serf or the hereditary subject of a noble, and no longer did anyone have to pay servile dues and obligations to a noble as recognition and consequence of his own hereditary inferior status, and the hereditary superior status of the nobleman. Now everyone was born free, now everyone was a subject of the state, and as a subject and citizen of the state everyone owed the same obligations to the state.

Freedom and equality were, of course, cardinal precepts of liberalism, the new foe and the ultimate conqueror of royal absolutism. Liberal ideologies, and liberal bureaucrats, and liberal revolutionary movements put pressure on rulers to end the servile status of the peasantry. The deciding factor, however, was the ruler's concept of his own best interests and of the best interests of the state. Only exceptionally, as in France, was the emancipation both initiated and carried out by a non-absolutist regime. During the brief revolutionary storm of 1848 newly formed and short-lived representative assemblies in some of the states of central Europe issued legislation that ended the servile order. But the way had been readied by earlier decrees of absolute monarchs, and when the absolutists regained control, as they quickly did, they carried out the revolution's agrarian reforms because these reforms suited their own interests.

The emancipations not only served the interests of the throne by reducing the power of the nobility; they also enabled the throne to hold the loyalty and support of the peasantry. The villagers had long looked to the sovereign as their protector against their seigniors, and now they owed

[373]

their freedom to the sovereign. The benevolence of the throne was, of course, not an altruistic gesture. Sovereigns more than ever needed the support of the peasantry to meet the challenges to their authority that came from within the realm—and also from without. Humiliating defeats in war revealed to the rulers of Prussia and Russia that their armies needed drastic reform, and that a servile peasantry blocked effective reconstruction of the military establishment.[30] When the youthful Franz Joseph ascended the Austrian throne in December 1848, his counselors advised him that the best interests of the dynasty dictated the implementation of the agrarian reforms initiated by the revolutionary assemblies. The strongest opposition to Hapsburg rule in years past had come from the Magyar nobles of Hungary and the Polish nobles of Galicia. The memory of the loyalty to the throne of the Galician peasants in 1846 was still fresh in the minds of the young emperor and his advisors. They saw, too, that the revolutions that had broken out in different parts of the realm had been successful only as long as the peasants had supported them. When the peasants gained their freedom they returned to their traditional loyalty and conservatism, and the revolutions found themselves in retreat. Serbian, Croatian, Slovak, and Romanian peasants in Hungary had put themselves at the disposal of the emperor against the Magyar lords who had risen in revolt against the throne. Finally, parts of the Monarchy had not yet been pacified. The peasantry's record of past loyalty, and the still existing uncertainties of the present, made it impossible to abandon the reform legislation and return the peasants to their hereditary subjection. And so the neo-absolutist regime carried out the emancipation with vigor and dispatch.[31]

The Russian rulers of Poland realized, too, that they had to show special favor to the peasants to protect their own interests. The Polish nobility had revolted in 1863 to obtain freedom from Russia. A fact-finding commission, headed by Nicholas Miliutin, informed Tsar Alexander II that the rebels had won peasant support by promising them full ownership of their holdings. To crush the revolt, the tsar had to meet this offer. And so on 19 February 1864 (a day purposely chosen as the third anniversary of the decree that freed the Russian serfs and the ninth anniversary of Alexander's coronation), the tsar issued a ukase that made the Polish peasants landowners, and ended the powers of the seignior over them. In the decree the tsar reminded the peasants of earlier efforts on their behalf by his father and by himself, and indicated that his benevolence was a reward for their "unswerving loyalty," which had enabled them to withstand the blandishments of the insurgents.[32] The stratagem worked. The peasants, with landownership a certainty and not just a promise from rebels, gave their allegiance to the tsar and the insurrection petered out.

[30] *Cf.* Craig (1955), 38-41; Ipsen (1954), 31; Rieber (1966), 24-29.
[31] Friedjung (1903), 113-114.
[32] Leroy-Beaulieu (1884), 198-229; 19 February 1864 decree in Rostworowski (1896), 46-47.

In the Danubian Principalities the *Realpolitik* of the European powers, and the nationalistic ambitions of Romanian leaders, combined to bring about the unification of the principalities and the emancipation of the peasantry. The Treaty of Paris in 1856, at the end of the Crimean War, did away with the Russian protectorate over the principalities. Instead, it placed them under the collective guarantee of the contracting powers (Austria, France, Great Britain, Prussia, Russia, Turkey, and Sardinia). The powers wanted a buffer state between Russia and Turkey, and wanted it to be strong enough to keep the Danube open to commerce, and to withstand the restoration of hegemony by a neighboring power. The delegates at the Paris conference realized that to accomplish these goals fundamental social and political reforms had to be introduced, including a reorganization of the lord-peasant relationship. That was essential in order to win and hold the support of the peasantry, who formed the great bulk of the population, and in order to establish a national political system in which all Romanians could participate. The conference decided to leave the details of the reconstruction to the Romanians themselves. It ordered the summoning of a special assembly in each principality, with representatives from all strata of the social order, to draw up proposals for reform and submit them to the powers. The divans (as the assemblies were called) met, but the boyars who dominated the meetings refused to make the concessions necessary for meaningful reform. The powers then decided to take matters in their own hands. In the Convention of Paris, signed on 19 August 1858, they drafted a new constitution to replace the Organic Statutes that Russia had imposed in 1831. The Convention joined the two principalities into the United Principalities of Moldavia and Wallachia, each with separate but identical administrations. Article 46 of the Convention ordered that "The Moldavians and Wallachians shall be equal before the law and in taxes. . . . All the privileges and monopolies still enjoyed by certain orders shall be abolished, and steps shall be taken without delay to revise the law which governs the relation of the proprietors of the soil with the cultivators, with the view of ameliorating the condition of the peasantry."[33]

The Convention provided for the election of a prince by the assembly of each principality. To the general surprise—and not least his own—each assembly in early 1859 chose Alexander John Cuza for the post. Member of a lesser boyar family, Cuza had studied in Paris and had participated in the failed revolution in 1848 in his native Moldavia. Once in office Cuza found himself confronted with the obstructionism of the new national assembly. This body, established in 1862, and supposed to share the rule with the prince, was controlled by the boyars. Cuza, a long-time advocate of agrarian reform, decided that he had to win the support of the peasantry in order to consolidate his own power. And so, after much wrangling, he seized power in a *coup d'etat* on 28 March 1864. A plebiscite in early May gave him an

[33] Martens (1860), xvi, pt. 2, 51, 58.

overwhelming mandate (683,928 yeas, 1,307 noes, 50,232 abstentions) to act on his own, and on 14 August 1864 he promulgated the decree that freed the peasants from their servitude.[34]

In their resolve to reform their realms, monarchs in all of the servile lands owed much to the counsels and persuasions of their close advisors. These men, advocates of the bureaucratic sovereign state, opposed the traditional order because it interfered with and impeded the welfare and the power of the state. Though nearly all of them were of noble birth, they dedicated their efforts and energies to the aggrandizement of the central power, thereby often winning for themselves the enmity of their fellow nobles. Some of them, like the Reventlow brothers or Christian Colbjörnsen or Count A. P. Bernstorff in Denmark, or Baron vom Stein and Prince Hardenberg in Prussia, were of foreign birth. Count Maximilian von Montgelas was the son of a Savoyard nobleman who had entered the service of the ruler of Bavaria. Men such as these had no hereditary or emotional bonds to the native nobility, and did not share its ambitions and frustrations. They were the king's men, and they depended upon him for their special eminence. Others like Nicholas Miliutin or Leopold von Schroetter had deep roots in their native land, and had important family connections that opened doors for them in their ascent to high places in government. Some were poor, like Miliutin or Stein. Others, like the Romanian Mihail Cogălniceanu or the Prussian von Schroetter, came of families of wealth. Some, like Montgelas, Stein, Schroetter and his colleague Theodor von Schön, Miliutin and Cogălniceanu, had become advocates of reform while still young men, before they had entered government service. Others, like the Russian General I. I. Rostovtsev, came late to reform but argued valiantly for it. Whatever their origins and background, these men, and others like them, insisted upon agrarian reform because they believed that it was indispensable to the growth in the power and unity of the state, and in the authority of the monarch they served.

[34] Emerit (1937), 357-401, 448-505; Riker (1931), 25-32, 437.

CHAPTER 17

The Reforms

I

THE release of the peasantry from their servile condition, and the termination of the privileges and administrative functions of the seigniors, inevitably involved the renovation of many of the institutions of social and political life in the servile lands. Law codes, courts, police, fiscal policies and taxation, military conscription, education, and the legislative and administrative apparatus of local and central government, all had to be recast. They had to suit the new social order in which all men were equal before the law, had freedom of movement and occupation, and were not bound by accident of birth to fixed social orders, each with its own privileges and responsibilities. The comprehensive reform movement went swiftly in some lands, and much more slowly in others. And when the era of reform ended, not all of the blemishes of the servile regime had been obliterated. It took longer—sometimes decades—for that to happen (as later pages will show).

It seems hardly coincidental that in many of the servile lands the era of reform followed soon after a change in the leadership of the state. In Denmark a bloodless coup worthy of *opera bouffe* drove out the reactionary regime led by the demented King Christian's stepmother, the Queen Dowager, her son (the king's half-brother), and Oeve Höegh-Guldberg, once the son's tutor and now the active head of the government. On a day in April 1784 the sixteen-year-old Crown Prince Frederick, confirmed after long delay as heir to the throne, attended his first Privy Council meeting. There, to the astonishment of all, he declared the end of government by cabinet and announced the appointment of four first-rate men to the Privy Council. King Christian signed the orders, and then fled from the Council chamber with his outraged half-brother in hot pursuit. Young Frederick next coolly informed Guldberg and his cabal that his father, the king, had no further need of their services. He then set out to find the king, who meekly signed the rescript that made Frederick, for all practical purposes, the regent of the kingdom. Thereupon the young prince immediately set into motion the men and the movement that produced the emancipation of 1788, along with other great reforms.[1] In France and Switzerland revolutionary governments that supplanted the old regimes were responsible for the reforms. In Bavaria the oppressive twenty-two-year rule of Elector Charles Theodore ended with his death in 1799. He was succeeded by

---

[1] *Cambridge Modern History* (1909), vi, 751-755. King Christian lived until 1808; only then did Frederick ascend the throne as Frederick VII.

[377]

Maximilian I Joseph, a man of very different stripe. The new ruler (who as Maximilian I Joseph became the first king of Bavaria in 1805) and his chief minister, Count Maximilian von Montgelas, set out to remake the state. Their achievements included a constitution issued in 1808. The first written constitution of any German state, it provided for the abolition of serfdom, equality before the law, liberty of conscience, and universal liability to taxation.[2]

In Prussia, too, the accession of a new monarch heralded an abrupt turn in state policy. Frederick William II, who ruled from 1786 to 1797, was adamant in his opposition to agrarian reform. In a statement on 5 September 1794 he declared that "The abolition of the labor obligations of the peasant could never be squared with the wise and just principles of government held by His Majesty." He promised that "His Majesty will never deprive the lords of the services of their subjects or to urge their cancellation or commutation into monetary obligations against the will of their owners."[3] His son and successor, Frederick William III (1797-1840), disagreed entirely with his father's position. In a cabinet order issued almost at the outset of his reign he said that the system of hereditary subjection was "ripe for the sickle." He was not a forceful man nor an especially discerning one, but, as the ardent reformer Hermann von Boyen said of him, "he had a genuine desire to free the lower orders from their burdens." Soon after his accession he instructed his officials to address themselves to the problem of the abolition of the servile system. Already in 1798 he had accepted a plan (which was never implemented) to free all minors and thereby gradually eliminate hereditary subjection.[4]

King William I of Württemberg (1816-1864) succeeded a reform-minded father, Frederick I (1806-1816). Frederick, however, had ruled in the tradition of the enlightened despots of the eighteenth century. William, thirty-five when he ascended the throne, was attuned to the new liberal ideas. When he took over rule, his kingdom was suffering from the effects of the wars of the Napoleonic era, and in addition was wracked by famine. William, a strong and able leader, decided that the best way to achieve recovery was to scrap the old order, with its hierarchy of privilege, and convert his realm into a constitutional monarchy.[5] In Hannover Count Ernst Münster, the all-powerful minister who dominated the government, was dismissed by his master, William IV King of England and of Hannover, on 12 February 1831 after widespread unrest that had been set off initially by news of the July Revolution in France. Order was quickly restored, and in March the government presented the reconvened diet with a proposal for

---

[2] *Königlich-Baierisches Regierungsblatt*, 1808, ii, 1933ff.
[3] Quoted in Epstein (1960), 370.
[4] Borcke-Stargordt (1954), 310; Borcke-Stargordt (1958), 123-124; Simon (1955), 10; Hintze (1896), 509, 509n.
[5] Weller and Weller (1971), 223-225.

sweeping agrarian reform. In Saxony, too, the revolutionary wave of 1830 had its repercussions. It compelled the aged King Anthony I to accept his nephew, Frederick Augustus, as his co-ruler. Soon, under the leadership of Frederick Augustus, legislation that included a written constitution and reforms of education, taxes, village communal organizations, and of the lord-peasant relationship, transformed many of the traditional institutions of the kingdom.[6]

In Russia the accession of Alexander II in 1855 marked the opening of the great era of reform in that vast empire. Alexander's inclinations had been against reform, but events compelled him to realize that the continued existence of his realm was threatened unless he initiated sweeping changes. In the Danubian Principalities, the election of Alexander Cuza as sovereign of the United Principalities opened a brand-new chapter in the troubled history of that region. Cuza and Mihail Cogălniceanu, his one-time schoolmate and now his closest advisor, were men of liberal outlook, who were determined to recast the institutions of their homeland, and especially the relationship between peasant and seignior.

Usually a series of preliminary reforms appeared in the years that immediately preceded the decree that freed the peasants from their servile status. In Denmark, where emancipation was ordered by the decree of 20 June 1788, a law of 30 October 1786 bestowed freedom of movement upon peasants who had completed their military service, or had been found unfit for it. Legislation of 28 June 1787 provided protection for peasant renters against possible exploitation by their landlords. In Schleswig-Holstein a series of lesser reforms foreshadowed the decree of emancipation in 1804. An edict of 28 July 1807 in Bavaria set norms for the labor service of peasants, limited fees charged by seigniors on the transfer of peasant holdings, and established the principle of redemption of servile obligations by mutual agreement of seignior and peasant. Nine months later the new constitution of Bavaria freed the peasants. In the canton of Basel, Abel Merian, a member of the Grand Council, on 21 September 1789 asked his confreres "if it would not conform to the dignity of the state and to present circumstances to free the serfs." Nothing came of his initiative at that time. Then on 20 July 1790 the town of Liestal presented the Grand Council with a petition, part of which concerned the grant of personal freedom. After some hesitation, the Council on 20 December 1790 voted unanimously to end serfdom in the canton of Basel. Actually, only remnants of the institution remained, so that its abolition was little more than a formality. In Schaffhausen canton a decree of 1 January 1798 abolished serfdom. A few months later the Legislative Council of the newly established Helvetic Republic ordered the end of all servile obligations.

The exclusively noble Hungarian diet in its session of 1839-1840 adopted

[6] Wittich (1896), 433-434; Kötzschke and Kretschmar (1965), 322-327.

legislation that permitted peasants, through voluntary agreement with their seigniors, to buy their freedom and to become landowners. Its supporters had high expectations for the law, but it soon became apparent that it would have little effect. And so at the diet that convened in 1847, reformers urged that redemption be made compulsory. Their efforts foundered on the opposition of a coalition of conservative lesser nobles and the great magnates. In the spring of the next year, however, revolution persuaded the diet to accept emancipation, and on terms much less favorable to the lord than those projected in earlier reform proposals. In Poland a tsarist ukase of 16 May 1861 ordered the commutation into money payments of the labor obligations of the peasants. By 1863, 96.1 per cent of the peasantry had commuted their obligations. Another decree of 5 June 1862 provided for improvements in rental contracts of certain groups of peasants, and ordered the establishment of local committees of landowners and government officials to determine the rent.

The freeing of the gypsy slaves in the Danubian Principalities preceded the emancipation in 1864 of the peasants. In Moldavia slaves of the state and of monasteries and bishops were freed in 1844 without indemnification. During the 1848 revolution the provisional government of Moldavia banned slavery, but the revolution was quashed before the decree could be implemented. In 1851 Barbu Ştirbei, hospodar of Wallachia, forbad the sale of slaves except to the state, and the state then freed the purchased bondsmen. Finally, in 1855 all slaves who belonged to private persons were freed by decree, with indemnification to be paid to the owners by the state.[7]

In Bavaria and in the Danubian Principalities (or Romania, as it was called from 1862), the state secularized church land shortly before it issued the decree of emancipation. In both countries the church had enormous holdings so that the seizure of its property provided the government with an ample base, in terms of land and peasants, from which to launch its agrarian reform. In Roman Catholic Bavaria the church owned 56 per cent of the 29,807 peasant homesteads when the new ruler, Maximilian I Joseph, began secularization in 1803. The conversion of these holdings into state property, plus the 13.6 per cent of peasant homesteads that already belonged to the sovereign, gave the government a free hand to apply reform to the largest part of the Bavarian peasantry. A decree of 27 June 1803 provided the peasants on secularized land with the right to become free proprietors of their holdings by making redemption payments.[8]

In Romania, where most of the people belonged to the Orthodox Church, an estimated one-fourth of all the land in Wallachia, and one-third

[7] Denmark: Nielsen (1933), 323-324. Schleswig-Holstein: Sugenheim (1861), 523. Bavaria: Sée (1921), 217. Switzerland: Rappard (1912), 138-139; Henne am Rhyn (1903), I, 456. Hungary: Benda (1948), 222. Poland: Leslie (1963), 118-119; Rostworowski (1896), 40-44. Danubian Principalities: Emerit (1937), 354-355; Emerit (1930), 133.

[8] *Churbaiersche Regierungsblatt*, 1803, 427-429; Brentano (1899), 260; Carsten (1959), 352.

in Moldavia, were owned by monasteries. It was the richest possession of any church in all of Christendom. The revenues from this enormous patrimony were supposed to be spent for education, hospitals, aid to the poor, and other charitable purposes. Instead, the monks used most of the income to support themselves in luxurious ease. There was also much graft and corruption connected with the farming out and the collection of the monasteries' revenues. Some of the monasteries were called "dedicated"; they were supposed to use some of their income for humanitarian purposes at home, and were "dedicated" to send the rest to support the Holy Places of the Orthodox church in Jerusalem and elsewhere. The monks of these institutions spent none of their revenues on the native population. They used as much as they needed to maintain themselves in fine style, and sent the rest abroad. The native rulers were, of course, aware of these abuses, but could do nothing to stop them because the Russians, who had the protectorate over the principalities, would not allow any infringements upon the monasteries. When the Treaty of Paris in 1856 terminated the Russian protectorate, and the principalities were united, the monetary needs of the new government aroused interest in secularization. The powers, who now collectively guaranteed the united principalities, instructed Prince Cuza to enter into negotiations with the monks. The churchmen refused to make any concessions, whereupon the government, by a decree of 29 December 1863, ordered the secularization of all monastic land. The government offered a large indemnity for the seizure, but the monks, hoping to gain more by winning foreign support, remained intransigent. Their obstinacy cost them what foreign support they had, and in the end they lost everything. The secularization, which brought great numbers of peasants directly under state control, made it easier to carry out the emancipation statute, which was issued seven months after the edict of secularization. The confiscated church properties also provided the state with an enormous reserve from which, after emancipation, it drew land for holdings for landless peasants.[9]

In some countries the sovereign appointed a special committee and charged it with the task of drafting the legislation that would free the peasant. That was the way it was done in Denmark, Prussia, and Russia.[10] In revolutionary France, the National Assembly (1789-1791) and its successor, the Legislative Assembly (1791-1792), each had a Feudal Committee to which was entrusted the preparation of legislation for agrarian reform. In October 1792 the National Convention (1792-1795) appointed a forty-eight-member Committee of Civil, Criminal, and Feudal Legislation. In revolutionary Austria in the summer of 1848 the emancipation bill was hammered out on the floor of the Constitutional Reichstag. That assembly,

[9] Emerit (1937), 471-486; Riker (1931), 354-356.
[10] Nielsen (1933), 322; Borcke-Stargordt (1958), 126-129; Blum (1961), 579-590.

elected by universal male suffrage, convened in Vienna in July. Ninety-two of its 383 delegates were peasants, and most of the other delegates sympathized with the peasant cause. At the third session on 24 July the youngest delegate, the twenty-five-year-old Hans Kudlich, son of a peasant, proposed the abolition of "all servile relationships together with rights and obligations coming therefrom." Debate on this motion began on 8 August, with indemnification of the seigniors as the principal point at issue. After heated discussions the assembly adopted a measure that included indemnification. On 7 September 1848 the emperor signed the bill as "constitutional Emperor of Austria" and it became law.[11]

In certain lands the estates took a leading part in the preparation of the emancipation legislation. Earlier pages have told of the initiative of the diets in the Baltic provinces of Russia in the landless emancipations in that region. When the seigniors of Schleswig-Holstein accepted the inevitability of emancipation, they decided, in 1795, to take the lead in preparing the legislation. A committee was appointed to study the problem. After several years of discussion and politicking, the proposed legislation was presented to the sovereign and the State Council. After making important changes, they gave their approval to the proposal. In Hannover the government in March 1831 presented the estates with a draft of a proposal for agrarian reform. The estates appointed a committee, whose leading member was Carl Stüve, bourgeois lawyer and long-time advocate of reform, to study the draft. The committee made significant changes, and then submitted the amended bill to the estates. After angry exchanges the bill passed, was signed by the sovereign, and was published on 10 November 1831.[12]

Sometimes, as in Swedish Pomerania and in Romania, the emancipation came as the dictate of the ruler. In Swedish Pomerania[13] the resistance of the local nobility to the exceptional war measures of King Gustavus IV Adolphus in 1806 angered that autocratic monarch. He therefore abolished the special privileges enjoyed by the province as part of the Holy Roman Empire (which, in any event, was disbanded later that year), disbanded the diet, and in a decree of 26 June 1806 extended Swedish constitutional arrangements to Hither Pomerania. In Sweden the peasants were free and formed the fourth estate with their own delegates to the national diet. Now the peasants of Swedish Pomerania had these rights and this freedom. To make it clear that the peasants were emancipated, a royal patent of 4 July 1806 specifically announced the abolition of serfdom. This edict ordered the peasants to continue to pay their dues and services to their seigniors until

[11] Caron (1924), 12-16; Grünberg (1893), II, 495.

[12] Hvidtfeldt (1963), 499-505; Wittich (1896), 434.

[13] Sweden acquired Hither Pomerania (Pomerania west of the Oder river) and the island of Rügen in 1648 by the Treaty of Westphalia. Farther Pomerania (Pomerania east of the Oder) belonged to Prussia. In 1720 Sweden had to give up part of Hither Pomerania to Prussia, and in 1815 relinquished the rest to Prussia.

1810. However, French occupation of the province in 1807 prevented application of the reform, and when the long war finally ended, the peasants of erstwhile Swedish Pomerania found themselves subjects of the Prussian king, and subject to his laws.[14] In Romania a plan for reform that offered no substantive relief to the peasants was adopted in 1862 by nearly a two-to-one majority of the boyar-dominated assembly of the united principalities. Prince Cuza, who wanted genuine reform, refused to give the bill his approval. Two years of wrangling followed, until Cuza executed his *coup* and issued his own law of agrarian reform.[15]

II

The multiplicity of the decrees of emancipation, and the seemingly infinite variety of their provisions, make it difficult, if not impossible, to present an ordered comparison of them. In many lands the legislation stretched out over decades: the first paragraph of the Prussian edict of 2 March 1850, which completed the emancipation process there, listed thirty-three laws issued between 1811 and 1849 that were now superseded by the 1850 decree. Then there is the length and complexity of some of the decrees. A modern collection of the legislation and administrative orders that dealt with the suppression of the "feudal order" in revolutionary France between August 1789 and July 1793 fills 180 closely printed pages. The decree of 17 March 1832 in the Kingdom of Saxony contained 317 articles and ran on for 81 pages. The Russian law of 19 February 1861 takes up 466 pages in a Soviet reprinting. The wide disparities in the condition of servitude and in the dues and services among peasants of different servile lands and within the same land, and the varieties of their tenures, present further obstacles to a comprehensive and systematic comparison.

Still, despite the difficulties, it is possible to filter out and compare characteristics and qualities possessed in common by the decrees.[16] The grant of

---

[14] Barton (1974), 277; Fuchs (1888), 228-238.   [15] Emerit (1937), 399-403, 453-469.

[16] Except where otherwise noted, the account of the emancipation legislation in this and the next chapter is based upon the following sources: Austria, law of 7 September 1848, Grünberg (1893), II, 495-497; law of 4 March 1849, *Allgemeines Reichs-Gesetz-und Regierungsblatt für das Kaiserthum Oesterreich*, 1849, 167-173: Bavaria, law of 31 August 1808, *Königlich-Baierisches Regierungsblatt*, 1808, 1933-1936, law of 4 June 1848, *Gesetzblatt für das Königreich Bayern*, 1848, 97-118: Baden, law of 23 July 1783, Franz (1963), 292-294: France, laws of 3 November 1789 to 17 July 1793, Caron (1924), 19-198: Hannover, law of 10 November 1831, Conze (1957), 177-183: Poland, law of 19 February 1864, Rostworowski (1896), 46-57: Prussia, law of 9 October 1807, *Sammlung Preussischer Gesetze und Verordnungen* . . . (1819), IX, 85-88; law of 14 September 1811, *Allgemeines Landrecht für die Preussischen Staaten* (1837), III, part 2. vol. 1, 456-468; law of 29 May 1816, *ibid.*, 468-486. Romania: law of 14 August 1864, Warriner (1965), 178-186; Russia, law of 19 February 1861, *Krest'ianskaia Reforma v Rossii 1861 goda* (1954), Savoy, laws of 19 December 1771 to 27 October 1792, Bruchet (1908), 55-226: Saxony, law of 17 March 1832, *Sammlung der Gesetze für das Königreich Sachsen*, 1832, 163-244: Schleswig-Holstein, law of 19 December

personal freedom was, of course, a feature of every emancipation edict. The legislation sometimes included an explicit statement of liberation of the peasants from their servile bonds and obligations, and sometimes implied but did not state it directly. For example, in the decree of 19 December 1804 the king of Denmark ordered that "From 1 January 1805 villeinage in Our duchies of Schleswig and Holstein is completely and forever abolished without any exception" (art. 1). The Prussian law of 9 October 1807 declared that "With Martinmas [11 November] 1810 all villeinage ends in Our entire state. After Martinmas 1810 there will only be free people . . ." (art. xii). The opening paragraph of the Russian General Statute of 19 February 1861 stated that "The serfdom of the peasants who live on seigniorial property and of the household serfs is abolished forever . . ." and ordered that henceforth they were "free, rural inhabitants" (p.39). The French National Assembly was less specific when, in the opening words of the decree of 11 August 1789 (promulgated on 3 November), it declared that "The National Assembly completely does away with the feudal regime." Similarly, the brief Austrian decree of 7 September 1848, drafted by the Constitutional *Reichstag*, began with the statement that the subjection of the peasantry, together with all of the laws regulating it, were abolished. In Romania the agrarian reform law of 14 August 1864 listed the servile obligations that it now abolished, and gave the peasant full ownership of his land, but it did not specifically state that the peasant was now a free man.

As a matter of fact, the decrees did not always give personal freedom to all the peasants simultaneously. In Denmark the law of 20 June 1788 granted full personal liberty only to peasants who were under fourteen and over thirty-six. Those between fourteen and thirty-six, the age group eligible for military service, had to remain serfs until they reached thirty-six, or until 1 January 1800, whichever came first. In Mecklenburg, to calm the fears of the proprietors that emancipation would create a labor shortage, the edict of emancipation of 18 January 1820 ordered that during the next four years seigniors need only free one-fourth of their serfs each autumn. Nor did the grant of freedom always give the peasant the right to move about as he wished. The Napoleonic legislation had declared that the peasant of the grand duchy of Warsaw was a free man. But if the peasant wanted to move, he had to get written permission from the mayor of his village, who after 1815 was also the seignior or his agent. In the Baltic provinces, too, where the peasants had been freed without land early in the nineteenth century, the villager had to get written permission from his lord if he wanted to leave his employ and take work elsewhere. He then had to

---

1804, *Kong Christian den Syvendes allernaadigste Forordninger og aabne Breve*, 1804, 301-306: Switzerland, law of 4 May 1798, *Tageblatt der Gesetze und Dekrete der gesetzgebenden Räthe der helvetischen Republik* (1798), i, 45-46; Württemberg, law of 18 November 1817, *Regierungs-Blatt für das Königreich Württemberg in Auszuge* (1841), ii, 98-107.

present the document to the new employer, who was required by law to inform the old employer that he was willing to hire the peasant. Only then could the peasant leave. In Russia the freed peasant could not leave his village for a prolonged absence unless he had permission from the head of his household and from his village commune.[17]

Along with personal freedom for the peasants, the emancipation decrees, or other legislation issued at or near the same time, provided for a greater or lesser degree of economic freedom. In Denmark laws of 6 June and 11 June 1788 allowed anyone to engage in the hitherto restricted grain trade, and gave everyone the right, until now held only by nobles, to fatten cattle for export and sell them abroad.[18] In France the National Assembly, especially in its rural code of 28 September 1791, struck heavy blows against the restrictive practices that had prevailed in the old order. Now anyone could grow whatever he wanted, could sell his grain freely at home or abroad, or store it if he so wished, could keep as much livestock as he felt he needed, and could freely enclose his fields.[19] The Prussian law of 9 October 1807 gave all subjects of the state the right to own land and do with it as they wished, and to follow any occupation of their choosing (art. I, II, V). The emancipation decree for Schleswig-Holstein declared that as of 1 January 1805 the freed peasants, like any freeborn subject, could do as he wished with his person and property, so long as he did not violate the laws of the land (art. 3). In Russia, too, the emancipation statute included freedom of choice of occupation for the peasant. Sometimes the legislation spelled out specific rights and liberties now possessed by the peasant. For example, the Schleswig-Holstein decree stated that the peasant no longer had to get his seignior's approval to wed or to learn a trade (art. 4). In Prussia the 1807 statute explained that the peasant now could freely become a burgher, and the burgher could freely become a peasant (art. II). The Russian statute included provisions that gave the peasant freedom to enter into contractual obligations, to sue and be sued in his own name, and to bear witness in court actions (General Statute, Title I, art. 21, 22, 24).

The grant of personal freedom did not always extend to one category among the peasantry, or at least not to the degree to which it applied to the rest of the peasantry. That category—and it was a large one—was that of the farm servants, the hired hand who lived in the home or on the holding of his employer. In Denmark a law of 1791 forbad unmarried male farm servants to earn their livelihood as hired day workers or at other employments. They had to remain in the permanent service of their employer, who had the right to give them corporal punishment if he deemed it necessary. This severe restriction on personal freedom, which affected a

[17] Scharling (1909), II, 579; Mager (1955), 349; Leslie (1955), 72-73; Kahk (1969), 135; *Krest'ianskaia Reforma* (1954), General Statute, Title II, ch, v, sect. 1.

[18] Scharling (1909), II, 579.   [19] Jeanneney and Perrot (1957), 36-38.

large number of Danish peasants, remained the law for another fifty years. Even then it was not entirely abolished. In 1840 legislation permitted the farm worker to seek other employment, but only after he reached the age of twenty-eight. Some of the German states also issued special legislation that made it difficult, if not impossible, for farm servants to leave their employer, and that imposed other limitations upon their freedom. Some of these restrictions persisted until the collapse of the German empire in 1918. In Poland a law of 1821 decreed that farm servants had to agree to serve for a full year. The employer could use corporal punishment to discipline the servant, and could dismiss him at any time. The servant, however, could not leave before the year's end, except in the case of maltreatment or extreme cruelty by the employer. In the Austrian Monarchy, too, the law limited the freedom of the farm servant during the term of his contracted service.[20]

Actually, in nearly every land the decree that is celebrated as the law that freed the peasants did not really end their servile status. Though the edicts solemnly declared or implied that henceforth the peasants were free men, much of the apparatus and the reality of servility remained. These decrees represented the breakthrough and prepared the way for the later legislation that completed the task, and so are justly honored. There was, however, nearly always a hiatus, often of many years, before the dues and obligations, the seigniorial privileges and jurisdictions, and other remnants of servility finally disappeared. Once the enthusiasm that had accompanied the initial decrees of emancipation had waned, there was a lag in the continuation of the process of liberation from servility, and of the redemption of servile obligations and of land. The opposition of seigniors to the continuation of reform, the reactionary posture of governments after 1815 that was inspired by their determination to stifle the ideological legacy of the French Revolution, and the political inertia of the peasantry, help to explain the lag.

Charles Emmanuel of Savoy won fame as the first of the emancipators when he issued his decree of 19 December 1771 (published in May of the next year). The final annulment of seigniorial privilege and peasant servility did not come, however, until 1792, and then, as pointed out earlier, at the instance of revolutionary France, which had annexed Savoy. In Baden, second among the servile lands to free its peasants, the initial decree appeared in 1783, but the abolition of all seigniorial privilege occurred sixty-five years later during the revolutionary year of 1848. In Denmark the decree of 20 June 1788 abolished serfdom for most Danish peasants, but they did not lose all traces of their servility until 1861. France, the next to free its peasants, was one of the few, and the only major exception to the long-

[20] Sugenheim (1861), 522-523, 527; Abel (1964), 100-101; Kieniewicz (1969), 76; Stölzl (1971), 34; Purs (1963), 53-56.

drawn-out process of granting full civil equality to the peasant. Less than four years elapsed between the first decrees of the National Assembly, promulgated by royal proclamation on 3 November 1789, and the law of 17 July 1793, which definitively ended all seigniorial rights and privileges. The Helvetic Republic's decree of 4 May 1798 freed Swiss peasants from many of their seigniorial obligations, but the last remnants of their servility were not banished until 1846. And though Napoleon freed the serfs of the grand duchy of Warsaw in 1807, their servile dependence upon their seigniors continued until 1864.

Prussia was first among the major states of Germany to abolish serfdom, in the famed decree of 9 October 1807. Actually, that edict left the peasants still subject to seigniorial dues and services, and did not affect seigniorial privileges and monopolies. In fact, it is unclear what the decree did abolish. Months elapsed before it was proclaimed in most provinces, and it was never proclaimed in Brandenburg. The French occupied that province when King Frederick William published the decree, and after it was regained by Prussia in 1809 the bureaucrats there did not bother to promulgate the decree.[21] On 14 September 1811 the king issued another decree, which prescribed the conditions by which peasants could redeem their obligations and their holdings. The stringent terms of this legislation, and the renewal of war against Napoleon—the so-called "War of Liberation"—prevented much use of this law. Victory in the war freed the rulers of Prussia from the need to make any further concessions to the peasantry. So on 29 May 1816 a new decree drastically amended the 1811 law to make it even more difficult for peasants to gain their freedom. In the succeeding years, the government issued a series of new laws and ordinances concerning agrarian matters, but these did not materially alter the existing state of affairs. Most Prussian peasants continued in their servile status, albeit no longer serfs, until 1850. Only then, in a delayed reaction to the bad fright that the 1848 revolutions had given to Prussia's rulers, the decree of 2 March 1850 allowed hitherto excluded peasants to gain freedom from servile tenures and servile obligations.

Less than a year after the initial Prussian decree of 1807, the king of Bavaria ordered the end of serfdom there. Title I, article 3 of the constitution of 1 May 1808, declared that "Serfdom where it still exists is abolished," and a decree of 31 August 1808 provided detailed guidance for the abolition of servility. However, the Bavarian peasantry continued to be burdened with servile obligations, and seigniors still retained privileges, until the fateful year of 1848, when a royal decree of 4 June abolished all servile obligations and seigniorial privileges, and granted the peasants full citizenship and full freedom of ownership. In the Austrian Monarchy sixty years passed before the reform movement initiated by Joseph II came to

[21] Ford (1922), 204-205; 205n.; Ziekursch (1927), 290-291.

fruition under the pressure of revolution, with the emancipation of the peasantry. On 11 April 1848, a month after the outbreak of revolution, the Hungarian diet, which had declared Hungary all but independent of the rest of the Monarchy, decreed the end of hereditary subjection and of its associated dues and services. The decree drafted by the Constitutional Reichstag, and signed by the emperor on 7 September 1848, ended the servile system in the German and Slav crown lands. Seven months later, on 4 March 1849 (15 August 1849 for Galicia, 12 March 1851 for Cracow, 23 October 1853 for Bukovina), the restored absolutism issued a patent that expanded on the September decree, and provided the mechanism needed to carry out the emancipation and redemption procedures. Later legislation provided specific instructions for each province. After the defeat of the Hungarian revolution, Hungary was reduced from a kingdom to the status of a province, and the revolutionary legislation was annulled. Imperial patents in 1853 and 1854 ordered the application of most of the provisions of the decrees of 7 September 1848 and 4 March 1849 to Hungary and Croatia.

III

Every emancipation operation, whatever the country, had to deal with the question of indemnification to the seigniors for their losses in dues, services, and land. As can be easily imagined, that was the thorniest problem that confronted the legislators. Perhaps that helps to explain why, with rare exception, the initial decrees of emancipation did not make redemption mandatory. Indeed, in some lands decades passed before governments decided to take that step. Instead, as mentioned in the preceding chapter, redemption was usually left to the voluntary mutual decision of lord and peasant.

The first, and possibly the most difficult, issue that had to be settled was to distinguish between obligations for which the seignior was to receive indemnification, and those which were abolished without indemnification. In most lands a line was drawn between charges that rose out of the servile relationship of the peasant to his lord, and those which rose out of the peasant's occupation of land that belonged to the seignior. The legislation usually annulled the former without indemnification, because they rose out of the now abolished servile status of the peasant. Therefore, seigniors did not receive indemnification for their loss of such things as the compulsory labor service of peasant children, the labor services of landless peasants and cotters, exit fees, and those monopolies which they had to relinquish. When the freed peasant received land along with his freedom, he had to redeem the land. In most states this was done by indemnifying the seignior for his loss of the dues and services that the peasant had paid in return for his occupation of the seignior's land. These dues and services were regarded as property rights of the seignior, and, therefore, he had to be paid for their loss. Often, however, the distinction between these two categories of obligations, sometimes called personal and real, were not clear, and this led to confusion, uncertainties, and bitter disputes.

Nowhere was the confusion greater, and the debate more intensive and divisive, than in revolutionary France. The decrees of 11 August to 3 November 1789 ordered indemnification for the real obligations, and no indemnity for the personal ones. But the legislation did not list the obligations in each category. The National Assembly was soon flooded with protests, and with queries it could not answer. The legislators worked long and hard at the problem without a resolution, though they did succeed in raising many hackles. Finally, the National Convention (1792-1795), longest-lived of the revolutionary assemblies, decided to cut the Gordian knot. A law of 17 July 1793 ordered the suppression without any indemnification of all the obligations owed by the peasants to their seigniors. To nail down the decree, the law further ordered the public burning of all records that related to these obligations. Later legislation, however, issued in 1793 and 1794, allowed proprietors, under certain circumstances, to add the yield of some of the abolished obligations to the rents they charged peasants for land.[22]

In other servile lands the seigniors received more consideration, though not always as much as might have been expected. The calculation of the indemnities to be paid them was based upon the annual cash value of the obligations. This presented no problem for dues that were paid at regular intervals in money, nor for dues in labor or kind. The annual value of the latter could be determined by the current market price for hired labor and goods, or at a specific date in the past, or by averaging these prices over a period of years, as, for example, in Hannover, where the legislation called for the average prices of the products used for payments in kind for the twenty-four years immediately preceding the redemption operation.[23] It was far more difficult to determine the annual value of obligations that recurred irregularly, such as the fees paid to the seignior when a holding changed hands.

In the Austrian Monarchy the initial decree of emancipation of 7 September 1848 had ordered that the seigniors were to receive indemnification only for the real obligations, that is, those dues in cash, kind, and labor which the peasants had paid to the seigniors in return for their occupation of the seignior's land. No indemnification was to be made for those seigniorial revenues which stemmed from the servile status of the peasantry, as, for example, the lord's right of jurisdiction (arts. 5, 6). The patent of 4

[22] Caron (1924), 197; Herbert (1969), 111-118, 128-130, 188-196; Mackrell (1973), 174-177.
[23] Wittich (1896), 438.

March 1849, which expanded at length upon the earlier decree, required the use of cadastral data to calculate the value of the payments in kind. These figures, collected in earlier years by the government for the purpose of tax assessments, were based upon prices of the early 1840's. These prices were considerably less than prices of the 1850's, when the indemnification process was carried out. That meant that the seigniors took a considerable loss. In addition, the law stated that the labor obligation could not be valued at more than one-third of the wage of hired labor—evidence of the general recognition of the inefficiency of the labor obligation. The law also ordered the deduction of one-third of the calculated income of the indemnifiable obligations, to discount the costs incurred by the seigniors in the administration of these obligations (arts. 9, 10, 11, 16). So the lords of the Austrian Monarchy received as indemnification only two-thirds of the calculated value of the obligations the law required the peasant to redeem, and the calculated value itself was well below the current market value. In Hungary in 1848, in the first flush of revolutionary enthusiasm, and spurred by the fear of peasant unrest, the diet on 11 April 1848 abolished all peasant obligations without indemnification. That edict never was put into effect. When the Hapsburg rule had been reestablished, the provisions of the imperial patent of 4 March 1849 were applied, except that the deduction of one-third from the calculated value of the obligation for administrative costs was not made there.[24]

In Romania, too, the charges imposed upon the peasant were much less than the value of the payments in kind, labor services, and other dues the peasant had paid to his seignior in return for occupying the seignior's land. The reform legislation of 1864 divided the freed peasants into three categories according to the number of cattle they owned. The average annual value of their obligations to their seigniors in Moldavia was calculated to have been 233 *lei* for the first category, 174 *lei* for the second, and 115 *lei* for the third. The corresponding figures in Wallachia were 236, 162, and 74 *lei*. Under the terms of the reform legislation, the Moldavian peasant in the first category had to pay his former seignior only 100 *lei*, the second category 74 *lei*, and the third category 44 *lei*; in Wallachia the amounts were 130, 62 and 3 *lei*, respectively. Thus, the redemption payments ranged between 38 and 55 per cent of the value of the servile obligations for all categories, save the third category in Wallachia. The redemption charges for these peasants was only 4 per cent of the calculated value of the obligations they had paid to their seigniors.[25]

In Russia the emancipation statute did not provide for the evaluation of individual obligations, nor did it concern itself with a determination of which obligations were to be indemnified and which not. Instead, the statute ordered that the peasants were to pay for the so-called allotment land,

[24] Evans (1924), 72.　　　　[25] Emerit (1937), 515-516.

that is, the land turned over to the peasants by the seigniors. The peasants did not have to pay for their personal freedom. That meant that the seigniors suffered a serious financial loss, since the serfs had a cash value that before the emancipation seigniors could realize by selling or mortgaging their serfs. However, the authorities in charge of the redemption operation placed a much inflated valuation on the allotment land. For the empire as a whole the value set upon the allotment land exceeded the free market price of land by 34 per cent. In the fertile black-earth provinces, where the peasants had to surrender some of their land to their lords, the redemption valuation was 20 per cent higher than the market price. In the less fertile non-black earth region, where the peasants kept all of their land, the redemption valuation averaged 90 per cent higher than the market price. The explanation of this striking difference was that in the black earth, where many lords engaged in agricultural production and wanted as much land as they could get, they received concealed compensation for the loss of their serfs in the form of the land the freed serfs had to relinquish. In the non-black earth region, where lords typically did not engage in direct agricultural production and did not want more land, the grossly inflated redemption price compensated the seigniors for the loss of their serfs. In the western provinces, however, redemption value and market price coincided.[26] The reason? Most of the seigniors in these provinces were Polish, and the tsarist regime was following its now customary punitive policy vis-à-vis the Polish nobility.

In most lands the legislation required the peasant to pay the entire costs of redemption. The payments were usually supposed to be made in annual installments, which included interest and amortization, though it was possible for the peasant to pay the entire capital sum at one time. In Russia the legislation allowed, but did not require, the peasant to give up three-fourths of his holding to the lord in lieu of indemnification payments. In Württemberg and in Hesse the legislation specifically ordered that the redemption payments had to be in cash; in some of the smaller German states the laws left the form of indemnification—whether cash or land—to the free agreement of the concerned parties.[27]

In a few lands the peasant paid only a part of the indemnification to the seignior, and in some places none of it. In the Austrian Monarchy the peasant paid half, and the government of the province in which he lived paid half out of its tax revenues. The central government paid the entire indemnity for the fees seigniors had charged when a peasant holding changed hands. The amount of this compensation was determined by averaging the payments of these fees for a holding over the thirty years that preceded the initiation of the redemption procedure (arts. 14, 18). An exception had to be made for Bukovina, where it soon became apparent that the peasants

[26] Gerschenkron (1965), 738-739.   [27] Lütge (1943), 381.

were too poor to pay their share. An imperial patent of 23 October 1853 declared that the provincial government of Bukovina had to pay the full indemnity, which proved to be beyond the fiscal capacities of the province. Matters dragged on until 1863, when the central government decided to provide the necessary financing. In Hungary, too, the state paid the entire indemnity to the seigniors; the peasants paid nothing.[28] In Württemberg the indemnification act of 1836 provided that the peasant would pay two-thirds of the indemnification for certain obligations, including the labor service. The state paid the remaining third. In Baden the state paid one-fifth of the indemnification for the tithe, abolished by a decree of 1833. In the duchy of Nassau, in western Germany, the government paid one-eighth of the indemnification for the tithe.[29] The agrarian reform law in Romania specified that the state would pay one-third and the peasant two-thirds of the indemnification.[30]

Whether or not governments obligated themselves to pay part or all of the redemption, the usual procedure was for a government agency to advance the capital sum of the indemnification to the seignior as soon as the indemnification was determined. The amount of the capital sum was determined by capitalizing the annual income received by the seignior from those obligations or land for which he now was to receive an indemnity. Thus, the capital sum paid to the seignior would provide him with a yearly income equal to the yearly income he would have received from the obligations or land. In many states the capitalization rate was set at 4 to 5 per cent, or 25 to 20 times the annual income; in Poland and Russia it was 16-2/3 times the annual income; in Romania it was 10 times the annual income. The payment of the capital sum to the seignior was made in the form of government bonds, which usually bore 4 to 6 per cent interest, and often were issued specifically for this purpose. The peasants were then responsible for making regular payments to the state over a fixed period of years to repay, with interest, the money the government had advanced for them. There were variations from this general pattern. In Poland the peasants paid a land tax, collected semi-annually. The state used the income from this levy to pay interest and amortization on the bonds it had given to the seigniors to indemnify them for their losses. The amount of the tax did not cover the full costs, so that the state had to provide a supplement from other revenues.[31] In Russia the government advanced 75 to 80 per cent of the capital sum of the indemnification. It made the larger advance when the peasant redeemed all of the land he had tilled before his emancipation, and the smaller advance when the peasant redeemed less land. The peasant had to make up the remaining 20 or 25 per cent by direct payment to the seignior. The government paid its share to the seigniors with a specially issued

[28] Grünberg (1901), 98; Macartney (1969), 462.   [29] Winkel (1968), 43, 52, 59.
[30] Emerit (1936), 506.   [31] Rostworowski (1896), 61.

redemption bond that bore 5 per cent interest, later raised to 6 per cent. In Romania the state proposed to raise the money needed to pay its one-third share of the indemnification by the sale of state land to peasants. The bonds issued by the state to indemnify the seigniors originally paid 10 per cent, but were later converted to 6, and finally to 4 per cent bonds.

The number of years given the peasants to pay back the state for its advance, plus interest, varied widely. In Romania the legislation set the term at 15 years, in the Austrian Monarchy 20 years, in Saxony 25 years, in Prussia $41^{1}/_{12}$ years or $56^{1}/_{2}$ years, depending upon whether the peasant opted to pay 5 per cent or $4^{1}/_{2}$ per cent interest, and in Russia 49 years. The frequency of the installments ranged from monthly in Prussia to annually in Russia.

In a number of states the government established special credit institutions to facilitate the peasants' redemption of their holdings. In Denmark the Royal Credit Bank opened in 1786, two years before the edict of emancipation. Its purpose was to promote the improvement of agriculture in general, and in particular to help peasants to commute their obligations. The bank lent to both peasants and lords, at first at only 2 per cent per annum, later increased to 6 per cent, of which 2 per cent was for amortization. About 850 peasants became proprietors of their land with the aid of this bank. Then the financial difficulties of the war period of 1807-1814, which included the bankruptcy of the state in 1813, ended the bank's activities. The first banks organized specifically to handle the indemnification operations opened in 1832 in Hesse and in Saxony. In both states the decrees that established these institutions were issued simultaneously with the decrees of emancipation. The banks paid the capital sum of the indemnification to the seignior, and the peasant paid back the bank over a period of years, with his debt considered a mortgage on his property. In 1841 the government of Hannover founded a bank of this nature, the Bavarian government followed suit in 1848, and so did nearly all the other states of Germany. The Prussian government ordered the establishment of such banks in each of its provinces on 2 March 1850, the same day on which it issued its final decree of emancipation. In 1850, also, the Danish government authorized the establishment of credit unions, or cooperative credit associations, under state control and audit, to make mortgage loans to peasants so that they could purchase their holdings.[32]

IV

The pattern followed in most states was for the peasants with holdings to continue in possession of their holdings. In Romania, however, the reform

[32] Scharling (1909), ΙΙ, 579; Blaschke (1965), 285; Sugenheim (1861), 491-492; Morier (1971), 385-386; Ashley (1924), 250; Judeich (1863), 226-227.

law did not specify that the peasants were to get the land they had occupied before emancipation. As a result, they often were allotted land of inferior quality, or without access to a road or river, or a holding broken into several pieces, each distant from one another, or not as much land as they were supposed to receive.[33] The law had ordered a set amount of land for each of the three categories into which it divided the peasants (p. 390). In Wallachia the holdings were supposed to range from 13¾ acres for the household with 4 oxen and 1 cow, to a bit more than 5 acres for the household with 1 or no cows. In Moldavia the range went from 19¼ acres down to 9¼ acres. The seignior was supposed to provide the peasants with the requisite amount of land, but did not have to give up more than two-thirds of his land to meet the requirements of the law (arts. I, III).

In France and in Poland peasants gained land in addition to the land they held when they were in a servile status. In France the revolutionary regime confiscated the land of the church and of the émigrés, the professed enemies of the revolution who had fled France. In some regions these expropriated estates amounted to as much as one-fourth or more of all the land in the district, in others it was of far less importance. The government sold this land, the so-called *biens nationaux*, to the highest bidders. Among the purchasers were nobles, agents of the émigrés, townsmen, professional men—and peasants. In some regions the peasants seemed to have gained more of this land than any other group; for the country as a whole it is unclear which sector of society gained the most land from the sale of the *biens nationaux*.[34] In Poland, as part of the government's punitive policy against the Polish seigniors, the law of 19 February 1864 required the return to the peasants of all land taken from them by the seigniors since 1846, without indemnification to the seignior. That added about 2½ million acres (approximately 8 per cent of the area of the Kingdom of Poland) to the land turned over to the peasants.

In Prussia and in Russia the legislation was much less favorable to the peasants. In Prussia the edict of 14 October 1811 had divided landholding peasants into two categories: those who held by hereditary tenure, and those who held at the will of the seignior or who were renters. The latter category formed by far the largest part of the seigniorial peasantry. The law allowed those who held by hereditary tenure to gain freedom from their obligations and become the owners of their holdings by giving up a third of their land to their seigniors. Those in the second category would have to surrender half of their land (arts. 10, 37). These conditions remained (with

[33] Emerit (1937), 509-510; Adăniloaie (1966), 100-105; Evans (1924), 41-42.
[34] Lefebvre (1928), 207, 209-211; Soboul (1958), 82; Cobban (1971), 87-89. Soon after the restoration of the Bourbon dynasty in 1814, confiscated land that the revolutionary and Napoleonic regimes had kept as national domain, notably forest land, was restored to returned emigrés. Forster (1967), 75-78.

certain minor exceptions)[35] until the law of 2 March 1850 banned the surrender of land and ordered, henceforth, peasants to redeem their land by
money payments.

In Russia the emancipation statute set minima and maxima in each region for the size of the land allotments assigned to each peasant household
of the commune. If the pre-emancipation holdings were larger than the size
prescribed by the statute the proprietor could reduce the holding to the
appropriate size. Furthermore, if the assignment of allotments of the prescribed size left the seignior with less than one-third of the land area of the
manor (without wasteland), the seignior could reduce the size of the allotments to raise his share of the manor up to one-third or one-half, depending upon the region, of the size of the estate. The law did forbid the proprietor to reduce the peasant allotments to less than one-third of the
maximum set for the region. Comparison of the amount of land held by
peasants before and after the emancipation showed that peasant-held land
decreased by only 4.1 per cent. However, nine-tenths of whatever increases
there were in peasant land took place in eight western provinces, where
most of the seigniors were Polish, and who were discriminated against in
the legislation. If these provinces were excluded, the loss in peasant land
increased to 13 per cent. Furthermore, most of this loss occurred in the sixteen provinces of the fertile black earth. The peasants there surrendered
23.3 per cent of their holdings to the seigniors as the consequence of the
terms of the emancipation statute. Another great loss of peasant land resulted from the provision of the statute that allowed the proprietor, by
agreement with his peasants, to give the peasants only one-quarter of the
land allotment to which the law entitled them. In return, the peasants were
relieved of all redemption payments. An estimated 6 per cent of the freed
serfs agreed to accept these so-called "gratuitous allotments." Most of
these people lived in the southern and eastern provinces. In four of these
provinces they accounted for 20 to 30 per cent of the freed serfs, in four
others between 30 and 45 per cent, and in the province of Orenburg as
much as 70 to 75 per cent.[36]

In most of the erstwhile servile lands the peasant who received land became the proprietor of his holding when he undertook its redemption. (In
France, the revolutionary regime by its decree of 17 July 1793 transformed
the landholding peasants into free proprietors, with no indemnity paid to
the seigniors.) In Denmark and in Schleswig-Holstein the laws ordered the

---

[35] In Posen a decree of 1823 allowed peasants to redeem their land and obligations in cash;
the holdings of the peasants there were so small that if the peasants had to surrender land they
would have been left with too little land to support themselves. In East Prussia some proprietors disregarded the law and permitted their peasants to pay a money indemnity. Lütge
(1943), 391; Borcke-Stargordt (1954), 318-321; Kieniewicz (1969), 64-65.

[36] Gerschenkron (1965), 729-730; Pavlovsky (1968), 73.

conversion of the serf into a free tenant with a hereditary lease that could not be for less than fifty years. Legislation, however, made it possible for the peasant to buy his holding, and with time the number who did so steadily increased; by 1901 of the 249,783 holdings in Denmark 84 per cent were owned by their occupants. In most of Russia the freed peasant did not become an independent proprietor, although the emancipation statute assigned a specific allotment of land for each household of the village. Instead, title to all of the village land went to the commune to which the peasant belonged. The commune could redistribute the land periodically to each household, or could allot holdings to each household in perpetuity, according to the decision of two-thirds of its members. In Great Russia over 96 per cent of peasant land was held by communes, and between 80 and 90 per cent in New Russia and in the eastern part of the Ukraine. Elsewhere in the empire communal landholding was far less important or was unknown.[37]

In nearly every land, the reform legislation did not provide holdings for landless peasants, for cotters, and in Russia for the household serfs who, on the eve of emancipation there, numbered nearly 1.5 million, or 6.8 per cent of Russia's serf population. Romania and Poland were exceptions to this usual pattern. In Romania the law of 14 August 1864 decreed, in an order that was never fully implemented, that every peasant was to get some land. Childless widows and peasants who were not able to do farm work or who were not engaged in farming were supposed to be given a house and a bit of land around it, and were to become the full owners of house and lot. As indemnity they were to pay the seignior who provided them with the land the modest sum of 11.75 *lei* in two installments. Peasants whose holdings did not come up to the minima set by the law, cotters, and landless or nearly landless newly wed couples, had the right to buy not more than fifteen acres of state land, to be paid for over fifteen years in equal installments without interest (arts. IV, VI, LIV, LVI). In Poland the tsarist bureaucrats who supervised the implementation of the 1864 legislation were concerned about the possibility of unrest among the disappointed rural proletariat. These peasants had been promised land by the leaders of the failed insurrection of 1863. The bureaucrats decided that it was politically expedient to distribute government land to some of these people, and so gave out about 130,000 small holdings.[38]

In both Prussia and Russia serious consideration had been given to the possibility of a landless emancipation. As might be expected, noble landowners were the leading advocates of this proposal. In Prussia a landless emancipation had the support of some men counted as friends of the peas-

[37] *Statistik Aarbog* 1916, table 38; Lamartine Yates (1940), 54; Gerschenkron (1965), 745-748.
[38] Leslie (1963), 239.

antry, including Albrecht Thaer, the famous agriculturist. These men argued that the freed peasant could not support himself as an independent farmer, so that it would be in the peasants' own interest to become day laborers employed by large landowners. In the end, in both Prussia and Russia the emancipation did provide land for peasants: when in the winter of 1860-1861 Tsar Alexander II presented the statute of emancipation to the council of ministers, he solemnly regretted that the peasants in the Baltic provinces had been freed without land.[39] However, the arguments of those who favored landless emancipation seems not to have been without effect. The terms of the emancipation in both Prussia and Russia were among the least generous of all of the emancipations of the era.

In Swedish Pomerania much peasant land had been appropriated by seigniors and converted into demesne. When in 1806 the Swedish king ordered the liberation of the peasants in his Pomeranian possession, his decree made no provision for land to the peasants. In 1815, when Prussia annexed the province, Prussian legislation that provided for peasant landownership was not applied to the new territory. A similar condition of landlessness prevailed in neighboring Mecklenburg, where, in the absence of a governmental policy of protection of peasant land from seigniorial expropriation, only a relatively few peasants had holdings. So legislation about peasant landholding there had little practical consequence, since it did not provide land for the broad mass of the peasantry.[40]

Separate legislation arranged for land and freedom for the unfree people who lived on land of the state, or of the crown. Peasants on the crown estates in the eastern provinces of Prussia had been given their personal freedom in 1804. In 1808 the Prussian government transformed over 30,000 of these peasants into proprietors of their holdings. The peasants of the Military Frontier, a narrow band of land that formed the southern boundary of Hungary, occupied their holdings of state land in return for military and other services to the state. In 1850 the Hapsburg regime made them free proprietors of their land, though with restrictions on their rights of ownership. The holdings, which went not to the individuals but to the *zadruga*, the extended family communes that prevailed in that region, were declared inalienable. Governmental approval was required to divide a holding, or to borrow against it, and then only up to one-third of its value. The peasants also had to continue their services for the state until, during the years from 1869 to 1881, they were gradually released from this obligation. In Russia a ukase in 1866 freed the state peasants (whose number exceeded that of the serfs), and provided them with permanent holdings. Nearly always these allotments were considerably larger than those received by the

[39] Leroy-Beaulieu (1884), 206; Knapp (1887), I, 147-150.
[40] Fuchs (1888), 238-239; Lütge (1967), 248-249.

freed serfs. The state peasants, however, did not become the owners of their land. Instead, they paid an annual rent to the state, with the size of the rent dependent upon the peasant's income, regardless of its source. Twenty years later new legislation converted the state peasants into proprietors. The annual rent was replaced by a somewhat larger annual redemption charge to be paid for the next forty-five years, after which the peasant would become the unencumbered owner of his holding. Imperial decrees in 1858 and 1859 had given the appanage peasants, who lived on the manors of the imperial court, their personal freedom. Legislation in 1861 and 1863 converted their holdings into their property, in return for payments to the state for the next forty-nine years. The average size of their allotments was less than that of the state peasants, but was larger than the average for the freed serfs.[41]

V

As the preceding pages have shown, the provisions for emancipation and redemption in some lands were much more favorable to the peasant than they were in others. The enactments that were most favorable to the peasants were those of the French revolutionary governments. In 1792, after the French annexation of Savoy, the remaining seigniorial rights and privileges there were suppressed without indemnification, and arrears in redemption payments owed by the peasants were cancelled. In France itself the decree of the National Convention of 17 July 1793 ordered the abolition without indemnification of all the servile obligations owed by the peasants to their seigniors. In all of the other servile lands, the legislation provided for indemnification to the seigniors. In general, the terms provided for in the statutes were easier on the peasant in the western lands than in those countries where the lord-peasant relationship had been more rigidly structured and demanding of the peasants. Among these latter countries, the legislation in the Austrian Monarchy and in the Kingdom of Poland offered the most advantages to the peasants. In both lands redemption was mandatory, unlike other states, where, for many years after emancipation decrees appeared, redemptions remained voluntary. In both lands patrimonial jurisdiction ended with emancipation; in other lands the lords often retained much of their judicial and police authority. The valuations placed upon the peasants' obligations for purposes of redemption were pegged at a lower level than in other countries, and neither the Austrian nor the Polish peasant had to surrender any of his land. Indeed, the Polish peasantry gained land. In both countries the state assumed part of the redemption ob-

---

[41] Borcke-Stargordt (1954), 308, 314; Katus (1961), 130-132; Robinson (1932), 89-90; Blum (1961), 599; Vasil'chikov (1881), 448-449.

ligation. In the Austrian Monarchy the low valuation of the obligations, the deduction of one-third of the valuation representing the overhead costs of the abolished seigniorial system, and the government's assumption of one-third of the redemption costs, sharply reduced the indemnification costs that the peasants had to pay.

At the other end of the scale were the landless emancipations in the Baltic provinces of Russia, and what amounted to landless emancipations in Swedish Pomerania and in Mecklenburg. The gross injustice and inequity of this kind of legislation was avoided in other lands. Their arrangements, however, held many serious disadvantages for the peasants. Except for Poland and Romania, their legislation made no provision of land for cotters and landless peasants. In Prussia until 1850 and in Russia the laws allowed the peasant to redeem his holding by surrendering a large part of it to the seignior. In Denmark the freed peasants became renters, rather than proprietors, and continued to pay servile obligations as rent for decades after the emancipation there. In Russia the valuations—and, therefore, the costs of redemption—of the allotments given to the peasants exceeded, often by a large amount, the current market price of the land.

Whatever favor was shown to the peasants was, of course, at the expense of the seigniors. In the Austrian Monarchy the lords took a considerable loss in the indemnification they received for the land they had to surrender to the peasants; in Hungary, for example, the lords were paid about one-third of the market price of the land.[42] In the Kingdom of Poland the seigniors suffered at the hands of the Russian bureaucrats who had the responsibility for the implementation of the reform—unlike Russia, where the responsible officials, the peace arbitrators, were selected from the local nobility. The Russian commissioners were strangers to the country and ignorant of local conditions, customs, and laws. Some of them had been sent off to serve in Poland because they were suspected of radicalism. Some of them came fresh from the university. Many of them were army officers who had fought against the Poles in their insurrection in 1863. All of them, whatever their background, were hostile to the Polish nobility. Reportedly, they routinely accepted the peasants' version in disputes with seigniors about obligations owed to the lords, or about rights of the peasants in the forests and pastures of the seigniors.[43]

Even when the legislation was strongly biased in favor of the seigniors, they sometimes came out as losers. Many of them, needful of cash to maintain their standard of living, or for capital expenditures to replace the animals and equipment hitherto furnished by the peasants on their labor services, hastened to sell the indemnification bonds they received from the

[42] Macartney (1969), 412.
[43] Leroy-Beaulieu (1884), 272; Rostworowski (1896), 58-61.

state. This forced down the prices of the bonds by as much as 30 to 40 per cent.[44] In Russia the government deducted from its payments to the seigniors the debts the seigniors owed to state lending agencies. That added up to a very considerable sum of money. By 1871, of the 543 million rubles credited to the seigniors for redemption payments the state had deducted 46 per cent (248 million rubles) to satisfy these debts. In addition the depreciation of the indemnification bonds cost Russian seigniors much money.[45] Losses such as these, on top of the losses for those services, goods, fees, and monopolies for which they received no indemnification, had a damaging impact upon the economic condition of the seigniors. Indeed, for many lesser proprietors, and for some middle-sized and even large ones, the emancipation proved to be an economic disaster (pp. 425-427).

Still, as later pages will tell, seigniorial privilege and seigniorial power and status continued long after the issuance of the decrees of emancipation. The old order did not die easily or gracefully. It was a difficult task to rid a culture of its centuries-old customs and traditions, and to erase the conviction shared by men of all orders of the natural superiority of the nobleman and the natural inferiority of the peasant (a conviction that has not yet entirely vanished). It was difficult, too, to overcome the natural inclination of the ruling segments of society to hang on for as long as they could to the privileges they had enjoyed for so many centuries.

[44] Kovacs (1961), 103-104; Rostworowski (1896), 60-61; Pavlovsky (1968), 100; Patterson (1869), i, 326.
[45] Anfimov (1969), 317.

CHAPTER 18

Pluses and Minuses

I

LORDS and peasants met the emancipation legislation with what can fairly be called a mixed reaction. Some, usually but not always peasants, liked it, and some, usually but not always lords, disliked it. In Savoy the peasants greeted the decree of 19 December 1771 with rejoicing, while their seigniors condemned it as a "spoliation," and prophesied that it would bring doom and disaster in its train. In 1790 a hundred proprietors of Jutland, in an address to Crown Prince Frederick, who headed the Danish government, complained bitterly about the damaging effects of the emancipation legislation of 1788. French peasants could not understand why they had to continue to pay obligations to their seigniors after the National Assembly on the famed night of 4 August had proclaimed, for all the world to hear, "the complete destruction of the feudal regime." There was much unrest, and sometimes open revolt in which peasants sacked and burned the chateaux of the proprietors. A Soviet scholar has counted 158 outbreaks of French peasants against their seigniors from September 1789 to July 1792.[1]

In Prussia the emancipation decree of 9 October 1807 stirred up antagonism among both lords and peasants. The resentment and opposition of some nobles traced back to the ancient struggle between throne and nobility. These nobles, whose chief spokesman was F. A. L. von der Marwitz, did not oppose the emancipation per se. Indeed, a number of them, including Marwitz, had voluntarily commuted some or all of the obligations of their peasants well before 1807. Their opposition was aroused by the fact that the throne had made a unilateral decision to free the seigniorial peasants and to allow them to become proprietors of their holdings. They held that by this action the throne had violated the rights of the provincial estates, who should have been consulted and asked for their approval. Nor was this the end of it. To Marwitz, and those who sympathized with him, the real enemy was individualism or, as Marwitz put it, the isolation of man. They longed to restore to full vigor the corporate society, in which they fondly believed that lord and peasant were held close to one another by a patriarchal bond of mutual regard, and in which agriculture was a way of life, rather than a rationalized, profit-making activity. Seigniorial opposition and pressure bore results in the decrees of 14 September 1811 and especially of 29 May 1816, which severely restricted the ability of peasants

[1] Bruchet (1908), lxvii-lxxi; Darmstaedter (1897), 50-53; Skrubbeltrang (1953), 45; Ado (1971), 415-435; Sée (1924), 231ff.; Aulard (1919), 117-150.

to redeem their land and obligations. In other German states, too, seigniors, fearful of economic loss, and of derogation of their superior social status, opposed as best they could the emancipation legislation.[2]

Open peasant resistance to the decree of 1807 occurred only in Silesia. Opposition to the decree was especially strong among the nobles of that province. Many of them kept their peasants uninformed about the new law, so that the peasants picked up a garbled version. This led them to believe that the king had freed them of all their obligations, and that the local bureaucrats and the seigniors had conspired to keep the truth from them. The confusion produced a minor revolt in 1808, and Silesian lords had to ask the French troops who occupied Silesia at the time to put down the rising. In 1811 eighty villages in Upper Silesia rose in a short-lived rebellion. They believed that the king had ordered the cancellation of the labor obligation, and that the seigniors, in league with the bureaucrats, had suppressed the royal decree. In the following decades there were only sporadic incidents of unrest, such as the refusal to perform services, or the threat of a strike at harvest time. None of these incidents reached serious proportions. But a movement for more freedom, led at first by liberals, the formation of associations to represent the interests of the peasants against the seigniors, and political agitation, gave witness to growing rural discontent. The failure of the potato crops in the mid-1840's, a general crop failure in 1846, and the hard times that followed upon these calamities exacerbated the discontent. The peasants, then, were ready to support the revolutions that erupted in Germany in the spring of 1848, and that brought about the final acts of emancipation.[3]

In Austria Field Marshal Prince Alfred Windischgrätz protested, not against the emancipation, but against some of its terms. Windischgrätz spoke only for a small group of noblemen, but they were men of much importance, and Windischgrätz himself was one of the Monarchy's most influential personages. He had led the imperial troops against the rebellious cities of Prague and Vienna in 1848, and with his brother-in-law, Prince Felix Schwarzenberg, had arranged the accession of the youthful Franz Joseph to the imperial throne in 1849. In a memorandum to the emperor of 22 February 1850 about redemption legislation, he declared that "the most outstanding of Communists has not yet dared to demand that which Your Majesty's government has carried through." Windischgrätz argued that the rate of indemnification set by the law of 1849 was unfair to the seigniors, and demanded a higher compensation for the rights they had to relinquish. He was also opposed to the provision of the law that required peasants who had become hereditary tenants on state land through the

[2] Lütge (1943), 361-362; Finckenstein (1960), 128, 129; Frauendorfer (1957), I, 276; Brentano (1899), 255-257; Weller and Weller (1971), 232.
[3] Ziekursch (1927), 292-296; Kieniewicz (1969), 62; Franz (1959), 188; Frauendorfer (1957), I, 333-334.

Raab reform (p. 211) to pay the entire costs of the redemption of their land. Unlike other peasants, they were not to receive any financial aid from the state or the province. Windischgrätz and his supporters condemned this as unjust and illegal. Despite this potent opposition the statute was not amended, and the government, under the leadership of Minister of Interior Alexander Bach (who was the grandson of a peasant), persevered in carrying out its provisions.[4]

The peasant unrest that followed the landless emancipations in the Baltic provinces of Russia was unique in that it found sympathy in the very highest levels of government. Tsar Nicholas I declared that he understood the unrest there, blaming it on the proprietors who were unwilling to do anything to improve the condition of the peasantry.[5] In Russia itself many nobles looked upon the emancipation statute of 1861 as a sellout, and accused their fellow nobles who participated in drafting the legislation as traitors, turncoats, and spoliators. As for the peasants, the government did not bother to prepare them for the terms of the emancipation. Rumors quickly spread through the villages of such beneficences as full and immediate freedom with land at no cost to the peasant and with no obligations to the seignior. When the cold facts became known, bitter disappointment, and the feeling of being cheated, replaced the euphoric visions. The pathetic myth of the benevolent sovereign's good intentions being thwarted by seigniors, abetted by corrupt officials, reemerged. Many believed that the true manifesto had been suppressed by these evildoers, who substituted a manifesto of their own devising. To make matters worse, the length and intricacy of the statute led to confusion, and sometimes serious misunderstandings. The mutterings of discontent quickly translated themselves into active and open resistance. More than 1,300 rural disturbances were reported for the first five months of 1861. These outbursts rarely involved violence. They were much more likely to be refusals by peasants to pay the obligations required by the statute during the two-year period of transition, during which the surveys and arrangements for redemption were to be made. The troubles reached their peak in the spring of 1861. Then, as the peasants realized that the published decree indeed represented the tsar's wishes, and as the newly appointed peace arbitrators undertook the implementation of the reform at the local level, the unrest gradually subsided.[6]

II

The promptitude with which the implementation of the emancipation legislation, and specifically the redemption arrangements, proceeded,

[4] Friedjung (1903), 106-107, 109-111.
[5] Zaionchkovskii (1968), 55; *Studia historica . . . Kruus* (1971), 329.
[6] Leroy-Beaulieu (1884), 65; Emmons (1968), 323-326; Philippot (1963), 246-250.

depended—as could be expected—upon the complexities involved in the operation. In those lands where the seigniors had small demesnes or no demesne at all, and where the peasants had light obligations, the procedure was relatively simple. In other states, the transfer of land, the great number of individuals involved in the operation, the variety and the huge cumulative total of the obligations to be redeemed, made the process much more difficult. In the German-Slav provinces of the Austrian Monarchy, 54,267 landowners had to be indemnified by 2,625,512 peasant households. These peasants owed their former masters 38,587,940 days of labor services per year without animals, and 29,442,387 days with one to four draft animals. They also had paid tithes in produce with an average annual value of 4,270,845 florins, dues in cash amounting to 3,892,348 florins a year, annual dues in kind that added up to 3.8 million bushels (2,176,250 lower Austrian *Metzen*), and fees paid on the transfer of their holdings with an average annual value of 2,251,103 florins.[7] Some of the obligations in labor and kind had been commuted into money payments during the servile era, but for purposes of redemption the commuted obligations were counted in their original form. For example, in Lower Austria the redemption data showed that the peasants owed 6,177,184 days of labor without animals, and 2,204,176 days with animals. The number of days of labor services actually performed by the peasants was much less than these figures indicated. As early as 1792 an official report stated that the labor services of the peasants on 1,600 manors in Lower Austria had been commuted into cash payments.[8]

In Prussia, peasants redeemed 6.4 million days of labor services with animals, and 23.6 million days without animals, between the decree of 1807 and the end of the century. The redemption cost them a total of 204.2 million marks, 415,298 *Scheffel* (672,783 bushels) of grain, mostly rye, and 1.67 million *Morgen* (1.05 million acres) in land. In Russia 9,795,163 (another figure is 10,682,400) adult males who had belonged to private proprietors received allotments totalling 35,779,014 desiatins (96.6 million acres). In Poland 694,747 peasant households on private and state-owned land became proprietors. Their holdings added up to about 12 million acres. In Romania, 406,898 peasant households became proprietors of holdings, and 60,651 were given land for house and garden.[9]

Despite the huge proportions of the operation, the work proceeded briskly and with reasonable smoothness almost everywhere. In the German and Slav crown lands of the Austrian Monarchy, arrangements for redemption were completed by 1853. In Hungary, where the redemption procedure began in 1853 and 1854, it was declared completed in 1859. In

[7] Mischler and Ulbricht (1906), II, 62-65.   [8] Blum (1948), 56; Lütge (1968), 190-209.
[9] Saalfeld (1963), 165; Vasil'chikov (1881), I, 448; Rostworowski (1896), 61-64; Adăniloaie and Berindei (1966), 121-122.

19. Newly emancipated Russian peasants. (*Velikaia reforma*, IV, Moscow, 1911.)

Germany, too, the redemptions, once under way, made relatively rapid progress. Even in Russia, where the emancipation legislation was inordinately detailed and replete with complex and sometimes contradictory provisions, and where, initially, redemptions were voluntary, most peasants had arranged for redemption of their allotments by 1881, when redemption was made compulsory. By then 84.7 per cent of the freed serfs had become the owners of their allotments. In Romania, in contrast to these other lands, there seems to have been a deliberate effort to impede or even evade redemption. The landowners there were hostile to the reform, and in a

[405]

country where bribery and corruption had been a way of life for centuries they found it easy to buy the cooperation of bureaucrats. The combined obstructionism of seigniors and officials served to delay the completion of the redemption process, and to give it a more limited character than had been intended by the framers of the law of 1864. The regulations were applied more equitably on state land, but the state dragged its feet, too, particularly on the sale of state land to peasants qualified by the 1864 law to purchase this land.[10]

Once the arrangements for redemption had been completed, the payments to the state required of the peasants usually stretched out over a long period of years. In some parts of Germany peasants were still making these payments in the 1920's.[11] In Romania, however, the legislation had given the peasants only fifteen years to pay off their debt. The double burden of redemption payments and taxes proved too heavy for many peasants, and so in 1874 the state was compelled to cancel the remaining redemption payments. In Russia, too, arrearages quickly piled up. To evidence its good will toward the peasants (whose support it needed), the government in 1881 forgave part of the accumulated arrears, and reduced the size of the payments. Still the arrears continued to mount, in no small part because of the unpopularity of the redemption payments among the peasants, who felt that they should have received their allotments at no cost to them. Mostly because of this resistance, it cost the state about five times as much to collect redemption payments as it did to collect taxes. This expense, swelling peasant discontent, and the fact that the payments amounted to only 6.4 per cent of the state's total net tax revenue, persuaded the government in late 1905 to abolish redemption payments as of 1 January 1907.[12]

III

Though emancipation decrees had categorically abolished servility, seigniors still continued to demand servile obligations from their peasants. Often this happened because the law permitted voluntary redemption of these services at the instance either of lord or peasant, instead of compulsory redemption. It is easy to imagine that ignorant or intimidated villagers would not initiate the process, though the law accorded them that right. Instead, they would continue to pay their traditional dues and services until, as happened everywhere, new legislation ordered the compulsory redemption of these obligations. It is possible, too, that (as mentioned earlier)

[10] Grüll (1952), 227; Lütge (1968), 204; Kún (1903), 103; Weller and Weller (1971), 232; Wittich (1896), 446; Lütge (1967), 245; Gerschenkron (1965), 738; Adăniloaie and Berindei (1966), 68, 76, 98-105, 121-122.
[11] *Cf.* Engels (1957), 126; Ford (1922), 219; Lütge (1967), 251.
[12] Ionescu-Şişeşti (1912), 2; Gerschenkron (1965), 769-770, 779, 786-787.

some peasants preferred payments in kind and labor, because they had a shortage of cash and a surplus of labor, and because they wanted to continue to benefit from the obligations that by law and custom, the seigniors owed them. In Denmark, in Poland, and in the Baltic provinces of the Russian empire, landowners demanded that the peasants who leased land from them had to pay their rent in labor, or part labor, part cash. The peasants performed their labor rents with the same reluctance and inefficiency that had marked their labor services when they were unfree. As time went on the proprietors realized this and commuted the labor rent into cash. By 1849 in Denmark only 13 per cent of all peasant holdings still paid a labor rent; of these, one-third paid all of their rent in labor. The other two-thirds paid a combination of labor and cash. In Poland, too, commutations increased, though far less rapidly than in Denmark. In 1810, three years after the Napoleonic emancipation, only an estimated 5 per cent of all peasant holdings paid their rent in cash. By 1859, on the 208,982 peasant holdings on land owned by private persons, about 25 per cent (52,506) paid their rent in cash; 15 per cent (31,636) paid a mixture of cash, kind, and labor; and 60 per cent (124,840) still paid by performance of labor services. Government data showed that cash rentals were most common among peasants who had larger holdings. Forty-one per cent of the peasants who rented more than 3 *morgi* (4 acres) paid money rents. Also cash rents were much more frequent among peasants who lived on state land; in 1859, 91 per cent of those who rented holdings of over 3 *morgi* of state land paid their rent entirely in cash.[13]

In Prussia and Russia, the emancipation legislation itself was responsible for the continuation of servile obligations. The Prussian edict of 14 September 1811 allowed peasants to redeem their holdings under certain specified and stringent conditions. Only a few of them had been able to make use of the law before the rules were tightened still more. In the wave of reaction that followed Napoleon's defeat, the government, as mentioned earlier, decided to make redemption even more difficult. The decree of 29 May 1816 stated that its purpose was "the clarification of the many proposals and uncertainties about the Edict of 14 September 1811," and proceeded further to restrict eligibility for redemption. Now only those peasants who had holdings large enough to support them, whose labor services included the use of draft animals, whose holdings were entered in the provincial tax rolls as peasant land and not seigniorial land, and who could prove that their holding had been held by peasants at a fixed date that ranged from 1749 to 1774, depending upon the province, could redeem their land and their obligations (arts. 4, 5). Local and provincial divergences in the determination of who met these qualifications placed additional barriers to re-

---

[13] Scharling (1909), I, 580; Kieniewicz (1969), 56, 145; Leslie (1963), 69-70.

demption. Thus, the minimum size of holdings eligible for redemption varied. So, too, did the requirement that the peasant had to use draft animals in his labor service. In some places this was interpreted to mean that he had to use a pair of animals; in other places, one animal satisfied the requirement.[14] Most of Prussia's peasants could not meet the standards of eligibility, whatever they were, and so they continued to pay their servile obligations to their seigniors until 1850, when the law finally allowed all peasants to redeem their land and their obligations.

The Russian statute of emancipation of 1861 required the freed peasant to continue for the next two years to pay their former masters the same obedience and the same obligations they had paid as serfs. Then the freedmen went into a status called "temporary-obligated." The seignior continued to own the land and to have extensive authority over the peasants, who paid them a rent in labor or in cash. The "temporary-obligated" peasant could choose the form of rent. If, however, he wanted to shift from labor to money rent, he had to announce his intention to the proprietor a year in advance, could not be in arrears in payments to the seignior or the state, and had to pay six months' rent in advance. The statute set the amount of both the labor rent and the money rent (arts. 168-241). The peasant left the "temporary-obligated" status when he redeemed his holding from the proprietor. This, however, required the consent of the proprietor, and many peasants of unobliging seigniors were trapped in the "temporary-obligated" status. Not until 1881 did the government make redemption obligatory.

Servile dues lingered on in many other places.[15] So, too, did many of the privileges and prerogatives of the seigniors. In some countries they managed to preserve their exemption from the land tax for decades after the act of emancipation. In Denmark they kept it until 1850. In the miniscule duchy of Lauenburg, acquired by Denmark in 1815, the seigniors enjoyed freedom from land taxes, as well as from tariffs and other fiscal burdens, until 1864, when Prussia annexed the duchy.[16] In Prussia after 1807, nobles had to pay tolls, taxes on consumption, and the new income tax of 1820. But they did not pay taxes on their land. Legislation in October 1810 had ordered such a tax. This and other provisions of these laws aroused so much opposition from the nobility that within less than a year new decrees tacitly reaffirmed the exemption of noble land from taxation. By and large, noble land, except in Altmark, remained untaxed until a decree of 21 May 1861 imposed such a levy. Altmark, that part of Brandenburg which lay west of the River Elbe, had been included in the Kingdom of Westphalia

---

[14] Kieniewicz (1969), 63; Knapp (1887), I, 258-259.
[15] Knapp (1902), 100; Schremmer (1966), 82; Sée (1921), 213; Lütge (1967), 252-255; Walter (1966), 30.
[16] Hovde (1948), I, 285; Meyer (1965), 21.

during the Napoleonic era. At that time the exemption of the nobility from the land tax had been cancelled, and it was not restored when Altmark rejoined the kingdom of Prussia.[17] In Russia, peasant allotment land was assessed at a much higher rate than was the land of private proprietors, who were chiefly nobles, and much privately owned land (84 million acres between 1871 and 1901 according to zemstvo statisticians) managed to escape all taxation. In Romania, too, peasant land was taxed much more heavily than the land of large proprietors.[18]

Seigniorial monopolies often persisted for years after the emancipations. In all of the German states, the lords retained their exclusive hunting and fishing privileges until the revolutions of 1848 compelled their abrogation.[19] Seigniors of the Austrian Monarchy kept a number of their monopolistic privileges until the end of the 1860's. These included the sole right to produce and sell spirits, and the obligation of the village tavern keeper to buy his beverages from the seignior. An imperial patent of 7 March 1849, which regulated the hunting privilege, ended the right of the seignior to hunt over the land of others, and also ordered the abolition without indemnification to the seignior of the compulsory hunting services of the peasants. The patent limited the hunting monopoly to properties of at least 200 contiguous yokes of land (284 acres). Possibly the government still feared the threat of an armed peasantry, and perhaps it also wanted to mollify the large landowners who had suffered from the operations of the emancipation. Later legislation extended the hunting right, but still kept it restricted.[20] In Poland, where the Russian rulers had no interest in mollifying the proprietors, the decree of 19 February 1864 gave peasants the right to hunt over the land in their villages and to fish in its streams (art. 16). In Russia, nobles kept certain economic privileges that included special rights in distilling and in the manufacture of beet sugar.[21]

The seigniors not only retained valuable services and privileges at the expense of the freed peasant; they also gained liberation from the obligations they owed to their peasants before emancipation. Now that the law declared that the peasants were free men, the seigniors no longer had these sometimes onerous and expensive obligations. Indeed, in places in central Germany the obligations of the seignior were worth more than the dues and services owed him by a small peasant. The laws that dealt with the redemption of obligations provided that in such cases the lord had to indemnify the peasant with land or money, to compensate the peasant for his loss.[22]

The emancipation decrees also struck down the restrictions on the ab-

---

[17] Hintze (1915), 59; Goldschmidt (1910), 27; Simon (1955), 58-62, 83-84.
[18] Yaney (1973), 348, 348n.; Mitrany (1930), 84.   [19] Judeich (1863), 230.
[20] *Allgemeines Reichs-Gesetz-und Regierungsblatt* . . . 1849, no. 154; Purs (1963), 38-39; Kravets (1966), 752; Benda (1948), 228-229; Stölzl (1971), 51-54.
[21] Korelin (1971b), 57.   [22] Lütge (1957), 286.

sorption of peasant land into seigniorial demesne that had been a feature of the agrarian policies of the absolute monarchs of the eighteenth century. Now the restrictions were ended. In Prussia an "Edict for the Improvement of Agriculture" was proclaimed on 14 September 1811, the same day as the decree that prescribed the conditions by which peasants could redeem their holdings and their obligations. The edict ended the distinction between seigniorial and peasant land, legalized free purchase and free alienation of land, and allowed the seigniors to acquire peasant land without hindrance.[23] In the German and Slav crown lands of the Austrian Monarchy the protection of peasant land from absorption by seigniors ended almost two years before the emancipation, with the decree of 18 December 1846. That act permitted the peasant to give up some of his land to his seignior as payment for the redemption of his obligations. In Prussia and Russia, too, arrangements for redemption allowed the peasant to surrender part of his holding to his seignior. In at least one jurisdiction, however, the restriction on seigniorial appropriation of peasant land was retained. The emancipation decree for Schleswig-Holstein forbad seigniors to add peasant land to their demesnes (arts. 15, 16).

IV

In contrast to the removal of restraints upon seigniorial liberty to acquire land, the emancipation legislation, or later statutes, often placed restrictions upon the property rights of the freed peasant. The intent of these constraints was to prevent fragmentation of holdings, on the one hand, and, on the other, to prevent the concentration of land in the hands of a few. In Germany, legislation in Baden, Nassau, Bavaria, and Saxe-Weimar forbad the division of a peasant holding into pieces smaller than a minimum size established by the legislation. In Lower Saxony the peasant could alienate or subdivide only one-third of his inherited land; the other two-thirds had to remain undivided. In the Austrian Monarchy the law limited the right of the peasant to subdivide his holding beyond a certain point, to bequeath his land as he wished, to borrow against his property beyond what the government deemed the maximum amount, or to acquire additional land. Widespread evasions quickly reduced the effectiveness of this legislation and it was repealed in 1868 and 1869. In Russia, where title to the land went to the commune and not to the individual peasant, the peasant had no rights in the disposition of his allotment. If he wanted to leave the village he received no reimbursement for his allotment. To make matters even more difficult, he had to have paid one-half of the redemption costs of his allotment, paid all tax arrears plus the tax for the current year for all members of his household, and had to waive his right permanently to communal

---

[23] Edict reprinted in Franz (1963), 368-373.

land allotments and the use of common land, before he could get permission to move away. The Polish peasant proprietor could sell the land he received by the 1864 decree only to another peasant, his farming methods had to conform to certain regulations, and he could not divide his holding among his heirs in shares of less than a prescribed size. In practice, peasants often subdivided their holdings into pieces smaller than the legal minimum, presumably without the authorities learning of it. In Romania the emancipation statute declared that for the next thirty years peasants (or their heirs) could not alienate or mortgage land they received by terms of the statute, except to another peasant or to the village community, and those who purchased state land could not alienate it for thirty years, except to other peasants.[24]

An integral part of the peasant economy everywhere had been the rights of use, or servitudes, possessed by the peasants in the fallow fields, forests, pastures, meadows, and wastes of the manor (p. 93). The servitudes provided the villagers with resources of critical importance. Understandably, they were reluctant to abandon these rights in any event, and certainly not without some compensation for their loss. The proprietors, for their part, wanted to end them, not only because they did not get paid for this use of their property, but also because of damage to field and forest caused by the servitudes, and because they hindered the introduction of improvements that would increase the lord's income from his property. The framers of the emancipation and redemption legislation had to face up to this conflict of interests, and, not surprisingly, the peasants usually lost out.

In France the revolutionary governments freed the forests of the landed proprietors from the rights of use long enjoyed by the villagers, and tried, albeit without much success, to end servitudes in pastures and fallow fields. The Austrian decree of emancipation of 7 September 1848 had cancelled the servitudes without indemnification to the peasants (art. 7), though the decree came out of the Constitutional Reichstag in which so many peasants and their friends sat. The restored absolutism, as part of its effort to keep the support of the peasantry, in the law of 4 March 1849 ordered the continuation of the servitudes until further arrangements could be made for their redemption (art. 4). An imperial patent of 5 July 1853 instructed the seigniors to indemnify the peasants for the loss of servitudes by a cash payment, or by turning over some land to them. The determination of the value of the servitudes and of a mutually acceptable indemnification quickly became a wellspring of discord and sometimes of peasant violence. It was especially difficult to reach agreement in regions of hills and mountains,

---

[24] Germany: Lütge (1966), 442-443. Austria: Stölzl (1971), 28n.; Purs (1962), 251. Russia: Gerschenkron (1965), 752-754. Poland: *Polish Encyclopedia* (1922), III, 590; Kieniewicz (1966), 180-181. Romania: arts. VII, LVII in Warriner (1965), 180-185.

where the peasants' livelihood depended upon his right to pasture his cattle on land of the lord. Most of the settlements, however, were completed by the 1880's. On the whole, the peasants fared poorly, receiving indemnifications that did not cover the losses they suffered. Many could no longer make ends meet, and had to abandon independent farming as their way of life.

In Prussia, the servitudes were made redeemable at the instance of the peasant or of the seignior. Legislation provided that the annual value of the servitude was to be determined by a specialist. The peasant received indemnification in land, or in a capital sum, or a cash annuity that could be cancelled by payment by the lord of twenty-five times the annual payment. In Lithuania, White Russia (except for the province of Mogilev), and in the Kingdom of Poland, the servitudes remained in effect after the emancipations. The lord could end them only through a voluntary agreement with the peasants, to whom he had to give land whose value equalled that of the servitudes. That turned out to be a difficult and disputatious task, accompanied by much litigation. Data for 1893 for 71 per cent (9,251) of all privately owned manors in the Kingdom of Poland showed that peasants had retained their servitudes on 48 per cent (4,446) of these manors. As late as 1922, settlement still had not been made on 28 per cent of the private estates in the then Republic of Poland. In Romania article ix of the 1864 statute specified that the peasants were to retain rights they had in the forests of the proprietors. However, after fifteen years the proprietor could end the servitudes, whether by private agreement with the peasants or by court order. The proprietors made full use of this provision, so that after the specified period the right of the peasants to fell timber and gather wood vanished almost everywhere. The reform legislation made no provision for the continuation of pasturing servitudes. The result was a sharp and rapid decline in peasant animal husbandry, for the holdings of the peasants were too small to allow them to grow food crops and also raise livestock.[25]

V

Emancipation ended the fragmentation of public authority that had characterized the old order. The seignior's administrative, judicial, and police authority at the local level had derived from, and had rested upon, the servile dependence of the peasantry. Now that the law had abolished that dependence, the way was opened for the state to expand its control over local government. In some lands that happened simultaneously with the emancipation, or within a short time of it. In France, legislation in August 1789

[25] Austria: Feigl (1964), 334-335; Kravets (1966), 752-756; Mischler and Ulbricht (1905), I, 72; Purs (1962), 250. Prussia: Judeich (1863), 43; Poland: Rostworowski (1896), 66-69; *Polish Encyclopedia* (1922), III, 406, 597-599. Romania: Grünberg (1889), 85-86; Economo (1911), 197-198. France: Denis (1957), 267; Cobban (1971), 100n.

ordered the abolition of seigniorial jurisdiction, but allowed it to continue until the National Assembly had provided for the establishment of a new judicial system. A law of 16 August 1790 provided for such a system, and on 6 September 1790 the Assembly decreed the definitive abolition of the seigniorial courts.[26] In the Austrian Monarchy, the emancipation statute of 7 September 1848 ordered seigniors to continue their judicial and adminis-trative functions until state officials could take over from them (art. 9).

In other states, some of the seigniors' public authority, particularly their police and judicial powers, persisted for decades. In Bavaria, Württemberg, and Hannover, proprietors retained their judicial and police authority until 1848, though the peasants of these lands had been freed in 1808, 1817, and 1831, respectively. In Prussia, reformers had demanded the end of seignio-rial judicial and police authority at the time of the emancipation in 1807. Determined opposition from the nobility, and from within the govern-ment, defeated these efforts. The seigniors of Prussia kept their courts and police powers until 1848, when, under the pressure of revolution, they were taken from them. However, after a short interval, police authority was returned to them, but not the judicial function. The proprietors were charged with the responsibility of maintaining law and order on their prop-erties, of approving the village's selection of its officials, and of overseeing the general administration of the village. Laws in 1872 and 1891 for the six eastern provinces of Prussia abolished patrimonial police power. However, the new arrangements were such that the lord of the manor doubled as a state official, and thereby retained his police authority, and still supervised the overall administration and operations of the village. The new legislation did transfer the lord's power to approve the selection of village officials to state authority. But this, too, was largely meaningless, since the official now charged with this function was a nobleman who represented the nobil-ity of the district.[27] Proprietors in Mecklenburg kept their judicial author-ity until 1877. Thus, for fifty-seven years after the peasants had been freed there, seigniors could still sentence villagers to up to 8 days in jail, and up to 25 blows of the cudgel. In Saxony the administration of local justice and police remained in the hands of the seigniors until 1855, or twenty-three years after the peasants had been emancipated. The decree of emancipation for Schleswig-Holstein in 1804 forbad seigniors to sit as judges over their peasants. Persons trained in the law had to preside over the court, and the government had to approve their appointment. However, the court re-mained the seignior's court. This arrangement continued in Schleswig until 1853-1854, when seigniorial jurisdiction was abolished. In Holstein the lord's court persisted until the annexation of the duchy by Prussia in 1866.[28]

[26] Herbert (1969), 144-145.
[27] Muncy (1944), 24; Anderson and Anderson (1967), 95.
[28] Mottek (1964), II, 23-24; Blaschke (1965), 286-287; Sering (1908), 230.

In Poland the French-imposed constitution of 1807 in the grand duchy of Warsaw had ended seigniorial jurisdiction. However, the new government lacked the means and the suitable personnel to establish a system of state courts and police. It therefore ordered its prefects to appoint a mayor for each manor in their districts, to perform these functions. In most instances the prefects chose the owner of the manor or his steward for the post. After Russia annexed the duchy, the tsar in 1818 decreed that the mayor of the village must be the seignior or his deputy. The mayor had extensive judicial and administrative authority that included jurisdiction over minor criminal cases and the power to sentence culprits to short jail terms and to beatings. The seigniors in Russia's Baltic provinces, where the peasants had been freed early in the nineteenth century, retained their police authority until 1865. The extent of the punishment they could impose was, however, reduced. In Russia itself, the emancipation statute of 1861 ordered the establishment of a court in each township (*volost*), composed of several villages, to replace the seigniorial courts. The judges, who served for one year, were elected by the peasants from among their own number. The legislation defined the competence of these courts; general courts staffed by imperial officials heard cases that fell outside the jurisdiction of the township courts. Apparently, however, the peasants preferred their own traditional village tribunals to the township courts. A survey made in 1871-1874 indicated that up to three-quarters of peasant disputes that were in the competency of the township courts were actually settled in the unofficial village courts.[29]

Though seigniors in some lands continued their public functions, the state everywhere intruded increasingly in local government. In some of the servile lands, that intrusion predated the emancipation of the peasants by many years.[30] Now the process accelerated in these lands, and was initiated, sometimes slowly and gradually, in other of the erstwhile servile states. In addressing itself to the problem of rural local government, the central administration often reshaped the structure of the local communal organization. In France, intervention of the state in local government, which began in the seventeenth century, reached its peak with the decree of 25 July 1787. That edict ended the democratic control of the commune by its members. It provided that a council, elected by a severely restricted suffrage and drawn from persons who paid at least thirty livres a year in taxes, was to run the commune. The revolutionary government's law of 14 December 1789 scarcely altered the terms of the 1787 statute. Membership in the general assembly of the village, formerly the principal voice of the community, was now restricted to taxpayers; the assembly met only in special circumstances, and only after a fixed number of the assembly mem-

[29] Kieniewicz (1969), 75; Tobien (1911), II, 148, 279-281; Czap (1967), 151-153, 157-158, 175-178.
[30] Cf. Babeau (1878), 26-28; Wittich (1896), 138; Steinbach (1932), 107; Winkler (1941), 52.

bers petitioned the council to meet. During the era of the Consulate
(1799-1804), new legislation abolished the election of the council. Instead,
officials of the central government appointed its members. Not until 1831
did villagers regain the right to choose their own council.[31]

In Saxony, on the other hand, the central power's intervention in local
government worked in the direction of greater democracy. Only peasants
with holdings had been members of the village communities there. A law of
1838 decreed that all persons living within the borders of the commune
were to be active members of it. In some lands the state created a two- or
three-tiered structure for local government. The Helvetic Republic assembled local communes into administrative districts, with the local organization shorn of many of its functions. In the Austrian Monarchy an imperial
patent of 17 March 1849 ordered the creation of three levels of local government: the local community, the district, and the county. The law
granted wide autonomy to each level. It provided for the election of the
council of the local community by the local inhabitants on a fairly wide suffrage base. The local councils elected the members of the district council,
who in turn chose the members of the county council. Elections for the
local councils were held early in 1851, but in March the absolutist regime
suspended elections to the two higher councils, and drastically reduced the
autonomy of the local councils. Eleven years later, however, the government issued a new law that was almost identical with the 1849 statute, and
so reinstituted the aborted reform of that year.[32]

In Russia, the emancipation statute established a two-tiered system of
local government. The basic unit, the village community, usually coincided
with the already existing village commune, though sometimes several villages combined to form one village community. Each community had its
own officers, elected by the village assembly, which was composed of the
heads of the village households. The village community looked after purely
local matters, and had no formal link to the central government. The villages were grouped together into townships, each with from 300 to 2,000
adult males, and with the member villages not more than eight miles away
from each other. The township, or *volost*, had its own assembly, also
elected by the peasants, with 1 representative from every 10 households.
The *volost* assembly and its officials concerned themselves with matters
that affected the township as a whole, and with the township court. There
were direct ties between the *volost* and the central government, with the
officials of the *volost* directly responsible to officials of the central government.[33]

[31] Babeau (1878), 29-30, 55; Parain (1945), 48.
[32] Blaschke (1967), 238; Winkler (1941), 56; *Allgemeiner Reichs-Gesetz-und Regierungsblatt . . . Oesterreich*, 1849, no. 170; Macartney (1969), 438-439, 531.
[33] Vucinich (1960), 191-192; Emmons (1968), 46-47.

In Poland the legislation in 1864 that finally freed the peasants included new arrangements for local government. As in Russia, a two-tiered system was introduced: the local settlement, called the *gromada*, and the township, the *gmina*, formed by neighboring settlements. The officials of both *gromada* and *gmina* were elected by assemblies in which only those who owned at least 3 *morgi* (about 4 acres) could vote; later the minimum was dropped to 1.5 *morgi*. In 1873 there were 1,313 townships in the Kingdom of Poland, their population ran from 1,203 to 10,087, and averaged at 4,016, and their average area was 13,839 *morgi*, or almost 30 square miles.[34]

The roles assigned to the seigniors in the restructuring of local government differed considerably. In Russia the law restricted membership in the village community and the township to peasants. Supposedly they were self-governing. However, the emancipation statute placed them under the supervision of a nobleman called the "peace arbitrator." Chosen by the local hereditary nobility from among their own number, the peace arbitrator had to be confirmed by the provincial governor (who was appointed by the emperor), and then by the Imperial Senate. There were between thirty-five and fifty of these arbitrators in each province. They represented in their persons the interests of the local nobility. Their task included the settlement of disputes between lords and peasants, approval of land allotments to the peasants and of compensation to the nobles, and other matters concerned with the operation of the emancipation, and the oversight of the organs of peasant local government. In this latter capacity they could subject village and township officials to reprimands, fines, and arrests, and could remove them from office. They also supervised the exercise of police and courts in their districts.[35] In addition, an imperial statute of 1 January 1864 established district and provincial assemblies, called zemstvos. They were formed to provide local public services, such as the construction and maintenance of roads, support of public education and health, veterinary services, charity, local taxation, and the like. The assemblies, whose members were elected, represented the peasants, town dwellers, and nobles, but the law tilted the suffrage in favor of the nobility. Thus, in the mid-1860's nobles made up 42.4 per cent of the deputies to the district assemblies, and 81.8 per cent of the members of the provincial assemblies, and in later legislation the imbalance was made even greater.[36]

In the Austrian Monarchy and in Poland, seigniors could participate freely and fully in the work and deliberations of the local assemblies and administration. However, their vote counted for no more than did that of a

[34] Rostworowski (1896), 81, 81n.

[35] *Akademiia Nauk* (1959), II, 32. This office was abolished in 1874.

[36] Zaionchkovskii (1968), 410. Initially only 19 provinces had zemstvos, 34 had them by 1875, and 43 (out of the 70 provinces of the empire) in 1914.

peasant, and they had to abide by the decisions of the peasant-dominated local administration. As can be imagined, that did not sit well with some—and probably most—of the seigniors. One haughty Austrian, Count Eugen Czernin, remarked bitterly that "the nobleman with thirty-two or sixty-four [noble] ancestors has to bow to that vulgar local council. . . . The ignorant peasant who often cannot write . . . becomes the superior of his cultured and wealthy lord."[37] Count Rostworowski, scion of one of Poland's old noble families, in his scholarly study of rural Poland, concluded his discussion of the nobility's loss of power in local affairs with the comment that "In this way the influence of the intelligent has been completely excluded." Nor did Rostworowski neglect to mention the prevalence of illiteracy among local officials. He cited a report of 1870 that claimed that 40 per cent of the head officers of the townships could neither read nor write.[38]

Nowhere in Europe did the seigniors retain greater control of local government than they did in the eastern provinces of Prussia. Each large manor there constituted an independent administrative district headed by a proprietor who, as one writer put it, "ruled as a sovereign." Though, as mentioned earlier, they lost some of their authority in 1872, they continued to exercise wide local authority until new legislation in 1891 provided for sweeping reforms. Even then the Junkers, who controlled political life in eastern Germany, managed to reduce the effectiveness of the reform.[39]

The persistence of these aspects of seigniorial authority and privilege could not, however, conceal the reality. The emancipation of the peasantry spelled the end of the old order, the order whose origins reached back a thousand years in European history. For the acts of emancipation, though directed to the reform of the relationship between seignior and peasant, had far wider significance. The abolition of the servile dependency of the peasantry necessarily involved the dissolution of the organic concept of society, the hierarchical arrangement of the estates, and the structure of hereditary privileges—all heritages of medieval civilization. The collapse of these ancient pillars of social organization spelled the end of the society of orders, and allowed the reconstruction of the social order upon the very different institutional arrangements of the class society. The character and the extent of these new arrangements are the subject of the next—and last—chapter.

[37] Quoted in Stölzl (1971), 37-38.   [38] Rostworowski (1896), 81-82.
[39] Eyck (1948), 49; Cavaignac (1894), 77-78; Muncy (1944), 24.

CHAPTER 19

From Order to Class

I

THE transition from the society of orders to the class society took place against a background of unprecedented economic changes and unprecedented growth in population. The 100 or so million people who had lived in the servile lands in the last quarter of the eighteenth century had increased to nearly 300 million by the first decade of the twentieth century. The most spectacular increases occurred in the second half of the nineteenth century and in lands where the bonds of servitude had been most oppressive.[1] Some have suggested that the emancipation had much to do with the explosion of population. In the old order, younger sons had not married because of sanctions against the division of holdings. The relaxation or abandonment of these restrictions after the emancipation is said to have encouraged marriages, for now peasants could subdivide their land and provide for all of their children. It has also been suggested that the abolition of dues and services owed to the seigniors raised the standard of living and the well-being of the peasantry and thereby contributed to a decline in the death rate.[2]

In the eighteenth century the overwhelming majority of the population had lived on the land. The proportion of rural dwellers declined as cities grew and as industry flourished, but in the early years of the twentieth century country people still made up the largest part of the population in all of the former servile lands save for Germany.[3] The idiosyncrasies of census classification, however, allow only approximations in comparisons of the relative proportions of the rural population. Data on employment provides

---

[1] Austria: 61.5% from 1850 (17,534,950) to 1910 (28,324,940). *Oesterreichisches Statistisches Handbuch*, 1916-1917, 3.

Denmark: 113.9% from 1840 (1,289,075) to 1911 (2,757,076). *Statistisk Aarbog*, 1916, table 1.

Hungary: 43.4% from 1847 (14,565,968) to 1910 (20,886,487). *Tafeln zur Statistik*, 1853, pt. 1. table 2; *Annuaire Statistique Hongrois* , XXII (1916), table 4.

Poland: 174% from 1858 (4,764,446) to 1913 (13,056,000). *Statisticheskiia Tablitsky Rossiiskoi Imperii* (1863), 187; Wunderlich (1918), 335.

Prussia: 82.5% from 1849 (20,432,748) to 1905 (37, 293, 324), *Statistisches Handbuch für das Deutsches Reich*, 1907, pt. 1, tables 3, 4-7.

Romania: 82.8% from 1860 (3,917, 541) to 1912 (7,160, 682). Roberts (1951), 355.

European Russia: 116.9% from 1858 (59,415,400) to 1914 (128,864,300), *Statisticheskii Ezhegodnik Rossii*, 1914, pt. 1, 58.

[2] Lütge (1967), 274, 274n., 285; Leslie (1963), 240; Zubrzycki (1953), 250.

[3] The percentages of rural dwellers were: Denmark in 1911, 59.7%, *Statistisk Aarbog*, 1916, table 5; France in 1911, 55.8%, Augé-Laribé (1925), 20; Germany in 1907, 41.9%, *Deutsche Landwirtschaft* (1913), 20; Hungary in 1910, 81%, *Annuaire Statistique Hongrois*, 1914, 8-10; Poland in 1901-1906, 60%, Ballerstedt (1939), 25; Romania in 1905, 81%, Ionescu-Şişeşti (1912), 109; Russia in 1914, 85.6%, *Statisticheskii Ezhegodnik*, 1914, pt. 1, 61.

a more precise measurement of the continued importance of agriculture. These show that, with the exception of Germany, far more people earned their livings from agriculture (including forestry and fisheries) than from any other sector of the economy.

		Per Cent of Total Labor Force Employed in		
		Agriculture	*Industry*	
Austria	(1910)	53.1%	22.6%	*Oest. Statistik*, 1916, III, 13.
Denmark	(1911)	37.6	21.8	*Statistisk Aarbog*, 1916, table 33.
France	(1906)	42.7	30.2	*Annuaire Statistique*, 1909, 188.
Germany	(1907)	37.8	43.0	Woytinsky (1926), II, 12.
Hungary	(1910)	62.5	17.1	*Annuaire Statistique Hongrois*, 1914, 23.
Poland*	(1900)	64.9	25.8	Gieysztorowa (1968), 14.
European Russia	(1897)	74.9	9.7	*Statisticheskii ezhegodnik*, 1913, pt. 1, 85-86.

*Includes the three zones of partition, i.e., Austrian, German, and Russian Poland.

II

Just as agriculture continued to be the leading sector of economic life, so did land continue to be the principal form of wealth. And though commoners used profits from trade, industry, and the professions to buy manors, up to 1914 noblemen remained the principal owners of estates. Instead of being privileged seigniors, however, the noble proprietors had been reduced to the status of mere landowners, possessed of no more rights and privileges than any other landowner. The loss of their role as seigniors stripped the concept of nobility of its essential meaning. For a thousand years the rationale for the privileged status of the nobility had rested upon the nobleman's leadership over, responsibility for, and protection of the peasants who lived in his seigniory. Now the state had taken over these functions and nobles were legally no different from any other subject. As the Danish constitution bluntly declared, "All privileges granted by law in connection with nobility, title, or rank are abolished."[4] The legislation of other states was usually less direct but had the same effect.

In real life the nobility, despite the laws, retained a superior status. The centuries-old acceptance of privilege was deeply imbedded in the consciousness of European society. It was still a "deference society" (to borrow F.M.L. Thompson's term for nineteenth-century England) in which the community paid habitual respect to the nobility, who, as Professor Thompson put it, "were superior by reason of their style, authoritative manner and air of gentility and who were acknowledged as such because

[4] Art. 92, Dodd (1910), I, 280.

they claimed the rights of their social position with self-assurance."[5] That was true above all of the high nobility, who by virtue of their wealth and titles were endowed in the public mind with that magical essence called "glamour" (a quality that, as the dictionary explains, "delusively magnifies or glorifies"). Their comings and goings, their romances, and their marriages were followed with breathless interest by enthralled millions, even as in our own time the daily routine of the widows of Greek shipping magnates holds a mysterious fascination for the multitude. They were the "beautiful people" of their era, and, for the most part, were as uninteresting and as superfluous as their modern counterparts.

Because of the persistence of the deference society, noblemen retained an importance in government that was out of all proportion to their numbers, their abilities, and their contributions to their societies. They surrounded their monarch, provided him with his confidants and closest advisors, and held a disproportionate number of the highest posts in the civil and military establishments. The diplomatic corps and the non-technical branches of the army, the infantry and cavalry, were their favored preserves. Their traditions and training and their self-assurance fitted them for these specialties. Even in France, where their power and influence ebbed more swiftly than in other lands, in 1900 they still dominated the ambassadorial corps, and 75 of the 300 French army generals were noblemen.[6]

The over-representation of the nobility extended to the legislative assemblies that became standard parts of European governments in the era before the First World War. In the last century of the old order, nobles, meeting in their provincial and national estates, had nearly everywhere exercised little political or legislative power. Now, ironically, because of their over-representation in both national and provincial assemblies in central and eastern Europe, they became a major political force. In the parliaments of these lands, most of the seats in the upper chambers, which had veto power over actions of the lower house, were reserved for noblemen, and often the lower house had many noblemen among its members. In 1913 three-quarters of the members of the upper house in the Prussian *Landtag* were nobles, and over a fourth (119) of the 443 members of the lower house were also noblemen.[7]

As the decades went by, however, the preeminence of the nobility diminished, drained by the ever-wider acceptance among Europeans of the concept of equality and by the increased self-assurance of the bourgeoisie.

[5] Thompson (1963), 184.

[6] Austria: Teifen (1906), 63; Macartney (1968), 714. France: Lhomme (1960), 20-26; Anderson and Anderson (1967), 188; La Gorce (1963), 20-21. Germany: Muncy (1944), 160-163, 175, 202-207; Dissow (1961), 5; Armstrong (1973), 77-78, table III, 91. Hungary: Gubernatis (1885), 260. Russia: Korelin (1971b), 70.

[7] Austria: Teifen (1906), 62; *Statesman's Year-Book*, 1914, 621. Germany: *Statesman's Year-Book*, 1914, 936, 939, 949, 974, 981. Hungary: *ibid.*, 637. Romania: Eidelberg (1974), 16-18, 21.

It was not so much a precipitous decline in the status and importance of the nobility as it was a dilution of their preeminence. By the eve of World War I—the great caesura of modern European history—the nobility had to share its leadership with men of common origin. Education and merit, instead of birth, became more and more the pass-key to high places. The always expanding scope of activity of the post-emancipation state created the need for more bureaucrats, and particularly for trained specialists. The nobility was neither large enough nor did it contain enough able men to meet the demand. Monarchs had, of course, long used commoners in important positions. Now, however, to meet their needs governments had to make themselves far more open to talent than ever before, and men of non-noble birth filled many high offices in all of the former servile lands. The ascent of commoners was most pronounced in the branches of administration that require special skills and training, such as the ministries of finance, justice, and agriculture, but they made deep inroads, too, in those favored preserves of the nobility, the ministry of foreign affairs and the army. In 1804 none of the major posts in the Austrian Foreign Office had a bourgeois incumbent; by 1918 burghers held 66 per cent of these appointments. In 1804 only 2 of the 37 generals in the Austrian army were of bourgeois origin. By 1908, 20 of the 39 generals and, in 1918, 42 of the 61 generals were of bourgeois birth. Out of the 7,000-8,000 officers of the Prussian army in 1806, only 695 were bourgeois, and only about 30 of these commoners held field-grade rank, that is, were majors or higher. In 1865 nearly half (3,997) of the 8,169 officers, and 14 per cent (in 1860) of the generals and colonels came from bourgeois families. By the end of 1913, by which time the army was more than twice as large as it had been in the 1860's, 70 per cent of the entire officer corps, and 48 per cent of the generals and colonels, were from bourgeois families. A survey made in Russia in 1895 found that nearly half (49.2 per cent) of 31,350 army officers were of non-noble birth. These men were concentrated in the line regiments; nearly all of the officers in the elite Guards regiments were of noble birth. In the navy the great majority of the technical officers, graduates of naval engineering and shipbuilding schools, were sons of commoners.[8]

The commoners who rose to high office were often rewarded with a patent of nobility. Commoners who distinguished themselves in business and the professions were ennobled, too, though in fewer numbers. In the old order the patent of nobility would have endowed these men with legal superiority over the lower orders. Now the patent was merely a recognition of achievement, a badge of honor granted with increasing frequency to men who attained high success in their callings, whatever their social origins. From 1871 to 1918 the Hohenzollern as kings of Prussia created 1,129 new

[8] Preradovich (1955), 46-47, 52-55, 65; Demeter (1965), 5-7, 28-29; Craig (1955), 233, 234-235; Zaionchkovskii (1973), 148-149, 149n.; Garthoff (1960), 326; Thomas and Znaniecki (1920), ɪᴠ, 314-315.

Prussian nobles, all of them from the bourgeoisie, and promoted 186 nobles to higher titles. William II (1888-1918), who was responsible for 836 of the creations, often granted patents of nobility to entire branches of a family, so that sometimes as many as 30 persons were ennobled by a single patent. In the 50 provinces of European Russia the number of hereditary nobles grew by 45 per cent between 1858 and 1897, from 609,973 to 885,754. A disproportionate number of these nobles infested the Baltic, White Russia, and Lithuanian provinces. If the swarms of Polish and German nobles in these 9 provinces are excluded, the hereditary nobility in the remaining 41 provinces more than doubled between 1858 and 1897, from 232,346 to 477,836. The French officially abolished the rank of nobility for the third time when they stumbled into the Third Republic. The first attempt at abolition had been made by the National Assembly in 1790, and the second by the short-lived Second Republic in 1848. The attempt by the government of the Third Republic was about as unsuccessful as the attempts by the revolutionaries of 1790 and 1848. The French nobility not only continued in existence after 1871; it actually grew. The end of the legal sanction for the existence of the nobility meant that anyone could assume a title without fear of running afoul of the law. So wealthy bourgeois families, especially in the provinces, called themselves marquises or counts, or simply added a "de" to their family names. Not only was there none to say nay to them, but, remarkably, instead of being lampooned for their presumption they were accepted as nobles if they adopted the style of life associated in the popular mind with the nobility.[9]

To employ the awkward but descriptive Marxist term, the nobility was being "bourgeoisified" by the elevation of families of common birth. The process of bourgeoisification (the French *embourgeoisement* sounds more elegant) was accelerated considerably by common political interests of old nobility and new wealth, by intermarriages, and by joint participation in business enterprise. Politically, nobles and wealthy burghers generally held the same conservative views, and shared the same suspicions of social and political reform. Marriages between scions of great noble houses and daughters of rich industrialists and bankers multiplied, especially in the last decades of the nineteenth and first years of the twentieth century.

The involvement of nobles in business enterprise reached back into the era of the traditional order, but, as earlier observed, it was an exceptional phenomenon. In the years after the emancipations, many noblemen, among them members of old and famous houses, became active participants or major investors in commerce and industry, or lent their names to add prestige to corporate ventures. By 1902 in France 30 per cent of the boards of directors of railroads and 32 per cent of the boards of large steel and banking firms were members of the nobility. In Germany and Austria

---

[9] Cecil (1970), 759-760, 767, 771; Korelin (1971a), 124, 129-135; Michels (1914), 157.

noblemen of the highest rank, including mediatized princes (one-time rulers who had lost their sovereignty in 1806 when the number of independent German states had been reduced from 360 to 39), invested heavily in established firms and founded new enterprises. Among the largest of the titled industrial magnates was Prince Christian zu Hohenlohe-Oehringen. The Hohenlohe fortune was estimated at 150 million marks, with four-fifths of it invested in industry and only one-fifth in land. Fifty million marks were in Hohenlohe-Werke AG, a coal and zinc complex founded by Prince Christian in 1905. The patent to establish the famed Austrian Credit-Anstalt in 1855 was granted to Princes Fürstenberg, Schwarzenberg, and Auersperg, and Count Chotek, each of them from the highest and oldest nobility, and three bankers, S. M. Rothschild, L. Lämel, and L. von Haber. Fürstenberg, Schwarzenberg, Auersperg, Chotek, and 5 other members of distinguished noble families, 3 bankers, and 2 industrialists founded the Austrian Syndicate for Chemical and Metallurgical Production. In 1874, 13 princes, 1 landgrave, 64 counts, 29 barons, and 41 other noblemen sat on the boards of Austrian railroad companies founded since 1866 (when a great wave of new company promotions got under way), and 1 prince, 16 counts, 6 freiherrs, and 2 other nobles were on the boards of other enterprises founded in Vienna since 1866. In Russia, too, wealthy nobles, among them members of some of the greatest families, participated in business enterprise. They sat on the boards and took part in the councils of management of the railroads and invested heavily in new and old enterprises. Even members of the imperial family were not above putting money into business enterprises; at his death in 1909 Grand Duke Vladimir Aleksandrovich, the uncle of the tsar, owned railroad shares worth 1,133,800 rubles that from 1904 to 1908 paid him an annual average dividend of 122,600 rubles.[10]

Central and eastern European noblemen had assumed leadership in brewing, distilling, and the refining of beet sugar in the decades before the emancipations and their domination continued into the twentieth century. The output in these industries, and particularly in beet sugar manufacture, grew so much after the middle of the nineteenth century that they assumed major importance in the industrial production of their respective lands. In 1886, 80 of the 120 beet sugar refineries in Bohemia (where most of Austria's beet sugar was produced) belonged to magnates, as did 500 of the 900 breweries, and 300 of the 400 distilleries. In Russia, in 1913-1914, nobles owned 2,377 of the 2,978 distilleries and turned out 55 per cent of all the spirits produced in the empire.[11]

The grandees who engaged in business, whether as active participants or

[10] Zeldin (1973), 405; Palmade (1972), 214; Jaeger (1967), 31-33; Gollwitzer (1964), 255-258; Winkel (1968), 36-38; Stölzl (1971), 80-81; Anfimov (1969), 255, 271-273.
[11] Macartney (1968), 622; Anfimov (1969), 256-257.

as investors or as ornaments to lend prestige, were, of course, a small minority of the nobility. Their entry into the bourgeois world of trade, industry, and banking brought them into contact with the topmost stratum of the bourgeoisie. The style of life and the self-assurance of the great capitalists differed hardly at all from that of the high nobility, and many were themselves ennobled. In a sense there was interpenetration of high nobility and high bourgeoisie, in which noble became bourgeoisified and bourgeois became feudalized. The rest of the nobility, less well endowed with earthly goods, followed other courses. Some managed to continue in their traditional way of life. Many others, deprived of much, or even all, of their income by the emancipations, could no longer afford to maintain the old noble way of life. They had to shift to bourgeois standards and to seek employment in government, in the bureaucracy, and in bourgeois occupations. Others, still imbued with the prejudices of the old order, looked down upon trade as a calling unworthy of a nobleman, and clung to their ancestral acres. It did not take long for many of these people to be reduced to the status of impoverished country squire or, as the Germans called it, *Krautjunker*.[12]

Robert Michels in 1914, in a long essay, provided an insightful sociological analysis of the fate of the nobility in Europe. "The nobility," he wrote, "inundated by a new nobility mainly of financial origin without a noble past and in part without aristocratic manners and way of life, stripped of its old prerogatives . . . and of its unwritten privilege of nearly exclusive possession of posts in the diplomatic corps and the highest ranks in army and government, is today, so to speak, déclassé. In short, it is no longer an order because it no longer possesses a special status guaranteed by law, nor is it a class, because even less does it possess any special economic characteristics."[13] Marcel Proust, in what has been called the great obituary of the French nobility, viewed the crumbling fabric of that nobility from a more sensitive perspective. In the slow-moving and endlessly detailed prose of his masterly (albeit at times seemingly interminable) *Remembrance of Things Past*, he recounted from his own experience the nobility's loss of its self-confidence and its exclusivity in the years before the First World War. In the account of the afternoon party given by the Princess Guermantes that takes up most of the twelfth and last volume of the novel, the protagonist finally realizes what has happened to the nobility: "Enfeebled and broken, the springs of the machine could no longer perform their task of keeping out the crowd; a thousand alien elements made their way in and all homogeneity, all consistency of form and color was lost. The Faubourg Saint-Germain was like some senile dowager now, who replies only with

[12] Muncy (1944), 55-58, 157; Lütge (1967), 271; Winkel (1968), 29-30; Gieysztor (1968), 532.
[13] Michels (1914), 151.

timid smiles to the insolent servants who invade her drawing rooms, drink her orangeade, present their mistresses to her."[14]

In Russia the division of society into orders was retained after the emancipation. Until 1917 people were legally defined by the order, the *soslovie*, to which they belonged. As the years went by, these forms gradually lost their significance, and by the end of the century people seemed no longer interested in knowing the *soslovie* of an individual. The increase in the urban, non-landowning nobles, swelled by the influx of proprietors who sold or lost their land, encouraged the adoption of this attitude among the nobility. These city dwellers tended to identify with interests other than those of the corps of the nobility. Prince B. A. Vasil'chikov, marshal of the nobility of the province of Novgorod, commented on this in a report he made in 1896. "The concerns of each section of the nobility," he wrote, "is much more completely expressed by the interests of the calling which it pursues than by the interests of its *soslovie*. . . . To expect an awakening of a caste self-awareness and solidarity in this diversified mass at the end of the nineteenth century is to delude oneself."[15] In the aftermath of the Revolution of 1905, nobles in 1906 organized the Council of the United Nobility as a political pressure group. The Council seized upon every opportunity to obstruct the advances of constitutional government and to oppose proposals that threatened the power and especially the land of the nobility. But even among this group there were men who recognized that the day of the nobility was nearly over. They called themselves aurochs, the last representatives of an almost extinct species.[16]

III

The dilution of the preeminence of the nobility was accompanied and to a considerable extent caused by economic reverses suffered by many noblemen. The emancipation of the peasants swept away the underpinnings upon which the economy of most noble landowners had rested. They lost the goods and services and cash dues paid to them by their peasants, they lost much of their land, and they lost their tax exemptions. Their indemnification fell short of compensating them for their material losses, and was further reduced by declines in the value of indemnification bonds, by long delays in some lands in the payment of the indemnity, and in Russia and France by the subtraction of outstanding debts.[17] So for many noble-

[14] Proust (1970), 345. [15] Korelin (1971a), 172-173.
[16] Williams (1914), 371. The aurochs is the European wild ox.
[17] In Russia, as mentioned earlier (p. 400), the state deducted the money owed by proprietors to state lending agency. In France in 1825 around 25,000 émigrés were indemnified by the restored Bourbon government for property confiscated by the revolutionary regimes, but with all obligations and liens against the property deducted from the indemnification. Sometimes the debts exceeded the value of the indemnification. Forster (1967), 81-82.

men, especially but not exclusively lesser proprietors, the emancipation turned out to be a calamity. Hardest hit of all were those seigniors who had little or no demesne, and who depended for their income upon the payments in cash and kind they had exacted from their peasants.[18]

The indemnification was supposed to provide the proprietors with the capital they needed to adjust to the new conditions. That seemed to have worked for some proprietors, and especially for great proprietors who received staggering sums as indemnification. In Bohemia, for example, the owners of the 93 largest estates received a total of 15,866,834 silver florins. Seven families who owned 31 of these 93 manors were paid nearly 7 million florins. Some of these men and a significant number of other proprietors used their indemnification to modernize and intensify their agricultural operations, including food processing, and to invest in non-agricultural enterprises. Others, and apparently the majority in some lands, spent their indemnification money on consumption instead of putting it to productive use. And, in any event, small proprietors and some medium-sized ones did not receive enough to cover the costs of improvements, even if they had wanted to make them.[19]

The difficulties confronting noble proprietors were compounded by the attitude and lack of knowledge and initiative of many of them, including some large proprietors. These failings were perhaps more common among the proprietors of Hungary, Galicia, Romania, and Great Russia than in other lands, though they certainly were not unknown elsewhere. Already in debt before the emancipations, these nobles borrowed more money from state lending institutions and from private lenders who charged them extortionate rates of interest. The high grain prices of the 1850s and 1860s enabled most of them to survive despite their inefficiency—though there were something like 20,000 foreclosures in Hungary within the first two decades after the emancipation there. When in the 1870's prices began their long downward slide, noble proprietors suffered severe losses. Many of them had to sell part or all of their land, or lost it to their creditors. By the end of the nineteenth century only one-third of the "knight's estates" (*Rittergüter*) in the Prussian provinces east of the Elbe were still owned by noblemen. In European Russia the amount of land owned by nobles in the 47 out of 50 provinces for which data are available fell by almost 45 per cent between 1861 and 1911, from 77.8 to 43.2 million desiatins.[20]

[18] Feigl (1964), 338; Macartney (1968), 466; Eddie (1967), 295, 297; Engels (1957), 158; Finck von Finckenstein (1960), 115, 117; Conze (1948), 10; Gieysztor (1968), 532; Eidelberg (1974), 71; Haufe (1939), 110; Pavlovsky (1968), 104, 111, 190-191; Anfimov (1969), 318, 323-327.

[19] *Sessional Papers*, LXVII (1870), pt. ii, 9; Purs (1962), 249; Purs (1963), 37-38; Feigl (1964), 338; Winkel (1968), 30, 38, 157; Jensen (1937), 49; Brugger (1904), 98-99.

[20] Germany: Winkel (1968), 31; Lütge (1967), 271; Finck von Finckenstein (1960), 118-120; Muncy (1944), 26; Lütge (1967), 271. Galicia: Warriner (1953), 183. Hungary: Eddie (1967), 296-297; Gubernatis (1885), 261; Patterson (1869), I, 325-326; Warriner (1965),

In Russia most of the land given up by nobles was purchased by peasants (see below). In Hungary large noble proprietors often bought the land sold by other nobles. Between 1867 and 1914 latifundia, defined in Hungary as estates of over 10,000 *hold* (14,300 acres), grew rapidly at the expense of smaller manors, particularly those in the middle-size range. In 1867 latifundia took up 8.5 per cent of the area occupied by landed properties. By 1914 that ratio had risen to 19.4 per cent, while the proportion occupied by estates of between 200 and 10,000 *hold* fell from 44.9 per cent to 31.6 per cent. Burghers everywhere bought land, too. Some purchased estates to gain the social cachet that went with ownership of a country seat. Others invested in land as a business proposition. In Prussia east of the Elbe, in Mecklenburg, and in France in the neighborhood of large cities, bourgeois proprietors became a major component among the landowners. In Prussia, bourgeois proprietors were most frequent as owners of medium-sized estates averaging around 500 hectares. Most estates larger than this belonged to nobles, old and new, with properties of over 5,000 hectares belonging almost exclusively to noblemen. In Austria, the number of bourgeois estate owners grew by the year, but the total area of land owned by them was relatively insignificant. In Russia, wealthy burghers had been the principal purchasers of noble land in the years immediately succeeding the emancipation. By 1877 they owned nearly 12 million of the 94 million desiatins owned by individuals (the rest of the land was owned by the state, peasant communes, and miscellaneous institutions, including the church). For a time it seemed as if burghers might supplant the nobility as the chief landowners of the empire. Then as land prices, which had been rising steadily since 1861, continued to go up because of the strong demand from peasants, bourgeois purchasers bought land for quick and profitable resale, while the rate of their permanent acquisitions slowed down. In Romania, burghers, many of them Jewish, rented noble-owned land. Around 1906, 56.88 per cent of the area occupied by all properties of over 50 hectares, and 72.43 per cent of the area occupied by estates of over 5,000 hectares, were rented. The renters, nearly all of them large-scale lessees, sublet the land in small pieces to peasants. In Hungary, too, there was much large scale leasing. In 1895 only 2.71 per cent of all farm enterprises there were leased, but they covered 19 per cent of the area of the country.[21]

Not all noble landowners lost out in the post-emancipation era. There were many proprietors who adjusted successfully, and there were still great magnates who owned enormous stretches of land and commanded great

33-34. Poland: Kieniewicz (1969), 185. Romania: Martonne (1902), 298-299; Haufe (1939), 109. Russia: Anfimov (1969), 289-293; Woytinsky (1926), III, 35; Iatsunskii (1966), 62.

[21] Austria: Teifen (1906), 22, 25, 30; Richter (1964), 64. France: Sée (1942), II, 126; Wright (1964), 7. Germany: Winkel (1968), 32; Rosenberg (1969), 15, 17-18. Hungary: Eddie (1967), 296; Puskás (1961), 198-199. Poland: Kieniewicz (1969), 185. Romania: Creangă (1907), I, 137-140; Roberts (1951), 14. Russia: Robinson (1932), 132-133.

wealth. In 1905 in European Russia 8.7 per cent (9,324) of the 107,237 noble proprietors there owned 72 per cent of the land still in the hands of nobles. One hundred and fifty-five of these grandees each had over 135,000 acres. Together they owned 43.5 million acres. That amounted to one-sixth of all the privately owned land in European Russia. The mediatized princes of Germany often had great land holdings, much of it in forest. In the Hapsburg empire the eleven largest proprietors in Silesia owned 20 per cent of that province, the 11 largest in Moravia owned 10.8 per cent, and the 13 largest in Lower Austria owned 9 per cent of all the land in their respective provinces. All of these largest proprietors were noblemen. The landholdings of the French nobility had not been substantially reduced during the revolutionary era. Many nobles had not emigrated and so had not had their estates confiscated, while returned émigrés recovered or bought land. However, large estates were exceptional in France. A property of more than 100 hectares was considered large, and estates of over 1,000 hectares were rarities.[22]

Great proprietors sought protection from future losses of family land and wealth, and therefore of family status, by entailing their properties. The creator specified the property to be entailed (nearly always land, though sometimes more liquid assets were entailed), and prescribed the manner in which the property was to devolve upon his descendants. The occupants had only a life interest in the entailed property and had to turn it over unencumbered and undiminished to their successors. The entail ended only when the family died out, or in Prussia when all the affected participants agreed to its dissolution.[23]

The right to entail was restricted to the largest proprietors and was a frequent target of liberal political action. In France the revolutionary government in 1792 abolished entails, Emperor Napoleon restored the privilege, the restored Bourbons loosened the rules, the government of King Louis Phillippe in 1835 forbad the creation of new entails and limited many of the existing ones to two generations, and, finally, after the revolution of 1848, entails were forbidden. In much of southern and western Germany entails had been abolished during the French occupation, were restored in 1815, outlawed again during the revolutions of 1848, and then once more restored in all save a few lands. In Prussia the constitution of 1850 abolished entails, but two years later the right was restored.[24] Thereafter the number of entails rose rapidly. In 1850 there had been 519 entails, covering 1,249,000 hectares. At the end of 1912 there were 1,277 with 2,449,000 hectares, amounting to 7 per cent of all of Prussia. Almost 46 per cent of

[22] Austria: Macartney (1968), 466; Teifen (1906), 21, 24-25, 27, 29, 32, 34. France: Labrousse (1954), 25-26; Augé-Laribé (1925), 21. Germany: Gollwitzer (1964), 254-255. Russia: Proskuriakova (1973), 68; Anfimov (1969), 28, 31.

[23] Except where otherwise noted the data on entails is from Dietze (1926), 991-1000.

[24] Tönnies (1912), 1057.

this land was in forest in 1900. Only 2.2 per cent of the entails were in bourgeois families; all the rest were in noble houses.

In Austria, on the other hand, the number of entails increased hardly at all in the decades before 1914. This was because the law now required the parliament to sanction new creations and the assembly grew reluctant to give its consent. There had been 292 entails in Austria in 1882, involving 1.14 million hectares, of which nearly two-thirds was in forest. Between then and 1910 only 6 new entails were established, with 65,257 hectares.[25] In Hungary until 1848 all inherited land had been inalienable and had to be passed on undiminished to the occupant's heirs. The abolition of this requirement during the 1848 revolution persuaded Hungarian magnates to gain permission from the crown to create entails. By 1914 there were 92 of them, covering 2.267 million hectares, or about 7 per cent of the country.[26]

In Denmark the constitution had forbidden the creation of new entails and had promised that future legislation would convert entailed land into freely transferrable property.[27] Despite this, about 10 per cent of the arable land in Denmark was the entailed property of old noble families. In the Russian empire, entails were most common among the German nobles of the Baltic provinces. By 1909 there were 266 entails there, many of them established in the second half of the nineteenth century. They covered a total of 991,000 desiatins, or 11.7 per cent of the area of the three Baltic provinces. In the Russian provinces the long tradition of partible inheritance militated against entails. In 1845 Tsar Nicholas I authorized their establishment but set the qualifications so high that only the very wealthiest proprietors could take advantage of the legislation. Few if any did until after the emancipation in 1861. Then the steady loss of land by nobles convinced some magnates to establish entails in order to avoid diminution of their family's patrimony in later generations. On the eve of the First World War they had entailed 3.5 million desiatins. That amounted to about 8 per cent of all the land owned by nobles at that time (excluding the Baltic provinces). In Romania, where partible inheritance had long been the rule, entails remained unknown.[28]

IV

Just as the traditional superior status of the nobility persisted after the emancipation, so too did the social and political inferiority of the peasantry. The passage from the old order of legally sanctioned privilege to the open society in which economic role and not birth determined status was too

---

[25] *Oesterreichisches Statistisches Handbuch*, 1910, table 9, 112.

[26] Blum (1948), 64-66; Földes (1894), 829; *Annuaire Statistique Hongrois*, XXII (1914), table 5, 72.

[27] Art. 93, 1849 constitution, Dodd (1912), I, 278.

[28] Anfimov (1969), 40, 42, 44-46; Jelavich (1962), 184.

From Order to Class

sudden for all of its implications to be understood and accepted by those whose values had been formed by the old order. It was a moral and psychological revolution that required a profound change in the social and mental climate that only time could bring.

The adjustment would have been swifter had governments used their authority to speed the process. Instead, they delayed the grant of full citizenship and of equal rights to the freed peasantry. For years after their emancipation, the peasants of Denmark, Prussia, Russia, and Romania paid the full land tax on their holdings while noble proprietors were assessed at a much lower rate or paid no land tax at all. In response to the demands of landowners, governments placed stringent restrictions on the freedom of movement and other civil rights of farm laborers, and particularly the live-in farm hands who were engaged by the year. The Hungarian Farm Servants Act of 1907, for example, forbad these workers to leave the farm or receive outside visitors without their employer's permission on pain of a fine and deduction from their wages; laborers under eighteen could be whipped for infractions of discipline; laborers were liable to fines, costs, and damages for any neglect of duty and wages and belongings, except food, fuel, and shelter, could be seized to meet the penalties; and heavy fines and imprisonment were ordered for those farm hands who encouraged fellow workers to take concerted action against the employer or who joined in a strike or other refusal of duty. A half century after the emancipation in Denmark, noble proprietors there claimed the right to flog peasants, and in Russia until 1904 courts could sentence peasants to whippings, a form of punishment long since banned for all other subjects. In Russia a host of restrictions hobbled the civil rights of the peasants until after the Revolution of 1905. That rising had badly shaken the autocracy and compelled it to grant reforms in succeeding years that removed many of the legal disabilities attached to the peasant status. These included the right to travel and live anywhere in the empire, to withdraw from the commune and become a private landowner with a consolidated holding, and to be tried only for acts recognized as crimes in the general criminal code. Even then the peasants did not have complete equality of rights with other citizens, though the most restrictive limitations upon their freedom had been lifted.[29]

Everywhere governments so arranged the franchise that a small minority, determined by social status and income, had a far greater voice in elections than did the rest of the electorate, and particularly the peasantry. In Denmark, where the peasants were not enfranchised until 1849, six decades after their emancipation, the votes of noble landowners and wealthy burghers were weighted to give them a majority of the seats in the upper chamber of the parliament. Not until 1915 was equal suffrage—that is, one

[29] *Sessional Papers*, 1870, LXVII, pt. 1, 201; Drage (1909), 319-321; Wunderlich (1961), 18-19; Roberts (1951), 12-13; Gerschenkron (1965), 787-797; Czap (1967), 177-178.

man one vote—introduced.[30] In Austria the upper house of the parliament was composed of princes of the imperial family, large noble landowners who inherited their seats, prelates, and life-members appointed by the emperor. The members of the lower house were chosen by an electorate divided into four divisions, called curials. The 5,402 large landowners, nearly all of them noblemen, who in 1891 made up the first curial chose 85 of the 353 deputies in the lower house, while the 1,387,572 rural voters who were the fourth curial elected 129. Not until 1907 did Austria get rid of this system in favor of universal manhood and equal suffrage. In Hungary restrictions on the right to vote disenfranchised most of the peasantry and left political power in the hands of the nobility.[31] The nearly 400 members of the Reichstag of the German empire were elected by universal manhood suffrage. In Prussia and the other states of the empire, however, property qualifications restricted the suffrage.[32] In Russia the peasants did not receive the franchise until October 1905. The First Duma, elected in 1906, had 64 peasant members, and the Second Duma, chosen in 1907 had 111, amounting to 24.8 per cent of that assembly. However, a decree of 3 June 1907 restructured the franchise so that the nobility, who were about 1 per cent of the population, elected nearly half of the Duma's members. In Romania, property and educational qualifications kept 98 per cent of the electorate from being allowed to vote for members of the upper house of the parliament. The lower house was divided into three so-called colleges, elected by different groups of voters. The first college, with 41 per cent of the deputies, was chosen by about 1.5 per cent of the electorate; the second college, with 38 per cent of the deputies, was chosen by 3.5 per cent of the electorate. College III, with 21 per cent of the deputies, was chosen by the remaining 95 per cent of the voters. Moreover, the poor and illiterate peasants who made up nearly all of this 95 per cent did not vote directly for their representatives, but chose electors who chose the deputies.[33]

The realities, then, did not come up to the great expectations that many had for the results of the emancipations. But the shortcomings were only one side of the story. Peasant freedom and civil equality, albeit still limited, opened hitherto closed doors to personal advancement and to human dignity. Rural illiteracy remained shockingly high, but the gradual increase in schools offered new opportunities for basic education. And an always growing number of peasant children found their way to higher education. In 1880 in Russia only 3.3 per cent of the university enrollment came from peasant families; by 1914 that ratio had risen to 14.5 per cent of the 35,695 students attending the universities.[34]

---

[30] Section IV, Constitution of Denmark, Dodd (1909), I, 271-273.
[31] Anderson and Anderson (1967), 319-320, 326-327.
[32] *Statesman's Year-Book*, 1901, 612ff.
[33] Levin (1966), 67n.; Eidelberg (1974), 15-16.   [34] Hans (1931), 238-239.

Most important of all, the peasantry emerged as a class with its own political and economic interests and programs. The proclivity to join together in common action was, of course, deeply rooted in peasant life. In the days of the traditional order, however, their cooperation had been limited to their own community, save when they joined with other peasants in sporadic and always shortlived risings. Compulsory military service and tax levies had provided almost the only sustained contact with outside society. "The peasantry is a myth," wrote Jean Valarché, "in the era when the only leaders whom the peasants can find among themselves are the leaders of jacqueries. The peasant class does not really exist so long as the manor house closes off the horizon and governs the village that cowers in its shadow."[35] The end of servility, the growing availability of schooling, the opening up of the rural world by improved communications, and the realization that they were still disadvantaged, awakened peasants to the need for organization and activism. Their organizations, some local, others regional and national, attracted many hundreds of thousands of members. Bourgeois reformers, radicals, conservatives, and reactionaries, each of whom wanted to use the peasant for their own ends, often supplied guidance and leadership in the establishment of these organizations.

In Germany and Austria the peasants tended to align themselves politically with reactionary noble landowners and with rightist political parties. In Denmark the peasants supported the liberal party called at first Friends of the Peasants and later renamed the Democratic Left. For most of the time from 1872 on, the peasants' party had a working majority in the lower house of the Danish parliament. In France the peasants made little use of their potential for political power. They scattered their votes across the political spectrum despite efforts by rival agrarian organizations to mobilize the peasant vote. In Russia radical political leaders in the revolutionary year of 1905 tried to win the support of the peasants by promises of land reform and by urging peasant seizure of the property of private landowners. For a time the peasants seemed to be attracted to the radical line. But soon the revolutionary movement ebbed among the peasants, hastened by massive governmental repression and by the reforms that gave the peasants new freedom.[36]

The successes of the peasants in economic cooperation overshadowed by far their political achievements. The emancipations had exposed the peasants to the money economy to a much greater extent than they had hitherto experienced. In the traditional society they had paid many obligations in kind and labor, most of them had been involved hardly at all in the

[35] Valarché (1959), 39-40.
[36] Austria: Buchinger (1952), 273-282; Knoll (1973), 182-187. Denmark: Howe (1921), 133-137. France: Wright (1964), 14-25. Germany: Haushofer (1963), 214-215; Pühle (1975), 37-40, 143-146; Tirrell (1951), 173-178, 331-332. Russia: Robinson (1932), 160-207; Walkin (1962), 207-208; Pares (1907), 442-448, 520-521.

market economy, and in many places it had been the seignior's obligation to tide his peasants over bad times. Now, as free individuals they became enmeshed in the cash nexus. They needed money for redemption payments, to carry them over a poor harvest, to improve their farms, and to buy or rent more land. They needed money, too, for less material reasons, such as to pay for a wedding or a funeral, events for which family pride demanded the greatest possible expenditure. One of the most serious shortcomings of the emancipations had been the failure of governments to provide credit facilities which would advance money to the newly freed peasants. They could not qualify for loans from reputable sources; for example, the mortgage department of the Austrian National Bank, established in 1855, was not permitted to make loans of less than 5,000 gulden, and private banks and charitable foundations preferred more credit-worthy borrowers. The usual peasant had no recourse other than to borrow from the village moneylender, or from the local large landowner. These lenders charged usurious rates; interest of 30 to 60 per cent was common, and in Austria-Hungary and Romania charges of 100 per cent and even more were said not to have been unusual. In Galicia and Romania landowners who lent money to peasants usually required repayment in the form of labor, and demanded much more working time from the borrower than the amount of the loan would have purchased on the open labor market.[37]

Many peasants borrowed beyond their capacity to repay and lost their holdings to their creditors. Many others, however, increasingly aware of what they could achieve as free men, organized credit unions and cooperatives. The movement began hesitatingly around the middle of the nineteenth century, swiftly gathered momentum, and by the end of the century had spread across the continent. It had its most spectacular success in Denmark, where cooperatives encompassed every branch of agriculture and where by 1914 the great majority of the rural population belonged to these organizations. Germany had 1,050 agricultural cooperatives in 1883 and 23,751 in 1910, most of them credit unions. European Russia, where the first credit cooperative had been established in 1869, had 10,422 of these associations by 1914, with 6,589,176 member households, or around a third of the country's population. In Romania the first peasant-owned and operated credit union was established in 1891 with 85 members. At the end of 1913 there were 2,901 of these Popular Banks, as they were called, with 583,632 members, or over half of all peasant landowning families. In France the cooperative movement, though popular, enjoyed less success than it did in these other lands.[38]

[37] Kravets (1966), 752; Ionescu-Şişeşti (1912), 123-124; Macartney (1968), 465, 625-626.
[38] Denmark: *Statistisk Aarbog*, 1916, tables 118, 119. France: Golob (1944), 84-98. Germany: Haushofer (1963), 217-219. Romania: Mitrany (1930), 377-384; Eidelberg (1974), 76, 79, 108. Russia: Petersen (1973), 132-133, 412. For Austria see Buchinger (1952), 251-259, 263-264; for Poland see *Polish Encyclopedia* (1922), iii, 312.

The emergence of the peasants as an independent force in their societies worked a dramatic change in the public image of the peasantry. Instead of the scorned and ignored bumpkin of the old order, the peasant became for many almost a folk hero. Political parties wooed him, and ideologues of right and left spun programs to win him to their views. Scholars labored long and arduously to produce thick books and long-winded articles about the peasantry in whom they had hitherto shown not the slightest interest. Politicians and demagogues and professors and philosophers extolled the virtues of the peasantry. French politicos called their country—only a century earlier the center and arbiter of noble style and elegance—a Peasants' Republic, and assured all who would listen that the peasants were the bulwark of the Third Republic. In Germany politicians and professors, disturbed by the changes brought on by the rapid industrialization that began in the 1870's, vigorously defended pre-industrial society and declared that the nation owed its special character to the peasant. "Rightly," wrote Professor Max Sering of the University of Berlin and a leader of the academic community, "we designate the people of the land as the source of eternal renewal of the physical strength of all classes. The fountain of youth of our national strength would be spent with the destruction of the peasantry."[39] In Russia a commission appointed to study the peasant problem in that land in its report declared that the peasantry "more than the representatives of any other part of the population, always stood and still stands on the side of the creative and positive foundations of community and state. . . ."[40]

There is good reason to suspect the motives of these celebrators of the peasantry. As Barrington Moore observed, "Reactionary social theories are liable to flourish in a landed upper class that manages to hang on to political power successfully although it is losing out economically or perhaps is threatened by a new and strange source of political power." There is much talk, he continued, about the need for moral regeneration; the peasant way of life is acclaimed because it is said to be an organic whole and therefore supposedly superior to the atomised world of urban civilization, and the peasant's alleged attachment to the soil becomes the subject of much praise and little action.[41] These strictures need not be limited to the landed upper class. Revolutionaries, too, and less radical but still confirmed antiestablishment types celebrated the peasantry. The populist movement in Russia that attracted so many youthful radical intellectuals in the decades after the emancipation championed the values of the peasant way of life, and saw the peasant commune not as a survival of the past that impeded agricultural progress, but as the vehicle that would allow Russia to escape the supposed evils of capitalism and enter directly into the promised land of socialism. The Socialist Revolutionaries, heirs of the populist doctrines, in

---

[39] Wright (1964), 13-14; Barkin (1970), 167-169.
[40] *Trudy redaktsionnoi kommisii* (1903), i, 12.   [41] Moore (1966), 490-492.

the party platform they adopted in 1905 called for the socialization of the land but with the retention of the world view, the traditions, and the way of life of the peasantry.[42] In Denmark admiration of, and faith in, the virtues of the peasantry and their way of life found perhaps its clearest expression in the Folk High School movement. The movement was founded by N.F.S. Grundtvig (1783-1872), clergyman, politician, and poet, and his chief disciple, Christian Kold. The first schools opened in the 1840's. By 1914 there were 80 of them with around 10,000 students, nearly all of them young peasant adults. The schools were privately owned, often by peasant organizations. The course of study ran for less than a year, so that there was an annual turnover of the student body. It was feared that longer residence would make the youths dissatisfied with the virtues and rewards of peasant life. From these schools came leaders of the Danish peasantry in politics and in the organization and administration of the cooperatives that distinguished Danish agriculture.[43]

V

The same decades that saw the growth of peasant self-consciousness, self-help, and political involvement also witnessed significant changes in the economic condition of the peasantry. Many of these changes arose out of an old problem that had long bedeviled the peasantry and that now took on new and far more serious proportions. That old problem was pressure on the land that resulted from population growth. The numbers of smallholders and of landless peasants had swelled during the last century of the old order, and the unprecedented increase in population during the nineteenth century aggravated the already grave situation. In response to the pressure, the supply of plowland was increased by reclamation and by cultivation of land that had hitherto lain empty, or had been used for pasture or meadow, or had been planted at infrequent intervals in the system of shifting cultivation with long fallows. In Prussia the amount of cropland more than doubled between 1805 and 1864. In Romania arable is said to have increased by 120 per cent between 1860 and 1905, from 2.5 to 5.5 million hectares.[44] Peasants also added to the stock of land available to them by purchases from noble and bourgeois proprietors. In 1877 Russia's peasants, either as individuals or in communes, owned 118.2 million desiatins. By 1905 they owned 148.7 million desiatins. Their holdings in 1905 amounted to 63 per cent of all the privately owned land in European Russia. Purchase of land from nobles, much of it financed by the Peasants' Land Bank, established by the government in 1882, accounted for nearly all of the increase in

[42] Scheibert (1972), 37.
[43] Fogt (1914), 16-35; Friend (1914), 12; Ravnholt (1947), 12-14.
[44] Finck von Finckenstein (1934), 13; Haufe (1939), 114.

peasant-owned land.[45] In Congress Poland peasants acquired 1,112,000 hectares from large proprietors between 1894 and 1909. They purchased much of this land through the Peasants' Land Bank, which extended its operations to Poland in 1894. They also acquired land from noble landowners as compensation for the servitudes they had agreed to relinquish. In France peasants had increased their landholdings during the Revolution by purchase of *biens nationaux* and they continued to buy land during the succeeding decades. At the end of the eighteenth century they had owned an estimated one-third of France's farm land; a hundred years later they owned nearly half.[46]

Peasants rented land, too. Sharecropping persisted in France, though it was much less extensive than it had been in the old regime, and in Romania. In Romania, too, landlords often demanded their rent in labor. Nearly everywhere else peasants paid their rents in cash. The proportion of renters and the area they rented differed widely among the former servile lands. Thus, in Denmark by 1905 only 10 per cent of all holdings were leaseholds. In France 23 per cent of all farms in 1892 were leaseholds and another 7 per cent were worked by sharecroppers. In 1907 in Germany 17.2 per cent of the 5.7 million farming enterprises there were leaseholds, and in another 9.7 per cent over half of the land was rented.[47]

Large as the additions were to the stock of land held by the peasants, they were outpaced by the increase in rural population that grew everywhere except in France. The continuing imbalance between available land and population brought on unceasing splintering of peasant holdings and a huge increase in the number of smallholders.[48] By the turn of the century, as the following table shows, from 5.3 (in Denmark) to 7.7 (in Romania) out of every 10 peasants had less than 5 hectares (12.4 acres). Altogether their holdings occupied only a small part of the farm area, in contrast to the large share owned by the small number of large proprietors.

The "less than 5 hectares" rubric conceals the fact that a large proportion

---

[45] Tsentral'nyi Statisticheskii Komitet, *Statistika zemlevladenie 1905g.* (1907), table II, 12, 16-17; table III, 78-79; table v, 130-131. In 1905 land owned by private individuals (nobles, burghers, peasants), plus land owned collectively by peasant communes, accounted for 60.9 per cent of all the land in European Russia. The remainder belonged to the state, church, and other institutions.

[46] Ballerstedt (1939), 28; *Polish Encyclopedia* (1922), III, 405-406; Labrousse (1966), 45-51.

[47] *Statistisk Aarbog*, 1916, table 39; International Institute of Agriculture (1939), 18; *Die deutsche Landwirtschaft* (1913), 34-38.

[48] In Denmark the number of holdings rose by 60.5 per cent between 1850 and 1905, from 180,090 to 289,130. Faber (1918), table 3, 161. In Congress Poland the number of holdings increased by almost 45 per cent between 1870 and 1904, from 697,998 to 1,011,240. Ballerstedt (1939), 25. In the nine provinces that made up the kingdom of Prussia before the territorial additions of the 1860's, the number of holdings went up by 180 per cent between 1861 and 1907, from 938.4 thousand to 2,628 million. Finck von Finckenstein (1934), 10. These figures are for all holdings and so include large non-peasant holdings. However, these holdings made up a very small proportion of the total number of holdings.

Distribution of Holdings[49]

		Less than 5 ha.		5 to 100 ha.		100 ha. and Over	
		% of Land- holders	% of Area	% of Land- holders	% of Area	% of Land- holders	% of Area
Austria	(1902)	71.8	—	27.5	—	0.7	49.5
Denmark	(1901)[a]	53.4	4.9	43.0	62.0	3.5	33.1
France	(1892)[b]	85.1	27.0	12.5	30.0	2.4	43.0
Germany	(1907)	74.2	15.3	25.4	61.5	0.4	23.2
Hungary	(1895)	72.6	16.1	26.9	42.1	0.5	41.8
Poland	(1905)	48.0	13.2	51.0	42.6	0.9	44.2
Romania	(1905)	77.2	25.7	22.1	25.6	0.6	48.7

[a] Rubrics for Denmark: less than 5 ha., 5 to 60 ha., over 60 ha.
[b] Rubrics for France: less than 10 ha., 10 to 100 ha., over 100 ha.

of the holdings in this category were of miniscule size. In Denmark 27.4 per cent, in Germany 32.7 per cent, and in Hungary 22 per cent of all holdings were less than one-half hectare; in France 39.2 per cent and in Romania 15.1 per cent were less than one hectare; in Austria 43.6 per cent were less than 2 hectares. Many of these dwarf holdings were market gardens, or small vineyards, or belonged to people whose main occupation was in a non-farming activity. Others belonged to peasants who had to hire themselves out as farm laborers, or had to rent additional scraps of land to make ends meet. Improved farming methods and resulting increased yields per unit of land enabled peasants in central and western Europe to support themselves from smaller holdings. More significantly, the growth of cities and of industry in Germany, France, Denmark, and Austria, and emigration to the New World, drained off much of the surplus rural population. In eastern Europe industrialization and urbanization lagged and unimproved agriculture was nearly universal. The result was chronic and unceasing pressure for land, and poverty for most of the peasantry. Their poverty prevented the peasants, who made up the greatest part of the population, from becoming a market for manufactured goods. This seriously retarded industrial growth, and therefore the opportunities for the employment of the surplus rural population in industry.

Yet, despite the splintering of holdings and the persistence of inefficient farming methods, the standard of living of much of the peasantry improved in the years after the emancipations. Though typically their incomes were less than those of the other sectors of the population, they shared in the economic growth of the era. They had a greater variety in their diets, they

[49] Austria: *Oesterreichische Statistik*, LXXXIII, 1909, table x, p. xx, table xx, p. xxvii. Denmark: *Statistisk Aarbog*, 1916, table 38. France: International Institute of Agriculture (1939), 15. Germany: *Die deutsche Landwirtschaft* (1913), 37. Hungary: *Annuaire Statistique Hongrois*, XXII (1904), 69. Poland: Woytinsky (1926), III, 58. Romania: Creangă (1907), I, 93.

ate more meat, white bread became more common, they dressed better, and their houses were larger and sturdier. Even in Russia, where real income per capita was about half that in Germany (and about one-third that in the United States),[50] peasants lived better after 1861. They built better houses for themselves, they acquired the habit of drinking tea, they bought samovars to brew the tea, they increased their consumption of sugar, took up smoking, and lighted their houses with kerosene. Despite heavy taxes levied on these commodities, the peasant demand for them continued to rise.[51]

There were many glaring exceptions to the general improvement in rural living standards. In Romania excessive exploitation of the peasantry continued unabated, and, indeed, probably increased after the emancipation there. Karl Grünberg in 1882 wrote that "the misery in which most of the Romanian peasantry live beggars all description." Later data make it clear that there was no amelioration until after a peasant rising in 1907, and then the improvements were minimal.[52] In the Austrian province of Galicia, where backward agriculture, lack of capital, absence of industrialization, and rapid population growth characterized the economy, the bulk of the peasantry suffered great poverty and deprivation.[53] Above all, farm laborers everywhere shared little, if at all, in improvements in living standards. In some lands these people made up a sizable portion of the rural population. In 1902 in Austria 13 per cent (1,187,310) and in Germany 16 per cent (1,579,000) of all persons engaged in agriculture were hired laborers. Some of these people owned a scrap of land, but the greatest number were landless. Thus, in Austria 70 per cent, and in Germany 84.4 per cent, of all farm laborers were live-in farm hands or farm servants.[54] The growth of cities and the improvements in transportation expanded the market for farm goods and thereby heightened the demand for farm labor; so did the labor-intensive improved farming techniques used increasingly, especially on large farms. Simultaneously, the growth of industry and of communications, particularly railroad construction, drew always increasing numbers of workers away from the land by the lure of higher wages. These developments combined to produce a serious farm labor shortage in the economically more advanced lands. In France the number of farm laborers fell from nearly 3 million in 1848 to 2.5 million in 1892. In Bohemia, the most industrialized province of the Austro-Hungarian empire, the farm labor force dropped from 1,189,770 in 1869 to 299,446 in 1902. Germany's rapid industrialization after 1871 attracted thousands from the villages to work in

[50] Goldsmith (1961), 475.

[51] Juillard (1953), 241-242; Sée (1942), 331-334; Kodedová (1967), 131; Kieniewicz (1969), 225; Yaney (1973), 38-39; *Village of Viriatino* (1970), 62-73; Samoilovich (1977), 11-14.

[52] Grünberg (1889), 77-78; Mitrany (1930), 67-90.

[53] Kieniewicz (1969), 210-214; Zubrzycki (1953), 253.

[54] *Oesterreichische Statistik*, LXXXIII (1909), XXXIX; *Die deutsche Landwirtschaft* (1913), 67, 68.

the booming factories. To meet their need, farm employers had to turn to migratory labor. In the quarter-century before 1914 there were huge seasonal movements of foreign workers, many of them women, into Germany, with most of them coming from Poland and Galicia. In 1911-1912 there were 397,364 of these migrants working on German farms. France imported seasonal laborers from Italy, Spain, Belgium, and from as far away as Poland.[55]

To hold workers, farm employers had to raise wages. Between 1850 and 1913 the money wage of German agricultural labor rose by 127 per cent, and that part of their wages paid in kind went up, too. In France farm wages went up by nearly 30 per cent between 1852 and 1862 and 10 to 15 per cent more during the next 20 years, while farm prices declined sharply. In Russia daily wages for farm labor in 1913 was 23 to 64 per cent higher than the 1901-1905 average; meanwhile the local market price for rye, the staple of peasant diet, had gone up by only 10 to 16 per cent. Hungary was an exception to this general trend. Wages there turned downward with the fall in grain prices that began in the 1870's and that continued until the 1890's. Wages rose after 1900 but generally only enough to reach the level of real wages of the early 1870's.[56] Even with the increases, all farm wages lagged behind those paid in industry. In large part this was because women made up a much larger part of the farm labor force than of the industrial labor force. Women received lower wages in both agriculture and industry, and their greater presence among farm labor pulled down the average for the entire farm labor force. And, despite better wages, all too many day laborers continued to live in direct poverty. Most of them found work for only part of the year and struggled to stay alive during the long months of unemployment. Their only alternative was to join the exodus from the land, along with the workers in cottage industry who could not compete with factory industry, and with the peasants whose holdings were too small to support their families. By the end of the nineteenth century the exodus had taken on flood proportions. Millions moved to the growing cities and industrialized regions of their own and neighboring lands, or migrated to overseas lands, or, in Russia, moved to Siberia, where they settled on land alloted to them by the state. The migrants came from all strata of rural society, and in much lesser numbers from other sectors of the population. By far the greatest number were those peasants who had dwarf holdings or had no land at all, and who had earned part or all of their livings as hired farm laborers.[57]

[55] Zeldin (1973), 170; Augé-Laribé (1925), 31; Kodedová (1967), 144; *Die deutsche Landwirtschaft* (1913), 82; Haushofer (1963), 180-183; Ballerstedt (1939), 54-55.

[56] Grantham (1975), 320; Toutain (1961), II, 188; Mitchell (1975), 191-192; Eddie (1967), 306-307; Volin (1970), 111.

[57] Teifen (1906), 44; Macartney (1968), 629, 716-717; Macartney (1962), 195; Kosa (1957), 503; Lévy (1951), II, 137-139; Lütge (1967), 284; Zubrzycki (1953), 251-257; Bilimovich (1930), 310; Woytinsky (1925), I, 128; Treadgold (1957), 89-93.

VI

The phenomenon of the rural exodus better perhaps than any other indicator revealed the difference between the old order and the new kind of society that was replacing it. It told of the freedom that the villager now had to come and go at his own will and to pursue his own self-interest. The exodus told, too, of the new opportunities opened up by the burgeoning of industry and of transportation. In the old order the peasant who fled from his village all too often had no alternative but to join the bands of beggars and vagabonds who haunted the streets and highways of town and country. Now he could journey by railroad and steamer to seek a new start in life, whether in the cities and mines and factories of the Old World or the New, or as a farmer in the broad and open plains of America or Siberia.

Individual freedom of these dimensions had not been possible in the old order. The old regime had been a corporate society, made up of estates each of which performed certain assigned social functions. The order had been paramount, so that the individual's rights depended upon the order to which he belonged. The structure of the society had been held together by bonds of loyalty and fealty among the orders. The hierarchical arrangement of the orders had reflected the prestige and the honor accorded by the society to the social function performed by each order. The inequalities and injustices implicit in this hierarchical arrangement, with its descending scale of status and privilege, had been accepted by the tacit consent of all of the people in the society.

Now all that was changed because of the acts of emancipation. These acts made everyone in the society equally citizens of the state. They were held together in an organized community by a common subordination of all citizens to the central authority. There was one law for all citizens, and (at least nominally) everyone was equal before the law. The hierarchy of privilege and preferred treatment, sanctioned by law and tradition in the old order, no longer prevailed. The personal relationships, the bonds of loyalty and fealty, and the servile dependence of the traditional society were replaced by impersonal relationships imposed by the rule of law.

Equality before the law carried with it the guarantee of equal civil, personal, and property rights to all citizens of the state. Absolute equality in these rights did not become a universal in the servile lands after the emancipations. Peasants often were still subjected to restraints and handicaps not imposed upon other citizens, and nobles still enjoyed status and privilege not accorded to others in the society. However, these lingering relics of times past were destined to disappear as the years went by. Of far greater significance, the grant of equality, even if incomplete, to everyone as a citizen of the state condemned the traditional society to oblivion. Now the individual had become paramount. Society was seen as an aggregate of individuals, rather than of orders. In this atomized society each individual pursued his own interests and made his own decisions, albeit within a framework determined by legal codes, constitutions, and agreed-upon usages. There were still strata in society but they were classes determined by common interests and economic roles, and not orders determined by birth. In the society of orders the distinctions had been between nobles and burghers and peasants. In the class society the distinctions were between rich and poor.

The liberties that were now extended to the individual provided him with important economic freedoms. He could enter any trade or profession, he could buy and sell as he pleased, he could make contracts freely, he could do as he wished with his property, he could move about freely in the pursuit of his own economic interests. These freedoms greatly facilitated the acceleration in the pace and scale of economic growth in the one-time servile lands in the years after their emancipation. Technological advances, new sources of energy, the growth of population, improvements in transportation and communication, and concentrations of capital were, of course, of critical importance in bringing about the material progress. But the institutional changes were at least of equal importance, for the economic advances would not have been possible without the changed institutional framework.

The war that came in 1914 and that engulfed Europe for four terrible years swept away monarchies and their trappings, and with them the last meaningful vestiges of the old order. Deprived of their old authority figures, the peoples of Europe have tried ever since to establish new and lasting forms of governance and of social organization. The story of their successes and failures is still unfolding, and will continue to unfold as long as men seek to increase individual freedom or to repress it. The beginning of that story—what has been termed "the opening act of a great and still unfinished social revolution"—was the freeing of the peasantry from the bonds of their servility.

List of Works Cited

Abel, W. (1966), *Agrarkrisin und Agrarkonjunktur*. Hamburg and Berlin.

Abel, W. (1967a), *Agrarpolitik*. 3rd ed. Göttingen.

Abel, W. (1964), *Die drei Epochen der deutschen Agrargeschichte*. 2nd ed. Hannover.

Abel, W. (1967), *Geschichte der deutschen Landwirtschaft vom frühen Mittelalter bis zum 19. Jahrhundert*. 2nd ed. Stuttgart.

Abel, W. (1955), "Schichten und Zonen europäischer Agrarverfassung," *Zeitschrift für Agrargeschichte und Agrarsoziologie*, III.

Abel, W. (1938), "Wandlungen des Fleischverbrauchs und der Fleischversorgung in Deutschland seit dem ausgehenden Mittelalter," *Berichte über Landwirtschaft*, N. F., XXII.

Achilles, W. (1965), *Vermögensverhältnisse braunschweigerischer Bauernhöfe im 17. und 18. Jahrhundert*. Stuttgart.

Adams, J. Q. (1804), *Letters on Silesia, written during a Tour through that County in the Years 1800, 1801*. London.

Adaniloaie, N. and D. Berindei (1966), *La réforme agraire de 1864 en Roumanie et son application*. Bucharest.

Ado, A. (1971), *Krest'ianskoe dvizhenie vo Frantsii vo vremia velikoi burzhuaznoi revoliutsii kontsa XVIII veka*. Moscow.

Ahrens, G. (1969), *Caspar Voght und sein Mustergut Flottbek. Englische Landwirtschaft in Deutschland am Ende des 18. Jahrhunderts*. Hamburg.

Akademiia Nauk Estonskoi SSSR, Institut Istorii (1958), *Istoriia Estonskoi SSR*. 2nd ed. Tallin.

Akademiia Nauk SSSR (1935, 1950), *Materialy po istorii krest'ianskoi promyshlennosti XVIII i pervoi poloviny XIX v.* I. V. Meshalin, ed. 2 vols. [Trudy Istoriko-Arkheograficheskogo Instituta, XV.]

Akademiia Nauk SSSR (1959), Institut Istorii, *Istoriia SSSR*. 2 vols. Moscow.

Albert, R. (1969), "Wie das Leben der Leibeigenen auf dem adeligen Gut Roest wirklich verlaufen ist," *Jahrbuch des Angler Heimatvereins*, XXXIII.

Allgemeine Landrecht für die Preussischen Staaten von 1794 (1970). Berlin.

Allgemeines Landrecht für die Preussischen Staaten (1837). A. J. Mannkopff, ed. Berlin.

Allgemeines Reiches- Gesetz- und Regierungsblatt für das Kaiserthum Oesterreich. Jahrgang 1849. Vienna.

Anderson, E. N. and P. R. (1967), *Political Institutions and Social Change* in Continental Europe in the Nineteenth Century. Berkeley and Los Angeles.

Anderson, M. S. (1961), *Europe in the Eighteenth Century, 1713-1783*. New York.

André, R. (1846), *Darstellung der vorzüglichsten landwirthschaftlichen Verhältnisse*. 5th ed., Prague.

Andrews, J. (1774), *The History of the Revolutions of Denmark*. 2 vols. London.

Andrews, R. H. (1935), *Les paysans des Mauges au XVIII siècle: la vie rurale dans une région de l'Anjou*. Tours.

Andrian-Werburg, V. von (1843-1847), *Oesterreich und dessen Zukunft*. 2 vols. in 1. 2nd ed. Hamburg.

Anfimov, A. M. (1969), *Krupnoe pomeshchich'e khoziaistvo evropeiskoi Rossii*. Moscow.

Annuaire statistique de la France.

Annuaire statistique hongrois.

Archives Parlementaires de 1787 à 1860, 1st ser. 1789-1799.

Argenson, R. L., Marquis d' (1859-1867), *Journal et mémoires*. 9 vols. Paris.

Arneth, A. von (1863-1879), *Geschichte Maria Theresia's*. 10 vols. Vienna.

Arion, C. C. (1895), *La situation économique et sociale du paysan en Roumanie*. Paris.

Armstrong, J. A. (1973), *The European Administrative Elite*. Princeton.

Arnim, V. von (1957), "Krisen und Konjunkturen der Landwirtschaft in Schleswig-Holstein vom 16. bis zum 18. Jahrhundert," *Quellen und Forshungen zur Geschichte Schleswig-Holsteins*, xxxv.

Ashley, W. J. (1928), *The Bread of our Forefathers*. Oxford.

Ashley, W. J. (1913), "Comparative Economic History and the English Landlord," *Economic Journal*, xxiii.

Ashley, W. J. (1924), "Memorandum IV. Denmark. Agricultural Tribunal of Investigation. Final Report," Great Britain. House of Commons. *Sessional Papers*, 1924, vii, 241-277.

Aubin, G. (1910), *Zur Geschichte des gutsherrlich bäuerlichen Verhältnisses in Ostpreussen*. Leipzig.

Augé-Laribé, M. (1925), *L'agriculture pendant la guerre*. Paris.

Augé-Laribé, M. (1955), *La révolution agricole*. Paris.

Aulard, A. (1919), *La révolution française et le régime féodal*. Paris.

Auroux Des Pommiers, M. (1762), *L'art de s'enrichir promptement par l'agriculture, prouvé par des expériences*. Paris.

Avenel, G. d' (1927), *Histoire de la fortune française*. Paris.

Avrich, P. (1972), *Russian Rebels, 1600-1800*. New York.

Babeau, A. (1883), *La vie rurale dans l'ancienne France*. Paris.

Babeau, A. (1878), *Le village sous l'Ancien Régime*. Paris.

Bailey, L. H. ed. (1922), *Cyclopedia of Farm Crops*. New York.

Balazs, E. H. (1956), "Die Lage der Bauernschaft und die Bauernbewegung (1780-1787)," *Acta Historica Academiae Scientiarum Hungaricae*, III.

Ballerstedt, K. (1939), *Erbrecht, Erbsitten und Grundbesitzzersplitterung in Polen*. Stuttgart, Berlin.

Baraboi, A. Z. (1964), "Posevy i urozhai khlebov, kartofelia, sakharnoi svekly v pomeshchich'em i krest'ianskom khoziaistvakh Pravoberezhnoi Ukrainy v pervoi polovine XIX v.," *Ezhegodnik po agrarnoi istorii vostochnoi Evropy, 1962g*. Minsk.

Barany, G. (1968), *Stephen Széchenyi and the Awakening of Hungarian Nationalism, 1791-1841*. Princeton.

Barkin, K. D. (1970), *The Controversy over German Industrialization 1890-1902*. Chicago.

Barth-Barthenheim, J.B.L.E. (1818-1820), *Das politische Verhältniss der verschiedenen Gattungen von Obrigkeiten zum Bauernstande im Erzherzogthume Oesterreich unter der Ens*. 2 vols. in 3. Vienna.

Barton, H. A. (1974), "Late Gustavian Autocracy in Sweden: Gustav IV Adolf and his Opponents, 1792-1809," *Scandinavian Studies*, XLVI.

Bauer, M. von (1907), *Die Landwirtschaft in Mähren vor Aufhebung der Untertänigkeit* (Erlangen, 1907).

Beauchet, L. (1904), *Histoire de la propriété foncière en Suède*. Paris.

Begtrup, H. *et al.* (1949), *The Folk High Schools of Denmark and the Development of a Farming Community*. 4th ed. London.

Behrend, H. (1964), "Die Aufhebung der Feldgemeinschaften," *Quellen und Forschungen zur Geschichte Schleswig-Holsteins*, XLVI.

Behrens, B. (1967), *The Ancien Régime*. New York.

Behrens, C.B.A. (1963), "Nobles, Privileges and Taxes in France at the End of the *Ancien Régime*," *Economic History Review*, 2nd ser., XV.

Beidtel, I. (1896-1898), *Geschichte der österreichischen Staatsverwaltung, 1740-1848*, 2 vols. Innsbruck.

Benda, C. (1948), "La question paysanne et la révolution hongroise en 1848," *Etudes d'histoire moderne et contemporaine*, II.

Berchtold, F. von (1842), *Die Kartoffeln*. Prague.

Berend, T. I. and G. Ránki (1974), *Economic Development in East-Central Europe in the 19th and 20th Centuries*. New York.

Bergmann, D. R. (1952), "Regrouping of Farm Holdings in France," *International Journal of Agrarian Affairs*, I.

Bernardt, J. (1848), *Handbuch der provinziellen Gesetzkunde von Mähren und Schlesien*. Olmütz.

Bernhard, H. (1915), "Veränderungen in der Bodenkultur des Kantons Zürich," *Jahresbericht der geograph.-ethnographischen Gesellschaft in Zürich*, XIV-XV.

Berthold, R. (1962), "Einige Bemerkungen über den Entwicklungsstand des bäuerlichen Ackerbaus vor den Agrarreformen des 19. Jahrhunderts," Deutsche Akademie der Wissenschaften. Institut für Geschichte. *Beiträge zur deutschen Wirtschafts- und Sozialgeschichte des 18. und 19. Jahrhunderts*. Berlin.

Beudant, F. S. (1823), *Travels in Hungary in 1818*. Transl from French. London.

Beyer, H. (1957), "Zur Entwicklung des Bauernstandes in Schleswig-Holstein zwischen 1768 und 1848," *Zeitschrift für Agrargeschichte und Agrarsoziologie*, v.

Bibikov, G. I. (1938), "Rassloenie krepostnogo krest'ianstva v barshchinnoi votchine v kontse XVIII i nachale XIX v.," *Istoricheskie zapiski*, no. 4.

Bibl, V. (1911), *Die niederösterreichischen Stände im Vormärz*. Vienna.

Bickel, W. (1947), *Bevölkerungsgeschichte und Bevölkerungspolitik der Schweiz seit dem Ausgang des Mittelalters*. Zürich.

Bilimovich, A. D. (1930), "The Land Settlement in Russia and the War," A.N. Antsiferov *et al.*, *Russian Agriculture during the War*. New Haven.

Billington, J. H. (1966), *The Icon and the Axe*. New York.

Bittermann, E. (1956), "Die landwirtschaftliche Produktion in Deutschland 1800-1950," *Kühn-Archiv*, LXX, no. 1.

Blackwell, W. L. (1968), *The Beginnings of Russian Industrialization 1800-1860*. Princeton.

Blaschke, K. (1955), "Das Bauernlegen in Sachsen," *Vierteljahrschrift für Sozial- und Wirtschaftsgeschichte*, LXII.

Blaschke, K. (1965), "Grundzüge und Probleme einer sächsischen Agrarverfassungsgeschichte," *Zeitschrift der Savigny-Stiftung für Rechtsgeschichte*, Germanistische Abteilung, LXXXII.

Blaschke, K. (1956), "Soziale Gliederung und Entwicklung der sächsischen Landbevölkerung im 16. bis 18. Jahrhundert," *Zeitschrift für Agrargeschichte und Agrarsoziologie*, IV.

Blaschke, K. (1967), "Vom Dorf zur Landgemeinde," H. Haushofer and W. Boelcke, ed., *Wege und Forschungen der Agrargeschichte*. Frankfurt a. M.

Blaschke, K. (1962), "Zur Bevölkerungsgeschichte Sachsens vor der industriellen Revolution," Deutsche Akademie der Wissenschaften. Institut für Geschichte. *Beiträge zur deutschen Wirtschafts- und Sozialgeschichte des 18. und 19. Jahrhunderts*. Berlin.

Bloch, M. (1966), *French Rural History*. Transl. from French. Berkeley and Los Angeles.

Bloch, M. (1930), "La lutte pour l'individualisme agraire dans la France du xviiie siècle," *Annales d'histoire économique et sociale*, II.

Bloch, M. (1966a), "The Rise of Dependent Cultivation and Seigniorial Institutions," *Cambridge Economic History of Europe*, 2nd ed., I.

Bloch, M. (1960), *Seigneurie française et manoir anglais*. Paris.

Bluche, F. (1973), *La vie quotidienne de la noblesse française au xviiie siècle*. Paris.

Blum, J. (1971a), "The European Village as Community: Origins and Functions," *Agricultural History*, XLV.

Blum, J. (1971b), "The Internal Structure and Polity of the European Village Community from the Fifteenth to the Nineteenth Century," *Journal of Modern History*, XLIII.

Blum, J. (1961), *Lord and Peasant in Russia from the Ninth to the Nineteenth Century*. Princeton.

Blum, J. (1948), *Noble Landowners and Agriculture in Austria, 1815-1848*. Baltimore.

Blum, J. (1943), "Transportation and Industry in Austria, 1815-1848," *Journal of Modern History*, XV.

Bobińska, S. (1970), "Les mouvements paysans en Pologne aux xviiie et xixe. siècles: Problèmes et méthodes," *Acta Poloniae Historica*, XXII.

Boelcke, W. (1957), *Bauer und Gutsherr in der Oberlausitz*. Bautzen.

Bois, P. (1960), *Paysans de l'Ouest*. Paris.

Bollinger, A. (1941), *Die Zürcher Landschaft an der Wende des 18. Jahrhunderts*. Zurich.

Boncerf, P. F. (1789), *Les inconvéniens des droits feodaux*. Paris.

Borcke-Stargordt, H. von (1958), "Aus der Vorgeschichte zu den preussischen Agrarreformen. Christian Jakob Kraus zum Gedächtnis," *Jahrbuch der Albertus-Universität zu Königsberg/Pr.*, VIII.

Borcke-Stargordt, H. von (1960), "Grundherrschaft-Gutswirtschaft. Ein Beitrag zur Agrargeschichte," *Jahrbuch der Albertus-Universität zu Königsberg/Pr.*, X.

Borcke-Stargordt, H. von (1954), "Zur preussischen Agrargesetzgebung der Reformzeit," *Mensch und Staat in Recht und Geschichte. Festschrift für Herbert Kraus*. Kitzengen.

Borders, K. (1927), *Village Life under the Soviets*. New York.

Borovoi, S. (1948), "K voprosu o skladyvanii kapitalisticheskogo uklada v Rossii XVIII v.," *Voprosy istorii*, no. 5, 1948.

Borovoi, S. Ia. and A. S. Kopievskii (1966), "Osnovnye momenty v razvitii sel'skokhoziaistvennogo proizvodstva i form ekspluatatsii krest'ian Stepnoi Ukrainy v doreformennyi period," *Ezhegodnik po agrarnoi istorii vostochnoi Evropy 1964g*. Kishenev.

Boserup, E. (1965), *The Conditions of Agricultural Growth*. Chicago.

Bosher, J. F. (1970), *French Finances 1770-1795*. Cambridge.

Boswell, A. B. (1953), "Poland", in A. Goodwin, ed., *The European Nobility in the Eighteenth Century*. London.

Bouchard, G. (1972), *Le village immobile; Sennely-en-Sologne au xviiie siècle*. Paris.

Bourde, A. J. (1967), *Agronomie et agronomes en France au xviiie siècle*. 3 vols. Paris.

Bourde, A. J. (1953), *The Influence of England on the French Agronomes 1750-1789*. Cambridge.

Bramsted, E. K. (1964), *Aristocracy and the Middle Classes in Germany*. Revised ed. Chicago.

Bratanić, B. (1952), "On the Antiquity of the One-Sided Plough in Europe, especially among the Slavic Peoples," *Laos*, II.

Bratianu, G. (1933), "Servage de la glebe et regime fiscal. Essai d'histoire comparée roumaine slave et byzantine," *Annales d'histoire économique et sociale*, V.

Braudel, F. (1967), *Civilisation matérielle et capitalisme (xve-xviiie siècle)*, I. Paris.

Braudel, F. and E. Labrousse, ed., (1970), *Histoire économique et sociale de la France*, II. Paris.

Braun, R. (1960), *Industrialisierung und Volksleben: die Veränderung der Lebensformen in einem ländlichen Industriegebiet vor 1800*. Zurich and Stuttgart.

Bremner, R. (1839), *Excursions in the Interior of Russia*. 2 vols. 2nd ed. London.

Brentano, L. (1899), *Gesammelte Aufsätze*. Stuttgart.

Brocard, L. (1970), *Les doctrines économiques et sociales du marquis de Mirabeau dans l'Ami des Hommes*. New York.

Brockhaus, F. A. and I. A. Efron, eds., *Entsiklopedicheskii slovar*. 41 vols. in 82. St. Petersburg, 1890-1914.

Bruchet, M. (1908), *L'abolition des droits seigneuriaux en Savoie (1761-1793)*. Annecy.

Bruford, W. H. (1935), *Germany in the Eighteenth Century*. Cambridge.

Brüggen, E. von der (1904), *Russia of Today*. London.

Brüngger, H. (1962), "Allmend und Bürgerrecht," *Heimatbuch der Gemeinde Pfäffikon*. Pfäffikon.

Brünneck, W. von (1890), "Die Aufhebung der Leibeigenschaft," *Zeitschrift der Savigny-Stiftung für Rechtsgeschichte*. Germanistische Abteilung, XI.

Brünneck, W. von (1887), "Die Leibeigenschaft in Ostpreussen," *Zeitschrift der Savigny-Stiftung für Rechtsgeschichte*. Germanistische Abteilung, VIII.

Brunner, O. (1949), *Adeliges Landleben und Europäischer Geist*. Salzburg.

Brusatti, A. (1965), *Österreichische Wirtschaftspolitik von Josephinismus zum Ständestaat*. Vienna.

Brusatti, A. (1958), "Die Stellung der herrschaftlichen Beamten in Oesterreich in der Zeit von 1780-1848," *Vierteljahrschrift für Sozial- und Wirtschaftsgeschichte*, XLV.

Buchinger, J. (1952), *Der Bauer in der Kultur- und Wirtschaftsgeschichte Österreichs*. Vienna.

Bull, E. (1930), *Vergleichende Studien über die Kulturverhältnisse des Bauerntums*. Oslo.

Burton, W. G. (1966), *The Potato: a Survey of its History and of Factors Influencing its Yield, Nutritive Value and Storage*. 2nd ed. Wageningen.

Buschen, A. von (1862), *Bevölkerung des russischen Kaiserreichs in der wichtigsten statistischen Verhältnissen dargestellt*. Gotha.

Calonne, A. de (1920), *La vie agricole sous l'ancien régime dans le nord de France*, Mémoires de la Societé des Antiquaires de Picardie, 4e series, IX.

Cambridge History of Poland (1941). II.

Campbell, J. C. (1948), "Eighteen Forty-Eight in the Rumanian Principalities," *Journal of Central European Affairs*, VIII.

Campbell, J. C. (1944), "The Influence of Western Political Thought in the Rumanian Principalities, 1821-1848: the Generation of 1848," *Journal of Central European Affairs*, IV.

Carman, E. A. et al. (1892), *Special Report on the History and Present Condition of the Sheep Industry of the United States*. Washington.

Caron, P. ed. (1924), "La suppression des droits féodaux. Instruction, receuil de textes et notes," *Bulletin d'histoire économique de la Revolution, 1920-1921*. Paris.

Carré, H. (1912), *La fin des parlements (1788-1790)*. Paris.

Carré, H. (1920), *La noblesse de France et l'opinion publique au xviiie siècle*. Paris.

Carsten, F. L. (1959), *Princes and Parliaments in Germany from the Fifteenth to the Eighteenth Century*. Oxford.

Cavaignac, G. (1894), "La féodalité en Prusse à la fin du xixe siècle," *Revue de Paris*, 1894, no. 3.

Cecil, L. (1970), "The Creation of Nobles in Prussia, 1871-1918," *American Historical Review*, LXXV.

Chambers, J. D. and G. E. Mingay (1966), *The Agricultural Revolution 1750-1880*. London.

Chatelain, A. (1956), "Dans les campagnes françaises aux xixe siècle: la progression de la faux," *Annales. E. S. C.*, XI.

Chatfield, C. (1949), *Food Composition Tables*. FAO Nutritional Studies, no. 3. Washington.

Chepko, V. V. (1959), "Polozhenie krest'ian i klassovaia bor'ba v Belorusskoi derevne v pervoi polovine XIX veka," *Ezhegodnik po agrarnoi istorii vostochnoi Evropy 1958g*. Tallin.

Chepko, V. V. (1964), "Rost tovarnosti pomeshchich'ego khoziaistva Belorussii v pervoi polovine XIX v.," *Ezhegodnik po istorii agrarnoi istorii vostochny Evropy 1962g*. Minsk.

Chérin, L.N.H. (1788), *La noblesse considérée sous ses divers rapports*. Paris.

Chevallaz, G. A. (1949), *Aspects de l'agriculture vaudoise à la fin d'ancien régime*. Lausanne.

Chombart de Lauwe, J. (1946), *Bretagne et pays de la Garonne, évolution agricole comparée depuis un siècle*. Paris.

Christensen, A. E. (1960), "The Development of Large-Scale Farming in Denmark, 1525-1744," *Scandinavian Economic History Review*, VIII.

Churbaierische Regierungsblatt 1803.

Churchill, W. (1938), *While England Slept*. New York.

Clapham, J. H. (1955), *The Economic Development of France and Germany, 1815-1914*. Cambridge.

Clark, C. and M. Haswell, (1970), *The Economics of Subsistence Agriculture*. 4th ed. New York.

Cobban, A. (1950), "The *Parlements* of France in the Eighteenth Century," *History*, XXXV.

Cobban, A. (1971), *The Social Interpretation of the French Revolution*. Cambridge.

Collins, E.J.T. (1969), "Labour Supply and Demand in European Agriculture 1800-1880," E. L. Jones and S. J. Woolf, eds., *Agrarian Change and Economic Development*. London.

Comité des k.k. Ackerbauministeriums (1899), *Geschichte der österreichischen Land- und Forstwirtschaft und ihrer Industrien, 1848-1898*. 4 vols. Vienna.

Commager, H. S. (1928), *Struensee and the Reform Movement in Denmark*. Unpublished Ph.D. dissertation, Univ. of Chicago.

Confino, M. (1963), *Domaines et seigneurs en Russie vers la fin du xviiie siècle*. Paris.

Confino, M. (1961), "Le paysan russe jugé par la noblesse au xviiie siècle," *Mélanges Pierre Pascal, Revue des études slaves*, XXXVIII.

Confino, M. (1969), *Systèmes agraires et progrès agricole. L'assolement triennal en Russie aux xviiiie-xixe siècles*. Paris.

Connell, K. H. (1950), *The Population of Ireland 1750-1845*. Oxford.

Constantiniu, F. (1973), "Fürstliche Reformen und Bojarenreaktion. Die Lage der rumänischen Bauernschaft im Zeitalter des aufgeklärten Absolutismus," D. Berindei *et al.*, *Der Bauer Mittel- und Osteuropas im sozio-ökonomischen Wandel des 18. und 19. Jahrhunderts*. Cologne.

Conze, W. (1940), *Agrarverfassung und Bevölkerung in Litauen und Weissrussland*. Leipzig.

Conze, W. ed. (1957), *Quellen zur Geschichte der deutschen Bauernbefreiung*. Göttingen.

Conze, W. (1948), "Die Wirkungen der liberalen Agrarreform auf die Volksordnung in Mitteleuropa," *Vierteljahrschrift für Sozial- und Wirtschaftsgeschichte*, XXXVIII.

Corfus, I. (1969), *L'agriculture en Valachie pendant la première moitié du xixe siècle*. Bucharest.

Coxe, W. (1802), *Travels in Poland, Russia, Sweden, and Denmark*. 5th ed. 5 vols. London.

Coxe, W. (1789), *Travels in Switzerland*. 3 vols. London.

Craig, G. A. (1955), *The Politics of the Prussian Army, 1640-1945*. Oxford.

Creangă, G. D. (1907, 1909), "Grundbesitzverteilung und Bauernfrage in Rumänen," *Staats- und sozialwissenschaftliche Forschungen*, CXXIX, CXL.

Creutzberg, H. (1910), *Die Entwicklung der kurländischen Agrarverhältnisse seit Aufhebung der Leibeigenschaft*. Königsberg.

Csaplovics, J. von (1829), *Gemälde von Ungern*. 2 vols. Pest.

Czap, P. (1967), "Peasant-Class Courts and Peasant Customary Justice in Russia, 1861-1912," *Journal of Social History*, I.

Czybulka, G. (1949), "Die Lage der ländlichen Klassen Ostdeutschlands im 18. Jahrhundert," *Beiträge zum Geschichtsunterricht*, XV.

Dansk Biografisk Leksikon (1933-1944). 27 vols. Copenhagen.

Darmstaedter, P. (1897), *Die Befreiung der Leibeigenen (mainmortables) in Savoyen, der Schweiz und Lothringen*. Strassburg.

Davidson, S. and R. Passmore (1966), *Human Nutrition and Dietetics*. 3rd ed. Cambridge and London.

Davies, A. (1964), "The Origins of the French Peasant Revolution of 1789," *History*, XLIX.

Debien, G. (1945), "Land Clearings and Artificial Meadows in Eighteenth-Century Poitou," *Agricultural History*, XIX.

Demangeon, A. (1927), "La géographie de l'habitat rural," *Annales de Géographie*, XXVI.

Demeter, K. (1965), *The German Officer-Corps in Society and State 1650-1945*. Transl. from German. New York.

Demian, J. A. (1809), *Tableau géographique et politique de Hongrie, d'Esclavonie, de Croatie, et de la grande principauté de Transilvanie*. Transl. from German. 2 vols. Paris.

Den Hollander, A. N. J. (1960), "The Great Hungarian Plain: a European Frontier Area," *Comparative Studies in Society and History*, III.

Denis, M. (1957), "Grandeur et décadence d'une forêt: Paimpont en xvie au xixe siècle," *Annales de Bretagne*, LXIV.

Dessmann, G. (1904), *Geschichte der schlesischen Agrarverfassung*. Strassburg.

Deutsches Museum (1780).

Die deutsche Landwirtschaft. Hauptergebnisse der Reichsstatistik (1913). Kaiserliche Statistische Amt. Berlin.

Dieck, A. (1954), "Über das Alter des Buchweizenanbaues in Nordwestdeutschland," *Zeitschrift für Agrargeschichte und Agrarsoziologie*, II.

Diederichs, H. (1870), "Garlieb Merkel als Bekämpfer der Leibeigenschaft . . . ," *Baltische Monatschrift*, XIX.

Dietze, C. von (1926), "Fideikommisse," *Handwörterbuch der Staatswissenschaften*, 4th ed., Jena.

Dinklage, K. (1965), "Gründung und Aufbau der theresianischen Ackerbaugesellschaften," *Zeitschrift für Agrargeschichte und Agrarsoziologie*.

Dion, R. (1934), *Essai sur la formation du paysage rurale française*, Tours.

Dissow, J. von (1961), *Adel im Übergang*. Stuttgart.

Dodd, W. F. (1912), *Modern Constitutions*. 2 vols. Chicago.

Dodge, W. R. (1950), *Abolitionist Sentiment in Russia*. Unpublished dissertation, University of Wisconsin.

Domar, E. (1970), "The Causes of Slavery or Serfdom: a Hypothesis," *Journal of Economic History*, XXX.

Dorn, W. L. (1940), *Competition for Empire*. New York and London.

Dorn, W. L. (1932), "The Prussian Bureaucracy in the Eighteenth Century," *Political Science Quarterly*, XLVII.

Dovring, F. (1969), "Eighteenth Century Changes in European Agriculture: a Comment," *Agricultural History*, XLIII.

Dovring, F. (1956), *Land and Labor in Europe in the Twentieth Century*. The Hague.

Drage, G. (1909), *Austria-Hungary*. New York.

Drake, M. (1969), *Population and Society in Norway 1735-1865*. Cambridge.

Drakokhrust, E. I. (1938), "Rassloenie krepostnogo krest'ianstva v obrochnoi votchine XVIII v.," *Istoricheskie zapiski*, no. 4.

Druzhinin, N. M. (1946-1958), *Gosudarstvennye krest'iane i reforma P.D. kiselev*. 2 vols. Moscow-Leningrad.

Duby, G. (1968), *Rural Economy and Country Life in the Medieval West*. Transl. from French. Columbia.

Ducros, L. (1926), *French Society in the Eighteenth Century*. Transl. from French. London.

Dupaquier, J. (1956), "La propriété et l'exploitation foncières à la fin de l'ancien régime dans le Gâtinais septentrional," *Commission de recherche et de publication des documents relatifs à la vie économique de la Révolution*, XI.

Dürst, E. R. (1951), *Die wirtschaftlichen und sozialen Verhältnisse des Glarnerlandes an der Wende vom 18. zum 19. Jahrhundert*. Glarus.

Economic Life of Poland. See *Polish Encyclopedia*.

Economo, D. (1911), *Les phases de la propriété foncière en Roumanie jusqu'aux lois agraires de 1907*. Paris.

Eddie, S. M. (1967), "The Changing Pattern of Landownership in Hungary, 1867-1914," *Economic History Review*, 2nd ser., xx.

Eggert, O. (1965), *Die Massnahmen der Preussischen Regierung zur Bauernbefreiung in Pommern*. Cologne-Graz.

Eidelberg, P. G. (1974), *The Great Rumanian Peasant Revolt of 1907*. Leiden.

Elvert, C. d' (1870), *Geschichte der k.k. mähr.-schles. Gesellschaft zur Beförderung des Ackerbaues der Natur- und Landeskunde*. 2 vols. Brünn.

Emerit, M. (1937), *Les paysans roumains depuis le traité d'Adrianople jusqu'à la libération des terres (1829-1864)*. Paris.

Emerit, M. (1930), "Sur la condition des esclaves dans l'ancienne Roumanie," *Revue historique du Sud-Est européen*, vii.

Emmons, T. (1968), "The Peasant and the Emancipation," W. S. Vucinich, ed., *The Peasant in Nineteenth-Century Russia*. Stanford.

Emmons, T. (1968), *The Russian Landed Gentry and the Emancipation of 1861*. Cambridge.

Encyclopédie Polonais (1920). Comité des publications encyclopédique sur la Pologne. Fribourg-Lausanne.

Engel-Janosi, F. (1924), "Über die Entwicklung der sozialen und staatswissenschaftlichen Verhältnisse in deutschen Österreich 1815-1848," *Vierteljahrschrift für Sozial-und Wirtschaftsgeschichte*, xviii.

Engelbrecht, E. (1913), *Die Agrarverfassung des Ermlandes und ihre historische Entwicklung*. Munich and Leipzig.

Engelmann, J. (1884), *Die Leibeigenschaft in Russland*. Leipzig.

Engels, W. (1957), *Ablösung und Gemeinheitsteilungen in der Rheinprovinz*. Bonn.

Ensminger, M. E. (1969), *Animal Science*. Danville, Ill.

Epstein, K. (1966), *The Genesis of German Conservatism*. Princeton.

Ermolov, A. (1878), *Mémoire sur la production agricole de la Russie*. St. Petersburg.

Ernst, F. (1935), *Kleinjogg der Musterbauer*. Zurich, Berlin.

Eszlary, C. d' (1960), "La situation des serfs en Hongrie de 1514 à 1848," *Revue d'histoire économique et sociale*, xxxviii.

Evans, I. L. (1924), *The Agrarian Revolution in Roumania*. Cambridge.

Eyck, E. (1948), *Das persönliche Regiment Wilhelms II*. Erlenbach-Zurich.

FAO. See Food and Agricultural Organization of the United Nations.

Faber, H. (1918), *Co-operation in Danish Agriculture*. London.

Falguerolles, G.-E. de (1941), "La décadence de l'économie agricole dans le consulat de Lempaut au xviie et xviiie siècle," *Annales du Midi*, liii.

Faucher, D. (1961), "L'assolement triennal en France," *Études rurales*, i.

Faucher, D. (1949), *Géographie agraire. Types de culture*. Paris.

Faucher, D. (1954), *Le paysan et la machine*. Paris.

Feldborg, A. A. (1824), *Denmark Delineated*. Edinburgh.

Festschrift zur Säcularfeier der Königlichen Landwirthschafts-Gesellschaft zu Celle am 4 Juni 1864 (1865). 3 vols. Hannover.

Festy, O. (1947), *L'agriculture pendant la Révolution franqise: les conditions de production et de récolte des céréales*. Paris.

Festy, O. (1950), *L'agriculture pendant la Révolution française. L'utilisation des jacheres 1789-1795*. Paris.

Festy, O. (1957), "Les progrès de l'agriculture française durant le premier empire," *Revue d'histoire économique et sociale*, xxxv.

Finck von Finckenstein, H. W. (1960), *Die Entwicklung der Landwirtschaft in Preussen und Deutschland 1800-1930*. Würzburg.

Finck von Finckenstein, H. W. (1934), "Die Getreidewirtschaft Preussens von 1800 bis 1930," *Vierteljahrshefte zur Konjunkturforschung*. Sonderheft, xxxv.

Flatrès, P. (1957), "Paysages ruraux de pays atlantiques," *Annales E. S. C.* xii.

Florinsky, M. T. (1953), *Russia. A History and an Interpretation*. 2 vols. New York.

Fogt, H. W. (1914), *The Danish Folk High Schools* (U.S. Bureau of Education. Bulletin no. 22). Washington.

Földes, B. (1894), "Das Familienfideikommiss in Ungarn," *Jahrbücher für Nationalökonomie und Statistik*, vii.

Food and Agricultural Organization of the United Nations. *Production Yearbook*. Rome.

Forberger, R. (1958), *Die Manufaktur in Sachsen vom Ende des 16. bis zum Anfang des 19. Jahrhunderts*. Berlin.

Ford, G. S. (1919), "The Prussian Peasantry before 1807," *American Historical Review*, xxiv.

Ford, G. S. (1922), *Stein and the Era of Reform in Prussia, 1807-1815*. Princeton.

Ford, W. C. ed. (1913-1917), *Writings of John Quincy Adams*. 7 vols. New York.

Forordninger. See Kong Christian den Syvendes.

Forster, R. (1971), *The House of Saulx-Tavanes*. Baltimore.

Forster, R. (1960), *The Nobility of Toulouse in the Eighteenth Century*. Baltimore.

Forster, R. (1961), "The Noble Wine Producers of the Bordelais in the Eighteenth Century," *Economic History Review*, 2nd ser., xiv.

Forster, R. (1970), "Obstacles to Agricultural Growth in Eighteenth Century France," *American Historical Review*, lxxv.

Forster, R. (1963), "The Provincial Noble: a Reappraisal," *American Historical Review*, lxvii.

Forster, R. (1967), "The Survival of the Nobility during the French Revolution," *Past and Present*, no. 37.

Fourastié, J. (1960), *The Causes of Wealth*. Transl. from French. Glencoe.

Franz, G. (1959), "Die agrarische Bewegung im Jahre 1848," *Zeitschrift für Agrargeschichte und Agrarsoziologie*, VII.

Franz, G. (1970a), *Geschichte des deutschen Bauernstandes*. Stuttgart.

Franz, G. (1970), "Johann Nepomuk Hubert (von) Schwerz," G. Franz and H. Haushofer, *Grosse Landwirte*. Frankfurt.

Franz, G. (1963), *Quellen zur Geschichte des deutschen Bauernstandes in der Neuzeit*. Munich and Vienna.

Frauendorfer, S. von (1957), *Ideengeschichte der Agrarwirtschaft und Agrarpolitik im deutschen Sprachgebiet*, I. Munich.

Freudenberger, H. (1960a), "Industrialization in Bohemia and Moravia in the Eighteenth Century," *Journal of Central European Affairs*, XIX.

Freudenberger, H. (1963), *The Waldenstein Woolen Mill. Noble Entrepreneurship in 18th Century Bohemia*. Boston.

Freudenberger, H. (1960), "The Woolen-Goods Industry of the Habsburg Monarchy in the Eighteenth Century," *Journal of Economic History*, XX.

Friend, L. L. (1914), *The Folk High Schools of Denmark* (U.S. Bureau of Education, Bulletin no. 5). Washington.

Fridman, M. B. (1958), *Otmena krepostnogo prava v Belorussii*. Minsk.

Friedjung, H. (1903), "Gegner der Bauernbefreiung in Österreich," *Vierteljahrschrift für Sozial- und Wirtschaftsgeschichte*, I.

Friis, A. (1905), *Die Bernstorffs*. Leipzig.

Friis, A. and K. Glamann (1958), *A History of Prices and Wages in Denmark 1660-1800*, I. Copenhagen.

Fuchs, C. J. (1888), *Der Untergang des Bauernstandes und das Aufkommen der Gutsherrschaften nach archivalischen Quellen aus Neu-Vorpommern und Rügen*. Strassburg.

Fussell, G. E. (1969), "The Classical Tradition in West European Farming: the Sixteenth Century," *Economic History Review*, 2nd ser., XXII.

Gagliardo, J. G. (1969), *From Pariah to Patriot. The Changing Image of the German Peasant, 1770-1840*. Lexington, Ky.

Gamperl, H. (1955), *Die Flurbereinigung im westlichen Europa*. Munich.

Garthoff, R. L. (1960), "The Military as a Social Force," C. E. Black, ed., *The Transformation of Russian Society*. Cambridge.

Gay, F. (1958), "Production, prix et rentabilité de la terre en Berry au xviiie siècle," *Revue d'histoire économique et sociale*, XXXVI.

Gay, P. (1959), *Voltaire's Politics. The Poet as Realist*. Princeton.

Georgescu-Buzau, Gh. (1965), *La révolution de 1848 dans les pays roumains*. Bucharest.

Gerschenkron, A. (1965), "Agrarian Policies and Industrialization: Russia 1861-1917," *Cambridge Economic History*, VI, pt. 2. Cambridge.

Gesetzblatt für das Königreich Bayern.

Gesetz-Sammlung für die Königlichen Preussischen Staaten.

Gieysztor, A. et al. (1968), History of Poland. Warsaw.

Gieysztorowa, I. (1968), "Research into Demographic History of Poland. A Provisional Summing-Up," Acta Poloniae Historica, XVIII.

Gitermann, V. (1941), Geschichte der Schweiz. Thayngen.

Gitermann, V. (1944-1949), Geschichte Russlands. 3 vols. Zurich.

Goethe, J. W. von (1901), Wilhelm's Meister's Apprenticeship. Transl. by T. Carlyle. 2 vols. Boston.

Goldschmidt, H. (1910), Die Grundbesitzverteilung in der Mark Brandenburg und in Hinterpommern vom Beginn des dreissigjährigen Krieges bis zur Gegenwart. Berlin.

Goldsmith, R. W. (1961), "The Economic Growth of Tsarist Russia, 1860-1913," Economic Development and Cultural Change, IX.

Gollwitzer, H. (1964), Die Standesherren. 2nd ed. Göttingen.

Golob, E. O. (1944), The Méline Tariff: French Agriculture and Nationalist Economic Policy. New York.

Goltz, T. von der (1902-1903), Geschichte der deutschen Landwirtschaft. 2 vols. Berlin.

Gonner, E. C. K. (1912), Common Land and Inclosure. London.

Goodwin, A. (1953), "Prussia" A. Goodwin, ed., The European Nobility in the Eighteenth Century. London.

Goodwin, A. (1965), "The Social Structure and Economic and Political Attitudes of the French Nobility in the Eighteenth Century," XIIe Congrès International des Sciences Historiques. Rapports, I. Vienna.

Goubert, P. (1969), L'ancien régime, I. Paris.

Goubert, P. (1960), Beauvais et le Beauvaisis de 1600 à 1730. Paris.

Goubert, P. (1956), "The French Peasantry of the Seventeenth Century: a Regional Example," Past and Present, no. 10.

Goubert, P. (1966), Louis XIV et vingt millions de Français. Paris.

Goubert, P. (1957), "Les techniques agricoles dans les pays picards aux xviie et xviiie siècles," Revue d'histoire économique et sociale, XXXV.

Grantham, G. W. (1975), "Scale and Organization in French Farming, 1840-1880," W. N. Parker and E. L. Jones, eds., European Peasants and their Markets. Princeton.

Gromas, R. (1947), Histoire agricole de la France. Mende.

Gruder, V. R. (1968), The Royal Provincial Intendants. New York.

Grüll, G. (1963), Bauer, Herr und Landesfürst. Linz.

Grüll, G. (1952), Die Robot in Oberösterreich. Linz.

Grünberg, K. (1901), "Die bäuerlichen Unfreiheitsverhältnisse und ihre Beseitigung in der Bukowina," K. Grünberg, Studien zur österreichischen Agrargeschichte. Leipzig.

Grünberg, K. (1909), "Die Bauernbefreiung in Rumänien," Handwörterbuch der Staatswissenschaften, 3rd ed., II.

List of Works Cited

Grünberg, K. (1893-1894), *Die Bauernbefreiung und die Auflösung des gutsherrlich-bäuerlichen Verhältnisses in Böhmen, Mähren und Schlesien.* 2 vols. Leipzig.

Grünberg, K. (1921), *Franz Anton von Blanc, ein Sozialpolitiker der theresianisch-josefinischen Zeit.* Munich.

Grünberg, K. (1889), "Die rumänische Agrargesetzgebung im Hinblick auf ihre Reform," *Archiv für soziale Gesetzgebung und Statistik*, II.

Gubernatis, A. de (1885), *La Hongrie politique et sociale.* Florence.

Guggisberg, K. (1970), "Philipp Emanuel von Fellenberg (1771-1844)," G. Franz and H. Haushofer, eds., *Grosse Landwirte.* Frankfurt.

Gurko, V. I. (1939), *Features and Figures of the Past.* Stanford.

Habakkuk, H. J. (1953), "England," in A. Goodwin, ed., *The European Nobility in the Eighteenth Century.* London.

Habernoll, P. (1900), "Die Versuche Friedrichs des Grossen, das englische System der Fruchtwechselwirtschaft in Preussen einzuführen," *Landwirtschaftliche Jahrbücher*, XXIX.

Hamerow, T. S. (1958), *Restoration, Revolution, Reaction.* Princeton.

Handbuch aller unter der Regierung des Kaisers Joseph des II. für die k.k. Erbländer ergangenen Verordnungen und Gesetze in einer sistematischen Verbindung. Vienna.

Handwörterbuch der schweizerischen Volkswirtschaft, Sozialpolitik und Verwaltung. 3 vols. in 6. Bern, 1903-1911.

Hans, N. (1931), *History of Russian Educational Policy, 1701-1917.* London.

Hanssen, G. (1880), *Agrarhistorische Abhandlungen.* 2 vols. Leipzig.

Hanssen, G. (1861), *Die Aufhebung der Leibeigenschaft und die Umgestaltung der gutsherrlich-bäuerlichen Verhältnisse, überhaupt in den Herzogthümern Schleswig und Holstein.* St. Petersburg.

Hantsch, H. (1962), *Gestalter der Geschichte Österreichs.* Innsbruck.

Harper, A. E. (1959), "Carbohydrates" in U.S. Dept. of Agriculture, *Food. The Yearbook of Agriculture 1959.* Washington.

Hassinger, H. (1964), "Der Stand der Manufakturen in den deutschen Erbländern der Habsburger-Monarchie am Ende des 18. Jahrhunderts," F. Lütge, ed., *Die wirtschaftliche Situation in Deutschland und Österreich um die Wende vom 18. zum 19. Jahrhundert.* Stuttgart.

Haufe, H. (1939), *Die Wandlung der Volksordnung im rumänischen Altreich.* Stuttgart.

Haun, F. J. (1892), *Bauer und Gutsherr in Kursachsen.* Strassburg.

Hauser, A. (1971), "Bäuerliche Wirtschaft und Ernährung in der Schweiz vom 15.-18. Jahrhundert," *Zeitschrift für Agrargeschichte und Agrarsoziologie*, XIX.

Hauser, A. (1962a), "War Kleinjogg ein Musterbauer," *Zeitschrift für Agrargeschichte und Agrarsoziologie*, IX.

Hauser, A. (1965), "Schweizer Bauern als Kolonisten in Preussen und Litauen," *Zeitschrift für Agrargeschichte und Agrarsoziologie*. XIII.

Hauser, A. (1961), *Schweizerische Wirtschafts- und Sozialgeschichte*. Erlenbach-Zurich.

Hauser, A. (1962), *Von Essen und Trinken in alten Zürich*. 2nd ed. Zurich.

Haushofer, H. (1963), *Die deutsche Landwirtschaft im technischen Zeitalter*. Stuttgart.

Hausmann, S. (1892), *Die Grund-Entlastung in Bayern*. Strassburg.

Haxthausen, A. von (1866), *Die ländliche Verfassung Russlands*. Leipzig.

Haxthausen, A. von (1847-1852), *Studien über die innern Zustände, das Volksleben und insbesondere die ländlichen Einrichtungen Russlands*. 3 vols. Hannover and Berlin.

Hazard, P. (1954), *European Thought in the Eighteenth Century*. Transl. from French. New Haven.

Heckscher, E. F. (1954), *An Economic History of Sweden*. Transl. from Swedish. Cambridge.

Heitz, G. (1960), "Feudales Bauernlegen in Mecklenburg im 18. Jahrhundert," *Zeitschrift für Geschichtswissenschaft*, VIII.

Helfert, J. A. von (1904), *Aufzeichnungen und Erinnerungen aus jungen Jahren*. Vienna.

Helleiner, K. F. (1967), "The Population of Europe from the Black Death to the Eve of the Vital Revolution," *Cambridge Economic History of Europe*, IV. Cambridge.

Henderson, W. O. (1963), *Studies in the Economic Policy of Frederick the Great*. London.

Henne am Rhyn, O. (1903), "Bauernbefreiung," *Handwörterbuch der Schweizerischen Volkswirtschaft, Sozialpolitik und Verwaltung*, I. Bern.

Henning, F.-W. (1969a), *Bauernwirtschaft und Bauerneinkommen in Ostpreussen im 18. Jahrhundert*. Würzburg.

Henning, F.-W. (1969b), *Dienste und Abgaben der Bauern im 18. Jahrhundert*. Stuttgart.

Henning, R. (1882), *Das deutsche Haus in seiner historischen Entwicklung*. Strassburg.

Herbert, S. (1969), *The Fall of Feudalism in France*. Reprint. New York.

Hintze, O. (1915), *Die Hohenzollern und ihr Werk*. Berlin.

Hintze, O. (1896), "Preussische Reformbestrebungen vor 1806," *Historische Zeitschrift*, LXXVI.

Hitchins, K. (1969), *The Rumanian National Movement in Transylvania, 1780-1849*. Cambridge.

Hlubek, F. X. (1860), *Ein treues Bild des Herzogthums Steiermark*. Graz.

Hodgskin, T. (1820), *Travels in the North of Germany*. 2 vols. Edinburgh.

Hoffbauer, J. C. (1793), *Naturrecht aus dem Begriffe des Rechts entwickelt*. Halle.

Hoffbauer, J. C. (1795), *Untersuchungen über die wichtigsten Gegenstände des Naturrechts*. Halle.

Hoffmann, H. (1969), *Handwerk und Manufaktur in Preussen 1769. Das Taschenbuch Knyphausen*. Berlin.

Hoffmann, A. (1952), *Wirtschaftsgeschichte des Landes Oberösterreich*, I. Salzburg.

Holborn, H. (1959), *A History of Modern Germany*, I. New York.

Hommaire de Hell, X. (1843-1845), *Les steppes de la Mer Caspienne, le Caucase, la Crimée et la Russie méridionale*. 3 vols. Paris, Strasbourg.

Hötzsch, O. (1902), "Der Bauernschutz in den deutschen Territorien vom 16. bis ins 19. Jahrhundert," *Jahrbuch für Gesetzgebung, Verwaltung und Volkswirtschaft*, XXVI.

Houston, J. M. (1963), *A Social Geography of Europe*. New York.

Howe, F. C. (1921), *Denmark, a Cooperative Commonwealth*. New York.

Hovde, B. J. (1948), *The Scandinavian Countries 1720-1865*. 2 vols. Ithaca.

Hrushevsky, M. (1941), *A History of the Ukraine*. Transl. from Ukrainian. New Haven.

Hufton, O. H. (1972), "Begging, Vagrancy, Vagabondage and the Law: an Aspect of the Problem of Poverty in Eighteenth-Century France," *European Studies Review*, II.

Hufton, O. H. (1974), *The Poor of Eighteenth Century France 1750-1789*. Oxford.

Hurst, W. M. and L. M. Church (1933), *Power and Machinery in Agriculture*. U.S. Dept. of Agriculture, Miscellaneous Publication, no. 157.

Hutcheson, T. B. and T. K. Wolfe (1924), *The Production of Field Crops*. New York.

Hvidtfeldt, J. (1963), *Kampen om ophaevelsen af livegenskabet i Slesvig og Holsten, 1795-1805*. Viborg.

Iatsunskii, V. K. (1958), "Osnovnye etapy genezisa kapitalizma v Rossii," *Istoriia SSSR 1958*, no. 5.

Iatsunskii, V. K. (1966), "Osnovnye momenty istorii sel'skokhoziaistvennogo proizvodstva v Rossii c XVI veka do 1917 goda," *Ezhegodnik po agrarnoi istorii vostochnoi Evropy 1964 god*. Kishenev.

Ignat'ev, A. A. (1955), *Piat'desiat let v stroiu*. 2 vols. Moscow.

Ilzhofer, H. (1942), "Die Deckung des Vitaminsbedarfes in früheren Jahrhunderten," *Archiv für Hygeine und Bakteriologie*, CXXVII.

Indova, E. I. (1955), *Krepostnoe khoziaistvo v nachale XIX veka po materialam votchinnogo arkhiva Vorontsovykh*. Moscow.

Industries of Russia (1893), Published by Department of Agriculture (Russia). Ministry of Crown Domains.

International Institute of Agriculture (1939a), *European Conference on Rural Life 1939. Land Reclamation and Improvement in Europe*. Rome.

International Institute of Agriculture (1939), *European Conference on Rural Life 1939. The Land Tenure Systems in Europe*. Document no. 2. Rome.

Ionescu, D. B. See Jonescu

Ionescu-Şişeşti, G. (1912), *Rumäniens bäuerliche Landwirtschaft*. Bucharest.

Ipsen, G. (1954), "Die preussische Bauernbefreiung als Landesausbau," *Zeitschrift für Agrargeschichte und Agrarsoziologie*, II.

Ivanova, O. E. (1966), "Agrotekhnika v Pol'she ot XVI do poloviny XVIII v.," *Ezhegodnik po agrarnoi istorii vostochnoi Evropy 1964 god*. Kishenev.

Ivany, B. G. (1960), "From Feudalism to Capitalism: the Economic Background to Széchenyi's Reform in Hungary," *Journal of Central European Affairs*, xx.

Jacob, W. (1826), *Report on the Trade in Foreign Corn and on the Agriculture of the North of Europe*. 2nd ed. London.

Jacob, W. (1828), *Tracts Relating to the Corn Trade and Corn Laws: including the Second Report*. London.

Jacob, W. (1820), *A View of the Agriculture, Manufactures, Statistics, and State of Society, of Germany, and parts of Holland and France*. London.

Jacoby, E. H., ed. (1959), *Land Consolidation in Europe*. International Institute for Land Reclamation and Improvement, publ. 3/E. Wageningen.

Jaeger, H. (1967), *Unternehmer in der deutschen Politik (1890-1918)*. Bonn.

Jahrbücher der preussischen Monarchie (1800). III. Berlin.

Jasny, N. (1940), *Competition Among Grains*. Stanford.

Jeanneney, J.-M. and M. Perrot, eds. (1957), *Textes de droit économique et social français 1789-1957*. Paris.

Jelavich, B. (1939), *Russia and the Rumanian National Cause. 1858-1859*. Bloomington.

Jelavich, C. and B., eds. (1962), *The Education of a Russian Statesman*. Berkeley.

Jensen, E. (1937), *Danish Agriculture, its Economic Development*. Copenhagen.

Johnston, R. (1970), *Travels through Part of the Russian Empire*. Reprinted from 1816 ed. New York.

Jonescu (Ionescu), D. B. (1909), *Die Agrarverfassung Rumäniens; ihre Geschichte und ihre Reform*. Leipzig.

Jordan-Rozwadowski, J. von (1900), "Die Bauern im 18. Jahrhunderts und ihre Herren im Lichte des neuesten deutschen Forschungen," *Jahrbücher für Nationalökonomie und Statistik*. 3rd ser., xx.

Judeich, A. (1863), *Die Grundentlastung in Deutschland*. Leipzig.

Juillard, E. (1952), "L'assolement biennal dans l'agriculture septentrionale. Le cas particulier de la Basse-Alsace," *Annales de Géographie*, LXI.

Juillard, E. (1953), *La vie rurale dans la plaine de Basse-Alsace*. Paris.

k.k. Direction der administrativen Statistik, *Tafeln zur Statistik der österreichischen Monarchie*.

Kahan, A. (1966), "The Costs of 'Westernization,' in Russia," *Slavic Review*, xxv.

Kahan, A. (1968), "Natural Calamities and their Effect upon the Food Supply in Russia," *Jahrbücher für Geschichte Osteuropas, N. F.*, xvi.

Kahk, J. (1969), *Die Krise der feudalen Landwirtschaft in Estland. (Das zweite Viertel des 19. Jahrhunderts)*. Tallin.

Kahk, J. (1961), "Ob istoricheskikh predposylkakh otmeny krepostnogo prava v Estliandskoi gubernii (1816g.)," *Ezhegodnik po agrarnoi istorii vostochnoi Evropy 1959g*. Moscow.

Kann, R. A. (1960), *A Study in Austrian Intellectual History*. New York.

Kant, I. (1968), "Über den Gemeinspruch," *Kant's Werke*, viii. Berlin.

Kaplow, J. (1964), *Elbeuf during the Revolutionary Period*. Baltimore.

Kaplow, J. (1972), *The Names of Kings*. New York.

Karamzin, N. M. (1959), *Memoir on Ancient and Modern Russia*. Transl. from Russian. Cambridge, Mass.

Kareev, N. I. (1899), *Les paysans et la question paysanne en France dans le dernier quart du xviiie siècle*. Paris.

Karpachev, A. M. (1964), "O primenenii naemnogo truda v pomeshchich'em khoziaistve Belorussii vo vtoroi polovine XVIII v." *Ezhegodnik po agrarnoi istorii vostochnoi Evropy 1962g*. Minsk.

Katus, L. (1961), "Hauptzüge der kapitalistischen Entwicklung der Landwirtschaft in den südslawischen Gebieten der Österreichisch-Ungarischen Monarchie," *Studien zur Geschichte der Österreichisch-Ungarischen Monarchie*. Studia Historica Academiae Scientiarum Hungaricae. No. 51.

Kellenbenz, H. (1962), "Bäuerliche Unternehmertätigkeit im Bereich der Nord- und Ostsee vom Hochmittelalter bis zum Ausgang der neueren Zeit," *Vierteljahrschrift für Sozial- und Wirtschaftsgeschichte*, IL.

Kellenbenz, H. (1960), "Die Betätigung der Grossgrundbesitzer im Bereich der deutschen Nord- und Ostseeküste in Handel, Gewerbe und Finanz (16. bis 18. Jahrhundert)," *Première Conference Internationale d'Histoire Économique, Stockholm 1960*. Paris, The Hague.

Kerner, R. J. (1932), *Bohemia in the Eighteenth Century*. New York.

Khoroshailov, N. G. (1956), "K istorii kul'turi klevera v SSSR," *Materialy po istorii zemledeliia SSSR.*, II. Moscow-Leningrad.

Khromov, P. A. (1950), *Ekonomicheskoe razvitie Rossii v XIX-XX vekakh 1800-1917*. Moscow.

Kieniewicz, S. (1969), *The Emancipation of the Polish Peasantry*. Chicago.

Király, B. K. (1969), *Hungary in the Late Eighteenth Century: the Decline of Enlightened Despotism*. New York.

Király, B. K. (1967), "Peasant Movements in Hungary in 1790," *Südost-Forschungen*, XXVI.

Kisch, H. (1964), "Growth Deterrents of a Medieval Heritage: the Aachen Area Woolen Trades before 1790," *Journal of Economic History*, XXIV.

Kisch, H. (1959), "The Textile Industries in Silesia and the Rhineland: a Comparative Study in Industrialization," *Journal of Economic History*, XIX.

Klein, E. F. (1797), *Grundsätze des natürlichen Rechtswissenschaft nebst ein Geschichte derselben*. Halle.

Klíma, A. (1961), "Ein Beitrag zur Agrarfrage in der Revolution von 1848 in Böhmen," *Studien zur Geschichte der österreichisch-ungarischen Monarchie*. Studia Historica Academia Scientiarum Hungaricae No. 51.

Klíma, A. (1959), "English Merchant Capital in Bohemia in the Eighteenth Century," *Economic History Review*, 2nd ser., XII.

Klíma, A. (1974), "The Role of Rural Domestic Industry in Bohemia in the Eighteenth Century," *Economic History Review*, 2nd ser., XXVII.

Kliuchevskii, V. O. (1937), *Kurs russkoi istorii*. 5 vols. Moscow.

Knapp, G. F. (1909), "Die Bauernbefreiung in den östlichen Provinzen des preussischen Staates," *Handwörterbuch der Staatswissenschaften*, II.

Knapp, G. F. (1887), *Die Bauernbefreiung und der Ursprung der Landarbeiter in den älteren Theilen Preussens*. 2 vols. Leipzig.

Knapp, T. (1902), *Der Bauer im heutigen Württemberg nach seinen Rechtsverhältnissen vom 16. bis 19. Jahrhundert*. Stuttgart.

Knapp, T. (1964), *Gesammelte Beiträge zur Rechts- und Wirtschaftsgeschichte vornehmlich des deutschen Bauernstandes*. Aalen.

Knapp, T. (1919), *Neue Beiträge zur Rechts- und Wirtschaftsgeschichte des württembergischen Bauernstandes*. Tübingen.

Knoll, R. (1973), *Zur Tradition der Christlichsozialen Partei*. Graz.

Knowles, L. (1919), "New Light on the Economic Causes of the French Revolution," *Economic Journal*, XXIX.

Kodedová, O. (1967), "Die Lohnarbeit auf dem Grossgrundbesitz in Böhmen in der zweiten Hälfte des 19. Jahrhunderts," *Historica*, XIV.

Kong Christian den Syvendes allernadigste Forordninger og aabne Breve for Aar 1804. Copenhagen.

Königlich-Baierisches Regierungsblatt, 1808. Munich.

Koniukhova, T. A. (1960), "Sel'skoe khoziaistvo gosudarstvennykh krest'ian Vilenskoi i Kovenskoi gubernii v period reformy P. D. Kiseleva

(1840-1857gg.)," Akademiia Nauk, Institut Istorii, *Materialy po istorii sel'skogo khoziaistva i krest'ianstva SSSR*. IV. Moscow-Leningrad.

Köppen, P. V. (1852), *Statistische Reise in's Land der donischen Kosaken durch die Gouvernments Tula, Orel, und Woronesh im Jahre 1850*. St. Petersburg.

Köppen, P. V. (1845), "Über den Kornbedarf Russlands," *Mémoires de l'Académie Impériale des Sciences de St.-Pétersbourg*. VIme série, Sciences Politiques, Histoire, Philologie, v.

Korelin, A. P. (1971a), "Dvorianstvo v poreformennoi Rossii," *Istoricheskie zapiski*. No. 87.

Korelin, A. P. (1971b), "Rossiiskoe dvorianstvo i ego soslovnaia organizatsiia (1861-1904gg.)," *Istoriia SSSR*, 1971, No. 5.

Korf, M. (1896), "Imperator Nikolai v soveshchatel'nykh sobraniiakh (iz sovremennykh zapisok stats-sekretaria barona Korfa)," *Sbornik Imperatorskago Russkago Istoricheskago Obshchestva*, XCVIII.

Kornilov, A. A. (1905), "Gubernskie komitety po krest'ianskomu delu v 1858-1859gg.," *Ocherki po istorii obshchestvennago dvizheniia krest'ianskago dela v Rossii*. St. Petersburg.

Koroliuk, V. D. *et al.* (1956), *Istoriia Pol'shi*. 2nd ed. Moscow.

Körösi, J. (1873), *Beiträge zur Geschichte der Preise*. Pest.

Korth, S. (1953), "Die Entstehung und Entwicklung des ostdeutschen Grossgrundbesitzes," *Jahrbuch der Albertus Universität zu Königsberg/Pr.*, III.

Kosa, J. (1957), "A Century of Hungarian Emigration, 1850-1950," *American Slavic and East European Review*, XVI.

Kostiushko, I. I. (1962), *Krest'ianskaia reforma 1864 goda v Tsarstve Pol'skom*. Moscow.

Kostiushko, I. I. (1954), "Razlozhenie feodal'nykh otnoshenii i razvitie kapitalizma v sel'skom khoziastve Tsarstva Pol'skogo," *Uchenye zapiski, Instituta Slavianovedeniia*, x. Moscow.

Kötzschke, R. (1953), *Ländliche Siedlung und Agrarwesen in Sachsen*. Remagen.

Kötzschke, R. and H. Kretzschmar (1965), *Sächsische Geschichte*. Frankfurt a. M.

Kovács, J. (1961), "Zur Frage der siebenbürgischen Bauernbefreiung und der Entwicklung der kapitalistischen Landwirtschaft nach 1848," *Studien zur Geschichte der Österreichischen-Ungarischen Monarchie*. Studia Historica Academiae Scientiarum Hungaricae. No. 51.

Koval'chenko, I. D. (1960), "K istorii skotovodstva v evropeiskoi Rossii v pervoi polovine XIX veka," Akademiia Nauk, Institut Istorii, *Materialy po istorii sel'skogo khoziaistva i krest'ianstva SSSR*, IV. Moscow-Leningrad.

Koval'chenko, I. D. (1961), "K voprosu o sostoianii khoziaistva pered ot-menoi krepostnogo prava v Rossii," *Ezhegodnik po agrarnoi istorii vostochnoi Evropy 1959g*. Moscow.

Koval'chenko, I. D. (1964), "O tovarnosti zemledeliia v Rossii v pervoi polovine XIX v.," *Ezhegodnik po agrarnoi istorii vostochnoi Evropy 1963g*. Vilna.

Koval'chenko, I. D. (1965), "Rassloenie obrochnykh krest'ian tsentral'no-promyshlennogo raiona vo vtoroi chetverti XIX v.," Akademiia Nauk, Institut Istorii, *Materialy po istorii sel'skogo khoziaistva i krest'ianstva SSSR*, VI. Moscow.

Koval'chenko, I. D. (1967), *Russkoe krepostnoe krest'ianstvo v pervoi polovine XIX veka*. Moscow.

Kovalevsky, M. (1909-1911), *La France économique et sociale à la veille de la Révolution*. 2 vols. Paris.

Kovalevsky, M. (1891), *Modern Customs and Ancient Laws of Russia*. London.

Kravets, N. N. (1966), "Krest'ianskoe dvizhenie na severnoi Bukovine vo vtoroi polovine XIX veka," *Ezhegodnik po agrarnoi istorii vostochnoi Evropy 1964g*. Kishenev.

Krest'ianskaia reforma v Rossii 1861 goda; sbornik zakonodatel'nykh aktov (1954). Moscow.

Krest'ianskoe dvizhenie 1827-1869 (1931). 2 vols. Moscow.

Krest'ianskoe dvizhenie v Rossii v 1826-1849gg. Sbornik dokumentov (1961). Moscow.

Krest'ianskoe dvizhenie v Rossii v 1857-Mae 1861gg. Sbornik dokumentov (1963). Moscow.

Krichauff, T.E.H.W. (1895), "The Tercentenary of the Introduction of Potatos into England," *Journal of the Royal Horticultural Society*, XIX.

Krug, L. (1970), *Betrachtungen über den Nationalreichtum des preussischen Staates*. 2 vols. Reprinted from 1805 edition. Darmstadt.

Krüger, H. (1958), *Zur Geschichte der Manufakturen und Manufakturarbeiter in Preussen. Die mittleren Provinzen in der zweiten Hälfte des 18. Jahrhunderts*. Berlin.

Krzhivoblotskii, Ia. (1861), *Materialy dlia geografii i statistiki Rossii, sobranye ofitserami General'nago Shtaba. Kostromskaia guberniia*. St. Petersburg.

Krzymowski, R. (1961), *Geschichte der deutschen Landwirtschaft*. 3rd ed. Berlin.

Kübeck von Kübau, C. F. von (1909), *Tagebücher*. 2 vols. in 3. Vienna.

Kuczynski, J. (1960-1972), *Die Geschichte der Lage der Arbeiter unter dem Kapitalismus*. 38 vols. in 40. Berlin.

Kuhn, W. (1955-1957), *Geschichte der deutschen Ostsiedlung in der Neuzeit*. 2 vols. Cologne.

Kulischer, J. (1971), *Allgemeine Wirtschaftsgeschichte des Mittelalters und der Neuzeit*. 2 vols. Vienna.

Kulischer, J. (1931), "Die kapitalistischen Unternehmer in Russland (insbesondere die Bauern als Unternehmer) in den Anfangsstadien des Kapitalismus," *Archiv für Sozialwissenschaft und Sozialpolitik*, LXV.

Kulischer, J. (1932), "Die Leibeigenschaft in Russland und die Agrarverfassung Preussens im 18. Jahrhundert," *Jahrbücher für Nationalökonomie und Statistik*, CXXXVII.

Kún, E. (1903), *Sozialhistorische Beiträge zur Landarbeiterfrage in Ungarn*. Jena.

Kurnatowski, G. (1933), "Les origines du capitalisme en Pologne," *Revue d'histoire moderne*, VIII.

Kusheva, E. N. (1951), "Proekt uchrezdeniia aktsionernogo 'Obshchestva uluchsheniia chastnogo sel'skogo khoziaistva' 30-kh godov XIX v.," *Istoricheskii arkhiv*, VII.

Labrousse, C.-E. (1944), *La crise de l'économie française à la fin de l'ancien régime et au début de la Révolution*. Paris.

Labrousse, C.-E. (1933), *Esquisse du mouvement des prix et des revenus en France au xviiie siécle*. 2 vols. Paris.

Labrousse, E. (1966), "The Evolution of Peasant Society in France from the Eighteenth Century to the Present," E. Acomb and M. Brown, eds., *French Society and Culture since the Old Regime*. New York.

Labrousse, M. E. (1954), *Aspects de l'evolution économique et sociale de la France et du Royaume-Uni de 1815 à 1880*. Les Cours de Sorbonne. 3 pts. Paris.

Lacroix, P. (1963), *France in the Eighteenth Century*. Reprinted from 1876 ed. New York.

LaGarde-Chambonas, A.C.L. (1831), *Journal of a Nobleman*. 2 vols. London.

La Gorce, P. M. de (1963), *The French Army*. Transl. from French. New York.

Lamartine Yates, P. (1940), *Food Production in Western Europe*. London.

La Monneraye, J. de (1922), *Le régime féodal et les classes rurales dans le Maine au xviiie siècle*. Paris.

Lane, F. C., and J. C. Riemersma (1953), *Enterprise and Secular Change*. Homewood, Ill.

Laubert, M. (1934), "Der Posener Adel und die Bauernbefreiung," *Jahrbücher für Kultur und Geschichte der Slaven*, N. F., x.

Lefebvre, G. (1949), "Le despotisme éclairé," *Annales historiques de la Révolution française*, XXI.

Lefebvre, G. (1973), *The Great Fear of 1789*. Transl. from French. London.

Lefebvre, G. (1972), *Les paysans du Nord pendant la Révolution française*. Paris.

Lefebvre, G. (1921), "La place de la Révolution dans l'histoire agraire de la France," *Annales d'histoire économique et sociale*, i.

Lefebvre, G. (1955), *Questions agraires au temps de la Terreur*. 2nd ed. La Roche-sur-Yon.

Lefebvre, G. (1928), "Les recherches relatives à la vente des biens nationaux," *Revue d'histoire moderne*, iii.

Lekhnovich, V. C. (1956), "K istorii kul'tury kartofelia v Rossii," Akademiia Nauk, Institut Istorii, *Materialy po istorii zemledeliia SSSR*, ii. Moscow-Leningrad.

Lengerke, A. von (1846-1847), *Beiträge zur Kenntniss der Landwirtschaft in den Königl. Preuss. Staaten*. 2 vols. Berlin.

Lennard, R. (1922), "The Alleged Exhaustion of the Soil in Medieval England," *Economic Journal*, xxxii.

Le Play, F. (1877-1879), *Les ouvriers européens*. 6 vols. Tours.

Leroy-Beaulieu, A. (1883), *L'empire des tsars et les Russes*. 2 vols. Paris.

Leroy-Beaulieu, A. (1884), *Un homme d'état russe*. Paris.

Le Roy Ladurie, E. (1966), *Les paysans de Languedoc*. 2 vols. Paris.

Leshchilovskaia, I. I. (1961), "Otmena krepostnogo prava v Khorvatii i Slavonii v 1848g.," *Ezhegodnik po agrarnoi istorii Evropy 1959g.* Moscow.

Leskiewicz, J. (1959), "Les debuts du capitalisme dans l'agriculture du Royaume de Pologne," *Acta Poloniae Historica*, ii.

Leskiewicz, J. (1965). "Les entraves sociales au développement de la 'nouvelle agriculture' en Pologne," *Second International Conference of Economic History 1962*. Paris.

Leslie, R. F. (1956), *Polish Politics and the Revolution of November 1830*. London.

Leslie, R. F. (1963), *Reform and Insurrection in Russian Poland 1856-1865*. London.

Levin, A. (1966), *The Second Duma*. 2nd ed. Hamden.

Lévy, M. (1951-1952), *Histoire économique et sociale de la France depuis 1848*. 3 vols. Paris.

Lévy-Bruhl, H. (1933), "La noblesse de France et le commerce à la fin de l'ancien régime," *Revue d'histoire moderne*, n.s. no. 8.

Lewis, W. H. (1953), *The Splendid Century*. New York.

Lhomme, J. (1960), *La grande bourgeoisie au pouvoir 1830-1880*. Paris.

Liashchenko, P. I. (1949), *History of the National Economy of Russia*. New York.

Liashchenko, P. I. (1956), *Istoriia narodnogo khoziaistva SSSR*. 2 vols. Moscow.

Liashchenko, P. I. (1945), "Krepostnoe sel'skoe khoziaistvo Rossii v XVIII veke," *Istoricheskie zapiski*, no. 15.

Liashchenko, P. I. (1913-1926). *Ocherki agrarnoi evoliutsii Rossii*. 2 vols. St. Petersburg.

Liebel, H. (1965), "Enlightened Bureaucracy versus Enlightened Despotism in Baden, 1750-1792," *Transactions of the American Philosophical Society*, n.s., LV.

Lincoln, W. B. (1971), "Russia's 'Enlightened' Bureaucrats and the Problem of State Reform 1848-1856," *Cahiers du monde russe et soviétique*, XII.

Link, E. M. (1949), *The Emancipation of the Austrian Peasant 1740-1798*. New York.

Lizerand, G. (1951), *Études d'histoire rurale*. Paris.

Lizerand, G. (1942), *Le régime rural de l'ancienne France*. Paris.

Löning, E. (1880), "Die Befreiung des Bauernstandes in Deutschland und Livland," *Baltische Monatschrift*, XXVII.

Loone, L. A. (1959), "O razvitii nekotorykh elementov kapitalizma v sel'skom khoziaistve severnoi Estonii v 20-50-kh godakh xix veka," *Ezhegodnik po agrarnoi istorii vostochnoi Evropy 1958g*. Tallin.

Loone, L. (1968), "Zur Entwicklung der landwirtschaftlichen Produktion in Estland und Livland im XVIII. und XIX. Jahrhundert," *Third International Conference of Economic History, 1965*, pt. 2. Paris, The Hague.

Lopez, R. S. (1953), "The Origin of the Merino Sheep," *The Joshua Starr Memorial Volume*. New York.

Louchitsky, J. (1911), *L'état des classes agricoles en France à la veille de la Révolution*. Paris.

Louchitsky, J. (1933), "Régime agraire et populations agricole dans les environs de Paris à la veille de la Révolution," *Revue d'histoire moderne*, n.s., no. 7.

Ludwig, T. (1896), *Der badische Bauer im achtzehnten Jahrhundert*. Strassburg.

Lütge, F. (1935), "Die Ablösung der grundherrlichen Lasten in Mitteldeutschland," *Jahrbücher für Nationalökonomie und Statistik*, CXLII.

Lütge, F. (1949), *Die bayerische Grundherrschaft*. Stuttgart.

Lütge, F. (1966), *Deutsche Sozial- und Wirtschaftsgeschichte*. Berlin.

Lütge, F. (1955), "Freiheit und Unfreiheit in der Agrarverfassung," *Historisches Jahrbuch*, LXXIV.

Lütge, F. (1967), *Geschichte der deutschen Agrarverfassung vom frühen Mittelalter bis zum 19. Jahrhundert*. 2nd ed. Stuttgart.

Lütge, F. (1968), "Die Grundentlastung (Bauernbefreiung) in der Steiermark," *Zeitschrift für Agrargeschichte und Agrarsoziologie*, XVI.

Lütge, F. (1957), *Die mitteldeutsche Grundherrschaft und ihre Auflösung*. 2nd ed. Stuttgart.

Lütge, F. (1967a), "Die Robot-Abolition unter Kaiser Joseph II," H. Haushofer and W. Boelcke, eds., *Wege und Forschungen der Agrargeschichte*. Frankfurt a. M.

Lütge, F. (1943), "Über die Auswirkungen der Bauernbefreiung in Deutschland," *Jahrbücher für Nationalökonomie und Statistik*, CLVII.

Lyall, R. (1970), *Travels in Russia, the Krimea, the Caucasus, and Georgia*. Reprinted from 1825 edition. New York.

Macartney, C. A. (1968), *The Habsburg Empire 1790-1918*. London.
Macartney, C. A. (1962), *Hungary: a Short History*. Chicago.
Macdonald, J. (1809), *Travels through Denmark and Part of Sweden*. 2 vols. London.
Mackrell, J.Q.C. (1973), *The Attack on "Feudalism" in Eighteenth-Century France*. London.
Maçzak, A. (1958), "Polnische Forschungen auf dem Gebiete der Agrargeschichte des 16. und 17. Jahrhunderts (1945-1957)," *Acta Poloniae Historica*, I.
Maçzak, A. (1967), "Zur Grundeigentumsstruktur in Polen im 16. bis 18. Jahrhundert," *Jahrbuch für Wirtschaftsgeschichte*, IV.
Mager, F. (1955), *Geschichte des Bauerntums und der Bodenkultur im Lande Mecklenburg*. Berlin.
Mailáth, J. (1838), *Das ungrische Urbarialsystem*. Pest and Leipzig.
Majors, K. R. (1951), "Cereal Grains as Food and Feed," *Crops in Peace and War. The Yearbook of Agriculture 1950-1951*. Washington.
Malthus, T. R. (1966), *Travel Diaries*, edited by Patricia James. Cambridge.
Mandrou, R. (1961), "Vie materielle et comportements biologique," *Annales E. S. C.*, XVI.
Marczali, H. (1910), *Hungary in the Eighteenth Century*. Cambridge.
Marion, M. (1968), *Dictionnaire des institutions de la France aux xviie et xviiie siècles*. Paris.
Marion, M. (1902), "État des classes rurales au XVIIIᵉ siècle dans la généralité de Bordeaux," *Revue des études historiques*, LXVIII.
Markina, V. A. (1964), "Dvizhenie tsen v magnatskikh latifundiiakh Pravoberezhnoi Ukrainy vo vtoroi polovine XVIII v.," *Ezhegodnik po agrarnoi istorii vostochnoi Evropy 1963g*. Vilna.
Marshall, T. H. (1964), *Class, Citizenship, and Social Development*. New York.
Marshall, T. H. (1929), "Jethro Tull and the 'New Husbandry' of the Eighteenth Century," *Economic History Review*, II.
Martens, G. F. de and C. Samwer (1860), *Nouveau receuil général de traités. . .*, XVI, pt. 2. Göttingen.
Martin, G. (1900), *La grande industrie en France sous le règne de Louis XV*. Paris.
Martiny, F. (1939), "Die Adelsfrage in Preussen vor 1806 als politisches und soziales Problem," *Vierteljahrschrift für Sozial- und Wirtschaftsgeschichte*, Beiheft XXXV.
Martonne, E. de (1902), *La Valachie*. Paris.

Martov, L. *et al.*, eds. (1909-1911), *Obshchestvennoe dvizhenie v' Rossii v' nachale XX-go veka*. St. Petersburg.

Masefield, G. B. (1967), "Crops and Livestock," *Cambridge Economic History*, VI. Cambridge.

Matis, H. (1967), "Die Grafen von Fries. Aufstieg und Untergang einer Unternehmerfamilie," *Tradition*, XII.

Matl, J. (1965), "Historische Grundlagen der Agrarsozialen Verhältnisse auf dem Balkan," *Vierteljahrschrift für Sozial- und Wirtschaftsgeschichte*, LII.

Matossian, M. (1968), "The Peasant Way of Life," W. Vucinich, ed., *The Peasant in Nineteenth-Century Russia*. Stanford.

Mayer, F. M. (1909), *Geschichte Oesterreichs*. 3rd ed. 2 vols. Vienna and Leipzig.

McCance, R. A. and E. M. Widdowson (1947), *The Chemical Composition of Foods*. New York.

McCloy, S. T. (1946), *Government Assistance in Eighteenth-Century France*. Durham.

McGrew, R. E. (1965), *Russia and the Cholera 1823-1832*. Madison.

McManners, J. (1953), "France," A. Goodwin, ed., *The European Nobility in the Eighteenth Century*.

Meier, E. von (1908), *Französische Einflüsse auf die Staats- und Rechtsentwicklung Preussens im 19. Jahrhundert*. 2 vols. Leipzig.

Merle, L. (1958), *La métairie et l'évolution agraire de la Gâtine poitevine, de la fin du moyen âge à la Révolution*. 1958.

Mésároš, J. (1961), "Die Expropriation des Bauerntums und die Überreste der feudalen Unterdrückung in der Slowakei in der zweiten Hälfte des 19. Jahrhunderts," *Studien zur Geschichte der Österreichisch-Ungarischen Monarchie*, Studia Historica Academiae Scientiarum Hungaricae, no. 51. Budapest.

Meshalin, I. V. (1950), *Tekstil'naia promyshlennost krest'ian Moskovskoi gubernii v XVIII i pervoi polovine XIX veka*. Moscow, Leningrad.

Meuvret, J. (1953), "Agronomie et jardinage au xvie et au xviie siècle," *Éventail de l'histoire vivante*, II.

Meuvret, J. (1947), "Circulation monétaire et utilisation économique de la monnaie dans la France du xvie et du xviie siècle," *Études d'histoire moderne et contemporaine*, I.

Meuvret, J. (1960), "Domaines ou ensembles territoriaux?" *Première conference internationale d'histoire économique. Contributions. Communications. Stockholm, 1960*. Paris, The Hague.

Meyer, G. (1965), *Die Verkoppelung im Herzogtum Lauenberg unter hannoverscher Herrschaft*. Hildesheim.

Meyer, J. (1966), *La noblesse Bretonne au xviiie siècle*. 2 vols. Paris.

Michels, R. (1914), *Probleme der Sozialphilosophie*. Leipzig and Berlin.

Miliukov, P. *et al.* (1932-1933), *Histoire de Russie.* 3 vols. Paris.

Miliukov, P. (1896-1903), *Ocherki po istorii russkoi kul'tury.* 3 vols in 2. St. Petersburg.

Millot, J. (1937), *Le régime féodal en Franche-Comté au xviiie siècle.* Besançon.

Mingay, G. E. (1963), "The Agricultural Revolution in English History: a Reconsideration," *Agricultural History*, XXXVII.

Mingay, G. E. (1969), "Dr. Kerridge's 'Agricultural Revolution': a Comment," *Agricultural History*, XLIII.

Ministerstvo Gosudarstvennykh Imuschestv (1858), *Materialy dlia Statistiki Rossii.* 2 vols. St. Petersburg.

Ministerstvo Gosudarstvennykh Imushchestv (1869), *Ob'iasneniia k khoziaistvenno-statisticheskomu atlasu evropeiskoi Rossii*, I. Vil'son, ed. 4th ed. St. Petersburg.

Ministerstvo Gosudarstvennykh Imushchestv (1861), *Statisticheskii obzor gosudarstvennykh imuchestv za 1858 god.* St. Petersburg.

Mirabeau, V. de Riqueti, Marquis de (1970), *L'ami des hommes.* Reprinted from 1756 ed. Aalen.

Mironov, B. N. (1973), "The 'Price Revolution' in Eighteenth Century Russia," *Soviet Studies in History*, XI.

Mischler, E. and J. Ulbrich, eds. (1905-1909), *Österreichisches Staatswörterbuch*, 2nd ed. 4 vols. Vienna.

Mises, L. von (1902), *Die Entwicklung des gutsherrlich-bäuerlichen Verhältnisses in Galizien (1772-1848).* Vienna.

Mitchell, B. R. (1975), *European Historical Statistics, 1750-1970.* London.

Mitchell, B. R. and P. Deane (1962), *Abstract of British Historical Statistics.* Cambridge.

Mitrany, D. (1930), *The Land and the Peasant in Rumania.* London.

Mittheilungen der k.k. mähr.-schles. Gesellschaft zur Beförderung des Ackerbaues.

Moericke, O. (1905), *Die Agrarpolitik des Markgrafen Karl Friedrich von Baden.* Karlsruhe.

Molesworth, R. (1694), *An Account of Denmark as it was in the Year 1692.* 3rd ed. London.

Moore, B. (1966), *Social Origins of Dictatorship and Democracy.* Boston.

Morier, R.B.D. (1971), "The Agrarian Legislation of Prussia during the Present Century," J. W. Probyn, ed., *Systems of Land Tenure in Various Countries.* Reprinted from 1881 ed. New York.

Morineau, M. (1971), *Les faux-semblants d'un démarrage économique: agriculture et démographie en France au xviiie siècle.* Paris.

Morineau, M. (1968), "Y a-t-il eu une révolution agricole en France au xviiie siècle?," *Revue historique*, CCXXXIX.

Mortensen, H. and G. (1955), "Über die Entstehung des ostdeutschen Grossgrundbesitzes," *Nachrichten der Akademie der Wissenschaften in Göttingen*, i, Philologisch-Historische Klasse.

Mottek, H. (1964), *Wirtschaftsgeschichte Deutschlands*. 4th ed. 2 vols. Berlin.

Mühlen H. von zur (1951), "Zur Entstehung der Gutsherrschaft in Oberschlesien," *Vierteljahrschrift für Sozial- und Wirtschaftsgeschichte*, xxxviii.

Müller, H.-H. (1964a), "Der agrarische Fortschritt und die Bauern in Brandenburg vor den Reformen von 1807," *Zeitschrift für Geschichtswissenschaft*, xii.

Müller, H.-H. (1965a), "Die Bodennutzungssysteme und die Separation in Brandenburg vor den Agrarreformen von 1807," *Jahrbuch für Wirtschaftsgeschichte*, 1965, pt. iii.

Müller, H.-H. (1969), "Christopher Brown—an English Farmer in Brandenburg-Prussia in the Eighteenth Century," *Agricultural History Review*, xvii.

Müller, H.-H. (1965), "Domänen und Domänenpächter in Brandenburg-Preussen im 18. Jahrhundert," *Jahrbuch für Wirtschaftsgeschichte*, 1965, pt. iv.

Müller, H.-H. (1964b), "Die Entwicklung der Ackerbauverhältnisse in der märkischen Landwirtschaft vor den Agrarreformen von 1807," *Jahrbuch für Wirtschaftsgeschichte*, 1964, pt. i.

Müller, H.-H. (1967), "Märkische Landwirtschaft vor den Agrarreformen von 1807," *Veröffentlichungen des Bezirksheimatmuseums Potsdam*, xiii.

Muncy, L. W. (1944), *The Junker in the Prussian Administration under William II*, 1888-1914. Providence.

Muyden, B. van (1898), *Histoire de la nation suisse*, ii. Lausanne.

Nabholz, H. *et al.* (1932-1938), *Geschichte der Schweiz*. 2 vols. Zurich.

Neumann, A. (1911), *Die Bewegung der Löhne der ländlichen "freien" Arbeiter*. [*Landwirtschaftlicher Jahrbücher*, xl, Ergänzungsband iii.]

Neupokoev, V. I. (1962), " 'Vol'nye' liudi Litvy v pervoi polovine XIX v.," *Ezhegodnik po agrarnoi istorii vostochnoi Evropy 1960 g*. Kiev.

Nielsen, A.E.H. (1933), *Daenische Wirtschaftsgeschichte*. Jena.

Nikishin, I. I. (1953), "Nekotorye voprosy ekonomiki krepostnogo khoziaistva pervoi poloviny XIX veka," *Istoricheskie zapiski*, no. 44.

Noyes, J. O. (1858), *Roumania: the Border Land of the Christian and the Turk*. New York.

Nuttonson, M. Y. (1958), *Rye-Climate Relationships and the Use of Phenology in Ascertaining the Thermal and Photo-thermal Requirements of Rye*. Washington.

List of Works Cited

Oechsli, W. (1903-1913), *Geschichte der Schweiz im neunzehnten Jahrhundert.* 2 vols. Leipzig.

Oekonomische Neuigkeiten und Verhandlungen.

Oesterreichische Statistik, published by k.k. Statistischen Zentralkommission. Vienna.

Oesterreichisches Statistisches Handbuch, published by k.k. Statistischen Central-Commission. Vienna.

Oţetea, A., ed. (1975), *The History of the Romanian People.* Transl. from Romanian. New York.

Oţetea, A. (1955), "Le second asservissement des paysans roumains (1746-1821)," Comité national des historiens de la République Populaire de Roumanie, *Nouvelles études d'histoire présentées au Xe Congrès des Sciences Historiques Rome 1955.* Bucharest.

Oţetea, A. (1960), "Le second servage dans les Principautés danubiennes (1831-1864)," Comité national des historiens de la République Populaire Roumaine, *Nouvelles études d'histoire publiées à l'occasion du XIe Congrès des Sciences Historiques Stockholm, 1960.* Bucharest.

Otruba, G. (1963), *Die Wirtschaftspolitik Maria Theresias.* Vienna.

Paget, J. (1839), *Hungary and Transylvania.* 2 vols. London.

Pallas, P. S. (1794), *Voyages du Professeur Pallas dans plusieurs provinces de l'empire de Russie et dans l'Asie septentionale.* Transl. from German. 8 vols. Paris.

Palmade, G. P. (1972), *French Capitalism in the Nineteenth Century.* Transl. from French. Newton Abbot.

Palmer, F. B. (1907), *Peerage Law in England.* London.

Palmer, R. R. (1959-1964), *The Age of the Democratic Revolution.* 2 vols. Princeton.

Papers of Thomas Jefferson, J. P. Boyd, ed. 18 vols. Princeton.

Parain, C. (1952), "Travaux récents sur l'histoire rurale du Danemark," *Annales de Normandie*, II.

Parain, C. (1945), "Une vieille tradition démocratique: les assemblées de communauté," *La Pensée*, 1945, no. 4.

Pares, B. (1907), *Russia and Reform.* London.

Patterson, A. J. (1869), *The Magyars. Their Country and Institutions.* 2 vols. London.

Pavlovsky, G. (1968), *Agricultural Russia on the Eve of the Revolution.* Reprinted from 1930 ed. New York.

Pazhitnov, K. A. (1940), "K voprosu o roli krepostnogo truda v doreformennoi promyshlennosti," *Istoricheskie zapiski*, no. 7.

Pedersen, O. K. (1958). *Dansk Landbrugsbibliografi*, I. Copenhagen.

Petersen, A. B. (1973), *The Development of Cooperative Credit in Rural Russia, 1871-1914.* Unpublished dissertation, Cornell University.

Petitpierre, A. (1971), *Un demi-siècle de l'histoire économique de Neuchâtel*, 1791-1848. Neuchâtel.

Peyrer, C. (1877), *Die Regelung der Grundeigenthums-Verhältnisse*. Vienna.

Pfeifer, G. (1956), "The Quality of Peasant Living in Central Europe," ← *Man's Role in Changing the Face of the Earth*. Chicago.

Philippe, R. (1961), "Vie matérielle et comportements biologiques," *Annales E.S.C.*, XVI.

Philippot, R. (1963), "L'application de la Réforme dans la province de Kharkov," R. Portal, ed., *Le statut des paysans libérés du servage 1861-1961*. Paris, The Hague.

Picheta, V. I. (1911), "Pomeshchich'e khoziaistve nakanune reformy," Obshchestvo rasprostraneniia technicheskikh znanii, Uchebnye otdel, Istoricheskaia komissia, *Velikaia Reforma*, III, Moscow.

Pintner, W. McK. (1967), *Russian Economic Policy under Nicholas I.* Ithaca.

Pintner, W. McK. (1970), "The Social Characteristics of the Early Nineteenth-Century Russian Bureaucracy," *Slavic Review*, XXIX.

Pipes, R. ed. (1959), *Karamzin's Memoir on Ancient and Modern Russia.* Cambridge.

Pokhilevich, D. L. (1952), "Perevod gosudarstvennykh krest'ian Litvy i Belorussii v seredine XVIII v. c denezhnoi renty na obrabotochnuiu," *Istoricheskie zapiski*, no. 39.

Pokhilevich, D. L. (1966), "Pomest'e Belorussii i Litvy vo vtoroi polovine XVIII v.," *Ezhegodnik po agrarnoi istorii vostochnoi Evropy 1964 god.* Kishenev.

Poliakoff, J. (1916), *Die bäuerlichen Loskaufszahlungen in Russland.* 2 vols. Munich.

Polish Encyclopedia, Economic Life of Poland, III (1922). Publication of the Polish National Committee of America. Geneva.

Pollard, S., and C. Holmes (1968), *Documents of European Economic History*, I. London.

Polnoe sobranie zakonov Rossiiskoi Imperii s 1649 goda. 1st series, 45 vols. in 48, St. Petersburg, 1839-1843; 2nd series, 1825-1881. 55 vols. St. Petersburg.

Portal, R. ed. (1963), *Le statut des paysans libérés du servage 1861-1961*. Paris.

Porter, R. K. (1809), *Travelling Sketches in Russia and Sweden 1805-1808*. London.

Preradovich, N. von (1955), *Die Führungsschichten in Österreich und Preussen (1804-1918)*. Wiesbaden.

Preyer, J. N. (1838), *Des ungrischen Bauer's früherer und gegenwärtiger Zustand*. Pesth.

Pribram, K. (1907), *Geschichte der österreichischen Gewerbepolitik bon 1740 bis 1860*, I. Leipzig.

Produktschap voor Gedistilleerde Dranken (1968), *Hoeveel Alcoholhoudende Dranken worden er in de Wereld gedronken*. Schiedam.

Proskuriakova, N. A. (1973), "Razmeshchenie i struktura dvorianskogo zemlevladeniia evropeiskoi Rossii v kontse XIX-nachale XX veka," *Istoriia SSSR*, 1973, no. 1.

Proust, M. (1970), *Time Regained*, transl. by A. Mayor. London.

Puhle, H.-J. (1975), *Agrarische Interessenpolitik und preussischer Konservatismus im wilhelminischen Reich*. Bonn.

Purs, J. (1962), "Die Aufhebung der Hörigkeit und die Grundentlastung in den böhmischen Ländern," *Deuxième Conference Internationale d'Histoire Economique 1962*. Congrès et Colloques, VIII.

Purs, J. (1963), "Die Entwicklung des Kapitalismus in der Landwirtschaft der böhmischen Länder in der Zeit von 1849 bis 1879," *Jahrbuch für Wirtschaftsgeschichte*, 1963, pt. iii.

Puskás, J. (1961), "Die kapitalistischen Grosspachten in Ungarn am Ende des 19. Jahrhunderts," *Studien zur Geschichte der Österreichisch-Ungarischen Monarchie*. Studia Historica Academiae Scientiarum Hungaricae, no. 51. Budapest.

Pyler, E. J. (1973), *Baking Science and Technology*. 2 vols. Chicago.

Quesnay, F. (1958), "Analyse de la formule arithmetique du Table au Économique," Institut National d'Études Démographique, *François Quesnay et la Physiocratie*, II. Paris.

Quirin, K. H. (1952), *Herrschaft und Gemeinde nach mitteldeutschen Quellen des 12. bis 18. Jahrhunderts*. Göttingen.

Radishchev, A. N. (1958), *A Journey from St. Petersburg to Moscow*, ed. by R. P. Thaler, Cambridge.

Raeff, M. (1966), *Origins of the Russian Intelligentsia: the Eighteenth Century Nobility*. New York.

Raeff, M. (1957), *Michael Speransky. Statesman of Imperial Russia 1772-1839*. The Hague.

Raeff, M. (1970), "Pugachev's Rebellion," R. Forster and J. P. Greene, eds., *Preconditions of Revolution in Early Modern Europe*. Baltimore.

Raeff, M. (1957), "The Russian Autocracy and its Officials," *Harvard Slavic Studies*, IV. Cambridge.

Rappard, W. E. (1912), *Le facteur économique dans l'avènement de la démocratie moderne en Suisse*. Geneva.

Rashin, A. G. (1940), *Formirovanie promyshlennogo proletariata v Rossii*. Moscow.

Rashin, A. G. (1956), *Naselenie Rossii za 100 let, 1811-1913*. Moscow.

Raveau, P. (1926), *L'agriculture et les classes paysannes. La transformation de la propriété dans le Haut Poitou au xvie siècle*. Paris.

Ravnholt, H. (1947), *The Danish Co-operative Movement*. Copenhagen.

Razgon, A. M. (1959), "Sel'skoe khoziaistvo krest'ian Ivanovskoi votchiny Sheremetevykh vo vtoroi polovine XVIII veka," Akademiia Nauk, Institut Istorii, *Materialy po istorii sel'skogo khoziaistva i krest'ianstva SSSR*, III. Moscow-Leningrad.

Razous, P. (1944), "L'évolution de l'agriculture française métropolitaine à travers l'histoire," *Journal de la Société de Statistique de Paris*, LXXXV.

Recordon, F. (1821), *Lettres sur la Valachie*. Paris.

Redaktsionnye komissii dlia sostavlenia polozheniia o krest'ianakh vykhodiashchikh iz krepostnoi zavisimosti, *Pervoe izdanie materialov*, 18 vols. St. Petersburg, 1859-1860.

Redlich, F. (1955), "Entrepreneurship in the Initial Stages of Industrialization," *Weltwirtschaftliches Archiv*, LXXV.

Redlich, F. (1953), "A German Eighteenth Century Iron Works during its First Hundred Years," *Bulletin of the Business Historical Society*, XXVII.

Regierungs-Blatt für das Königreich Württemberg in Auszuge, 1841, II.

Règlement organique de la Principauté de Moldavie. (1834). Brussels.

Reinhard, M. (1956), "Élite et noblesse dans la seconde moitié du xviiie siècle," *Revue d'histoire moderne et contemporaine*, III.

Revesz, L. (1964), *Der osteuropäische Bauer*. Bern.

Richard, G. (1962), "La noblesse de France et les sociétés par actions à la fin du xviiie siècle," *Revue d'histoire économique et sociale*, XL.

Richter, K. (1964), "Über den Strukturwandel der Grundbesitzenden Oberschicht Böhmen in der neueren Zeit," *Problème der böhmischen Geschichte*. Veröffentlichungen des Collegium Carolinum, 16. Munich.

Rieber, A. J. ed. (1966), *The Politics of Autocracy. Letters of Alexander II to Prince A. I. Bariatinskii, 1857-1864*. The Hague.

Riemann, F.-K. (1953), *Ackerbau und Viehhaltung im vorindustriellen Deutschland*. Jahrbuch der Albertus-Universität zu Königsberg/Pr. Beiheft, III. Kitzingen-Main.

Rigaudière, A. (1965), "La Haute-Auvergne face à l'agriculture nouvelle au xviiie siècle," *Études d'histoire économique rural au xviiie siècle*. Travaux et recherches de la Faculté de Droit et des Sciences Économiques de Paris, "Sciences Historiques" no. 6. Paris.

Riker, T. W. (1931), *The Making of Roumania*. Oxford.

Ritter, G. (1936), *Friedrich der Grosse*. Leipzig.

Roberts, H. L. (1951), *Rumania, Political Problems of an Agrarian State*. London.

Robinson, G.T. (1932), *Rural Russia under the Old Regime*. New York.

Rogin, L. (1931), *The Introduction of Farm Machinery in its Relation to the Productivity of Labor in the Agriculture of the United States during the Nineteenth Century.* Berkeley.

Romanovich-Slavatinskii, A. (1870), *Dvorianstvo v Rossii ot nachala XVIII veky do otmeny krepostnago prava.* St. Petersburg.

Roos, H. (1971), "Der Adel der Polnischen Republik im vorrevolutionären Europa," in R. Vierhaus, ed., *Der Adel vor der Revolution.* Göttingen.

Rosdolsky, R. (1951), "The Distribution of the Agrarian Product in Feudalism," *Journal of Economic History*, xi.

Rosdolsky, R. (1954), "Die ostgalizische Dorfgemeinschaft und ihre Auflösung," *Vierteljahrschrift für Sozial- und Wirtschaftsgeschichte*, xli.

Rosenberg, H. (1958), *Bureaucracy, Aristocracy and Autocracy.* Cambridge.

Rosenberg, H. (1969), "Die Pseudodemokratisierung der Rittergutsbesitzerklasse," H. Rosenberg, *Probleme der deutschen Sozialgeschichte.* Frankfurt a. M.

Rostworowski, A.J.F.C. von (1896), *Die Entwicklung der bäuerlichen Verhältnisse im Königreich Polen im 19. Jahrhundert.* Jena.

Roupnel, G. (1922), *La ville et la campagne au xviie siècle. Étude sur les populations du pays Dijonais.* Paris.

Rozdolski, R. (1961), *Die grosse Steuer- und Agrarreform Joseph II.* Warsaw.

Rozier, F. ed. (1785-1800), *Cours complet d'agriculture . . . ou dictionnaire universel d'agriculture.* 10 vols. Paris.

Rudé, G. (1956), "La taxation populaire de Mai 1775 à Paris et dans la région parisienne," *Annales historiques de la Révolution française*, no. 143.

Rudé, G. (1961), "La taxation populaire de Mai 1775 en Picardie, en Normandie et dans le Beauvaisis," *Annales historiques de la Révolution française*, no. 165.

Rudloff, H. L. (1915), "Beiträge zur Geschichte der Bauernbefreiung und der bäuerlichen Grundentlastung in Kurhessen," *Jahrbücher für Nationalökonomie und Statistik*, 3rd ser., l.

Ruffmann, K. H. (1961), "Russischer Adel als Sondertypus der europäischen Adelswelt," *Jahrbücher für Geschichte Osteuropas.* ix.

Rumler, A. (1921-1925), "Die Bestrebungen zur Befreiung der Privatbauern in Preussen 1797-1806," *Forschungen zur Brandenburgischen und Preussischen Geschichte*, xxxiii, xxxiv, xxxvii.

Rusinski, W. (1960), "Hauptprobleme der Fronwirtschaft im 16. bis zum 18. Jahrhundert in Polen und den Nachbarländer," *Première Conférence Internationale d'Histoire Économique. Stockholm, 1960.* Paris, The Hague.

Rusinski, W. (1973), "Veränderungen in der Struktur und ökonomischen Lage der polnischen Bauernschaft an der Wende vom 18. zum 19. Jahrhundert," D. Berindei *et al.* eds., *Der Bauer Mittel- und Östereuropas im sozio-ökonomischen Wandel des 18. und 19. Jahrhunderts.* Cologne.

Russkie istoriko-etnograficheskii atlas (1967). Moscow.

Rutkowski, J. (1953), *Ekonomicheskaia istoriia Pol'ski.* Transl. from Polish. Moscow.

Rutkowski, J. (1926-1927), "La régime agraire en Pologne au xviiie siècle," *Revue d'histoire* économique et sociale, xiv, xv.

Saalfeld, D. (1960), *Bauernwirtschaft und Gutsbetrieb in der vorindustriellen Zeit.* Stuttgart.

Saalfeld, D. (1964), "Die Bedeutung des Getreides für die Haushaltsausgaben städtischer Verbraucher in der zweiten Hälfte des 18. Jahrhunderts," H. G. Schlotter, ed., *Landwirtschaft und ländliche Gesellschaft in Geschichte und Gegenwart.* Hannover.

Saalfeld, D. (1963), "Zur Frage des bäuerlichen Landverlustes in Zusammenhang mit den preussischen Agrarreformen," *Zeitschrift für Agrargeschichte und Agrarsoziologie,* xi.

Saint-Jacob, P. de (1962), *Documents relatifs à la communauté villageoise en Bourgogne du milieu du xviie siècle à la Révolution.* Paris.

Saint-Jacob, P. de (1960), *Les paysans de la Bourgogne du nord au dernier siècle de l'ancien régime.* Paris.

Salz, A. (1913), *Geschichte der böhmischen Industrie,* Munich.

Sammlung der Gesetze und Verordnungen für das Königreich Sachsen vom Jahre 1832. Dresden.

Sammlung Preussischer Gesetze und Verordnungen (1819), arranged by C.H.L. Rabe, ix. Halle and Berlin.

Samoilov, S. I. (1955), "Narodno-osvoboditel'noe vosstanie 1821 g. v Valakhii," *Voprosy istorii,* 1955, no. 10.

Samoilovich, V. P. (1977), *Narodnoe arkhitekturnoe tvorchestvo.* Kiev.

Scharling, W. (1909), "Die Bauernbefreiung in Dänemark," *Handwörterbuch der Staatswissenschaften,* 3rd ed. ii.

Scharling, W. (1894), "Die Bestrebung zur Sicherung des Kleingrundbesitzes in Dänemark," W. Hasbach, *Die englische Landarbeiter in den letzten hundert Jahren und die Einhegungen.* Leipzig.

Scheibert, P. (1973), *Die russische Agrarreform vom 1861.* Cologne.

Scheibert, P. Ed. (1972), *Die russischen politischen Parteien von 1905 bis 1917.* Darmstadt.

Schiemann, T. (1904-1919), *Geschichte Russlands unter Kaiser Nikolaus I.* 4 vols. Berlin, Leipzig.

Schiff, O. (1924), "Die deutschen Bauernaufstände von 1525 bis 1789," *Historische Zeitschrift,* cxxx.

Schiff, W. (1898), *Österreichs Agrarpolitik seit der Grundentlastung.* Tübingen.

Schlögl, A. ed. (1954), *Bayerische Agrargeschichte. Die Entwicklung der Land- und Forstwirtschaft seit Beginn des 19. Jahrhunderts*. Munich.

Schlözer, A. L. (1793), *Allgemeines Stats Recht und Stats Verfassungs Lere*. Göttingen.

Schmidt, G.V.L. (1932), *Der Schweizer Bauer im Zeitalter des Frühkapitalismus*. 2 vols. Bern.

Schnabel, G. N. (1846), *Statistik der landwirtschaftlichen Industrie*. Prague.

Schnitzler, J. H. (1866), *Les institutions de la Russie depuis les réformes de l'empereur Alexandre II*. Paris.

Schönebaum, H. (1917), "Agrarrechtliche Reformen in Sachsen seit der Mitte des XVIII. Jahrhunderts bis 1840," *Landesbauernschaft Sachsen Wochenblatt*, LXV.

Schorer, H. (1904), "Das Bettlertum in Kurbayern in der zweiten Hälte des 18. Jahrhunderts," *Forschungen zur Geschichte Bayerns*, XII.

Schremmer, E. (1966). "Die Auswirkung der Bauernbefreiung hinsichtlich der bäuerlichen Verschuldung, der Gantfälle und des Besitzwechsels von Grund und Boden," K. E. Born, ed., *Moderne deutsche Wirtschaftsgeschichte*. Cologne-Berlin.

Schremmer, E. (1963), *Die Bauernbefreiung in Hohenlohe*. Stuttgart.

Schröder-Lembke, G. (1964), "Englische Einflüsse auf die deutsche Gutswirtschaft im 18. Jahrhundert," *Zeitschrift für Agrargeschichte und Agrarsoziologie*, XII.

Schröder-Lembke, G. (1954), "Entstehung und Verbreitung der Mehrfelderwirtschaft in Nordostdeutschland," *Zeitschrift für Agrargeschichte und Agrarsoziologie*, II.

Schröder-Lambke, G. (1956), "Die mecklenburgische Koppelwirtschaft," *Zeitschrift für Agrargeschichte und Agrarsoziologie*, IV.

Schröder-Lambke, G. (1959), "Wesen und Verbreitung der Zweifeldwirtschaft im Rheingebiet," *Zeitschrift für Agrargeschichte und Agrarsoziologie*, VII.

Schumpeter, J. A. (1939), *Business Cycles*. 2 vols. New York.

Schwabe, A. (1928). *Grundriss der Agrargeschichte Lettlands*. Riga.

Schwerin von Krosigk, L. (1957), *Die grosse Zeit des Feuers*. 2 vols. Tübingen.

Sclafert, T. (1941), "Usages agraires dans les régions provençales avant le xviiie siècle," *Revue de géographie alpine*, XXIX.

Sée, H. (1906), *Les classes rurale en Bretagne, du xvie siècle à la Révolution*. Paris.

Sée, H. (1921), *Esquisse d'une histoire du régime agraire en Europe aux xviiie et xixe siècles*. Paris.

Sée, H. (1939-1942), *Histoire économique de la France*. 2 vols. Paris.

Sée, H. (1923), "La mise en valeur des terres incultes défrichements et dessèchements à la fin de l'ancien régime," *Revue d'histoire économique et sociale*, XI.

Sée, H. (1924), "Les troubles agraires en Haute Bretagne (1790-1791)," *Bulletin d'histoire économique de la Révolution, 1920-1921*. Paris.

Sée, H. (1924), *La vie économique et les classes sociales en France au xviiie siècle*. Paris.

Seebohm, F. (1890), *The English Village Community*. 4th ed. London.

Semevskii, V. I. (1881-1901), *Krest'iane v tsarstvovanie imperatritsy Ekateriny II*. 2 vols. St. Petersburg.

Semevskii, V. I. (1888), *Krest'ianskii vopros v Rossii v XVIII i pervoi polovine XIX veka*. 2 vols. St. Petersburg.

Sering, M. (1908), *Erbrecht und Agrarverfassung in Schleswig-Holstein*. [*Landwirtschaftlicher Jahrbücher*, XXXVII. Ergänzungsband V.]

Sessional Papers, House of Commons, LXVII, 1870, part 1, "Reports from Her Majesty's Representatives respecting the Tenure of Land in the several Countries of Europe, 1869."

Shchepetov, K. N. (1947), *Krepostnoe pravo v votchinakh Sheremetevykh*. Moscow.

Shcherbatov, M. M. (1969), *On the Corruption of Morals in Russia*, transl. by A. Lentin. Cambridge.

Sheppard, T. F. (1971), *Lourmarin in the Eighteenth Century*. Baltimore.

Shepukova, N. M. (1964), "Ob izmenenii razmerov dushevladeniia pomeshchikov Evropeiskoi Rossii v pervoi chetverti XVIII-pervoi polovine XIX v.," *Ezhegodnik po agrarnoi istorii vostochnoi Evropy, 1963 g*. Vilna.

Shlossberg, E. P. (1959), "K voprosu ob izmenenii feodal'noi renty v Belorussii XVII-XVIII vekov (po dannym inventarei feodal'nykh vladenii)," *Ezhegodnik po agrarnoi istorii vostochnoi Evropy, 1958 g*. Tallin.

Shtrange, M. M. (1956), *Russkoe obshchestvo i Frantsuzskaia Revoliutsiia 1789-1794 gg*. Moscow.

Siegert, H. (1971), *Adel in Österreich*. Vienna.

Sievers, K. D. (1970), *Volkskultur und Aufklärung im Spiegel der Schleswig-Holsteinischen Provinzialberichte*. Neumünster.

Simkhowitsch, W. G. (1899), "Die Bauernbefreiung in Russland," *Handwörterbuch der Staatswissenschaften*, 2nd ed., II.

Simon, W. M. (1955), *The Failure of the Prussian Reform Movement, 1807-1819*. Ithaca.

Sinclair, J. (1831), *The Correspondence of the Right Honourable Sir John Sinclair*. 2 vols. London.

Sion, J. (1909), *Les paysans de la Normandie Orientale*. Paris.

Sivkov, K. V. (1962), "K voprosu o rassloenii krest'ian v krupnom imenii tsentral'no-chernozemnoi polosy Rossii," Akademiia Nauk, Institut Istorii, *Materialy po istorii sel'skogo khoziaistva i krest'ianstva SSSR*, v. Moscow.

Sivkov, K. V. (1959), "Nekotorye itogi zernovogo proizvodstva v Evropeiskoi Rossii na rubezhe XVIII-XIX vv.," *Ezhegodnik po agrarnoi istorii vostochnoi Evropy 1958 g.* Tallin.

Sivkov, K. V. (1961), "Novye iavleniia v tekhnike i organizatsii sel'skogo khoziaistva Rossii vo vtoroi polovine XVIII v.," *Ezhegodnik po agrarnoi istorii vostochnoi Evropy 1959 g.* Moscow.

Sivkov, K. V. (1951), *Ocherki po istorii krepostnogo khoziaistva i krest'ianskogo dvizheniia v Rossii v pervoi polovine XIX veka.* Moscow.

Sivkov, K. V. (1952), "Voprosy sel'skogo khoziaistva v Russkikh zhurnalakh poslednei treti XVIII v.," Akademiia Nauk, Institut Istorii, *Materialy po istorii zemledeliia SSSR*, I. Moscow.

Skalweit, A. (1942), *Das Dorfhandwerk vor Aufhebung des Städtezwangs.* Frankfurt am Main.

Skene, J. H. (1854), *The Danubian Principalities.* 2 vols. London.

Skerpan, A. (1964), "The Russian National Economy and Emancipation," A. Ferguson and A. Levin, eds., *Essays in Russian History.* Hampden.

Skovgaard, K. (1950), "Consolidation of Agricultural Land in Denmark," B. O. Binns, ed., *The Consolidation of Fragmented Agricultural Holdings.* Washington.

Skrebitskii, A. (1862-1868), *Krest'ianskoe dielo v tsarstvovanie imperatora Aleksandra II.* 4 vols. in 5. St. Petersburg.

Skrubbeltrang, F. (1953), *Agricultural Development and Rural Reform in Denmark* (FAO UN, Agricultural Studies no. 22). Rome.

Skrubbeltrang, F. (1961), "Developments in Tenancy in Eighteenth-Century Denmark as a Move towards Peasant Proprietorship," *Scandinavian Economic History Review*, IX.

Slicher van Bath, B. H. (1963), *The Agrarian History of Western Europe A. D. 500-1850.* Transl. from Dutch. London.

Slicher van Bath, B. H. (1969), "Eighteenth Century Agriculture on the Continent of Europe: Evolution or Revolution?" *Agricultural History*, XLIII.

Slicher van Bath, B. H. (1965), "Die europäischen Agrarverhältnisse im 17. und der ersten Hälfte des 18. Jahrhunderts," *A. A. G. Bijdragen*, XIII.

Slicher van Bath, B. H. (1960), "The Influence of Economic Conditions on the Development of Agricultural Tools and Machines in History," J. L. Mey, *Mechanization in Agriculture.* Amsterdam.

Slokar, J. (1914), *Geschichte der österreichischen Industrie und ihrer Förderung unter Kaiser Franz I.* Vienna.

Smith, A. (1937), *An Inquiry into the Nature and Causes of the Wealth of Nations.* New York.

Smith, A. (1969), *The Theory of Moral Sentiments*. Reprinted from 1759 edition. New Rochelle.

Smith, C. T. (1967), *An Historical Geography of Western Europe before 1800*. London.

Soboul, A. (1958), "Les campagnes Montpelliéraines à la fin de l'ancien régime. Propriété et cultures d'après les compoix," Commission de recherche et de publication des documents relatifs à la vie économique de la Révolution, *Mémoires et documents*, XII.

Soboul, A. (1970), *La civilisation et la Révolution française*, I. Paris.

Soboul, A. (1957), "La communauté rurale (xviiie-xixe siècle)," *Revue de Synthèse*, 3rd ser., LXXVIII.

Soboul, A. (1960), *La France à la veille de la Révolution*, I. Paris.

Solov'ev, Ia. A. (1880-1884), "Zapiski Senatora Ia. A. Solov'eva o krest'ianskom dele," *Russkaia starina*, XXVII, XXX, XXI, XXXIII, XXXIV, XXXVI, XXXVII, 1884, no. 2.

Sombart, W. (1928), *Die moderne Kapitalismus*. 3 vols. in 6. Munich and Leipzig.

Soreau, E. (1937), *La chute de l'ancien régime*. Paris.

Sozin, I. V. (1959), "Pomeshchich'e khoziaistvo Pol'shi v 70-90-e gody XVIII v.," *Istoricheskie nauki*, I.

Speier, H. (1936), "Militarism in the Eighteenth Century," *Social Research*, III.

Spira, G. (1968), "La dernière génération des serfs de Hongrie: l'exemple du comitat de Pest," *Annales É. S. C.*, XXIII.

Springer, A. (1863), *Geschichte Oesterreichs seit dem Wiener Frieden 1809*. 2 vols. Leipzig.

Springer, J. (1840), *Statistik des österreichischen Kaiserstaates*. 2 vols. Vienna.

Stamm, F. (1856), *Verhältnisse der Volks-, Land- und Forstwirthschaft des Königreiches Böhmen*. Prague.

Stark, W. (1952), "Die Abhängigkeitsverhältnisse der gutsherrlichen Bauern Böhmens im 17. und 18. Jahrhundert," *Jahrbücher für Nationalökonomie und Statistik*, CLXIV.

Stark, W. (1957), "Der Ackerbau der böhmischen Gutswirtschaften im 17. und 18. Jahrhundert," *Zeitschrift für Agrargeschichte und Agrarsoziologie*, V.

Stark, W. (1937), "Niedergang und Ende des landwirtschaftlichen Grossbetriebs in den böhmischen Ländern," *Jahrbücher für Nationalökonomie und Statistik*, CXLIV.

Starr, S. F. (1972), *Decentralization and Self-Government in Russia 1830-1870*. Princeton.

Statens Statistike Bureau (1874), *Résumé des principaux faits statistique du Danemark*. Copenhagen.

Statesman's Year Book. London.

Statistisches Handbuch für das Deutsche Reich (1907), pt. 1. Berlin.

Statisticheskiia tablitsy Rossiiskoi Imperii. Nalichnoe naselenie imperii za 1858 god. A. Buschen, ed. St. Petersburg, 1863.

Statisticheskii ezhegodnik Rossii. publ. by Tsentral'nyi statisticheskii komitet. St. Petersburg.

Statistisk Aarbog, publ. by the Statistiske Departement. Copenhagen.

Steensberg, A. (1951), "Modern Research of Agrarian History in Denmark," *Laos*, 1951.

Stein, R. (1918-1934), *Die Umwandlung der Agrarverfassung Ostpreussens durch die Reform des neunzehnten Jahrhunderts*. 3 vols. Jena.

Steinbach, F. and E. Becker (1932), "Geschichtliche Grundlagen der kommunalen Selbstverwaltung in Deutschland," *Rheinisches Archiv*, xx.

Stekl, H. (1973), *Österreichs Aristokratie im Vormärz*. Vienna.

Ştirbu, S. (1955), "Les rapports de collaboration entre Tudor Vladimirescu et les mouvements de libération des pays de l'est européen," *Nouvelles études d'histoire présentées au Xe Congrès des Sciences Historiques Rome 1955*. Bucharest.

Stolz, O. (1940), "Die Bauernbefreiung in Süddeutschland im Zusammenhang der Geschichte," *Vierteljahrschrift für Sozial- und Wirtschaftsgeschichte*, xxxiii.

Stolz, O. (1936), "Weistum und Grundherrschaft," *Vierteljahrschrift für Sozial- und Wirtschaftsgeschichte*, xxix.

Stölzl, C. (1971), *Die Ära Bach in Böhmen*. Munich.

Storch, P. (1848-1850), "Der Bauernstand in Russland in geschichtlicher, statistischer, staatsrechtlicher und landwirtschaftlicher Hinsicht," *Mittheilungen der Kaiserliches Freien Ökonomischen Gesellschaft zu St. Petersburg*.

Strakosch, S. von (1917), *Die Grundlagen der Agrarwirtschaft in Österreich*. Vienna.

Strazdunaite, R. Iu. (1961), "Sel'skoe zapasnye magaziny, vspomogatel'nye kassi i krest'ianskie sudy v Litve v pervoi polovine, XIX v.," *Ezhegodnik po agrarnoi istorii vostochnoi Evropy 1959 g*. Moscow.

Strod, G. P. (1962), "Merinosovoe ovtsevodstvo v Latvii v pervoi polovine XIX v." *Ezhegodnik po agrarnoi istorii vostochnoi Evropy 1960 g*. Kiev.

Strod, G. P. (1963), "Nachalo primeneniia sel'skokhoziaistvennykh mashin v Latvii (konets XVIII -nachalo 60-kh godov XIX v.)," *Ezhegodnik po agrarnoi istorii vostochnoi Evropy 1961 g*. Riga.

Strod, G. P. (1959), "Perekhod ot parovoi sistemy zemledeliia k plodosmenu v Latvii v pervoi polovine XIX veka," *Ezhegodnik po agrarnoi istorii vostochnoi Evropy 1958 g*. Tallin.

Struve, P. B. (1913), *Krepostnoe khoziaistvo*. Moscow.

Studia historica in honorem Hans Kruus (1971). Tallin.

Stulz, P. and A. Opitz (1956), *Volksbewegungen in Kursachsen zur Zeit der Französischen Revolution.* Berlin.

Sugenheim, S. (1861), *Geschichte der Aufhebung der Leibeigenschaft und Hörigkeit in Europa.* St. Petersburg.

Sutton, A. W. (1896), "Potatos," *Journal of the Royal Horticultural Society*, XIX.

Swinton, A. (1792), *Travels into Norway, Denmark and Russia in the Years 1788, 1789, 1790 and 1791.* London.

Szabó, E. (1947), "Les grands domaines en Hongrie au début des temps modernes," *Revue d'histoire comparée*, XXV.

Tafeln zur Statistik. See k.k. Direction der administrativen Statistik.

Tageblatt der Gesetze und Dekrete der gesetzgebenden Räthe der helvetischen Republik, I, 1798. Bern.

Tarlé, E. (1910), *L'industrie dans les campagnes en France à la fin de l'ancien régime.* Paris.

Tarlé, E. (1942), *Napoleon's Invasion of Russia 1812.* New York.

Tarlé, E. (1943), *Nashestvie Napoleona na Rossiiu* 1812 god. Moscow.

Tarvel, E. (1964), *Fol'vark, pan i poddannyi.* Tallin.

Tautscher, A. (1947), *Staatswirtschaftslehre des Kameralismus.* Bern.

Tcherkinsky, M. (1941), "The Evolution of the System of Succession to Landed Property in Europe," International Institute of Economics, *Monthly Bulletin of Agricultural Economics and Sociology*, XXXII.

Tebeldi, A. (1847), *Die Geldangelegenheiten Oestreichs.* Leipzig.

Tegorborski, L. (1852-1854), *Études sur les forces productives de la Russie.* 3 vols. Paris.

Teifen, T. W. (1906), *Die Besitzenden und die Besitzlosen.* Vienna.

Thaer, A. (1809-1812), *Grundsätze der rationellen Landwirthschaft.* 4 vols. Berlin.

Thirsk, J. (1967), "Enclosing and Engrossing," H.P.R. Finberg, ed., *The Agrarian History of England and Wales*, IV. Cambridge.

Thomas, W. I. and F. Znaniecki (1918-1920), *The Polish Peasant in Europe and America.* 4 vols. Chicago and Boston.

Thompson, F.M.L. (1963), *English Landed Society in the Nineteenth Century.* London.

Thorpe, H. (1951), "The Influence of Inclosure on the Form and Pattern of Rural Settlement in Denmark," *Transactions of the Institute of British Geographers*, 1951, no. 17.

Tirrell, S. (1951), *German Agrarian Politics after Bismarck's Fall.* New York.

Tobien, A. (1899-1911), *Die Agrargestzgebung Livlands im 19. Jahrhundert.* 2 vols. Berlin and Riga.

Tobien, A. (1880-1882), "Zur Geschichte der Bauernemancipation in Livland," *Baltische Monatschrift*, XXVI-XXIX.

Tocqueville, A. de (1955), *The Old Regime and the French Revolution.* Transl. from French. New York.

Tönnies, F. (1912), "Deutscher Adel im neunzehnten Jahrhundert," *Neue Rundschau*, XXIII.

Toennies, F. (1953), "Estates and Classes," R. Bendix and S. M. Lipset, eds., *Class, Status and Power.* Glencoe.

Tooke, W. (1799), *View of the Russian Empire during the Reign of Catherine II to the Close of the Present Century.* 3 vols. London.

Topolski, J. (1962), "La régression économique en Pologne du xvie au xviiie siècle," *Acta Poloniae Historica*, VII.

Torke, H.-J. (1967), "Das russische Beamtentum in der ersten Hälfte des 19. Jahrhunderts," *Forschungen zur osteuropäischen Geschichte*, XIII.

Toutain, J.-C. (1963), *La population de la France de 1700 à 1959.* Cahiers de l'Institut de Science Économique Appliquée, suppl. no. 133. Série AF no. 3.

Toutain, J.-C. (1961), *Le produit de l'agriculture française de 1700 à 1958.* 2 parts. Cahiers de l'Institut de Science Économique Appliquée, no. 115, July 1961, Série AF, no. 1.

Transehe-Roseneck, A. von (1890), *Gutsherr und Bauer in Livland im 17. und 18. Jahrhundert.* Strassburg.

Treadgold, D. W. (1957). *The Great Siberian Migration.* Princeton.

Troinitskii, A. G. (1861), *Krepostnoe naselenie v Rossii po 10-ii narodnoi perepisi.* St. Petersburg.

Trudy redaktsionnoi kommisii po peresmotru zakonopolozhenii o krest'ianakh (1903), I. St. Petersburg.

Trusova, N. S., and O. A. Bliumenfel'd (1959), "Iz istorii . . . Moskovskogo Obshchestva Sel'skogo Khoziaistva. . . ," *Materialy po istorii sel'skogo khoziastva i krest'ianstva SSSR*, III. Moscow.

Tsentral'nyi statisticheskii komitet (1858), *Statisticheskiia tablitsy Rossiskoi Imperii za 1856-i god.* St. Petersburg.

Tsentral'nyi statisticheskii komitet (1863), *Statisticheskiia tablitsy Rossiiskoi Imperii.* St. Petersburg.

Tsentral'nyi statisticheskii komitet (1907), *Statistika zemlevladeniia 1905 g.* St. Petersburg.

Tugan-Baranovsky, M. I. (1970), *The Russian Factory in the 19th Century.* Transl. from Russian. Homewood.

Turgot, A.R.J. (1913-1923), *Oeuvres*, 5 vols. G. Schelle, ed. Paris.

Turnbull, P. E. (1840), *Austria.* 2 vols. London.

Ulashchik, N. N. (1962), "Izmeneniia v khoziaistve krepostnoi Litvy i zapadnoi Belorussii v sviazi s vvedeniem novykh kul'tur (kartofel')," *Materialy po istorii sel'skogo khoziaistva i krest'ianstva SSSR*, V.

Ulashchik, N. N. (1961), "Orudia proizvodstva i sistemy zemledeliia v pomeshchich'em khoziaiste Litvy i zapadnoi Belorussi. . . ," *Ezhegodnik po agrarnoi istorii vostochnoi Evropy 1959 g.* Moscow.

Urlanis, B. Ts. (1941), *Rost naseleniia v Evrope.* Moscow.

U.S. Dept. of Agriculture (1974), *Agricultural Statistics.* Washington.

U.S. Dept. of Agriculture (1880), *Report on the Culture of the Sugar Beet and the Manufacture therefrom in France and the United States.* Special Report no. 28. Washington.

U.S. Department of Agriculture. Foreign Agricultural Service (May 1977), Foreign Agricultural Circular, FLM 2-77. Washington.

Vaillant, J. A. (1844), *La Romanie.* 3 vols. Paris.

Valarché, J. (1959), *L'économie rurale.* Paris.

Valjavec, F. (1951), *Die Entstehung der politischen Stroemungen in Deutschland, 1770-1815.* Munich.

Valran, G. (1899), *Misère et charité en Provence au xviiie siècle.* Paris.

Vandenbroeke, C. (1971), "Cultivation and Consumption of the Potato in the 17th and 18th Century," *Acta Historiae Neerlandica*, v.

Van Regemorter, J.-L. (1968), "Deux images idéales de la paysannerie russe à la fin du xviiie siècle," *Cahiers du monde russe et soviétique*, ix.

Varga, J. (1965), "Typen und Probleme der bäuerlichen Grundbesitzen in Ungarn 1767-1849," *Studia Historica Academiae Scientiarum Hungaricae*, no. 56.

Veit, R. (1841), *Lehrbuch der Landwirtschaft.* Augsburg.

Venard, M. (1957), *Bourgeois et paysans au xviie siècle.* Paris.

Vermale, F. (1911), *Les classes rurales en Savoie au xviiie siècle.* Paris.

Vidalenc, J. (1952), "L'approvisionnement de Paris en viande sous l'ancien régime," Revue d'histoire économique et sociale, xxx.

Vierhaus, R., ed. (1971), *Der Adel vor der Revolution.* Göttingen.

Vilfan, S. (1973), "Die Agrarsozialpolitik von Maria Theresia bis Kudlich," D. Berindei *et al.*, *Der Bauer Mittel- und Osteuropas im sozio-ökonomischen Wandel des 18. und 19. Jahrhunderts.* Cologne.

Village of Viriatino (1970), transl. from Russian and edited by S. Benet. New York.

Vil'son, I. See Ministerstvo Gosudarstvennykh Imuschetv (1869).

Violand, E. (1850), *Die sociale Geschichte der Revolution in Oesterreich.* Leipzig.

Volin, L. (1970), *A Century of Russian Agriculture.* Cambridge.

Vollrath, P. (1954), "Das landwirtschaftliche Beratungs- und Bildungswesen in Schleswig-Holstein am Ende des 18. und in der ersten Hälfte des 19. Jahrhunderts," *Zeitschrift für Agrargeschichte und Agrarsoziologie*, ii.

Voltaire, F.M.A. de (1816), *Dictionnaire philosophique.* 14 vols. in 7. Paris.

Vucinich, A. (1960), "The State and the Local Community," C. E. Black, ed., *The Transformation of Russian Society*. Cambridge.

Wahlen, H. and E. Jaggi (1952), *Der schweizerische Bauernkrieg 1653 und die seitherige Entwicklung des Bauernstandes*. Bern.

Walkin, J. (1962), *The Rise of Democracy in Pre-Revolutionary Russia*. New York.

Wallace, D. M. (1877), *Russia*. New York.

Walter, E. J. (1966), *Soziologie des alten Eidgenossenschaft*. Bern.

Walter, G. (1963), *Histoire des paysans de France*. Paris.

Wangermann, E. (1959), *From Joseph II to the Jacobin Trials*. Oxford.

Warriner, D. ed. (1965), *Contrasts in Emerging Societies*. Bloomington.

Warriner, D. (1953), "Some Controversial Issues in the History of Agrarian Europe," *Slavonic and East European Review*, XXXIII.

Warszawski, M. J. (1914), *Die Entwicklung der gutsherrlichbäuerlichen Verhältnisse in Polen und die Bauernfrage im XVIII. Jahrhundert*. Zurich.

Watters, F. M. (1968), "The Peasant and the Village Commune," W. S. Vucinich, ed., *The Peasant in Nineteenth Century Russia*. Stanford.

Weber, F. C. (1738-1740), *Das veränderte Russland*. 3 pts. Frankfurt, Leipzig.

Weber, M. (1953), "Class, Status, Party," R. Bendix and S. M. Lipset, eds., *Class, Status and Power*. Glencoe.

Weber-Kellermann, I. (1966), "Betrachtungen zu Wilhelm Mannhardts Umfrage von 1865 über Arbeitsgerät und bäuerliche Arbeit," *Zeitschrift für Agrargeschichte und Agrarsoziologie*, XIV.

Weidmann, W. (1968), *Die pfälzische Landwirtschaft zu Beginn des 19. Jahrhunderts*. Saarbrücken.

Weinzerl-Fischer, E. (1954), "Die Bekämpfung der Hungersnot in Böhmen, 1770-1772," *Mitteilungen des österreichischen Staatsarchiv*, VII.

Weller, K. and A. (1971), *Württembergische Geschichte im südwestdeutschen Raum*. Stuttgart.

Wellmann, I. (1968), "Esquisse d'une histoire rurale de la Hongrie depuis la première moitié de xviiie siècle jusqu'au milieu du xixe siècle," *Annales E. S. C.*, XXIII.

Widding, O. (1959), *Markfællesskab og Landskifte*. Copenhagen.

Wiese, H. (1966), "Die Fleischversorgung der nordwesteuropäischer Grossstädte vom XV. bis XIX. Jahrhundert unter besonderer Berücksichtigung des interterritorialen Rinderhandels," *Jahrbücher für Nationalökonomie und Statistik*, CLXXIX.

Wiese, U. (1935), *Zur Opposition des ostelbischen Grundadels gegen die agraren Reformmassnahmen 1807-1811*. Berlin.

Wiessner, H. (1946), *Beiträge zur Geschichte des Dorfes und der Dorfgemeinde in Öesterreich*. Klagenfurt.

Wilkinson, W. (1971), *An Account of the Principalities of Wallachia and Moldavia*. Reprinted from 1820 edition. New York.

Williams, H. W. (1914), *Russia and the Russians*. New York.

Winkel, H. (1968), *Die Ablösungskapitalien aus der Bauernbefreiung in West- und Süddeutschland*. Stuttgart.

Winkler, E., ed. (1941), *Das Schweizer Dorf*. Zurich.

Wittich, W. (1896), *Die Grundherrschaft in Nordwestdeutschland*. Leipzig.

Woytinsky, W. (1925-1928), *Die Welt in Zahlen*. 7 vols. Berlin.

Wright, G. (1964), *Rural Revolution in France. The Peasantry in the Twentieth Century*. Stanford.

Wright, W. E. (1966), *Serf, Seigneur, and Sovereign. Agrarian Reform in Eighteenth-Century Bohemia*. Minneapolis.

Wunderlich, E. (1918), *Handbuch von Polen (Kongress-Polen)*. Berlin.

Wunderlich, F. (1961), *Farm Labor in Germany 1810-1945*. Princeton.

Wuttke, R. (1893), *Gesindeordnungen und Gesindezwangsdienst in Sachsen bis zum Jahre 1835. (Staats- und sozialwissenschaftliche Forschungen*, xii, pt. 4.) Leipzig.

Wyczański, A. (1960), "Le niveau de la récolte des céréales en Pologne du xvie au xviiie siècle," *Première Conférence Internationale d'Histoire Economique. Stockholm 1960*. Paris, The Hague.

Wyss, F. (1852), "Die Schweizerischen Landgemeinden," *Zeitschrift für schweizerisches Recht*, i.

Young, A. (1970), *Travels during the Years 1787, 1788 and 1789*. 2 vols. Facsimile of 2nd edition, 1794. New York.

Zablotskii-Desiatovskii, A. P. (1882), *Graf P. D. Kiselev i ego vremia*. 4 vols. St. Petersburg.

Zailer, V. (1903), *Die Land- und Alpenwirtschaft in den österreichischen Alpenländern*. Vienna.

Zaionchkovskii, P. A. (1968), *Otmena krepostnogo prava v Rossii*. 3rd ed. Moscow.

Zaionchkovskii, P. A. (1973), "Soslovnyi sostav ofitserskogo korpusa na rubezhe XIX-XX vekov," *Istoriia SSSR*, 1973, no. 1.

Zajaczkowski, A. (1963), "En Pologne: cadres structurels de la noblesse," *Annales E. S. C.*, xviii.

Zeldin, T. (1973), *France 1848-1945*. Oxford.

Zelenin, D. K. (1926), *Russische ostslavische Volkskunde*. Leipzig.

Zenker, E. .V. (1897), *Die Wiener Revolution 1848 in ihren socialen Voraussetzungen und Beziehungen.* Vienna, Pest, Leipzig.

Ziekursch, J. (1927), *Hundert Jahre schlesischer Agrargeschichte. Vom Hubertusburger Frieden bis zum Abschluss der Bauernbefreiung.* 2nd ed. Breslau.

Zink, A. (1969), *Azereix. La vie d'une communauté rurale à la fin du xviiie siècle.* Paris.

Zlotnikov, M. (1935), "K voprosu ob izuchenii istorii rabochego klassa i promyshlennosti," *Katorga i Ssylka*, I.

Zolla, D. (1893-1894), "Les variations du revenu et du prix des terres en France au xviie et au xviiie siècle," *Annales de l'École Libre des Sciences Politiques*, VIII, IX.

Zopfi, H. (1947), *Das Bauerntum in der Schweizergeschichte.* Zurich.

Zorn, W. (1963), "*Unternehmer und Aristokratie in Deutschland,*" *Tradition*, VIII.

Zubrzycki, J. (1953), "Emigration from Poland in the Nineteenth and Twentieth Centuries," *Population Studies*, VI.

Zytkowicz, L. (1968), "An Investigation into Agricultural Production in Masovia in the First Half of the 17th Century," *Acta Poloniae Historica*, XVIII.

INDEX

absentee ownership, 158
absolutism, and agrarian reform, 373; in
  Savoy, 216-217; pro-peasant policy, 197,
  205-208; protection of peasants, 373-374
Achard, Franz Karl, 296
Adams, John Quincy, 170, 179, 183, 281
agrarian codes, Austrian Monarchy, 55,
  222-223, 226, 267, 311, 360
agrarian communism, 123-124
agrarian reform, absolutism and, 373-374;
  arguments against, 330-331; Austrian
  Monarchy, 222-223, 360, 364-365;
  capitalism and, 371-372; Denmark, 219-
  220; drafting of legislation, 381-382; effects of French Revolution, 367-368;
  example of other lands as stimulus, 368;
  follows political changes, 377-379; impact
  of 1848 revolutions, 370-371; intellectuals
  and, 366; land-labor ratios and, 372; military defeat as stimulus, 370; peasants and,
  359-360; Poland, 365-366, 374; profitable
  agriculture as stimulus, 368-369; rural
  unrest and, 360-366; Russia and the Crimean War, 365; seigniorial opponents and
  supporters, 357-358. *See also* emancipations
agrarian reform movements, 310-315
agricultural education, 251-252, 283, 291-
  292
agricultural implements, 131-133, 135-136,
  278
agricultural improvements, 277-278; clergymen as innovators, 290-292; England,
  250-251; government encouragement of,
  283-284; hindrances to, 117-120, 136-
  137, 262-263; peasant opposition to, 292-
  293
agricultural industry, 295-297, 423
agricultural manuals, 247-248
agricultural revolution, 303
agricultural societies, 282, 287-290
Agricultural Society at Vienna, 289
Agricultural Society of the Kingdom of Poland, 359
Agricultural Society of Paris, 282, 287, 288
agricultural treatises, 251
agriculture, dominant sector of the economy,
  116, 138-139, 419; new interest in, 247-
  248, 250
agromanie, 248

Aiguillon, Armand de V.D.R., duke d', 158,
  358, 368
Alexander I of Russia, 326; agrarian reforms, 236; Baltic emancipations, 229-
  230; ends noble landowning monopoly,
  19; repeals tax on nobles, 22
Alexander II of Russia, 228; accession of,
  379; opposes landless emancipation, 359,
  397; plans to free serfs, 328, 365, 370;
  Polish emancipation, 374
Alföld, 255
Allgäu, 264
allotment land, 390-391, 395, 404
Alsace, 126, 136, 137, 139, 140, 293
altyn, 46n
"americans," 271, 271n, 277
andramaa, 95
anglomania, 250-251, 265
animal husbandry, *see* livestock
Anthony I of Saxony, 379
Anton, Karl Gottlob von, 286
Appanage, Department of the, 214
Appanage peasants, 43, 214
arable, increase, 257; increase post-
  emancipation, 435
Argenson, Marquis Marc-René d', 147
Arles, 343
arpent of Paris, 212
arrearages, 406
arrendators, 217
Artois, 52
assignat ruble, 70n, 169, 243
assigned peasants, 340-341, 347
Auersperg, Prince Vinzenz Karl, 423
Auerstädt, battle of, 370
Aunis, 165
Auroux des Despommiers, Mathieu, 178,
  249
Austrian Monarchy, 84, 432; agrarian codes,
  222-223; agrarian reforms, 73, 211, 221-
  226, 316-317, 360, 364-365; agricultural
  and industrial labor force 1910, 419; agricultural societies, 288-289; arable area,
  254; banks, 168; bourgeois proprietors
  post-emancipation, 427; bourgeoisie in
  high offices post-emancipation, 421; compulsory child labor, 57-58; conscription,
  69; cottage industry, 172, 175; cotters and
  landless peasants, 106; criticism of seigniorial privileges, 309-311; defense of

Library of Congress Cataloging in Publication Data

Blum, Jerome, 1913-
   The end of the old order in rural Europe.

   Includes bibliographical references and index.
   1.   Europe—Rural conditions.   2.   Peasantry—
Europe—History.   3.   Feudalism—Europe—History.
4.   Social classes—Europe—History.   I.   Title.
HN373.B55   309.2'63'094   77-85530
ISBN 0-691-05266-2
ISBN 0-691-10067-5 pbk.